John Ray

SAMS
Teach Yourself

Dreamweaver MX
Application
Development

in 21 Days

SAMS

201 West 103rd St., Indianapolis, Indiana, 46290 USA

Sams Teach Yourself Dreamweaver MX Application Development in 21 Days

Copyright ©2003 by Sams Publishing

International Standard Book Number: 0-672-32403-2

Library of Congress Catalog Number: 2002103160

Printed in the United States of America

First Printing: 2002

04   03   02   4   3   2   1

Trademarks

Warning and Disclaimer

ACQUISITIONS EDITOR
Betsy Brown

DEVELOPMENT EDITOR
Jonathan Steever

MANAGING EDITOR
Charlotte Clapp

PROJECT EDITOR
Matthew Purcell

COPY EDITOR
Kezia Endsley

INDEXER
Kelly Castell

PROOFREADER
Linda Seifert

TECHNICAL EDITOR
Robyn Ness

TEAM COORDINATOR
Amy Patton

INTERIOR DESIGNER
Gary Adair

COVER DESIGNER
Aren Howell

PAGE LAYOUT
Rebecca Harmon

GRAPHICS
Oliver Jackson
Tammy Graham

Contents at a Glance

Contents

About the Author

JOHN RAY is an award winning developer and technology consultant with more than 16 years of programming and administration experience. He has worked on projects for the FCC, The Ohio State University, Xerox, and the State of Florida, as well as serving as IT Director for a Columbus, Ohio-based design and application development company. John has written or contributed to more than 11 titles currently in print, including *Mac OS X Unleashed.*

Dedication

This book is dedicated to TiVo—my ever-patient, ever-thoughtful, digital video recorder. Thank you for remembering to record for me. Even though I never watched most of what you stored, please know that I appreciated your tireless efforts nonetheless.

Suggestions for my next dedication will be accepted through http://dedications.poisontooth.com/.

Acknowledgments

Many thanks to the helpful people at Sams Publishing who made this revision possible, and helped to ensure the quality and accuracy of the text. Betsy Brown, Jon Steever, Matt Purcell, Kezia Endsley and Robyn Ness have all been instrumental in keeping this book moving through all the changes and re-writes required with each new Dreamweaver MX beta release.

We Want to Hear from You!

As the reader of this book, *you* are our most important critic and commentator. We value your opinion and want to know what we're doing right, what we could do better, what areas you'd like to see us publish in, and any other words of wisdom you're willing to pass our way.

You can email or write me directly to let me know what you did or didn't like about this book—as well as what we can do to make our books stronger.

Please note that I cannot help you with technical problems related to the topic of this book, and that due to the high volume of mail I receive, I might not be able to reply to every message.

When you write, please be sure to include this book's title and author as well as your name and phone or email address. I will carefully review your comments and share them with the author and editors who worked on the book.

E-mail: webdev@samspublishing.com

Mail: Mark Taber
            Sams Publishing
            201 W. 103rd Street
            Indianapolis, IN 46290

Reader Services

For more information about this book or others from Sams Publishing, visit our Web site at www.samspublishing.com. Type the ISBN (excluding hyphens) or the title of the book in the Search box to find the book you're looking for.

Introduction

About This Book

Comprised of the combination of Dreamweaver with Dreamweaver UltraDev, Macromedia's latest offering, Dreamweaver MX, is poised to bring dynamic application development to the masses. Dreamweaver MX offers easy-to-use tools that can very quickly connect to databases and Web pages in a logical and visual manner.

This book walks you through the Dreamweaver tools, from design to application development, and includes several sample projects that you can build as you read through the chapters. The book also takes into account the cross-platform and cross-server nature of the product. Dreamweaver can *design* interactive sites on Windows and Macintosh computers, but *deploy* the appropriate code to run the sites on Unix, Linux, BSD, Windows, Macintosh, and dozens of other operating systems. Keeping this in mind, the exercises in the book are designed to be as portable as possible and stay within the Dreamweaver MX interface as much as possible.

This is *not* a reference book for experienced Web programmers. It is a step-by-step tutorial for those who understand the basics of HTML, want to learn Dreamweaver, and want to exercise the features of MX to build maintainable dynamic Web applications. I once read a Dreamweaver review that stated "until there are Dreamweaver books on demand (customized books for each reader), there will be no perfect book." I agree. Dreamweaver MX covers a *lot* of ground. It is my hope that this book will serve as your guide for getting started with Dreamweaver MX and provide ideas on how you can use the software to bring your Web development plans and ideas to fruition.

 Note

> Sample pages, graphics, and databases for each lesson in the book are available from `http://downloads.cutelittledogs.com`—the book's support site. (Yes, it is a tribute to my dog, who has put up with hours of waiting by her leash as I type through the pages of this book.)

The Early Favorite

In 1997, Macromedia released the Dreamweaver HTML editor for the Macintosh and Windows. It quickly became the standard by which other editors were judged. Combining the power of the full HTML language and an interface that made publishers and designers feel at home, it brought cross-platform HTML development to the world.

Macromedia has upgraded Dreamweaver to keep it current with the HTML specification and introduce new features such as group Web site collaboration, site management, and JavaScripting. Dreamweaver continues to win numerous awards for ease of use and technical superiority.

The world, however, isn't standing still, and neither is Dreamweaver.

The Web Elite

With HTML in the hands of the masses, Web page design is available to anyone. This has pushed the elite HTML programmers to move onward and upward to the next big thing. This "big thing" is creating sites that interact with the users. Rather than just presenting static pages to the site's visitors, today's Web sites store and process information, creating an experience that can be unique for every person. These are no longer just Web sites; they are Web "applications."

Online stores, catalogs, and bidding services are everywhere. Programmers who were writing HTML have now moved on to write the server-based code that drives these dynamic sites. A plethora of languages and technologies is used to drive these custom sites—ColdFusion Markup Language, PHP Hypertext Preprocessor, Active Server Pages, and Java Server Pages—to name a few.

Similar to the birth of HTML and the WYSIWYG editor, dynamic Web applications have led to tools to help nonprogrammers design Web site logic. These tools have been very lacking—supporting very few server technologies, which are limited to a single platform for development and created for people who already know how to program.

The power of Web application development is in the hands of the few. Or is it?

Enter Dreamweaver MX

Macromedia rose to the challenge of creating an environment for designing Web applications that combines the power of dynamic sites with the Dreamweaver point-and-click interface— Dreamweaver MX.

Dreamweaver MX supports not one, but five server technologies (JSP, CFML, ASP, PHP, and ASP.NET) with the capability to expand to new technologies through plug-ins. Furthermore, Macromedia is supporting this product on both Windows and Macintosh platforms, enabling Mac users to author ASP and CFML code in a rich visual environment for the first time.

Unlike other Web development packages, Dreamweaver MX offers the designer the ability to preview data in real-time within a document design. Guessing how a product catalog is going to look in your browser and seeing it laid out before your eyes is the difference between a two-hour and a two-day job. Dreamweaver MX makes life even easier by allowing the person designing the application logic to work on the database side while designers work on the page layout. The days of handing files off to another person are over.

As you make your way through this book, you will learn how to use the capabilities of Dreamweaver MX to their fullest. Whether you've never used Dreamweaver, or have never even used an HTML editor, you'll be creating your own database-driven Web sites in 21 days. The only prerequisite for reading the book is an understanding of HTML and access to a Windows-based or Mac OS–based computer.

The Coming Weeks

Before we get started, let's take a look at how this book is structured.

- The first week focuses on the HTML editing capabilities of Dreamweaver MX and introduces the basics of database-driven sites. You'll learn the tools for managing and editing HTML, and will become a pro in the WYSIWYG environment. After the interface features are covered, the real fun begins. Learn about the fundamentals of database design and the different server technologies supported in Dreamweaver MX.

- In week two, the power of Dreamweaver MX becomes apparent. After successfully connecting to a database, you'll start including dynamic data in your Web applications immediately. You'll also discover the data visualization tools and prebuilt server behaviors. Near the end of the week, you'll learn several fundamental techniques that are commonly used in Web application design.

- By week three, you'll be ready to start building real applications. The many of the last days are dedicated to creating and maintaining real-life projects. You can take these applications, extend them, and put them to work immediately. You'll also learn some tips for debugging your finished applications in case something doesn't appear to be working as you had planned.

When you're finished with the book, you'll be able to create a variety of Web applications and use the Dreamweaver MX tools to interact with your database and application servers. Now you'll be the one with power!

WEEK 1

At a Glance

Part of the appeal of the Dreamweaver MX environment is that it isn't just a powerful application builder; it is also a first class Web page authoring environment as well. Macromedia has included all the features of the popular Dreamweaver application in Dreamweaver MX. This enables the users to design visually appealing dynamic applications within a reliable and consistent interface.

The first week of work focuses primarily on using these tools to create and manage Web pages. In order to create engaging dynamic applications, you must first have the knowledge and background to create the HTML that the pages use.

Even if you're an experienced HTML author, it is a good idea to read through the first week. Although easy to use, Dreamweaver MX has many hidden features that, if used correctly, can help reduce your Web page development time exponentially. Here are just some of the features you'll learn about:

Flash Buttons and Text—Quickly add Flash-based text and buttons to your documents, without a need for the Flash authoring tools.

Use DHTML to Animate—Without the need for plug-ins, you can add animation and even simple games to your pages.

Pixel Point Positioning—Position elements in your document with pixel-point accuracy using layers and the unique Layout Mode offered in Dreamweaver MX.

Advanced Site Management Tools—Design your site in a multi-user environment using Dreamweaver MX's other built-in file and version management systems.

The first several days contain a lot of information, but should provide a valuable reference during the remaining few weeks. Because I'm sure that most everyone is interested in the dynamic server-based components of Dreamweaver MX, the first week will end with several important lessons to prepare you for Weeks 2 and 3.

If this is your first foray into dynamic Web programming, it's unlikely that you have a database design background. Don't worry; you're going to have one in a few days. Although it might sound silly now, you're going to learn that the most powerful part of your Web application environment is your database server. The more work your database server can do, the faster your site will operate and the faster your application server will respond.

What if you don't even have an application server yet? Don't worry. Week 1 ends with a look at all the servers that Dreamweaver MX's dynamic tools support and what each has to offer, and then takes you through the steps of setting up servers for Windows XP and Mac OS X.

Good luck, and feel free to email me (jray@poisontooth.com) if you have any questions.

DAY 1

Getting Started

Whether your interest lies in developing a few static Web pages or a complex database-driven application, you must familiarize yourself with the Dreamweaver MX interface. Numerous windows, panels, and menus await your exploration. In today's lesson, you'll:

- Learn how to find your way around the Dreamweaver MX environment.
- Explore the myriad of panels and windows that you'll use everyday with Dreamweaver.
- Discover ways to customize the Dreamweaver system, such as creating new keyboard shortcuts.
- Understand the Dreamweaver MX preferences to quickly customize tools and features.

The Dreamweaver MX Interface

In many ways, Dreamweaver MX is two applications in one: a Web page design tool (Dreamweaver) and a utility for connecting Web pages to dynamic database-driven information (that's the MX part). These components are integrated into the same interface, but are used independently. If you want to create a Web site with a few simple pages, you won't be forced to use any of the MX-specific features. Likewise, if you have an existing Web site that you'd like to connect to a database system, you can easily do so without delving into the design tools.

The first week of *Sams Teach Yourself Dreamweaver MX in 21 Days* will help you get up to speed with all the Dreamweaver MX tools and prepare you for the dynamic application development in the rest of the book. Becoming comfortable with the basic tools and palettes is the first step in creating documents that both look *and* work great.

Today's lesson will give you a general overview of the Dreamweaver MX interface so that you'll feel at ease finding the different features later in the week. Like many modern applications, Dreamweaver MX provides a customizable environment that gives the user numerous ways to accomplish a single task. As you work with Dreamweaver in the coming days, you might find certain techniques that work better for you than those described in the book. I continually find myself refining the ways I create pages and discovering new shortcuts for interacting with the program.

Dreamweaver MX's interface is as flexible as the program itself—you've never seen a program that gives you as many ways of looking at your data. The document design view shows you a general overview of how your completed Web page will look in a Web browser, whereas the Property panel lets you get close and personal with the attributes for individual objects within your design. For those who prefer a more "nitty-gritty" approach, the application gives you full access to the underlying source code with an HTML editor, Quick Tag Editor, and hierarchical tag view. A plethora of supporting panels will allow you to add custom JavaScripts, database connectivity, and many more features.

Starting Dreamweaver MX for the first time can be a bit overwhelming. Tool panels and windows cover the screen, just waiting for the click of a mouse. Figure 1.1 displays the typical startup Dreamweaver MX workspace. The first time the application starts, Windows users are prompted to choose between viewing the workspace in one of two modes: Integrated and Floating. Figure 1.1 shows the Integrated Workspace mode, which places all the Dreamweaver windows and palettes within a single "master" window with a single menu bar. This is convenient if you often find yourself switching between applications and want to quickly minimize your current Dreamweaver MX project.

Macintosh users are "limited" to the Floating Workspace mode, in which the individual windows intermingle with those of other applications, as seen in Figure 1.2. Users of the UltraDev software might recognize this as the standard working mode of the older program. Windows users can switch to the Floating workspace by opening Preferences from the Edit menu, choosing the General category, and then clicking the Change Workspace button.

FIGURE 1.1

The Dreamweaver MX interface layout is quite extensive. The Integrated Workspace mode contains all the available palettes within a single master window.

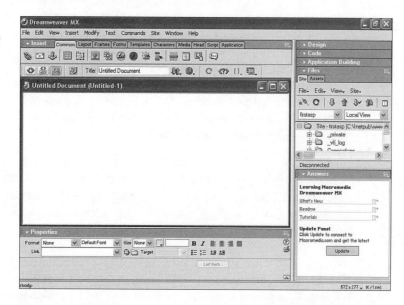

FIGURE 1.2

The Floating Workspace view (seen on Mac OS X) allows Dreamweaver application windows to intermingle with other active software.

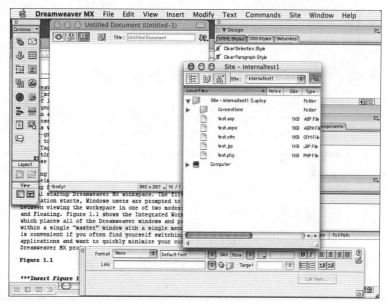

Tip

> If you're a Macintosh user (like myself), don't fret. The Integrated Workspace mode is easily replicated on the Mac by hiding all active applications but Dreamweaver MX. Just choose Hide Others from the Dreamweaver MX application menu in Mac OS X, or the application switcher menu in Mac OS 9.

Regardless of the workspace mode you choose, without a reference you can quickly find yourself digging through the menus and windows to find the functions you need to perform a simple task. Dreamweaver MX's job is to make your Web editing life easy; spending five minutes looking for the right button or menu item to italicize text or create a Web link is more than slightly counterproductive.

In order to make life a bit easier, let's take a look at the panels and menus that you'll commonly use when working with Dreamweaver MX. This will help you locate the tools you need to start composing HTML—which we'll jump into on Day 2, "Creating Your First Web Site." Don't worry if you're not sure exactly what a given item does. We'll cover the tools and panels again as we use them.

Tip

> For those of you who like to explore, be sure to take advantage of the extensive use of tooltips throughout the Dreamweaver MX interface. Positioning your cursor over an icon will often show a short description of the function of that tool.

The Interface Components

Dreamweaver MX organizes the workspace into sections or "panels," each containing tools that can be applied to accomplish certain tasks. Figure 1.3 once again shows the workspace, this time with callouts to the relevant components. If you're using an installation of Dreamweaver MX that was set up by a previous user, you might notice some differences. Don't worry, you can quickly drag and rearrange the components however you like.

Let's go ahead and get started with a tour of each of these elements. Feel free to click around at will. In Day 2, you'll build a simple Web site; the more familiar you become with the interface, the easier the subsequent days will be.

Insert panel   Menu bar

FIGURE 1.3

These are the components you'll use every day in Dreamweaver MX.

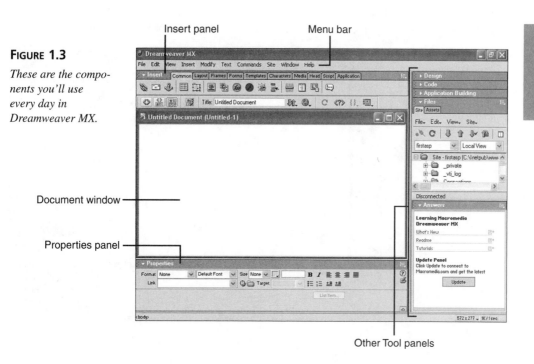

Document window —

Properties panel —

Other Tool panels

The Document Window

When you start Dreamweaver MX, the largest area on your screen will be the document window. This is where you compose your Web pages in the *WYSIWYG (what you see is what you get)* interface. As you build your page, you'll immediately see the results of each change, just as it would appear in a Web browser.

There are three parts that make up the document window. The top of the window contains the toolbar, which holds shortcuts to many common commands and functions (you'll learn about these as needed), the middle is the content area, and, at the bottom, is the status bar. In Integrated mode, these elements are arranged a bit differently on the screen. Figure 1.4 shows the document window with a few sentences added.

To add to your page layout, you can type directly into the document window or use the Insert panel or Insert menu to add text, graphics, or links to the page. The flashing cursor in the document window shows where the current insert point is located. You can move this point by clicking with your mouse or using the arrow keypad to move it around. Wherever the cursor is, that's where your text or object will be inserted. Try typing into the document window now. Enter a few sentences. You won't be saving this document, so it isn't important what you type, just that you give it a try.

Toolbar

FIGURE 1.4

The document window is where you will do most of your Web page editing.

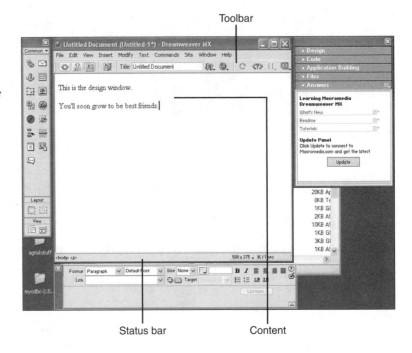

Status bar   Content

Note

Unlike modern word processors such as Word 200x and WordPerfect, Dreamweaver MX, by default, will allow you to position your cursor only within the text or object stream you've already created. You cannot, for example, click at the bottom of the window and start typing. However, using the Layout view mode, discussed in detail tomorrow, you can create arbitrary regions within a page to which you can add content. It isn't quite as simple as clicking where you want to start typing, but close.

Manipulating Objects

Anything that has been added to the document window can easily be removed, cut, copied, or pasted—much like your standard word processing software (Notepad or TextEdit, anyone?). You can select text by clicking and dragging your cursor over the letters. To select an object like an image, click it once. You can choose multiple items by moving the insertion point to the beginning of the group of objects you want to select, and then holding Shift and clicking where you want the selection to end. Single selected objects are designated by a darkened outline, whereas multiple objects are darkened completely.

After an object is selected, you can use the Copy, Cut, Paste, and Clear commands under the Edit menu to move, duplicate, or delete the selection. The Backspace key also works in a pinch to delete a selection. Two additional Copy and Paste methods are located in the Edit menu—Copy HTML and Paste HTML. These are rather counter-intuitive operations that might not perform exactly how you'd expect. As you might know, HTML is the underlying language that forms Web pages. Simple "tags" define the way a page looks when it is presented in a browser. Each tag usually has a "start" tag and an "end" tag to define what a particular style applies to.

For example, the "bold" tag is used make text appear bold in your Web browser. In the following sentence, the word "bold" is defined using HTML tags to appear in a bold typeface onscreen:

```
I like to emphasize words with <b>bold</b>.
```

The Copy HTML selection will copy the underlying HTML behind what you see onscreen. You can then paste the HTML into other applications. If you simply used the Copy command, you'd end up just pasting the text version of what you see onscreen. Paste HTML works similarly with the Paste operation. If you've copied HTML code from another program, you can use the Paste HTML function to paste it into Dreamweaver MX with all the styles intact. The standard Paste operation would end up pasting the HTML code itself. A good rule of thumb is to use these special forms of Copy and Paste only when working with external programs; otherwise you might find the results confusing. The tags themselves will be pasted as part of the onscreen text, rather than being recognized as HTML.

Dreamweaver MX has provided several shortcuts that make selecting objects even easier. To select a line of text or an object, click in front of the object near the left window border. The cursor will change to an alternate arrow style to show that it is in the line-select mode. You can extend this technique to select multiple objects by clicking and dragging down the left border of the screen.

Tomorrow, you start working with some of the more advanced page designs. You'll learn even more ways to precisely select objects in the document window. As I said earlier, it's rare that you'll find just one way to do something in Dreamweaver MX!

Status Bar

At the bottom of the window is the document status bar. This provides a few simple controls for interacting with the document view.

Tag Hierarchy

The left side of the status bar contains a listing of the HTML tags surrounding the current cursor position. Because you're just getting started, this won't be of much use just yet. To get an idea of what this is good for, let's use the sentence from the previous example. Type the following words into your document window:

```
I like to emphasize words with bold.
```

Next, select the word bold and choose Style, Bold from the Text menu. You should now see the sentence with the word "bold" highlighted.

Finally, click so that your cursor is inside the word "bold." The left side of the status bar will show:

```
<body><b>
```

This indicates that you're currently working inside of a "bold" tag, which is inside of a "body" tag. As you work with more complex Web page designs, you'll appreciate how quickly this can help you determine exactly where you are.

Note   You might not remember inserting a body tag in your design. Never fear, you didn't! The body tag (which indicates the "body" of the page content) is inserted automatically by Dreamweaver MX.

Design Size

The next component in the status bar (working your way from the left) is the current size of the document window in pixels (*width*×*height*). As you're almost certainly aware, Web sites often are designed without any attention paid to the size of the screen on which they will display. Pages scroll off to the side or down with seemingly no end. Dreamweaver MX makes it simple to preview how a page will look at different window dimensions simply by resizing the document window. The current size is displayed in the status bar of the window. You can quickly set several preview sizes by clicking and holding on the display of the current window size in the status bar. A pop-up menu will appear with a list of common preset sizes that you can choose, including the maximum window size for WebTV viewers. Other sizes can be added through the Dreamweaver MX "Status bar" preferences. As you change the value, the status bar will reflect those changes.

Don't Discount the Little Guys

It's important not to guess what your audience is going to be using to view a site. I recently participated in a review consultation for a Web site that was created for the reselling of homemade crafts and recipes. A surprisingly large number of the customers on the site (over 35%) were WebTV users. Luckily, the site was built with a small window size in mind, and all viewers were capable of fully enjoying the site. The same holds true for the growing handheld marketplace. Pocket PCs and Palm-based systems can display very limited amounts of information onscreen at once. Accommodating these devices is often frustrating, but, if they represent a large portion of your target audience, leaving them in the cold might not be the best idea.

It is important to note that the size of the document window is not necessarily the size that the output HTML will be. It is simply a method of previewing your work at various sizes. If you insert an object (such as an image) that is 800 pixels wide, but are designing in a screen that is 600 pixels wide, it will not automatically be resized to fit the design screen. Likewise, if you're designing for a small screen, be sure to preview at various sizes in order to ensure that users with larger browser windows will also have a visually pleasing display.

Download Time and Page Size

Next to the browser size setting is an estimation of the page size and the time it will take to download. Most site developers target a particular class of user—dial-in/network/modern browsers, and so on. Creating beautiful pages that take 10 minutes to download is not a good idea. The default speed that is used to estimate the download time is a 28.8Kbps modem. You can adjust the speed in the Dreamweaver MX preferences, which are discussed at the end of the day.

Toolbar

The final portion of your design area is the toolbar. Located directly above the design window itself, the "document" toolbar (as it is called by Macromedia) contains quick-click shortcuts for switching between HTML, split HTML/Design, Design (the default), and Live data views as well as a very convenient way to set the title of the current document. You'll learn more about these features tomorrow and over the next week.

Tip

If you're familiar (and happy) with the Microsoft Word toolbar for accessing the basic file operations (open, save, print, and so on), you might want to activate the "standard" toolbar by choosing Edit, Toolbars, and then Standard. Even though this is labeled the "standard" toolbar, it isn't on by default.

The Insert Panel

The grand daddy of all the Dreamweaver panels is the Insert panel. This is a floating window that appears in the upper-left corner of your screen the first time you start Dreamweaver MX. As you design pages, you'll frequently refer to this panel, shown in Figure 1.5, and its toolbox of Web elements.

FIGURE 1.5

The Insert panel is your Web design toolbox.

> **Tip**
>
> Unlike most other Dreamweaver MX windows, the Insert panel can change orientation from a horizontal arrangement to a vertical layout by clicking the small rectangular button at the right side (in horizontal mode), or in the lower-right corner (in vertical mode) of the panel. You must be in floating window mode to change the orientation.

If you're using the Insert panel in horizontal mode, you should see several categories of elements that you can work with, represented by tabs. In its vertical orientation, the tabs are replaced by a single pop-up menu at the top of the panel. Using either the tabs or the pop-up menu, you can access these types of tools:

Common—This is the most common of the design elements. This includes images, tables, embedded objects, and composite constructs such as navigation bars and image rollovers. This is the default palette shown.

Layout—Tables, layers, and other elements for creating complex page layouts.

Text—Text formatting functions; no visual HTML objects. Useful mainly to those working directly with source code.

Tables—Inserts the table object (also available in the Common panel) and provides shortcuts for inserting the HTML source for each table element (<tr>, <td>, and so on).

Frames—Preconstructed framesets for laying out sites without the need to manually design the commonly used frame schemes

Forms—Text fields, radio buttons, and everything you need to put together input forms.

Templates—Elements for building template Web pages to distribute editing responsibilities.

Characters—Special characters and symbols that cannot be typed directly into the design view.

Media—Java applets, ActiveX plug-ins, and browser plug-ins.

Head—Some of the most important parts of a Web page are the elements contained in the `<head>` tags. These items help you define the metatags (such as keywords and descriptions) that will help search engines classify your site or automatically redirect the users to another page.

Script—Tools for inserting server-side includes and adding JavaScript or VBScript.

<Server Platform>—If you're working on a dynamic page, you might see a tab related to your server platform. This tab will contain shortcuts for inserting common server code into the HTML source.

Application—When creating dynamic Web sites, Dreamweaver MX makes it simple to set up certain types of pages based on a pre-made template. The panel contains several dynamic templates to quickly add to your page.

Note

> Many of the Insert panel categories correspond to the Insert menu's Object submenus. The Tables tab corresponds to Table Objects, Form to Form Objects, and so on.

When looking at the Insert panel in the vertical orientation, there are two additional features that remain constant for all the different categories—the layout and view mode. (Consequently, the Layout panel is not a separate panel.) These icons are used to switch between a traditional and free-form layout design view. You'll become more familiar with these tools tomorrow, but be aware of where they're located—you'll find them immensely useful in the near future.

The next few pages will visually document the different objects in each of the Insert panels' categories. Let's get started.

Common Elements

Of all the design elements, you're likely to spend the most time using the "common" category. Here you can insert the basic building blocks for most pages. The common elements portion is displayed in Figure 1.6.

Hyperlink—Adds a common Web link to a page.

Email link—Inserts a link into the document, which enables the users to send e-mail to a specified address. This is implemented using a `mailto:` tag, which launches your e-mail client and starts a new message.

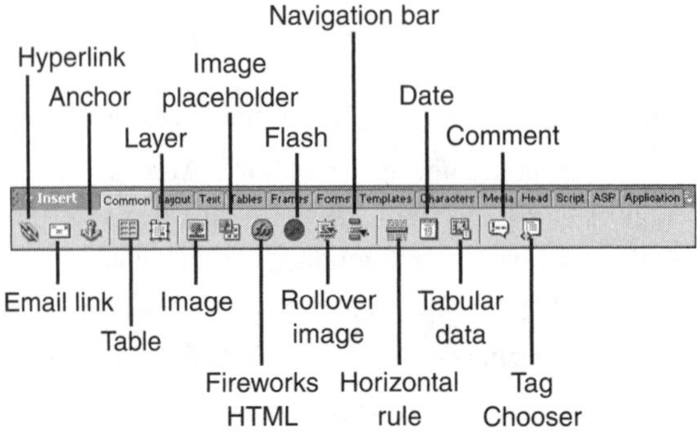

FIGURE **1.6**

Insert images, tables, and other objects with a single click.

Navigation bar

Hyperlink　　Image
　Anchor　placeholder　　　Date
　　　　　Layer　　Flash　　Comment

Email link　Image　Rollover　Tabular
　　　　　　　　　image　　data
　　Table
　　　　　Fireworks　Horizontal　Tag
　　　　　HTML　　rule　　Chooser

Anchor—Inserts an invisible "anchor" into a document so that a link can be created that attaches directly to a specific portion of a page. You've probably seen long pages that include a table of contents that links to portions of the same page. Named anchors, sometimes called *bookmarks*, are used to create these points.

Table—Tables have many purposes in HTML: aligning images and objects, presenting data, creating navigation bars, and so on. The use of tables can give you true control over the final look of your document while maintaining high browser compatibility. Clicking the table icon will prompt you for information about the table (size, width, height), and then automatically inserts it into your document.

Layer—Layers can be used to position elements to exact pixel coordinates, resulting in *extremely* precise layouts. Unfortunately, this technology is not supported in early 3.0 browsers. To create a new layer, click this icon, and then click and drag in the document design view to draw a rectangle in the size and location you want your layer to appear.

Image—Using the image tool, you can quickly insert an image into your document.

Image placeholder—Know you want to add an image, but don't have the file ready yet? Just add a placeholder for the time being.

Fireworks HTML—The Macromedia Fireworks image optimization program generates its own HTML for rollover images, menu bars, and other special effects. To insert an HTML file built by Fireworks into your HTML, click this icon.

Flash—Easily insert Macromedia Flash elements into a document. Macromedia Flash is the leading vector animation package used online.

Rollover image—Although not exactly an HTML element, rollover images are universally used to signal on/off states of buttons on Web sites. Rather than forcing you to write the JavaScript to do this yourself, you can simply click the rollover icon, tell Dreamweaver MX what the on and off state images are, and away you go.

Navigation bar—A truly wonderful Dreamweaver MX feature is the navigation bar constructor. Clicking this icon enables you to quickly create a rollover navigation bar out of a series of on and off images. Although this would also be possible using the table and rollover image tools, it's a great timesaver to have it all located in one easy-to-use interface.

Horizontal rule—Typically used to divide pages into sections, clicking this icon will insert a horizontal line into the document.

Date—Inserts the date and/or time into the document. Includes an option to automatically update the date as soon as the document is saved.

Tabular data—A common use of tables is to create an online display of existing data, such as spreadsheet calculations. In order to simplify the creation of these Web page elements, Dreamweaver MX allows you to import a text file containing data directly into your Web site. Click this icon, choose a file, and the table is automatically generated to your specifications.

Comment—Allows the insertion of text that won't be visible on the page when viewed with a browser. Comments are typically used by the designer or programmer to document complex page structures and coding.

Tag Chooser—A hierarchical HTML/PHP/ASP tag browser, used for picking tags to insert into the HTML document.

Layout

The Layout category is used to access the HTML features that can be used to format information in a Web page. These functions are also available in the Common group, if you're using the Floating Workspace mode and the panel is in the vertical orientation. Figure 1.7 displays the Layout icons.

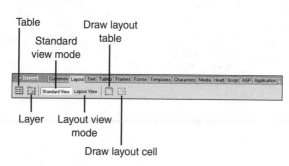

FIGURE 1.7

The Layout tab groups the features that can be used to create sophisticated Web page designs.

You'll learn how to use many of the Layout tools tomorrow and the next day.

Text

The Text category of the Insert panel, shown in Figure 1.8, is primarily an HTML code tool. It can be used to insert text-related HTML pages into your documents.

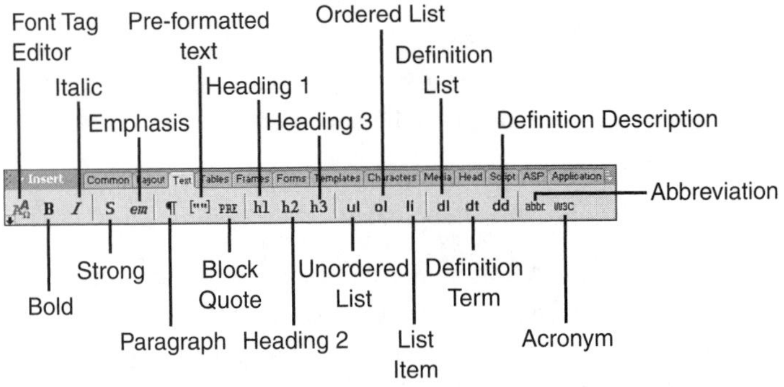

FIGURE 1.8

Use the text panel to insert HTML text-related tags.

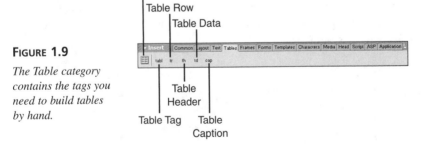

Of note is the font tag editor, located on the far left of the Insert panel. The editor can be used to construct `<font>` tags for inserting into the pages. This is a specialized use of the Tag Editor, discussed in Day 3.

Tables

Like the Text category, the Table items are used mostly for interacting directly with HTML. This category of the Insert panel, shown in Figure 1.9, adds any of the table available table tags to your document.

FIGURE 1.9

The Table category contains the tags you need to build tables by hand.

Frames

Frames are used to divide up a browser into separate virtual "screens," each of which can contain an individual Web page. This is a convenient way to keep page navigation and content in individual documents, yet composite them into a single Web page. Unfortunately, frames are more useful in theory than in practice. Many developers find frames difficult to use, and users find them frustrating to understand. Figure 1.10 shows the Frames category, which is used to quickly add common frame divisions to a page.

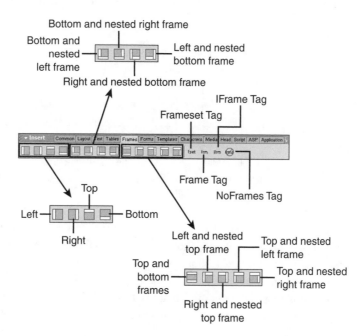

FIGURE 1.10

Most of the common frame layouts are easily handled by this palette.

The folks at Macromedia seem to have gone slightly overboard with this collection of framesets. Because these are all so similar, let's just focus on how you can decode the Dreamweaver MX terminology.

Each of the frameset names is based on the *opposite* of where the primary page content is displayed (or, if you prefer, where the *navigation* elements are displayed). The Left frameset displays the main content in the right side of the screen, whereas the Top frameset uses the bottom of the screen. The Top/Left, Bottom/Left, and so on framesets move the content into one of the corners of the screen. Obviously you have quite a selection to choose from—and, if you want something different, you can easily modify the framesets once they're added to the page.

At the far right of the Insert panel's Frame category are four icons that can be used to insert the tags required to manually work with frames.

Forms

Forms are most commonly used in interactive applications, which you'll be learning about next week. The elements of a form enable the users to input data in a simple and familiar way. Let's take a look at what you can add to a form using the Dreamweaver MX interface. In Figure 1.11, you can see the elements available for form design.

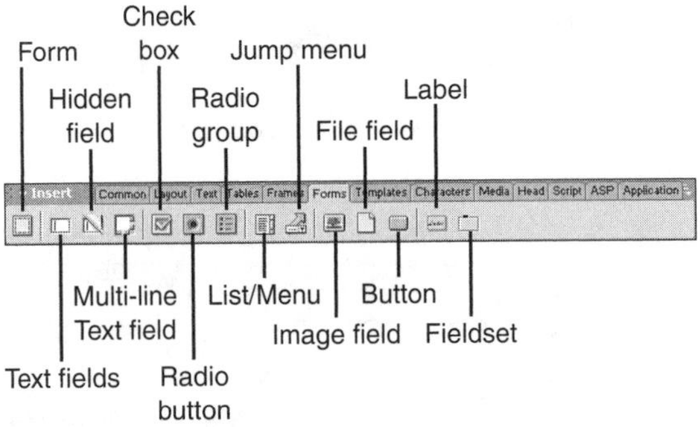

FIGURE 1.11

All elements you need for form design are in a single place.

Form—The most important tag in any form is the `<form>` tag itself. This tag is used to tell the remote server what to do with data that it receives from the users. This is the first element that you should use when defining a form. Although the tag itself is considered an invisible element (meaning that it doesn't show up on the displayed page), it is represented in the Dreamweaver MX document design window as a dotted red rectangle. The rectangle expands to encompass all the form elements that you put in it.

Text fields—These are single line text fields. These are the most common type of input on HTML forms. You can set this element to be either of type text or password—the latter of which hides user input as it is typed into the field.

Hidden field—Hidden fields are used to store data that is needed by the program processing the data, but does not necessarily need to be shown to the user such as the email address that a feedback form will be sent to.

Multi-line text fields—Like normal text fields, these are used to collect information from the browser. Multi-line text fields, however, span several lines and can collect large amounts of data in a single form field.

Check box—Check boxes are commonly used on forms to represent multiple possible options; that is, "Choose all that apply."

Radio button—The radio button is similar to the check box, but instead of being used for multiple selections of several attributes, it is used to choose a single option from a set of options; that is, "Choose the option that best suits your needs."

Radio group—A single radio button is a reasonably rare (in fact, unseen) element. You'll typically see groups of radio buttons on pages, representing different possible options. The radio group feature adds and organizes multiple radio buttons on your Web page automatically.

List/menu—Selection lists are one of more unusual of the HTML language. Depending on how you set the attributes for a selection list, it can appear as a single pop-up menu allowing for one item to be selected, or as a scrolling list of options from which multiple items can be chosen. In some browsers, these two variations of the same element can have drastically different appearances.

Jump menu—The Jump menu is a composite of JavaScript and the List/Menu option. It is not intended to be used with a data submission form. Its purpose is to provide a convenient pop-up navigation menu that can be used on any page to help the users maneuver through the site. There is no need to add a form tag before adding a Jump menu—one is added automatically.

Image field—Image fields are commonly used as form submit buttons, and they do work very well for that function. The data returned from an Image field, however, is a bit more complicated. Not only do they return the name of the image clicked, but they also return the coordinates of where the mouse clicked. There are several "click the secret location" prize games that use this technique to find their winners.

File field—The File field is rarely used, but can be extremely useful for some applications. File fields add a Browse button to the form that can be used to select a file from the user's local drive. The file is then uploaded along with the other fields when the form is submitted. An example of its use is a design company that allows its clients to upload artwork for use in the design and layout process.

Button—Buttons are used to submit or reset the contents of a form.

The final two panel icons, Label and Fieldset, are used to insert the `<label>` and `<fieldset>` tags into the HTML document. They have no "visual" effect on the design, but are used to logically group and label elements.

Templates

Templates are a unique element of Dreamweaver MX that are useful when you want to build a Web site without content, and then pass off the task of filling in the pages to someone else. The problem with this process has typically been entrusting the page layout to other people. It's *easy* to mess up a complex Web page, and there's nothing worse than having to fix pages that were perfectly fine when you originally created them. Templates solve this problem by allowing the author to lock down parts of the content.

The Template category of the Insert panel, demonstrated in Figure 1.12, provides a few common tools that are used with templates.

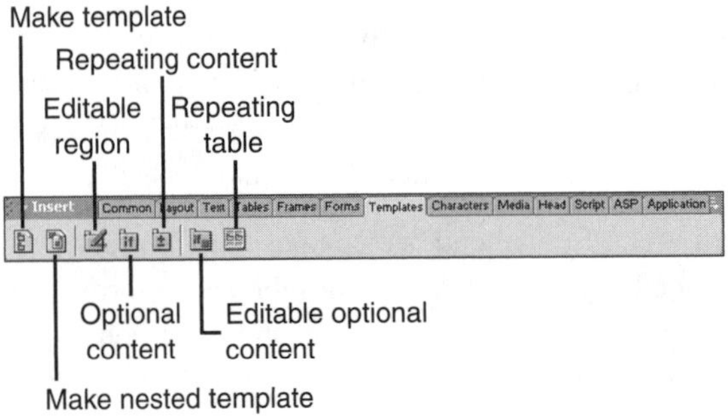

FIGURE 1.12

Template elements are used when adding template constraints to a page.

Make template— Create a new template from the document that is currently open in the design window.

Make Nested template—A nested template is a template that is defined based inside a parent "base" template. This is used to create a very general "site template" with headers and footers, then nest specific templates within this base template for different portions of your side.

Editable region—Defines an area of the template Web page that is "optional." It can either be hidden or displayed based on certain conditions.

Optional content—Adds a content region that might not be displayed on pages based on the template.

Repeating content—Sets up an area of content in the template that will be repeated multiple times. Typically used with tables.

Editable optional content—Identical to the Editable region, but defines the optional content as "editable" within the template.

Repeating table—Inserts a table of repeating content. This is a shortcut for applying the Repeating Content tool to tables.

Templates are a great feature for anyone who works in a distributed Web production environment and wants to retain control over their design. You'll learn how to make templates from existing Web pages later this week.

Characters

To insert a character wherever the insertion point is located, click the appropriate button in the Character panel. The panel's icons are shown in Figure 1.13.

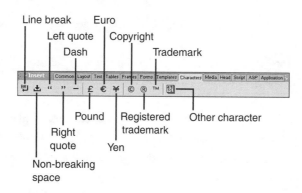

FIGURE 1.13

Click a character to insert it into the Web page.

> **Tip**
>
> Typing a return in the design view is not the same as inserting a line break. Pressing Return will insert <p> </p> into the HTML. This is the equivalent of a double space and will not result in elements that fall directly under one another. To insert a line break without clicking anything, hold down Shift and press Return. Additionally, you might want to simply use two line breaks in a row to create double-spaced lines. The tags

 are a bit cleaner than the paragraph markup with a nonbreaking space stuck in the middle.

If you don't see the characters you need listed in the main panel, click the Other Character button. This will open another window with a large selection of special characters.

Media

Today's Web sites are continually adding new forms of media. Images are passe, Flash is in! If you want to add Flash, Java, ActiveX, or other special content to your Web page, the Media elements, displayed in Figure 1.14, provide what you need to get the job done.

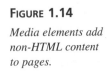

FIGURE 1.14

Media elements add non-HTML content to pages.

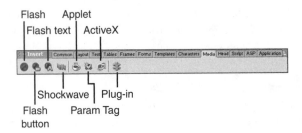

Flash—Inserts a Flash animation file into the page. You'll need Macromedia Flash to create these files.

Flash button—Inserts a Flash animated button with a custom label into the document. This button is created on-the-fly and does not require Flash to be present on your system.

Flash text—Inserts Flash vector text into the document. Unlike standard HTML text, you can use any font you prefer in the document. Again, Flash is *not* required.

Shockwave—Inserts a Shockwave animation into the HTML. Macromedia Director is used to author Shockwave files.

Applet—Java applets are programs that provide desktop-application style functionality, but are platform independent and can run in a browser window.

Param—Used to construct an HTML <param> tag using the Tag Editor tool.

ActiveX—Similar to the Netscape plug-in tool, but is intended for Internet Explorer site development.

Plug-in—Allows custom plug-ins to be inserted for viewing specialized data.

Head

The Head elements are some of the most important elements to include for a successful Web site deployment. These elements aren't actually seen in the document design view, but they are visible to search engines. Not using these features can mean the difference between clients being able to find your Web site and turning up as site 10,109 out of 2,534,222. Figure 1.15 displays the available Head elements.

FIGURE 1.15

Head elements are invisible, but important.

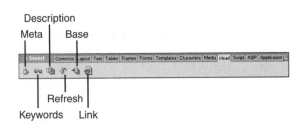

1

Meta—Inserts an arbitrary metatag and lets you define the contents. Certain tags aren't handled directly in the Dreamweaver MX environment, such as content rating. You can use this generic element to insert the tags in your page.

Keywords—Sets a list of words that can be used to define your site. Many search engines use these keywords to categorize and classify your site. Many Web sites count on the search engine to classify the site correctly based on the contents of its pages—yet the information on pages varies from one to another. Setting keywords guarantees consistency and positions your site using its strongest properties.

Description—This is a description of the contents of a page. Similar to the keywords, this is used by some search engines when displaying summary information for a URL.

Refresh—Allows you to create a Web page that will automatically reload, or load a new URL after a specified number of seconds. This is useful for creating a Welcome To page that transfers visitors to the main site—or for displaying information that changes with time on a dynamically generated page.

Base—Sets a base URL to which all links on a page are relative. If you are creating a page containing a list of links to `http://mysite.com/`, you could specify that as the base. Then your link tags only need to reference the documents themselves, rather than the entire URL.

Link—Used to define a relationship to another document. Most frequently you will use this to link a cascading style sheet into your document.

Scripts

The Scripts category contains a total of three items, as seen in Figure 1.16. This panel is used to insert JavaScript/VBScript and server-side includes into HTML documents.

Script

Server-Side Includes

FIGURE 1.16

Use the Scripts category to insert server-side includes or your own JavaScript/VBScript code.

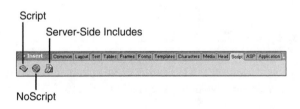

NoScript

Script—The Scripts object inserts JavaScript or VBScript into the current document. As a bonus, it also adds the appropriate supporting `language` and noscript tags automatically. This is useful for programmers or those inserting pre-made JavaScript into their pages.

NoScript—To insert alternative content for those who can't run embedded scripts, use the NoScript element.

Server-Side Includes—A server-side include is a piece of code executed by your Web server—usually to include headers and footers. SSIs aren't dependant on a programming language, rather special tags defined by your Web server.

Server Platform

If you're building a dynamic application and have chosen a server platform, you might see a twelfth tab named after the platform you've chosen (such as ASP). This tab will contain shortcuts for inserting server code into your document. It is mainly of use to programmers wishing to access common language functions and constructs.

Application Objects

Because Dreamweaver MX is a dynamic authoring tool, obviously you'll spend a great deal of time working with dynamic pages. Rather than starting from scratch each time, you can use these built-in objects to get a quick start on your pages (see Figure 1.17).

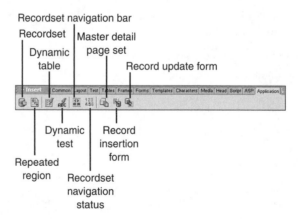

FIGURE 1.17

Application objects add functionality beyond what is possible using standard HTML and JavaScript.

Recordset—A recordset is a collection of information pulled from a database. The first step in creating a dynamic page is adding a recordset that will be used to drive the content of the page.

Repeated region—Repeating regions are used to display multiple records stored in a recordset. Rather than adding every single piece of information to a page individually, Dreamweaver can cycle through each record in a database and add it automatically.

Dynamic table—Quickly inserts a database table into a page. This is a very common design element, and the Dynamic table makes it very easy to set up.

Dynamic text—Adds text from a database table field into a document. This tool is actually a more convoluted way of doing something that is simple to begin with.

Recordset navigation bar—Browsing records in a database is made possible by a navigation bar that lets you step forward and backward through the records. The navigation bar provides this functionality.

Recordset navigation status—Used in conjunction with the recordset navigation bar, the status shows the users where they are (record 3 of 10, and so on) within the database.

Master detail set—Many dynamic pages are built from a master page that lists the records in the database and a detail page that shows details of a record after clicking it. This object provides a basis for this type of site.

Record insertion form—Sets up a basic form for inserting data into a database.

Record update form—Sets up a basic form for updating existing data in the database.

The Properties Panel

Each element that you add to a Web page, be it image, text, or any other object, has properties that can change how it looks in a Web browser. Text can be set to certain colors; images can be altered to different widths or heights. Rather than create a different configuration dialog box for each object that you can edit, a single floating palette, called the Properties panel, handles everything. Whatever item is currently selected on your screen is configurable through the Properties window. As you switch from one element to another, the contents of the property window change as well—automatically. Try, for example, selecting some text that you've typed into your document design window. Figure 1.18 shows the properties for basic page text.

FIGURE 1.18

The Properties panel shows the attributes that can be modified for the selected object.

The Properties window itself has a few different modes that can be activated depending on the level of detail you want to work with. If you're a beginner, you might want to view the properties in the simple mode. To do this, collapse the window to its smallest size by clicking the up arrow in the lower-right corner of the window. If the arrow is pointing down, the window is already collapsed, and clicking the arrow will toggle into expert mode, providing several additional options. Most of this book will refer to the Properties panel in this mode.

Two other features provide useful shortcuts to additional Dreamweaver MX functionality. The first is the Help icon located in the upper-right corner of the Properties window. This will launch the help system and display information about the attributes you are editing. This is an excellent way to get context-sensitive information about an object without resorting to a reference manual.

The Quick Tag Editor

The second feature, in my opinion, is one of the greatest features of the Dreamweaver MX environment. Clicking the icon directly below the help icon launches the Quick Tag Editor. The Quick Tag Editor simply brings up a pop-up window that contains the HTML for the tag being edited. You can change any of the HTML in the tag directly. Although this might not seem like a very big feature, sometimes you know exactly what you want to change on a tag, but you don't want to search through the source code or deal with going through an interface to find it. The Quick Tag Editor gives you exactly what you want and doesn't force you to use a GUI interface to make your changes.

If you're working in the document design window and have an item selected, you can bring up the Quick Tag Editor by choosing Quick Tag Editor from the Modify menu. This enables you to directly access the HTML you need without needing the Properties window.

 Tip

Control+T (Windows) or Command+T (Macintosh) can be used to easily access the Quick Tag Editor. Because this is a handy feature, you might want to make a mental note of the keyboard shortcut.

The Menu System

The menu system under Dreamweaver MX is very simple to understand. Most of the functionality of the tool palettes is replicated under the available menus, so you'll probably spend very little time with the menu system, and most of your time in the document and panel windows. Here is a brief overview of what you can expect to find under the menu system:

    File—Open and Save HTML documents. Anything related to opening files, importing data from external sources, or saving HTML is located here. You'll notice that there are some options you probably don't immediately recognize, such as Templates and Design Notes. For now, if you aren't sure of what an item does, don't worry about it. You'll learn everything there is to know about the Dreamweaver MX features as the week progresses.

Edit—Cut, Copy, Paste, and Search objects within Document view. From within the Edit menu, you can also adjust the Dreamweaver MX preferences. Later today you'll learn about these preferences and which settings can help you during your design.

View—What optional elements are being displayed in your document design view? The View menu controls what is currently visible. As you begin to add elements to your HTML, you'll find this menu very helpful in hiding guidelines and table borders so that you can get a better feel for how the final page is going to look.

Insert—If you'd rather use a menu to add items to your page, the Insert menu can be used to add images and other elements corresponding to the tool palettes directly to your HTML. There is no difference between using this menu and the Insert panel icons.

Modify—The Modify menu enables you to change items on your page. This menu is most useful when you have selected an item on the page and want to modify it. You can use Modify to change a selection to a link and to alter the layout of certain elements, such as tables.

Text—From the Text menu, you can control the attributes of the text you are typing or the text of a selection box. These selections are similar to their word processing counterparts: Font, Size, Style, and so on. Despite the name, the Text menu also contains a number of functions, such as alignment, that can be used to adjust other onscreen elements.

Commands—The Dreamweaver MX command menu puts you in control of an easy-to-use macro-creation system. Record sequences of events and play them back to create new commands. Additionally, you can download libraries of commands free from Macromedia. Also, a few miscellaneous commands are included in this menu that can be used to clean up HTML and alter your page's color scheme, among other things. Day 5, "Creating Reusable Components," will teach you how to make your own commands.

Site—Although Dreamweaver MX can be used to build single Web pages, its capability to manage entire Web sites makes it an extremely powerful tool for beginners and pros. The Site menu controls the definition of Web sites and their attributes. Day 6, "Introduction to Dynamic Web Applications and Database Design," will document the site tools and explain how they can be used to manage sites of any size.

Window—Hide or show any of the windows and palettes that are discussed in this text. If the book is discussing a certain window that seems as if it should be on your screen, but isn't, this is where you should look to find it.

Help—The Dreamweaver MX Help system can be launched at any time from the Help window. The Help system is HTML and Java-based and runs from your Web browser, so it might seem a bit strange at times to switch between different applications in order to read help screens. Luckily, the online manual is quite extensive, and more than makes up for the awkward interface. You also have access to a wide variety of tutorials that can help you immediately get started with the system.

Tip

Contextual menus exist for many of the functions that you use to edit objects. To access the contextual menu, select an object, and then right-click (Windows) or Control-click (Mac) on it.

Keyboard Shortcuts

As you're certainly accustomed to seeing in other large applications, Dreamweaver MX has a number of keyboard shortcuts that can save you a significant amount of mousing time. What *isn't* common to many programs is the capability to assign new keyboard shortcuts to menu functions. To assign a new shortcut, choose Keyboard Shortcuts from the Edit menu. The shortcut window is shown in Figure 1.19.

FIGURE 1.19

Keyboard shortcuts can save you time and your mousing hand.

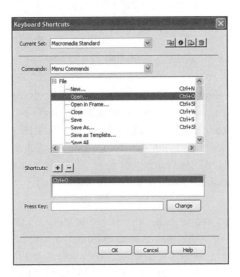

At the top of Keyboard Shortcuts window is the Current Set pop-up menu containing prebuilt shortcut sets. You might recognize several of these sets as mirroring popular editing packages. You can use the four buttons at the top of the window to duplicate, rename, export, or delete sets.

Editing a Shortcut

To edit a shortcut in the current set, follow these steps:

1. Choose the type of commands you want to edit from the Commands pop-up menu.
2. Navigate through the hierarchical list of possible functions in the scrolling window in the middle of the window.
3. Click on a function to select it.
4. Click the + button to add a new shortcut for the selected function.
5. In the Press Key field, press the key combination you want to use to activate the selected function.
6. Click the Change button to active the new shortcut.
7. If necessary, use the - button to "unattach" a shortcut from a function.

When you've created or changed all the shortcuts you need, click the OK button to continue using Dreamweaver MX.

The Other Windows and Panels

The other panels used in the Dreamweaver MX environment are important, but have a very limited range of relevance. As you work through the book, their functions will be discussed where appropriate. To get an idea when you'll be seeing these panels, here is a short list of the other panels you'll be using. These are located in the panel groups on the right side of your screen, or under the Windows menu.

Data bindings—Defines and edits connections to live data sources. This will be used extensively in Weeks 2 and 3 when we start to build dynamic Web sites.

Server behaviors—Also necessary for dynamic sites, Server Behaviors control how information is processed by the remote Web server.

Databases—Databases provide the information used inside a dynamic site. The Databases panel is used to define and view databases connected to the current site.

Components—Used to add JavaBeans or Web services to the application. This panel mainly of use to advanced developers.

Site—The site files window contains the tools you need to keep track of your Web site's files and synchronize them with remote servers.

Site Map—Although part of the Site window, the Site Map is an entirely separate tool. One of the hardest parts about maintaining a site is keeping track of how the pages connect and the paths that the users can take to reach different pieces of information. Dreamweaver MX can generate a map of your Web site for easy reference.

Assets—Site Assets are all the images, colors, and other objects in use on your site. You do not need to manually create the Assets panel—Dreamweaver MX will update it for you. The Assets panel is an excellent way to keep track of everything on your site.

Behaviors—The Behaviors panel is used to add JavaScript actions to objects on a Web page. The behaviors are generated automatically, without any need for knowledge of the JavaScript language.

Code Inspector—Want direct access to the HTML and JavaScript? This is the option you need. This is largely redundant considering the HTML view mode of the design window.

CSS Styles—*Cascading style sheets (CSS)* are the w3C standard for controlling the look and feel of your Web site down to the pixel size of the font being used. This panel contains all the defined styles and allows you to edit and apply them.

Frames—If you're creating a Web site that uses frames, you'll probably want an easy way to control them. The Frames panel lets you select and modify individual frame attributes.

History—If you've ever used Photoshop, you'll recognize the History panel immediately. The History contains a list of all the changes that you've made to the Web document. You can immediately back up to any state that the document has been in since it was last saved. The history can hold between 2 and 99,999 steps, with the default being 50. You can reset this value in the General section of the Dreamweaver MX preferences.

HTML Styles—Unfortunately, CSS Styles only work in browsers that support them (4.0 or greater). Luckily, Dreamweaver MX gives you a similar functionality to CSS by using HTML styles. HTML styles are simply standard HTML tags (`<font>`,`<b>`), but can be applied all at once to a selection of HTML.

Layers—Layers are a very powerful tool, but because they can exist on top of one another and be entirely invisible, it's often difficult to find the layer you want to edit. The Layer panel shows you a list of all the defined layers in a single location.

Reference—The Reference panel is an extremely detailed reference for cascading style sheets, HTML, and JavaScript. If you're interested in the technology behind the code you create, everything you need to know is right here.

Sitespring Tasks—Dreamweaver MX integrates with Macromedia Sitespring collaboration server software to provide a seamless Web production environment. The Sitespring Tasks panel is used for managing connections to the server.

Snippets—The Snippet panel holds small code fragments that you can use with your site.

Timelines—Through the use of JavaScript and layers, portions of a Web page can be animated over time. The Timeline panel enables you to visually set the position of layers against time.

Tag Inspector—Displays a hierarchical view of the current Web page. HTML tags can be collapsed or expanded to show detail. Much more useful than the Code Inspector.

Answers—Provides quick access to the Dreamweaver MX help system, online Macromedia resources, and tutorials.

With all the different windows and panels you can have open at a time, your screen can quickly become filled with all the different elements of the Dreamweaver MX environment. You can quickly collapse all the panels by clicking the center of the divider bar that separates the panels from the main content area of the screen.

By default, Dreamweaver MX arranges different panels into panel groups, which contain similar features, as seen in Figure 1.20.

FIGURE 1.20

The Dreamweaver MX interface organizes elements into groups of related panels.

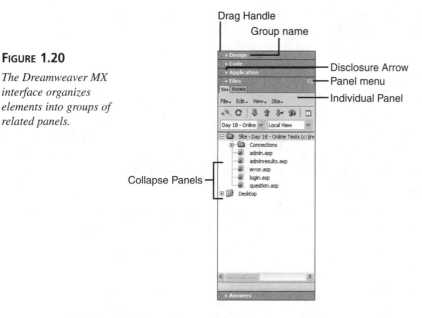

You can collapse panel groups into a single line or expand them to show the entire panel by using the disclosure arrow in front of the panel name. These groups are then listed as part of the complete panel collection, usually located down the right side of your screen.

You can move individual panels between groups by bringing up a contextual menu for their respective tab, or by using the panel menu and choosing the appropriate "Group With" options.

The "Group With" submenu contains a list of all of the available panel groups. Choosing one of the group names will immediately transfer the current panel into the chosen group. If you don't like Macromedia's predetermined groups, you can easily rearrange them as you please. If you want to create a brand new group and place panels under it, use the Group With submenu's "New Panel Group" selection. This will add a new group name to the list and let you add one or more panels to it.

With the number of panels and panel groups available, things can very quickly get confusion. To hide individual panel groups, deselect them under the Window menu, or use the Hide Panels option to hide all of them at once. If you'd like to straighten-up your panel arrangement, choose "Arrange Panels" from the Window menu. Dreamweaver MX will attempt to arrange the floating windows as best it can (Floating Workspace mode only).

Also available for Floating Workspace users is the ability to edit Dreamweaver MX preferences so that certain panels can float above or be hidden by other windows. In the default state, all panels float to the top, covering anything underneath them. Use the Preference's Panel category to set the float state for each panel individually.

Getting Help

Dreamweaver MX has extensive help for almost all the functions, windows, and buttons you see on the screen. As you already learned, tooltips are prevalent throughout the interface, but the primary help system contains far more detailed information on using the software. Choosing Using Dreamweaver MX from the Help menu displays the online help system, demonstrated in Figure 1.21.

In addition to the general usage information, Dreamweaver MX also provides extensive reference information and can easily locate anything you'd ever want to know about HTML, ASP, PHP, and the other built-in languages. When we start looking at HTML code this week, you'll learn more about this feature.

 Tip

Another source for help is the Answers panel, accessible by choosing Window, Others and Answers from the menu bar. This panel provides quick links to tutorials, help, and online resources.

FIGURE 1.21

The Dreamweaver MX help system provides detailed instructions for finding your way around the system.

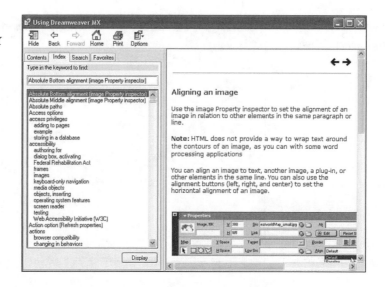

Customizing the Dreamweaver MX Preferences

Today ends on a short discussion of the Dreamweaver MX preferences. There are more than a few attributes of the default Dreamweaver MX settings that you might want to change before you start using the program full-time. For example, the panel windows can be configured to fall beneath other windows, rather than remain on top. This is useful for smaller screens so that they don't overwhelm the main design view. Let's take a look at the available preferences now by selecting Preferences from the Edit menu (or the Dreamweaver MX application menu in Mac OS X). Figure 1.22 shows the initial Preferences window.

Twenty (yes, you read that right!) different categories of settings can alter the function and appearance of Dreamweaver MX. Here's what you can set in each of the preference areas:

General—Configures the dictionary, look and feel of the Dreamweaver environment and panels, and options to be used when saving or opening files. If you want to change the tool panel so that it displays text labels with the icons, this is where you do it. Additionally, you can configure the number of stored history steps here.

Accessibility—Dreamweaver can add important accessibility attributes to HTML objects as they are added to your design. Use these settings to choose which objects will display additional attributes in their dialog boxes when being defined.

FIGURE 1.22

Many options can be configured in the Preferences window.

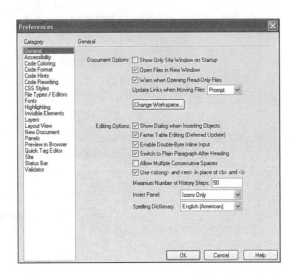

Code coloring—Dreamweaver MX lets you set up the colors that are used to highlight the source HTML for a Web page. In the default configuration, only a few tags are defined—you might want to define colors for some of the other tag types.

Code format—You can configure how the HTML is generated for elements by setting the attributes in this section. If you are deploying from a Macintosh system, you can adjust the "end of line" characters so they show up correctly on Windows computers and vice versa. The Override case option lets you tell Dreamweaver MX to override the case of tags and attributes that you add to the code. This makes the code much cleaner, easier to read, and compliant with the HTML 4.0x recommendations and XHTML spec.

Code hints—If you code HTML by hand, you'll love the code hints feature. Code hints are used to automatically complete HTML tags and display hints about the tag that you are typing (tag names, attributes, and so on).

Code rewriting—Dreamweaver MX will attempt to fix problems with HTML that is loaded into the editor. You can configure the program to *never* fix potential problems by disabling all the rewrite rules. I often create files that are included in other HTML files at the server level, and, as such, are *not* valid HTML. If I open these files in Dreamweaver MX, they become functionally broken. Because of this, I make sure that all the rewriting is turned off.

CSS styles—Controls how Dreamweaver MX writes the CSS styles. You can select a shorthand style rather than the traditional format. Unfortunately, although easier to read, this format is not compatible with some browsers. There is little need to change the options on this screen.

File types/editors—Configures how Dreamweaver MX interacts with external editors. You can add and configure the default editors for different file types, such as GIFs, JPEGs, and other file formats that are likely to be used in your Web site.

Fonts—These options are similar to the Font preferences in standard Web browsers. Configure the default screen fonts for the design view as well as the HTML source editor.

Highlighting—Highlights are used to denote editable and non-editable items in template-based files. Here you can set the colors that are used for these highlights.

Invisible elements—When invisible elements are inserted into the HTML, Dreamweaver MX inserts an icon into the design view. These can be a bit annoying, so you are given the option of shutting them off. Turn them on and off here if you prefer.

Layers—As you add layers to your document, you might want to set some of the default attributes for the layer. These preferences control the initial state of a layer when it is created. If you're interested in changing the default background color, width, or height, you've found the right place. Otherwise, I recommend that you leave the default settings alone.

Layout view—Choose how Dreamweaver MX maintains cell spacing in the tables created within the free-form Layout mode. You can also set the manner in which layout tables are displayed onscreen. You'll learn more about the Layout mode tomorrow.

New document—Used on a per-site basis to determine what type of document the New command will create.

Panels—The floating panels can be toggled from the default Stay On Top state to behave more like traditional windows. At the same time, you can also add any of the object panels to the launcher panel at the bottom of the document design window. This is a good way to quickly create a fast and easy way to get to your most frequently used tools.

Preview in browser—Configures the browsers that are available for previewing your creation. Add browsers to the Preview in Browser menu and set command keys to launch a preview at the touch of a button.

Quick tag editor—Adjusts a few options for the Quick Tag Editor.

Site—Sets attributes for the network FTP connection to your production server and the display of the site files. If you are not using FTP, many of these options are not likely to be useful.

Status bar—Adds items to the browser window size options and toggles the default speed setting for estimating page download times.

Validator—Dreamweaver MX can validate your Web page code against a large number of standards. The validator settings determine the standards that will be used as a basis for your documents.

If you want more information about the individual options available in the preferences, just click the Help button—each of the preference options is extremely well documented in the online help. The options that I typically change are documented as they are used, but you might want to click through the different screens to see whether there is something that can make your life easier.

Summary

Today you familiarized yourself with the Dreamweaver MX environment. If you have any problems finding your way around, take time to look around the interface and explore the available tool panels and control windows. In the next few days, you'll create Web pages and become familiar with using the tools on real HTML documents.

Don't feel overwhelmed by the Dreamweaver MX interface. It encompasses a huge range of tools and can take a while to get used to. I still find myself having to scan through the menus occasionally to locate options.

Workshop

The Workshop area is meant to reinforce your reading with a series of questions, answers, and exercises.

Q&A

Q I've been going through the Dreamweaver MX interface on a shared computer at work, and the options do not look anything like they do in the book. What's wrong?

A The Dreamweaver MX interface is completely open for editing and expansion. If you're using a copy that has been customized, it's entirely possible that it bears little resemblance to the default state. You'll need to re-install the software to replace the customized layout with the original configuration.

Q I can't remember what the palette icons refer to, and I hate the tooltips. What can I do?

A Use the General preferences to change the Object Panel view type to Text or Icons and Text. This will keep a constant label on the screen and make it easier to pick out the tools you need.

Q **I've started to add to a Web page, but I keep getting a message saying I need to define a site. What is the problem?**

A Tomorrow you'll define your first Web site. For now, if you choose to play around, just ignore this message and click Cancel. Dreamweaver does not function well as a single-page editor and bases its operation on the editing of *sites* rather than pages.

Quiz

1. Which window is used to adjust the attributes of objects that are added to your pages?

2. The floating palettes are great, but you switch between the design view and a panel. The panel window keeps floating on top. How can you fix it?

3. How can you set a new shortcut for a Dreamweaver MX menu item?

Quiz Answers

1. The Properties window provides a one-stop-shop in order to pick and choose the attributes you want to set for a particular element.

2. Turn off the Always On Top attribute of the panel by editing the Dreamweaver MX Panel preferences.

3. Choose Keyboard Shortcuts from the Edit menu.

Exercises

1. Add highlight colors to the HTML tags used in the source editing view. This will help you find your way around when you have to go into the HTML directly.

2. Configure the browsers that are available for previewing your Web site. It's useful to have both Internet Explorer and Netscape installed to make sure that your pages look reasonably similar on both platforms.

DAY **2**

Creating Your First Web Site

Now that you understand the basics of the Dreamweaver MX workspace, you're ready to get down to business. The tools for creating stunning and easy to manage Web sites are just itching to be used. In this chapter, you will:

- Learn the steps that you should take before you create your first Web site.
- Use the Site Files window to organize and add files to your Web site.
- Insert images and links, and use the Properties window to adjust their attributes.
- Discover how to use tables for precise positioning of elements.

Design Considerations

I know what you're thinking; you're ready to start using the Dreamweaver MX tools and design your Web site…so why aren't we jumping right in? Before you get started, there are a few points of Web design that I'd like to stress—most notably that every attractive and successful Web site starts with research and planning.

Know Your Customer

Creating a site can be a tremendous amount of fun, but it also requires some forethought. You should determine whom your site is for before you start building it. If, for example, you're trying to sell yourself as a Web designer, you shouldn't put up a plain gray screen with a text copy of your resume (or one exported from Microsoft Word…yick!). At the opposite end of the spectrum, there is no reason to include heavy graphic elements on a page that is designed to quickly provide mainly text-based information to its visitors. The best site is balanced and uses some graphical elements to supplement the textual information, not just for looks.

Plan for the Lowest Common Denominator

If the purpose of your Web site is providing information, be sure to take into account the different browsers that might be trying to access the information. Coming from a UNIX background, I often find myself at a command prompt needing access to a piece of information on a site. In a snap, I can use the Lynx text-based Web browser to call up a Web page and find what I'm looking for. For example, here is copy of the Apple (www.apple.com) home page in a text browser:

```
#home index

Apple The Apple Store iTools iCards QuickTime Apple Support Mac OS X
Hot News Hardware Software Made4Mac Education Creative Small Biz
Developer Where to Buy

Double feature.
                The Dual 1GHz Power Mac G4 Power Mac G4

NVIDIA GeForce4 Graphics - SuperDrive (CD-RW/DVD-R) - L2 and L3 Cache
                - Gigabit Ethernet - $2,999

                Hot News Headlines Hot News Ticker

   The new iMac. iPhoto. Free download. The missing link in digital
photography. 14-inch iBook New apps. Developers deliver for Mac OS X.

                                          Search
                    Site Map | Search Tips
```

As hideous as this might seem to those accustomed to styled text, colors, and animation, all the navigation and supporting text is clearly visible. It is a perfect example of a Web site that was designed to support any type of browser technology—not just the latest and greatest plug-ins.

HTML was written with the lowest common denominator in mind. Although graphics are everywhere on the Internet, many of them could easily be replaced with descriptive text. By setting an `alt` attribute within an image tag, you can set a line or two of text that is displayed when the page is loaded. This feature is absolutely critical in creating pages that are accessible to the blind—who are often *read* the contents of a page via special software.

Keep It Clean

No, I'm not talking about the contents of your site, but the HTML. If you're comfortable with editing HTML by hand (which you'll learn about today), it's very tempting to add and tweak tags yourself. If you do this, remember to keep the HTML clean. Dreamweaver MX does everything it can to make sure there are end tags and that the code is correct. Unfortunately, it can still make mistakes. Depending on your coding habits, you might end up confusing Dreamweaver MX and having your HTML automatically rewritten in ways that you didn't intend—think of it as a Microsoft Word-like "Autocorrect" feature. This can be turned off in the Dreamweaver "Code Rewriting" preferences, but doing so can increase the likelihood of manual errors.

Develop a Site Map

Planning is one of the most important phases in the design of a Web site. Much like "painting yourself into a corner," designing a Web site opens the possibility of creating "dead ends" for the user in terms of navigation. If multiple people are designing the site, it becomes even more critical to carefully plan its construction to avoid any chance of differing styles in layout and navigation.

As I'm sure you've all experienced, it's too easy to get lost on a Web site. Navigation bars switch sides, links disappear and reappear, and the design of the pages themselves might vary from section to section. Some Web sites even feature someone else's content, contained within a frame on their pages.

Proper planning can eliminate these problems and more, and a site map is a great place to start. Much like a storyboard "maps" out the scenes of a play or film, a site map is a visual representation of the pages, sections, and links within a Web site. It doesn't contain the content of the site, just a guideline of how to get from a good idea in your head to a logical, functional, Web site.

Throughout this book, we're going to work to build a Web site dedicated to dogs. Each day will introduce new features to the site, all of which can be viewed online at `day#.cutelittledogs.com`. For example, today's lesson can be found at `day2.cutelittledogs.com`.

> The Web site for each day (with the obvious exception of Day 1 and a few other informational days) comes in two versions. For Day 2 there are two folders, "Day 2" and "Day 2 Complete." The "Complete" version of the site has all the finished HTML. You should work with the basic "Day x" version so you can follow the steps and build the day's examples on your own.

Figure 2.1 shows the map for what we are going to be developing today—a simple four-page site that includes a basic home page and three internal pages whose content should be obvious based on the names in the site map.

FIGURE 2.1

A site map can ease the process of designing and linking pages in a Web site.

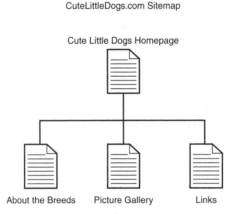

In the site map, pages are grouped by category, and links between these categories are shown with lines. By laying out your site visually before it's built, you can determine the best way for the users to navigate. You can also avoid the problem of having *orphan pages* that are not linked to directly from the rest of the site.

> *Orphan pages* occur when someone designs content for an area of a Web site. It gets built, but is never linked into the bulk of the pages.
>
> I've experienced this firsthand on several occasions when a site has been created without a proper site map. I recently constructed a site following the guidelines that the client had prepared, only to find that it was impossible to reach the About This Company portion of the Web site from any of the other pages. Taking the time to create a simple site map would have solved this problem.

File Layout

Site maps also aid in the actual directory structure that you use while building the site. It is all too common to take over the maintenance of a site and find that every single page is located in the same directory, regardless of its position on the site. The process of creating a site map involves defining the relationships between the pages on the site. Later, when you create the site itself, related pages can be grouped under common directories. This makes finding and manipulating them much easier.

Typically, sites are created with directories for each of the major categories on the site, and an image directory for the images on the pages within that category. You might find that a different layout works better for you. I've had many occasions in which the number of images on an individual page warranted creating a separate image directory for that document. The most important thing to keep in mind is that the structure you're creating will probably have to be maintained by someone else someday.

Lecture over; let's get started!

Creating Your First Web Site

Today, you'll build a small site called `cutelittledogs.com` that contains four pages. Two of these pages we'll build together; two are left as an exercise for you:

- Home
- About the Breeds
- Photo Gallery
- Links

Before you can start authoring Web pages, you must first define a site so that Dreamweaver knows where to find all the files it will need, and where it should save the HTML that you generate. If you tried to create a page in the first day, you might have run into problems when the software asked you to define a site root. Although it is possible to work with the tools without going through this process, you're likely to find problems with the pages you create.

All links created in your document, whether to other pages or to images, should be added relative to the document you are creating. For example, you don't want your images to be linked to `C:\myproject\images\cutepuppy.jpg`. This would cause a broken image link to appear in the browser after uploading the page to a remote Web server. Instead, images should be linked in relation to the location of the HTML file itself: `images\cutepuppy.jpg`. If you attempt to work on Web pages outside of a Dreamweaver "site," it will *not* use relative links and more often then not will "break" the page you're editing. Creating a site enables Dreamweaver MX to keep track of where the files are in relation to each other. If you edit an HTML file and save it to a new folder within the site, Dreamweaver MX will automatically rewrite the links in that page so that they continue to work, even though the document is now located in a new place.

Defining a Site

To start with, you'll need to define a Web site. This is simply a directory on your desktop computer where all the HTML files will be created. From the Site menu, choose Edit Sites. Figure 2.2 shows the Edit Sites dialog box.

FIGURE 2.2

The first thing you'll need to do is define a site to work in.

By choosing Edit Sites rather than New Site, you open a simple manager for all the sites that you've set up on your system. Here you can create a new site, edit/duplicate existing site definitions, import or export sites, and, of course, remove sites. Click the New button to start a new site definition.

 Note

> One of the themes throughout this book is that there are multiple ways to do *everything*. You can certainly just choose New Site from the Site menu, but the Edit Site dialog box gives you the same option and several more.

Those of you who were frustrated with the Site Definitions in the previous "UltraDev" applications (the earlier versions of Dreamweaver MX) will be pleased to see that the Site definition is now set up as a wizard (or an assistant in Mac lingo). You can see the Site Definition dialog box in Figure 2.3.

First, decide what you want to name your site, and type it into the Site Name field. This is an arbitrary name that is only used to identify the site to you; it won't show up on any of the Web pages. For our purposes, use "Day 2" as the site name. Click Next to move on.

FIGURE 2.3

The Site Definition dialog box requires a site name.

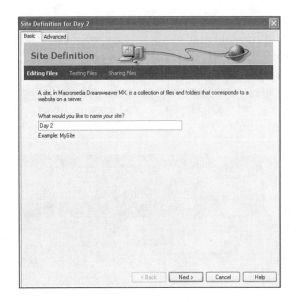

Dreamweaver MX will now prompt you if you want to work with a server technology (to build dynamic database driven pages), as seen in Figure 2.4. Because we aren't to that stage yet, choose "No, I do not want to use a server technology", and then click Next.

FIGURE 2.4

We aren't going to use server-based technologies. Yet.

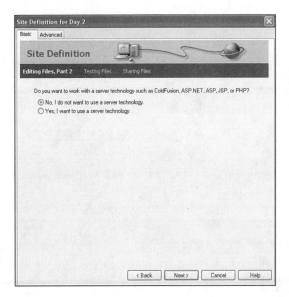

On the third screen of the site definition, Dreamweaver will ask where it should store files on your local computer, and how it is going to connect to a remote server. We're going to get to remote servers tomorrow, so, for now, choose the top option ("Edit local copies on my machine, then upload to server when ready"), as seen in Figure 2.5. Enter in a path where all the site's data will be stored. This is called the *local root folder*. Rather than typing into the field, you can also click the folder button at the end to choose a folder on your local drive.

FIGURE 2.5

Choose to edit the copies on your local computer and pick a directory on your hard drive.

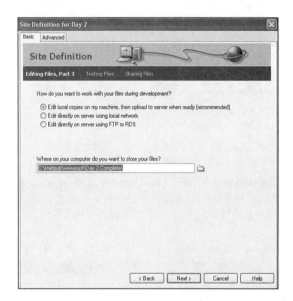

Click Next again, and Dreamweaver MX will prompt you for how you are going to connect to your remote server. We haven't talked about this yet, so, for now, choose None from the pop-up menu, and click Next one last time.

Dreamweaver MX will display a summary of the site definition. Click Done to save the information for your site to your hard drive.

You've just created your first Dreamweaver MX Web site (albeit slightly "light" on content).

How Do I Import an Existing Site?

If you aren't starting from scratch and already have a Web site that you want to work with, there are a number of ways to import it into Dreamweaver MX. The easiest solution is to copy the files to a folder on your local hard drive using external tools (file sharing, FTP, and so on), and then set this folder as your local root folder during the site definition process.

Alternatively, you can define an empty site locally, and then use the remote site access tools to copy the files to your computer. You'll learn about the remote site access methods tomorrow.

Site Files

After you've saved your site definition, Dreamweaver MX will automatically update the Site panel to show the site contents. In the Integrated Workspace mode, the files are in a small panel on the right side of the screen—you must expand this view using expand/collapse icon at the right side of the panel toolbar. The expanded window is shown in Figure 2.6. If the window does not open automatically, choose Site Files from the Window menu. Here you can work with the files needed to build your Web site, much as you would within the Windows Explorer or Macintosh Finder. It's a convenient way to organize things without having to switch in and out of Dreamweaver MX.

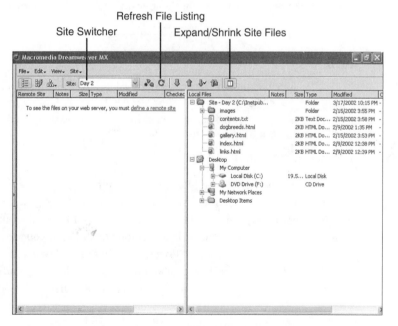

FIGURE 2.6

The Site panel is used to view and manipulate files that are associated with your Web site.

By default, the Site panel displays both the files located locally on your computer, and those that are on a remote server. In Floating Workspace mode, click the arrow in the lower-left corner of the window to hide the remote file listing (not visible in Figure 2.6).

The Site panel is the easiest place to get to the files that make up your site. From the Site panel, you can move files around by clicking and dragging, sort them by clicking the column headings, and open them by double-clicking. New files and folders can be created using Site Files View options located under the Site menu.

Tip

> Dreamweaver MX makes extensive use of contextual menus. Right-clicking (Control-clicking on the Macintosh) on items in the file list lets you perform many basic file functions on the selected object—including deleting and renaming.

The files for the currently active site are shown near the top of the window. Before them is an object called "Computer," which is a hierarchical listing of all the files on your desktop computer and its attached drives. To prepare yourself for the activities of Day 2, use your browser to connect to http://downloads.cutelittledogs.com and download the Day 2 project archive for your computer platform. Unarchive the project files and then drag them into the site folder you've defined for today. You should do this for every lesson in the book, but I'll prompt you, just to make sure you remember!

Note

> For each book project, the http://downloads.cutelittledogs.com/ Web site also includes a version of the project files labeled "completed." These are the finished exercises and should *not* be copied to your site, because you're going to be building them by hand.
>
> If you get stuck, you can always refer to the completed files for each lesson, but be sure to try it yourself first!

An interesting note about the Site Files view is that it is an "intelligent" means of managing your files. Unlike the file system on your computer, when you drag a file from one folder to another in your site, the Dreamweaver MX file manager understands that this move might have consequences. It will automatically scan your documents and make sure that any links to or from the document being moved will still work. With these conveniences (and others you'll learn about later), you're likely to find that the site window quickly becomes one of your most frequently visited screens.

Creating and Editing the Home Page

Now you're ready to get started. As defined in the site map earlier, the basic Web site is going to consist of four pages:

- Home
- About the Breeds
- Photo Gallery
- Links

The Home page is defined as the top of the Web site—the first page that a users see when they go to your Web address. Typically this page will provide a welcome message to the readers, a general overview of the site, and links to the appropriate content areas.

Although the names of all the other files in your site are arbitrary, the home page often has a special name that is designated by the server that is hosting the site. Most Windows servers, for example, use the name `Default.htm`. Mac, Linux, and UNIX servers typically use `index.html` or `index.htm`. Your server manager will know for sure. For this example, I'll be using `index.html`.

Note   Don't spend too much time worrying about the default home page name. As long as you use the Site window to rename your files, there will be no problem changing the name in the future.

To create a new page, choose New from the File menu. Dreamweaver MX will display the New Document dialog box, as shown in Figure 2.7.

FIGURE 2.7

Choose the type of document to create.

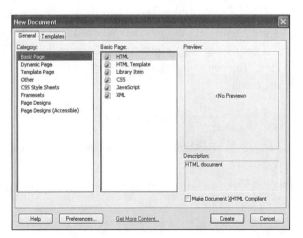

The Category selection allows you to choose between blank documents, templates, and stationrry. We want to start with a Blank Document, so be sure that it is highlighted. Next, in the category items list, pick HTML Page. Finally, click the Create button.

In the lower-right corner of the new document dialog, you'll see a check box labeled Make Document XHTML Compliant. Checking this box will force Dreamweaver MX to write code that is compliant with the W3C's XHTML 1.0 specification (http://www.w3.org/TR/2001/WD-xhtml1-20011004/). XHTML is HTML 4.0 defined using XML. As the world moves toward XML for data exchange, XHTML is the next step in advancing HTML to a modern an extensible standard.

If you're authoring pages for a modern audience, you might want to activate this option. If you have existing software that parses Web pages (search engines, link checkers, and the like), they might not yet be updated to work with the new standard.

Your new document will open in the workspace. (You could also create a new file in the site files window using the Site Files menu or contextual menu, as discussed earlier.)

Before doing anything else, choose Save As from the File menu, enter the appropriate name for your home page, and save the file into your Web site directory.

Until a file is saved, Dreamweaver MX will not recognize that it is part of a site and might miswrite links to other documents.

You should now have a blank HTML document open in your editor, waiting anxiously for content. Figure 2.8 displays the new, named document (index.html). Finally, to set this document as your home page, right-click its icon in the Site Files listing and choose Set as Home Page. You can also choose Set as Home Page from the Site Map View submenu of the Site menu.

FIGURE 2.8

Your home page is now ready and waiting for content.

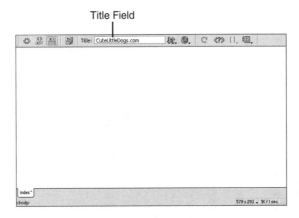

As a final step in preparing the page, be sure to set the title that will appear in the browser's title bar when the page is opened. My home page, for example, is titled `CuteLittleDogs.com`. This is a quick-and-dirty method of setting the `<title>` tags for the page.

| Tip | Get in the habit of setting page titles as you create the documents. It's very easy to end up with sites that are all labeled "Untitled"—which can be very annoying to users trying to bookmark your site. |

2

Adding Basic HTML Objects

So, now that we've got a page, it would probably be a good idea to add something to it. Point your Web browser to the site `day2.cutelittledogs.com`—this should give you a good idea of what we're trying to create.

The first thing we need is content. Because this is a site about cute little dogs, perhaps something related to that topic would be appropriate. If you'd like to type something, just click inside the document window and start typing. If you want to follow the example exactly, you can copy the content from the file `content.txt` inside the Day 2 archive available on `http://downloads.cutelittledogs.com/`, or simply re-type what's here:

```
Cute Little Dogs

Most dog owners believe theirs is the most wonderful pet in the world —

But for the owners of small dogs, that belief is confirmed every time
they bring them out in public and are surrounded by people pointing and
calling out: "What a cute little dog!"

Who are we to disagree?

(Maddy, the four-year-old Pomeranian shown here, has often been compared
to a stuffed animal by passing admirers.)

Click on the links below to see more dog pictures, to visit other pages
about dogs, and to learn more about small dog breeds.
```

Setting Text Attributes

You should now have a page with some text on it, but nothing terribly exciting to look at. Let's see how you can add some styles to the page. It's time to open the Properties window; choose Properties from the Window menu. The Properties window is shown in Figure 2.9.

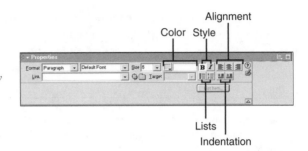

Color Style Alignment

Lists

Indentation

FIGURE 2.9

The Properties window is used to add style to the text content.

Moving from left to right, these are the properties that can be set for text within your document:

Format—This is the style of the text entered (heading sizes and so on).

Default Font—This is the font face of the text.

Size—This is the font size of the text, in either absolute or relative numbers.

Color—Sets the color of the text. You can either use the color picker or enter an HTML color directly into the field to the right of the color square. We'll look at the color picker shortly.

Style—Bold or Italic options are available.

Alignment—Chooses left-, center-, right-, or fully-justified text.

Link—If the text is part of a link, it will be shown on the second line. We'll look at link options shortly.

Target—The target is the name of the window or frame that should contain the content of the link after it is clicked.

Lists—Inserts unordered or ordered lists into the current text.

Indentation—Indents the current text.

These properties will be very important in editing text and objects in the future. You can also use the Text menu to access these and even more text formatting options.

To apply formatting to the home page for `cutelittledogs.com`, start with the heading, "Cute Little Dogs." Use your cursor to select it in the document, and then choose Heading 1 from the Format pop-up menu. Then, click the Align Center button in the Properties panel. Your document should now have a large centered heading. Behind the scenes, Dreamweaver has inserted the appropriate `<h1>` and alignment tags into the document.

Work your way through the rest of the text in the page, setting attributes using the Properties panel. For my example page, I used the Size attribute to set the majority of the text to a size of 5, along with the bold and italic attributes to set off certain sentences.

Colors

If you checked out the sample home page online, you might have noticed that the heading is in color. To set a color for the heading, use the Dreamweaver MX color tools. The color picker is common for all HTML elements that support a color attribute, so you'll end up using this even if you don't want colored text.

To set a color using the Property panel, click in the color square. A Web safe color palette is displayed that lets you pick a color from the 212 available. You can alter the way that the available colors are displayed by clicking the pop-up menu arrow in the upper-right corner of the Color palette.

Two other options make life easier if you find yourself feeling too constrained by the Web color palette: the eyedropper and the system color pickers.

To use the eyedropper, just click the color square—your cursor will change to an eyedropper. Wherever you move the eyedropper, the color will be selected. This will allow you to choose a color from anywhere on the screen, including your desktop background. If, at any time, you want to return to the default color setting, click the default color icon (a square with a line through it) in the upper-right corner of the Color palette.

A more precise way of choosing colors is by using the system's color pickers. Once again, open the color-safe palette and click the right-most icon in upper-right corner. This will bring up the color picker that is native to your system. Using the system's color picker will not necessarily result in a Web-safe color.

Note

Web-safe colors are guaranteed to display correctly on 256-color systems. Using Web-safe colors is the only way to ensure that your images will look even remotely correct on an 8-bit system.

Today's computers ship with graphics cards that run in either 16- or 24-bit color—eliminating the need to worry about selecting colors from the Web-safe palette. If you are designing a site using new technologies targeted for the most recent browsers, you really don't need to worry about choosing Web-safe colors. In a few years, they'll be nothing but a distant memory.

Images

There are still a few elements missing from the home page—most notably, the image of my dog Maddy. This image is named maddyincape.jpg and is stored in the images directory of the Day 2 project archive.

To insert an image, make sure your cursor is located where you want the image to appear (before the word "most" on the sample page), and then click the image button in the Common section of the Insert panel or choose Image from the Insert menu. Choose the `maddyincape.jpg` image from your site directory, as shown in Figure 2.10.

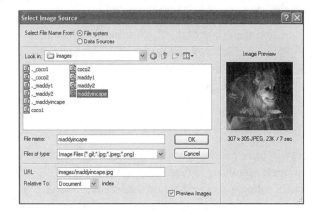

You'll see a few options related to dynamic data when selecting the image from your drive. You can ignore these for now—we'll see them again next week. One option you *will* want to take a look at is the Relative To: setting. This pop-up menu determines how Dreamweaver MX will write the links to the image. Usually you'll want to use the "relative to document" setting. This means that the links will be created relative to one another. If an image is located two directories above the current document, the link in the document will be set to look for an image two directories above it, no matter where you happen to store the file. Linking that is "relative to the site root" will reference the files based on the top of the Web site—moving the linked files anywhere else within the site will break the link.

If you choose an image outside of your folder, Dreamweaver MX will give you the option of copying it into your site. You can also specify a URL to an image that is located remotely. Unfortunately, Dreamweaver MX will only display local images, so the design view might become a bit confusing if you link all your images into the site via remote URLs.

Caution

If linking to a remote image, be sure you have properly secured the rights to display the image and use of the remote server to transfer the image. If not, you may be breaking copyright law and inadvertently *stealing* the service.

I Know I Want an Image Here, But I Don't Have One Yet!

If you want to insert an image, but you don't have one ready yet (waiting on the graphic designers again, huh?), you can insert a placeholder using the Image Placeholder object rather than an image. You can drag the handles (black squares) around the placeholder to size it in your document view. Later, you can assign an image file to the placeholder by selecting it and providing an image filename or URL in the Properties panel.

Tip

To save yourself some time, you can open the site window, navigate to the image file you want, and then drag its icon into the document where you'd like to see it inserted.

Setting Image Attributes

As with any HTML object that is inserted into a page, you can set certain attributes for an image. This is done by opening the Properties panel (from the Window menu) and selecting the image in your document. Figure 2.11 shows the available image properties available in Dreamweaver MX.

Note

As you work more and more with the application, you'll begin to recognize many of the attributes without needing a reference. Many HTML objects share more than a few common attributes, so in future chapters, we'll only show the Properties panel when introducing something new.

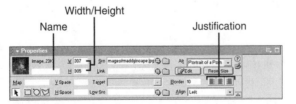

FIGURE 2.11

Set the appropriate image attributes through the Properties window.

From left to right, these are the properties that can be set for images on your page:

Name—Directly below the image size is a name that can be used to refer to it programmatically. This is typically used in JavaScript.

Width/Height—The W and H fields set the width and height of the image as it will appear on the page.

Src—The URL to the image that will be displayed.

Link—If an image is to be used as a link, you can quickly add all the appropriate `<a href>` tags around it by just typing the destination URL in this field.

Alt—Alternative text to be displayed in case the image can't be viewed or is to be read aloud by browsers for the visually impaired. You should try to use `alt` attributes whenever possible.

V Space/H Space—Set vertical and horizontal padding around the image.

Target—The target window or frame to be set as the target if the image is being used as a link. This should usually be left blank.

Low Src—Rarely used, this sets a URL to a low resolution (usually black and white) version of the image. This allows a version of the image to be displayed quickly, while the high-resolution version loads.

Border—Sets a border around the image.

Align—Determines where an image will lie in relation to objects that are next to it.

Justification—The three justification alignment buttons in the lower-right of the Properties panel control where the image is placed in relation to the HTML text around it.

Using the alignment properties to position text and graphics is beneficial when creating Web pages that must be accessible to a variety of computers and browsers. If you are positioning text exactly (with tables or layers—something you'll learn tomorrow), you inevitably will create pages that display poorly on low resolution screens, or displays that have different font settings. Using alignment properties allow the images and text themselves to drive the display of the page. If text is too long, it will wrap around the image and fill the screen (or the parent object) as much as necessary.

> **Note**
>
> To change the size of an image (or other HTML object that supports resizing), select it within the document window, and then use the small square handles on the sides of the element to shrink or expand it.
>
> It is important to note that resizing an image does *not* make its file size smaller. Even when you resize a 1024×1024 image down to a 10×10 icon, the browser must still load the large image to display it.

If you don't have complex image alignment requirements, allow the text to wrap around images on your pages. Any time you can design a page to take advantage of the cross-platform and cross-browser nature of HTML, it's a good thing.

For our page, we need to make sure that the image of Maddy is located to the left of the content on the page. Click on the image file that you've inserted, and then choose Left from the Align attribute pop-up menu.

 Tip Remember to fill in the `alt` attributes for as many images on your site as possible if you intend it to be viewable from text-only browser systems.

Horizontal Rules

There are only a few more elements missing from our first page. The home page, in particular, is missing a horizontal rule and a few links. The horizontal rule is a common object that separates different types of content. In the case of the sample home page, it divides the content region from the links to other pages. Go ahead and use the horizontal rule object in the Insert panel to add a rule to the bottom of the document you've been building. Like an image or any other object, it will be inserted wherever your cursor is located. In this example, the horizontal rule directly follows a line break; otherwise it would jut out from the right side of the image, along with the HTML text.

After inserting the horizontal rule, be sure to select it and check out the Properties panel. You'll see some familiar attributes, such as width, height, and alignment, as well as an option to enable or disable shading of the rule.

Links

A link is a "hot spot" that takes readers from one page to another or to a specific spot within a given page. There are three links on the home page for `cutelittledogs.com`: `Photo Gallery`, `Links`, and `About the Breeds`.

Because there are a number of ways to create these links, let's take a look at the most useful. Before we begin, however, it's a good idea to create the files that we'll be linking *to*. Although this isn't absolutely necessary, it is good form. Use the Site Files submenu of the Site menu (or choose New from the File menu) to create these three new HTML documents:

`gallery.html` (Photo Gallery)

`links.html` (Links)

`dogbreeds.html` (About the Breeds)

To add the first link, position your cursor where it should appear, and then click the Hyperlink object in the Insert panel. You should see a dialog box similar to that shown in Figure 2.12.

FIGURE 2.12

The Hyperlink tool will insert everything you need for a link.

Type Photo Gallery into the Text field. This will set the text of the link that is displayed onscreen in the browser. Next, type gallery.html into the Link field. Alternatively, click the folder icon at the end of the field and choose the gallery.html file directly from your site directory.

> **Tip**
>
> Anytime you see a folder icon at the end of a URL or file path field, you can click the icon and use your standard system file chooser to graphically pick the file.
>
> Remember that you'll also be asked whether or not to use absolute or relative linking. Relative linking is the easiest to manage in most cases.

Leave the Target field empty, unless you want to open the link in a new window or a frame (which we'll look at tomorrow). The remaining settings are useful and can be defined however you'd like:

Tab Index—Setting a tab index chooses the order in which the link will be highlighted when users press Tab to navigate the page.

Title—Link titles do not show up in the page itself, but appear as tooltips in Internet Explorer and a few other browsers.

Access Key—This is a keyboard shortcut that can be used to access the link directly.

When you've finished filling in the dialog box, click OK to create the link and add it to the Web page.

Perhaps it's just me, but this seems like an incredible hassle, just to add a link or two to a page. Guess what? Dreamweaver MX provides a myriad of other ways to link documents together—some of which are much faster.

To create the second link, position your cursor after the newly inserted Photo Gallery link, and then type | to give the links some breathing room. Pipes are commonly used to separate horizontal lists of links, like we're creating now. Next, type the text for the second link: Links.

If you remember from the text attributes we set earlier, there is a "Link" attribute for any selected text. Carefully highlight the word Links in your Web page, and then, using the Link field in Properties window, enter in links.html and press Enter. Congratulations, you've just entered your second link!

For the third and final link, we'll try something a bit more exciting. Again, enter a space and pipe character to give yourself some working room. Then type the phrase About the Breeds and select the text in the document view. Open and position your Site Files window so that you can see the file (dogbreeds.html) you want to link to. Now look at the Properties panel—just to the right of the Link field. You should see a little icon of crosshairs.

The crosshairs are used to "target" a link to a particular file. Use your mouse to drag from the crosshairs to the dogbreeds.html file. As you drag, an arrow will be drawn from the crosshairs to the file in the Site window. That's it; you've just created a link by pointing to a file! Pretty nifty, huh?

Tip

You can use this same technique on text that you've selected in your document. Highlight the text to turn into a link, and then click and drag from the highlighted words. The arrow will appear, just as if you had used the crosshairs in the Properties window.

There are actually even *more* ways to make links with Dreamweaver MX. Using the Insert menu, or selecting the link-to-be-text and using the contextual menus will also suffice. You can go back at any time and edit existing links through the Modify menu's Change Link option, or by editing the Link field in the Properties window.

You've just completed the first page of the http://day2.cutelittledogs.com site. To preview it in your Web browser, choose your browser from the Preview in Browser option of the File menu; the results should look similar to the document shown in Figure 2.13.

You might now want to check the online "About the Breeds" page to see how it is formatted (http://day2.cutelittledogs.com), and then build it using the content.txt file from the Day 2 project archive. You can save it for later if you'd like—it uses the same techniques you've already seen.

You're now ready to move on to a slightly more complex topic—HTML tables.

FIGURE 2.13

*Behold the finished
page!*

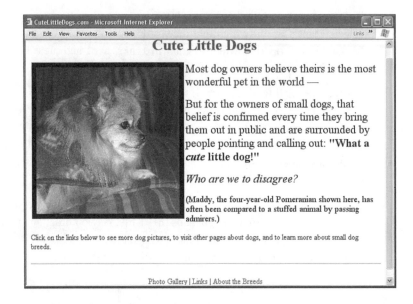

Positioning with Tables

Although you can create simple functional pages with the text and image alignment
properties that you've already seen, you can't create a page that "holds together" and
keeps a certain type of layout no matter what browser is being used to view it.

For the second page we're going to look at today, there are several pictures that would be
nice to lay out in a gallery format. Unfortunately, just adding images to a document will
give you a jumbled mess—a table can create a more organized layout, as seen in
Figure 2.14.

In its most basic form, a table is nothing more than a grid of cells, each of which can
contain whatever content you'd like: text, images, other tables, and so on. What makes
tables complicated are the number of attributes and operations that can be performed on
them and the cells that make them up. You can merge cells to create irregularly shaped
tables, set padding values to space the cell contents apart, and the like. If you haven't
used tables before, it might be a good idea to consult an HTML reference to get an idea
of everything they can do.

Let's start looking at the Dreamweaver MX table tools by creating the `cutelittle-`
`dogs.com` photo gallery page. Assuming you've already created an empty version of the
page, open it now. My version of the page has a few headings, the table in the middle,
and the links at the bottom. You can go ahead and insert the headings and links—you
should already know how to do it. The table in the middle is the focus for the remainder
of our exercise for the day.

FIGURE 2.14

Tables can create neat orderly views.

Inserting a Table

The gallery page has a two-row-by-two-column table to hold the images and their captions. To insert a table in the HTML, position your cursor where you want it to appear, and then click the table icon in the Insert window, or choose Table from the Insert menu. You'll be prompted for the initial attributes of the table, as shown in Figure 2.15. These values can be changed at any time using the Modify menu, or using the Properties window in conjunction with the selected table.

FIGURE 2.15

You can set most of the attributes of a table as it is being added.

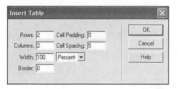

The initial attributes you can set when inserting a table are as follows:

Rows/Columns—The number of rows and columns the table should have.

Cell Padding—How many pixels of padding are around the inside edges of a table cell.

Cell Spacing—The number of pixels of padding to be added to the *outside* edges of a table cell.

Width—The width of the table in percent or pixels. Widths specified as percentages grow and shrink with the overall size of the browser window.

Border—The width, in pixels, of the border (if any) to be drawn around the table.

For the gallery table, choose a table with two rows, two columns, a Width of 100% and a Cell Padding of 5 pixels. The Cell Spacing is 5—keeping an ample amount of room between the navigation and content portions of the table. Click OK when you're ready, and the table will be added to your document.

When examining a table in the Properties window you'll notice a number of additional attributes and functions you can work with. Most notable is a set of six buttons in the lower half of the window, used to reset column widths/heights and to convert pixel widths/heights to percentages. Position your cursor over each of the buttons to see its function in a tooltip. Additionally, you can define a background color, border color, or background image to spice up the table's appearance.

Adding Content

Your document will now have a dotted outline of a four-cell table inserted wherever your cursor was. Clicking inside the table cells will move your cursor into the cell and allow you to start adding content. You can think of each cell as being a tiny little Web page; almost any content that can go into a page can also be added directly to a table cell.

Note that the property window changes when you move into a table cell—this is because a cell (a <td> tag) is a separate object from the table itself. You can choose where the cell's content is added by using the Horz and Vert alignment pop-up menus, set individual cell widths in pixels or percentages, define the cell as a "header" cell, turn off text wrapping, and set individual color attributes for the cell! The same goes for table row elements, which hold the table cells in each row.

For the gallery page, there is a line of text that accompanies each image in the layout. These serve as simple captions for the pictures, and are centered in the cells. Go ahead and type each of the captions into the cells, starting in the upper-left corner and moving down to the lower-right corner:

```
Maddy, a Pomeranian, at 2 years old.

Coco, a miniature American Eskimo, at 8 weeks old.

Maddy at 4 years old.

Coco at 1 year old.
```

As you click into a table cell to type in the captions, use the Properties panel to set the horizontal alignment to Center, the vertical alignment to Middle, and the Width to 50%.

This will make the text center itself within the cell, and will cause each of the cells to take up half of the total horizontal width of the page.

Once the captions are added, go ahead and insert the images just as you did for the home page. There are four pictures located in your site's images directory that correspond to the headings:

```
maddy1.jpg
coco1.jpg
maddy2.jpg
coco2.jpg
```

Because the table cells were already set to align content to the center of the cell, the images will fall into place as they are added. Within a few seconds, you will have built the gallery page and used your first Dreamweaver MX table.

This leaves (assuming you completed the About The Breeds" page) one additional page (Links) to be completed. As before, the Links page uses the same elements you've used in the Gallery. If you haven't already, log into the Web site to retrieve links.html from the project archive, and then build your own version of the page.

Selecting and Resizing Tables, Cells, and Rows

Tables are remarkably complex creatures and there are a number of additional operations you might want use as you get more comfortable with incorporating tables into your site. I urge you to test these functions while building your links.html page for the cutelittledogs.com sample site.

Let's start with a common activity—visually selecting and resizing tables and their cells. To change the size of a cell, move the cursor to the edge of the table's boundary wall until the cursor turns into two vertical lines with outward pointing arrows. You can then click and drag the boundary so that it moves into the position you want.

To resize tables themselves, apply the same procedure as with an image. Choose the object, and then drag the small square handles around the border to shrink and grow the table.

As you practice working with table cells, you might notice that it is sometimes difficult to select a table cell rather than its contents. To force Dreamweaver MX to choose a table cell rather than what is inside of it, hold down the Control (Windows) or Command (Mac) key when clicking on the cell.

Likewise, you can select a row of table cells (and thus have access to the table row <tr> attributes) by holding down the Shift key while selecting each of the cells in the row.

This, however, can be painful on extremely large tables. To quickly select a row, move your cursor so it is *just* touching the dotted border in front of the table row you want to select. The cursor will change to a horizontal-pointing arrow, which, when clicked, will highlight all the cells in the row.

Tip

In addition to working directly with objects in the document, there are two very easy ways to select objects within the HTML hierarchy. In the status bar of the document window, you'll see a listing of the hierarchy of tags that contain the object you're currently editing. For example, if you're editing inside a table's data cell, you might see something like this:

<body><table><tr><td>

This list indicates that you are inside of a <td> (table cell) element, which is inside of a <tr> (table row), which is inside of a <table> (table), which, in turn, is inside of the main <body> (page body) tag. This is an excellent view of the parent/child relationship of tags. The leftmost tag is the top "parent", whereas the tag to the immediate left is a child of that parent, and so on.

You can immediately select the table cell containing this link by clicking the <td> in the list. You can extend this up as far as you want: Select the table row by clicking <tr>, the entire table with <table>, or even the whole HTML body with <body>. This is a convenient and intuitive way to make selections.

You can also use the Select Parent Tag and Select Child options in the Edit menu to select the child and parent objects within the hierarchy.

Precise Positioning

If you are in a situation where you must position images precisely with other elements (images, text, and so on), the alignment tags will be of little use to you. Instead, you can define a table that contains the components you need to position. With the ability to define the precise width in pixels of individual cells, you can control the alignment of your page elements exactly.

To use a table for positioning, the best way to control your layout is to set exact widths for the table and its cells. Also make sure that the table you are using to force the positions has Border, Cell Spacing, and Cell Padding attributes set to zero. Setting these values to zero in the Properties panel will ensure that the contents of your table cell will be exactly where you want them—not slightly skewed by the border and spacing attributes of the table cells. Make sure that your table widths always add up to the width of the table itself. If the values are off, the resulting table can look strange after it's loaded into a browser.

Joining Cells and Nesting Tables

HTML tables require that the width of table cells be consistent for each row in the entire table. Likewise, the height of a row must be consistent across the entire row. Although this might seem as if it limits where items can be placed, it actually doesn't. In each cell of a table, you can insert another table. This lets you further subdivide tables into smaller units.

Additionally, you can combine multiple cells of a table into a single cell, or split a cell into multiple cells. To join cells, select the cells you want to combine by holding down the Command key on the Macintosh or the Alt key on Windows and clicking in the cell to select. (They must be contiguous blocks of cells.) Then choose Merge Cells from the Modify menu. The selected cells will "become one."

Under the Modify menu's Table option, you'll notice that there are quite a few commands to combine and reconfigure a table layout. Here's a description of the effects you'll see when these are applied to a table cell:

Split Cell—Using the split cell option will create new cells in the selected table cell. You will be prompted for the number of rows or columns to create.

Insert Row/Column—The insertion features will insert a new row or column directly before the currently selected cell. Choose the Insert Rows or Columns item to choose what you want to insert and where (before or after the current selection) you want to insert it.

Delete Row/Column—Removes the row or column that contains the currently selected item.

Increase Row/Column Span—The row span and column span for a cell can be increased with these options. This will connect the selected cell with the cell directly below or to the right of it. This affects the cell immediately below or beside the current cell. You do not need to have multiple cells selected for this feature. In fact, if you do, it won't work.

Decrease Row/Column Span—If a cell is spanning multiple columns or rows, decreasing the row or column span will shrink the current cell back towards its original position.

Through a combination of multiple nested tables and combining existing cells, you can create layouts that position your elements in very complex arrangements.

The Positioning Compromise

With all the options for percentage and pixel based layouts that span multiple rows or columns, you can create layouts that vary from being extremely loose to being pixel-point precise. Unfortunately, you might be designing tables that lock you into a particular browser size. Let's take a look at one way that tables can be used to position elements in a manner that will accommodate multiple browser sizes.

Setting exact pixel sizes for tables and their cells lets the page designer position everything perfectly. If, however, the elements only need to be positioned relative to one another, the table can be set up using percentages instead of exact values. Cells based on percentages will expand as the size of the browser is increased. The designer can still position how elements are laid out with respect to one another, but not with pixel-level accuracy. Unless you're using a table to position pieces of an image, percentages will probably work well for your project.

You can take this one step further by not setting any widths or heights for table cells. This lets the content of the table drive its own layout. As I've mentioned before, HTML was designed to present information on as wide a variety of computers and platforms as possible. Giving the browser the control over how items are positioned is always the most favorable option.

If you've already set up your tables using hard-coded widths, you can quickly convert your widths between percentages and pixels by using the Convert Widths to Pixels or Convert Widths to Percent options of the Table submenu under Modify. To get rid of the widths and heights completely, use the options Clear Cell Heights and Clear Cell Widths under the same menu. You need to select the entire table to do this using the Modify menu and Table submenu.

Tip

> Be sure to practice using tables before attempting to do a large-scale production using tables for control. Tables are a useful tool, but can be extremely tricky unless you're used to their eccentricities.
>
> For example, you might notice that inserting images in table cells that are *supposed* to follow one another often results in a small amount of whitespace being inserted between images. If this happens, open the HTML source and check for spaces between the <td> tags and your <img> tags. Dreamweaver MX sometimes seems to insert spaces in places you'd rather not have them.

Using the Table Layout Mode

Now that you know everything about the complexities of creating table designs, let's look at a tool that makes these important elements significantly easier to work with. Dreamweaver MX includes a layout mode that makes it simple to create complex layouts

using tables. Typically, you would manually position the cells in a table to lay out information—subdividing and merging as necessary. Layout mode lets you define your content regions without needing to worry about manually determining spacing information.

To switch to layout mode, use the icons in the Layout tab of the Insert panel, as seen in
Figure 2.16, or use the Table View Option on the View menu.

Note   These options are always available at the bottom of the Insert panel when
displayed in vertical mode of the Floating Workspace view.

Draw Layout Table

Standard View

FIGURE 2.16

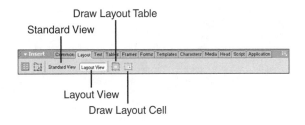

*Use the view icons to
toggle to and from
layout mode, and the
layout icons to draw
layout cells.*

Layout View

Draw Layout Cell

After switching to the layout mode, there are two new tools you can use—the Layout
Table and Layout Cell objects, both located in the Layout section of the Insert window.

Think of a layout table as a free-form area on the page where you can do anything that
you want. Using the Layout Table, you can click and drag across an area of the design
view to add an empty layout region to the screen. An example of an empty layout region
is shown in Figure 2.17.

FIGURE 2.17

*Draw a layout table on
the screen wherever
you want to precisely
position page content.*

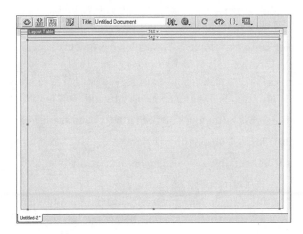

Within the layout table, you can add in a layout cell, much the same way you added the layout table to page. This cell can be positioned anywhere—with pixel point accuracy—on the entire page. Figure 2.18 shows the layout table with an added layout cell.

FIGURE 2.18

Adding a layout cell to the layout table lets you add content to a page anywhere you want.

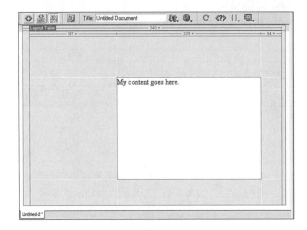

Layout cells can be moved and resized after they are added to a layout table. Clicking and dragging the edge of a cell will move it within the table region. Clicking the border of the cell a single time will highlight the cell and add resizing handles to it. This will let you resize the cell at any time to add room or remove extraneous space.

As you draw layout cells, small menus showing the current column width are added to the top of the layout table. These menus give you even greater control over what is happening in the columns. Clicking one of the menu headings reveals a pop-up menu with options to control the cells and how they are generated:

Make Column Autostretch—Sets the column so that it will automatically grow as needed to fit the available content.

Add Spacer Images—Some browsers have problems keeping table cells set to the right size unless the cells actually hold something. To get around this, people (and Dreamweaver) use "spacer" images to fill the cells. These are single pixel transparent images that are stretched to the appropriate width and height.

Clear Cell heights—Removes all height information from the cells in the table.

Make Cell Widths Consistent—Generates equally sized cells within the layout table.

Remove All Spacer Images—Removes any spacer images that have been added to the table.

Remove Nesting—If Dreamweaver MX has nested multiple tables to create the given layout, the remove nesting option will flatten the layout to a single table.

It's important to remember that the table layout mode is really just creating a table structure based on the position and size of the cells you're adding. You can, at any time, switch back to the normal design view by clicking the left-most button (Standard View) in the View portion of the Insert panel. This is an absolutely wonderful tool to use to create precise table layouts especially when using tracing images, which you'll learn about tomorrow. Unfortunately, it also leads to Web pages with very difficult-to-read HTML code, and are (usually) fixed to a certain screen size. If this is unimportant for your application, however, don't hesitant to use layout tables!

Other Important Functions

To round out today's lesson, let's take a look at two functions you might want to use while you're composing your pages and content—Spell Checking and Previewing.

Spell Checking

You've finished your first few pages in Dreamweaver MX, but you might want to double-check your work using the built-in spell-checking capabilities of the editor. There's nothing more embarrassing than making a silly spelling error and exposing it to the world.

To launch the Dreamweaver MX spell checker, choose Check Spelling from the Text menu. This will open the Check Spelling dialog box, seen in Figure 2.19—this should seem familiar to most anyone with experience using a word processor.

FIGURE 2.19

You can spell check your Web site from within Dreamweaver MX.

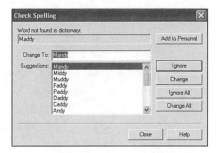

If an unknown word is found, you can choose to add it to your personal dictionary, ignore it, or change it. If you are building computer-related Web sites, you'll find that you end up adding many words to your personal dictionary. It seems that dictionary programs can't keep up with the ever-growing list of computer jargon. Be aware that spell-checking is not a substitute for proofreading. You should always proofread and have others proofread your site before going live.

Assuming you've created a perfect page (in terms of layout and spelling!), the final thing you'll want to do before declaring it "done" is to preview it in a browser.

Previewing

Although the Dreamweaver MX environment does an excellent job of giving you a preview of the final product, sometimes it doesn't exactly match what you're going to see in the browser. To preview your work in an actual browser, use the Preview in Browser submenu within the File menu. It's best to preview in both Internet Explorer and Netscape; otherwise you might be in for a big surprise down the road.

The preview system in Dreamweaver MX is a bit different from other HTML editors. Instead of launching the browser with the file you are editing, Dreamweaver MX creates a temporary HTML file each time you use the preview option. This eliminates problems with browsers caching the page you're viewing and not updating correctly between previews.

By default, only Internet Explorer is listed as a browser in the preview submenu. To add additional browsers, open the Dreamweaver MX preferences and select the Preview in Browser category. The preference window shown in Figure 2.20 should appear.

FIGURE 2.20

Add browsers to the preview system.

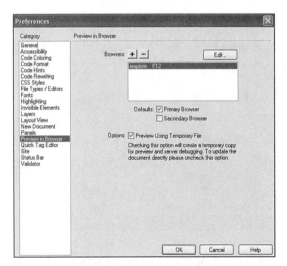

Click the + button to open a window that will allow you to choose an alternative browser from your computer's drive. To remove a browser from the listing, highlight it, and then click the – button.

Caution

> Dreamweaver MX normally previews your document by saving it to a temporary file and opening in your browser of choice. This lets you test changes without saving them to your working document.
>
> If you'd prefer that the *real* HTML file is used for previews, uncheck the Preview Using Temporary File box. All changes will be saved back to the original document, which will then be opened in the browser.

2

Summary

Today you learned many of the tools that you need to create complex Web sites. Images, links, tables, and the Properties panel should no longer hold any mystery. These tools, although not necessary for creating dynamic Web sites, are an important part of Dreamweaver MX's capability to maintain all aspects of a Web site—from the application logic to the look and feel.

Workshop

The workshop area is meant to reinforce your reading with a series of questions and exercises.

Q&A

Q I need greater control of the fonts and styles in the document; is this the best Dreamweaver can do?

A Absolutely not! Dreamweaver offers a full-featured style sheet editor, which you'll learn all about in Day 5, "Creating Reusable Components."

Q What kinds of images can I insert into the documents I create?

A The most common types of images used are GIF and JPEG formats. JPEG images are *lossy*—meaning they lose detail information as they are saved—but are great for most photographs. GIFs are limited to 256 colors, but do not lose any detail when saved for the Web. Elements that must remain clear and legible are a prime candidate for the GIF format.

Q What happens if I use a non-Web-safe color and view it on a 256-color display?

A The color will be mapped to one of the available Web-safe colors—this can lead to some rather ugly displays.

Q I've tried to use the crosshairs target tool to pick files for linking, but it doesn't seem to work very well. Am I doing something wrong?

A The crosshair tool is a neat feature, but is often difficult to use. The Site Files window scrolls a bit too easily to make precision "targeting" easy. Choosing the file directly or typing the name of a file to link to is often more effective.

Quiz

1. What is the easiest way to set a page's title?

2. Where can you define the colors for a selected chunk of text?

3. What is the crosshair icon for?

4. Why should you define a site before editing pages?

5. How can you use a table to create pixel-point accurate layouts without resorting to layers or time-consuming manual cell spacing?

Quiz Answers

Use the Title field at the top of the document window.

2. The Properties window can define attributes for any selected object.

3. The crosshair icon is used to visually link to files in the Site Files window.

4. Unless you define a site, Dreamweaver MX doesn't know how to correctly link files to one another. This can result in problems when you try to publish your pages online.

5. The Layout mode uses tables to transparently allow you to position cells anywhere you'd like on the screen. This is an excellent alternative to layers.

Exercises

1. Create the About the Breeds and Links pages as discussed in the day's lesson. Test the final site and compare it to http://day2.cutelittledogs.com/.

2. Practice positioning elements on your page using tables. Tables are the most complex element you've seen thus far, and are one of the most important HTML objects used in the book.

DAY **3**

Advanced HTML and Site Tools

In yesterday's lesson you learned that the basics of designing a simple Web site consisting of text, images, links, and tables. So what else is there? Plenty. Although you now know the tools necessary to construct most basic sites, there are a number of additional functions that can aid in advanced page layout, navigation, and site management. With the advanced features come numerous additional support tools, windows, options, dialog boxes, and so on. There's a great deal of information contained here, so be patient and take the time to work with the tools. Among other things, you'll work with:

- Dreamweaver's navigation tools
- Layers for precise control over Web page content
- Framesets that can divide a Web browser window into multiple components
- Cascading style sheets for precise control of fonts, margins, and other page elements
- HTML code editing tools
- Additional site-management features

Advanced Navigation

Yesterday you learned how to make simple links by selecting objects and using the Properties panel or Insert menu to add links to other pages. Now let's look at alternative ways of navigating through pages, such as image maps, named anchors, and other special tools.

To explore these tools, we'll look at creating alternative versions of the Web site that we worked with yesterday. As a first step, you should create a new site named Day 3 (using the same steps as yesterday) using the Day 3 files archive available at http://downloads.cutelittledogs.com/.

After setting up the site files, open the home page (index.html) by double-clicking the file in the Site Files window, or choose Open from the File menu.

We're now ready to try some alternative navigation methods.

Drawing Image Maps (Hotspots)

Images can easily be made into links by selecting them and using the Make Link option under the Modify menu, or by simply filling in a URL in the Link field of the Properties window. This is fine, but it requires multiple images in order to link to multiple pages. To link a single image to several pages, you can set up an "image map" using the Dreamweaver MX tools.

An image map (or Dreamweaver MX "Hotspot") is defined visually by drawing regions within a single image—these regions can then be linked to other files, anchors, and so on—the same as any other link. When the Web was still in its infancy, image maps were confusing and complicated to make—in fact, image maps initially required the server to process information, rather than the client. With Dreamweaver MX, however, you simply draw the shapes that you want to represent links, and then connect them to other pages using the same tools you've already seen.

For example, let's take a look at the links on the home page that we made yesterday, seen in Figure 3.1.

As we look at the different navigation tools, we'll use the home page as the testbed for alternatives. Examples of the changes are online at http://day3.cutelittledogs.com.

Open the file index.html in your Day 3 site and scroll down to the bottom where the links are. I've removed them from this file because you're going to replace them with a single image-mapped graphic.

FIGURE 3.1

Let's try to do something a bit more exciting with these links.

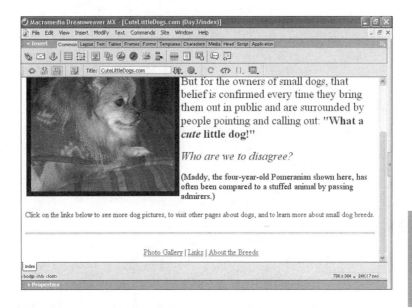

Using the Insert panel or the Insert menu, (or one of the many other ways to add an image to a document), add the file `imagemapnav.jpg` from the site's `images` directory to the bottom of the page. Your document should look a bit like the window in Figure 3.2.

FIGURE 3.2

Add the navigation image to your page.

3

Image maps are created through the use of the Properties panel (much like everything else in Dreamweaver). When an image is selected, tools for "drawing" a map appear within the panel, demonstrated in Figure 3.3.

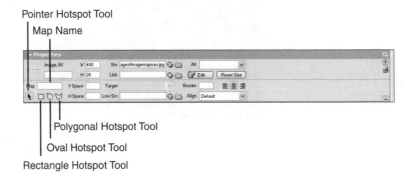

FIGURE 3.3

Use the Properties window drawing tools to "draw" an image map.

Follow these steps to create an image map.

1. Select the image in the design view, and then open the Properties panel.

2. Enter a name for the image map in the Map Name field. This is an arbitrary name used to name the map coordinates in the HTML file.

3. Use the rectangle tool to draw "hotspots" around each of the buttons in the image. Depending on the type of image you're working with, the oval or polygon tools might be better choices, but for rectangular buttons, a rectangle tool is a reasonably good fit.

4. After you draw several regions for the image map, you can use the pointer arrow to highlight an individual region or hotspot for resizing or defining its link.

Once completed, each mapped area can be linked by selecting highlighting it and using the Properties panel, shown in Figure 3.4.

Choose the hotspots, and then using the Link field (or crosshairs or folder icon) in the Properties panel to pick the files that they will connect to. These should be identical to the links you created yesterday.

After you define all the hotspot links, the image map is ready. Save this version of the home page as `index2.html` and preview it in your browser. Clicking one of the hotspots should take you to page you've defined.

FIGURE 3.4

Define the link for the region by selecting the hotspots and filling in the fields in the Properties panel.

Rollover Images

Image maps are fine, but how about a bit more pizzazz? You've all seen images that change as your mouse moves over them—these are "rollover" images, and are extremely simple to create in Dreamweaver MX. Besides looking pretty, rollover images also provide a visual indicator so that users know what is (and isn't) navigation.

Open the base `index.html` file again, scroll down to the bottom of the page, and position the cursor where the navigation is needed. This time we're going to add a few rollover images to provide links to other pages.

To add a rollover image link, follow these steps:

1. Click the rollover image button in the Insert panel, or use the Insert menu.

2. The Insert Rollover Image dialog box, displayed in Figure 3.5, will be displayed.

3. Enter a name for the rollover image. This is used by the JavaScript that "powers" the rollover and can be anything you like, as long as it is unique.

4. Choose the "original" image (this is the default state of the rollover graphic) by filling in the supplied field, or by clicking the Browse icon and choosing an image from your site.

5. Choose the "rollover" image using the same method. The rollover image is the graphic that's displayed when the mouse is over the image. Click the Preload check box to ensure that the rollover image loads when the page loads. This eliminates "lag" in the rollover effect.

6. Enter any alternative text that you want to appear in nongraphical browsers.

7. Enter the URL that the image should link to when clicked. You can simply fill in the field or click the Browse button and choose it from your site.

8. Click OK when you're finished.

FIGURE 3.5

Generating rollover images is a matter of filling in a few fields.

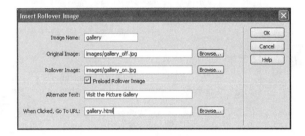

For your home page, there are several predefined images that you can use to test the rollover features:

`about_off.jpg, about_on.jpg`

`gallery_off.jpg, gallery_on.jpg`

`links_off.jpg, links_on.jpg`

Go ahead and add them to your document. When you're finished, save it as `index3.html` and preview it in your browser. Because there really isn't any way to show a rollover in a figure, I recommend visiting `http://day3.cutelittledogs.com/` to get an idea of how it should work.

Navigation Bar

If you worked through the previous exercise, you might have noticed that the steps you took to create your navigation elements were quite repetitive. You have also noticed that if you resize your browser to a size smaller than what the images can fit in, they'll wrap to another line. You can get around this by inserting the images into the table, but we're lazy, aren't we? It would be nice if there were a way for Dreamweaver to do all of this for us…

There is—the built-in navigation bar tool.

The navigation bar tool is a link-management tool. It automatically creates rollover images, links, and stores it all in a convenient table. You can easily modify the navigation bar at any time—even change it from a horizontal to vertical orientation with a single click. To test the tool, open the `index.html` file yet again. You'll be creating one more version of the home page using the navigation bar tool. Position your cursor where you'd like the navigation to be inserted and click the navigation bar icon within the

Insert panel. Dreamweaver MX will open the Insert Navigation Bar dialog box, displayed in Figure 3.6.

FIGURE 3.6

The navigation bar builds a table of links, complete with dynamic images.

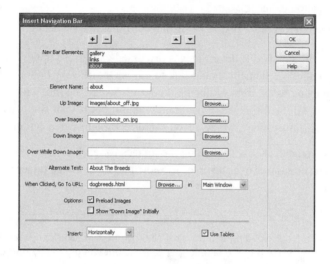

The Nav Bar Elements field is a list of the different "units" (links and their associated images) that make up the navigation bar. Clicking the "+" button adds a new element, whereas "-" deletes the selected element. The up and down arrows to the right of the list move the selected element's position within the list.

Tip

> These controls (the "+"/"-" and arrow buttons) are common throughout the Dreamweaver MX application. If you understand their use here, you'll know what to do when you see them elsewhere.

By default, there is a single element unnamed1 added to a default navigation bar. You can change the name of this element by highlighting it in the element list and then changing the Element Name field. The name is *not* displayed in the browser, so it isn't necessary to use names that would make sense to the client.

After filling in the element name, you can then add up to four images that will be displayed as the client's cursor moves over the graphic:

Up Image—The default image that is displayed.

Over Image—The image that is displayed as the mouse "hovers" over an image. (This is the same as the "on" image in a rollover graphic.)

Down Image—An image that is displayed when the user first clicks the graphic.

Over While Down Image—A graphic to show if the user continues to hold down on navigation element.

Alternative Text—Text to be displayed if the images cannot be displayed.

As with the standard rollover images discussed earlier, fill in the Go To URL field with the page that the element should link to, or use the Browse button to make a choice. The pop-up menu to the right of this field controls where the link will be take the users. By default it will be displayed in the main window, but if your site is using frames (we'll get to frames shortly, don't worry!), you can direct the link to a certain frame.

Finally, you can choose to preload the images for each element so that they react quickly when a user mouses over them, or to show the down image rather than the up image by default.

 Tip

> Preloading images is usually a good idea. On slow connections it can cause the page to take longer to load, but will ultimately result in a more "snappy" user experience.

After defining all the elements used for the navigation, use the Insert pop-up menu to choose whether the bar will be laid out horizontally or vertically and be sure to check the Use Tables check box so that the elements will stick together if the browser is resized.

Go ahead and test the navigation bar's capabilities by using the same images from the basic rollovers you created earlier:

`about_off.jpg`, `about_on.jpg`

`gallery_off.jpg`, `gallery_on.jpg`

`links_off.jpg`, `links_on.jpg`

The Up images correspond to the "off" files, whereas the Over image (or the Down image, if you'd like a slightly different effect) should be set to the "on" files. Figure 3.7, for the sake of being different, shows the navigation bar laid out vertically.

After you create a navigation bar, you can select it in the design window and choose "navigation bar" from the Modify menu to add/delete or rearrange its elements. Alternatively, you can click the navigation bar icon again, as if to add a new bar. Dreamweaver MX only allows one bar per document and will offer to open the existing bar.

FIGURE 3.7

How about a vertical navigation bar?

Advanced Layout and Document Control

There are a few HTML constructs that behave a bit differently from images, tables, and other simple objects. Layers and frames, for example, have their own panels for fine-tuned control, whereas style sheets can be used to alter the appearance and behavior of existing HTML objects. Let's look at these features now.

Positioning with Layers

By this point in time, you should be able to use tables to position your content and navigation. Unfortunately, although tables are a good way to create consistent layouts, they are also cumbersome to use and maintain. Additionally, the complex table sets that are created within the Dreamweaver MX interface are very difficult to edit by hand. Digging through 10 or so nested tables can be a nightmare. To get around the limitations of positioning elements using tables, Netscape created the Layer tag. This tag was designed to form a floating layer that could contain HTML and be positioned on a Web site wherever the author felt necessary.

Although a good idea, the folks at Netscape had jumped the gun. There was no corresponding standard in the HTML specification for the Layer tag, and only users who were browsing with Netscape could make use of it. Designing completely separate Web sites for Netscape and everyone else didn't make much sense, so the Netscape-designed version of layers didn't live a very long or fruitful life.

Luckily additional tags were added to the HTML specification that, when coupled with style sheets, gives the author the sort of cross-browser and cross-platform support that was impossible to achieve previously.

Before you get too excited, there is one slight drawback to the use of layers: The users must have a modern browser in order to see them displayed properly. If they're viewing with an older browser, the display isn't going to look *anything* like you intended. For most people, this is a design decision that can be made without stepping on too many toes. Looking at the statistics from several Web sites that I oversee, fewer than 2% of the visitors to these sites use older than a 4.0 browser.

Tables can be constructed with precise cell and column widths to construct a very "tight" layout. With layers, you can accomplish the same thing in much less time, and with significantly fewer problems.

Assume you have a table with images and want to change the width of one of the images so that it extended slightly beyond the cell where it currently lies—all without changing the width of the cells underneath it. With standard HTML tables, this gets to be quite a headache because cells would have to be split, or new tables would need to be inserted.

With a layer it's very easy. For example, take a look at Figure 3.8. As you can see, it certainly isn't very consistent with a table-based layout. The images are not spaced consistently down the length of the table, and the text cells don't line up with what would be columns or rows. In fact, if you look closely, you'll see that the images are actually overlapping on the page. This isn't a specially edited graphic or any sort of trick—it's just an example of the sort of flexibility that comes with the use of layers.

FIGURE 3.8

Layers let you create some pretty complex page designs without much trouble.

To add layers to your own page, click the Layer tool in the Common category of the Insert panel, and then move your cursor to the document design view. Next, draw a rectangle about the size of the layer you want to create. Don't worry; you can always resize it later.

Selecting Layers

You'll notice that two things were inserted into your design view: the rectangle that holds the layer contents, and a tag that represents the layer itself. To add items to the layer, click inside it and begin typing or adding HTML objects from the Insert panel. On the top-left corner of the layer is a small square handle. The handle can be used to select the layer itself (rather than its contents). This allows you to move (either through dragging or the arrow keys) and resize the selected layer.

Additionally, you can click the layer tag icon itself to select a layer. This is actually a useful way of getting to a layer. Because layers can be overlapping, or even invisible, it's often difficult to find them when you're looking.

Viewing Layer Properties

After you've added a layer to your page, open the Properties panel for the layer, as seen in Figure 3.9.

FIGURE 3.9

Layer properties include attributes that are not shared with any other HTML object.

Layers have several attributes that are not shared with any other object:

L/T/W/H—These are Left, Top, Width, and Height. The Left and Top fields specify the coordinates of the upper-left corner of the layer. The width and height of the layer are given in the other two fields.

Z-index—The Z (depth) ordering of the layers on the page controls the overlapping of the layers on the HTML page. If you'd like a layer to be above another layer, enter a value that is greater than the "underneath" layer. If you don't understand what this value does, it's best to leave it set at the default.

Vis—This is the initial visibility of the layer. If you're going to use JavaScript to control the visibility of your layers, you might have reason to set a layer to be hidden when it is first drawn on the screen. You can use JavaScript to make the layer appear—this is frequently used to create pop-up windows within a Web page.

Tag—The tag used to create the layer. The default tag is `<div>`, which works across different browsers. The `<span>` tag will also work with other browsers, but the `<layer>` tag is Netscape only.

Overflow—The overflow attribute does not apply to the Netscape-only layers. On `<div>` and `<span>` based layers, setting the overflow determines how the browser handles situations in which the contents of a layer are larger than the layer itself. The visible setting displays all the layer's contents. Hidden clips the contents that extend beyond the viewable area of the layer. The last two options, scroll and auto, will display scrollbars either constantly, or only if the content exceeds the amount of space available.

Clip L/T/W/H—These are similar to the coordinates for defining the layer, but are used to define the visible portion of the layer. Also, instead of giving coordinates in terms of the page, these coordinates are specified in relation to the layer itself. This is mostly useful for JavaScripting layer-based effects.

The rest of the layer attributes should, by now, be familiar.

Using the Layers Panel

Layers are an important enough object that Macromedia felt they deserved their own tool panel. To see what I mean, insert a few layers into a design window. You can even nest layers within each other by holding Alt (Windows) or Option (Macintosh) when inserting subsequent layers in a document. Open the Layers panel from the Others option of the Window menu. Shown in Figure 3.10, this panel lets you arrange the Z ordering of all the available layers (the higher Z numbers are displayed on top of lower numbers).

FIGURE 3.10

The Layers panel gives you a quick view of the layers in your document.

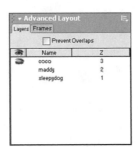

In addition, you can click within the "eye" column to toggle between visible and invisible modes (open and shut eyes). To change the layer names and ordering, just click the text you want to change and the field will become editable. If you have layers that are nested within one another, these will appear as a hierarchical indented list. You can remove nested layers from their parent list by dragging them within the panel.

Near the top of the tool panel, you'll see the Prevent Overlap check box. Choosing this will prevent *new layers* that you add to the document from overlapping. Now let's see why you'd even want to use this option.

Converting Layers to Tables and Vice Versa

If you like the ease of design that layers give you, but don't want to sacrifice support for other browsers, Dreamweaver MX gives you an option that will make you jump for joy: the capability to convert layer-based pages to tables and vice versa. You can design your pages using the free-form layer approach, and then convert to tables for the final deployment of your site. The only problem is that you can't convert overlapping layers to a table—thus the option that you saw in the last section. To test this function, add a few layers (with content) to a new page, and make sure that you don't have any overlap. Choose Convert Layers to Table from the Convert option of the Modify menu. Figure 3.11 shows the resulting dialog box.

FIGURE 3.11

The conversion between layers and tables is painless.

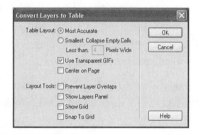

3

From my experience, your best bet is to go with the dialog box defaults. If you aren't concerned about the exact positioning of the cells in the resulting table, you might want to use the Smallest option rather than Most Accurate. When Dreamweaver MX generates the accurate tables, it creates enough cells to exactly position the contents of the layers within a table cell. The Smallest setting, however, will snap to the nearest cell if it is within the given number of pixels (default is 4). This cleans up small spaces and produces a less complicated table—if possible. The other available options are listed here:

Use Transparent GIFs—Forces the use of transparent GIFs in the newly generated table. These GIFs will force spacing of the table to be correct on any browser.

Center on Page—Centers the resulting table on the HTML page.

Prevent Layer Overlaps—Toggles the layer overlap checking.

Show Layer Palette—Displays the layer panel after creating the table.

Show Grid—Displays the document design grid after the table is created.

Snap To Grid—Toggles the snap to grid settings once the table is generated.

In addition, if you have an existing site that is based on tables and want to convert it to layers, Dreamweaver MX will let you do this as well. Just choose the Tables to Layers option. You'll probably notice that this does not create a perfect conversion. Using

Dreamweaver MX to go back and forth between layers and tables is a good example of the shortcomings of this feature. If you've used transparent GIFs to force the layout of layers into a table and then translate back to layers, each GIF will be in its own layer. Still, even with these drawbacks, this is a very useful feature that makes it possible to design pages with layers, and then convert them to a table format viewable in older browsers.

Creating Persistent Elements with Frames

Although similar to Layers in the level of control they provide over a page's layout, frames have an entirely different purpose. If you've started to link pages together in your site, you've probably duplicated the navigation bar on each page. Providing a consistent way to navigate through a Web site is very important in creating a pleasant and seamless user experience. If your navigation is built using rollover images, the process of loading new pages can take quite a while. Even if the individual images of the rollover navigation are cached, the load time still suffers.

One potential way to get around this is to use a *frameset* to define a navigation frame and a content frame. These frames each contain their own HTML document and only the portions of the page that actually *need* to change have to change. An added benefit of frames is that although the content of one frame might move as the page is scrolled, the other frames do not. This means that your navigation bar stays in the same place on the screen at all times—no need to scroll around and find it when you're done with a particular page.

I'm sure you've seen the Target attributes that you can set as you specify links on your pages. Now those attributes are going to come into play. Each frame in a frameset has a name—when you want a link to attach to that frame, you set the Target to the destination frame's name. If you'd like a linked page to be loaded into the same frame that contains its link, there is no need to set a target.

Defining a Frameset

Setting up a frame isn't one of Dreamweaver MX's strong points—if you find this at all confusing, don't feel too bad. The frameset tools are not as intuitive as one might hope. First, create a new document to hold your frames. Next, select the frame category in the Insert panel. I'm going to insert the Left Frame frameset in order to provide a constant navigation element down the left side of the screen.

After inserting the frameset, you should see that your design view is now broken into a few segments, similar to a table. Clicking in any of these areas results in live editing of the HTML document that is contained in that frame. It's important to make the distinction that you aren't editing cells similar to a table—instead you're editing entire HTML files that will be loaded into the frame. However, before you do any editing, it's best to set up the frameset the way you want. You can click on the outline of the frame dividers in your design view to select them. Holding the mouse over one of the frame's borders will change the cursor to a resizing tool. You can click and drag to change the position of the frame borders to fit your particular application. Selecting the outer-most border will select the frameset itself. Go ahead and do that now, and then open the Properties Inspector so that you can see the frameset's information. Figure 3.12 shows the properties for a left-navigation based frameset.

FIGURE 3.12

Select the frameset to edit properties for the individual frames.

After you have the properties open, you can edit the size of the frames by hand. In the lower-right corner of the frameset properties is a small graphical representation of the frames that are available on your screen. Click between them to see what this is actually doing. To adjust one of the frames, just click the one you want to change, and then edit the properties of the frameset:

Borders—If you want a visible border around your frames, set this option.

Border width—This is the width in pixels of a border, if any.

Border color—This is the color of the border, if any.

Column/Row sizes—Sets the exact pixel size or percentage of the browser that a frame should occupy.

With these properties adjusted, you can add some content to your frames. The easiest way to do that, assuming you already have HTML documents you want to insert into the frameset, is to open the Frames panel by choosing Other, Frames from the Window menu. Shown in Figure 3.13, the Frames panel provides a very simple means of selecting the individual frames that make up a frameset. The names of each frame are shown inside the content area of that frame within the panel. Clicking a frame selects it in the design view and allows you to easily adjust its properties in the Properties panel.

FIGURE 3.13

Choose a frame to edit its properties.

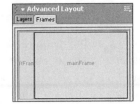

The Frames Properties

After selecting a frame within a frameset, the Properties panel will display the specifics for that frame. In particular, you can modify these attributes:

Frame Name—This is the name by which the frame will be referenced in a `target` attribute. If a link's target is set to this value, the contents of the link will be displayed in this frame.

Src—This is the HTML that will fill this frame. For my example, the filename is `navigation.html` for the left frame and `content.html` for the right.

Scroll—Sets whether the frame will scroll if necessary. If you are using a frame as a holder of a static graphic such as a navigation table, you don't want scroll bars to appear.

No Resize—If you'd like the user to be able to drag frame borders around and resize content areas, make sure that this selection is turned off.

Border—To draw a border around the current frame, set this to Yes. This setting takes precedence over the frameset settings.

Border Color—If you want a border, what color would you like it to be?

Margin Width/Height—Sets a margin for the frame.

Choosing the source (Src) in the Properties panel is the easiest way to attach a document to a particular frame within the set. Although it is possible to edit documents directly within the onscreen frames, this can be confusing because you can't navigate within the frameset—you can only view the initial documents that are displayed.

When you've finished setting up your frames, save the frameset by choosing Save Frameset from the File menu.

The NoFrames Content

Within a frameset definition, a special part of the HTML will be shown if the browser does not support frames. Within this area, you can place an alternate "frameless" version of the page, or inform the viewers that they must upgrade their browsers before continuing. You can access this special content by choosing Edit NoFrames Content from the Frameset option under the Modify menu.

Complex Framesets

The Insert panel's potential framesets is only a starting place for designing your own frames. Similar to tables, you can nest framesets inside of one another to create subdivisions of a given frame. You can also use the Split Frame options under Frameset in the Modify menu to subdivide a frame. This will let you set up your frames within the current frameset rather than embedding multiple frames within one another—which can lead to some nasty code.

Tip

> There is one good reason to embed multiple framesets within one another. As it stands now, a link can only target a single frame, or the top of a frameset. In order to refresh multiple frames within a page, those frames can all be embedded within a single frameset, and the top of that frameset itself can be the target of a link.

To Frame or Not To Frame?

There is some debate whether frames are a good idea for Web sites. I've recently worked on a few projects in which the goal was to redesign an entire site so that it worked outside of frames, even though the layout was originally designed to be included in a frameset.

The trouble with frames is that they can get confusing depending on how a user interacts with them. Suppose that a user goes to a page and finds content in one of the frames that he'd like to bookmark. Depending on the browser, it might bookmark the frameset (which doesn't necessarily include the page the user navigated to), or it might bookmark one of the frames in the frameset if the user highlighted it. For new users, this can be confusing and more than a little distressing.

For dynamic applications, if variables are being passed around to programs that generate the content of the frames, these programs might get out of sync with each other. Instead of having to generate a single page, the software needs to update multiple pages in multiple frames. On the flip side, this means that program functionality, in some cases, can be divided among multiple programs, with each program only knowing how to generate content for its frame.

No matter what route you choose, you'll find reasons for and against it. Frames are an HTML tool, and much like layers and tables, they have their benefits and their drawbacks. Go with what works best for you.

Cascading Style Sheets

Cascading style sheets, or CSS, can make your life as a Web designer much simpler. CSS allows far greater control over the objects in your document and can adjust attributes that aren't accessible from standard HTML.

3

Because of their complexity, editing a CSS manually isn't much fun. Understanding the syntax isn't difficult, but remembering all the attributes that you can set is. For example, here is a simple style sheet that alters the <td> and <th> tags:

```
<style type="text/css">
<!—
td {  font-family: Arial, Helvetica, sans-serif;
      font-size: 10pt; color: #0000CC}
th {  font-family: Arial, Helvetica, sans-serif;
      font-size: 12pt; font-weight: bold; color: #660000}
—>
</style>
```

This style sheet sets the font rendering preference for <td> elements to Arial, Helvetica, sans serif and also assigns a default size and color. Likewise, the <th> tag is also redefined to the same font face, but a larger font size and a different color. Any page that contains this style sheet or is linked to a style sheet containing these attributes will inherit the properties of these tags.

 Note   When you see a list of fonts used in style sheets or within a font tag, it indicates the preferred font rendering order. If the first font in the list is available, it is used, if not, the browser moves to the second, and so on.

The Dreamweaver MX interface makes defining tag attributes very simple—just a few points and clicks and you're set.

Working with Style Sheets

The CSS Styles panel, found under the Window menu or in the Design panel group, is the one-stop shop for creating, modifying, and linking to style sheets. Go ahead and open the CSS Styles panel now. It is shown in Figure 3.14.

FIGURE 3.14

CSS Styles can be applied across a single page or an entire Web site.

The CSS panel starts out empty. If you have an existing style sheet, you can immediately attach it to your document by clicking the first icon in the lower-right of the style sheet panel (rectangle with chain line). You'll be prompted to choose the style sheet within your site directory.

To create a new style, click the New icon in the lower-right corner (the pad of paper with "+" symbol), or choose New Style from the panel's pop-up menu in the upper-right corner. You should now be at the New CSS Style dialog box, shown in Figure 3.15.

FIGURE 3.15

Choose the type of style you want to define and click OK.

Three types of styles you can create are as follows:

Custom Style—The custom style can be applied to HTML objects, but must be explicitly specified when you want to use it. Custom styles are named starting with a period (.).

Redefined HTML Tag—By redefining a tag, you set the default style for that tag when it is used in the document. In order to override this default, you'll need to apply a custom style to the document.

Use CSS Selector—A CSS Selector is a combination of several tags.

The most powerful of these tools is the ability to redefine an HTML tag—suddenly your document can inherit a look without having to change any of the HTML.

You can create your styles in two places—an external file, or in the document that you are working in. If you want to add the style to a new style sheet, choose New Style Sheet File from the pop-up menu in the Define in section of the style creation screen. If you've already attached a style sheet to your document, you can select that sheet instead of creating a new one.

If you prefer to keep the styles defined directly within a document, make sure that This Document Only is selected.

Creating a Style

To create your first style, try redefining a tag like <b>. Click the Redefine HTML Tag button and choose <b> as the tag name. Click OK to continue:

1. Eight categories of attributes can be set for each style. The most common one is Type, which controls font attributes. If the type category is not selected, choose it now. The CSS Style definition dialog box is shown in Figure 3.16.

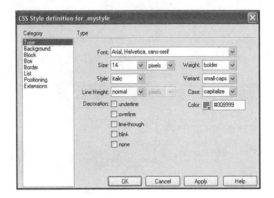

2. Set a sans serif font face, forced to a 72 pixel size, with a bold weight. If you don't want to follow this example exactly, you can choose any of the attributes you prefer to use, including color, style, and line height. In fact, the number of attributes is quite overwhelming. Because of the volume of options, I'm including a short reference immediately following this simple tutorial.

3. When you've finished deciding what your bold tag is going to look like, click the OK button.

4. Before trying the style, go through the same process again; except this time define a custom style for yourself.

5. The process of defining a custom style is exactly the same, except for choosing Make Custom Style (class) instead of Redefine Existing Tag. Name the new custom style `.heading`, and set it as you did the previous font. I choose a size of 128 pixels and an oblique style.

6. Close the style definition window when finished.

After your two styles are created, you should be able to look at the HTML source code for your document and see the style definitions in the <head> section:

```
<style type="text/css">
<!--
b {  font-family: Arial, Helvetica, sans-serif;
       font-size: 72px; line-height: normal; font-weight: bold}
.heading { font-family: Arial, Helvetica, sans-serif;
       font-size: 128px; font-style: oblique; font-weight: bold }
-->
</style>
```

Open the style panel again and take a look at the listed CSS styles that are available. Notice that only superbold is listed. The reason for this is that the only listed styles are custom styles. Styles based on redefined HTML tags are applied automatically and don't need to be listed.

Applying a Style

To apply a CSS-based style that redefines an existing HTML tag, you don't need to do anything except use that tag in your document. Try using the HTML tag you redefined in the previous example. If you followed the example and defined the <b> tag, just enter some text in the design view and choose Style menu under Text.

Notice that all of a sudden the bold tag doesn't behave the way it used to. Anytime you use it in the document where it has been redefined, it will appear using the attributes that you set.

To set text to a custom style, you can use either the CSS Styles panel or the CSS Styles menu under Text. Simply select what you want to apply a style to, and then click the style in the panel or choose it from the appropriate menu. If the auto-apply check box in the lower-right corner of the panel is not checked, you'll need to click the Apply button in the panel before the style will be applied. The None style will remove any applied styles from the current selection.

For precise control over where the style is applied, you can use the pop-up menu at the top of the CSS Style panel to choose any of the containing tags of the current selection.

Tip

> If you've set up styles that aren't appearing correctly in your document design view, it might be that Dreamweaver MX doesn't support rendering that particular style attribute. Check the CSS definition screens for an * by your missing attribute. If you see an *, you'll need to preview your document in a browser to see that style attribute rendered correctly.

Editing and Linking to External Style Sheets

Defining styles within a document is perfectly fine, but doesn't make the best use of style sheets. Instead of redefining styles each time they need to be used, you can create a master style sheet that is linked to by every page that needs it. This is a more efficient means of keeping your site consistent. The most direct way to link to a style sheet is using the Attach Style Sheet icon in the lower-right corner of the CSS panel, as mentioned earlier. This, however, doesn't give you the greatest amount of control over the style sheets—you can use the Edit Style Sheet panel menu to manage linked styles in your document.

To create an external style sheet, use the panel menu, or choose CSS Styles, Edit Style Sheet from the Text menu. The Style Sheet editor seen in Figure 3.17 should appear.

FIGURE 3.17

You can edit and link to style sheets from this window.

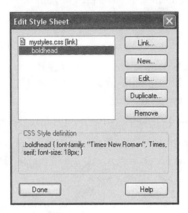

From this view, you can create new styles or duplicate, edit, and remove selected styles. The item that we're mostly interested in right now is the Link button. Go ahead and click it now. You'll be prompted for a file or URL to link to and given the option to link or import the targeted style sheet. The Link External Style Sheet dialog box is shown in Figure 3.18.

FIGURE 3.18

Link to an existing style sheet or provide a new name to create a new file.

If you have a style sheet created, enter its location in the URL. If not, supply a new file-name in the URL field and click OK. This creates a new empty style sheet.

Note   The Style Sheet *import* function only works on Internet Explorer. You should always *link* to external style sheets so that you maintain the greatest cross-platform compatibility.

The Edit Style Sheet dialog box will reappear listed with the linked-to style sheet. To start working with the new style sheet file, select it in the list and click Edit. An empty copy of the edit window will appear. This window references the linked style sheet. Here you can add all the styles you prefer. They'll be saved to the external file, but will be accessible in your current document. On subsequent Web pages, you can simply link to this newly established style sheet and instantly have access to all your styles.

Tip

Dreamweaver MX does not currently offer the ability to copy styles between sheets. If you want to merge two existing style sheets, open them in a text editor and copy the contents from one into the other.

A reference to the supported Dreamweaver MX CSS elements is included in Appendix C.

A Final Word on Styles

When you start using CSS, don't get carried away. CSS is a great idea and a fantastic tool, but it does not always work the way you would think. There are inconsistencies between Internet Explorer and Netscape, and between the same browsers on different platforms.

In my experiences with CSS, I've found that it is very useful for maintaining consistent text attributes across pages and keeping sites as cross-platform as possible. Don't expect things to look exactly as they do in the Dreamweaver MX design view, however. Be sure to preview in your browser frequently and have more than one browser platform to use in your tests.

Customizing the Document Design Window

To better use the advanced layout tools, Macromedia has provided several ways to customize the Dreamweaver MX design window so that you can create a more layout-oriented design experience.

Page Properties and Tracing Images

As you've seen, you can edit the title of your page by using the Properties panel on the appropriate tag within the page heading or directly from within the design window toolbar. Dreamweaver MX also provides another means of accessing common page properties, including the page title, margins, and default link/background colors. To access these attributes for any page, choose Page Properties from the Modify menu. The Page Properties dialog box is shown in Figure 3.19.

3

FIGURE 3.19

*The Page Properties
dialog box allows you
to set a variety of
attributes within the
head and body sections
of the HTML.*

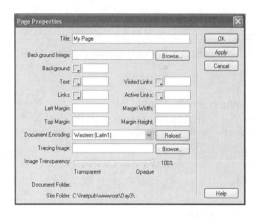

As you can see, there are several useful items here:

Title—This is the title of the current page.

Background Image—Don't confuse this with the tracing image. The background
image is a repeating tiled image that is displayed in the background of the Web page.

Background—Sets a background color for the page. You can either type a standard
HTML hexadecimal color code into the appropriate field, or click the color square to
pop up the color picker. You'll learn more about the color picker shortly.

Text—Controls the color of the text on the Web page.

Links—Sets the colors of links, active links, and visited links.

Margins—A page's margins are set using the four margin fields. If you want the contents of a page to adjoin the upper-right corner of the browser window, set these to 0.
There are four attribute settings because margin widths are set with different attributes
in Netscape (width/height) and Internet Explorer (left/top). You'll need to set all four
of these fields in order to have full cross-browser compatibility.

Document Encoding—This is the default language for the document.

Tracing Image/Image Transparency—The tracing image and its corresponding
transparency setting allow you to pick an image which will be displayed in the background of the document design window while you work.

Although most of these features are simply attributes that you can set by directly editing
the <body> and <head> document tags, the tracing image isn't actually a part of the final
HTML design—it is simply a graphic that is displayed in the back of the design window.

Tracing Images

If you've ever had to layout a Web page based on an existing piece of art, you know how
hard it is to make everything line up exactly as it did in the original artwork. To make

life easier, Dreamweaver MX includes the ability to add tracing images to the background of any document. This image floats behind the actual page and can be used to align elements so that the HTML stays true to the original designer's vision.

To add a tracing image to the document window, choose Tracing Image, and then Load from the View window. You will be prompted to select an image file to use. Once chosen, the image will be displayed in your window aligned to the upper-right corner of your HTML. Figure 3.20 shows a Web page with a tracing image turned on.

FIGURE 3.20

The tracing image floats behind the Web page and allows the designer to use it as a guide.

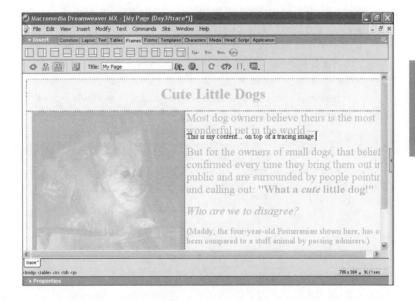

You might find that you don't want the tracing image located at the origin point of the HTML. To move the tracing image, you can use Adjust Position option under the View and Tracing Image menus to enter exact pixel coordinates or move the image around using the arrow keys. You can also align an image with an existing object (useful for using a tracing image to layout a table) by selecting the object and choosing Align with Selection from the same menu. At all times, the tracing image can be reset to its original position with the Reset Position option.

You might be thinking to yourself, "Isn't that image going to get in the way of my design process?" The answer is almost certainly, "yes." Luckily, Macromedia has this under control. The Tracing image also has a transparency control that lets you ghost the image so that it can barely be seen on your display. Setting the tracing image to be nearly invisible keeps it from overwhelming the display and interfering with the design process. To set the transparency, choose Page Properties from the Modify menu and use the Image Transparency slider to adjust the image from fully visible (100%) to invisible (0%).

To quickly hide the tracing image at any time, just deselect Show from the View, Tracing Image menu.

Grids and Rulers

If you need visual alignment cues, you can also add grid guidelines and rules to the design window. From the View menu, choose Grid and the Edit Grid option. This option lets you create a grid, specifying the spacing of the cells, color, style, and snap to.

Rulers can also be used to help position items. Once again, go to the View menu. Choose Rulers and Show. From the Rulers submenu, you can also adjust the units that the rulers are shown in. If you'd like to change the origin of the ruler, just click and drag from the upper-right corner of the onscreen rulers to wherever on the page you want the 0,0 point to be located. Choose Reset Origin from the View, Rulers menu to reset this point to its original location. Figure 3.21 shows the design window with grid and ruler options active.

FIGURE 3.21

Grids can aid in the layout of HTML elements.

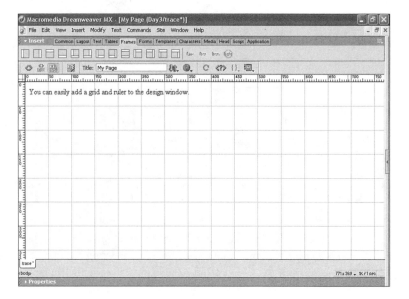

Forms: A Brief Introduction

An HTML component that you haven't seen yet is the form. Forms are used to create the interactive elements of Web sites. As such, it isn't something you'll really get a chance to use until you've reached the dynamic portions of Dreamweaver MX. If you need to create forms that connect to existing dynamic applications, you'll have to learn the tools, so let's do that now.

There really isn't a good way to demonstrate the use of form elements until they come into play later in the text, so this will just serve as a reference until later.

Here is a summary of Insert panel form objects, and what they're used for:

Form—The <form> tag set *contains* the other elements in the form and determines how they will be transmitted to an application for processing. Just as a <table> object holds rows and cells, the <form> holds input fields, buttons, and so on.

Text Field—Text fields are used to collect information from the users. Although text fields are single-line elements, Dreamweaver MX abstracts the text field to a point where it can instantly be converted to and from a multiline field (actually a <textarea>).

Hidden Field—Hidden fields are used to carry data along with the form that you might not really want the user to see. Check out Day 6, "Introduction to Dynamic Web Applications and Database Design," for more information on variable passing. Hidden fields should never be used to pass sensitive information. Users can always create a local copy of a form with hidden fields and manually edit the fields to contain whatever data they want. A bank, for example, wouldn't want to pass a user's current balance around through a hidden field. The users could potentially edit the value and drastically increase their net worth.

Text Area—Text areas, like text fields, are used to collect information from the users. Text areas, however are multiline text fields and can collect several lines of information. Dreamweaver MX can convert text areas to text fields and vice versa.

Check Box—The check box is used to create a group of items that can be turned off or on. This is usually used on a form to select multiple attributes that apply to something (implying an AND state). The most common misuse of the check box is applying it to OR states, such as "Click yes OR no."

Radio Button—Similar to the check box, the radio button also enables users to choose among several attributes on a form. Unlike the check box, however, the radio *should* be used when an OR state is implied. If two radio buttons share the same name, they are mutually exclusive of one another. (Both cannot be selected at the same time.) Radio buttons are sometimes used in the place of check boxes. If each radio button is named differently, this *almost* works. When a radio button is set, it cannot be unselected unless a Reset button is supplied for the form.

Radio Group—Because radio buttons are usually added in groups, the Radio Group tool automates the process. This is used to create a collect of like-named radio buttons and their labels.

List/Menu—The list/menu is a rather bizarre construct because it behaves very differently between its two forms. In one configuration, it is simply a pop-up menu that can

3

be used to choose one option among several choices (for example, choose your state from the list). In its other incarnation, it displays as a rectangular scrolling list in which multiple items can be highlighted. In my opinion, although they take more room, check boxes are better suited to providing the "pick all that apply" functionality than lists are.

Jump Menu—The jump menu is not a form element, but is a JavaScript construct that you can use on any page, regardless of whether it is part of a server-processed form. Creating a jump menu in your document creates a simple pop-up menu that visitors can use to quickly jump to different parts of your Web site.

Image Field—Image fields are typically used as graphical form submit buttons, yet they also transmit back information to the server in the form of the X and Y coordinates where the click took place—just like an image map.

File Field—The file field is finally starting to be useful now that all modern browsers support it. If you've seen one of the "Upload your files to 20MB of free remote storage" Web sites, you've probably seen the file field in use. The file field enables a Web page to submit an entire file to a server for processing. Some of the more interesting uses of this feature have been on Web pages that allow retailers to customize their merchandise by uploading a logo that is then mapped to their product catalog.

Button—Button elements are most frequently used to submit the contents of a form, or reset them to their default values.

Label/Fieldset—The final two buttons in the form category of the Insert panel—label and fieldset—simply insert the `<label>` and `<fieldset>` tags into the document. They do not add anything to the design window.

As you work with form elements, you'll start to understand the common elements between them. Most form elements, for example, submit information, have a default value, and a name.

Text Fields

For example, let's take a look at the most common element you'll see—text fields. Add in a text field by clicking the Text Field icon in the Tool panel or by choosing Text Field from the Form Object submenu under Insert. A single field should be inserted into the document. Select the field in the design view and open the Properties panel, shown in Figure 3.22.

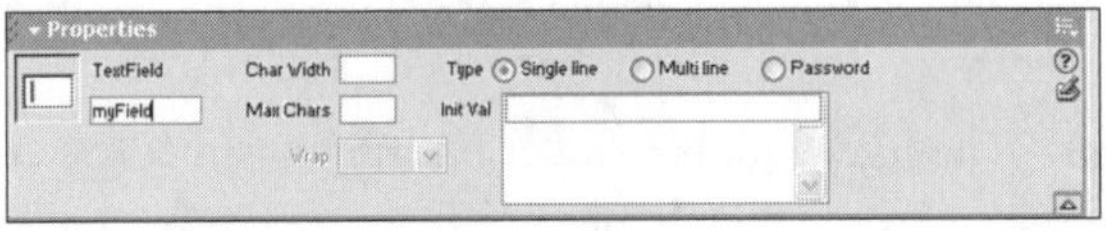

FIGURE 3.22

Form objects have properties, just like everything else.

Here you can change the attributes of the text field that is being used in the document. The three variations of fields available from the one Text Field tool are as follows:

Single line—Inputs a single line of text at a time. Although you can use this to input long sentences and even paragraphs, it's mostly useful for gathering one or two words from the users. This is the default text field type.

Multi line—Lets the users type multiple lines of data in a more free-form style. This field type does not allow styles as in a traditional word processor, but does give the same cursor control that users are accustomed to. Although accessed using the same Text Field tool, this form element is actually quite different from the other two options.

Password—The password field is just what it sounds like, a field for entering passwords. This field type is identical to the single line field, but it replaces the user input with symbols so that it can't be read. In all honesty, there is very little protection offered by using this field on a page. It does not secure a site and only offers a very basic visual form of protection.

Besides setting a field type, you also need to set a name for each field. This name will be used by the Dreamweaver server behaviors to receive and process incoming data.

A few other fields can be set in order to restrict the user's input or change the way the field is displayed onscreen. They are as follows:

Char Width—The character width attribute determines the number of characters that can be entered into the field and displayed onscreen at a time. This does *not* affect the number of characters that the field can hold; only the number that can be seen.

Max Chars (Single line and Password only)—The maximum number of characters a field can hold. Use this value to set an upper limit on the typing that a user can perform. This is useful for keeping data within the defined size limits of the fields.

Num Lines (Multi line option only)—For multi-line displays, this attribute replaces the Max Chars option. The Num Lines determines the number of rows of text that will be visible to the users when they enter information. There is no way to set the maximum number of characters in a multi-line field, other than checking its size with JavaScript.

Init Val—The initial value that the field will contain. This value will show up in the form when it is first displayed. This value can be edited by the person viewing the form.

Caution

Be careful when using initial values. Users have a tendency to skip over already filled-in fields. You might end up with bad data unless you force them to choose a value.

Wrap (Multi line option only)—The Wrap attribute controls how text is wrapped when the end of the line is reached in a multi-line form element. The Off setting will scroll the text area horizontally when the user reaches the edge of the text area. Pressing Return is the only way to start a new line. Virtual will automatically place the cursor on the next line when it reaches the edge of the text area but doesn't add an EOL (End of Line) character to the text. Physical behaves the same way as a Virtual wrap, but it does insert an EOL at the end of each line.

Submit Buttons

Another common form element is the button. Buttons are usually used to trigger the processing of form information. Clicking the button object in the Insert panel will add a basic Submit button to the form at your present cursor position.

The properties of a simple Submit button are shown in Figure 3.23.

FIGURE 3.23

You can name your button from the Properties panel.

If you're just using the button to submit a form, most likely all you need to set is the label. The *button label* is the text that is actually drawn inside the button graphic on the page. Don't confuse this with the *button name*, which provides a form field name for the button object.

Tip

What good is a field name for a button? Actually, buttons are just as valid an input device as any other field on a form. For example, assume that you have a form collecting data on your inventory of video tapes. Rather than having a radio button or text field that needs to be set each time for the rating (G, PG, PG-13, R, or NC-17), you could set the value as part of the submit process. You would just create five submit buttons sharing the common name "rating." Each would submit a different value for the movie's rating when it is clicked. Don't discount the usefulness of the button as an input device.

There are two other actions that a button can take on. The action you've probably seen before on other pages is the reset action. A button defined as a reset button and added to a form will automatically change all field values to their defaults when it is clicked. This provides a convenient way for a user to start over without having to manually clear out data from the fields in the form.

Caution

Be careful when labeling and placing your Submit and Reset buttons on the page. If a user spends 15 minutes filling out a form on a page, only to click the Reset button because it is featured more prominently than the Submit button, he or she is likely to give up.

Note

The reset action resets the form to its initial empty state. If you used initial values for your fields, however, those values are restored as well.

The other type of button action, None, is no action at all. This is generally used in conjunction with JavaScript to provide client-side behaviors.

Image Buttons

If you want to be fancy with your presentation, there is another type of button you can use to submit data: an image button. This button is a bit strange in that it doesn't submit data to the server in exactly the same format as the standard HTML Submit button. To add an image button to your document, click the Image Field item in the Forms panel. As with any image, you'll be prompted for the location of the image file. This is a pure HTML construct and doesn't use any JavaScript, so it is *just* an image—there is no down or rollover state for it.

The behavior of the Image Field starts out the same as a standard Submit button—it submits the contents of the current form to the server for processing. However, it also sends additional data about where the user clicked on the image button in order to cause the submit to take place. This additional information is encoded into two additional variables named with the original image field name, but with a X and a Y on the end, and it contains the X and Y coordinates of the user's click in the image.

This information can be used for processing real-time image maps of images that are generated on-the-fly, or for guessing games in which the user must click somewhere on an image in order to win a prize.

The drawback to using image fields as buttons is that they don't offer the same level of feedback as traditional buttons, and they are difficult to maintain. Every time you want to change a button on your page, you have to edit the graphic of the button—not just edit its label. On a positive note, I find that graphical buttons are "prettier" and offer a friendlier browsing experience. They can be laid out on the screen precisely as you want them, rather than you relying on the browser to render a button with the same dimensions you happened to have in mind.

Although this is but a short introduction to forms, you shouldn't worry about not getting to use them later. We'll use make of the form objects once we reach the dynamic portions of this book.

Direct Access to the HTML

There comes a time, no matter what you're doing, when you need to have access to the HTML itself, rather than just the WYSIWYG interface. It's often easier to change a few tags by hand than to select the objects, open the Properties panel, find the appropriate attribute to change, and change it.

To view HTML within the document design window, you have two choices—either a straight code view (Code), or a code and design view (Code and Design). Switch to these modes by choosing the appropriate option from the View menu or by clicking the icons in the design window toolbar. The Code and Design mode is shown in Figure 3.24. You can toggle between all three window modes by using Switch Views from the View menu.

FIGURE 3.24

The Code and Design view lets you edit the HTML directly or visually.

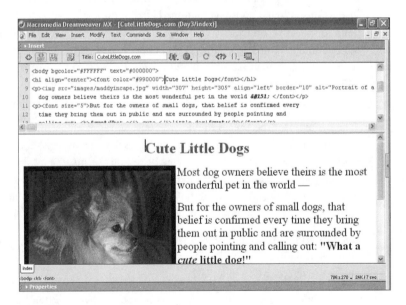

The editor is easy to use, but offers advanced features such as syntax highlighting, automatic indentation, and code completion (for those writing server-side code). The Edit menu has several features specific to working in the code view—Indent/Outdent Code to adjust indentation, Balance Braces for JavaScript programming, and Code Hints for those writing server-side code.

Note If you're a programmer, you'll greatly appreciate code hints, which are active by default. These "hints" appear after typing a few characters of a server language function, allowing you to quickly auto-complete the code.

Transferring Selections Between Views

As you are editing the HTML in either the code or design view, you can select the HTML text or the objects themselves within the design view. Once selected, if you switch views, the selection also appears in the alternate view. For example, if you graphically select a table in the document design view, the `<table></table>` tags (and everything in between) will also be selected in the code view. On very complex pages, this makes it simple to find what you're looking for in the HTML.

Similarly, as you update HTML code, the design view is immediately updated and vice versa. If the views get out of sync, you can force a reload with the circular arrow icon in the toolbar.

Changing Line Options

Text in the HTML code display can be displayed with line numbers by selecting the appropriate options from the top-right menu of the toolbar. Line numbers are mostly useful for debugging source code of dynamic applications. You probably won't use it much while editing standard HTML.

Lines can be displayed wrapped to the length of the size of the editing window by using the Word Wrap menu selection. Although displaying the window in a non-wrapping mode makes it easier to understand the structure of the HTML, it means that you often have to scroll horizontally to find the tags you're looking for.

From this same menu, you can also choose to auto-indent code as it is entered, highlight invalid HTML tags, and color your code syntax.

Using the Quick Tag Editor

The Quick Tag Editor lets you quickly edit the HTML from within the standard design-editing mode. Selecting an object in the design window, opening the Properties panel, and clicking the icon directly below the help icon launches the Quick Tag Editor. The Quick Tag Editor simply brings up a pop-up window that contains the HTML of the tag being edited. You can change any of the HTML in the tag directly. Although this might not seem like a very important feature, sometimes you know exactly what you want to change on a tag, but you don't want to search through the source code or deal with going through an interface to find it. The Quick Tag Editor gives you exactly what you want and doesn't force you to use a GUI interface to make your changes.

3

If you're working in the document design window and have an item selected, you can also bring up the Quick Tag Editor by choosing Quick Tag Editor from the Modify menu. This enables you to directly access the HTML you need without needing the Properties panel.

| Tip | Control+T (Windows) or Command+T (Macintosh) can be used to easily access the Quick Tag Editor. |

Referencing Tag Information

To use the extensive reference capabilities of Dreamweaver MX from within the editor, you can select a tag that you want to look up, and then click the <?> button in the toolbar. Within a few seconds, Dreamweaver MX will open the Tag Reference panel and show you all the available options for a specific tag. This is a fantastic way to find additional attributes to fine-tune your HTML manually. Figure 3.25 shows the Tag Reference panel.

FIGURE 3.25

The Tag Reference panel contains complete information on every document tag.

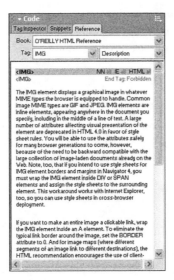

| Note | The Tag Reference panel can be used at any time, not just in the design view. You can access it from the Window menu's Reference option. |

Exploring Search Features

If you need to search for text or tags within the HTML, you can use the built-in find and search/replace options. The search and replace features are somewhat extensive, and should allow you to find very complex patterns within the HTML. The Edit menu contains your search options:

Find and Replace—Performs a search and replace operation on the HTML. This option also allows for Find without replace, so it can be used for all your searching needs.

Find Again—Finds the next occurrence of the search item and highlights it in the HTML.

Let's go ahead and take a look at the Find and Replace window now. Figure 3.26 shows this window in its fully expanded form.

FIGURE 3.26

A wide variety of options are available in the Find and Replace window.

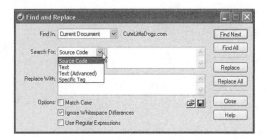

In this example search, I've chosen to search the Current Document for the tag <td> that does not have the bgcolor attribute set. The bottom of the window shows a list of the files where a match was found and what the matching tag looks like. This detailed section of the window is normally hidden and can be toggled on or off by clicking the expansion triangle in the lower-right portion of the window.

The search and replace options are varied and can be adapted to match patterns rather than just literal strings or tags. Here's how you can modify the search and replace options so that they fit your needs.

Search Scope

Adjusting the Find In attributes lets you change what files are going to be checked. You can check the current document, the entire local site, selected files in the site, and the contents of a folder. Being able to update hundreds of files simultaneously enables you to easily fix problems that would be a nightmare otherwise. For example, if your site has hundreds of links to an external site spread throughout the source, updating those links would take an eternity if the domain name changed. A properly defined search and replace on the entire site will fix the problem in a matter of seconds.

Search Criteria

The next thing you'll need to do is specify exactly what you're searching for by choosing the appropriate option from the Find What section. The following search types are available:

Text—A text search operates only on the body text of the document—not the text within any of the tags.

Source Code—This search examines the contents of the HTML tags themselves. This is the opposite of the Text search.

Text (Advanced)—The Advanced text search lets you check the text inside and outside tags. Using the "+" and "-" buttons, you add and delete attributes that you want, or don't want to find.

Specific Tag—The Tag search is similar to the advanced search, but it only searches the inside of tags.

Actions

After a search has been defined, you can click the Find Next or Find All button to perform the search, or define a Replace action that will take place on the items that are located.

Most of the search types provide a simple Replace With field to enter your text or tags. This will do exactly what you expect. If you are using the Tag search type, you can specify an attribute change action. For example, you can easily change the value of bgcolor, width, and height globally.

Search Modifiers

A few options are available that can alter a search in very dramatic ways:

Match Case—The text being searched for must *exactly* match the text that is found based on capitalization.

Ignore Whitespace—Because the HTML language condenses strings of spaces, it is very likely that words aren't necessarily next to each other. This will ignore extra spaces if they exist between words.

Use Regular Expressions—Regular expressions enable patterns to be searched for, rather than literal text. These will require some additional explanation.

The most powerful type of search is one in which you aren't just matching literal characters, but patterns of characters. For example, if you wanted to match anything in the text that appears to be a phone number of the format ###-###-####, there is no way to do this with a traditional search string without testing for every single possibility. Through the use of regular expressions, you can easily match that sequence of numbers with "\d{3}-\d{3}-\d{4}". This might look a bit confusing at first, but it's quite simple. By inserting certain characters into your search string, you can create a search pattern that matches many variations of a string.

Here is a list of the regular expressions available, and an example of their use:

\w—This is an alphanumeric character. \w\w\w would match any three character string containing letters or numbers. To match anything *but* an alphanumeric character, use \W.

\d—This is any number. \d\d\d-\d\d\d-\d\d\d\d is an alternative version of the pattern to match a simple phone number. As with the previous tag, the \D variation of this expression matches anything that isn't a number.

.—This is any character except a newline. h.ppy will match happy, hoppy, or any other character in the second position.

\s—This is a whitespace, such as a tab or space. happy\sday will match the word happy and day as long as there is a space between them. To match something that isn't a space, use \S.

\t—This is a tab. Field1\tField2 matches the word Field1 followed by a tab and then Field2.

\r,\n,\f—This is return, newline, and form feed. Depending on the platform that the HTML was originally created on, you might need to use one or more of these matches.

a|b—Matches either the pattern on the right or the left side. left|right will match either left or right.

[xyz]—Matches any of the characters within brackets. [012345] will match the numbers between 0 and 5. To negate this pattern, put a ^ at the front of the character list. For example, [^012345] will match any number that *isn't* 0–5.

—Matches the preceding character zero or as many times as possible. test\d will match the string test followed by as many digits as it can, or none if no digits are available.

+—Matches the preceding character at least once. test\d+ will match the string test followed by at least one digit.

?—Matches the preceding character at *most* once. ca?t will match cat and ct.

{x}—Matches the preceding character a specific number of times. The initial phone number pattern we looked at, \d{3}-\d{3}-\d{4}, uses this construct.

{x,y}—Forces a match of at least *x* repetitions, but no more than *y*. \d{5,10} will match between 5 and 10 digits.

^—Matches the beginning of a line. ^Line 1 will match the string Line 1 only if it occurs at the *start* of a line.

**$**—Matches the end of a line. Line 1$ will match the string Line 1 only if it occurs at the *end* of a line.

\b—Matches the border of a word. \bpaste will match the word paste but *not* the word toothpaste. Likewise, \B is the inverse and will match a position that *isn't* a word boundary.

By constructing searches using regular expressions, you can efficiently find patterns that match multiple items in a single pass. This is far more efficient than having to deal with conducting multiple searches for similar items.

> **Tip**
>
> If you define a particularly complicated search pattern, you might not want to have to type it over again the next time you use it. To save your query, click the disk icon in the Find/Replace window. Saved queries can then be reloaded by clicking the folder icon.

Searches can be performed at any time, regardless of whether you are in the HTML source view. Be aware that you cannot run a Search and Replace on files that aren't open. You should always make a copy of your site before performing a potentially destructive search and replace.

> **Note**
>
> Although staying within a single program for editing purposes is nice, sometimes the advanced features of other text editors can come in handy. Dreamweaver MX can launch your favorite text editor by choosing the Edit with option from the Edit menu. You can set the preferred editor within the File Types/Editors Preference category.

Tag Inspector

Another way to look at an overview of the HTML in your document as it is created through the Tag Inspector panel. This tool, shown in Figure 3.27, displays the documents HTML as a hierarchical list of basic tags.

FIGURE 3.27

The Tag Inspector presents a hierarchical view of the document's HTML.

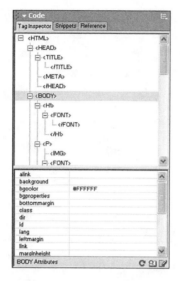

The Tag Inspector does not show all the document at once, or all the attributes for every tag. In order reveal more information, you must expand the tags that contain the objects you want to see. For example, the <body> tag contains everything in the design view—expanding it will display the objects (tables, images, and so on) you've added to your document. To view the attributes that have been set for a particular tag, highlight the tag in the Tag Inspector and the attributes will appear in the lower part of the panel. You can even edit the values for the attributes by double-clicking the fields beside their names, or by selecting a tag and clicking the Edit icon in the lower-right corner of the panel.

Tag Library Editor

The Tag Library Editor is invoked by clicking the middle icon at the lower-right corner of the Tag Inspector. This tool is probably best left as-is for beginners. It allows you to browse the tags that Dreamweaver MX supports, expand the tags, and edit the individual attributes that the program recognizes. Tag libraries are available for HTML and all the supported development languages. The Tag Library Editor is displayed in Figure 3.28.

Tag Chooser

A more appropriate way to view and insert tags (rather than digging through the Library Editor) is to use the Tag Chooser—accessible by choosing Tag from the Insert menu. The Tag Chooser, shown in Figure 3.29, divides tags into functional groups, such as Lists, Tables, and so on, and allows you to easily find the HTML you want to use, and then insert it into the document.

FIGURE 3.28

The Tag Library Editor can be used to edit the very tags that Dreamweaver MX recognizes.

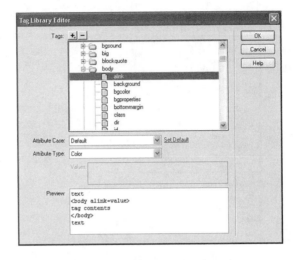

FIGURE 3.29

The Tag Chooser allows you to browse the available tag libraries.

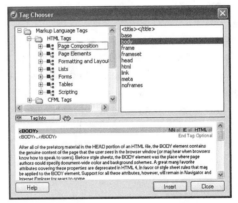

Drill down through the different tag libraries, groups, and so on, to reach the individual tags, which will be displayed in the right pane of the panel. Highlighting one of the available tags and clicking Insert will add it to your document.

To see more information about a selected tag, click the Tag Info button to see the usage information for the highlighted tag. Alternatively, using the <?> button will open the reference information for the tag.

As you can see, Dreamweaver MX offers a number of ways to view your HTML, insert tags directly, and explore the available attributes for modifying each tag.

Site-Management Tools

The final section of today's lesson will investigate the advanced Dreamweaver MX site-management tools. Yesterday you learned how to define a site; today you'll learn how to upload it to a remote server.

Configuring Remote Server Access

You already know the steps required to define a static site. Let's take that a step further, and look at how we can access remote files in Dreamweaver MX.

Begin the site definition as you normally would. Immediately after answering the "Would You Like To Use a Server Technology" (which you should answer "no"), you'll be presented with the choice of determining where your files are located. This dialog box is displayed in Figure 3.30.

FIGURE 3.30

This step determines where the files are going to be stored.

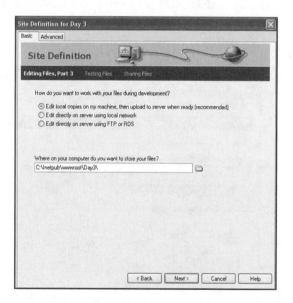

You have three choices for how Dreamweaver MX treats your files—either storing them locally and uploading them when needed, editing the files on your local network (this is the same as mounting and editing from a network drive), and, finally, editing directly on an FTP or RDS (ColdFusion) server. It is highly recommended that you choose the first option, as it provides the best control over your files and is least prone to accidents.

If you choose to edit files directly on the server using a mounted volume, choose the second option. You will be prompted for the path to the server volume. From

Dreamweaver's perspective, this is any folder that your computer has access to—it doesn't care, as long as it can see it. If you're *writing* the site on the server itself, you can use this option and simply choose the folder the pages should be published to.

If you choose to edit the files directly on the FTP or RDS server, you'll *still* need to pick a local folder to hold a local copy of the files—they *aren't* being edited on the remote server, despite the misleading dialog box. In order to edit a file, Dreamweaver MX will download it first, and then allow you to edit it. The "Automatically Upload files to the server every time I save" check box, when activated, keeps the local files automatically synchronized with the server. If this box is *not* checked, there's no difference between choosing this route, or storing the files locally and uploading them when needed (the first option for where the files will be stored).

If you choose the local Network option, click Next and you're done!

Assuming you chose to use FTP/RDS or store the files locally and connect as needed, the next setup dialog box is identical. (No, I don't particularly understand this either.) Figure 3.31 shows the remote connection setup dialog box.

FIGURE 3.31

*The Sharing Files dia-
log box allows you to
configure the setup of
the remote server
connection.*

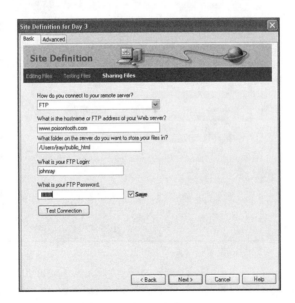

Regardless of how you got here, you have five possible choices for how to connect to a remote server:

None—There is no server connection. This is what you used yesterday.

FTP—Connect to a remote FTP (File Transfer Protocol) server for exchanging files.

Local/Network—Connect to the remote server using a mounted server volume or just save it to a local folder.

RDS—Use a Remove Development Services server to store the remote files.

WebDAV—Connect to a Web Distributed Authoring and Versioning server.

Whatever option you choose, you'll need to contact your server administrator or ISP to find out exactly what information you need to enter for the configuration options. If you choose WebDAV or RDS, click the Settings box to open a configuration window and enter the share point information for these protocols. The FTP configuration is displayed directly within the setup window and features a Test Connection button for verifying the settings. This is *only* available if you're using FTP.

After configuring the connection with the information provided by your server administrator, click the Next button.

The final setup dialog box, not shown in this section, is for configuring the Check-In/Check-Out system for sharing editing with others. You'll learn how to set up Check-In/Check-Out in Day 5, "Creating Reusable Components." For now, set these options to "Do Not Enable Check-In and Check-Out."

Advanced Settings

A more straightforward way to edit remote server settings (especially if you've already created a site and want to upload it to a remote server) is to click the Advanced tab within the site definition and select the Remote Info category. Shown in Figure 3.32, this is similar to what you saw when choosing your server access method.

FIGURE 3.32

The Remote Info category provides direct access to your remote server settings.

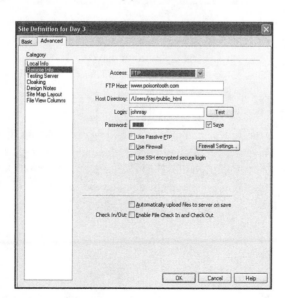

Use the Access pop-up menu to choose between FTP, WebDAV, Local/Network, and RDS settings. RDS, WebDAV, and Local/Network offer no more features than available when doing a simple setup. FTP, however, provides additional settings for getting through firewalls. If you are behind a NAT or network-connection-sharing device, click the Passive FTP option, or your connections are likely to fail. Likewise, if your administrator uses a firewall, click the Use Firewall button, and then click the Firewall Settings box (the same as choosing Site in the Dreamweaver MX preferences). As with the basic connection information itself, I can't tell you what the firewall values will need to be—it's dependent on your network setup.

Two additional options are available for the all the connection methods:

Automatically upload files to server on save—Each time a file is saved locally, it is uploaded automatically to the remote server.

Enable File Check In and Check Out—The File Check In/Out system is used during distributed editing to keep from overwriting files that others are working with. You'll learn more about it in Day 5.

What Is a Testing Server?

You might have noticed that there is a category for Testing Servers in the Advanced Site Definition. This is a *third* location that your files could potentially inhabit. It is typically called a "staging" server and is used to test files before they are sent to the final remote server. The testing server is configured exactly like a remote server and is accessed through the Site panel, which you'll learn about next.

Cloaking

When working with your site files, you might have to deal with files and folders that aren't directly related to your pages (Photoshop files, content folders, or server files such as .htaccess files on Apache). To "hide" these files, you can use the Cloaking feature of the advanced site definition, shown in Figure 3.33.

After enabling cloaking, you can also choose to enable cloaking files with a particular ending. More frequently, you'll choose to cloak an object by right-clicking it in the Site panel and choosing Cloak from the Cloaking menu, or using the Cloaking submenu in the Site menu. This menu can also be used to quickly enable or disable cloaking for a file, folder, or deactivate cloaking for everything.

FIGURE 3.33

Use a cloak to hide files not related to your site.

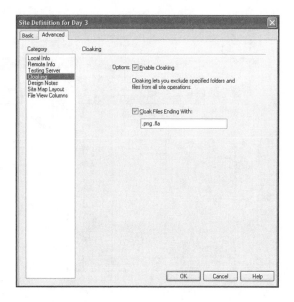

Using the Connection

If you've set up a connection you're ready to try the file transfer features of the Site panel. Go ahead and connect to the remote site by clicking the Plug Connect button at the top of the screen. Figure 3.34 demonstrates a live connection between my local computer and a remote FTP site (with the site window expanded).

 Note

If you are working in the single-paned panel view, you can switch to the remote site by choosing Remote View from the pop-up menu on the right side of the panel.

If your screen only shows the local files, click the small triangle in the lower-left corner of the file window so that it points to the right. You're now ready to transfer files between your local and remote sites.

 Note

When the Dreamweaver Site panel is maximized and the Site Files icon is clicked, you'll see the local files on the right and the remote server files on the left. If you're using the "third" server (a testing server), you can switch to a view of the local files and testing server files by clicking the Testing Server icon.

FIGURE 3.34

A live connection is made.

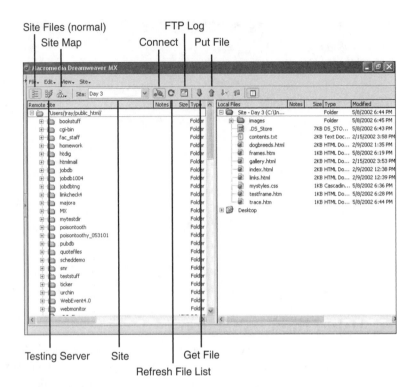

Site Files (normal)
Site Map
FTP Log
Connect
Put File

Testing Server
Site
Get File
Refresh File List

Manually Transferring Files

The easiest way to move files between the different locations is to click and drag. An extremely beneficial feature of this process is that Dreamweaver MX will determine what the selected file(s) dependant files are, and it will offer to transfer them. This saves you the trouble of trying to find everything that goes with a certain file—it will be done automatically. You can drag individual files, multiple files, or even entire folders between these views.

Alternatively, you can follow the FTP model for file transfers and use the Put button (up arrow) to put files from the local directories onto the remote servers. The Get button (down arrow) retrieves files and folders from the remote server. A status bar in the lower-right corner of the Site Files window shows the progress of the files as they are transferred. Clicking the red stop sign by the status bar cancels the current action in progress.

If something goes wrong during the FTP process, you can view a log of the FTP commands sent to the remote server with the FTP Log option found in the Window menu or in the Site panel toolbar. There's a good chance you can find the solution to your problems here.

Refreshing the File View

If a file changes (is added or deleted) on the local or remote side without the knowledge of Dreamweaver MX, it probably won't show up in the file listing. If you feel that something isn't appearing on either side of the connection, you can refresh the files that are shown by clicking the refresh button—the circular arrow at the top of the site view. This will reload both sides of the display.

If you'd specifically prefer to force the local or the remote file lists to refresh, you can choose Refresh Local or Refresh Remote from the Site Files View submenu located under Site. This forces only the appropriate file listing to be reloaded.

Synchronizing Files

The most useful way of transferring files is through synchronization. Instead of trying to find all the updated files you need to transfer manually, you can ask Dreamweaver MX to help you determine what has changed. If you'd just like a list of what has changed, use the Select Newer Local and Select Newer Remote commands from the Site Files View menu. This highlights all the files in the respective list that are newer than the corresponding file at the other end of the connection. You can then drag the files over to the opposite side to synchronize the file listing. This, coupled with Dreamweaver MX's capability to also transfer dependent files, makes this a great way to keep things in sync without turning complete control over to Dreamweaver MX.

If you prefer to let Dreamweaver MX do all the work for you, choose the Synchronize selection from under the Site menu. As you can see in Figure 3.35, just click Preview, and Dreamweaver MX will compile a list of files that should be updated. If you'd like to modify the files being transferred, select/deselect the files you'd like. When ready, click OK to perform the synchronization process.

FIGURE 3.35

Synchronize your local and remote sites instantly.

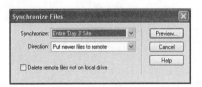

With the Synchronize command, you can choose what you want to transfer (the entire site, or only selected files) and which way you want the transfer to take place (from local to remote, remote to local, or both). The final option—Delete Remote Files not on Local Drive—removes any files from the remote server that don't match something on the local side. Be very careful in choosing to select this option. If anything on the remote site doesn't have a corresponding local file, it will be deleted.

When you've finished transferring files to your site, click the Disconnect button to close the connection between your computer and the remote server.

Generating a Site Map

The final feature we'll look at in the Site panel is Dreamweaver's Site Map feature. Site maps become extremely handy as the number of files in your site increases. It provides a different view of the files that comprise your Web presence.

If you have defined a site and created a few pages, go ahead and switch to that site using Open Site under the Site menu. If you haven't yet worked with a site, you can use one of the Dreamweaver MX tutorial sites to see how the site map function works.

You can switch to the Site Map view by clicking the site map icon (the third icon from the top left) in the Site panel. Alternatively, you can just select Site Map from the Window menu to automatically switch to this mode. For example, choose the Day 3 site in the Site pop-up menu, and then switch to the Site Map view. Your display should look similar to the one shown in Figure 3.36. Nice feature, isn't it? What makes it even better is that this view is actually very useful besides being pretty. Let's go through the parts of the site map screen and their uses, and then take a look at the things you can do from within this view.

FIGURE 3.36

The site map view gives you a visual overview of your site's layout.

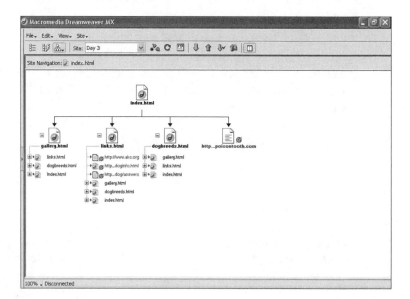

The Dreamweaver MX site map tool is very similar to a hand-created site map, but offers some definite benefits from having direct access to the HTML itself.

Understanding the Icons

Each of the icons in the site map display represents a page that it is linked to in the site. Two primary types of icons are local and remote. Local site documents are shown using the standard Dreamweaver MX document icons. Documents that are linked to remotely are shown as a generic text style icon with a small globe in the lower-right corner.

These two icons are the primary placeholders for a page on your site map. You can take the map one step further and display all files that are linked into your site (images, style sheets, and so on), by choosing Show Dependent Files from the Site Map View under the Site menu. This can be a bit overwhelming and rarely seems to be of much use—on Windows platforms this is accessible directly from the View menu in the site window.

By default, the names of the icons are set to the name of the HTML file. You might find it more intuitive to switch the files to display the name of the HTML page (derived from the `<title>` tag) rather than its file system name. To switch to this view, visit the Site menu again and choose the Show Page Titles option from the Site Map View submenu. You can also set these options from within the Site Map Layout section of the Site Definition dialog box.

Tip

> Titling your HTML documents is very important in providing a perfect browsing experience to your viewers. Without page titles, bookmarking a page is more or less useless. Properly defined page titles help the users navigate and find previously saved information quickly.
>
> Using the Show Page Titles option makes it easy to locate the files that don't have their `<title>` tags set. Just scan for the Untitled label.

If there is a file that you don't want displayed in your site map, you can mark it as hidden under the Site menu using Show/Hide Link options. Unfortunately, if you hide a link, it's difficult to select it to use the Show option. Luckily, you can choose Show Files Marked as Hidden to show everything. This is another one of those strange Dreamweaver MX interface elements that doesn't seem to be completely intuitive. Hidden files will be shown in italic.

One last feature of the icon view is the coloring of the icon label. Broken links are highlighted using red—this makes it very simple to find problems with your site just by looking for the highlighted icons.

Viewing Links

As you've already seen, the connecting lines represent the links between files. Often lines are not spaced as carefully as one would hope. You can change the spacing between linked files by positioning your cursor over the vertical spacing lines and using your mouse to drag the lines over. Near each icon representing a local page is a small target icon, similar to what you've seen for making links from the Properties panel to other files on your site. You can add links between pages by clicking and dragging between the target and the page you want to link to. This will add a simple text link at the bottom of the HTML page to the target page. You'll need to open the page and put the link where you want it—don't expect it to automatically show up in your nice graphical navigation system. An alternative way to perform this function is by choosing the Make Link option under Modify.

If you want to change the spacing of the icons in the site map view, just position your mouse over one of the connecting arrows and drag.

If your site is more than a single layer deep, you've noticed that pages are missing from the map. The Dreamweaver MX mapping tool only shows the main level of the site. The lower levels of links can be revealed by clicking the plus and minus icons located near every document icon. You can collapse and expand the tree of links to show or hide as much of the site as you need.

If you'd like to move down the tree, you can select another file to be the root node of your site map. Clicking one of the icons in the site map and selecting View as Root from the Site, Site Map menu (or the contextual menu) will move that icon to the top of the site map display window. The top of the site map shows where in the site hierarchy you're currently viewing, as seen in Figure 3.37. You can click the levels shown in the window header to move up in the site tree.

Similarly, if you'd like to redefine which file is the home page of your site, you can select the file in the local file listing and use the Set as Homepage selection. You can also use the New Home Page option to create a new HTML file that will become the root of your site. Personally, I've never found an applied use for these options.

A few useful options are Change Link and Remove Link. If you select an icon and then Change Link, Dreamweaver MX will bring up the standard link selection dialog box. Selecting a new link will replace all links in your site that referenced the old file so that they point to a new location. Choosing Remove Link will remove links in the site that point to that file. It might seem a bit confusing at first, but you're not really modifying the file that is selected, you're modifying the files that point to the selected file.

FIGURE 3.37

Use the top of the site map window to navigate through the levels of the site hierarchy.

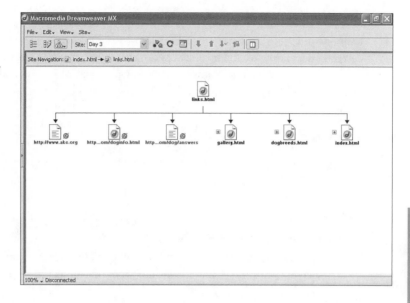

Selected Files

Within the site map, you can use a standard file selection rectangle to select multiple (or single) local files. Cumulative statistics for these files will be shown in the status bar of the site map window. As you select files within this view, notice that the corresponding site files are selected in the file list on the right side of the panel.

Miscellaneous Site Map Options

A few other options can be set that alter the display of the site map. Choosing Layout from the Site Map View menu will open the Layout portion of the site definition window. Again, the Dreamweaver MX interface is a bit confusing here. The only settings found here that you haven't seen already are Number of Columns and Column Width. The Number of Columns parameter is used for configuring how many columns of icons are shown in each row of the site map. Column Width is a value, given in pixels, that will be used to set the default width of an icon and its label as shown in the site map view.

Summary

Today's lesson covered a great deal of ground, and wrapped up the HTML and site-management tools available in Dreamweaver MX. You should now have the background necessary to create and upload Web sites to remote servers.

You've learned about advanced objects like layers, style sheets, and frames. Although tempting to use, these are some of the more "peculiar" elements that might not render correctly depending on the browsers being used by your target audience. Some alternative browser's are making headway (such as Opera and Mozilla), so don't assume that everyone will always be able to see your pages in the same way.

Workshop

The Workshop area is meant to reinforce your reading with a series of questions and exercises.

Q&A

Q How are layers typically used?

A Layers are *barely* handled correctly in 4.x level browsers. Rather than using them for layout, most layer-based sites use them for animation—which you'll learn about tomorrow!

Q How can style sheets be used to create cross-platform/cross-browser compatible Web sites?

A Besides setting spacing/margin attributes in pixels, style sheets can be used to force *pixel* font sizes for text in the design view. This enables you to develop a Web page that is pixel-per-pixel identical (or as close to identical as possible) between browsers and platforms.

Q What's the best way to get files to my server?

A I prefer to use Network/Local server access—this won't require anything more than mounting a server volume on your computer and choosing the folder using the standard file-browsing tools.

Q Why do forms require server behaviors to work?

A Forms submit information back to a server. It is up to the server to process the form's information and produce a result. Alternatively, you can write JavaScript to process the contents of a form, but this is best left to books on JavaScript!

Quiz

1. What does the Cloaking option do?
2. What is the Z value in reference to layers?
3. What does a frameset hold?
4. What is a testing server?

5. What advantage does a navigation bar offer over simply inserting navigation elements?

Quiz Answers

1. Cloaking hides files and folders that should not be considered an "active" part of the Web site.

2. The Z index is refers to the level of the layers. If a layer appears above another layer, it has a higher Z value.

3. A frameset contains the individual frames that, in turn, contain their own full HTML pages.

4. Dreamweaver MX supports three types of file locations—local, remote, and testing. The testing (or "staging") server is used as an intermediate testing ground before moving files to the remote server.

5. The navigation bar allows you to insert and manage navigation elements, including re-ordering and changing their on-page orientation.

Exercises

1. Assuming you have an ISP or server, try setting up a remote connection and uploading the Day 1 site to the remote server.

2. Practice using the tools and techniques (specifically style sheets and layers) discussed in the chapter. There are many things to explore—take your time.

3

WEEK 1

DAY 4

Web Sites with Action— Client-Side Behaviors

Everything we've covered, up until today, has been related to making Web sites that are static, both in terms of appearance and content. Although you've learned about the prebuilt JavaScript objects, they remain the only way to add actual programmatic functionality to your HTML—until today. Today the Dreamweaver MX environment comes to life with DHTML. Today, you will learn

- DHTML basics, pros, and cons.
- The Client Behaviors tool and how to use it to attach functionality to objects and edit the functionality of the prebuilt JavaScript-based objects in your site.
- How layers, coupled with DHTML, can be used to create unique Web applications.
- The Dreamweaver MX timeline's use as a scripting tool to add time-based actions to your Web site.
- Other technologies for creating client-side effects and functionality.

DHTML—What It Is and Isn't

DHTML is a bit of a misnomer. Standing for Dynamic HTML, it implies that the HTML itself provides dynamic behavior to a Web page. Seeing the letters DHTML for the first time, you might think to yourself, "Darn it, not *another* language to learn." In fact, DHTML is nothing more than the fusion of HTML, cascading style sheets, and JavaScript.

 Caution   If you're interested in building universal sites that are accessible by anyone using any browser, DHTML might not be appropriate for your needs. By adding DHTML content to your pages, you're greatly increasing the browser requirements (versions 4 or greater) needed to view your content.

Cascading Style Sheets

Cascading style sheets, which you learned about yesterday, are a means of controlling the precise appearance and placement of objects on your page. Layers, in particular, make use of cascading style sheets for just about everything. If you've added any layers into your HTML and adjusted any of their properties, you've actually been editing a style for the layer.

Because style sheets can define positions for objects with pixel point perfection, they're necessary for adding DHTML-based animation and effects to Web pages. Without style sheets, it would be impossible for the JavaScript to control the object attributes necessary to create DHTML actions.

JavaScript

JavaScript provides a client-side programming language that can access all the objects that are on a Web page and manipulate them. JavaScript can modify the properties of an object only in relation to the HTML and CSS specifications. It can't for example, take an image and modify its brightness or contrast. If you can't access an object's attributes through HTML or with style sheets, don't expect JavaScript to save the day.

This, however, doesn't mean that JavaScript isn't useful. The capability to alter an object's properties means that a Web page can change itself within a viewer's browser. It can change, resize, or even move images and text with only a few lines of code. Providing these effects on the user's computer free the server from needing to process anything beyond sending the initial page and graphics.

The DHTML Problem

If DHTML sounds like a great idea, you're right. In theory, it is a great way to provide custom interaction with a user without needing to write any server-side code. Unfortunately, the reality is that DHTML is not as friendly as one would have hoped.

In this book's introduction, I made a point of discussing the evolution of the Web browser and the problems with differing HTML standards. This, for the most part, has been cleared up with Internet Explorer 5/6 and Netscape 6—HTML is settling down. The JavaScript implementation in each browser, however, still leaves much to be desired.

If you've ever written a JavaScript program for a Web page, you've probably managed to get it working in Netscape or Internet Explorer. At that point, you probably also sat back in your chair, quite proud of yourself, and sent off a quick e-mail to your friends, colleagues, and boss telling them to take a look at your new JavaScript-powered page. Regardless of what browser you chose to use to preview your JavaScript creation, inevitably every person who looks at your page will be using the opposite browser, and the JavaScript will, of course, fail to operate correctly.

This isn't just incredibly bad karma; it's the major downfall of successfully deploying cross-browser and cross-platform DHTML Web sites. JavaScript just isn't the same between different browsers. The primary problem lies with the *Document Object Model (DOM)* that is employed by the JavaScript implementation on each platform.

DOM describes how the different objects within JavaScript are referenced and manipulated. The differences between the Netscape DOM and Internet Explorer DOM are remarkably large. Keeping JavaScript portable between browsers requires no small amount of forethought and planning. Many times, it means keeping two slightly different versions of the code available for each of the browsers.

For an interesting description of the DOM differences between Internet Explorer 5.x and Netscape 6.x, take a look at `http://www.netscape.com/browsers/future/standards.html`.

Using DHTML in Dreamweaver MX eliminates this problem by auto-generating code that is compatible with both browser systems. You can even specify which version of the browsers you want to support. Depending on your target, your available options change. If you're bold and target your Web site specifically for Internet Explorer 6.0, the list of available client actions is very long.

To "D"(HTML) or not to "D"(HTML)?

DHTML is definitely high in the "wow" factor, but it also limits your audience. Without a 4.0 or greater browser and JavaScript enabled, a Web page that relies on DHTML to provide its content becomes useless to other viewers. I often find that DHTML is over-done on some sites to the extent of making them very difficult to use and quite hard on the eyes. For example, you might have noticed a recent trend using cute images that follow your cursor around, such as `http://www.wickedmoon.net/trail.htm.`:

In my opinion, DHTML should be used to supplement a page's content. If it can add to a page's content while not completely overwhelming the reader, by all means, use it. However, if you're just trying to work DHTML into your page because it's there, you're better off without it.

Note

Many types of animation can be used on a Web page—GIFs, Flash, Shockwave, Java, QuickTime, and so on. These types of animation (excluding animated GIFs) require browser plug-ins to operate and exist outside of the HTML page that contains them. DHTML animation is contained inside a page's HTML and does not require anything beyond the browser itself.

DHTML, however, cannot produce all the effects capable in plug-ins. Most browsers have the Macromedia Flash plug-in already in place, so you might want to consider using Flash for your complex animations.

Introducing Client Behaviors

The tool we're going to look at today is the Client Behaviors Panel. Like yesterday, we'll use the client behaviors to build a few examples. It's impossible to create a site that includes every feature of Dreamweaver MX, so hopefully the examples will suffice.

This small window lets you attach behaviors to HTML objects—that is, it lets you define how something should react when certain events, such as mouse clicks, take place. In essence, a behavior is one or more "events" and the "reactions" to these events.

The easiest way to introduce this tool is to view it in action. To do this, you'll need to add a JavaScript element to a page—so let's get a site created and start playing.

Create a new folder on your system called `Day 4` and then download the `Day 4` materials from the site `http://downloads.cutelittledogs.com`. Unarchive them and copy them to the folder. Finally, define a static site to point to the new `Day 4` folder.

Now, create and save a new HTML document within your site called `behaviortest.html`.

Add a simple rollover image named `MyRollover` to the page using the images `image_on.jpg` and `image_off.jpg` found in the `images` folder of your site, as seen in Figure 4.1. There's no need to supply a destination URL.

FIGURE 4.1

Add a rollover image to the empty document.

Now, select the image within the design view, and choose Behaviors from the Windows menu.

The Behaviors Panel

The Behaviors panel should appear with two JavaScript actions defined: `onMouseOver` and `onMouseOut`, as demonstrated in Figure 4.2.

Add/Remove Events

FIGURE 4.2

Behaviors are a list of JavaScript actions and reactions.

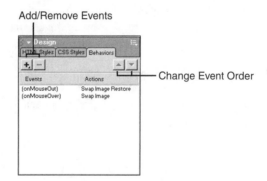

Change Event Order

4

The Behaviors panel displays a list of the currently assigned events and their corresponding actions. For the example of a simple rollover image, there is an `onMouseOut` event that will trigger Swap Image Restore. Likewise, `onMouseOver` triggers Swap Image. These two events combine to swap the existing image with another image when the mouse is positioned over it, and restore the original configuration when the mouse moves outside the image.

The Dreamweaver MX `rollover image` object is just a shortcut for inserting these two server behaviors.

Creating a Behavior

The Behaviors panel is simple to understand. The "+/-" buttons are used to add or remove behaviors and actions, whereas the up and down arrows on the right side of the panel rearrange the events and actions.

Using the "+" button, you can also show events for a particular browser platform. Click the "+" button, and then choose from the Show Events For submenu. The smaller the browser number you choose, the fewer events you'll have access to. The more specific you are, the more restrictive you are on your audience.

I suggest using 3.0 and later for the greatest compatibility or 4.0 and Later for the greatest compatibility and largest feature set.

Let's go over the basic steps in creating a behavior, and then take a look at a few examples that you can use on your Web site.

Adding Actions

Although it might seem a bit backward, before you can define the event that triggers something, you must first define the action that will be triggered. When manually creating an image rollover, for example, you first define the Swap Image action, and then choose onMouseOver as the event. Strange, isn't it?

Behaviors (actions and events) are created only after you've added the objects you want to work with to your Web page. If you want to swap an image, that image needs to be on the page and selected in order to create a behavior that works with it.

To add a behavior to an object (Image, Layer, and so on), be sure that the object is selected in the document design window. Then, click the "+" button and choose an appropriate action from the pop-up menu. Some of these will probably seem quite obvious—such as Play Sound. Others will need a bit of explanation.

A list of the actions that you can choose from is shown in Table 4.1.

TABLE 4.1   JavaScript Functions and Their Uses

Function Name	Description
Call JavaScript	If you've written a custom JavaScript function, this action will let you call it.
Change Property	Alters the properties for an object. This is useful for adjusting layer attributes, and so on.
Check Browser	Redirects the user's browser between different URLs depending on the type browser type and version number.
Check Plugin	Checks for the existence of a plug-in and redirects the browser appropriately.
Control Shockwave or Flash	Controls the playback of Shockwave or Flash presentations.
Drag Layer	Sets up a layer so that the users can move it around the screen. We'll take a closer look at this feature in a little bit.

TABLE 4.1   continued

Function Name	Description
Go To URL	Moves the browser to a new URL.
Jump Menu	Changes the functionality of a jump-to menu.
Jump Menu Go	Alters the Go button of a jump-to menu. This JavaScript element is found in the form area of the tool palette.
Open Browser Window	Opens a new window in the browser containing a certain URL.
Play Sound	Plays a sound on the end user's browser.
Popup Message	Shows a simple text message in a separate pop-up window within the browser.
Preload Images	Loads images into the cache so that they can quickly be switched out without additional load time. Images for Dreamweaver MX-created rollovers are preloaded by default.
Set Nav Bar Image	Changes the image that is being used on the current navigation bar.
Set Text	Adds text to layers, frames, text fields, and the status bar.
Show-Hide Layers	Changes the visibility of layer objects.
Swap Image	Swaps one image for another. If you're building rollover-type functionality by hand, this is what you should be using.
Swap Image Restore	Restores the images that were swapped using the Swap Image function.
Timeline	Although you haven't seen the timeline yet, you can probably guess what it does: It lets you define actions that happen at a certain time. The Timeline actions let you jump to points in the timeline or otherwise control the flow of time.
Validate Form	If you have a form that has required fields of data, this JavaScript action can be useful in configuring auto validation before forms are processed by the server.

Tip

Most of the actions described in Table 4.1 require that the object they are working on is a named object; that is, it has a name= attribute set. If you haven't set the names for the objects in your document yet, be sure to do that before defining behaviors. Click the object, and then open the Properties panel. The object name field is the text field in the upper-right corner of the panel.

If you're a JavaScript programmer already, you're probably looking at this list of actions and thinking, "These aren't JavaScript functions." You're right. The actions library is a group of prewritten JavaScripts that is designed to be cross-browser and cross-platform in nature. At the bottom of the list of actions is a Get More Behaviors function. This takes you to an area on Macromedia's Web site where you can download new and exciting actions for your pages.

For every behavior action, there must also be an event that triggers it.

Adding an Event

After you've added an action to your behavior list, you need to attach an event that will trigger the action. As luck would have it, Dreamweaver MX does this for you, and attaches an event to the action. When adding a Swap Image action, for example, Dreamweaver takes it upon itself to add a onMouseOver automatically, as if reading your mind. And it doesn't stop there. When adding an action that usually comes as part of a pair (Swap Image usually comes with Swap Image Restore in rollovers), it will add the send action and event for you. Of course, sometimes you might not *want* the extra behavior, so you can select it and click the "-" button to make it disappear.

You're also likely to find that Dreamweaver doesn't always pick the right event for an action. To set your own event, select the behavior you want to work on, and then click the down arrow in the right side of the selected item's event field. A pop-up list of the available events will appear, as seen in Figure 4.3.

FIGURE 4.3

Choose the event that you want to trigger your action.

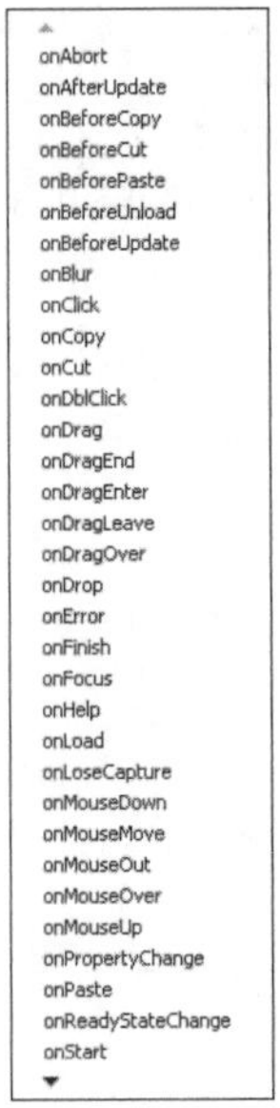

```
onAbort
onAfterUpdate
onBeforeCopy
onBeforeCut
onBeforePaste
onBeforeUnload
onBeforeUpdate
onBlur
onClick
onCopy
onCut
onDblClick
onDrag
onDragEnd
onDragEnter
onDragLeave
onDragOver
onDrop
onError
onFinish
onFocus
onHelp
onLoad
onLoseCapture
onMouseDown
onMouseMove
onMouseOut
onMouseOver
onMouseUp
onPropertyChange
onPaste
onReadyStateChange
onStart
```

You'll notice that in some cases the events are surrounded by parentheses. This indicates that the object itself does not support the event, but an object can be added that *does*. For example, images do not natively support onMouseOver—in fact, images by themselves support almost no useful events. In order to detect a mouse-over event, Dreamweaver MX will automatically stick an anchor tag around the image (<a href><img></a>), which gives the appearance of the image supporting the necessary functions and saves you the headache of having to remember which object supports what events.

If you are seeking further information on supported events in Netscape or Microsoft browsers, you can learn more from their Web sites:

Microsoft: http://msdn.microsoft.com/scripting/jscript/default.htm

Netscape:
http://developer.netscape.com/docs/manuals/index.html?content=javascript
.html

Some of the common events for 4.0 or greater browsers are listed here:

onMouseUp—The mouse button has been released over the object.

onMouseOver—The mouse cursor is located over the object.

onMouseDown—The mouse button is down while the cursor is over the object.

onMouseOut—The mouse cursor has moved outside of the object.

onClick—The user has clicked on the object.

onDblClick—The user has double-clicked on the object.

onKeyDown—The user has pushed down on a key.

onKeyPress—The user has pressed and released a key.

onKeyUp—The user has released a key.

onBlur—An object (such as a text field) has *lost focus*, which means the cursor has moved out of the field.

onChange—The contents of an object have been changed (such as a pop-up selection field).

onFocus—An object has received focus.

Most JavaScript is triggered based on mouse events, so you'll probably want to pay the most attention to using those as your triggers.

Modifying Behaviors

As you add more actions and events to your document, more and more lines are added to the Behaviors panel. To modify a behavior, click and select the line with the action and event that define it, and then use the panel buttons to change it.

If you add actions that are triggered by the same event, you can use the up and down arrow buttons at the top of the Behaviors panel to adjust the ordering of the execution of the events. The events execute in a top-down fashion.

To alter an event, you can always reassign it using the pop-up menu. The action itself can be redefined by double-clicking the action field for that behavior. To delete the entire behavior, just select it in the behavior list and click the "-" button. Suddenly, it's gone.

This is all fine and dandy, but what does it actually mean? Let's try building a behavior and see if that doesn't clear things up.

Creating a Status Bar Behavior

Let's start exploring client behaviors by doing something simple—creating a behavior for a rollover image that also displays a description of what clicking the image does in the status bar of the browser. This is a convenient way of providing informative feedback to the user without having to alter the current HTML display or pop up a new browser window.

Create a duplicate of the behaviortest.html document you used earlier, and name the new file showstatus.html. If you didn't follow the earlier example, create a new file named showstatus.html and add a simple rollover image to it. The images directory contains image_on.jpg and image_off.jpg, which should do nicely.

As discussed previously, two behaviors are already defined for a rollover image based on the events onMouseOver and onMouseOut. In order to set the status bar message, you'll need to add a third behavior that also reacts to the onMouseOver event.

Adding the Set Text Action

Highlight the rollover image in the document design window. This is the object to which you want to add a new action/event (that is, the behavior).

Next, click the "+" button in the Behaviors panel and choose Set Text of Status Bar. A pop-up window, shown in Figure 4.4, appears to let you enter the text you want to be visible in the status bar.

FIGURE 4.4

Enter a line of text you want to be visible in the status bar.

Into the dialog box, type **This link goes nowhere, it's just an example of a status bar message**, and then click OK.

Almost every Dreamweaver MX action includes its own dialog box for configuring how the action will be carried out. The Set Text dialog boxes are among the simplest actions to configure.

Adding the onMouseOver Event

The default event for the Set Text action is onMouseOver—so actually, if this is what you want, you don't need to set a thing. When the mouse is over the image, the Set Text action is executed, and the text you entered a few moments ago is displayed in the status bar. Obviously nothing is stopping you from using onClick or any of the other defined events. The final Behaviors panel should look very similar to Figure 4.5.

FIGURE 4.5

Three actions are now defined for the rollover image.

Don't worry that two onMouseOver events are defined in the behavior list. The ordering of the events (top to bottom) indicates their execution order. In the current configuration, the images will be swapped first, and then the text of the status bar will be set. Because this happens too quickly to be discernable, the ordering isn't important. If, however, you would like the status bar text to be set first, select that behavior line, and then click the up button to move it up in the execution list.

Note

The order of execution is only adjusted within a particular event type. You can't move an onMouseOver event to be higher in order of execution than an onMouseOut event because they are independent. Two instances of onMouseOver however, can be adjusted in relation to one another.

When you've finished setting up your behavior, try previewing it in your Web browser. As you move your mouse over the image, it will toggle to the alternative "over" image as well as place your customized message in the status bar, displayed in Figure 4.6. It's that simple.

FIGURE 4.6

The status bar text is set to your message!

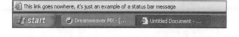

4

Tip

> You might want to check your behaviors in multiple browsers. You're likely to find that the results are not quite the same, thanks to the inconsistencies in JavaScript implementations.

How Does Dreamweaver MX Work this JavaScript Magic?

Each behavior that you add to the document will add a new JavaScript function to perform its action. Even if you aren't a JavaScript programmer, you should be able to determine what code was added by what behavior just by looking at the function names. For example, the `swapImage()` and `swapImgRestore()` actions are based on two JavaScript functions:

```
function MM_swapImage() { //v3.0
  var i,j=0,x,a=MM_swapImage.arguments;
  document.MM_sr=new Array;
  for(i=0;i<(a.length-2);i+=3) {
   if ((x=MM_findObj(a[i]))!=null){
     document.MM_sr[j++]=x;
     if(!x.oSrc) x.oSrc=x.src; x.src=a[i+2];
    }
   }
 }
function MM_swapImgRestore() { //v3.0
  var i,x,a=document.MM_sr;
  for(i=0;a&&i<a.length&&(x=a[i])&&x.oSrc;i++) x.src=x.oSrc;
 }
```

As you can see, these functions are named after the behaviors that they perform. Although you don't need to be a JavaScript programmer to understand what JavaScript code was added to your pages, if you *are* a developer, you can easily customize and use these routines by hand.

Creating Pop-Up Help

Changing the text in the status bar is a reasonable way to provide user feedback, but it doesn't really grab a person's attention. Something a bit more obvious would be better. Undoubtedly, you've seen the tooltips that are so prevalent in today's software. Wouldn't it be great to provide that functionality on a Web page through JavaScript? (Of course it would.)

Start by creating and saving a new document to the site called `tooltip.html`. You'll implement a behavior-based tooltip or two in this document.

Note

> You can quickly implement tooltips in Internet Explorer by setting name attributes for elements. This, however, doesn't give you the same flexibility that you're about to see, but, depending on your audience, is a fast and easy way to add similar functionality.

Setting Up a Tooltip

Before setting up a tooltip, you obviously need to create some objects that you'll be attaching tooltips to. There are two images in the images folder that you can use for this purpose—pomeranian.jpg and eskimo.jpg (you should have downloaded these files from the http://downloads.cutelittledogs.com Web site earlier in the day. These images show representatives of the two dog breeds. When the cursor moves over each image, we'll make some information about the pictured dog appear. You can attach a tooltip to any object you want, as long as it supports the onMouseOver and onMouseOut events, but because images are easy to work with, they make a perfect example.

The tooltips themselves will be drawn in layers. Because I have two images, I'm going to create two layers—one for each of the tooltips used on the page. Create layers named pomeranian and eskimo to correspond to each image. Fill in the contents of these layers with whatever text you want to appear when the cursor is over the object. For my page, I've used:

```
pomeranian - Maddy is a four-year-old Pomeranian.
She has a wonderful personality, rarely barks,
and is extremely good at fetch. She has accidents from time to time,
but not very often.
eskimo - Coco, a year-old American Eskimo,
exhibits the typical traits of her breed.
She is cute, cuddly, and hyperactive.
```

Position the layers as you would like them to appear when they "pop" onto the screen, and set any additional attributes you'd like. For my tooltips, I've set the background color of the layers to #FFFFCC.

Figure 4.7 shows the example page set up with two layers.

After the layers are positioned correctly and have the content that you want, open the properties for each of the layers and set the Visibility to Hidden. This will make sure that when a user visits your page for the first time, only the images being displayed are visible. You're now ready to make the behaviors to make your layers appear as tooltips for the images.

4

*Position the tooltip
layers as you want
them to appear when
the mouse is over the
corresponding images.*

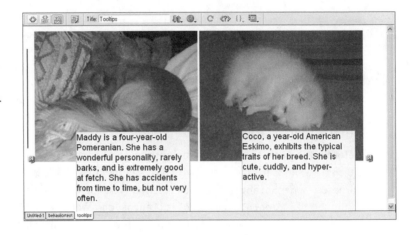

Adding the Hide/Show Behaviors

For each of the tooltips to appear and disappear, you will need to add a Show/Hide Layers action that will activate when `onMouseOver` and `onMouseOut` (respectively) are called for each image. When the user moves the mouse over the image, the appropriate layer should be displayed. When the mouse moves out, the layer needs to be hidden.

Select the first image (`pomeranian.jpg`) in the document design window. Next, open the Behaviors panel and click the "+" button. From the list of available actions, choose Show/Hide Layers. A list of the available layers and options for those layers will be shown, as shown in Figure 4.8.

*Choose the layer to
hide or show, and then
click the appropriate
button.*

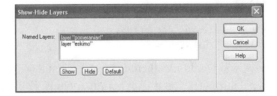

Select the `pomeranian` layer and then click the Hide button. Highlight your newly added behavior and change the event so that it reads `onMouseOut`—this ensures that the layer/tooltip is hidden when the users moves their cursors off of the button.

Immediately repeat these steps, adding a new Hide/Show Layer action for the `pomeranian.jpg` image, but choosing the Show button this time. You should now have two Hide/Show events (one Hide and one Show) for the layer containing your image's tooltip. For the second behavior's triggering event, choose `onMouseOver`. This will show the layer when the user's cursor is over the image. The final Behaviors panel for your image should look similar to Figure 4.9.

FIGURE 4.9

*You should now have
two behaviors defined
for the image.*

For the second image, eskimo.jpg, follow this same procedure, except choose the layer
that is appropriate for that image—eskimo. The tooltips are done and can immediately be
previewed in your browser.

In a matter of minutes, you can make your Web pages come to life with instant information that appears only when needed.

Tip

Some people use onMouseOver to create a tooltip effect by swapping out
images on the screen with an informative graphic containing text. This is a
less efficient method of providing information about an object's function
than the hide/show layer approach you just implemented. Graphic-only
tooltips take longer to load and don't provide the positioning flexibility
offered by layers. If you have to use graphics in your tooltips, remember, layers can hold anything—including graphics.

Pop-Up Browser Windows

A popular way of providing information when clicking a button is to "pop it up" in a
window outside the main browser. This is typically used when the information being displayed is relatively small and supplements the information in the main browser. You can
actually create a pop-up window without defining any behaviors by setting a unique *target* name for the link that you want to appear in a new window. This, however, will open
the default browser window with the navigation bar, toolbar, menus, and so on. Besides
not providing a very controllable solution to showing additional information, it often
obscures the main browser window and can be rather confusing to the viewer.

The Open Browser Window Action

One of Dreamweaver MX's actions is the capability to create a new browser window
with or without any of the browser's standard graphical components. As a basis for the
example, we'll use a single image this time. We're interested in trapping the user's mouse
click event and using it to open a new window. Create and save another new document in
the Web site; name this one openwindow.html.

Unlike the previous examples where the content for the pop-up information has been stored in the same HTML document you're authoring with the behaviors, the Open Browser action will point the new window to a URL containing the content you want to display. You'll need to author a new HTML document that contains what will be displayed in the pop-up. I've created a new file called help.html for this purpose. It should be stored in the Day 4 folder that you copied to your local system.

To open the help.html file in a pop-up window, first you need something that will trigger the action. Edit the openwindow.html document to include the image openhelp.gif that is found in the site's images directory. Select the image and then open (or switch to) the Behaviors panel. Click the "+" button to add a new action, and then choose Open Browser Window from the available items. The configuration screen is shown in Figure 4.10.

FIGURE 4.10

Choose how (and what) the new browser window will open.

Enter or browse to the URL that you want displayed in the new pop-up window. If you'd prefer to constrain the window size to a certain dimension, enter the height and width in pixels. For my help screen, for example, I'm using a 400×400 pixel window so that it doesn't hide the other browser window. If the pop-up screen is designed to supplement the main page, make sure that it is subordinate in size and can be positioned by the users so that it doesn't obstruct the content of the main page. Next, set the attributes that you want shown when the window opens: navigation toolbar, menu bar, location toolbar, scroll bars, status bar, and window resize handles.

Tip

It's best to leave the users with the capability to resize the window even if you are forcing the browser to a certain size. Users always have the final word in their browser configuration and can override the display of even the most carefully designed screens. Without the ability to resize, you'll inevitably end up with someone who can't see the content you've created.

As a last step, you might want to name the window. Providing a name for the window will enable you to use that window as a target for other links. If the user closes the window, however, its name is released and any use of it in other links will result in a new regular browser window being created.

To see the pop-up window in action, save the `openwindow.html` document, and then preview or open it in your browser and click on the image. The results are shown in Figure 4.11.

FIGURE 4.11

The infamous pop-up browser window; now it can be yours too.

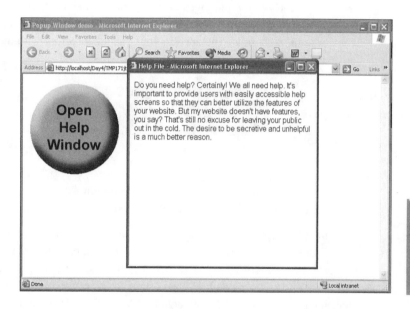

4

Tip

You might have noticed that many Web sites pop up a new window when you first go to their home pages. Sometimes this is informative; other times it's irritating. If you want to implement the same functionality on your site, you need to attach the Open Browser Window action to the `onLoad` event of the HTML `<body>`. Although this is useful in *some* cases, don't do it on every page of your site—hundreds of little browser windows aren't much fun to deal with.

Drag and Drop on a Web Page?

Yes, it's true. You can implement a full drag-and-drop system on your page using only the Dreamweaver MX development tools. This example will round out your exploration of the Behaviors panel and provide a close look at one of the more interesting actions built into Dreamweaver MX.

By now you've learned that layers can be positioned with pixel-perfect accuracy, and JavaScript actions can be used to control the attributes of layers. So, it stands to reason that a behavior could be created to actually move a layer around the screen.

Although this can't be used to develop full applications, it is possible to create simple tutorials or educational material that provides feedback to the users. For example, let's take a look at how you'd put together a draggable behavior to implement a simple "Stages of Life" application. I've prepared the graphics shown in Figure 4.12 for the behavior to use—these are included in your images directory with the names puppy.gif, adolescent.gif, and adult.gif.

FIGURE 4.12

With these graphics, you'll learn how to implement a simple game application.

The goal of this exercise is to create an application in which the user drags the three images into the correct order (from puppy to adult) on the Web page.

Get started by creating and saving a new HTML document named simplegame.html. Into this document you should add four layers named puppy, adolescent, adult, and receiver. Into each of these layers, add the corresponding image. The layer sizes should be set to 150px wide×100px high (*px* is short for pixel); the exact size as the images. The receiver layer will be the "drop target" for the different images (the place that the user drags each of the images into) and doesn't hold an image itself. Because it is going to hold the images, it should be large enough to contain all of them (150px wide×300px tall). I've also set my receiver layer to a light blue color (#DDDDFF) so that it stands out against the background, as shown in Figure 4.13.

Adding the Drag Layer Action

The Drag Layer action works by defining how a layer can be dragged onscreen, and where its final resting spot or *target*, should be. To make life easier, Dreamweaver MX allows you to "grab" the current location of a layer and use that location as the target. So, the first thing you want to do is move all of the layers with images onto the receiver layer in the order they should be in when the user has successfully completed the puzzle. Figure 4.14 shows the correct arrangement.

With the graphics in place, it's time to start implementing the dragging behavior. Each of the layers must be set up individually, but the steps should become simple after we walk through this first example.

FIGURE 4.13

Four layers—three for the images, and one to define the drop area—are used for the example.

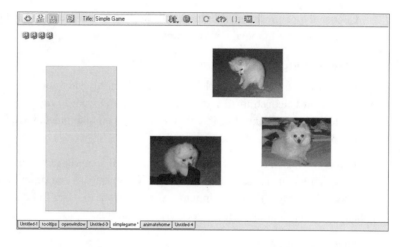

FIGURE 4.14

Drag the layers into their appropriate target location.

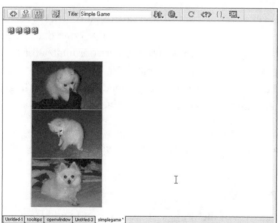

4

Switch to the Behaviors panel. Click the "+" button and select Drag Layer from the pop-up menu. You'll see a dialog box similar to the one in Figure 4.15.

FIGURE 4.15

You can define how the layer can be dragged and an appropriate drag target.

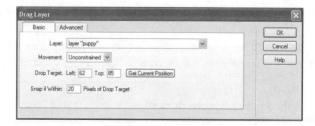

Choose the puppy layer from the Layer pop-up menu. Next decide how you'd like the layer to be able to move on your page.

Constraining Drag Motion

If you want the user to be able to drag the layer anywhere on the screen, you can leave the default Unconstrained setting. If, instead, you want to limit the amount of motion to the left, right, up, and down that the dragging can take place, switch the movement pop-up menu so that it reads Constrained.

If you've chosen to constrain the motion, you'll see four new fields appear: Up, Down, Left, and Right. These fields contain positive numbers that describe how far the layer is allowed to move from its original position. I want the user to be able to drag the layer anywhere, so I'm using the Unconstrained setting.

Drop Targets

Next, you can set a Drag Target for the layer you're working with. Earlier I told you to move each layer to its final destination. If you've done that, you can click the Get Current Position button to retrieve the correct coordinates for the drag target. You'll probably also want to set the Snap if Within field. This is a number of pixels that the drop can be off from the target but will still be snapped back into the target location. I've chosen 20 pixels as a reasonable Snap If Within value.

If you don't set a Snap value, users are likely to be frustrated with your interactive sites. Humans aren't perfect, especially when it comes to dragging objects around with a mouse.

Advanced Properties

Advanced properties of the drag action can be set to add even more interactivity to the layer dragging. By default, the entire layer is used as a handle for dragging around the screen—the user can click anywhere in the layer and drag it. Alternatively, you could provide a handle on the image that would be appropriate for the application you are building. For example, if you are creating draggable windows, you might want to define a title bar at the top of the layer and use that as the drag handle. To do this, switch Drag Handle to Area Within Layer. You'll be given four new fields to define the area within the layer that can be used for dragging. The Drag Handle fields are specified in relation to the left and top coordinates of the current layer using the height and the width of the handle.

Figure 4.16 shows the advanced properties for a draggable layer.

FIGURE 4.16

If you want to provide a drag handle or run other JavaScript functions, you can do it in the advanced preferences.

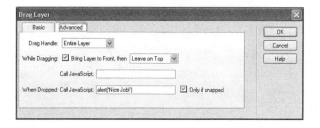

The While Dragging options control what happens to the layer as the drag process is taking place. The default action is to bring the layer to the top of all the other layers, and then Leave on Top when the drag is finished. You can also use the pop-up menu to reposition the layer back to its starting level. Additionally, the Call JavaScript field can contain JavaScript that is executed while the object is in the drag process, such as playing a noise during the drag, or updating other onscreen elements with the user's progress.

Finally, the When Dropped JavaScript settings are used to provide additional actions when the user is done dragging the layer. If the Only if Snapped check box is selected, the JavaScript action will only be executed if the layer is snapped into its final position. For your layers, add the JavaScript alert('Nice Job!') into this field and be sure the Only if Snapped option is selected.

Tip

> If it isn't entirely obvious, Only if Snapped can be used to validate if the user dropped the object in the right place. If the object is snapped, it has been appropriately positioned and has found its drop target.

When you've finished setting up your draw layer, click the OK button. You're almost done with the first layer, but not quite. In order for the page to work the way you want, you must change the triggering event to onMouseDown. The default trigger, onClick, would require that the user *click* on the image and then start dragging. Finally, within the design window, drag the puppy layer to a random starting location on the screen. This is where it will appear when the page is first loaded.

You should now be able to preview the resulting drag-and-drop application in your browser. To add the same functionality to the rest of the images, simply repeat the steps for the adolescent and adult layers.

Drag and Drop functionality is a powerful tool that would be very difficult to program in JavaScript by hand. Although you're not going to use it to write the next Microsoft Word, you can easily use it to create simple and effective learning games. I highly recommend that you look at the aforementioned JavaScript references to fully understand the myriad of events that you have at your disposal.

If you've successfully completed this section of the chapter, you should be equipped with everything you need to add object behaviors to your Web applications. There is, however, one final way to add dynamic behavior that you will find both easy to use and very powerful.

Using Timelines

If you've used Flash or a QuickTime editor, you've seen a timeline editor. Timelines are used to coordinate actions to a specific time, rather than a user action on a Web page. With Dreamweaver MX you can create timelines that execute when the page is loaded, or when a particular behavior is triggered. How you use timelines is up to you. The only warning I have is that they can be a bit overwhelming if used everywhere on your page. We'll take a look at a simple way to animate the logo of a Web page upon its initial loading.

The Timelines Panel

The Timelines panel is most often (and effectively) used to animate layers. You can also use it to animate images, but you won't have the same level of control that you have with a layer. I suggest that you use layers for animations and insert graphics into those layers.

To demonstrate the timeline, we're going to create an alternative home page for www.cutelittledogs.com. The page will feature the name of the Web site along with a bouncing tennis ball ('cause dogs like 'em!). Create a new document called animate-home.html and enter some basic text for the page, such as www.CuteLittleDogs.com with a few descriptive sentences, at the top.

Next, add a new layer called ball, and then insert the image tennisball.jpg from the images folder into the layer. Drag the layer into the upper-left corner of the document, directly under the text. Your page is now set up for a basic animation, and should resemble Figure 4.17. We're going to animate the ball falling and bouncing. It will fall from its initial position, bounce a few times, and then bounce into the position directly beside the title text.

Open the Timelines panel from the Window, Other menu. The default empty timeline window should resemble the one in Figure 4.18. Before adding anything to the timeline, it's best to understand how it operates.

FIGURE 4.17

Set your animate-home.html *page up to look like this.*

FIGURE 4.18

The timeline lets you create actions that are triggered by the passage of time.

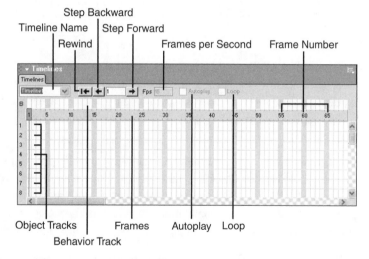

The first thing you'll notice in the timeline is the row of numbers listed horizontally in the window. These are the *frames* of animation that can be set. You can move to any point in the timeline by clicking the frame number that you want to move to. A red marker shows the current location in the timeline. There are different tracks down the left side of the timeline. Each of the tracks can hold objects that are being animated simultaneously with the current timeline. There is also a special track labeled B, which is the behavior track. When a frame in the B track is selected, you can open the Behaviors panel and add an action to that frame. Using this technique, you can have the timeline perform any of the actions normally triggered by clicks and mouseovers or other events.

Across the top bar of the timeline window are the controls for moving within that timeline and controlling how it plays. The first field is the name. You can create multiple timelines—that are triggered by behaviors—for each HTML document, so it's important to name your timelines so that you won't get them confused with one another. The pop-up menu to the right of the name lets you quickly choose which timeline you're working on.

The next group of controls is similar to working with a VCR. The Rewind button moves the current frame being viewed back to the beginning. The left and right arrows move through the frames one at a time. To quickly jump to a particular frame, you can key in the frame number between the two arrow buttons and the timeline will immediately center on that frame.

> **Tip**
>
> To quickly view an animation, click and drag the red frame marker over the timeline. This will let you preview your animation in real-time.

To control the fluidity of the animation, you'll need to adjust the FPS setting. The default selection is 15, meaning that in one second, 15 frames of animation will be shown. If the animation on your screen seems a bit too jumpy, try increasing this number to 30. This gives you more space on the timeline to design your animation and results in an overall increase in its smoothness.

The last two features of the timeline window are the Autoplay and Loop check boxes. Clicking the Autoplay check box makes the animation appear onscreen when the page is first loaded. This does nothing except add a behavior to the page's <body> onLoad event to play the timeline. The Loop button will cycle the animation once it finishes with the timeline—by adding a Play Timeline behavior to the last frame in the current timeline.

> **Tip**
>
> To create a decent looping animation, you must try to have the last frame of an object's animation *end* exactly where it *starts*. Otherwise, the object will appear to jump around the screen.

Setting Animation Keyframes

To create a simple animation with only a few clicks, you can set the location of your layer at certain points in the timeline, and the Dreamweaver MX supporting JavaScript will generate all the frames between them.

For example, to animate the bouncing ball, select the `ball` layer in the design window. Then, from the Modify menu, contextual menu, or the pop-up menu at the top right of the Timelines panel, choose Add Object. On track one of your timeline, you should now see the `ball` layer. You can drag it between different tracks on the timeline, if you so desire, but working with track one should be all you need for a simple animation. By default, two keyframes are set: the starting keyframe and the ending frame. These are represented on the timeline by white dots within the track you are editing.

Adding and Removing Keyframes

For your first animation, drag the ending keyframe out to around 60. The timeline window should now look like Figure 4.19.

FIGURE 4.19

Drag the end frame to 60 to give yourself some working room.

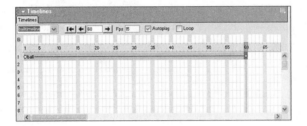

This will give you some area to work in. Next click on the 15th frame in the timeline *on the track you are editing*, and choose Add Keyframe from the panel pop-up menu or the Modify menu's Timeline option. Continue adding keyframes at the 30th and 45th frames. Each of these points will be at the top or bottom of the ball's bounce cycle. A keyframe is necessary where the object being animated changes direction.

If you accidentally add too many keyframes, you can use the Remove Keyframe menu option to remove them. Your timeline display should now resemble Figure 4.20.

FIGURE 4.20

Add keyframes where the ball will change direction.

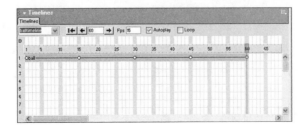

Now you're ready to define the `ball` layer positions based on these keyframes. The starting keyframe is already defined as the original position of the layer. We just need to define the 15th, 30th, 45th, and 60th (final) frames. Within the Timelines panel, click to highlight the 15th keyframe. Next, drag the `ball` layer to the bottom of the design window. This will be the first bounce. Highlight the 30th keyframe, and then drag the layer up toward the top of the window—this will be the position for the top of the first bounce. Repeat this same process for the 45th and 60th frames. The 60th frame will be the final resting spot for the ball, so be sure it is located exactly where you want the ball to appear when the animation is complete.

As you're adding the keyframes for your animation, you'll see that a path is drawn on the design view to represent how your image is going to move. Until you set the final, the path may look a bit strange, because the default frame for the last keyframe is the same as the first frame—causing the path to loop as it is built. The path for the final image animation is shown in Figure 4.21.

Tip

Be sure to click the Autoplay button in the timeline window so that the animation will start when the page first loads in the browser.

FIGURE 4.21

Create a simple animation using the Timelines panel and keyframes.

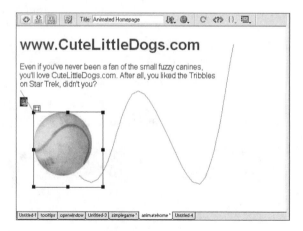

Easily Defining a Complex Path

Well, that wasn't so bad, but it isn't the easiest way to create an animation. If you know exactly how you want to animate an object and have a steady hand, you can drag the object in the path you want it to take, and the keyframes will be generated for you automatically.

To animate using this method, start from a clean slate. You can either create a new document with a layer, or use your existing document and delete the currently defined path in the timeline. To delete the animation in the current timeline, select the appropriate track by clicking on it, and then choosing Remove Timeline from the panel pop-up menu, or the Dreamweaver MX Modify menu.

Recording a Path

To record a path, make sure that the layer you want to record is selected in the design view (such as `ball`) and choose Record Path of Layer from the panel or Modify menu. Move back to the design view, and very carefully drag the layer around the screen in the path that you want the final animation to take.

As you drag the object, dots will be drawn onscreen to record the points where your mouse changed directions. After you're done drawing, the path will be filled in and smoothed out. Chances are that it's very unlikely that you managed to draw the path perfectly on your first try. Dreamweaver MX inserts more keyframes than you probably need, so you'll want to click through the keyframes in the timeline and delete those you don't need. Additionally, you can select a keyframe and reposition the layer so that it's positioned exactly where you want.

Additional Timeline Functions

Most of the options under the timeline pop-up menu should be self-explanatory. The functions that we haven't covered directly are listed here:

Add Frame—Not to be confused with adding a keyframe, the Add Frame function adds a frame to the timeline. If you find you've run out of space and don't want to manually reposition all your keyframes, you can insert frames until you have enough space.

Remove Frame—This function deletes a frame from the timeline.

Change Object—To change the object being animated without changing the animation path, you can use this option. You'll be prompted for the object you want to switch to.

Add/Remove Object—This function adds or deletes an object from the timeline.

Add/Remove Behavior—This is actually one of the more powerful capabilities of the timeline system. Pop-up windows, other timelines, or any action that you can normally write a behavior for can be added to the timeline.

Add/Remove/Rename Timeline—This function adds, deletes, and renames timelines. If you aren't using multiple timelines on your site, these features won't be of much use to you.

Timelines are best explored by playing with them. You can create effects that previously were limited to people using Flash or other plug-ins. The possibilities are almost unlimited. Using behaviors you can trigger sounds to be played during the animation process—all from within a single HTML file.

Instant Flash

Dreamweaver MX provides the ability to add some special dynamic elements to your pages as easily as creating HTML. Flash is a popular design tool that can easily create small and fast vector animations. Unlike traditional animated GIFs or embedded movies, Flash takes a fraction of the space and can produce dramatic results.

In order to easily create some simple Flash files, Macromedia has added two tools under the Media category of the Insert panel that enable Web developers to add Flash content without any Flash authoring skills or the Flash development environment:

Flash Buttons—Flash buttons work like rollover image links, but sport multiple highlight colors, customizable size, and the use of any font on your system.

Flash Text—Flash text takes over where HTML text leaves off. Instead of limiting you to a small range of fonts and sizes, Flash text enables you to add any font in any size to your document. In addition, you can use any of the added text as an HTML link.

Let's take a look at how each of these features work. You'll be surprised at how easy it can be to start using Flash on your site. Because these really are standalone features, I'll just show you how they work—it's up to you to find a place to use them!

Flash Buttons

To add a Flash button to your document, click the Flash Button icon in the Media tab of the Insert panel or choose Flash Button from the Interactive Media submenu of Insert. Don't worry if your cursor isn't exactly where you want the button—you have full control over it, even after it is added to the page.

After choosing to insert the button, Dreamweaver MX will display the setup dialog box shown in Figure 4.22. This is where you configure the behavior of the button you are adding.

The Sample section shows a pregenerated version of what the button will look like. This sample will *not* change as you adjust the parameters. Choose the style of button you want from the Style scrolling list. A wide variety of buttons are available—from artistic to e-commerce related.

FIGURE 4.22

Choose the appearance and label for your Flash button.

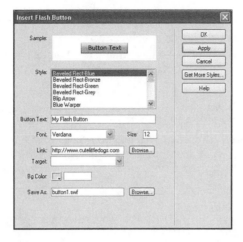

After selecting a style you prefer, enter the label for the button in the Button Text field. You can also choose the font that the button will be rendered in, as well as its size.

To create a link, simply fill in the appropriate field, or click Browse to choose a file in the site. A target for the link can be chosen with the Target pop-up menu.

Next, choose the background color for the button. The Flash file you insert will not necessarily be the same size as the button itself (the edges of the button may be rounded, and so on). If you want to set a color for the portion of the Flash that falls outside the body of the button, change the Bg Color selection appropriately. When you're satisfied with your results, you can choose a filename to hold the Flash button. If you're not picky, Dreamweaver MX will happily choose a name for you. Click the Apply button to apply your settings to the new button. Figure 4.23 shows a Flash button within the design window.

FIGURE 4.23

Flash buttons are a quick-and-dirty means of adding navigation to your site.

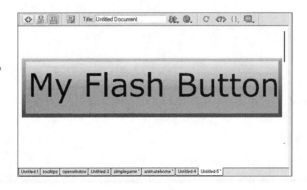

4

After the Flash button is added to the document, you can click to select it, and then use the resize handles to stretch it however you prefer. Being vector-based, the Flash button will maintain its high resolution no matter what. Double-clicking the button will jump back to the Flash button configuration screen—allowing you to make changes at any time.

> **Tip**
>
> When Flash content is selected in Dreamweaver MX, you can open the Properties panel and activate the Flash animation by clicking the Play button.

Flash Text

Operating much like the Flash button, Flash Text is a very simple way to add a high-quality vector text to your document design. Click the Flash Text button or choose Flash Text from the Interactive Media menu to begin. The Flash Text configuration screen can be seen in Figure 4.24.

FIGURE 4.24

Flash Text adds high-quality vector text to your document.

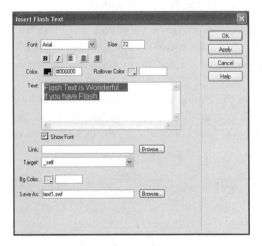

The Flash Text controls are similar to a standard word processor. You can choose the font, size, style, color, and justification. If you want to make the text into a link, you can also choose a rollover color.

Type the text you want to turn into a Flash file into the Text field. If the Show Font check box is selected, the text will be shown in the selected font as it is being entered.

If you want to turn the text into a link, be sure to fill in the Link field and set a link target, if necessary.

Similar to the Flash button, you can choose a background color for the Flash file so that it blends with your Web page. Finally, pick a filename. Chances are, however, that the given name is more than sufficient.

Unlike standard HTML text, the Flash Text is fully resizable and stretchable in the document design view. You can also double-click the text to edit it or adjust its style parameters.

Figure 4.25 shows a document design with Flash Text added.

FIGURE 4.25

Flash text and buttons allow you to use high-quality vector-based objects directly in the HTML authoring environment.

> **Caution**
>
> Be absolutely certain that your target audience members support Flash before using these features. If, for example, you build the majority of your navigation using Flash, your Web site might be inaccessible to those who don't have it. The number of non-Flash capable systems, however, is getting smaller every day. Check out Macromedia's Web site for JavaScript to detect Flash capable browsers— http://www.macromedia.com/.

Other Dynamic Elements

There are many other ways to get dynamic elements onto your Web pages—such as full-blown Flash animations or Java. Using Java can add a fully interactive program to your Web site. There is very little you can't do with these other animation/programming languages. The biggest difference is that these elements require plug-ins, or additional work outside of the Dreamweaver MX environment. You also have the disadvantage of not being able to see the content after it is added to your design view.

Use the Media option from the Insert menu to add Flash, ActiveX, Java applets, Shockwave, or other plug-ins to your document. These elements are also accessible from the Insert panel.

For example, choose Flash to insert a Flash movie into the HTML. You'll initially only see a gray rectangle to represent the dynamic element, but using the Properties panel, you can Play the element or set any special parameters that are passed to it—including database-driven values. The Properties panel for a Flash animation is shown in Figure 4.26.

FIGURE 4.26

Use the Properties panel to set attributes (and view) dynamic media.

Advanced JavaScript Programming and Debugging

Many of the features we've looked at in this chapter have required JavaScript to work their magic. Although this book isn't about learning JavaScript, Dreamweaver MX does offer several features for JavaScript programmers that make it a breeze to navigate and debug scripts within your documents. If you're a programmer, you'll recognize these functions as being standard within most programming IDEs. Try inserting a few behaviors into a new Dreamweaver MX Web page, and then switch to the code view of the page.

Within the toolbar, you'll see a menu represented by a bracket icon {}—this menu lists all the available JavaScript functions and gives you the opportunity to set a breakpoint within the code. Selecting a function jumps your cursor immediately to that area of the code.

If you want to set a breakpoint wherever your cursor is, choose Set Breakpoint from the menu. A red dot will appear in front of the line where the breakpoint is located. A *breakpoint* is a pausing point in the code where the execution of the program will momentarily stop. At this point, you can view the contents of variables to help determine where problems might be occurring. To clear all the breakpoints, choose Remove All Breakpoints from the pull-down menu.

After you've set the breakpoints in your code, you can choose Debug in Browser from the File menu, or from the pull-down World icon menu in the design view toolbar.

Within a few moments, your browser will launch and begin executing the JavaScript code. At the same time, the JavaScript debugger window will open, as seen in Figure 4.27.

FIGURE 4.27

Control your debugging session from the debugger window.

Along the top of the window are several icon functions that control how the debugger steps through your code. As you already know, it will stop as it reaches breakpoints, but you can use these icons for even greater functionality. From the left, these controls are as follows:

Run—Runs the script. Restarts the script execution from the beginning.

Stop Debugging—Ends the debugging session and exits the debugger.

Add/Remove Breakpoint—Toggles the breakpoint status of a line. If a breakpoint exists, it will be turned off. If there is no breakpoint, one will be added.

Remove All Breakpoints—Clears all the breakpoints in the script.

Step Over—Steps over a line or function, skipping its execution.

Step Into—Moves into a function and begins executing.

Step Out—Moves out of a function (the opposite of step into).

Additionally, you can monitor any of the variables in your functions by adding their names to the list of variables to monitor. Click the "+" button to add a new variable, and then type the name of the variable in the line you've added. As the program executes, the value stored in the variable will appear next to the variable name in real time.

For advanced programmers, the JavaScript debugger is an excellent addition to Dreamweaver MX. JavaScript remains one of the trickiest languages to work with in terms of cross-platform compatibility and the number of "gotchas" that can quickly lead to late-night caffeine-enhanced debugging sessions. I recommend *Sams Teach Yourself JavaScript in 21 Days* for those wishing to learn more.

Summary

Dynamic Web sites are everywhere these days. If you don't have something moving on your site, you're behind the times.

Although the world hasn't quite reached that point yet, it's getting there. Understanding how to create DHTML Web sites is becoming more and more important. Today you learned how Dreamweaver MX can automatically create JavaScript behaviors for your Web pages that would otherwise take extensive JavaScript programming.

Additionally, you learned how to create complex animation sequences and drag-and-drop programs all within the HTML of your Web pages—and all from within the Dreamweaver MX point-and-click interface.

For those who want to adopt basic Flash technologies, Dreamweaver MX gives you the ability to add buttons and text directly in the design view. Unlike HTML text/images, Flash graphics are vector based and can be resized without any loss of quality, but require a plug-in to do so.

Workshop

The Workshop area is meant to reinforce your reading with a series of questions and exercises.

Q&A

Q Will JavaScript *ever* work right?

A In a large part, the troubles of JavaScript have been eased in recent (5.x+) versions of Internet Explorer and Netscape 6.x. In fact, if we could convince the world to stop using the Netscape 4.x series, we'd avoid a number of Web design hassles.

Q The JavaScript action I want isn't available. How can I add it?

A You can check the Macromedia Web site for additional actions. Alternatively, if you're a programmer, you can read the "Extending Dreamweaver" documentation that is supplied in the Dreamweaver MX help system.

Q Can I cut and paste DHTML into Dreamweaver MX and edit it?

A No. You certainly can paste new JavaScript code into the Dreamweaver MX environment, but it isn't going to be editable using the timeline or any of the other tools.

Q Which should I use, a plug-in or DHTML?

A That's up to you. Do you want to rely on the users having a plug-in, or having a 4.0 or greater browser? You might want to survey your target audience before making a decision.

Quiz

1. What are behaviors?

2. Some Dreamweaver MX events are shown inside of parentheses. What is different about these events?

3. If you want to constrain the movement of a draggable layer to left and right, what values do you put in the constraint fields?

4. How can you increase the fluidity of the animation defined in the timeline?

5. Which tool lets you create fully scalable, vector-based text?

Quiz Answers

1. Behaviors consist of an action and a triggering event. They can be used to play sounds, create animation, and even make drag-and-drop applications.

2. These events aren't supported "natively" by the object. In order to work, Dreamweaver MX must insert additional HTML code around the object.

3. You should put zeros in the Up and Down fields.

4. Increase the FPS setting for the timeline.

5. The Flash Text tool lets you create vector text in a document without any additional authoring tools.

Exercises

1. Create a behavior that toggles two separate images based on a single image rollover. The built-in rollover tool can only change the image directly under the mouse.

2. Create your own version of a bouncing ball DHTML animation, similar to the example. Extend this bouncing ball to include a bounce sound that is triggered on the appropriate frames of the animation. The sound file bounce is included on the http://downloads.cutelittledogs.com Web site.

3. Take some time to research the other types of animation that can be generated through the use of plug-ins. For some interesting examples, look at the Gamelan Java collection (`http://www.gamelan.com/`) and Joe Cartoon's Flash animations (`http://www.joecartoon.com/`). Macromedia's Web site is a good starting point for other resources (`http://www.macromedia.com/`).

DAY 5

Creating Reusable Components

For the first four days, you've learned most everything you need to create Web sites using the entire spectrum of Dreamweaver MX tools. Now you'll find out how you can use these tools as infrequently as possible. No, this doesn't mean you should put Dreamweaver MX away—you should learn how to use it as efficiently as possible. Macromedia has provided tools for sharing resources between pages, sites, and people. Today, you will learn:

- Techniques on planning for code reuse. Learn how to best structure your site for reusing HTML.

- How to use the Dreamweaver MX Site Assets, which lets you store HTML for reuse across your site.

- How to use templates to create a work environment in which designers can maintain the page design, and content editors can worry about content.

- The Check-in/Check-out system's features for working on a single site with multiple team members.

- Ways to create macro command sequences by recording your actions while editing Web pages.

Planning for Code Reuse

If you've worked on large Web sites, you've probably found yourself cutting and pasting code between the different pages to create a consistent look and feel across your Web pages. There are many ways to try to keep your site as efficient as possible, including server-side includes and frames. In some cases they are completely legitimate techniques, but if your server doesn't support server-side includes, or you don't want to use frames, what do you do?

> **What Is a Server-Side Include?**
>
> Server-side includes are a means of including the contents of one file in another. They are used to include a standard header and footer in multiple Web pages. Server-side includes, however, are dependent on the Web server software—not on an application server.

Dreamweaver MX provides tools for minimizing the amount of editing you have to do while keeping the site completely compatible with any server. Before we get into those tools, however, you need to know what they are and how to best plan for their use on your site. By taking these steps and planning ahead, you'll be creating a site that will be easier to maintain and update in the future—both for yourself and the people who inherit the site from you.

Identifying Repetitive Formatting

Take a look through your source code. Do you use <font> tags to set the font face, size, and attributes throughout your documents? If you're using tables, setting the font for each cell can quickly grow tiresome and eat up a great deal of space as well. Keeping the font sizes and types correct across different pages is even more troublesome.

Most formatting and stylizing attributes are easily controllable with *cascading style sheets (CSS),* which you learned about in Day 3, "Advanced HTML and Site Tools." A style sheet is a way of defining and redefining style information in browsers that support CSS (Netscape and Internet Explorer 4.0 or later).

Style sheets can be embedded directly into the HTML document you're working on, or, better yet, be maintained in a separate document that is linked to by any of the HTML files in your site. Using this technique, changes to fonts or other formatting information can be applied directly to a single file and immediately carried across the entire site. If you're designing pages that, for one reason or another, can't support CSS, you can save time by defining HTML Styles. HTML Styles allow you to set up common combinations of fonts and font attributes that can be applied by selecting an item from a menu.

Finding Common Components

Most Web sites have common components used across multiple pages. Headers, footers, and navigation bars are very commonly repeated in HTML. This is fine for small sites, but on sites with hundreds of pages, keeping these objects current is a definite chore.

As an example of how this can be a problem—take, for example, a site I recently worked on that is updated with new event information every year. On the site is an archive of the event pamphlet artwork created each year. The artwork is located on a page specifically for that year—but also includes links to all the other pamphlets for other years. When a new year is added, all the other years must also be updated to include the new link. On a site with 20 years, I needed to update 20 individual pages just to add a single link.

Planning for Libraries

The repetition of constantly copying and pasting code from one page to another can be avoided by using the library tools in Dreamweaver MX. A *library* is a collection of HTML that can be used across many different pages. After a library item is created, it can be used on any of the pages of your site, but it can be edited from a single location.

If you're planning on using server technologies—such as *server-side includes (SSI)*—to provide the same library sort of functionality on your site, you need to identify what is possible before you start building your site. If you don't know what your deployment platform is going to be, stick to using the Dreamweaver MX library system.

 Tip

> If they're available on your system, server-side includes are the preferred way of creating reusable components. Using SSI results in smaller files—the reused HTML is kept in its own file and only visible in the final served page. Libraries offer the same flexibility, but the HTML from the library is automatically copied and pasted into other files on the Web site. Larger files are possible, but no dependence exists on the server platform.
>
> If you can't use server-side includes, look for a similar function in your deployment platform. PHP, for example, uses the `include` command to perform the same feat.

5

As you plan your site and navigation, make note of which components are repeated on your pages. Any common information that might need to change is a good candidate for use in a library.

Standardizing with Templates

Templates are a bit different from libraries, but they provide for additional code-reuse possibilities. Templates are exactly what they sound like—a template for a Web site. If you have a common Web site layout for content that is frequently added to your pages, you, as the Webmaster *extraordinaire* don't want to have to edit these new pages to add content. A good example would be a real-estate Web site. Although you might have designed the content layout for the site, you'd rather have the agents themselves add new house listings to the site. What you can do is create a template that lets the other people in your organization add content to pages without having to worry about the HTML.

A template contains the important parts of the page as locked-down code. The parts that should be editable remain accessible. Using a template can help create an efficient environment for editing pages by distributing the workload among multiple people. Combining a CSS with a template gives you even greater control over the content.

HTML Font Styles

Let's start our look at reusable coding by looking at HTML style definitions.

If you want to create font styles that will work on browsers that don't support cascading style sheets, you can use HTML styles using the standard font attributes. The styles that you create are included in the HTML Styles under the Text menu and can be used again and again just by choosing them from the menu. Just select the text that you want to apply the style to, and then choose the style from the menu.

 Caution
> The World Wide Web Consortium (W3C) strongly recommends that HTML Styles (such as <font> tags) be dropped in favor of cascading style sheets. In some cases, however, this isn't possible because of browser limitations and a lack of control over your target audience.

Adding HTML Styles

Styles are defined by choosing the New Style option under the HTML Styles menu. The configuration screen shown in Figure 5.1 will be displayed.

You'll need to set a few attributes before your new style becomes usable:

Name—This is the name of the style you're creating. This will be shown in the HTML Styles submenu of the Text menu for easy access.

Apply To—This chooses how the style is applied to the HTML: either to a selection or to a parent paragraph element (the enclosing <p></p> tags).

When Applying—Add to Existing Style keeps the added style within the context of whatever style you're currently using, whereas the Clear Existing Style option will apply the new style to the default browser style.

FIGURE 5.1

You can define HTML styles that will work in any browser.

Font Attributes—These are the Font face, Size, Color, and Style of the HTML style you're creating.

Paragraph Attributes—If you're applying the new style to paragraphs, you can also set a default format and alignment for the style.

Click the OK button when you're done and the HTML style will be created.

Tip

An alternative way of creating an HTML style is to format the text in your document the way you want. Then, select the properly formatted text before choosing the New Style option. The attributes of the selected text will automatically be reflected in the HTML style definition.

HTML Styles Panel

Besides the HTML Styles menu, you can also access styles from within the HTML Styles panel. Choose the HTML Styles selection from the Window menu. If you've looked at the Cascading Style Sheet panel, this, seen in Figure 5.2, will seem quite familiar. The paragraph symbol and letter a denote paragraph and character styles, respectively.

You can apply the listed styles to your HTML in two ways. By default, auto-apply is turned on by the small check box in the lower-left corner. Whenever you select text in the design view and then click on one of the HTML Styles, it will automatically be applied to the selection. If you uncheck this box, the Apply button in the panel will become active—you must then use the Apply button to force an HTML style to be added to the document.

5

Auto Apply

Create New Style

FIGURE 5.2

*The HTML Styles
panel gives easy
access to defining,
applying, deleting, and
editing styles.*

Apply   Delete Style

In the lower-right corner of the panel are two other functions that might be of use.
Clicking the pad of paper icon defines a new style. The trash can icon deletes the currently selected style. Editing a style is as simple as double-clicking the style in the list.
Be careful. If you're set to auto-apply styles, you might end up applying a style when
you only meant to edit it. If you don't like this behavior, click the Auto-apply button so
that it is unchecked.

 Tip

> HTML styles are site-wide attributes—you will need to copy the `styles.xml`
> file to the Library directory within other sites in order to make it available in
> other locations.
>
> The formatting of the styles, however, will show up in the HTML document,
> regardless of the `styles.xml` file.

Clear HTML Styles

There are two "clear" styles that can be applied to a given selection or paragraph. These
show up in the HTML Styles menu and panel, and can be used to clear styles that have
been applied to a given paragraph or selection. Alternatively, you can view the source
code for the page and remove the appropriate `<font>` tags.

Note

> Clearing a style will not work if the style is being generated by a cascading
> style sheet. You must edit the appropriate style sheet to remove or change
> the style.

Managing Site Assets

The majority of reusable components we'll look at fall generically under the title "Assets." An asset is exactly what you would expect, something that is used to build your site. You can store, reuse, and delete assets whenever you'd like. There are nine basic types of assets:

Images—Any image referenced in your site is included in the Images assets.

Colors—Color assets contain any HTML colors used on your site.

URLs—URLs linking pages to other pages or resources.

Flash—Macromedia Flash files used in the site.

Shockwave—Macromedia Shockwave files.

Movies—Any movies (embedded or otherwise) are listed in the Movie assets.

Scripts—JavaScript or VBScript code.

Templates—Template pages for creating a consistent look and feel.

Library—Library elements are commonly used portions of pages.

As their names suggest, each type of asset stores a particular type of information. The URLs asset stores URLs for links; the Colors asset stores HTML color codes, and so on. Each of the categories is accessed through the Assets panel, accessible from your Window menu or the Files panel group, and shown in Figure 5.3.

FIGURE 5.3

The Assets panel stores many types of reusable elements.

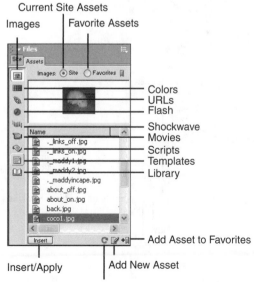

Current Site Assets

Images | Favorite Assets

Colors
URLs
Flash
Shockwave
Movies
Scripts
Templates
Library

Add Asset to Favorites

Insert/Apply

Add New Asset

Refresh Site Assets

5

Assets fall into two categories—Site Assets and Favorite Assets. Site assets are any assets you use to create your site. They're added automatically to the Asset Manager as you build your pages. The second category, Favorites, is a special class of assets accessible from any site. The icons at the bottom-right corner of the panel are used to refresh the site asset listing, add new assets, or save a selected asset as a favorite.

To add an existing asset to a Web page, highlight it in the list and click the Insert/Apply button in the lower-left corner of the panel.

Only Libraries and Templates assets are created by hand. When creating a site with images, for example, each of the images is automatically added as an image asset. If you drag new images into your site folder, they too will be added as soon as you click the Refresh Site Assets button in the panel.

Using Favorites

By default, when you work with the Assets panel, you are working with Site assets. To switch to the Favorites assets mode, click the Favorites radio button at the top of the panel. Favorites mode, pictured in Figure 5.4, works a bit differently from the standard Site mode.

FIGURE 5.4

Favorite assets span multiple sites and are a great place to store commonly used objects.

New Favorite Folder

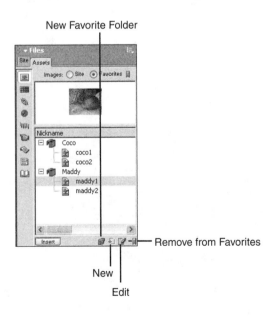

Remove from Favorites

New

Edit

Unlike Site Assets, Favorite Assets can be organized and arranged by folder. Click the New Favorites Folder button in the Assets panel to add a new folder to the list. Assets can be dragged in the panel and added to the folders as you see fit.

Of the different types of assets, Libraries and Templates have a few features beyond just storing basic information and files. These assets can be used to keep very large Web sites up-to-date and provide benefits for collaborative Web site editing. The rest of the assets, for all intents and purposes, manage themselves. Let's focus on the two very important Libraries and Templates assets.

Working with Libraries

A *library* is just a collection of HTML objects that you use frequently within your site. These pieces of HTML can be used wherever you need them and can be maintained in a common location. A good example of a component that you might want to reuse is a navigation bar. Because just about every page on a Web site has navigation, creating a navigation Library "object" would allow you to quickly add the same links to every page.

Creating a Library Item

The easiest way to put an item into a library is to create the object that you want to turn into a component inside your document design window. On Day 2, "Creating Your First Web Site," for example, each of the pages for the example site had a navigation bar with options for the Photo Gallery, Links, etc., as seen in Figure 5.5.

FIGURE 5.5

Navigation elements are a prime candidate for storing in a library.

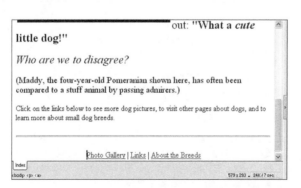

5

Let's turn this simple navigation bar into a Library object. Download the Day 5 folder from http://downloads.cutelittledogs.com onto your hard drive, unarchive it, and then define a Day 5 site that uses the folder as its local root folder (see Day 2 for more details on static site definitions). Within your newly defined site, you should see the file gallery.html. This is the same file shown in Figure 5.5.

Tip

For complex library items, defining all the components inside of a table or a layer provides a convenient way to group things together.

Open the `gallery.html` file and scroll to the bottom so that you can see the navigation bar. Add the navigation bar to the library by selecting it in the document design window and choosing Add Object to Library from the Library submenu of Modify menu, or by clicking the New Library Item button in the Assets panel.

The navigation bar should now be included in the Library portion of the Assets panel, as seen in Figure 5.6. Selecting the new asset will cause a preview of the navigation bar to be shown near the top of the panel. Click twice on the name of "Untitled" item in the list and give it a more meaningful title, such as "`navigation`." You can now insert the new library item into any file you'd like by highlighting it in the list and clicking the Insert button or dragging it into the design window.

FIGURE 5.6

The Library portion of the Assets panel contains all the items you've added.

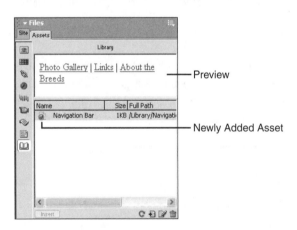

Note

If you don't have the HTML for a library item defined yet, you can start from scratch. To do this, make sure that a document design window is selected but none of its contents are highlighted. Next, open the Library area of the Assets panel and click the New icon (notepad with "+" symbol) in the lower-right corner. A new empty item will appear in the library list. Double-click the entry to open and edit it using the Dreamweaver MX tools.

Not surprisingly, the Library item you've created is stored as nothing more than simple HTML. If you double-click a library object or use the Edit icon in the panel, it will open the corresponding .lbi file in your site and allow you to edit it with the Dreamweaver MX tools. Saving the file will update *all* files that use the Library element. When viewing files that contain a library item, the item is highlighted to differentiate it from the rest of the document.

Exploring Other Library Functions

There are a few other Library functions that you can access from the Library submenu under the Dreamweaver MX Modify menu or the Panel group menu.

The Update Current Page menu item will update the currently opened page with any changes that have been made in the library. Usually, however, you'll want to work on an entire site and update all the pages with your changes. To do this, use the Update Pages selection.

Update Pages will open the dialog box seen in Figure 5.7. From here you can tell Dreamweaver MX to Look in an entire site, or choose to only look in pages that reference a particular library item and update the library items that it finds in those pages. A running log is kept of all the changes in case you what to review the modifications.

Figure 5.7

Update all the pages in your site in a single sweep.

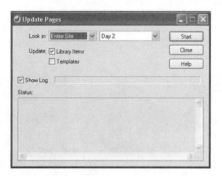

Library items can be deleted by selecting them in the panel and clicking the trash can icon, or choosing Delete from the panel menu. Library files themselves are kept in the Library directory within your site's root folder. These items are labeled with the .lbi extension, and, as previously mentioned, can be edited directly in Dreamweaver MX.

Working with Templates

Another important tool for code reuse and distributed editing is the Assets panel's Templates asset.

Templates are a special form of file that behave differently from the standard HTML files in the site. A template is used to create pages with a fixed look and feel but with varying content.

Where this comes in handy is in keeping things straight when files are constantly being opened and closed. With standard HTML files, you'll find that as files are passed around, things will mysteriously break—table dimensions will change, links will break—and no one will have any idea how it happened. If you set up your files as templates, you can safely give the files to content editors without worrying about them disturbing the layout of the page. In distributed editing environments, this is a must.

Another way to think of template files is as an inverse of the Library function. Instead of providing portions of HTML that are inserted into documents, you provide documents in which portions of HTML can be inserted.

Creating a Template from an Existing Page

Because a template is actually a layout of an entire Web page, it's easiest to create one from an existing page. That way you can design the page in Dreamweaver MX without having to worry about defining your editable areas until you are done. For example, open the gallery.html file in the Day 5 site again. This is a simple table-designed screen that features images in four cells of the table, shown in Figure 5.8. Suppose that you've designed this screen and you want to lock it down so that only the four table cells with text and images can be modified.

FIGURE 5.8

Assume we want to make the images in this simple table layout the only editable part of the document.

You'll first need to save the page as a template using Save as Template from the File menu. Unlike the normal Save As dialog box, this one looks a bit different. Templates are

saved in a special Templates directory inside of each Web site and have the extension
.dwt. From the Save As Template dialog box, shown in Figure 5.9, you can select the
site that will receive the template and the name of the template you're creating—by
default Dreamweaver MX will pick a template name based on the existing filename. In
this case, the template will be named gallery.dwt. After the template has been saved,
you can start defining the editable regions in the document.

FIGURE 5.9

*Templates are saved to
a specific site.*

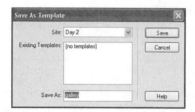

> **Caution**
>
> You don't have to save the document as a template before you start defin-
> ing editable regions. It does help prevent accidentally editing the original
> HTML.

By default the entire area of a template file is locked. You have to pick out the areas that
are editable. Select the first cell in the table and choose Editable Region from the
Templates Objects submenu of Insert. You'll be prompted for a name for the editable
area, as shown in Figure 5.10. This name distinguishes this section from other regions
while importing content. For the case of the four-cell table, upperleft should be fine.
You can change the names at any time by selecting the region and using the Properties
panel.

FIGURE 5.10

*Choose a name for the
editable region.*

As you add new editable regions to the document, the region will be highlighted in aqua
and its name will be displayed in a tab directly above it. When the template is opened to
create a new Web page, the locked portion of the page will be highlighted in yellow,
whereas the editable portion won't be highlighted.

To finish the template for the gallery page, repeat the process of choosing a table cell and
making an editable region until all four cells are defined as editable.

5

If you make a mistake and need to unmark a region, just select the region by clicking its tab, and then choose Remove Template Markup from the Template option of the Modify menu. Take note that the menu items for adding and removing template regions are found within the Insert and Modify menus, respectively; not under a single menu, as you might think.

Tip   If you don't like the colors of the editable/locked portions of templates, you can adjust them in the Highlighting portion of the Dreamweaver MX preferences.

When you've finished creating the template, make sure that all your changes have been saved, and then close the Template window. You can now create new pages based on this template by choosing New from the File menu, and then clicking the Template tab, and the Day 5 site.

Note   If you want, you can also create Templates from scratch. Choose New from the File menu, and then click the Template subcategory. Alternatively, click the new icon in the Assets panel (the same as in the Library section) to create a new template, and then double-click the new item to edit the template, or click the edit icon. You should recognize all these features from working with the Library.

When designing a template from scratch, you have access to all the same tools as when creating standard HTML pages. The difference is the ability to insert editable and other template specific regions into the document.

Advanced Template Features

You've seen two types of template content so far—locked content (the default content of any template) and editable content (which can be changed by anyone basing a document on the template). There are, however, several additional advanced content types that you can insert into your templates for even greater control.

Repeating Regions

Macromedia realized that while defining simple regions of editable content is great for many content pages, it is of little use to lists or other elements that continue to grow in length, rather than simply having a few sentences or images change around. In previous versions of Dreamweaver, the only way, for example, to be able to add a new content row to a table was to define the entire table as an editable region, and then hope that the editing process wouldn't accidentally screw up any of the table attributes, sizing, and the like.

In Dreamweaver MX, you, as the author, have the ultimate control by being able to define regions of HTML code that the editors can repeat as many times as they'd like. Repeating regions can contain editable regions as well, making it possible to design ever-expanding templates that can be easily updated by those who are maintaining content.

For example, create a new template in your Day 5 site named expandtable.dwt. Within the document design window, insert a simple two-column-by-two-row table. This will be our ever-expanding list of dogs and their owners. Into first row, column one, insert the heading Dog Name, and into the second heading position add Dog Owner.

To make the template functional, we want the remaining two cells of the document to be editable regions, but we also want them to be regions that can repeat as new dogs and owners are added to the list. Click inside the cell directly below the Dog Name heading and use the Insert panel or Insert menu to add a new editable region named Dogname. Do the same for the next cell, but name it Ownername. You now have a template with two editable cells, but that's not enough.

Finally, select the bottom row that contains both editable regions and choose Repeating Region from Insert, Template Objects, or from the Template category of the Insert panel. Your template should now look like Figure 5.11.

FIGURE 5.11

Repeating regions can include editable content.

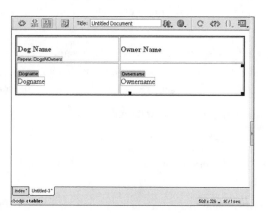

5

When editing a document that is based on a template with a repeating region, the Repeating Region tab includes four small button controls: "+", "-", up, and down (as arrows). Using the plus or minus button adds or subtracts a copy of the repeating region to the document. The up and down arrows move the active content up and down within the region. These features are also available by choosing Modify, Templates, and then choosing one of the Repeating Entries selections when editing a template-based document.

> **Tip**
>
> If your primary use for repeating regions is to add repeating tables, you can quickly generate a properly configured table by using the Repeating Table tool under Insert, Templates in the menu bar or in the Insert panel.

Optional Regions

Another advanced region type is the Optional Region—these regions are unusual in that you can create several "options" that can be valid on different pages. If there are several categories within a Web site, with each sharing a common format but different headers, an optional region could be created in the template that holds all the possible header options.

Optional regions can either be editable or noneditable, depending on your needs. These regions are not necessarily displayed in a document—they're available only if certain Dreamweaver parameters (variables) evaluate to a "true" condition for the region. Dreamweaver parameters are simply variables that are local to the Dreamweaver application and are evaluated when using templates. For full documentation on use of Dreamweaver MX parameters, consult your application documentation. Based on JavaScript, these parameters allow you to evaluate conditions on-the-fly, and change the template accordingly.

Parameters are set in the <head></head> area of a document. For example, assume you have a template that should (sometimes) display one header graphic when the Macromedia parameter header is set to equal 1 or another if the header equals 2.

You'd insert the following into the template file's <head>:

```
<!— TemplateParam name="header" type="number" value="1" —>
```

This essentially says that you have a parameter (variable) named header that is equal to 1.

Now, you can use the header parameter value to insert an optional region. As with any template feature, you can insert an optional region by using the Modify menu's Template Objects selection, or the Insert menu's Template objects. For example, to insert an optional header, you would add *both* potential header graphics to the document, and then select one at a time and choose Optional Region from the Insert menu or panel. Figure 5.12 shows the basic optional region insert dialog box.

FIGURE 5.12

The basic optional region settings allow you to set a default on or off content region.

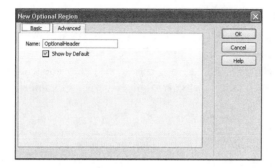

When adding a basic optional region, you can choose whether to Show by Default. If you choose this check box, the region will be visible by default in the template. If not, it will be hidden. What this is doing is actually inserting a parameter based on the name of the region into the <head> region. This parameter is toggled between true or false using the check box or by editing the <head> content.

To enter in your own parameter checking code (what you need to turn one header image on for header==1 and another for header==2), you'll need to switch to the Advanced tab, shown in Figure 5.13.

FIGURE 5.13

Advanced optional region parameters allow you to enter your own parameter-checking code.

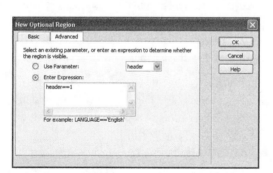

Under the Advanced tab, you can choose to use an existing parameter (this is good for linking multiple basic regions), or to enter your own expression. For two optional headers, you would enter header==1 for the first image and header==2 for the other. These regions could then be toggled for any page based on the template by editing the header parameter in the template's <head> code.

> **Tip**
>
> Use Check Template Syntax from Modify, Templates to verify that your template parameters have been entered correctly.

Editable Attributes

If you want to allow editors to fine-tune your page, you can make individual tag attributes, rather than an entire region, editable. For example, if you want to make the bgcolor attribute of a single table cell editable, choose the cell in the template, and then select Make Attribute Editable from Modify, Templates. The Editable Tag Attributes dialog box is seen in Figure 5.14.

Attributes of individual HTML tags can be made editable in a template.

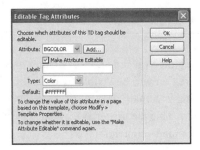

Click the Add button to add a new editable attribute, or, if you've already set the attribute to a default value in the template code, you can choose it from the Attribute pop-up menu. Click Make Attribute Editable so that template users will be able to modify the attribute on their pages. Next, set a label to identify the attribute, such as "my cell bgcolor" and pick a type for the attribute, such "color." This will determine the interface the users see when they modify the attribute.

Finally, enter a default value for the attribute in the Default field and click OK. The template now "knows" the attribute, and your editors will be able to change it on template-generated pages by choosing Template Properties from the Modify menu.

Employing Templates

You've got the basic background to make templates, so how do you use them once they've been created? The easiest way to use a template is to select New from the File menu, and then click the Templates tab at the top of the screen. This will let you select one of your already defined sites and its corresponding templates, and then create a new HTML file based on a template, as seen in Figure 5.15.

As you'd expect, only the editable regions can change. Other users who have access to this template can now safely create Web pages without having to worry about changing HTML or disturbing the layout.

Another way to use a template is to apply the content of an existing file to the template. This will actually insert the template into the document and position the content into one of the editable regions of the document. You can use the Apply button in the Assets panel to perform this action.

FIGURE 5.15

Use the Templates tab of the New Files dialog box to create a page based on a template.

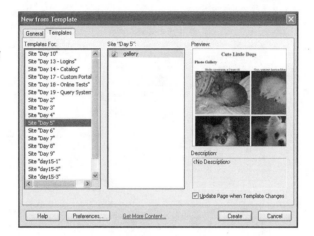

As with the Library items, you can update a Template file and apply the changes to all the files that use the template from the Template submenu of the Modify menu. This feature enables you to quickly change the entire layout of similar pages in your Web site from a single location. Hurray!

Tip

It is critical that all the users working on a site understand how templates and libraries work before they start using them. If a user just uses a template as a standard HTML document, the benefits of a global update and document content control will be lost.

If you find that you want to make additional changes to a template-based page that would violate the template, you can use Modify, Templates, Detach from Template to remove the template restrictions from the file while leaving its content.

Caution

Be aware that if you detach a page from its template, changes you make to the template will not be reflected in the page.

5

Working with Snippets

Similar to the library of components that you can build in the Site Assets panel are the snippets. A *snippet* is a piece (or pieces) of HTML code that you frequently apply in your document. Rather than typing it each time, you can quickly insert a chunk of code into your page, or around a selected object in your document. Open the Snippets panel by choosing Snippets from the Windows menu. The Snippets panel is shown in Figure 5.16.

FIGURE 5.16

Snippets are pieces of code that you can quickly insert into your documents.

At the bottom of the panel are the usual buttons: insert (to add a snippet to your document), new snippet folder, new snippet, edit snippet, and remove. The lower portion of the display contains folders of prebuilt snippets. You might want to check these out, as they contain a wide variety of useful code, from breadcrumb navigation to no-cache metatags.

To add a snippet, simply highlight it in the list, and then click the Insert button. It will be added wherever your cursor is in the document. Some snippets do more, however, than insert a single chunk of code. Wrap snippets insert code on each side of a selected piece of text, allowing you to wrap a selection between code sections of your making.

Creating a snippet is simple; simply click the New Snippet (+) icon at the bottom of the panel. The snippet definition window will appear, as demonstrated in Figure 5.17.

Use the Name and Description fields to provide an apt name and brief description of the snippet you're about to create. Next, decide whether you're creating a Wrap Selection or Code Block snippet. A code block is simply a chunk of HTML that will be inserted onto your page. The Wrap Selection however, is a bit more useful in that it can be used to modify other elements you've already added to your page.

FIGURE 5.17

Define your own snippets with ease.

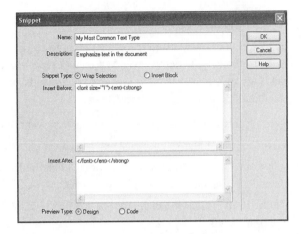

Assume, for example, I want to add `<font size="1"><em><strong>` before some selected text in my document, and then add `</font></em></strong>` after it. To define a snippet that can do this, I'd make sure that Wrap Selection was chosen, and then I add `<font size="1"><em><strong>` in the Insert Before text field and `</font></em></strong>` in the Insert After field.

Finally, use the Design and Code buttons to choose how to view the code. The Design button will show the code as it will appear in the design window, whereas the Code button shows the straight HTML code. Because many Wrap Selection snippets often don't render anything on the screen (nor do JavaScript functions) the Code option is the most useful for that type of snippet.

Recording Dreamweaver MX Commands

The Dreamweaver MX environment is very extensible—beyond what this book can document without taking an extra two or three weeks worth of text. The entire menu system is editable, and new commands written in JavaScript can be added to the system in a way that completely integrates with the rest of the application.

Take a look under your Commands menu. Several external commands are already installed on your system such as Clean up HTML and Clean up Word HTML. This functionality is not compiled into Dreamweaver MX but exists as an add-on file.

If you aren't a programmer and don't have any desire to write JavaScript extensions, there are two ways that you can add functionality to the Dreamweaver MX environment—recording commands and installing external prebuilt extensions, which you'll learn about in Day 21, "Advanced Dreamweaver MX Features."

5

Recording Commands

The easiest way to add your own custom functionality is to record a command you can use repetitively. Unfortunately, Dreamweaver MX cannot repeat mouse selection actions, so your commands are mostly restricted to keyboard commands and object inserts. To create a new command, perform the following steps:

1. Type, Insert, or perform the series of actions that you want to record.
2. Open the History panel and select the steps that you want to save.
3. If you want to immediately replay these options, click the Replay button or panel pop-up menu to verify that they do what you want.
4. If you like the results, click the disk icon, or use the Save as Command option from the pop-up menu.
5. Enter a name for the new command.
6. Presto! The command is inserted in the Commands menu.

Figure 5.18 shows the History panel with a simple series of actions ready to be saved as a command.

FIGURE 5.18

Select the actions you want to save as a command.

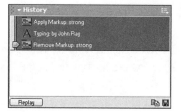

If you find yourself typing and retyping styled sequences of text, or inserting tables repeatedly, you can record these actions as commands and replay them any time you want.

To rename or delete commands that you've created, choose Edit Command List from the Commands menu. From the dialog box shown in Figure 5.19, edit the name of the command by clicking it or delete it with the Delete button.

There's also another way to quickly create a command sequence that you can use repeatedly without having to save a command—recording a temporary command.

Figure 5.19

Edit and delete commands you've created.

Recording Temporary Commands

To create a sequence of actions that can be replayed during the current Dreamweaver MX session, select Start Recording from the Commands menu. You can interact with Dreamweaver MX while it records what you do. Once again, you're bound to the rule of not being able to make mouse selections. When the recording is finished, choose Stop Recording.

The Play Recorded Command becomes active once a temporary command is in memory—use it to replay your actions at any time.

Creating a Distributed Editing Environment

If you have a group of people who are working together on a site, the need will eventually arise for people to edit files simultaneously. Unfortunately, the problem is that two people might try to edit the same file at the same time. In the normal editing mode, the last person to save the file will overwrite the changes made by the first person. Constantly having to tell your colleagues what file you're working on is not an efficient way of solving the problem either. As usual, Dreamweaver MX has a tool that makes this a nonissue.

Using a Check In/Out system, you can exert ownership over a file, and other people will not be able to access the file you have "checked out." It's similar to checking a book out of a library. When you check the book out, it's in your possession until you're done. People can look up who has it, but can't access it. When you're done, you check the book back in and other people can check it out.

Several systems implement Check In/Out systems, such as MS SourceSafe and WebDAV. If you aren't running either of these systems, Dreamweaver MX can't be certain what the remote system is running; it must keep track of who has the file using a simple file-locking system.

5

Enabling Check In and Check Out

The first thing you need to do if you want to use the Check In/Out system is adjust the site definition for the Web site that you want to use it with. Open the site definition window, and then choose Remote Info and click the Enable File Check In and Check Out button, as seen in Figure 5.20.

FIGURE 5.20

The Check In/Out options are very sparse.

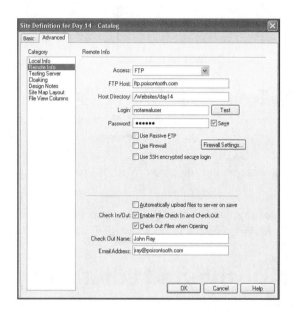

At the very least, you'll want to enable the Check In/Out system, and provide a name and e-mail address that will be attached to the file when you check it out. Finally, it's a good idea to select the Check Out Files when Opening option. This will automatically check files out as you open them.

 Note

In order to use the Check In/Out functions within Dreamweaver MX, you must be using a server access method other than None.

Using the Check In/Out System

Using the tracking system is very simple. If you've chosen the Check Out on Open option in the Check In/Out setup, you can operate the system as you normally would. Any file you open will be automatically checked out. Dreamweaver MX users who are properly configured will not be able to check out files once another user has control.

You can also use the Check Out (down arrow with checkmark) and Check In (up arrow with lock) buttons at the top of the Site Files window to control the process of gaining and relinquishing control of the site's files. The files that are checked out on the system are displayed along with a Check Mark icon and a field showing whom currently is using the file. Clicking on the user's name who has the file checked out will open your e-mail program so you can send them a nasty "give me back my file" message. Figure 5.21 demonstrates the check out system in action.

FIGURE 5.21

Files that are checked out show the user who is currently controlling them.

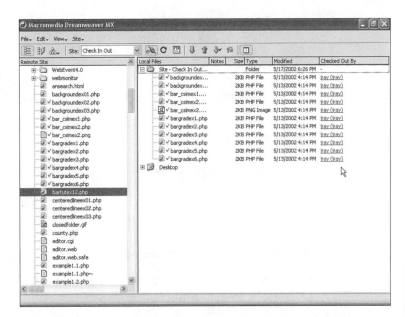

If you are creating Web sites in a distributed editing environment, you'll find the check in/out system invaluable. The only other options are clearly defining who should be editing what files, and when, or partition your Web site so that each portion of the site is defined separately within each person's copy of Dreamweaver MX.

Adding Design Notes

A final tool that is useful for multiuser editing are design notes. Design notes are pieces of information that can be attached to each Web page during the editing process. These notes are stored in XML in a folder named_notes found within the site root. When users check out a file that has design notes attached to it, they can look at the existing notes and add new notes. Because the notes are separate from the HTML, there is no need to worry about the XML getting in the way of code for the pages.

To attach a note to an open page, choose Design Notes from the File menu. To open the notes from the site files view, select the file you want to work with, and then open the contextual menu and choose Design Notes. The design notes definition screen is shown in Figure 5.22.

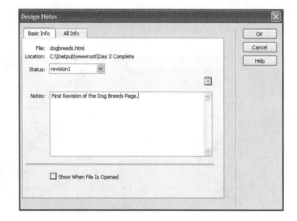

From the Basic Info tab, you can set a status for the file from a predefined list of some common project status settings. You can also type in a short note or two (clicking the calendar icon inserts the current date), and turn on an option to have the note displayed when its corresponding HTML file is opened.

If you'd like to store more information in the design note, select the All Info tab. Without getting into too much detail of XML, each of the design note attributes is stored as a name/value pair. The Info field shows all these defined pairs. The Name and Value can be changed by picking one of the lines in Info and altering the values in these fields. As with all Dreamweaver MX's property lists, the "+" and "−" buttons add and delete items from the list.

If you'd like to edit the design note directly, open the notes directory in your site and find the .mno XML file that matches your HTML file. For example, the design notes for news.html are stored in notes/news.html.mno.

Here is an example of the XML for a page's notes:

```
<?xml version="1.0" encoding="iso-8859-1" ?>
<info>
    <infoitem key="author" value="John Ray;" />
    <infoitem key="notes" value="16 June, 2002;" />
    <infoitem key="status" value="revision1" />
    <infoitem key="showOnOpen" value="true" />
</info>
```

As you can see, the information is open and very accessible. Many of Dreamweaver MX's configuration files are written in XML, making customization quite simple.

Summary

To create an efficient environment for editing any sort of code, the most important thing to do is make sure that you reuse as much previous work as possible. Dreamweaver MX has several tools that make this possible.

Cascading style sheets keep pages consistent across a site, across browsers, and across different computer platforms. The use of a CSS can cut down significantly on the amount of HTML formatting that you need to use in a site. If you're targeting a browser that doesn't support CSS, you can use HTML Styles in their place.

Libraries and templates are Dreamweaver MX's way of providing code-reuse facilities. Libraries store commonly used HTML that can be inserted anywhere and changed from a single location. Similarly, templates implement a look for a page that can be applied across many different pages. Once again, changes in a single location are reflected across the entire site.

Dreamweaver MX is extendable—both by recording your own command sequences and downloading new commands from the Internet. A few clicks and you have new functionality that didn't ship with the software.

Workshop

The Workshop area is meant to reinforce your reading with a series of questions and exercises.

5

Q&A

Q Will I ever really need reusable components?

A As you build larger and larger Web sites, you'll come to appreciate the Asset Manager and reusable components. For small sites, it's easy to overlook these Dreamweaver features and simply copy and paste between pages. When you're working on a site with hundreds of pages, however, the added organization provided by the Dreamweaver's assets can't be beat.

Q What are the best candidates for library items?

A Navigation bars, obviously, but also some of the smaller elements on the site might be subject to change such as mailto links, lists of outside links, and seasonal graphics. If it changes and you don't want to dig for it, build it into a library.

Q Are templates secure?

A Absolutely not. You can't distribute a template based Web site and completely protect the files from being changed. You should train your team members on how to use Dreamweaver MX effectively without going beyond the bounds that the software enforces.

Quiz

1. What are HTML Styles?

2. What's a library good for?

3. How can an existing HTML page be turned into a template?

4. What is a Wrap Selection snippet?

Quiz Answers

1. An HTML Style is a combination of font attributes that can stored and reused without having to insert all of the corresponding tags by hand.

2. Storing commonly used page components such as navigation.

3. By using the Save as Template option from the File menu, and then defining template regions as is appropriate.

4. A snippet defined as a Wrap Selection consists of two pieces of code, one that is inserted before a selection in the document window, and another that is inserted after it.

Exercises

1. Practice using the Library and Template assets. Create templates based off your existing pages and try adding data to them.

2. Browse the available premade templates and snippets. Macromedia has provided quite a collection of attractive and useful code samples.

DAY 6

Introduction to Dynamic Web Applications and Database Design

What are database-driven sites, what are they good for, and what background do you need to create your own site? By the end of the day, you'll be able to answer these questions and more. Today is a good day to sit back and take a breather from sitting in front of your computer. What you'll learn is a lesson in dynamic Web pages and the concepts behind them. It's mostly theory, but it's important to know:

- What types of sites make good database-driven sites? What can be driven dynamically?

- Which technologies are used to make Web sites dynamic and how does the HTTP protocol support these concepts?

- How are database-driven sites built? What planning needs to take place before a good site can be built?

- What are the basics of database design and normalization? How can efficient and easy-to-maintain database structures be created?

Dynamic Web Sites

It *is* tempting to just sit down and try to build database-driven sites without understanding how the sites really work. Unfortunately, this inevitably leads to poorly written and designed applications. Over the past year I've met with a number of Dreamweaver MX users to see how they use the application, and what they've found frustrating.

The overwhelming majority is disappointed with Dreamweaver MX's database connections and is confused with the process of putting together the databases themselves. There are tools built into the application for developing program logic, querying databases, saving data to databases, and so on, but absolutely nothing for creating the databases. Everything you do with Dreamweaver MX from now on will require a working and correctly structured database to be in place.

This chapter gives you a background in what dynamic sites are good for, and why you should take the time to develop your database skills now, rather than in the middle of building a dynamic site.

So, what is a dynamic site anyway?

A dynamic Web site is one in which the information contained on the pages changes. It is generated dynamically as the users browse the page. You've learned how to create Web sites that move and change as the users interact with its objects. Is that a dynamic Web site? Not really. The information needed to create those displays is contained within the Web page itself. All the processing power that takes place on the Web page comes from the computer of the person browsing the site.

On a truly dynamic site, the Web pages are generated by running a program on the Web server itself. This program, or *Web application*, builds a page using dynamic information and then delivers it to the client for display. From the client computer's perspective, the dynamic page is the same as any other Web page—it can contain all the same elements that you've used to build your own static pages throughout the week—images, style sheets, JavaScript, and so on.

More often than not, dynamic Web sites are powered by some sort of a database backend. This provides a place to store data and an easy access point for Web site administration. You can sometimes tell pages that are generated dynamically by the extension of the filename you are requesting, such as `.cgi`, `.php`, `.jsp`, or anything that varies from the `.htm` and `.html` standard.

Although a file extension itself doesn't guarantee that a site is database driven, it is a good indicator. It is also indicative of the technology that is used to drive the Web site. There are two commonly used approaches to creating dynamic Web sites: CGI and embedded programming.

Traditional Web Application Programming

Traditional Web application programming centered on writing a single "do-all" application called a *CGI (Common Gateway Interface)*. A CGI application is the equivalent of a local application that you run on your desktop, but instead it is hosted on a Web server. It is programmed similarly to a traditional application except for using an HTML interface.

The problem with many CGIs is that they require a lot of resources on the computer hosting the Web site. A typical execution of Perl (a popular CGI programming language) takes about 5MB of RAM. For systems such as Mac OS X and Windows XP, this isn't a huge problem, but the constant loading and unloading of the program in memory is. Because of this constant context switching, CGI applications require resources above and beyond the embedded languages, which we'll take a look at in a few seconds.

Note My comments on Perl are a bit of a generalization, there are several ways around its problems. The mod_perl library for Apache and ActiveState's Perl add-on for IIS can attach a Perl interpreter to the active Web server—saving them the need to launch a separate Perl process when a CGI is run.

One of the largest limitations of traditional CGI programming languages is that they were designed for programming—not necessarily programming Web applications. What takes dozens of lines in a CGI application might take only a single line in an embedded language. Passing information in and out of a CGI and communicating with databases often takes a large amount of additional code or external libraries. If you've worked with CGIs before, you'll find that switching to an embedded language will shorten your source code dramatically.

HTML Embedded Languages

Embedded HTML languages are the successor to the CGI languages. They provide functionality above and beyond CGIs—both in terms of ease of use as well as power. The biggest difference between CGIs and embedded HTML languages is how the code is structured. In a CGI, the programming language must generate the HTML; you cannot (easily) separate the two. In an embedded language, standard static HTML code remains the dominant force behind how the page is laid out. Instead of writing the application logic of the program, and then writing more code to generate HTML, you first write the HTML and then fill in the application logic wherever it is necessary. In essence, embedded languages separate a Web application's interface from the programming that makes it work its magic.

6

The method in which embedded programs are executed is also different. These languages are executed by the server as the page is sent to the client. No external software (such as Perl) is executed. The interpreter for the language is attached to the server itself. This makes the embedded languages extremely efficient in terms of execution and resource usage.

Another fantastic benefit of embedded languages is that they offer direct access to database systems. Most programming languages have added database support as an afterthought. The creators of embedded languages realized the potential of database access from within HTML source code and built it directly into the language. Speed and ease of use are only a few of the advantages of embracing these complimentary technologies.

Obviously, there are great advantages to using HTML embedded programming languages. In the past three years, embedded languages have taken off and there is a plethora of them to work with. Dreamweaver MX supports four embedded models, making it a very flexible tool, and one of the first of its kind to support real-time viewing of database-driven information.

Understanding Dynamic Sites

Although it might seem as if building a dynamic Web site would be no different from programming a standard application (except for the need to provide an HTML interface), it's actually a very different process. The HTTP protocol makes life a bit difficult for Web application creators. For example, what happens if you want to accept input from a user, process it, collect a bit more information, process it, and compile the results? In a standard desktop application, this wouldn't be a problem; you'd just structure the program exactly as you want the tasks to be performed.

For Web deployment, you need to take a different approach to solving the problem. The reason for this is that only a single step of the program can be implemented at a time and those steps must somehow be linked together. However, the HTTP protocol is a stateless protocol, and there is no continuation between the user's computer and the server over the interim that falls between each page of a dynamic site. Every page that is loaded, if it is generated dynamically, is an individual execution of a program on the server.

When a user submits a form, it goes back to the server and is processed, and a results page is usually shown. That's it for the server's involvement with the data. After the results are returned, no connection exists between the client and the server. So, what happens if you want to continue working with data that has been returned?

In order to maintain a connection between different accesses to a Web page or to subsequent pages in a site, you must use some kind of *session management*. Simply put, session management is a way to maintain a persistent virtual connection between the user and a remote Web server, even though no real connection exists. There are two ways that session

management can be maintained—through variable passing and through cookies.
Dreamweaver MX uses both of these techniques to build applications for your Web server.

Variable Passing

Variable passing is a way of passing values of individual variables between pages.
You've almost certainly seen URLs that tack extra information on to the end, and look
similar to this:

```
http://www.cutelittledogs.com/showname.php?firstname=John&lastname=Ray
```

In this example, the variables firstname and lastname are passed to the remote program
showname.php with the values John and Ray, respectively. If a program wanted to pass
data between different elements, it could embed the links between different pages with the
appropriate variables so that when they were clicked, the data is passed to the next page.

 Tip

Try testing the previous example (it *is* a working URL) with your own name.
Following the pattern set up for the first and last names, see if you can successfully pass the variable middlename to the application as well.

This method of passing variables is called the GET method. It is very common, but it also
leads to ugly URLs that display some of the inner workings of a Web site. If users bookmark a page that was retrieved using a GET method, they will end up bookmarking the
passed variables as well. Each time they go to the page, they will send the data that was
passed to the page the first time it was retrieved. The nice thing about the GET method of
variable passing is that it is easy to program by hand. You can quickly set up links to include parameters retrieved from a database or data that the users have input on another page.

The alternative way to pass data in the URL is through the POST method. This is traditionally used with forms to send data to the remote server without putting all the parameters of the form in the URL field when it is submitted. If, for example, you have a form
that accepts a large amount of data, you certainly don't want to pass that data with the GET
method. Instead, POST passes the data as part of the connection request on the remote server.

```
POST /showname.php HTTP/1.0
Host: www.cutelittledogs.com:
Content-type: application/x-www-form-urlencoded
Content-Length: 28

firstname=John&lastname=Ray
```

As you can see, the differences are subtle, but not the effect. Unlike GET, the users never
see the variables being sent, resulting in a much cleaner URL. In addition, one also gains
the benefit of being able to pass larger amounts of data from a form to the program.

6

Note

> Although it's not trivial, you can actually test this second example to experience firsthand how the POST method works. Telnet into port 80 of www.cutelittledogs.com, and then issue the commands, *exactly* as shown. On most systems, you'll need to type telnet www.cutelittledogs.com 80 at the command line.

The POST method, however, cannot be used directly in the HTML to pass values unless a form is present. You cannot manually create URLs that use this method. This requirement seriously limits use of this method. However, if you have a sequence of forms that the users need to fill out, the POST method is quite useful for carrying the data from one form to another. You'll see this in action next week.

Session Variables

No matter what method of variable passing you're using, there's still the problem of managing your data. For example, if you're creating a shopping cart application and you want to maintain a list of all the items that the users purchased, it isn't going to be terribly efficient to keep passing them from page to page in the URL. Instead, many embedded programming languages offer session variables to track information.

Session variables are virtual variables that exist while a user browses a Web site. They can be used to store anything, and their value is specific to a particular user's session. Because there really isn't a way to identify when a user is finished with a site, session variables typically expire after a user quits the browser. Sometimes sessions are created that automatically expire after a certain length of time. This will effectively log users out and forget all information that has been stored about them. Have you ever gone to an online store and picked out a few items, only to decide you're not going to buy them? Rather than go to the shopping cart and remove the items, you probably closed your browser window. If you returned to the site the next day, chances are your shopping cart was empty. This is an example of session expiration.

Note

> Another variable type used in dynamic applications is an *application* variable. This is a variable that persists across all user sessions and is accessible from anywhere within a Web application.
>
> Many people view application variables as a bad idea, just as are global variables in a programming language, but they can be very useful for maintaining internal statistics within an application.

Session variables, when used efficiently, are a great benefit to the user and programmer. They allow more complex and secure applications to be built than traditional variable passing. Improperly used, however, they can have significant drawbacks. Most languages that support session variables allow you to store complete data structures in a session variable. For example, you might store an entire shopping cart structure in a single variable. Although this works, it also eats up server resources. Each complex structure that is stored as a session variable must first be *serialized*—or converted into a stream of data that is easily stored on the server. Likewise, when that information is again requested, it must be converted back to a useable format. With thousands of simultaneous transactions, this eats up server time and resources.

A more appropriate approach is to store only what is absolutely necessary in session variables and keep the rest stored in a database based on the *session ID* of the current user.

A session ID is a unique identifier for a user's session. It is used to trigger the server to remember information about that user. From the perspective of the programmer, you might need to transfer the session ID from page to page, but that's it. Unfortunately, there's still a problem with this. The user is likely to bookmark a page that includes the session ID variable in the URL. Depending on how the Web application is configured, this could result in a `Session Expired` error or other unpredictable behavior when the user attempts to go back to that Web page.

What would be helpful is a way to handle session management that doesn't require any custom programming to pass variables between pages and is handled transparently to the user *and* programmer. Luckily, there is one—cookies.

Cookies

You've heard of cookies—they're a constant source of irritation among some, and a savior to others—in reality, they're small pieces of text information stored on the client browser.

A cookie provides a means by which a Web site can read and store information on your computer. To some, this is a very scary thought. If a cookie can store information on your computer, what is keeping it from writing a harmful program on your system that destroys your data? The answer is size. Cookies are limited to only a few thousand bytes—barely enough space to store anything useful, let alone a program. Secondly, cookies are all stored within a special Cookie file on your computer. At any time, you can open up the cookies in your browser and alter their contents or delete them.

For example, if you're a Netscape user, search your computer for a magic cookie file. Internet Explorer users should look for the Cookies folder within the Windows directory. A small snippet of my cookie file is shown here:

6

```
# Netscape HTTP Cookie File
# http://www.netscape.com/newsref/std/cookie_spec.html
# This is a generated file!  Do not edit.


free.aol.com     FALSE    /tryaolfree    FALSE    993674880    user    31031923
.excite.com      TRUE   /    FALSE    1057815167    mesp_popup    y2k%fDyes
.excite.com      TRUE   /    FALSE    1057815167    UID    9A7BF6F2Df023B94
.excite.com      TRUE   /    FALSE    1057815167    registered    no
.doubleclick.net    TRUE   /    FALSE    1920499223    id    8bccs8ce
.deja.com        TRUE   /    FALSE    1102550463    GTUID    04.48861.3.0.f.4363
```

Almost any consumer-oriented Web site uses cookies for one reason or another. I have more than 400 cookies currently set in my cookie file, and I spend most of my time browsing technology-oriented sites, not shopping online.

Another fear of cookies is that they can be used to track a user's actions across multiple Web sites. For some sites this is true, but only through a collaborative effort. Cookies are designed so that their information is only available to the site that set the cookie. This prevents information stealing. It is possible, however, for a single site to use cookies to track your actions. In fact, that's exactly what we're after—a way to correlate a specific set of Web accesses to a single user.

Using cookies, a programmer can set a variable that is accessible from any Web page in the site, without needing any special programming. Cookies are set with a specific path for your site. Any Web page that falls under this path has access to the cookie. For example, here is the actual code that is sent to a browser from a Web site that asks for a cookie to be set:

```
Set-Cookie: SESSION=3424; path=/shopping
```

After this cookie is set, anytime the client computer requests a URL from the Web site that falls under the shopping directory, the client computer automatically sends back the following code to the remote computer:

```
Cookie: SESSION=3424
```

By using a path of / when the cookie is set, the Web site creates a condition in which the client browser will send the cookie information back to the Web site for any page that is visited.

Dreamweaver MX automates the process of working with all types of data passing methods. It supports using cookies as a form of global variable and also allows the creation of links between pages that will pass all the variables on one page to the new page. One of the application's most important features—user authentication and security aren't possible without session variables and cookies. You, the application designer, won't need to remember all of this verbatim—much of it will be handled transparently behind the scenes. In some advanced cases, however, you'll be glad that you know what's happening on the server—it can aid in both development and debugging.

Creating Dynamic Sites

Determining when and if a site should be made dynamic is not a decision to be made hastily. I've worked with sites that, when first created, were designed as static sites for one reason or other. Now, performing monthly content updates requires several hours of editing to change the various pages on which the set of updates must occur. The larger such sites become, the harder they are to maintain and the more difficult they are to transition to a database-driven model. Decisions made in the early phases affect management of a site long into the future. Be sure to maintain a site map for every multi-page site that you create, regardless of how trivial it seems at the time. Chances are, you'll be glad you did.

Types of Dynamic Sites

If a site is subject to constant change, it is an excellent candidate for becoming database driven. The advantage of a dynamic design is that it removes the burden of updating the HTML of elements that change frequently. Instead, a centralized database interface can be developed that is as easy to use as any desktop application.

Another good candidate for the database-driven model is any site that collects data. It's surprisingly common for user feedback forms and surveys to be collected and sent in email. Literally thousands of CGI applications are dedicated to formatting the results of forms and sending them in email to a human for interpretation. Interestingly enough, programs are available for the receiving end of Web-generated emails that place the collected data in a database for easy manipulation. Obviously, if you can get the data into the database to begin with, it's going to be much, much easier than moving from survey to email, and then from email to database.

Several large commercial sites that I've been asked to revamp accept product information requests and other data through email sent from a form on the Web site. On the receiving end, the system administrators print the email and distribute it among the customer service personnel so that they can handle the various requests. If the printers jam, the orders are lost! This is not the sort of system you hope to develop as you create your Web sites. Once again, the longer a system like this is allowed to "live," the more difficult it becomes to exterminate.

6

The final type of site ideal for database integration is the site that hosts an enormous amount of information (and needs to provide ways for the users to navigate through it). Enabling the users to search and sort complete books is a much more useful approach than just supplying the information on a Web page. By letting the users query the data in ways that they define, a simple Web database can become a fantastic research tool.

Planning for Dynamic Sites

The first step in creating a dynamic Web site is planning for it. Making a good decision before you begin can save you from headaches later—it isn't an easy task to take a static site and re-integrate its content into a database. In fact, about the worst thing you can do is build and deploy a Web site as static HTML, and then decide that you want to turn it into a dynamic site. As the site grows and matures, the more interwoven the content becomes with the HTML itself. Usually transitioning from a static site to a dynamic site takes a complete rewrite of the site.

To plan for a dynamic site, follow these steps.

Create a Site Map

Create a detailed site map that includes all the areas on the Web site and a basic description of the content that they maintain. This is one of the most important steps in creating any Web site. For dynamic Web sites, the importance is exponentially higher. Identifying all the pages and how they are related aids in determining the relationship between the data that they contain.

Find Duplicate Information

Identify regions that include similar information. These areas of the pages, if significant in size or number, can be drawn from a database. Use common sense when marking out these regions. Just because the word "the" is repeated 19 times on a page doesn't mean that you should store the word in a database and dynamically query the database for it. Addresses, contact information, personnel bios—they're all prime candidates for being stored in a database.

Locate Lists

Locate lists of information that contain more than a few items. Lists of items are already a database of sorts—they're just not stored in a database yet. Typically Web sites contain pages that are a list of links or a list of industry news releases. Someone outside of the Web group often maintains these lists. In most organizations I've dealt with, lists are generated by the PR and HR departments and handed off to the people maintaining the sites. Depending on the number of items in the list, there can be a great amount of redundancy in the work.

Find Frequent Changes

Locate regions of the pages that will need to change on a frequent basis. For example, a book of the week or other temporary item is perfect for being pulled from a database. In the case of a book of the week, after the book is finished being featured, it can easily be switched to an archive section of a Web site, providing information to those who might have missed it the first time around.

The most important thing to remember when designing a database-driven site is to keep it in perspective. No hard and fast rules define when a site should be attached to a database or remain as static HTML. If your site is only two or three pages long, it doesn't make much sense to invest the time in setting up a database or application server in order to deploy it. Keeping lists and information up-to-date manually on sites this size is usually the easiest thing to do.

On the other hand, if you're designing sites commercially, your customers will often request that their sites be built to be as maintenance free as possible. Even with the Web in high gear as it is today, many people still would rather not concern themselves with the "hows" and "whys" of HTML. Setting up a database backend to a client's Web site can provide a simple centralized point to administrate all the information on a site—eliminating the need for them to even know HTML in order to update their site.

Why to Stay Static

Finally, there is a tendency for people to follow trends just because "they're cool." The trend of Web sites is to move to database-driven solutions and abandon simple static HTML altogether. I've been less than pleased when working with sites developed by those in this mindset. They fail to realize that the benefits might not justify the inconveniences. For instance, instead of going into a Web page to change a few lines of copy in the HTML, you might need to connect to a database, find the record with the target content, and change it there. In addition to requiring added steps, database-driven Web sites might also hinder maintenance because of their technology demands. With access to a Mac OS X (UNIX) account and something as simple as Palm Pilot, I could easily connect to a remote server and edit a Web page without any additional equipment. If the data is located in a database, however, that isn't necessarily the case.

Just use your best judgement when making the decision. Never use a technology just because other people say you have to. You might design sites as static HTML that you later wish had been designed as database-driven applications. However, you might also design database-driven sites that would have been simpler to manage if they were static HTML. The trick is making the latter mistake as little as possible.

6

Database Design

Now that you know *why* you want to create a database driven site, it's time to take the first step toward making one—designing the foundation of your site—the database.

For there to be any sort of database-driven site at all, there must be a database backend that drives it. Dreamweaver MX does not supply this backend, nor does it pick one out for you, or help you design one. One of the first things that you'll need to do before you can start designing sites using the dynamic tools of Dreamweaver MX is to set up a database system and learn how to create a functional structure to house your information.

Let me make this absolutely clear: there can be no dynamic Web site without a robust and capable database backend. A poorly designed system can lead to failures in stability, scalability, and security.

Because many readers don't have any experience with database systems, I'm going to give you step-by-step instructions on how to set up the MySQL database tomorrow. This database system is free on Windows, Mac OS X, Linux, and many UNIX-based OSes—allowing it to be deployed as a backend system on just about any platform you can find.

Why Aren't You Using MS Access as Your Database?

There are two reasons for this decision:

MS Access is not a robust enough database system for high volume Web sites (that's why Microsoft makes SQL Server, after all!). Almost all moderate-high volume dynamic sites feature an industrial-strength SQL server as their backend system. MySQL offers many of the features of commercial servers such as Oracle or MS SQL, at an infinitely more attractive price. Although you can certainly use MS Access for your database system, you should ultimately plan on moving to something more scalable as your site grows.

Not everyone has access to, or wants to invest in, Microsoft Access. Remember, Dreamweaver MX can author Web sites on Windows and Mac OS, and deploy on Windows, Mac OS, Linux, UNIX, and so on. For a grand total of $0, you can deploy a Linux Apache server with MySQL and run enterprise-class applications. With IT budgets tightening, this is a solution that should seriously be considered by anyone—no matter what your Dreamweaver MX design platform is.

Before you set up MySQL tomorrow, you need to know something about database design. Creating a database is not as easy as saying, "Here are the fields I need—let's put them in a file and call it a database." Instead, you need to find the most efficient way to store the data. This will enable you to easily work with information after it has been stored.

Let's work through an example of creating a solid database structure from start to finish.

Data-Modeling Terminology

Before you can create a database, you need to understand some of the terminology that is common to database creation. Starting with the "Holy Grail" of database design: normalization.

Normalization

Normalization is the process of simplifying a collection of data to remove redundancy. Flat file database systems lend themselves to storing more data than is actually needed. Normalization breaks up this monolithic data structure into smaller, more efficient collections of information.

There are several levels of normalization that you will look at today. These levels can be thought of as stepping stones that, one-by-one, prepare a collection of data for the final form it will take within the database.

Entities

Entities are individual objects that you want to store data about and are equivalent to tables within a database system. In fact, you'll eventually end up using these entities to name your tables in the final database. A "dog," for example, could be (and will be!) and entity we want to store information about.

Attributes

Entities contain attributes. Switching to traditional database terminology, this just means that tables contain fields. An *attribute* is a field within an entity. They are called attributes because they should describe the entity. For example, a "dog" entity might have an "AKC name" or "fur color" attribute.

Unique Identifiers

A *unique identifier* is an attribute, or group of attributes, that can be used to locate a particular piece of data and *only* that data. There are three rules for choosing a unique attribute:

- It must always contain a value. The identifier must always be defined—it can never be an empty (null) value.
- The identifier must be unique across all instances of data contained in an entity. You cannot create two instances of an entity that have the same identifier. For example, if two dogs have the same birthday, the birthday cannot be used as the unique identifier.
- The identifier can never change. This requirement might seem a bit strange, but you'll soon see why it is necessary. You cannot use a value that will ever change to be the unique identifier for an entity. Once a dog's AKC name is registered, for example, it can't be changed. If it could, it wouldn't uniquely identify the animal.

6

Relationships

A *relationship* is exactly what it sounds like—a way of relating (or connecting) different pieces of information. Three types or degrees of relationships that can exist between entities are as follows:

one to one—For each instance of one entity, there exists one instance of another entity. This is actually a very rare occurrence because a one-to-one relationship is usually just represented within a single entity, rather than splitting into two entities. One dog, for example, usually has one "handler."

one to many—For each instance of one entity, there can be multiple instances of the other entity. The class and room entities are in a one-to-many relationship. For example, there can only be one instance of a particular room, but there can be multiple classes held in that room. This is the relationship most of your data should fall into. For the dog show example we'll be looking at shortly, an example of a one-to-many relationship is "Breed" to "Dog." There can be many dogs in a show for any one given breed.

many to many—A many-to-many relationship is a relationship in which multiple instances of each entity are related to multiple instances of another entity. You cannot model a many-to-many relationship because there is ambiguity in matching the data from one entity to the data in another. If you find that you've accidentally defined a many-to-many relationship, you need to rework your entity model.

A Normalization Example

Assume that you want to create a database for a local dog show so that you can keep track of each breed's "Best of Breed" winner. The dog show's database must contain information about the dogs—what breed they are, the handlers, and the winner. Specifically:

- Breed
- Dogs
- Handlers
- Winner

At first glance, you might want to set up the database as a simple table of information, based on what you want to try to track. Just laying out a few sample records should quickly show you what the problem is with this approach. You can see a sample of this in Table 6.1.

TABLE 6.1   A Simple (But Incorrect) Approach to a Dog Show Database

Breed	Dogs	Handlers	Winner
15" Beagle	Grand Old Fuzzy, Kibbles, Tassle Master	Paul Nestle, Mr.Jim Cornston, Jeff Lazenby	Grand OldFuzzy
Irish Wolfhound	Small Doggy, Shaggy old beast, Don't eat the baby	John Ray, John Smith, Robyn Ness	Don't eat the baby
Pomeranian	Maddy the Magnificent, Coco the Imposter, Jack the sloth	John Ray, Robyn Ness, Sam Smith	Coco the Imposter

As you can see, this table easily stores the available data, but it does it in a way that would make life very difficult for anyone who wants to work with it. For example, how can you match a handler to a particular dog? Or a dog to a certain medal (other than first place)? How would you deal with the handlers named "John Smith"? How can you tell them apart?

In order to do this the right way (so you can answer questions like this), you need to normalize the data. There are three normal forms that you're going to use today—first, second, and third. In reality, there are several more normal forms, but the first three are the most important, and are about all the everyday mortals will ever need. Each level increases the amount of normalization.

First Normal Form

The first step in setting up data in a normalized form is to define the data entities. For example, the initial entity is the `Breed`, and you want to the names of the `Dogs`, `Handlers`, and the `Winner` for each of the `Breed` competitions. Figure 6.1 shows the `Breed` entity defined so far.

FIGURE 6.1

The Breed *entity is flawed.*

Breed
Breed Name
Dogs
Handlers
Winner

6

The first normal form requires that all the entities be singular without any repeating attributes. A simple way to tell if your entity has any repeating attributes is to look for plurals in the attributes. It's obvious that we've got quite a bit to be worried about:

- Dogs

- Handlers

These are repeating attributes and cannot be stored in the Breed entity in order to reach the first normal form. You must break each of these attributes into their own separate entity table. Additionally, you need to make sure that all attributes are broken into their smallest meaningful entities. For example, names should be broken into both first and last name fields. Figure 6.2 shows the new collection of entities with some additional added attributes.

FIGURE 6.2

Break the repeating attributes into their own tables.

Breed	Dog	Handler
Breed Name	Short Name	First Name
Winner	AKC Name	Last Name
Win Date	**Birth Date**	
	Breed Standard	

There are now three tables: Breed, Dog, and Handler. I've taken the liberty of adding some additional attributes to the entities to flesh things out a bit:

- Breed—Breed Name, Winner, Win Date

- Dog—Short Name, AKC Name, Birth Date, Breed Standard

- Handler—First Name and Last Name

Each of the entities is singular and does not contain any repeating attributes. The entities, however, are now self-contained and have no relationship to one another. This makes it difficult to extract any information from the data model other than what is described by one of the entities—in fact, the entire model will be useless. In order to form relationships between the data, you need to define unique identifiers for the data.

Let's take a look at the entities, one at a time, to see what can be used as a unique identifier.

- The Breed entity is in good shape. Each breed has a unique name that refers to *only* that breed.

- The Dog entity is in reasonably good shape, as long as you *don't* accidentally choose the "short name" to be the unique identifier. Dogs are typically identified by a short name that they use daily. The AKC registered name, however, is like a social security number for dogs—it is unique for each animal. Using the AKC name for the unique identifier will make everything A-Okay.

- The Handler entity, however, needs to be addressed. The initial reaction is to use the handler's name as the unique identifier. Be sure to ask yourself, however, is this value *always* unique, and will it ever change? Because the attribute is a name, the answer to these questions is no. It doesn't matter if it's unlikely that these conditions might exist, they must never be violated in your data model for the model itself to be correct. Because of this, a unique identifier must be added to the Handler entity. Thankfully, a handler ID is assigned during shows. This number, which we'll just call the Handler ID, uniquely identifies each handler in the show.

Note | If you can't find a unique identifier for a piece of information, most database systems offer auto increment or auto sequence fields that automatically generate a unique incrementing number for each record that you add. This value can then be used as your unique identifier.

The three entities (Breed, Dog, Handler), shown in Figure 6.3, are now in first normal form.

FIGURE 6.3

Once the entities have no repeating values and a unique identifier, they are in first normal form.

Breed
Breed Name
Winner
Win Date

Dog
Short Name
AKC Name
Birth Date
Breed Standard

Handler
Handler ID
First Name
Last Name

From here, you can start to define relationships between the different entities. This will provide a better visual model of the data and will help locate inconsistencies, if there are any.

For example, consider the entities Dog and Handler. Try looking at the different entities and saying "has a" between them. For Dog and Handler, this becomes "each dog has a handler." This is the first relationship.

In the current model, the following relationships can be defined:

- Breed/Dog (one-to-many)—One breed can have several dogs in it.

- Handler/Dog (one-to-many)—One dog can have one handler, but one handler can work with many dogs.

6

In designing some databases, this is the step where you might run into a few problems. In some cases you might discover that you've created a many-to-many relationship, and need to re-evaluate your entities. For example, assume you were showing your dog in a special dog show that featured a number different competitions, such as agility, speed, intelligence, and so on—rather than just the Breed. Each of these competitions could have many dogs registered in them, and you could register your dog in many competitions—suddenly you'd have a many-to-many relationship.

To "fix" the problem, you must break it down into a dual one-to-many relationship. To do this, you need to define a third entity that will form the middle of the relationship. This entity must have a one-to-many relationship with the two other entities. In the case of the hypothetical dog show I just mentioned, one could add an Entry entity, and define two new relationships:

- Competition/Entry (one-to-many)—Each of the special competitions can have many entries.

- Dog/Entry (one-to-many)—Each dog can be entered into many of the special competitions.

Breaking information down like this can help if you run into trouble. It takes a while to get used to, but can be a life-saver in the long run. Let's move on now, with the original three-entity model.

Second Normal Form

The first normal form is the toughest part of normalization, so if you've made it this far, you're home free. Now it's time to get entities into second normal form. In order to be considered in second normal form, the entities must be defined so that all the attributes of the entity (disregarding the unique identifiers) describe the unique identifier.

For example, if any of the attributes are identical in multiple separate instances (pieces of information) in an entity, those attributes are not entirely dependent on the unique identifier. Another way to determine this is to ask yourself the question, "If the data in this instance were to change, would it have to change in multiple instances of the entity?" Work your way through the different attributes in the entities we have defined, and you should notice a problem—the Dog table, for some reason, contains the field Breed Standard. Breed standards are *very* specific descriptions of dog breeds. For each dog we add to the system that is of the same breed, we'd have to re-enter the same information, over and over. Like-wise, if the breed standard *changed* it would have to be fixed for every dog in that breed.

In this case, you can solve the problem quite easily by realizing that the breed standard is unique to the Breed entity, and not to the Dog entity, and simply moving the attribute from one to the other. The new, happier, data model is shown in Figure 6.4.

FIGURE 6.4.

Moving the Breed Standard *attribute to the* Breed *entity puts the model in second normal form.*

Breed
Breed Name
Winner
Win Date
Breed Standard

Dog
Short Name
AKC Name
Birth Date

Handler
Handler ID
First Name
Last Name

We're now in second normal form; in each entity, all the attributes are dependent on the unique identifier. Each instance of each entity is truly a unique piece of data. There's only one more step to being fully normalized.

Third Normal Form

The third normal form is reasonably easy to understand. In order to be third normal form, the entity must already be in the second normal form and must not contain any attributes (other than the unique identifier) that are dependent on one another. This is generally very easy to spot. Let's take a look at the current entities and their attributes:

- Breed—Breed Name, Breed Standard, Winner, Win Date
- Dog—Short Name, AKC Name, Birth Date
- Handler—Handler ID, First Name, Last Name

In the Breed entity, we have Winner and Win Date attributes. These two attributes are, without a doubt, dependent on one another. This entity needs to be modified in order to reach third normal form. To do this, you'll need to add another entity, Result, which contains this information. Because there can only be one winner for a breed on a given day, the Win Date and Breed can be used together as the unique identifier. Making this tiny adjustment will finish the normalization and allow you to track more that just a single dog show!

> **Note**
>
> It is acceptable to use a combination of attributes to define an entity's unique identifier, as long as all the other rules of normalization are followed.

6

The final data model for the dog show is shown in Figure 6.5.

FIGURE 6.5

The data model is finally in third normal form.

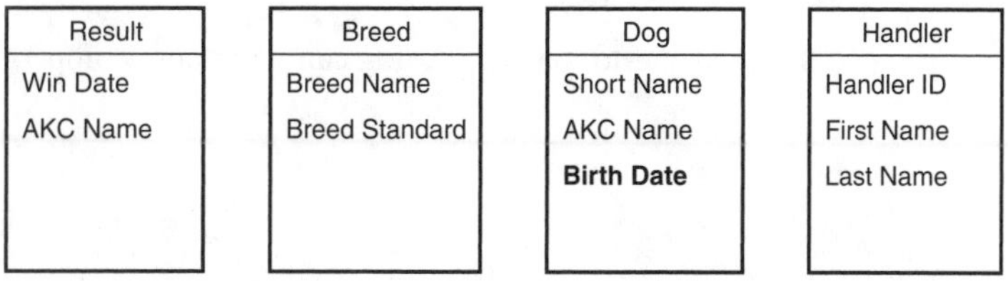

Result
Win Date
AKC Name

Breed
Breed Name
Breed Standard

Dog
Short Name
AKC Name
Birth Date

Handler
Handler ID
First Name
Last Name

You now have the following entities defined in the data model:

- Breed—Breed Name and Breed Standard
- Result—Winner and Win Date
- Dog—Short Name, AKC Name, Birth Date
- Handler—Handler ID, First Name, Last Name

This, coupled with the relationship information between them, is all you need to define a database for use with a Web site.

From Model to Database

Having a database model on paper isn't the same thing as actually having a database properly defined. You need to manipulate the information you have now in order to create the physical database structure. This structure is similar to the entities you've defined, but it needs a way to define the existing relationships between the different entities. Obviously, creating several tables with the attributes we've chosen will not magically link the tables together. Instead, you need to encode information about the relationships into the data held in the table. In order to do this, you need to understand the concept of *keys*.

Defining Database Keys

Two types of keys exist that you need in order to complete your database model. The first key is a *primary key*—this is nothing more than the unique identifier created for each of the entities in the model. The primary key enables the database system to determine what constitutes a unique record.

The primary key is simple. You already set it up when you defined your unique identifier for each entity. The second key that you need is the *foreign key*. This is the key that will "make magic" and define the relationships between the entities. The foreign key is nothing more than another entity's primary key that is stored in order to officially define a relationship between two entities.

All relationships must have a foreign key defined on the "many" side of the relationship. The following relationships have been defined for the data model so far:

- Breed/Dog (one-to-many)—One breed can have several dogs in it.
- Handler/Dog (one-to-many)—One dog can have one handler, but one handler can work with many dogs.
- Dog/Result (one-to-many)—A dog can win many competitions over time.

In each of these cases, the many instances must inherit the primary key of the one instance. This primary key is considered the foreign key when it is stored in the table that it didn't originate from. For example, in the Dog entity, we need to add the Breed Name from the Breed entity. This will complete the one-to-many entity. This same process needs to be repeated for all the entities in the data model.

If you want to, try this yourself. Do so now. You might find that subconsciously, we've defined some of the matches without even knowing it, and, in turn, created additional relationships. For example, the Result entity contains a winner. It has been my intention all along to store the dog's AKC Name in this field. This will allow you to create the relationship:

- Dog/Result (one-to-many)—One dog can have multiple wins over time.

Because of this "subconscious" normalization, I will have two foreign keys in the Result table—Breed Name and AKC Name.

The final representation is shown in Figure 6.6. When this process is finished, you have all the information necessary to create a proper SQL database.

FIGURE 6.6

The model is finally complete.

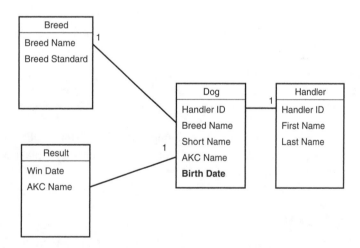

The Final SQL

Later in the book (on Day 12, "Writing Advanced Database Queries"), you'll learn about the SQL programming language. For now, let's take a look at how the model that we just set up translates into SQL. The entities in the data model translate directly into tables in the database. Additionally, the attributes make up the field names of the tables. You should easily be able to see how the SQL relates to the model in Listing 6.1.

LISTING 6.1   The SQL Database Structure for the Dog Show Database

```
1 create table tblBreed {
2       BreedName varchar(250) not null,
3       BreedStandards text,
4       primary key (BreedName)
5 }
6
7 create table tblResult {
8       AKCName varchar(250) not null,
9       WinDate date not null,
10       primary key (BreedName,WinDate)
11 }
12
13 create table tblDog {
14       ShortName varchar(100),
15       AKCName varchar(250) not null,
16       Birthday int,
17       HandlerID int,
18       BreedName varchar(250),
19       primary key (AKCName)
20 }
21
22 create table tblHandler (
23       HandlerID int not null,
24       FirstName varchar(150),
25       LastName varchar(100),
26       primary key (HandlerID)
27 )
```

It's interesting to compare the resulting database structure to the original database model that was proposed. You've moved from a single table that contained a bunch of data to a well-structured system of four tables.

Summary

The process of setting up a database-driven site requires more than just opening up Dreamweaver MX and coding. A considerable amount of time must be applied to the planning process. It's easier to sit down with a piece of paper and design the database correctly than to immediately start coding and end up needing to reinvent the database later.

Several types of Web pages lend themselves to being database driven:

- Lists—Lists of information can easily be pulled from a database and displayed in a table.

- Repeating information—Information that is used in several places on a site can be stored in a database allowing easy access for easy changes.

- Information that needs updating—If a piece of information needs updating on a frequent basis a database can provide a user-friendly interface to the site updates.

Creating a site map and then locating these types of sections on a Web site are the first steps in successfully planning a site.

If you already have the information needed for creating your site, you can prepare by building a model for your data. The process by which redundant data is eliminated from the model is called *normalization*.

Three levels of normalization exist that you should go through in order to prepare your data model for translation into an actual database.

- The first normal form defines the entities used in the data model and their attributes. It also makes sure that these attributes are singular and any repeating attributes are moved to their own table. After the initial entities are defined, the relationships between them can be defined. Relationships are defined by their degree: one-to-one, one-to-many, and many-to-many.

- The second normal form assumes that the data is in first normal form and extends the definition by saying that all the attributes must be dependent on the unique identifier for each instance.

- Finally, the third normal form takes entities that are in the second normal form and modifies them one step further. If attributes in an entity are dependent on one another rather than the unique identifier, they must be broken into their own table in order for the third normal form to be reached.

As a final step in database design, you will need to set up the database structure itself. The database structure is based on the data model that has been developed, but must include extra information in order to encode the relationships between entities.

Workshop

6

The Workshop area is meant to reinforce your reading with a series of questions and exercises.

Q&A

Q What's the best reason to create a database-driven site?

A The *only* real reason to create a database-driven site is because it is the most efficient way to build a site. All too often, sites are built just to use a particular technology, not because of any actual necessity. Only use a backend database if it benefits the function of the site and its upkeep—not because it's "the thing to do."

Q **How can a database provide an easier interface to a Web page than just plain HTML?**

A From what you've seen so far, you might be wondering why in the world a database-driven site would be considered easier to maintain than a site built using plain HTML. Using a tool such as MS Access, or a programming language such as RealBASIC, you can easily create a front end to the data that is as simple to use as any other desktop application.

Q **Can I create a database without normalizing data?**

A Yes, but it isn't usually recommended. Normalizing the data results in an efficient data model that offers consistent relations and eliminates redundancy. In some cases, a little bit of redundancy isn't much of a problem and you can skip the normalization. If you're working on a professional site, however, I suggest that you spend the time to develop a proper normalized model.

Q **What problems will I find if I don't normalize the data?**

A If you don't normalize your data, you'll find that you're going to have to spend *a lot* of time keeping your database up to date. A database that isn't normalized has redundancy and cannot be accurately queried. In order to update a database with redundant data, you have to update multiple pieces of data. In a five- or six-record database, this isn't going to be a problem. In a system of millions of records, the time expended searching for records that need to be updated can be very significant.

Quiz

1. What portions of a Web site are best translated into a dynamic site?

2. What does normalizing a database do?

3. What is the first normal form?

4. What is the second normal form?

5. What is the third normal form?

Quiz Answers

1. Repeating information, lists, and commonly updated information are best translated into a dynamic site. These three components make up most of the dynamic data found on sites. You can certainly explore other areas of dynamic data, but these are the most prominent.

2. Normalizing a database removes redundancy from the existing data model. Redundancy can lead to problems when inserting, deleting, or updating records because multiple records might be affected by the change.

3. The first normal form of a data model is met when all the defined entities are devoid of repeating attributes. All repeating attributes must be broken out of the entity and placed in a new entity.

4. An item is considered to be in the second normal form when all the attributes are dependent on the entity's unique identifier. If attributes between different instances of an entity are dependent on one another, these attributes must be broken out into a new entity.

5. The third normal form exists when an entity is in the second normal form and does not possess any attributes that are dependent on one another. If any of an entity's attributes is dependent on another attribute, those items must be placed in a newly defined entity.

Exercises

1. Visit sites that you've created, or draw a site map of a site that you want to create. Look for areas that would be more efficient if they were database driven. Don't just look for the obvious spots such as a personnel database or a video library. Instead, try to find information that lends itself to being manipulated in a database.

2. Create a data model in third normal form from the pet store data that is shown in Table 6.2. The hypothetical store wants to be able to create targeted mailings for customers who have purchased similar pet supplies in the past.

TABLE 6.2   Create a Normalized Database for This Pet Store

Product Name	Price	Previous Customers	Category
Meaty Dog Chews	$10.95	Sally Rider, Paul Neblitz, Jessica Teem…	Dog Food, Dog Toys
Super Dog Chow	$15.55	Jessica Teem, Terry Poltzer, Quinn Daug…	Dog Food
Rubber Ball	$2.50	Tim Letry, Paul Nastercin, Julie Vujevich…	Dog Toys, Cat Toys

6

DAY **7**

Preparing a Server for Dreamweaver MX

If you don't have a Web server yet, or even a deployment platform, what do you do? Dreamweaver MX supports several scripting languages and servers. Unless you have a good idea of what these languages do, where they can be used, and how to use them, you're going to be stuck before you even start. To help address these concerns, today you will learn:

- Which programming models are supported in Dreamweaver, and the implications of choosing one over another.
- The servers that support the scripting platform of your choice.
- How to set up a deployment platform on your Macintosh or Windows system. This will be the basis for everything else you do in the book.

The Dreamweaver MX Application Server

Before you can set up a dynamic site, you'll need to decide which language will be used to generate the embedded source code. This will also control what server OS you can use to deploy your applications. It's a decision that you don't want to make lightly.

What Is an Application Server?

The scripting platforms are typically called "application servers." Throughout the text, you may see references to the scripting languages, server platforms, and application servers. For our purposes, you can assume they all refer to the same thing.

They are not, however, to be confused with a Web server. The application server processes and controls the dynamic Web site, whereas the Web server sends the information back to the client browser. Application servers often support multiple Web servers running on multiple operating systems.

As you can see from Figure 7.1, there are several supported server platforms and technologies:

- ASP (Classic /.NET)—All of Microsoft's Active Server Page technologies are fully supported, including .NET's C# development language.
- JSP (Java Server Pages)—Java Server Pages are programmed using the popular object-oriented Java programming language (*not* JavaScript).
- CFML (ColdFusion Markup Language)—The ColdFusion Markup Language is not exactly a traditional programming language, but it does make Web-based application creation extremely simple.
- PHP (PHP Hypertext Preprocessor)—PHP is a relatively new language that offers remarkable features for zero cost.

Which choice is right for your application; which is the best long-term investment? If you have no preference, which should you choose?

Note

For the projects in this book, I chose the ASP application server. IIS/ASP is widely available and can easily be installed on any Windows 2000/XP computer in a matter of minutes.

Understanding that there are a large number of Mac users out there, we'll also take a look at installing the PHP application server on Mac OS X. PHP is easy to understand and available for whatever operating system you are using. Unfortunately, the PHP implementation in Dreamweaver MX is not yet complete, so there will be a few rough spots when using it.

If you don't plan to deploy on ASP or PHP, don't worry. The point of Dreamweaver MX is to make developing dynamic Web sites a point-and-click operation. Once the server is set up, you rarely (if ever) need to touch the code.

FIGURE 7.1

Choose the language that will be used to generate your pages.

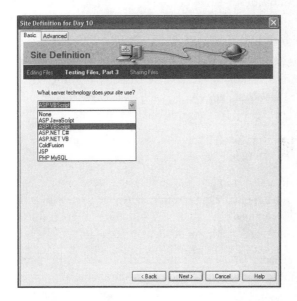

Active Server Pages

The Active Server Pages platform was developed by Microsoft, and was one of the first technologies to implement an embedded programming model. Rather than writing a traditional application in which the HTML is generated by the program, embedded languages let you embed the program directly within HTML.

The ASP model is a bit confusing in that it doesn't represent a programming language, rather a group of technologies that can be used from within a wide variety of languages. Still confused? Look at it this way.

Embedded programming languages include the capability of moving information in and out of databases, managing sessions, storing cookies, and so on. The Active Server Page model defines routines to work with all these features, and then makes them available to any programming languages written to take advantage of the ASP model. Although not supported in Dreamweaver MX, you can download Perl and install it as an ASP language.

7

The biggest drawback to the ASP platform is that it is proprietary technology and is available on only two platforms.

Anyone running MS Windows can download the Personal Web Server (PWS) and install the Active Server Pages components. This is not an ideal platform because it is relatively slow and limited in the number of simultaneous users that can access the server. Windows NT 4, Windows 2000, and Windows XP make far better deployment platforms.

Such is the trouble of ASP. In order to deploy on an ASP server, you are usually limited to Microsoft platforms. If you're a Mac user or a fan of the Open Source movement, this might not be your first choice for deployment platforms.

Luckily, there is a solution for those who *have* to use Active Server Pages, but don't or can't deploy on a Windows NT/2000/XP based platform. Using a product called iASP ("Instant" ASP), you can add the Active Server Pages model to several UNIX-based systems. Visit `http://www.instantasp.com/` for more details.

This is certainly a reasonable solution, but it isn't for everyone. If you're just starting out, it's probably best to pick a server and scripting platform based on their merits.

That said, Active Server Pages is a very flexible development platform that offers a wide range of features. Typically the scripting language used with ASP is VBScript, although JavaScript is sometimes used. ASP.NET introduces support for dozens of languages, including C#, VB, and JScript in the default package.

Many experienced developers consider working with ASP a painful experience. The ASP platform is full featured, but suffers from feature bloat and sometimes convoluted code. This has improved with ASP.NET, but, at the time of this writing, ASP.NET had not reached an official 1.0 release.

Java Server Pages

JSP, or Java Server Pages, is a relatively new embedded programming technology that is based on the Java Servlet Engine, which, in turn, is based on the Java programming language.

Java servlets were initially created to address the need for a Java-based method of writing the equivalent of CGIs within the Java programming language. A *servlet* is a piece of Java code that is compiled and used to generate an HTML page, process Web page input, and so on. Servlets are written entirely in the standard Java programming language, but take advantage of classes specifically designed for writing dynamic Web page applications.

Although it is possible to embed HTML into a servlet, you can't do the reverse—you can't embed a servlet into an HTML page. In order to overcome this limitation, servlets evolved into Java Server Pages. JSP is nothing more than a means of embedding the Java programming language into HTML pages. What makes this even more interesting is that the JSP system actually compiles each JSP document into a servlet before it is executed. Don't worry; you don't need to know this in order to use JSP; it all happens behind the scenes on your server.

Note

> Before you start saying, "The JSP to Servlet process must really slow things down," let's take a closer look at the translation process. When the JSP is translated into a servlet, that servlet is cached on the server. Only when the JSP is changed is the corresponding servlet regenerated. Although a slight delay might exist the first time a page is accessed, there is really no need for speed worries.

One of the best features of JSP is that it *is* Java. Anything that you can do in Java (except GUI applications, of course) can be done in JSP. Therefore, if you're a Java programmer, you can immediately jump into JSP page creation. Java is a fully modern language whose growth continues to outpace other languages for the past several years and shows no signs of slowing down.

Another benefit of Java is that it is a fully cross-platform language that knows no barriers. Any Web server that supports Java Server Pages can run a JSP page without changing the code. This includes everything involved in the page programming, including database access. JDBC drivers allow you to access databases using a single driver file. Copy the JDBC driver to another JSP server on a completely different platform; it will work exactly the same.

Deploying JSP applications is a bit more flexible than deploying Active Server Pages or ColdFusion applications. In fact, it's actually possible to deploy for *free* using Java Server Pages. The Apache Software Consortium has implemented and released an Open Source Java-based JSP server that is downloaded for free.

This server, known as Tomcat, is a product of the Apache Jakarta project, and is a full implementation of Java Server Pages 1.1 specification. Experiencing an almost exponential growth in popularity, Tomcat is rapidly becoming one of the most widely used JSP servers available.

You can get started immediately with JSP by downloading Tomcat from the Jakarta project Web site at `http://jakarta.apache.org/`.

7

Because Tomcat is under heavy development, it does come with a few drawbacks—the most notable being less-than-perfect documentation and a not-so-friendly installation process. If you can get over these deficiencies, you'll find that Tomcat is an almost universal deployment platform that can be used on almost any platform that includes a Java implementation—from Windows XP to Mac OS X.

If you'd prefer to stick with commercial software, you have a few choices to satisfy your serving needs. Several JSP servers are available for Windows and UNIX platforms. This is a partial listing:

- Macromedia JRun— `http://www.macromedia.com/software/jrun/`
- Oracle 9i Application Server—`http://www.oracle.com/`
- IBM WebSphere Application Server—`http://www.software.ibm.com/`
- iPlanet Web Server—`http://www.iplanet.com/`

The playing field for JSP servers is constantly changing. You can find the latest server information at Sun's Web page `http://java.sun.com/products/jsp/industry.html`.

Although JSP is a rapidly growing and standards-based server platform, it also carries with it the baggage of Java. Java is a modern object-oriented programming language that is, for beginners, extremely complex. Unless you're a Java developer or want to become one, this isn't the greatest place to start for your first Web application server.

ColdFusion

The easiest language to work with is the ColdFusion Markup Language. Bearing little resemblance to a programming language at all, CFML is more like an extended version of HTML that includes database access.

By creating a coding environment that is powerful enough for professional developers, but so user-friendly that casual HTML coders can easily pick it up, Macromedia made Web application development available to a very wide audience.

Rather than requiring custom programming code to be embedded within special delimiter tags in HTML (as is the case with ASP, JSP, and PHP), ColdFusion simply adds a new range of tags to the existing HTML tags. This extended authoring environment was almost stunning the first time I saw it. ColdFusion breaks out of the traditional programming mold and boldly treads into territory that makes database access almost as simple as writing HTML.

Note

> If you've never looked at ColdFusion before, I urge you to do so. I've always programmed in more traditional languages such as Java, Perl, and C, but after spending time working with ColdFusion, I was quite impressed. The designers of the CFML took into account almost every feature a Web application author could want, and then threw in a few dozen more.
>
> Despite its simplistic approach to embedded programming, it can be used to create truly powerful applications that perform very quickly and are a cinch to debug.

As with other platforms, there are drawbacks to using ColdFusion. The first problem is one of mindset. If you've spent time programming before, you have a general idea of what you're looking for when exploring a new language. You look for `for...next` loops and `if...then` style conditionals. What you *don't* expect is to find a series of tags to represent all these more traditional style constructs. Who would think that the complexities of loop syntax would be replaced by something as simple as a `<loop>` tag? Because of a needed shift in thinking, experienced programmers might find themselves running into more difficulty than those who have never programmed before.

Additionally, ColdFusion suffers from the similar platform limitations as Active Server Pages. Although it is available on a number of UNIX platforms, including Linux, the inability to *truly* run anywhere, coupled with a pricey deployment license, are two of the shortcomings of this otherwise tremendous package.

PHP Hypertext Preprocessor

The final supported application server is PHP, which strangely enough, is short for PHP Hypertext Preprocessor (the name is recursive). PHP is a free add-on that is available for Macintosh, Windows, and UNIX platforms. It can author anything from hobby Web sites to enterprise-level applications.

PHP is unique in that it is a very easy language to use if you're accustomed to Perl, JavaScript, or C-style constructs, and it provides an absolutely huge feature set without costing a dime. For example, PHP has ties into a huge number of free add-on products, such as graphing packages, PDF generators, and databases. Although these same tasks can be accomplished with ASP, Java, and the like, the learning curve is much larger.

As evidence of its growing popularity, you might want to check out the Apache module survey. Apache is the world's most popular Web server by roughly three times the volume of Microsoft's offerings (`http://www.netcraft.net/survey/`). Of those sites, 45% are running PHP. This means that there are actually *more* installed PHP-ready Apache

7

servers than there are Microsoft servers total. Check out the previously mentioned NetCraft site and Security Space (`http://www.securityspace.com/`) for more information.

> **Tip**
>
> In case you can't tell, I like PHP. It's a wonderful thing to be able to write a Web application with database access that performs *identically* on Windows, Mac, and UNIX systems with no changes.
>
> What many people don't realize is that PHP will happily co-exist on Web servers that support other languages. I run PHP, ColdFusion, and ASP applications from a single machine. Because PHP is free, your system administrator can almost certainly add PHP support to your Web server if it isn't there already.

PHP is a less developed platform than JSP, CFML, and ASP, and it is lacking in some of the object-oriented features supported on other systems. Although these issues can easily be worked around, the platform is not yet fully supported in Dreamweaver MX. This is obviously going to improve with subsequent releases, but for now, PHP is best left for those who don't mind editing code from time to time.

For more information, check out `http://www.php.net/`.

Choosing a Server

If you've decided on an application server technology to use, the next obvious choice is what type of server *operating system* will you use? There are two primary options to explore: UNIX and Windows NT/2000/XP.

> **Note**
>
> If you're a Mac user, be aware that "UNIX" now includes Mac OS X. You can easily deploy a stable and full-featured server on Apple's latest operating system.

This is the type of question that is batted around for days without a reasonable answer. I've read a number of magazine articles that discuss the plusses and minuses of UNIX versus Windows and, although claiming "The definitive results" on the front cover, they never bother to claim a preference for either one, nor declare one or another truly better at something than the other. So, if no one is willing to choose a winner, how are you expected to be able to pick the server operating system that you want to use to deploy your Web site?

Choosing a server is largely becoming as "religious" an issue as choosing between Windows and Macintosh operating systems. The recent increase in Linux's popularity has sparked the rebirth of UNIX and UNIX-like operating systems that were, for a time, considered "down for the count" in the wake of Microsoft Windows.

User Friendliness

The primary advantage of using Windows NT/2000/XP can be summed up quite succinctly—user friendliness. Anyone, regardless of previous computer experience, can have a server up and running on a network in a matter of minutes. Microsoft makes it very simple to set up the basic services required to become your own Internet server. The integration between different system components makes it easy to get different pieces of software working together and to develop complex network architectures from within an easy-to-use interface.

UNIX operating systems aren't standing idly by while this happens. In the past three years, Linux and FreeBSD have gone from operating systems with a lack of a consistent user interface, to featuring some of the most advanced interface tools available. Thanks to the work of users on the GNOME (http://www.gnome.org/) and KDE (http://www.kde.org/) projects, UNIX users now enjoy the same point-and-click setup as their Windows counterparts. Unfortunately, the quality of the service-configuration tools has yet to reach commercial quality.

> **Note**
>
> Although Linux is sometimes referred to as a different beast than UNIX, they are really very much the same thing. Linux is an Open Source implementation of a UNIX-like operating system. This is merely a matter of semantics, and you can feel free to read UNIX or Linux wherever I use either word.

What might take some readers by surprise is that there is one UNIX platform that is arguably easier to use than Windows, and just as capable a server—Mac OS X. Mac OS X is easy to install, simple to configure, and offers all the advantages of its UNIX heritage.

Type of Services Offered

The type of services that each operating system offers is another point to consider when making your OS choice. Windows, out of the box, offers basic Internet serving capabilities, file sharing, print sharing, Active Directory features, and so on.

Likewise, UNIX operating systems offer the Open Source equivalent of all these services, and many more. The MySQL database server, for example, is an extremely

7

powerful relational database server that, while running industry standard benchmark tests, competes head to head with commercial offerings from Oracle and Microsoft.

As mentioned earlier, the Apache Web server that comes with Mac OS X and Linux has consistently experienced more growth and development than the Windows-only IIS Server. You can check out the latest statistics in server popularity at `http://www.net-craft.com/survey/`.

In the area of number of available services and cross-platform compatibility, Windows and UNIX are roughly equivalent. The UNIX software is often more difficult to configure than its Windows counterparts, but is usually available at a drastically lower price point.

Reliability

The reliability of Windows has significantly increased in the past few years, culminating in a remarkably stable Windows XP. Overall, however, the advantage is the UNIX court. Commercial UNIX operating systems such as Solaris and AIX provide the most stability for mission critical applications. It is very difficult to document the stability of one platform in relation to another, and, unfortunately, most of the evidence is anecdotal. For example, here are the uptime statistics from a highly trafficked e-commerce site run on AIX (a UNIX distribution):

```
www3:/> uptime  10:38AM   up 285 days,  17:59,  1 user,
➡   load average: 0.26, 0.48, 0.45
```

This is a full production site under a reasonably heavy load. The development server for this site happens to be an NT 4.0 computer that has very light use. The NT 4.0 server must be rebooted at least once or twice a week in order to keep it online.

I highly recommend that you ask around and find out the statistics relevant to the hardware and application server platform that you are using. Finding the right combination of hardware and software to keep your servers online will save you from having to deal with phone calls at 3 a.m. because your Web site has crashed.

Performance/Cost Ratio

For many years, Windows has led the performance/cost ratio by running on relatively low-cost, Intel-based hardware. Traditionally, if you were going to run UNIX, you'd run it on hardware dedicated to that particular platform. Linux has changed that entirely.

Running on the same hardware as Windows (and *many* platforms Windows doesn't run on), Linux requires far fewer resources than NT and operates smoothly on low-end Pentium systems. The price of ownership ($0) for the Linux operating system also tips the scales in favor of the Open Source operating system.

Commercial UNIX systems, such as Mac OS X, have started to take after Linux and be priced affordably for even small organizations. In addition, rather than include proprietary software for their various services, commercial UNIX boxes have embraced the Open Source movement, making the initial hardware/operating system investment the largest (and often the only) cost in creating an Internet server presence.

Support

This is the big sticking point for many people thinking about using Open Source solutions —"How can I use a product that has no real support?" This is a valid question often asked within the enterprise environment.

Windows, without question, has the power of an incredibly large corporation backing it. As bugs are found, they are rapidly documented and addressed. Rarely do you find yourself wandering the Internet searching for someone who knows what you're talking about. Unfortunately, Windows systems have recently been the target of a *huge* number of attacks, such as Code Red. Unless your server is kept up to date with the latest patches, you're likely to find yourself wiping and reinstalling the system software.

Because of these problems, many industry analysts have urged Web masters to consider Apache-based servers, such as Apache on Linux. Unfortunately Open Source systems know no "real" ownership and cannot be "fixed" by the vendor who sold you your copy. Most times, you'll find that a simple post on a newsgroup will generate hundreds of helpful responses, but there are some instances when the lack of someone to turn to can become frustrating.

If you're interested in a low-cost UNIX solution without the hassle of Linux and including support of a large company, Mac OS X is a great choice. Apple's new dual-processor architecture and UNIX-based operating system are capable of handling large loads, and are as easy to maintain as, well, a Macintosh.

The Final Decision

So, by weighing the advantages and disadvantages of the platforms, can you decide which one is right for you?

First, the Windows choice. Choosing Windows as a server platform is a *safe* bet. You get a reasonably stable system that is easy to configure and maintain. You should be prepared to make a large initial investment to purchase the software components you will need to develop your Web site, unless you use components like MySQL and PHP (which we'll install in a few minutes). This is the best choice for someone who already has a great deal invested in the Windows platform and wants the server to integrate seamlessly into the existing network.

7

Second is UNIX, or Mac OS X. The UNIX decision gives you a very fast and flexible platform that can get you online and serving for no more money than the cost of your hardware and Internet connection (Linux). This is a great setup for the budget-limited or technically savvy. Support is a mixed bag, but you won't usually run into trouble if you stick with mainstream hardware. Mac OS X is a great UNIX choice for those who want the flexibility of an Open Source operating system with real support backing it up.

So, What System Do I Use?

Surprisingly enough, over the past year, I've migrated all of my Windows and Linux Web servers to Mac OS X, save one—a Windows ColdFusion server. The easy maintenance, flexibility of UNIX, and overall stability are hard to beat. That's just my preference; your mileage may vary.

Creating an ASP Application Server on Windows XP

If you're using Microsoft Windows XP or 2000, you're about 5–10 minutes away from having a real Web application server. You'll need to download a few files and install the Windows IIS service, but nothing to get bent out of shape over. If you happen to be using Windows 98 or Me, you can follow basically the same instructions, but you'll need to use the Microsoft Personal Web Server rather than the IIS.

These are the components you'll be adding to your system:

IIS—The Microsoft Internet Information Server is the Web server powering your site.

MySQL (optional)—The SQL database backend for your server. This free database engine can power anything from simple hobby sites to enterprise wide applications.

MS Access data files (optional)—If you don't want to use the MySQL platform, we're including MS Access files for all the examples in the book.

Data sources—To prepare for the rest of the examples in the book, you'll set up ODBC data sources for all the databases you'll be using. This will take a while, but keep things rolling in subsequent chapters.

Let's go ahead and get started.

Adding the Internet Information Service

Microsoft Internet Information Service is the default Web server for the Windows platform. It's easy to set up, well supported, and, better yet, included on your Windows XP CD-ROM.

Making sure that your Windows XP install CD is in your CD-ROM drive:

1. Click Start, and choose Control Panel from the pop-up menu.

2. Once the Control Panel icons have appeared, double-click the Add or Remove Programs icon.

3. Finally, click the Add/Remove Windows Components option on the left side of the screen. Within a few moments, the Windows Components Wizard will appear, as seen in Figure 7.2.

FIGURE 7.2

Use the Windows Components Wizard to add the IIS service.

4. Be sure that the check box in front of Internet Information Services (IIS) is checked, and then click the Next button.

5. Follow along with the default prompts and Windows will install the Web server component, IIS.

   IIS adds a folder hierarchy to your system under the directory C:\Inetpub. Within this directory is wwwroot, which will hold all the Web sites you'll be building in this book. You should also notice a new icon within the Administrative Tools portion of the control panels. This icon, labeled Internet Information Services Shortcut, can be used to gain access to all the administrative controls within IIS.

6. As a final step, you'll need to set the IIS server's permissions so that you can execute ASP code you create within the wwwroot directory. To do this, double-click the Internet Information Services shortcut. The IIS manager will start, showing the available services on the left side of the window. Expand the service hierarchy by clicking "+" in front of the name of your computer, followed by the Web Sites folder. Your display should now resemble Figure 7.3.

7

FIGURE 7.3

Expand the service hierarchy until you can see Default Web Site.

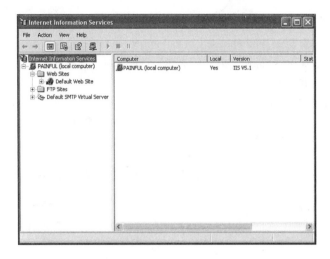

7. Next, right-click on the Default Web Site option, and choose Properties from the contextual menu that appears. Within the Properties dialog box, click the Home Directory Tab, and then change the Execute Permissions setting (located near the bottom of the dialog box) to read Scripts only, as shown in Figure 7.4.

Turn on Script Execution

FIGURE 7.4

Turn on script access for the default Web site.

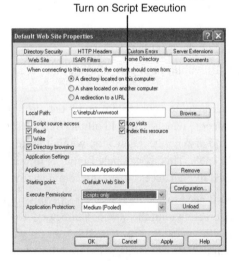

Note

This book doesn't cover the configuration of IIS beyond this basic setup. You should refer to your operating system documentation for more information.

8. Finally, click OK to save the settings, and then close the Internet Information Services window. Your Web server is now ready to go. It's time to install a database system (MySQL or MS Access, your choice).

Installing MySQL (Option A)

The next step is installing the MySQL database system for Windows. Although I highly recommend using MySQL for your database platform and it does form the basis of the examples in the book, you don't *have* to use it. MS Access files for all the databases are available on `http://downloads.cutelittledogs.com/`. Beginners might want to skip this step and move on to the section "Setting Up MS Access Databases."

A few years ago, setting up MySQL was a somewhat scary experience. Today, it is as simple as double-clicking an icon, but still requires some configuration. Download the Windows MySQL installer from `http://www.mysql.com/` or find a link to the installer on `http://downloads.cutelittledogs.com/`.

After downloading the latest MySQL distribution, double-click the "setup" program to start the installer. You will find yourself within another Windows wizard that will guide you through the setup, as shown in Figure 7.5.

FIGURE 7.5

Use the MySQL installer to add the database backend to your system.

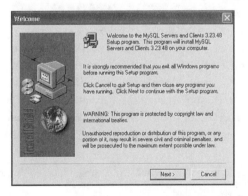

There won't be any complicated configuration during the install. Choose the default installation path and the Typical installation type, and then just keep clicking Next until the installer finishes. This will create a directory `C:\mysql` on your system that contains all the files necessary to run and configure the database server.

Setting Up the Default MySQL Databases

Once MySQL is installed on your computer, you will need a way to start and stop the server process, as well as seed the system with the default information required to run. Happily, there is a point-and-click solution for most of this.

7

Using the Windows explorer, navigate to the C:\mysql\bin directory. You should see an icon labeled winmysqladmin, as demonstrated in Figure 7.6.

FIGURE 7.6

The winmysqladmin *software will install a Windows XP service for MySQL and allow you to view active databases.*

Double-click the winmysqladmin application. It will automate the process of getting MySQL up and running on Windows. The first time it is run, you will be prompted for a username and password to be used with the system. Enter dreamweaver as the user and 21days as the password. Be sure to enter these *exactly* as shown here—you'll be using them to connect to the server for the remainder of the book. Figure 7.7 displays the username and password selection screen, shown the first time you run winmysqladmin.

FIGURE 7.7

Enter dreamweaver *as a username and* 21days *as the password.*

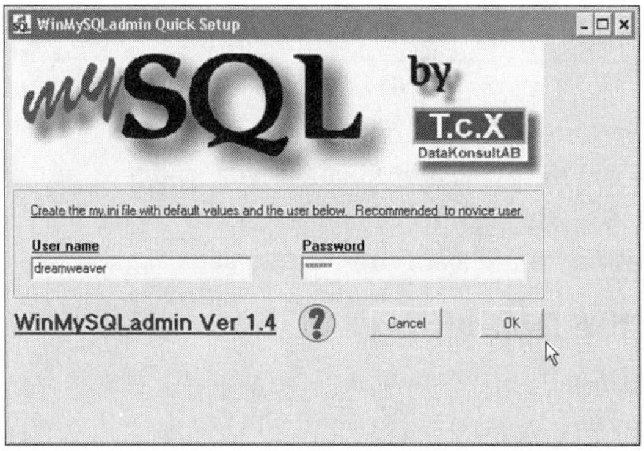

After typing in the password used to access the database server, the admin application will disappear—this is entirely normal. It has been minimized into the Windows tray, and is displayed as a small "stoplight" icon.

FIGURE 7.8

Use the tray icon to control the MySQL service.

Clicking the icon in the Windows tray will let you install/remove MySQL as a Windows service, shut down the admin tool, or start/stop the service as a standalone process, as shown in Figure 7.8. By default, MySQL will be installed as a service, so it should always start when your computer boots. One final option in the pop-up menu is Show Me, which will open a window that displays statistics for your database server and the databases it is using. You can learn more about the MySQL manager tools on http://www.mysql.com/; you won't really be needing them from now on.

To verify that your MySQL server is running, use the command mysqladmin version, which displays information about the version of the server that is running. Start the Command line by clicking Start, choosing Run, typing **cmd.exe**, and then pressing Enter. Type c:\mysql\bin\mysqladmin version at the command line now. You should see something similar to this:

```
C:\c:\mysql\bin\mysqladmin version
./bin/mysqladmin  Ver 8.23 Distrib 3.23.49, for Win95/Win98 on i32
Copyright (C) 2000 MySQL AB & MySQL Finland AB & TCX DataKonsult AB
This software comes with ABSOLUTELY NO WARRANTY. This is free software,
and you are welcome to modify and redistribute it under the GPL license

Server version          3.23.49-nt
Protocol version        10
Connection              . via named pipe
UNIX socket             MySQL
Uptime:                 2 days 9 hours 10 min 13 sec

Threads: 1  Questions: 5  Slow queries: 0  Opens: 5
Flush tables: 1  Open tables: 0 Queries per second avg: 0.000
```

To access the MySQL server, you'll typically use a simple command-line tool called, appropriately enough, mysql. You can invoke MySQL from the command line by typing C:\mysql\bin\mysql. This lets you interact with SQL directly. We'll take a look at this later in the book, but you'll need to use it once right now to load all the sample data required for the projects in the book.

7

Follow these instructions to add all the project data to your system:

1. Download the Day 7 archive from `http://download.cutelittledogs.com/` and unarchive it. Place the files on your drive. For this example, I'll assume it is located in `C:\day7` (change it as necessary on your computer).

2. Click the Start button and choose Run. Type **cmd** in the Run field and press Enter.

3. At the command prompt, type **cd c:\mysql\bin** and press enter.

4. At the next prompt, enter **mysql < C:\day7\dreamweaverSQL.txt**, as shown in Figure 7.9.

5. Close the command window.

FIGURE 7.9

Use the command line to configure load the Dreamweaver project information into MySQL.

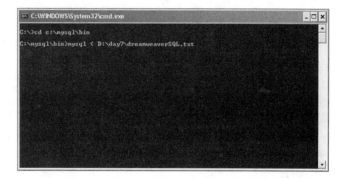

Don't worry, you won't be seeing the command line much after this point. Many popular SQL servers are much more difficult to operate, so don't think you're getting short end of the stick.

If you see *any* error messages during the setup of MySQL, you should retrace your steps and be sure you entered the information exactly as shown in the text. You can always add the records needed for the projects later, but that requires some typing that you probably don't want to do!

Setting Up MS Access Databases (Option B)

If you've chosen *not* to use MySQL, you can use the MS Access files that are included in the Day 7 archive. You don't actually need to have Access on your machine to use these files (Windows includes drivers to read them natively), so that makes this route a bit easier for beginners.

Copy these files from `http://downloads.cutelittledogs.com` archive into an appropriate directory on your Windows application server, such as `C:\databases`. Now, let's work on setting up data source names for the data you've installed on the system, be it

MySQL or Access. If you intend on following the examples in each day's lesson, this is perhaps the most important part of the book, so be sure to read it completely.

Setting Up the Data Sources Names

No matter which database you've installed on your computer (MySQL or Access), you'll need to provide a common way to access the data. Because we're using ASP for the application server, the easiest approach is to create a "data source name" (or *DSN*) that is attached to the database and provides a simple name that all connections can be based on. For example, rather than having to tell Dreamweaver MX that you're connecting to a MySQL server at 10.0.1.250 with the username dreamweaver and password 21days and a database name of day8, you can define a data source name that contains all of this information and allows you to refer to the whole mess as day8.

The beauty of this approach is that it's regardless of the type of database you're using. If you set up MySQL, you'll still refer to the same DSN as if you set up the Access databases.

Note

> If you plan to use a server model other than basic ASP, you might not have access to Windows DSN. PHP, for example, connects directly to the MySQL database. Tomorrow's lesson will discuss the other connection methods for alternative server platforms. If you're using another system, you might want to read through Day 8 to determine whether data source names are the way to go for your server platform.

Setting Up Data Source Names for MySQL

In order to set up a DSN for MySQL, you need to download the MyODBC driver from http://www.mysql.com/downloads/api-myodbc.html. At present, two versions of MyODBC are available—a development version and a stable version. Be sure to pick the stable version, and then choose one of the full setup downloads targeted for your system (Windows 95/98/Me or NT/2000/XP).

After you've downloaded the ODBC driver, run the included install program:

1. After the Welcome screen, click the Continue button.

2. At the Install Drivers screen, shown in Figure 7.10, be sure to highlight the MySQL driver. If you don't, it won't be installed. Click OK.

3. After the driver has installed, it will prompt you to set up a new ODBC data source. You can safely close out of this process. We'll be setting one up using the Windows ODBC control panel.

7

FIGURE 7.10

Be sure to select the MySQL driver; otherwise it won't be installed.

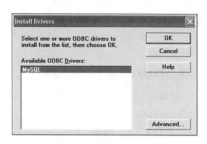

Note

If you get an error message telling you to reboot and try again, you probably need to adjust the installation process a bit. Click the Advanced button on the Install Drivers screen, choose Do Not Install Driver Manager, and then click OK. This seems to cure any installation problems.

After the driver is installed, you'll need to set up data sources for *each* of the examples used in this book. This process can be a bit time consuming, but it will pay off later. Be absolutely sure that you're setting up the DSNs on the same machine you've configured to be your application server (the same computer you've installed IIS on). If you don't, your Web applications will fail to run properly.

Set up a new MySQL-based DSN by following these instructions. You don't need to reboot after setting up a data source.

1. Click Start and choose Control Panel.

2. In Windows XP, switch to Classic View, and then click Administrative Tools, and then Data Sources (ODBC).

3. Click the System DSN tab.

4. Click Add.

5. Choose the MySQL driver from the list, and then click Finish.

6. Fill in the appropriate information for the driver configuration, shown in Figure 7.11. Then click OK.

Ack! That sounds simple enough, but what is "the appropriate information?" Don't worry; there are only a few fields you really need to configure:

- **Windows DSN name**—The data source name is an arbitrary name that you will use to refer to the data source. For this book, I've named the databases stored in MySQL *identically* to the DSNs I create. For example, if you're setting up a DSN for a MySQL database called day8, you should enter a Windows DSN of day8.

Figure 7.11

Set up the fields required to connect to the MySQL server.

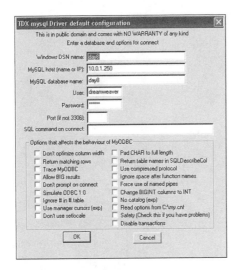

- **MySQL host**—The hostname of the database server. You should be running the MySQL server on the same machine you're working on right now. Enter `local-host`. Note: this isn't a requirement in a real deployment environment. If MySQL is on another computer, enter its IP address here.

- **MySQL database name**—The name of the database on the MySQL server. I'll provide a list of these shortly, but, except for one or two special cases, the database is named after the day it is used (lowercase and no spaces). For example, Day 8's database is `day8`.

- **User**—The username to connect to the MySQL server with. The MySQL data imported in this book sets up a username `dreamweaver`, which you should use for all the example connections.

- **Password**—The password for the database. Again, the import script has set this up as `21days`, so you should enter that value for all the DSNs.

After you've properly configured a connection to the database, you can immediately start using its Windows DSN name as a data source name within Dreamweaver MX connections, which you'll start working with tomorrow.

So, now that you know how to create a DSN for a MySQL database, let's go ahead and do it for everything you'll be using in this book. Using the previously discussed steps, configure DSNs for the databases shown in Table 7.1.

7

TABLE 7.1 Example MySQL Databases and the Corresponding DSNs

MySQL Database Name	DSN to Create
day8	day8
day9	day9
day10	day10
day11	day11
day12	day12
day13	day13
day14	day14
day15banner	day15banner
day15feedback	day15feedback
day15timeimages	day15timeimages
day16	day16
day17	day17
day18	day18
day19	day19

As you can see, there are few surprises in the list. For each MySQL database, there should be a corresponding DSN. Once you've created these entries, you're free to work solely within the Dreamweaver MX environment. No more database interaction required!

Setting Up Data Source Names for Microsoft Access

Many users will want to skip the step of using MySQL and turn to the simplicity of MS Access while learning Dreamweaver MX. I, personally, don't recommend using Access databases for production Web sites, but your needs might vary.

If you've decided to go with MS Access, use these steps to set up DSNs for use in Dreamweaver MX. Be absolutely certain that you're performing these steps on your application server (the same machine running IIS), otherwise Dreamweaver might not be able to connect correctly in subsequent exercises.

To add a DSN for a MS Access database, follow these steps:

1. Click Start and choose Control Panel.
2. In Windows XP, switch to Classic View, and then click Administrative Tools, and then Data Sources (ODBC).
3. Click the System DSN tab.
4. Click Add.

5. Choose the Microsoft Access driver from the list, and then click Finish.

6. Fill in the appropriate information for the driver configuration, shown in Figure 7.12. Then click OK.

If you attempt to configure the driver according to these instructions and do *not* see an Access ODBC driver, you can load it from your Office CD-ROM.

FIGURE 7.12

Setting up an Access database for ODBC access requires nothing more than a data source name and a database file.

Don't worry because you don't know the specifics for the different configuration options! These are the only settings that you'll need to configure for the examples in the book:

- **Data Source Name**—An arbitrary name that you will use to refer to the data source. For this book, I've named the MS Access databases *identically* to the DSNs I create. For example, if you're setting up a DSN for an Access database called day8.mdb, you should enter a Windows DSN of day8.

- **Description**—A basic description of the purpose of the connection. This is for your use and will not be needed by Dreamweaver MX.

- **Database**—Click the Select button to choose an existing database. Assuming you copied all the Access databases to C:\databases, you should simply browse to the file on your drive, such as day8.mdb, and select it. You can use the other buttons (Create, Repair, and Compact) as you would within Access—they are not related to the function of the ODBC driver.

As with the MySQL driver, as soon as you've set up the Access driver, the data source should be immediately accessible in Dreamweaver MX. You should repeat these steps for all the book's MS Access database files, creating DSNs for each, as defined in Table 7.2.

7

TABLE 7.2   Example MS Access Databases and the Corresponding DSNs

MS Access Database File	DSN to Create
day8.mdb	day8
day9.mdb	day9
day10.mdb	day10
day11.mdb	day11
day12.mdb	day12
day13.mdb	day13
day14.mdb	day14
day15banner.mdb	day15banner
day15feedback.mdb	day15feedback
day15timeimages.mdb	day15timeimages
day16.mdb	day16
day17.mdb	day17
day18.mdb	day18
day19.mdb	day19

Be sure to create all these data sources before moving to tomorrow's readings. I make the assumption that you've gotten past this stage in the rest of the book, so you won't guided through the setup of DSNs in the future.

Creating a PHP Application Server on Mac OS X

Setting up a Web application server in Mac OS X requires the same steps as on Windows, except that Mac OS X includes PHP rather than ASP, so all you'll need to do is activate it. As I've said before, PHP is not fully supported in Dreamweaver MX, but if you've got a Mac, it's the easiest solution for creating a compatible application server.

Even if you don't want to use Mac OS X as your application server, you can still use MySQL as the backend database for a Windows or UNIX server. Installing MySQL isn't completely trivial—you'll need to type a few extra commands at the command–line— but it's nothing you can't handle. Just be sure to follow the instructions provided here exactly.

Installing and Activating the Apache Web Server

The first step of getting the application server up and running is starting the Apache Web server. This is remarkably simple, as Apple has decided to include Apache with every copy of Mac OS X, including the client version. All you need to do to turn it on is to open the System Preference panel, click the Sharing panel icon, and then click the Start button in the Web sharing section, as seen in Figure 7.13. Mac OS X Server users should consult their manuals—it's just as simple, but slightly different.

FIGURE 7.13

Activate Apache by clicking Start. Simple, isn't it?

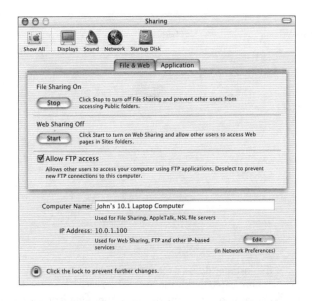

Now on to the tough part—getting the database backend installed and ready.

Installing MySQL

There are a number of MySQL distributions for Mac OS X. Some, such as the one available through www.mysql.com, require a great deal of command-line work to install. Others, such as the one you're going to look at today, are almost entirely automated.

The version of MySQL that you're going to use today is located at http://www.entropy.ch/software/macosx/mysql/. If you look closely at the page, you'll notice that there are two download links, one for mysql.pkg and another for mysql-startupitem.pkg. You should get *both* of these files before starting the install process. The main MySQL package contains the database and everything that it needs to run. The second package (with "startupitem" in its name) installs a special system service in your /Library/StartupItems folder so that the MySQL service will start each

7

time your server boots. Download both of these files and unarchive them now. You can also find links to these files on the `http://downloads.cutelittledogs.com/` site.

To start the installation, double-click the `.pkg` files, beginning with the main MySQL package. The installer process, shown in Figure 7.14, will guide you through adding MySQL to your system. There are no special options to configure or questions you'll need to answer. Just be sure to choose your Mac OS X hard drive when prompted, and then click install.

Figure 7.14

Use the Mac OS X installer to add MySQL to your system.

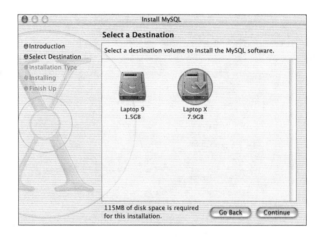

> **Caution**
>
> If the installer doesn't seem to want to work for you, make sure you've "authenticated" with the installer by clicking on the little lock icon. You will be prompted for an administrator username and password, and then allowed to continue.
>
> Because the MySQL installer adds software to a privileged directory on your system, it must have administrative access in order to work.

When finished with the first package, move on to the next (the startupitem `.pkg` file). Follow the exact same procedure. You should now be a few short minutes from running your very own MySQL-enabled Mac OS X computer.

Creating the MySQL User

It's usually considered bad form to run a critical system service as an administrative user. If the service is somehow compromised, the entire system could be damaged. MySQL, thankfully, will happily run as another user, but you must first create the user account it will run under. In this case, this will be the user `mysql`.

To add `mysql` to your system, simply open the Users panel within the Mac OS X System Preferences application, and then follow these steps:

1. Click New User.

2. Fill in all the information under the Identity tab. Most importantly, you *must* enter a short name of `mysql`. This will set the user account name for the database server.

3. Click over to the Password tab and enter a password for the new user. It doesn't matter what you use for the value.

4. Be certain that the Allow user to administer this computer button is *not* checked.

5. Click Save to save the account.

The basic user setup is demonstrated in Figure 7.15.

FIGURE 7.15

Add a MySQL user to your system.

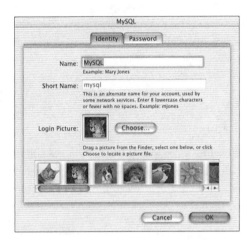

All that remains is to set up the initial MySQL databases and import the data file that you'll be using throughout the remainder of the text.

Setting Up the Default Databases

The final step in preparing MySQL for your system is installing the default databases. This, unfortunately, can be performed only from the command line. Go ahead and open up the terminal applications (in your Mac OS X Utilities folder) now.

When you've reached the command prompt, follow these steps:

1. Type `cd /usr/local/mysql`. You will now be inside the MySQL directory.

2. Type `sudo ./scripts/mysql_install_db`. Pay close attention; the computer will ask you for your password so that it can grant administrative rights to the process. Type in your password; then press Enter again.

7

3. Type **sudo chown -R mysql:staff /usr/local/mysql***. This command will set ownership of the MySQL directory so that it is owned by the newly created MySQL user.

4. Finally, **enter sudo ./bin/safe_mysqld – user=mysql &**. This starts the server and puts the process in the background.

You can test your MySQL distribution using the command mysqladmin version, which displays information about the version of the server that is running. Type **sudo mysqladmin version** at the command line now. You should see something similar to this:

```
[client0:~] root# sudo mysqladmin version
./bin/mysqladmin  Ver 8.23 Distrib 3.23.49, for apple-darwin5.2 on powerpc
Copyright (C) 2000 MySQL AB & MySQL Finland AB & TCX DataKonsult AB
This software comes with ABSOLUTELY NO WARRANTY. This is free software,
and you are welcome to modify and redistribute it under the GPL license

Server version          3.23.49-entropy.ch
Protocol version        10
Connection              Localhost via UNIX socket
UNIX socket             /tmp/mysql.sock
Uptime:                 42 sec

Threads: 1  Questions: 2  Slow queries: 0  Opens: 5
Flush tables: 1  Open tables: 0 Queries per second avg: 0.048
```

Congratulations, your Mac OS X computer is now running a high-powered SQL server, and you didn't have to spend a dime. Before quitting the terminal application, there is one small step that you need to perform—seeding the MySQL database with the data used for examples in the book.

This information is stored in a file called DreamweaverSQL.txt in the Day 7 archive on http://downloads.cutelittledogs.com. Download the archive to your system, uncompress it, and then copy the DreamweaverSQL.txt file to your home directory by finding it on your drive, Control-clicking its icon and choosing Copy from the contextual menu. Next, open your home directory by pressing Command+Option+H inside the Mac OS X Finder. Finally, choose Paste from the File menu.

Note

Yes, you can just drag the file to your home directory, but because the idea of a home directory might be new to many Mac users, this might be confusing for some.

Finally, to seed the database with the information contained in the DreamweaverSQL.txt file, just type **sudo mysql < ~<*username*>/DreamweaverSQL.txt** at the command line, replacing the *<username>* portion with your personal username. This is the same name that appears at the top of the window when viewing your home directory.

Now you're done. You've just set up MySQL with several days worth of project information as well as a username of dreamweaver and a password 21days, which you can use to access all the databases.

Note

You might have noticed that the Windows folks have a nice GUI to view their SQL databases. If you'd like something similar for the Mac, check out the 4X SQL manager software at http://www.macosguru.de.

Setting Up the Data Sources

Because Mac OS X does not support ODBC data sources nor ASP, you won't be setting up data sources if you use the PHP platform on the Macintosh. PHP speaks directly to the database server, and will simply use the names of the databases in MySQL as the data source. You'll learn more about making MySQL connections tomorrow.

Adding PHP Support

The final step in preparing Mac OS X to be used as an application server is adding PHP support. Thankfully, Apple has already taken care of this for you, so all you need to do is turn it on in the Apache configuration file. *Unfortunately*, the configuration file you'll need to change is set so that only the root user can edit it. Once again, you'll need to open the terminal application and type the following two lines at the command prompt:

```
sudo chown -R root:admin /etc/httpd
sudo chmod -R 774 /etc/httpd
```

This will adjust the permissions so that any administrative user can edit the Web server configuration. This is entirely reasonable, so don't worry about your system security being compromised.

You're finished with the terminal application; you shouldn't need it for the rest of the book.

Now that the Apache file is editable, go ahead and open it in your system's text editor application, TextEdit. Because the file is located in a UNIX directory, you'll need to type the path manually. Choose Open from the File menu, and then enter /etc/httpd/httpd.conf in the Go To field, as shown in Figure 7.16.

7

FIGURE 7.16

Enter the path to the httpd.conf *file.*

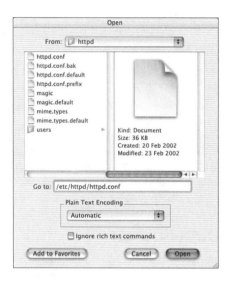

Once the file is open, search for the line:

```
#LoadModule php4_module        libexec/httpd/libphp4.so
```

Remove the # sign from the front of the line—this uncomments the instruction so that the Web server will load PHP when it starts.

Next, search for the line:

```
# AddModule mod_php4.c
```

And, again, remove the pound sign from the front of the line. Finally, save changes to the file and quit TextEdit.

Testing PHP

After changing the Apache configuration file, you'll need to restart the Web server process. You can do this by rebooting your computer, using the Start/Stop button in the Sharing System Preference panel, or by typing **/usr/sbin/apachectl restart** at a command line. Whichever way you choose, do it now.

Once you're restarted the Web server, you'll be ready to test PHP. Open your favorite text editor and create a simple text file with a single line that reads:

```
<?php phpinfo(); ?>
```

Save this file as test.php in the directory /Library/Webserver/Documents, and then try load it in a Web browser. You should see a screen similar to that of Figure 7.17.

FIGURE 7.17

FIGURE 7.17

If everything is installed correctly, you'll see this screen.

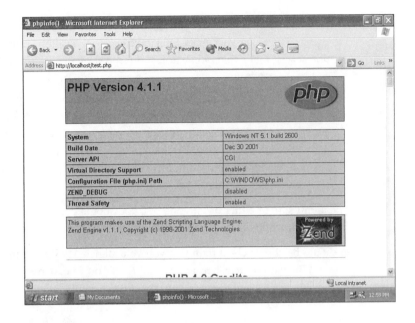

Note

When attempting to load the `test.php` page, if you're using the server running PHP, simply enter `http://localhost/test.php` as the URL. If you're using another machine, you'll need the IP address or hostname of the PHP/Apache/MySQL server computer. On my network, for example, I type `http://10.0.1.250/test.php`.

Your Mac OS X computer is now ready to run PHP-based projects that you create with Dreamweaver MX. Remember, PHP is a *new* language in Dreamweaver MX. Although this is the easiest solution for getting an application server running on the Macintosh, be aware that you're likely be missing a few features found in Dreamweaver's implementation of other application servers.

Other Things You'll Need

Surprisingly enough, you now have everything you need for a reasonably high volume server. There are still a few very important pieces of information you should gather before proceeding. Unfortunately, I can't really help you with this, because I don't know how your network is configured or the specifics of your operating system. Before moving to the other chapters, you should know two points:

7

- How to access your newly configured application server over a network. If you're going to be using your main Dreamweaver MX desktop computer as the application server, that's fine, you can just refer to it by the hostname `localhost` or the IP address `127.0.0.1`.

- How to access files on the application server. On the Mac, you'll need to access files in the `/Library/Webserver/Documents`, whereas Windows users will want to get at `C:\Inetput\wwwroot`. Because both Mac OS X and Windows have very simple means of sharing files, I'll assume you can figure this out on your own. Again, if you're using the same computer for your application server as you are for Dreamweaver MX, this won't matter.

If you aren't sure of either of these points, you should consult your network administrator or the instructions for your operating system. They are beyond the scope of this text.

You should be absolutely certain that you've installed MySQL or the Access databases and set up the data sources before continuing. If you've experienced any errors, visit `http://help.cutelittledogs.com` to see if there are updated installation instructions.

Summary

Today's lesson tied up all the loose ends that we needed to discuss before proceeding. A wide variety of potential development platforms and server platforms can be used with Dreamweaver MX, but, if you're a beginner, it can be difficult to decide what is right for you.

We've looked at the different embedded languages, their benefits and drawbacks, and the server operating systems that they run on. Hopefully you can now make a decision about what makes the most sense from both usability and performance/cost perspectives.

Finally, we've covered setting up your own application server on both Mac OS X and Windows. From this point, the book is going to pick up steam, and, within the next week, you're going to be well on your way to building complex dynamic Web-based applications.

Workshop

The Workshop area is meant to reinforce your reading with a series of questions and exercises.

Q&A

Q Why haven't I heard of PHP?

A PHP is a reasonably new language, but its adoption rate is phenomenal; so much so that Macromedia added it in Dreamweaver MX. It, like many other popular Internet technologies, is developed as a collaborative effort, not as a company's product. Unfortunately, until Macromedia fully supports the language, it isn't the best choice for beginners.

Q Why are there so many different embedded languages?

A Everyone has a favorite language. Embedding those languages into HTML is the next logical step for creating Web applications. JSP is aimed at Java developers. ASP is aimed at those who have worked in Visual Basic. ColdFusion and PHP are two of the few "original" languages born solely for the purpose of creating Web sites.

Q Are you saying I shouldn't run a Windows-based server?

A Not at all. The IIS product is excellent and much easier to use than Apache. Its greatest drawback is the number of exploits (bugs) that have appeared in recent months. As long as you keep your system up–to-date, you'll have no problems!

Q You can't seriously use a Macintosh as a real server, can you?

A Yes. Mac OS X is based on a very robust kernel architecture and UNIX base. Previously, running a server on the Macintosh was a less-than-enjoyable experience. Today it is just as reasonable as using Windows XP or any other commercial UNIX system for a standalone solution.

Quiz

1. What does ASP stand for, and who created it?
2. What features does PHP offer that ASP doesn't?
3. Which three components form a Web application server?
4. What directory does IIS use for the default Web site?

Quiz Answers

1. Active Server Pages; Microsoft created it.
2. The primary features of PHP are its cross-platform capabilities and very low entry cost.
3. The Web server, development platform/language, and database are the three components of a Web application server.
4. IIS uses C:\Inetput\wwwroot.

7

Exercise

Today's exercise is an easy one. Install the appropriate software for the Web application server, as discussed in this chapter. You'll need it for the rest of the book!

WEEK 1

In Review

The past seven days have been a crash course in the Dreamweaver MX authoring environment. A great deal of information was covered, so let's take a look at the important things that you should have learned. If any of this remains unclear, you should review these portions of the text before continuing. Understanding the Dreamweaver MX environment and available HTML tools is of paramount importance in using the dynamic behaviors.

HTML Design Tools—The Dreamweaver MX Insert panel lets you quickly add and manipulate objects in the Dreamweaver MX design window. Clicking an item in the Insert panel will either directly add the item to the design, or present the users with a configuration dialog box so that they can choose the parameters needed to create the object. There are two modes of design—the standard mode and the layout mode. Using the layout mode, you can quickly define content regions within your document with pixel accuracy. Be sure that you are comfortable with using this mode and the other tools at your disposal to lay out HTML documents.

Properties Panel—The Properties panel lets you view and modify almost any attribute of an HTML tag from within the graphical Dreamweaver MX environment. This eliminates much of the need for an HTML reference because everything you would want to modify is presented visually. If you need a quick reference, Dreamweaver MX includes an extensive online help area for HTML, cascading style sheets, and JavaScript.

Timelines and DHTML—Dynamic HTML is a powerful combination of JavaScript and layers that makes it possible to create dynamic applications that run from within the client browser. Using the timeline, you can create time-based animations, or add actual interactivity with the Drag Layer behavior. Understanding these features, although not necessary for writing server-based behaviors, is important for deciding which portions of your code should run on the client and which should run on the server.

Database Design—The final days of the week introduce the concepts behind database design. In order to author effective database-driven applications, you must be able to create the data structures that drive the Web site. Being able to normalize your data is critical for the rest of the text. Without this information, you'll be unable to design an efficient backend for Dreamweaver MX to communicate with.

Again, it's very important that you're comfortable with these functions before proceeding—even though this is a 21 day book, it doesn't necessarily have to be completed in that length of time.

WEEK 2

At a Glance

With the document design tools out of the way, we can
quickly move forward to the dynamic server-based tools in
Week 2. Dreamweaver MX takes five very different programming languages and provides a common interface to using
them all. With a simple point-and-click interface, you can create custom database driven Web sites that require almost no
programming knowledge.

That said, one of the largest mental leaps that new users need
to make in order to use Dreamweaver MX needs to be made
by people who *are* programmers. The dynamic tools,
although simple to use, are more focused on designers than
programmers and require some getting used to. Week 2 will
provide straightforward information to nonprogrammers, and
also introduce programmers to the application in such a way
that they can incorporate it into their existing programming
knowledge.

Dreamweaver MX creates dynamic applications using a series
of behaviors along with data that is *bound* to HTML objects.
These behaviors accomplish very specific tasks, such as
querying a database or inserting into a database table. By
itself, a server behavior won't make your site into a dazzling
dynamic masterpiece. Combined with other behaviors, however, you can create something that is, indeed, very complex.
Some of the available behaviors you'll work with include the
following:

- Showing/hiding information conditionally
- Displaying/updating/deleting information from a
  database

8

9

10

11

12

13

14

- Authenticating user information based on usernames and passwords
- Passing information from page to page

By the end of the second week, each of these behaviors (and several others) will be discussed in depth. You'll also learn how to use these features together to build common elements of dynamic Web sites. In fact, almost every aspect of Dreamweaver MX will be explained by the end of the second week.

You should feel completely comfortable with each behavior by the time you're done. What's missing, however, is the applied knowledge that you get only by *doing*. With this in mind, I've designed most of the lessons in the final week so that by the end of each day, you've created a new and different Web application based on the Dreamweaver tools.

DAY 8

Defining a Dynamic Site

You've got an application server platform and a database. Now what? The next step, and one of the most critical, is setting up the database connection for a Web site. If the settings are off by a misplaced space or stray period, the connection will fail, and you're likely to find yourself swearing at the computer for hours on end. In short, if you *don't* get the connection right, none of the Dreamweaver MX dynamic functionality will work. Today's lesson addresses this issue by:

- Demonstrating how a dynamic site is defined
- Uncovering the different database connection dialog boxes that are you will see
- Showing how you will know when your definition is in place and working

Interacting with the Application Server

Because we're dealing with multiple platforms today, beyond this introduction the text will be divided into sections that are either universal or platform specific and will be denoted as such. Additionally, some sections only apply to

ASP (Active Server Pages), JSP (Java Server Pages), ColdFusion, or *PHP* development. You might want to skip to the section that applies to you, as the information is relatively repetitive.

> **Note**
>
> Today's assumption is that you already have a database server up and running. If this isn't the case, turn back to yesterday's lesson for installing and preparing MySQL. It's fast, free, and perfectly suited for Web application deployment. For beginners, database files are provided for MS Access so that you can get up and running without anything extra.

When authoring dynamic sites within the Dreamweaver MX environment, the application provides a number of interactive tools that let you view live data and design your pages around the actual information in your database. These features, however, rely on being able to talk to a database server in real-time. To establish this link, you must create a Dreamweaver MX database connection, which describes to the application how it will be contacting the database server. In many cases, this is just an IP address, a username and password, and the name of the database.

So, why is it so difficult to do this correctly?

In all fairness, it isn't difficult. Creating a database connection will usually only take a few seconds after you've figured out what you're doing. The problem is that Dreamweaver MX supports *two* types of connections on the Windows platform. Macintosh users are limited to one connection type, and (surprise) it's a much less confusing setup process.

The first type of connection uses a *remote* data source. This is the default (and *only*) connection type available on the Macintosh, or when using the ColdFusion application server. Rather than connecting to a database that is housed locally, Dreamweaver MX will connect to a remote database server. What's unique about this process is that Dreamweaver doesn't actually connect to the database directly. Instead, it writes a small program and quietly transfers it to the application server. This program is capable of talking to the database and returning the results to the Dreamweaver MX application. This allows Macintoshes to talk to databases on Windows machines, and so on. As long as the application server can see the database, so can the users running Dreamweaver, no matter where they are.

8

Note

A big benefit of the remote database access method in Dreamweaver is that as soon as you've made the connection, you're virtually guaranteed that your Dreamweaver MX application will execute correctly. If Dreamweaver has successfully transferred and executed the files it needs to retrieve the initial information from the database, it will have no problem doing the same for your pages.

The second type of connection is a *local* data connection. This is where things get funky. The local data connection is a Windows *data source* that has been defined on the computer you're using Dreamweaver MX with. What's often confusing, however, is that a "local" windows data source means that the connection to the data is defined locally. The database itself can be located on a computer in another room, building, and so on. To make things worse, this data connection is an entirely different data source definition than the one on the application server itself. At the same time, the data connection must be configured identically to the application server; otherwise the Dreamweaver code will break.

What the user typically sees is that Dreamweaver MX can talk to the database with no problem, and everything *appears* to work in the design window. As soon as you attempt to preview your work or transfer it to the server, however, the dynamic functionality will break. If the local data source isn't consistent with the data source you'll be using to deploy the Web site, trouble awaits.

Setting Up a Dynamic Site Definition

Before you can even begin to think about connecting to a database, you must first define the remote application server, and how you will be accessing it. Remember, for many of the connection methods, Dreamweaver transfers files to the server and executes them. This means that the connection to the application server is priority one. After that, we'll worry about database connections.

For today's lesson, let's define a dynamic site called Day 8. If you're using the sample data that you created data source names (DSN) for in the last chapter, you'll even be able to make a real data connection in a matter of minutes.

Note

Setting up a DSN connection is a cinch. If you're following the book exactly, you won't have any trouble.

To set up the dynamic Web site, define a site as you normally would: create a folder on your drive called Day 8, and then start a new site definition. Click the Basic tab so that you can get the setup Wizard/Assistant to do most of the work for you. Fill in the first screen as you normally would, as seen in Figure 8.1.

FIGURE 8.1

Define the initial screen exactly the same as a static site.

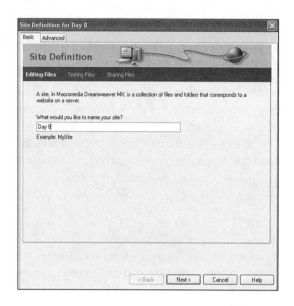

Click Next to move on to the dynamic/static choice screen displayed in Figure 8.2. In all the previous days, you've used the No (Static Site) option. Today (and for the rest of the days in the book), you should pick Yes (Dynamic Site). The screen will change slightly and present a list of available application servers.

Assuming you're using the basic ASP server set up in this book, go with the ASP VBScript choice. This will set the default document-type for the site definition. Click Next to continue.

Note

> Surprisingly enough, Dreamweaver MX will let you have pages for different application servers within a single site, and different types of database connections for the servers as well. This is useful if you combine technologies on a single server machine (PHP/ASP, PHP/CFML, ASP/CFML, and the like).

Now you've reached a very important setup screen—connection information for the *testing* server—this is the application server that is used to test code. This is where things get a bit confusing. Macromedia assumes that you'll be uploading your pages to a testing (or staging) server, *then* the application server. If you're just using a single server, think of the testing server as being the same as the Remote server that you configured in Day 3.

FIGURE 8.2

Today you start your first dynamic site.

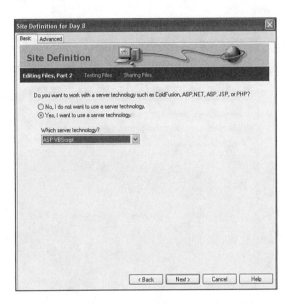

Shown in Figure 8.3, this screen is used to set up a connection to the Web application testing server. This is the same machine that you configured yesterday, and you can use any of the connection methods that you learned about in Day 3, "Advanced HTML and Site Tools" to send files to it.

You *must* configure this setting correctly, or you'll run into trouble down the road. Refer to Day 3 for more information on the connection methods. Click "Next" to choose the connection information specifics, just as you did in Day 3.

When complete, click Next (yes, again).

Believe it or not, you *are* approaching the end! For most users, this will be the final step—specifying the URL that will reach the root level of the project on your application server, demonstrated in Figure 8.4. Click the Test URL button to determine whether the specified remote URL is working.

If this doesn't make sense, look at it this way:

On your local machine you have a site that sits a directory, such as `C:\Projects\Day 8`.

On the remote server, the files in this site are copied to a folder that the Web server has access to—this is the URL of the Web site. For example, the `C:\Projects\Day 8` file could end up being served from the URL `http:\\www.cutelittledogs.com\day8`. In that case, you enter the complete address (including the `http://`) that it required to reach the top of your Web site.

FIGURE 8.3

Choose the location of the testing server on which you are going to deploy your application.

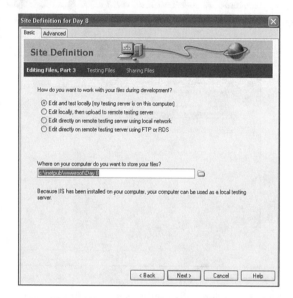

FIGURE 8.4

Enter the URL required to reach the root level of your Web site.

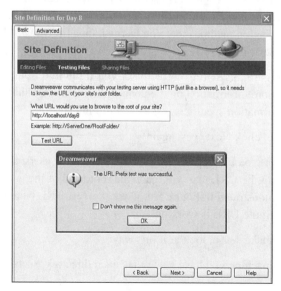

> **Note** The Dreamweaver MX instructions for this step mention that you should speci-
> fy the URL for a hypothetical page `MyPage.htm`. You don't need to do this; you
> can just enter the URL up to the end of the root directory of your Web site.

Click Next one more time. If you've chosen to use your local machine as the testing
server, you now have the option of setting a *remote* server. Figure 8.5 shows the remote
server configuration; the step that seems to trip up many readers!

FIGURE 8.5

*Remote server? Say
what?*

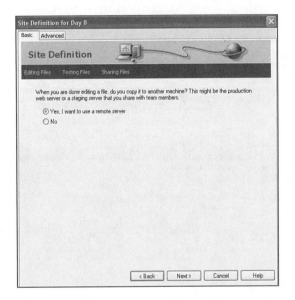

The confusion is that Dreamweaver MX is prompting you to configure a remote server,
not a *testing* server—this is really just a matter of semantics, and what button you'll need
to click on to display the remote files. In order to get to this screen you had to tell
Dreamweaver MX that your local workstation is the testing server. Thus, it thinks that
you might want to add in a remote (presumably your final deployment server) server and
prompts you.

Click Next to move to the final step. If you chose to use a remote server, on the last
screen of the setup (not pictured here) you can set file check-in/check-out attributes, just
as you learned in Day 5, "Creating Reusable Components" and click Next.

When you've completed the configuration process, a final display of the site-setting particulars is displayed, as shown in Figure 8.6. Click Done. Your settings will be saved.

Tip

There are a few (very few) extra site definition options that you might need to access, depending on your connection method. If you need better control of the setup, such as configuring firewall information, click the Advanced tab of the setup dialog box. There are three sections to review:

Local Info—Includes the site's name and location on your hard drive.

Remote Info—Defines the deployment server access method.

Testing Server—Sets the default application staging server and access method. Most of your work should take place on the testing server.

In addition, you might want to configure the application server to use UltraDev 4–style connections. Choosing this feature in the Application Server advanced configuration will alter the database connection dialog boxes a teensy bit so that older-style connections can be made.

FIGURE 8.6

The final site definition is displayed.

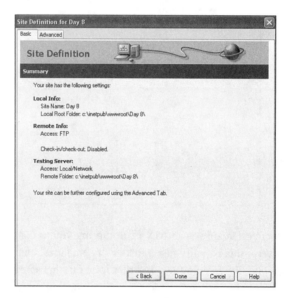

Once the dynamic setup is completed, you can view the files on the application server connection by clicking the second button from the left in the toolbar of the Site Files window, as seen in Figure 8.7.

If the remote server and application server are one and the same (more likely than not), this button will *not* add any functionality.

Remote (Deployment) Server
Application Testing Server

FIGURE **8.7**

Click the lightning bolt icon to view the application testing server files, or the icon to the left of it for "remote" (deployment server) files.

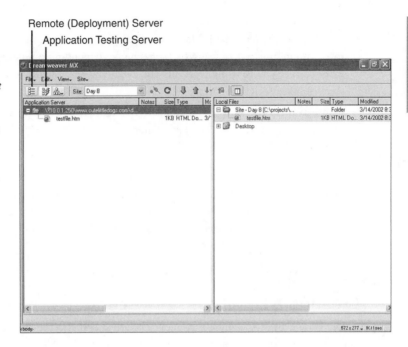

Database Connections

After you've defined your Web site using the appropriate server model, you can define a database connection. Several data access methods are supported by Dreamweaver MX—you will be guided by the program into choosing the right one for your server deployment platform:

Data Source Names—As you learned yesterday, using the ODBC controls, you can "abstract" a database so that the server system references it by a simple name, called the data source name. Once the ODBC connection is installed, using the database in Dreamweaver MX becomes simple. Yesterday you set up all of the necessary DSNs for the MySQL and MS Access databases used in the book.

Connection Strings—Provide another means of specifying a data source name and pertinent connection information in the form of a text string. These are somewhat confusing to configure, but result in faster access to the database if an OLE DB provider is used rather than ODBC. If you're a beginner, you're probably better off avoiding this until later. OLE DB connections are available only on NT/2000/XP machines with MDAC 2.6.

JDBC—Java Database Connectivity. A fully cross-platform means by which a database can be queried. Much like the connection strings, setting up JDBC drivers involves entering a text string that can change depending on the type of database and JDBC driver you're using. Not difficult once you find the documentation, but sometimes it takes some digging.

ColdFusion Data Sources—A data source that has been defined in the ColdFusion administration package. This data source is specific to the ColdFusion model and is only used on the server connection.

As mentioned earlier, there are often two forms of each type of connection for Windows machines. You could, for example, choose to use a local ODBC data source or one on the server. I highly recommend using the *server* data source, as it will avoid problems with differences in naming conventions, and the like. We'll be using the server-based source for all the examples in this book.

Let's see how these connections work.

Creating a Database Connection

In Dreamweaver MX, database connections are specific to the site you're working on. Once a connection is defined for the site, it is available to all the other pages (using the same application server language) within the site. Although this is, in fact, a wonderful feature, the interface for creating a database connection is slightly counterintuitive.

Rather than using the Site menu (which acts on the site as a whole), you must create a connection by first opening a new Web page and defining the connection through that page. For example, let's assume you've created the project `Day 8` and are using the `ASP VBScript` application server.

Create a new document for the site called `myconnection.asp` using the New option under the File menu. Choose ASP VBScript as the page type, as seen in Figure 8.8.

Be sure to save the document after creating it. This ensures that Dreamweaver knows the new document is part of the site. Now, open the Databases panel from the Window menu. This is usually located in the Application panel group. The panel should look similar to Figure 8.9.

Looking at the panel, you can see that it lists the steps necessary to connect to the database. You can use the hyperlinks in the description to skip to or edit any of the steps in the process. To add a database connection, click the "+" button. A list of possible connection methods will be shown, as in Figure 8.10.

FIGURE 8.8

Create a new ASP VBScript document.

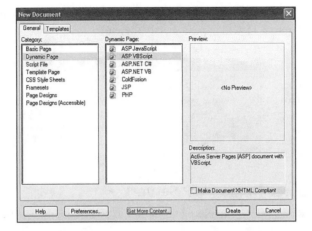

FIGURE 8.9

The Databases panel is used to add database connections.

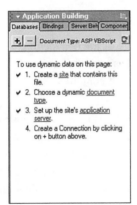

FIGURE 8.10

Click the "+" button to display a list of possible database connection methods for your chosen application server.

Choose Data Source Name (DSN) from the pop-up menu. The configuration dialog box
shown in Figure 8.11 will appear shortly thereafter.

FIGURE **8.11**

*The Data Source Name
connection dialog box
will be displayed.*

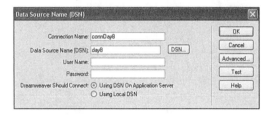

Data Source Name (ASP Server)

You're now ready to configure a connection to one of the data source names that you
configured yesterday (day7).

Five fields need to be configured for a basic connection:

- **Connection Name**—This is the name of the connection. You'll want to make sure
  this accurately but succinctly describes how the connection is used. It is suggested
  that you prefix your selected name with conn to show it refers to a connection. For
  today's lesson, just use connDay8.

- **Data Source Name (DSN)**—This is the Data Source Name for the ODBC data
  source that you want to connect to. If you are using a data source on the application server, which you *should* be, click the DSN button to poll the available sources
  from the remote server. You should see all the data sources defined yesterday.
  Choose day8 from the list. Windows users who are using a local data source can
  use the pop-up menu in this field to select the data sources that have been defined
  on that computer.

 Tip

> In addition to the DSN pop-up menu, Windows users also have access to a
> Define button to open the ODBC control panel. Click this button to define a
> new DSN for your local machine.

- **User Name**—This is the username to pass to the database for the connection.
  Because you configured the appropriate usernames/passwords in the DSNs themselves, you should leave this field *blank*.

- **Password**—This is the required password for the connection. As with the username, you can leave this field blank as long as you set the username and password
  when configuring the data source names yesterday.

- **Dreamweaver MX Should Connect**—You need to tell Dreamweaver MX whether to connect to the DSN through the application server or using a local source. You should be using the *application server* setting, as it will limit the configuration problems you encounter later. Macintosh users do not have this option and are forced to connect using the remote server's data source.

> As you are going through the different database connection dialog boxes, you might notice an Advanced button on the side of the window. Use this button to set a certain Catalog/Schema for the database you're connecting to. By default, Dreamweaver MX will show *all* the tables and views in a given database. This will often include system tables and other information you'd rather not see. By limiting the view to a particular Catalog/Schema, you can eliminate a bit of screen clutter.
>
> These settings are dependant on the database system you're using. If you don't know what to fill in, just ignore them.

After entering each piece of information, click the Test button to determine whether Dreamweaver can connect to the remote server. Remember that the connection is made by copying files to the application server and then running them and retrieving the results. The initial connection can sometimes take several seconds to establish. *Any* mistakes are likely to cause a failure.

If your test is not successful, you will usually get a message describing exactly what went wrong. Common problems include:

- Invalid usernames/passwords
- Incorrect hostname/IP addresses for remote DB servers
- Improper database names
- Invalid driver names
- Access blocked at the database server

If you experience any errors, double-check the connection information. Once the connection test succeeds, that's it! You're done.

There is, however, the matter of the *other* connection types supported. If you're using a different application server, you'll see different choices when you click the "+" button in the Databases panel. Let's look at these options now.

Custom Connection Strings (ASP Server)

The connection string method of configuring database access is a bit less friendly than using a DSN. Connection strings, however, give you greater flexibility in choosing the location of the database and other parameters without having to define an ODBC data source on your machine. Because the parameters of the connection string vary with the database server being used, you will need your database documentation to fully use this type of connection. Figure 8.12 shows the connection string fields.

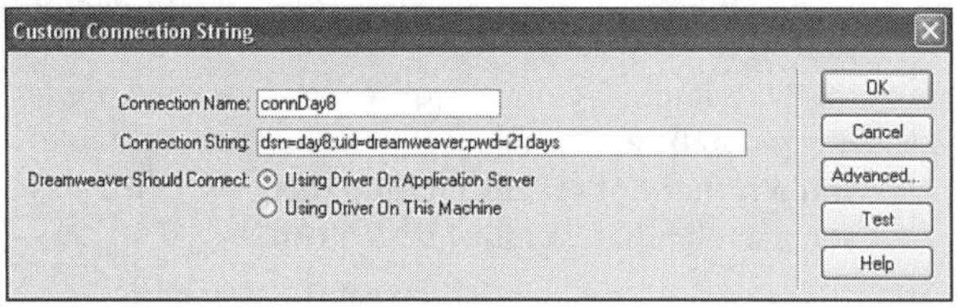

FIGURE 8.12

Connection strings provide a way to connect to a database without requiring that a DSN be predefined.

For this type of connection, there are only two fields that you need to define—the Dreamweaver MX connection name and the connection string. You will need to check your database documentation in order to determine the appropriate syntax to use for the ADO connection string. Two types of connection strings can be set—DSN and DSN-less. A DSN connection is just a variation of the connection you already learned about. Rather than defining all the information about the database, and so on, it just uses the data source name and an optional username/password to create the connection.

For example, a connection string to an ODBC data source named `mydatabase` with the username `myname` and password `mypassword` would look as follows:

```
dsn=mydatabase;uid=myname;pwd=mypassword;
```

A DSN-less connection string contains more information—everything that would normally be needed in an ODBC data source. For example, to connect to an Access database called C:\mydatabase.mbd with a DSN-less connection string, you might use

```
DRIVER={Microsoft Access Driver (*.mdb)};DBQ=c:\mydatabase.mdb
```

Unlike a predefined data source, the connection string is dependent on the specific database features you want to use. Read your database documentation for more information on the connection string attributes that it supports.

As with other connection methods, you can also choose whether you're connecting using a driver on the Application server or on the local computer. Macintosh users can only connect using the Application server.

When the configuration is complete, you can click OK to exit or click Test to verify the connection.

OLE DB Connection Strings (ASP.NET Server)

OLE DB connection strings are similar to the custom connection strings you've already seen. Each string defines an OLE DB "provider," which *provides* access to data sources on your system. This is faster than ODBC, but is only available on NT/2000/XP platforms. In addition, some databases might not allow OLE DB connections to be created. In those cases, you can use ODBC as an OLE DB provider. To make this process a bit easier, the OLE DB connection dialog box, shown in Figure 8.13, provides templates of common types of connections you can create.

FIGURE 8.13

OLE DB connection strings bypass ODBC and result in faster database transactions.

As with the other connection methods, you need to provide a name for the connection and then enter the connection string. Clicking the template button will open a small window and enable you to choose from several connection templates.

For example, choosing the Microsoft Access template will populate the connection string with:

```
Provider=Microsoft.Jet.OLEDB.4.0;
Data Source=[databaseName];
User ID=[username];
Password=[password];
```

You'll still need to fill in the name of the database and the username/password to access it, but the template should provide enough information to get you started. If you're on a Windows computer and need a helping hand, click the Build button. This will open the Microsoft Data Link builder and provide a more interactive approach to creating the connection. (Note: this is a feature of MS Windows, not Dreamweaver MX. Refer to Microsoft's documentation for more details.)

Again, what you enter here is a function of the database system you're going to use. It could be one of hundreds of different variations—only the documentation for your database can provide this information.

When the configuration is complete, you can click OK to exit or click Test to verify the connection.

ColdFusion Data Sources (ColdFusion)

ColdFusion manages databases in a manner that is slightly different than the rest of the software. Databases are defined within ColdFusion and are made available to ColdFusion applications, rather than the entire system.

To connect to a ColdFusion database, you must define the RDS (Remote Development System) login information. If you previously set up remote site access using RDS, this is already finished. If not, click the RDS Login link in the Databases panel, and then set the username and password for the ColdFusion server, as seen in Figure 8.14.

FIGURE 8.14

ColdFusion stores its database connection information on the central CF server.

Dreamweaver will attempt to log in to the ColdFusion server using the supplied information. After successfully connecting, you can click the pencil/paper icon in the upper-right corner of the Databases panel to create a new connection.

UltraDev 4–Style Connections (DSN/DSN-Advanced)

If you're developing your site using UltraDev 4–style connections, the Databases panel will look a bit different, and will include the standard "+" and "-" icons to add and delete connections. You will *not* see this behavior unless you've explicitly chosen to support UltraDev 4 when setting up the site.

The standard data source name connection dialog box is almost identical to the ASP data source name dialog box. You must specify the name of the data source (the *ColdFusion* data source name), as well as the username and password information required to access the data.

In addition to this basic connection, you can create the morbidly complex Data Source Name—Advanced setup by clicking "+" and choosing the advanced options. The advanced dialog box is shown in Figure 8.15.

This dialog box lets you provide the basic connection name, data source name, and username and password required to access the database on the application server. By default, your local copy of Dreamweaver will connect to the database using the data source as it is configured on the ColdFusion server. If, however, you want to connect directly, you can click the Connect Using JDBC Driver On This Machine radio button.

FIGURE 8.15

If you want complex, this is it.

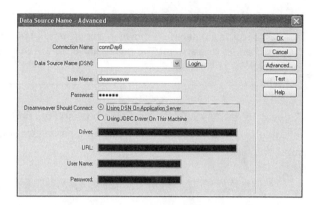

When connecting using a JDBC driver, you'll need to:

- Actually have the JDBC driver installed on your system.
- Know *how* the driver is referenced.

If you're scratching your head at this point, just use the Connect Using DSN on Application Server choice. It's easier and won't require you to install additional software on your machine.

If you do want to go ahead with using a JDBC driver, read through the next section, "JDBC Connections (JSP Server)." Although this is specific to configuring JDBC connections for the JSP application server, the configuration is *identical* to what you need to provide when using JDBC on your local computer to connect to ColdFusion.

When the configuration is complete, you can click OK to exit or click Test to verify the connection.

Dreamweaver MX is designed to work best with ColdFusion MX. If you're developing for ColdFusion MX and have no ties to old UltraDev code, you're never going to see these screens. That's a good thing.

JDBC Connections (JSP Server)

The next type of connection that you might see is the JDBC connection. If you choose JSP as your server platform, you'll need to create a JDBC connection to your database. Clicking the "+" button will show you a list of JDBC driver templates for the connection. If what you want isn't displayed, you can choose Custom JDBC Connection for a blank configuration.

Note   Just because a database is shown in this list *doesn't* mean the driver is installed on your system! This is very similar to the OLE DB templates noted earlier.

Shown in Figure 8.16, the MySQL Driver dialog box is very similar to an OLE DB connection string. It allows you to specify the connection parameters that are needed to access a remote database.

FIGURE 8.16

The MySQL Driver dialog box offers more obscure parameters to find and configure.

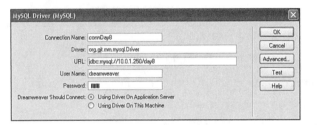

As with the other types of connections, you need to define the name of the connection as Dreamweaver MX will see it. You'll also need to set the username and password to access the data source. There are two new fields, however, that require some explaining:

- **Driver**—Although the other types of connections require drivers, they are integrated into the system components. Java still behaves as an add-on to most operating systems, so you'll need to explicitly tell the program what the driver is called. Java database drivers are implemented as Java classes that can run on any system (if implemented as 100% pure Java). For example, the name of the driver for the MySQL database is `org.gjt.mm.mysql.Driver`. If you have the documentation that came with your database server and it supports JDBC connections, the driver should be very well documented.

- **URL**—Roughly equivalent to the OLE DB connection strings, the URL field sets where and how the connection is made. This is specific to the database, so you'll have to check your documentation to determine what you need to use. The URL for MySQL's JDBC connection is structured like this `jdbc:mysql://10.0.1.250/day8`.

It can be very frustrating to try to find the right driver name and connection URL to use with a JDBC driver. Sometimes it's pasted at the start of the driver documentation, other times is seems that the developers want to keep it a mystery. Such is the complexity of working with a development tool that supports half a dozen languages and an outrageously huge combination of databases and server platforms.

After the configuration is complete, you can click OK to exit or click Test to verify the connection.

MySQL Connections (PHP)

The final connection type is to a MySQL database from PHP. MySQL connections are very easy to make because there are no drivers associated with the connection. PHP itself handles the communication. If, for example, you followed yesterday's instructions, you should be able to connect to day8 already set up on your PHP server. There are a few fields to fill out, shown in Figure 8.17, but nothing you can't handle.

FIGURE 8.17

MySQL connections require no additional drivers, making them one of the more trouble-free connection types.

Connection Name—This is the name of the connection. You'll want to make sure this accurately and succinctly describes the connection. The recommended practice is to prefix the connection name with conn, such as connDay8.

MySQL Server—The network address (or hostname) of the MySQL database server. If you're using your local computer, just enter localhost into the field.

User Name—A username that will be used to make a connection to the database server. The name used in the MySQL import files introduced yesterday is dreamweaver.

Password—The password for the connection. As with the username, if you used the import file discussed yesterday, the password is automatically set to 21days.

Database—Finally, the name of the database stored in MySQL. For today's lesson, this should be day8.

As always, after the configuration is complete, click OK to exit or click Test to verify the connection.

The Databases Panel

Although the Test button in the database connection dialog boxes *does* determine whether the information you've entered is correct, it provides a rather anticlimatic finish to the endeavor of defining a database connection. To see something a bit more viscerally stirring, you can use the Databases panel.

The Databases panel is used to add database connections and view their basic layout. After a database has been added, it is displayed in the panel list and can be expanded to show the three database components to which Dreamweaver MX has access: tables, views, and stored procedures. In turn, each of these elements can be expanded to show the available tables, and so on, that they contain.

If you defined the connection to the MySQL day8 database as described in this chapter, you should be able to manipulate your Databases panel view to look like Figure 8.18. Double-clicking a database within the Databases panel will edit the connection information you used to define it.

FIGURE 8.18

The Databases panel is used to browse the elements in your active database connections.

You'll grow to appreciate the Databases panel in upcoming days. It helps you organize and keep track of the data your applications are talking to. This is a very welcome addition to Dreamweaver MX that was greatly missed in earlier versions.

Summary

Today's lesson covered setting up connections to the databases that will drive your dynamic Dreamweaver MX sites. You can connect to databases either locally or through your deployment application server.

Depending on the application server, many different technologies are available for connecting to a database: OLE DB, ODBC, ColdFusion, JDBC, and MySQL. Macintosh users can use these connection types, but rather than relying on local database drivers, they can take advantage of drivers on the application server itself. The exception to this is when using JDBC or legacy UltraDev 4 ColdFusion configurations. Both of these connection types offer Mac users the capability to connect using JDBC drivers.

Setting up a database connection is probably the most important part of creating with Dreamweaver MX applications. No connection, no application! I strongly urge you to try the MySQL database system discussed yesterday, as it provides a robust backend for the development projects in the book.

Workshop

The Workshop area is meant to reinforce your reading with a series of questions and exercises.

8

Q&A

Q What databases can be used with Dreamweaver MX?

A Almost any modern database includes both ODBC and JDBC drivers—even Microsoft's SQL server. You'll have no problem finding a way to connect to almost any database.

Q How can connections be transferred between computers?

A Connections are stored directly with the site files in a Connections directory. Any user who defines his or her site using the same parameters will have access to the same connection definitions.

Q Why can't you use other databases from PHP?

A You can, but not in the Dreamweaver MX environment. Don't look at this as a serious limitation, however. MySQL recently outperformed many commercial systems in an *eWeek* database server shootout, and it's a bit cheaper than the alternatives.

Q How do I determine the address/hostname of my database server?

A If you set up the database/Web server combination described yesterday, it is the same as the network address of that computer. If you're running *everything* on the same computer, you can use the address 127.0.0.1 or localhost.

Quiz

1. What database connection types are available?
2. How can you determine whether a database connection is correct?
3. Where should you get the information needed to set up connection strings or JDBC connections.
4. Which operating systems can use OLE DB connections?

Quiz Answers

1. Too many to remember! If you know the answer to this, you're working too hard. ODBC, OLE DB, JDBC, MySQL, ColdFusion, and so on.
2. Use the Test button in the connection configuration dialog box, or determine whether you can browse the contents of the database in the Databases panel.
3. From your database documentation! Part of the trouble of trying to document

Dreamweaver MX is that it is *too* flexible. It's therefore impossible to cover every single server, database, and application platform combination.

4. Windows NT/2000/XP operating systems only.

Exercises

1. Try setting up a connection to the day8 data source and testing it.

2. If you're going to be using a database server other than MySQL or MS Access, make absolutely certain you can define databases and connect to them from Dreamweaver MX.

DAY 9

Introducing the Dreamweaver MX Dynamic Tools

Whether you're used to database design, are an expert with Dreamweaver, or can create a custom MS Access or Filemaker application in the blink of an eye, you're still going to need to get used to the tools that Dreamweaver MX uses to keep track of dynamic data. Macromedia does an excellent job of providing an interface that merges traditional database tools into a Web-centric authoring environment. Today, you will learn:

- The Dreamweaver MX terminology for connecting to databases, making queries, and displaying results.

- The purposes of the Server Behaviors and Data Bindings panels.

- How to work with the supplied tools efficiently and choose the right techniques for your authoring style.

Traditional Databases on the Web

Traditional database systems are slightly different from Web-based databases. You have instant access to the data and full control of the flow that the application takes. As you've already learned, the Web is a stateless environment. It does not remember what you've done from one moment to the next. In order to fully use the Dreamweaver MX environment, you must understand the use and limitations of the Dreamweaver MX dynamic authoring tools.

Today's lesson will provide a "catalog" of the available Dreamweaver MX tools and building blocks for online application development. Much like Day 1, "Getting Started," introduced you to the tools used to build static Web sites, here you'll learn their dynamic counterparts.

If you've used Microsoft Access or many other desktop database systems, you should recognize some of the constructs that Dreamweaver MX uses to represent data within the system. Three primary tools can be used to get your database from the desktop to the Web: Connections, Data Bindings, and Server Behaviors.

Connections

Connections were introduced in Day 8, "Defining a Dynamic Site," and are used to connect both Dreamweaver MX and the application server of your choice to a database server. Connections operate on a site wide basis and are specific to the projects that you create. The data for connections are stored in the Connections folder within your site directory.

Because connections are stored with the site, they are available on any machine where the site has been defined with the same parameters.

To access the tools that are discussed in the rest of the book, you'll need to have a database connection in place—that's why connections received their own chapter! You might want to define a database connection for this chapter (connDay9) simply so you can access the tools and see their setup screens as they are introduced.

Server Behaviors

After you've created a database connection, the next step in creating a dynamic site is setting up a server behavior to work with the connection. Server behaviors are added and manipulated using the Server Behaviors panel, shown in Figure 9.1.

FIGURE 9.1

The Server Behaviors panel is used to add and reconfigure behaviors in your document.

You can think of the Server Behaviors panel as a more advanced version of the standard behavior panel that you use when creating standard HTML pages. The difference is that, instead of relying on the client program to execute the behavior, it is executed on the server. This means that you're no longer relying on unreliable technology such as JavaScript to power the pages; you're using the processing power of your server to add dynamic functionality.

No matter what you program using server behaviors, your application will operate on any browser platform regardless of whether it has JavaScript turned on. As long as your server is configured correctly, you can author dynamic applications without the need to worry about the deployment platform. Unfortunately, this also has implications for maintaining server and database security—but those issues are well beyond the scope of this book, or even the topic of Web design and development.

Note

Server behaviors aren't *always* client independent. If the server behavior relies on cookies, it must be enabled in the client browser. This, however, is more reliable than a JavaScript-based solution.

Server behaviors are code fragments that Dreamweaver MX uses to construct a working program. These are prewritten pieces of code pieced together so that the end result is a complete working section of embedded code.

Note

If you're interested in seeing how these puzzle pieces are put together, look through the Dreamweaver MX Configuration directory. You'll see many files representing all the different server actions. Written in JavaScript, these routines drive everything that Dreamweaver MX does. If you edit the configuration files, however, understand that the stress-tested Macromedia code will

no longer be used in your final applications. If you're an experienced programmer, you probably won't care about this. If you're a beginner, think of
changing the code as "voiding your warranty"—it will become extremely
difficult to find other Dreamweaver MX users who will be able to help you.

Data Bindings

The most common server behavior is a query that retrieves information from the database. After being retrieved, the data is made available to Dreamweaver MX through the
Bindings panel. Besides database information, you can also add session variables and
cookies and other pieces of dynamic information to the Bindings panel. It keeps and
organizes all of the information that Dreamweaver MX has available for use on your
Web pages. Figure 9.2 shows the Bindings panel in use.

FIGURE 9.2

*The Bindings panel
tracks available data
and binds it to HTML
objects.*

Besides simply tracking this data, the Bindings panel, true to its name, *binds* data to
HTML objects. If, for example, you have a list of names in a database, you can bind
them to the cells of an HTML table to display them on your screen.

Although your interaction with the Bindings panel is usually limited to the design phase
of building your Web site, it is one of the most important and intuitive tools in the
Dreamweaver MX dynamic arsenal. You'll use this tool frequently over the course of the
next week and a half.

Standard Server Behaviors

At a basic level, Dreamweaver MX's dynamic Web functions are really very simple—
they let you display and change information in a database. The magic is in the way that
you combine the available behaviors. Let's take a look at the base-level server behaviors

that are available for (almost) all of the application servers in Dreamweaver MX. You'll use all of these, in one way or another, throughout the rest of the book.

Recordsets (Query)

A *recordset* is a construct that represents all the records returned after the database is queried. Within Dreamweaver MX, you define a recordset by supplying the application with the SQL code that you want it to execute (or by pointing and clicking to develop a simple query), and then sitting back and letting it do the work. The results are returned to the Bindings panel.

9

Although a recordset can contain multiple records, only the first record is accessible after the recordset is created. In order to access other records, you'll need to use additional server behaviors that operate on the recordset that you've defined.

Two modes of recordset definition exist—the most basic is the simple query, shown in Figure 9.3.

FIGURE 9.3

A simple query is used for noncomplex recordsets.

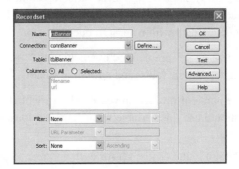

The simple query is used to select a group of records from a database table with as little work as possible. You can use this mode of the recordset creation to select records based on parameters passed in the URL line and sort the final query using a column in the table. Simple mode constrains you to automatically generated SQL statements. Sometimes, however, this isn't enough to work with.

By clicking the Advanced button, you can switch to a far more flexible recordset creation window, as seen in Figure 9.4.

From the advanced recordset creation screen, you can enter SQL queries directly into the server. This is the only mode in which you can truly harness the power of your database server. Here you can access tables, views, and stored procedures. It also introduces the Dreamweaver MX query variable.

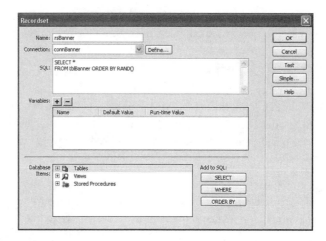

FIGURE 9.4

Advanced queries give much greater control over the application.

Dreamweaver MX variables are a way of attaching outside information—such as request values, cookies, and session variables—to a local variable within Dreamweaver MX that can be used within a query. Impossible in the simple query, these Dreamweaver MX creations let you include outside data within an SQL query.

Dreamweaver MX query variables are defined by clicking the "+" button and adding specifying a variable name, default value, and a runtime value:

variable name—The name of the Dreamweaver MX variable that will be taking on dynamic data. You should use this variable within single quotes to add its value to the SQL view.

default value—A default value can be set for each variable so that if dynamic data isn't available, it takes on the default value. This is useful for making certain that a query always runs, regardless of whether a user supplied the appropriate information.

runtime value—The value that the variable will take on with the application is run on the server. A runtime value is usually set to the value of a form variable, or another piece of dynamic data.

If you plan on implementing anything complicated within Dreamweaver MX, such as searches or other queries that process user input, you'll be using Dreamweaver MX's query variables.

Insert Record

Adding information to a database is accomplished through the Insert Record server behavior. This behavior takes the result of an HTML form and inserts it into a table within a database connection that you have defined. This function only operates on an HTML form—but with some creative programming, you can use this for more than just asking users to type in some information.

Before you can insert, update, or delete records in a database table, you must define a form within your Web pages. Each of the server behaviors that modifies database information is triggered from the input of a form. Figure 9.5 shows the Insert Record behavior configuration screen.

9

FIGURE 9.5

The Insert Record behavior stores data from an HTML form into a database table.

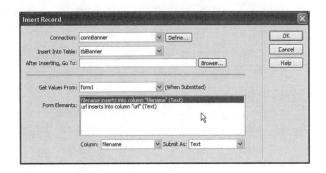

Note

Although we aren't really creating a Web application at this time, you can view these server behaviors if you add a form to an empty document.

The Insert Record behavior configuration is similar to most of the server behaviors, in that it requires you to set a connection and a table to operate on. After that, it requires a bit of explanation:

Form—Because a page can have multiple forms, you'll need to tell Dreamweaver MX what form will be supplying the information for the database table. You must be sure that the form contains all the fields necessary to fill the table, however.

Form Elements—All the Form fields are shown in the Form Elements list. In order for Dreamweaver MX to match up the elements of a form with their database counterparts, you must click through the list of elements, and then use the first Column pop-up menu to choose a database column, and the second pop-up to set the type of data (Text/Numeric) that the field will be returning.

Go To URL—After data has been inserted into the database, the server behavior will redirect the user's browser to a new page. This is the URL that the user should be sent to. Yes, you can send the user back to the same page.

You'll find that the other database-access behaviors bear a striking resemblance to the Insert Record behavior.

Update Record

Although it might seem as if an Insert behavior is identical to an Update, they're two very different behaviors. In order to change information in a database, you must use the Update Record server behavior. This server behavior's setup screen is shown in Figure 9.6.

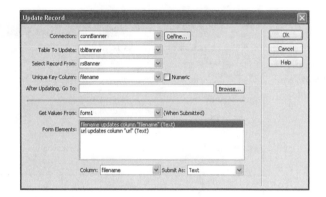

The similarities between the Insert and Update server behaviors are obvious—in fact, they're virtually identical. There are, however, two new values you'll need to set above and beyond an Insert Record behavior:

Select Record From—Unlike an Insert, an Update must operate on an existing record. Where do we get records? From recordsets. The Select Record From field chooses the recordset that contains the record you want to update.

Unique Key Column—The unique field that identifies the record being inserted. Unfortunately, Dreamweaver MX only supports single value primary keys, so you'll have to take this into consideration during your database design. If you want to learn more about keys, Day 6, "Introduction to Dynamic Web Applications and Database Designs," is the place to go.

Delete Record

Because you can add information to the database, you should also have the ability to delete it. This server behavior does just that. Nothing more. Nothing less. Figure 9.7 shows the Delete Record behavior's configuration.

The configuration of the Delete Record behavior is a combination of the other behaviors—you define a recordset that chooses the record to delete, provide a form that will trigger the action, and then add it to your page.

FIGURE 9.7

The Delete Record behavior deletes records upon submitting a form.

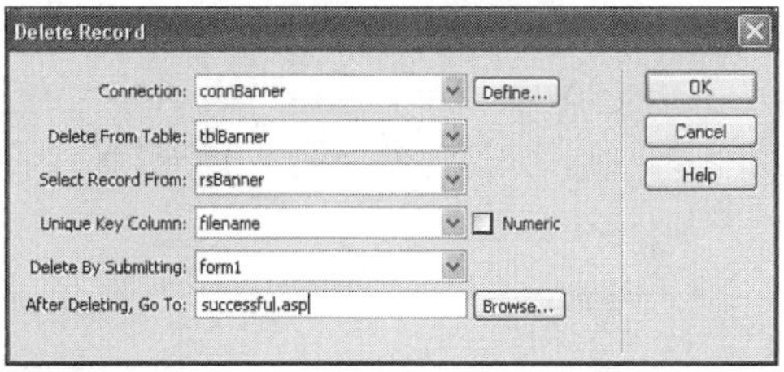

Command

The catch-all server behavior is the Command behavior, which is shown in Figure 9.8. This behavior lets you execute a stored procedure or straight SQL and return a recordset (if necessary). What makes this different from other behaviors is that it includes the capability to tie the behavior to Dreamweaver MX variables in ways that are otherwise impossible.

FIGURE 9.8

The Command behavior lets you execute stored procedures or other pieces of SQL on the server.

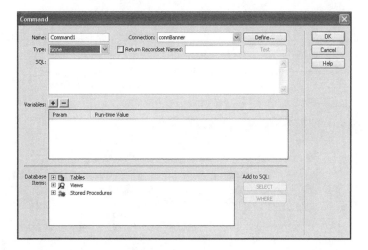

When defining a command, you'll recognize that it is very similar to the Insert Record and Recordset behaviors. After naming the command, you must choose the type—either one of several standard SQL commands (Insert, Update, and so on) or a stored procedure. If a recordset is returned after the command is executed, you must click the Return Recordset Named check box, and choose a name for the new query.

To make this tool even more flexible, you can use the Dreamweaver MX variables in the same way as a standard recordset. This means that you can use session data, cookies, or anything you want inside the body of the command. Unlike the standard Insert behavior, a Command behavior can take URL parameters and other pieces of data and use them in an INSERT statement. If you're interested in one of the more advanced features of the Dreamweaver MX authoring environment, this is it. Coupled with Day 12, "Writing Advanced Database Queries," this behavior can be used to directly access your database and its stored functions.

Why Is This Different from Any Other Database Application Development?

Assuming that you've worked with databases before, you're probably saying to yourself "sounds just like a normal database, so what's the big deal?"

The difference between a traditional database and these server behaviors is that the action is not immediate. Each time you use a server behavior, it is expecting information from a Web page, and it uses that information to execute the server behavior. What makes this confusing is that the code for each server behavior is stored in the page that is submitting the data—even though that page is not likely to be the page displayed after the behavior is executed.

Here's how it works:

1. An HTML page is created that will feed information from a form to the database. This information can be a record number to delete, information to insert, and so on.

2. A server behavior to work with the data is inserted into the document. This is typically one of the Insert, Update, or Delete behaviors.

3. The behavior is configured to redirect the user's browser to another Web page after it is executed.

4. The Web page is deployed.

5. When the users browse the page, they fill out the form and click Submit.

6. The form submits the data *back to the same page* that contains the server behavior, which is then executed.

7. After finishing, the behavior redirects the browser to another page, or even another Web site.

Hopefully that helps clarify things a little bit. It's a somewhat bizarre sequence of events, but it is the model you need to become accustomed to in order to author effective multi-page sites.

Not all server behaviors, however, store information in a database, or redirect the user to a separate Web page.

Let's take a look at some of the other behaviors you'll need for your applications.

Recordset Navigation Server Behaviors

Displaying and modifying information in a database is the primary purpose of Dreamweaver MX. Using the four primary server behaviors that we've discussed is a good start, but not enough for a significant Web application. For example, the recordset that we've defined contains 20 records—so how can we display all of them on the screen?

Better yet, what if the recordset contained 2,000 records? How can we give the users access to all the records without dumping 2,000 entries to a single HTML page?

Everything you need to solve these problems (and several others) is covered by a series of additional server behaviors that work with the recordset data to alter and control its display.

Repeat Region

The Repeat Region server behavior operates as a loop over a recordset. You can use this to display multiple records within a recordset—as many as are available, or limited to a certain number. The behavior doesn't just repeat field values, but everything that falls within a region.

For example, fields from a database table are typically displayed in an HTML table to keep them aligned. To use the Repeat Region behavior in this manner, you would add the fields you want to repeat to a row in a table, and then select the row and apply the behavior. All the data in the design view that you've selected will be repeated over the range of records you've chosen to display. Figure 9.9 shows the Repeat Region server behavior configuration screen.

FIGURE 9.9

The Repeat Region behavior is used to display multiple records.

After selecting a region of text to repeat, you will need to set the recordset that you will be looping through, as well as the maximum number of records to display.

Recordset Paging

Most people don't want to display 2,000 records on a screen. In fact, most browsers couldn't handle rendering a table with 2,000 lines. If you limit the number of records displayed based on the Repeat Region behavior, you'll also need some way to provide Next and Previous links to display additional information in the database.

The Recordset Paging behaviors can be employed to provide navigation within an existing recordset. These behaviors are found under the Move To submenu of the Server Behaviors panel:

Move To First Record—No matter which record was last displayed, this server behavior will move just to the start of the recordset.

Move To Previous Record—Move backward through a recordset. If you want to move back to a previous screen of records, use this behavior.

Move To Next Record—Similar to the previous record, this behavior advances the recordset one page forward.

Move To Last Record—Jumps to the last record in the recordset. Between the Move To First Record and Move To Last Record behaviors, you can quickly provide your users a way to navigate from one end of a database to another.

Move To Specific Record—Rather than moving relative to the current record, this behavior moves a record based on an identifier that you supply in the URL.

 Note
> It's important to realize that these behaviors operate on a specific recordset, not a complete table in the database. *Recordsets* are queries that contain data from one or more tables. If you use the Move To Next Record behavior, for example, the next record might not be the next record in the database table—but it is the next record within the recordset.

The Move To behaviors all feature the same basic configuration—you choose a recordset and a link that will activate the server behavior, and you're in business. Figure 9.10 shows a Move To Next Record behavior.

FIGURE 9.10

The Move To behaviors take a link and a recordset, and then move within a defined recordset.

Show Region

Although not needed for displaying records from the database, the Show Region behavior set is actually my favorite server-based behavior set. This collection of behaviors does exactly what you would expect from its name—it shows a region within a document. What could that possibly be good for, you ask?

The obvious use, and the only one documented in Macromedia's own materials, is the use of the behavior to conditionally show a region on the screen based on the contents of a recordset. The Show Region behavior is triggered based on the contents (or lack thereof) of a recordset.

For example, suppose that you have a Next button that takes you to the next page in a group of records (using the Move To Next Record behavior). When you reach the end of the recordset, the Next button becomes pointless. You can add the Show Region If Not Last Record behavior to show the Next button only if the last record hasn't been reached.

Shown in Figure 9.11, the configuration of the Show Region behaviors is very simple.

FIGURE 9.11

Choose the right condition to test, and then the recordset to test.

9

Tip

Showing Next and Previous buttons is indeed an obvious use of the Show Region behavior, but they aren't the most useful choices.

The Show Region behavior can be used to show *and* hide information—creating Web pages whose content changes completely, based on the results of a recordset. Remember, if you want to hide information based on a condition, you can accomplish the same thing by showing the region when the opposite condition is true. It's also important to keep in mind that this is a server behavior, meaning that the "hide" effect takes place on the server. The information is *not* transferred to the client, and then hidden.

In a few days you'll learn how to use this behavior to authenticate user logins, and several other interesting techniques.

Dynamic Elements

The Dynamic Elements server behaviors are probably one of the most common behaviors that you'll use, as they are used to add dynamic information directly to your Web documents.

There are five types of dynamic elements:

Dynamic Text—Inserts a database table field value directly into the Document Design view.

Dynamic List/Menu—Fills a pop-up menu or selection list with items from a database table. Also allows the database to drive the initial selection in the list or menu.

Dynamic Text Field—Inserts a recordset field into the value attribute of an HTML input field. Often used for restoring user values that were entered previously.

Dynamic Check Box—Takes an existing check box and determines if it should be rendered as checked by comparing a database value to a known value.

Dynamic Radio—Similar to the check box; the dynamic radio buttons are set to selected, based on a value in a database.

Coupled with a Repeat Region behavior, the Dynamic Text behavior will be used to generate most of your online database information displays.

User Authentication

The User Authentication behaviors provide a means of restricting Web page access based on usernames, passwords, and access levels stored in a database table. Dreamweaver MX's authentication behaviors compare input from an HTML form to the database information. If they match, a session variable called MM_Username is set. On subsequent pages, this session variable can be checked to see whether the user has access to the page. There are a total of four authentication behaviors, which we'll take a look at now.

Log In User

The Log In User behavior, shown in Figure 9.12, has a rather large configuration screen, but is really very easy to set up. This behavior should be added directly to a login screen. Everything is handled automatically—all you need to do is supply a form.

FIGURE 9.12

Configure the login behavior so that it can compare form fields to database fields.

To set up the login page, complete the four regions of the behavior configuration screen based on your site and database:

Get Input From Form—Choose the HTML form that will supply input to the authentication behavior. You also need to tell Dreamweaver MX which field contains the username, and which contains the password.

Validate Using Connection—Select the database connection as well as the table and table columns containing the username and password that you've stored for a user. These must be stored as plain text—not encrypted.

Go To—If the username/password from the form matches what is in the database, you can direct the user's browser to a URL of your choice. You can also select the Go To Previous URL option, which will send the users back to a page they tried to load but were denied access to. For login failures, you can supply another URL that the users will be sent to.

Restrict Access Based On—There are two options for this area—to restrict based on username and password, or username, password, and access level. The former is self-explanatory, whereas the latter allows you to set multiple levels of users who can access different pages (guest, administrator, user, and so on). If you are implementing user levels, you must select the column in your database table that includes the access level.

That's all you need to log in a user. After processing the server behavior, the user will be redirected to the screen of your choice. It is up to you to design these screens!

Restrict Access To Page

If a user is logging in, there usually is a reason for it—such as restricted access to certain pages. The Restrict Access To Page behavior allows you to verify that a user has the proper credentials to access a Web page before it is displayed on the screen. It is assumed that you would have already added a Log In User behavior to your document before you start using the Restrict Access behavior.

To use this behavior, simply add it to a page that you want only certain users to have access to. As shown in Figure 9.13, the behavior consists of nothing more than a choice of how to restrict the user's access (based on just a valid login, or a valid login and a user level). If the user has not logged into the site correctly, the user is redirected to the URL supplied in the If Access Denied field.

FIGURE 9.13

Restrict access to a page based on a user-name and password, or a username, password, and access level.

If you want to restrict a user's access based on level, the user must have logged in using a Log In User behavior with the same restriction technique. If it is the first time you've used access levels, you must click the Define button to add levels to the selection list. Use the "+" button to add a level and "–" to remove one. Be very careful when creating the levels; they must match up perfectly with their database counterparts.

Assuming that your levels are defined, just choose a level from the list you've created, and *only* users with corresponding database records including that access level will be allowed to view the page.

Log Out User

The Log Out User behavior does exactly what it implies. This behavior really isn't necessary in your Web site, but it does have its uses. When a user logs in, a session cookie is set to the browser. This cookie only lasts the length of time the browser is running. If the user quits Netscape or Internet Explorer, the user has effectively logged out of the system without any need for the Log Out User server behavior.

If you want to give a user the ability to log out of an account and then log back in under a different account, all in one session, you'll need to implement the Log Out User behavior, shown in Figure 9.14.

FIGURE 9.14

Choose when the logout should occur and the page to go to after it is done.

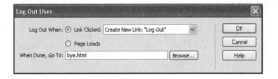

Configure the behavior by defining when the logout action occurs (after clicking a link or when the page with the behavior loads), and then choose a page that the user should be directed to when the logout action is complete.

Again, this behavior is not at all necessary. It is very unlikely that you'll have many users who even pay attention to a logout link on your page—such is the way of the Web.

Check New Username

Sometimes a Web site needs to have a Register Online section to enable users to create their own accounts from within their browser. Usually this involves picking a username and password. The trouble is that after you have a few thousand users on your site, the chances that they pick a unique username are slim to none. (If you've ever tried to get a personalized Hotmail or Yahoo account, you know what I'm talking about.)

The Check New Username behavior eliminates this condition by verifying that a username is unique before it is saved to a database. Used in conjunction with an Insert

Record behavior, the Check New Username behavior takes just two parameters to work: the database field containing the username field, and a page to redirect the browser to if the username already exists. A sample of this behavior is seen in Figure 9.15.

FIGURE 9.15

Choose the column that holds the user- name and where to send the user if the name already exists.

9

As you develop registration pages, you'll find this extremely useful, and a great way to eliminate INSERT errors.

Data Bindings

Although the server behaviors define what your Web application does *with* and *to* data- base information, the Bindings panel provides more design-centric control over your data. This panel is your central resource for determining what data you have access to, which portions of the HTML it is attached to, and how you can display it.

Sources

The first use of the Bindings panel is to create "sources" of information for use inside your Web application. These sources include recordsets, request variables, session vari- ables, and more. Each source can then be used to move data into your application design.

Note

You might notice that a recordset can be created and used as a data source. This is *identical* to the "recordset (query)" server behavior—adding either one accomplishes the exact same thing—they're two routes to the same result.

To add a Bindings source, click the "+" button and choose from the available options. By far, the most frequently used source will be the Recordset source, but the others are equally functional.

For a quick example, let's try to author a page that does the exact same thing as the showname Web example in Day 6. If you don't remember, this example demonstrated how parameters are passed on a URL line. Specifically, we passed two variables: firstname and lastname, to the following URL:

http://www.cutelittledogs.com/showname.php?firstname=John&lastname=Ray

Which, in turn, printed the first and last names. Nothing complicated, but it demonstrated how input can be provided to a Web application through the URL. Using the Bindings panel, you can re-create this simple application in a matter of seconds.

Make sure you've defined a site for the day (Day 9—no database connection is necessary for this example). Create and save a new ASP document called showname.asp.

Now, you want to accept the variables firstname and lastname as input into the page, and then display them on the screen. To do this, you must first declare each variable as a Bindings source.

1. Click the "+" button in the Bindings panel. Choose Request Variable from the pop-up list.

2. Set the Type field to Request, which is a "generic" class for many types of incoming data.

3. Enter firstname into the Name field, and then click OK, as seen in Figure 9.16.

4. Repeat the process for the lastname variable.

FIGURE 9.16

Set the Type to Request and enter the name of the URL parameter.

Your Bindings panel should now contain an object called Request, which contains both of the defined source variables. Click the disclosure arrow or "+" symbol in front of the Request object to reveal the two sources, as shown in Figure 9.17.

FIGURE 9.17

The firstname *and* lastname *variables should now be available in the Bindings panel.*

To finish the simple application so that firstname and lastname are displayed onscreen when showname.asp is loaded, simply drag their names from the Bindings panel into your document design window. They will show up as {Request.firstname} and {Request.lastname} in the HTML view. When accessed through your Web server and supplied the appropriate firstname and lastname variables through the URL, however, the page will substitute the appropriate values into the document.

When dragging the two Request variable sources to the design window, you inadvertently discovered the *other* use for the Bindings panel—binding a source to an HTML object. In the case of the two URL parameters, you simple bound them to text in design window.

Design Window Bindings

Design window bindings extend well beyond dynamic text. For example, rather than adding a server behavior to dynamically generate a pop-up menu or selection list, you can bind an existing pop-up menu to a recordset database table field.

You can bind to literally hundreds of attributes—names, colors, selected items, and so on. Anything that Dreamweaver MX recognizes as an attribute of the object can be bound to dynamic data. The bound attribute can be set at any time by selecting the Data Bindings source and using the Bind To pop-up menu to select an attribute of the currently active HTML object in the Design window.

Data Formats

For each bound piece of data, you can select a format in which it will be made available to Dreamweaver MX—either for display, or other data binding use. The formats are accessible by clicking the pop-up menu arrow in the Format field next to a Bindings source. Several categories of formats are available:

Date/Time—If the data being bound is a date or time, you can choose the way it is displayed by using one of these formats.

Currency—The Currency formats are used to represent money. Employing a currency format eliminates the need to add currency symbols (such as $) manually to the display.

Number—If you're working with numbers, the Number formats can be used to handle rounding, decimal places, and signed values.

Percent—Identical to the Number formats, but geared toward percentages.

AlphaCase—Alters text data so that it is in uppercase or lowercase.

Trim—Many pieces of textual information stored in databases (especially legacy systems) are padded with spaces. The Trim formats remove spaces from one or both ends.

Other types of formats include URL encoding that encodes string data so it can be passed through a URL. (Special characters are changed to their hex equivalents.)

If you can't find a format that you want, you can use the Edit Format List option from the bottom of the Format list to add a new format, or edit an existing format. The Master Edit Format List screen is shown in Figure 9.18.

FIGURE 9.18

You can edit or add formats to Dreamweaver MX.

To add a new format:

1. Click the "+" button.
2. Choose the type of format you want to add (Number, Currency, Percent) from the pop-up menu.
3. Set the attributes for the format that you are creating—such as the number of leading zeros, decimal places, and so on.
4. Click OK.

You'll immediately be able to access the new format from within the format pop-up menu of the Bindings panel. A sample format configuration screen is shown in Figure 9.19.

FIGURE 9.19

Customize formats for your Web application needs.

Indirect Data Bindings

In some cases data bindings are created through other means than directly accessing the Bindings panel. Prevalent throughout the Dreamweaver MX interface are "lightning bolt" icons. Clicking one of these icons, seen in Figure 9.20, opens a separate window that lists the available data bindings sources and allows you to bind to available sources, just as you would in the Bindings panel.

FIGURE 9.20

Lightning bolt icons are used to bind the associated field, attribute, or element to a data bindings source.

You'll see the lightning bolt icon used in the Properties panel, Tag Inspector, and many other places in the interface. Just one more example of the many methods that Dreamweaver MX provides for accomplishing a task.

Summary

Similar to the first day of the first week, today introduced you to the tools that you will be using for the rest of the book. I know you're anxious to get your hands on the Dreamweaver MX tools and create some sites, so we'll dive right in tomorrow. Later in the week, we'll take an in-depth look at the SQL language itself so that you can write advanced queries beyond what the simple point-and-click interfaces can get you.

You should come away from this lesson with an understanding of what server behaviors are, where they are located within the Dreamweaver MX interface, and how you'll be using them. Additionally, the purpose of the Bindings panel should be clear.

Used to provide an interface to your database queries and other dynamic data sources, you'll use the Bindings panel frequently when creating dynamic Web sites. The Bindings panel also provides a means of binding an HTML object in the document design view to a data source.

Finally, you've seen that Dreamweaver MX gives you the ability to format data on-the-fly as it is pulled from the database. Because you're likely to encounter data that varies from record to record, this will, in many cases, be a godsend.

Although the purpose of every tool might not be obvious, you'll learn by doing throughout the rest of the book. Don't worry, we'll cover the behaviors in-depth when you meet up with them again; there is no need to memorize everything we've covered today.

Workshop

The Workshop area is meant to reinforce your reading with a series of questions and exercises.

Q&A

Q What limits are there on advanced queries?

A The limits are likely set by your database server. Dreamweaver MX sends the query you define directly to your server; it does not parse the SQL itself. Extremely large queries have been known to "confuse" earlier versions of Dreamweaver MX, so be sure to test large queries before saving.

Q Is this all there is?

A Unless you want to start programming by hand (which we'll get into in Day 21, "Advanced Dreamweaver MX Features"), yes. Dreamweaver MX provides a very limited set of dynamic features. What you see here is essentially *all* you get. Don't be discouraged—it's actually pretty easy to combine these behaviors into some interesting Web applications, which you'll start learning about tomorrow.

Q What does the Get More Formats menu selection do when I choose a format for a data binding?

A Anytime you see "Get More…" in a menu, you can choose it to launch your Web browser and instantly be taken to Macromedia's download site for Dreamweaver MX extensions.

Quiz

1. What does the recordset behavior do?
2. How do you execute an Insert command directly on the server?
3. Does Dreamweaver MX support multiple value primary keys for a query?
4. Is there another way to add dynamic features to your site rather than adding server behaviors?
5. How can you control the format of the output of a field?

Quiz Answers

1. The recordset behavior performs a query on your database server—the results are made accessible through the Bindings panel.
2. The Command server behavior is the only way to execute an insert directly.
3. Nope. Not currently. If you have control over your database, define the tables so that they only have a single value primary key. All examples in this book are designed in this manner.
4. Yes, the Bindings panel can be used to directly bind HTML objects to information in a database and other data sources.

5. Setting a format value in the Bindings panel will force the data being used into a predefined format—such as a date or percentage.

Exercises

1. View each of the screens that you learned about today, and experiment with connecting them to one of the database connections that you created yesterday.

2. Explore the Bindings panel. You can work with the `showname.asp` example described in the chapter.

3. If you've programmed Web applications before, try to relate your existing programs to the server behaviors you have available. You'll find that, although different from traditional programming languages, the Dreamweaver MX programming environment is flexible enough to handle a wide variety of authoring tasks.

9

DAY **10**

Creating Database-Driven Web Pages

With the appropriate connections to a database server in place, Dreamweaver MX becomes a powerful visual development tool. The first step in developing dynamic applications is getting information out of the database and onto your Web page. In yesterday's lesson you learned how to create a connection to a database and verify that it was active. Today, you will take this a step further by:

- Pulling information from a database and putting it online using server behaviors.

- Formatting dynamic information with the Dreamweaver MX HTML tools.

- Adding graphics that are driven by your database design in order to completely customize your display.

From Database to Web

Databases, as you know, store information. Web pages display information. Connect the two, and you have a Web page that displays the information stored in a database. This is the essence of dynamic Web sites, and is what you will learn to do today.

Note
> Almost every other project that you will work on in the book will pull from today's lesson, so be sure to pay attention!

Pulling information from a database and displaying it onscreen is often called *reporting* in database lingo. Although a Web version of a report *is* what we're aiming for, it would be nice to go beyond the general conception of what a report page should look like.

One of the biggest problems with many database-driven sites is that they *look* database-driven. This doesn't have to be the case.

Careful design using the Dreamweaver MX tools can produce a Web site that uses a database for its backend information, but maintains a free-flowing approach and doesn't alienate the viewer. It's simple to dump a few hundred names and pictures onto a screen, but it takes finesse to do it in a manner that a person can easily use.

By the end of the day, you'll be a wizard with Dreamweaver's basic database server behaviors and will be ready to move on to more challenging tasks.

Throughout the day's lesson, we'll work with several databases and create a number of test pages. Before continuing, you should connect to `http://downloads.cutelittle-dogs.com/` and download the files for the Day 10 projects. You'll be setting up sample projects that require the files and folders in the archive.

A Table of a Table

A collection of information in a database is called a *table*. As you might guess, a table of data from a database is easily represented as a table within HTML. Dreamweaver MX makes it convenient to design a program that does just that—however, without a little work, you'll find that your information is probably lacking a bit on the style end.

Today's database, named `day10`, contains a few tables that we'll work to put online. If you followed the instructions in Day 7, "Preparing a Server for Dreamweaver MX," this data should already be accessible in either a MySQL or Access data source on your test server. If not, create your own `day10` database, and populate it with the sample data that is presented throughout the chapter. It is important that we're all working with the same information; otherwise things will get mighty strange mighty quickly. Don't worry; the chapters are laid out so that it should be very difficult to *not* have the right information and files in place at any given time. If you don't skip around too much, you won't get lost.

Table Definitions

The first table of sample data we'll display on the Web is a listing of dogs for www.cutelittledogs.com. My girlfriend and I have two dogs between us, if we decided to start allowing other owners across the country and around the world to share stories of their dogs, one of the first steps would be creating a database like this. For our purposes a simple table will do. Table 10.1 shows the definition of the database table tblSimpleDoglist. Make sure that this is defined in your day10 database before continuing.

10

TABLE 10.1 The Definition of the tblSimpleDoglist Table

Fieldname	Description	SQL Data Type
AKCname	The registered AKC name of the dog.	varchar(250)
shortname	A short "family" name that the dog is typically called.	varchar(250)
breed	The dog's breed.	varchar(250)
birthday	The dog's birth date.	date
owner	The name of the owner.	varchar(250)

This table holds a few pieces of information similar to what you saw in Day 6's database normalization example. The dog's AKC name, short name, breed, birthday, and owner's name are stored. If you read Day 6, "Introduction to Dynamic Web Applications and Database Design," you know that the AKC name is unique for each animal, so it will be the primary key.

Note

Normalization fanatics might want to break owner's name into a separate table. For our purposes, however, the dog's owner is just another simple attribute describing the dog and can be left as is.

Don't get me wrong, normalization is a good thing, but in some cases it can actually make a project and its maintenance more difficult than if a few rules are broken here and there. Shhh...don't tell anyone!

Sample Data

Having defined tblSimpleDoglist, we're ready to go, right? Not quite. Having a table defined is the first step, but if you want pull information from the table and display it onscreen, it is wise to actually add information into the system. If you've gone the MySQL or Access route, this has already been done for you. If not, you can use the SQL statements in Appendix B, "MySQL Quick Function Reference," or the sample data in Table 10.2 to populate the dog list.

TABLE 10.2 Sample Data for the tblSimpleDoglist Table

AKCname	Shortname	Breed	Birthday	Owner
Maddy The Great	Maddy	Pomeranian	12/23/98	John Ray
Coco The Barking Queen	Coco	American Eskimo	11/12/00	Robyn Ness
Abull King of the Danes	Abull	Great Dane	5/5/95	Kama Dobbs
Shamrock of Wilmar	Sham	Irish Setter	2/13/97	Jack Derifaj
Mojo bearded charcoal	Mojo	Scottish Terrier	7/4/98	Anne Groves

Tip

If, at any time, you want to verify that the data for a project is indeed in MySQL, you can use the mysql <database name> command-line utility to open the named database, and then a SELECT command to view the contents. For example, to view the contents of tblSimpleDoglist, type **SELECT * from tblSimpleDoglist \G** at the MySQL prompt:

```
mysql> select * from tblSImpleDoglist \G
*************************** 1. row ***************************
  AKCname: Maddy The Great
shortname: Maddy
    breed: Pomeranian
 birthday: 1998-12-23
    owner: John Ray
*************************** 2. row ***************************
  AKCname: Coco The Barking Queen
shortname: Coco
    breed: American Eskimo
 birthday: 2000-11-12
    owner: Robyn Ness
*************************** 3. row ***************************
  AKCname: Abull King of the Danes
shortname: Abull
```

```
        breed: Great Dane
     birthday: 1995-05-05
        owner: Kama Dobbs
*************************** 4. row ***************************
      AKCname: Shamrock of Wilmar
    shortname: Sham
        breed: Irish Setter
     birthday: 1997-02-13
        owner: Jack Derifaj
*************************** 5. row ***************************
      AKCname: Mojo bearded charcoal
    shortname: Mojo
        breed: Scottish Terrier
     birthday: 1998-07-04
        owner: Anne Groves
5 rows in set (0.01 sec)
```

If you're using MS Access, you should be able to open the database files directly in Access and view the contents.

Let's get this data onto the Web.

Implementing a Dreamweaver MX Front End

With the database sitting pleasantly in the back end, it's time to create the Web front end. You'll need to set up a connection to the database system. Refer to Day 8, "Defining a Dynamic Site," for detailed information on creating database connections. We'll still cover the basic steps, but if you need more information, read through Day 8.

Macintosh and Windows, Friends at Last

In the first version of this book, I used a Macintosh PowerBook as my design tool, with a MySQL and NT IIS Server doing the dirty work. For this revision, I've turned the tables. Windows XP is the design tool and a Mac OS X Server is the deployment application server. Whatever your choice of design/serving platforms (within reason!), Dreamweaver MX can make them work together.

Prepare your system by completing each of these steps.

1. Define a new dynamic ASP site using the Edit Sites option in the Site menu. Name the new site Day 10.

2. Copy the contents of the Day 10 folder archive, downloadable from http://downloads.cutelittledogs.com/.

3. Be certain that the remote server is ready—this was covered in Day 7. Also check to make sure that your site definition includes all the information it needs to send and retrieve files from the remote server.

4. If you aren't using the MySQL or Access databases we defined and seeded in Day 6, create the day10 database as discussed earlier today.

If you've successfully followed all these preparation steps, everything is ready for your first database-driven Web page.

Connecting to the Database

The first step in getting data from the day10 database onto the Web is *connecting* to the database. In order to define a connection, you must first create a new document.

Use the New option from the File menu to create an empty ASP file on your computer. Save the file to your site with the name simplelist.asp.

Next, open the Databases panel using the Window menu. Click the "+" button and choose Data Source Name (DSN) connection, as seen in Figure 10.1.

FIGURE 10.1

Click the "+" button in the Databases panel to add a new database connection.

The connection dialog box will appear. Here you must fill in the necessary information to connect to the day10 data source. If you're using another application server, the configuration will be slightly different (see Day 8 for more information). Figure 10.2 displays the connection setup.

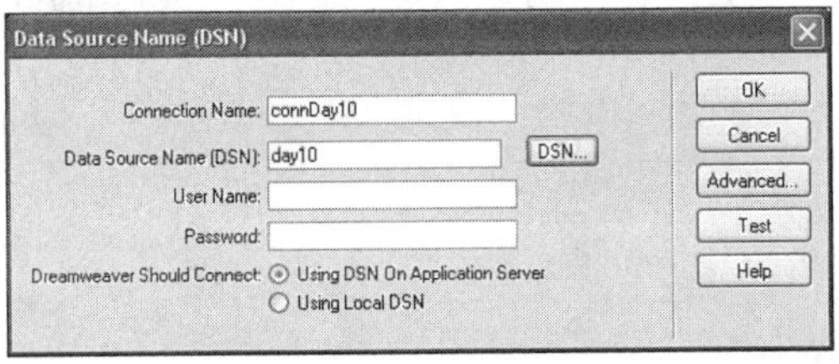

FIGURE 10.2

Create the connection to the Day 10 data source.

Complete the connection setup by entering the connection name connDay10 and the name of the data source (day10). Be sure to connect using the DSN on the application server. Click OK to save the connection.

You should now be able to expand the Day 10 and Tables objects in the Databases panel to view the tblSimpleDoglist table. The connection is complete.

Why Do I See Other Tables in the *day10* Database?

There are several variations of the example we're working on now that will be uncovered throughout today's lesson—each uses a slightly different table. In general, I've broken tables out into separate databases only when they're completely different exercises. You'll usually see one database per chapter, with a few tables inside. Only once or twice will a chapter cover a wide enough spread of information to warrant multiple databases.

10

Creating a Recordset

There's only one table that we're worried about right now—tblSimpleDoglist—so there's really only one recordset that needs to be created to display the contents of the table. Open the Bindings panel now, by choosing Data Binding from the Window menu.

Click the "+" button to add a new binding, and then choose the Recordset (Query) option from the pop-up menu that appears. Figure 10.3 shows the Recordset setup window.

FIGURE 10.3

Create your new recordset for tblSimpleDoglist.

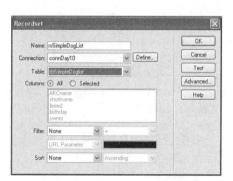

All we want to do with this recordset is select all the records in the tblSimpleDoglist table so that we can display them. Fill in the fields of the Recordset dialog box with the following information:

Name—A name for the recordset you're generating. I usually prefix my recordset names with `rs`, so let's call this one `rsSimpleDoglist`.

Connection—Choose `connDay10` from the Connection pop-up menu.

Table—Make certain that the table `tblSimpleDoglist` is selected in the Table pop-up menu.

Columns—You can choose to display all the fields in the `tblSimpleDoglist` table, or only those that you've selected in the Columns list. Pick All for now.

Leave the Filter and Sort settings alone—we'll get back to them in a few minutes. Click the Test button to see if information is retrieved from the database. You should see the five sample records appear almost instantly; click OK to dismiss the test window.

Tip

If, even with my incessant hounding, you managed to get here without setting up the `connDay10` database connection, you can click the Define button from within the Recordset dialog box to define a new connection "on-the-fly."

Why Does My Screen Look Different?

Aside from the various possible interface layouts, there's a good chance your screen looks different from what's here because the Recordset dialog box is in Advanced mode. If you see a button labeled Simple, click it!

Click the OK button to save the recordset and then switch to the Bindings panel where you should see the new `rsSimpleDoglist` recordset listed. Click the expansion arrow or "+" button in front of the recordset to view a list of all the fields that will be retrieved and ready for your use in Dreamweaver MX. Your display will look like Figure 10.4.

Adding Recordset Data to Your Page

For starters, drag each of the fields from the `rsSimpleDoglist` recordset into your `simplelist.asp` document design window. The page you create will have several special chunks of text in it that resemble `{rsSimpleDoglist.AKCname}`—these strange-looking strings will actually be replaced with information from the database.

Figure 10.5 shows a basic document with all the fields from the recordset displayed on the page.

FIGURE 10.4

The finished `rsSimpleDoglist` *recordset will look like this.*

FIGURE 10.5

Drag fields to the document design view to add them to the Web page.

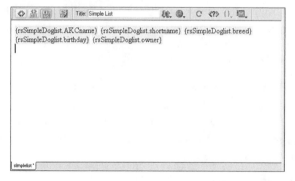

> **Note**
>
> You might notice a few items in the recordset that are not part of the database schema. There are three extra fields that will be useful later on: first record index, last record index, and total records. Total records is the number of records in the recordset, the last record index is a value for the last record on the page, and the first record index is the value for the first record shown. You'll be using these values in future projects.

As you drag the fields from the recordset, you're actually creating server behaviors. If you switch to the Server Behaviors panel for a second, you'll see that the recordset and several "dynamic text" elements are part of the system, as seen in Figure 10.6. Anything "dynamic" that you add to a page is a server behavior, whether or not you use the Server

Behaviors panel to do it. Of course, the more "interesting" behaviors are accessed directly from the Server Behaviors panel, but we'll get to those later.

FIGURE 10.6

You're adding server behaviors without even knowing it!

Back to the document… Designing pages using abstract field tags is certainly possible—just use them as you would any other text. If you choose to do this, however, you're going to miss out on what is undoubtedly Dreamweaver MX's most powerful feature: the capability to preview data from the database *directly* in the design view.

Other design tools use tags similar to the ones you currently see in order to represent data in the database server. Being able to connect to remote databases on multiple design platforms using different server operating systems is certainly not easy. Macromedia, however, has developed a very effective and novel approach to providing live data access from within the design window.

Live Data Previews

To provide a live preview of a Web page (complete with information from your database), Dreamweaver MX uploads the page to the application server. It then has the server render the page as it would in real-live production, downloads the resulting Web page, matches it up with the page in the design view, and inserts the dynamic data in the appropriate places—all in less than a second (on a reasonably fast connection).

To set up your computer to use the Live Data Preview option, all you need to do is select the Live Data option under the View menu or click the lightning bolt icon at the top of the document design window. Go ahead and do that now. If you've set up your page up exactly as described, your screen should resemble Figure 10.7.

Stop
Loading ¬ ┌Reload

Auto Refresh   Variable   Variable
Live Content   Field   Settings

FIGURE 10.7

*The abstract field tags
are now replaced with
actual data from the
database.*

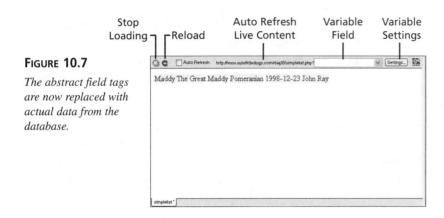

There are several controls for working with live data previews:

Stop Loading—Stops Dreamweaver MX from attempting to load live data.

Reload Data—Reloads the live data on the page.

Auto Refresh—Auto-reloads the page when the changes are made.

Variable Field—Supplies variables to the application via the URL line. Find out
more about variable passing in Day 6.

Variable Settings—Sets variables and their values that will be sent to the application
server each time the page is loaded. This will be covered later in the text.

If you have any problems viewing live data in your document, be sure to check all your
site definition information, especially the settings under Application Server and Remote
Info. Be certain that the URL Prefix field contains the proper URL for the remote Web
site. If not, quite simply, the Live Data isn't going to work.

If you're connecting to a remote server over a dial-in or very slow connection, using the
remote server to generate your live data view is going to be quite painful. The solution is
to set up a *staging* server on a local network and use it as a development platform.
Because that's what we devoted Day 7 to doing, I'll assume you've figured out your
server situation by now. Be aware, however, that you cannot switch server platforms in
the middle of creating a site. If you set up a local server running ASP, build your site,
and then want to deploy it on a PHP server, you'll have to rewrite all the pages.
Dreamweaver MX is *not* capable of translating from one server platform to another.

When you have the live data view functioning properly, you can reload the page using
the circular arrow Reload button in the upper-left corner. If a reload is taking longer than
planned, click the stop sign icon, which will cancel the current update. To automatically
update the Web page as changes are made to the design view, click the Auto Refresh

10

check box. Any changes you make (adding other fields, and so on) will be immediately updated in the design view. Otherwise you'll need to click the Reload button or choose Refresh Live Data from the View menu each time you want to view the progress of your work.

Displaying Multiple Records

You've noticed by now that only a single record is being displayed in the design view, but the database has multiple (a grand total of five) records currently available. So, how can you set up the system to display those records instead of just one? You could set up multiple recordsets that retrieve one record from the database. That, however, would be a little ridiculous.

It's easier to use Dreamweaver MX's Repeat Region server behavior to add multiple record functionality to your site. A repeating region will add all, or a portion of, the records in a recordset to your Web page. You select the data that you want to repeat, and Dreamweaver MX does the rest.

A repeat region works by generating the equivalent of a Do...Until or a For...Next loop to your document. If you choose to display all the records in the recordset, the repeating region will repeatedly display an area in the HTML, fetch the next record, and then display that area using the new data until all the records are shown. If you, instead, choose to only show a subset of the entire recordset, the repeating region will count how many times it has executed and stop when it hits the limit that you have defined.

 Tip   Before adding a repeating region, make sure that there is a line break after the end of the dynamic data currently in your site—otherwise, all the records in the table will be listed on a single line.

Let's go ahead and set up the simplelist.asp document to use the repeat behavior. Turn off the Live Data view for now (under the View menu).

Next, insert a line break after the last field in the simplelist.asp document. You're now ready to add your first "real" server behavior.

1. Select the fields that you want to repeat for each of the records in the table—or, in the case of our sample document, the entire line of fields.
2. Open the Server Behaviors panel.
3. Click the "+" button and choose Repeat Region from the pop-up menu.

You'll need to define the particulars of the region you're repeating. Figure 10.8 shows the Repeat Region dialog box.

FIGURE 10.8

Define the recordset you're repeating from and the number of records you want to display.

Choose the rsSimpleDoglist recordset, and then click the radio button in front of All Records. This will display all the records in the tblSimpleDoglist.

When you've picked your settings, click OK. As shown in Figure 10.9, the non-Live Data preview doesn't make an attempt at showing what the multiple records would resemble. Instead, Dreamweaver MX boxes the region that is going to be repeated and places a Repeat label at the upper-right corner of the region.

10

FIGURE 10.9

Without Live Data pre-viewing turned on, the display is less than beautiful.

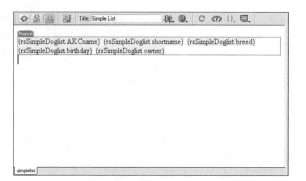

When you switch to the Live Data view, you will see all the records in the database one on each line. The live data portions of the display are highlighted in yellow, showing that they've been successfully translated into real data by the remote or local server. You can change this highlighting color by editing Dreamweaver MX's highlighting preferences.

> **Tip**
>
> After you've become accustomed to the Dreamweaver MX environment and the idea of having live data populate your screen, you might want to turn off highlighting of translated Live Data by clicking the appropriate Show Translated check box in the Highlighting section of the preferences. I find that the highlighting is distracting and gets in the way of the design process.

Organizing with Tables

Okay, so your data is being displayed, but it certainly isn't very pretty. In fact, it's quite ugly. Five records of varying lengths are displayed with no formatting information at all. How can you correct this? As I mentioned earlier, an HTML table is a great device for displaying a table of database information. We have five fields of data, so we could create a five-column table that would hold everything. Let's give it a shot.

Start a new document named `simpletable.asp` that will be built around a table. You'll need to re-create the recordset (`rsSimpleDoglist`) that you used in the previous example or copy the `simplelist.asp` document and delete all the server behaviors except the recordset. If you choose the latter route, open the Server Behaviors panel, select each behavior, and click the "-" button to remove it.

> **Caution**
>
> If you are reusing or editing a document that has server behaviors applied to it, *do not* use the document design view to remove the behaviors. You can certainly select and delete, for example, a repeating region within the document design view, and this will *appear* to work. However, changes made in design view won't necessarily delete all the Dreamweaver MX support code from the region. (You'll usually be warned about this.) If you then go on to add another repeating region to your document, it will fail when you attempt to run it. The only way to recover a document with this problem is to edit the embedded scripting directly in the HTML. Because we're trying to avoid this, I recommend starting from scratch rather than reusing documents—it only takes a few seconds to redefine your data bindings, and it will eliminate any possibility of residual code in the document.

Add a table to the document design view. For the `tblSimpleDoglist` recordset, add a table with five columns and two rows. The five columns are for the fields being displayed. You might be a bit confused about the two rows, however. Because the database has five records, shouldn't the table have at least five rows? The answer is simple: Yes, it should, but you don't have to worry about it—Dreamweaver MX's Repeat Region behavior will do the work for you.

The table we're adding really only needs a single row to hold the field elements. In a two-row table, however, the first row can be used to hold the names of the fields. That will help "neaten" things up a bit. Go ahead and create a simple table layout now using these steps:

1. Turn off Live Data during the design phase. You don't have to do this, but I find it easier to set up the document initially without viewing live data.

2. Insert a five-column, two-row table into the document design view.

3. Add the names of the fields being displayed to the cells in the first row. These will serve as headings for the rest of the table: AKCName, shortname, breed, birthday, and owner.

4. Drag the appropriate fields from the rsSimpleDoglist recordset in the Data Bindings panel over to the second row of cells in the table.

5. As a last step, highlight the row of cells that contains your data fields, and then add the Repeat Region server behavior for the defined recordset and all the records.

If you've successfully followed these steps, your display should resemble the one in Figure 10.10.

FIGURE 10.10

Laying out the data in a table format is amazingly simple—just design...

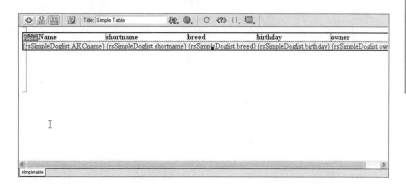

As a final test, switch to a Live Data mode or preview the page in your browser. Shown in Figure 10.11, all five records are in the table, just as you might expect.

FIGURE 10.11

...Then preview.

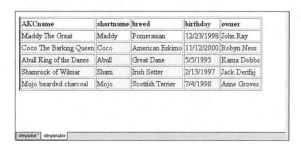

Although this might seem almost magical, in fact, it's really no different than the previous example in which the data was listed with each record on a single line. Dreamweaver MX will automatically write the code necessary to repeat a group of fields and HTML until all the records are shown. In the first example, the only thing that needed to be repeated was the dynamic data (the fields), and the <br> at the end of each line.

This example worked the same way, but the section being repeated was a table row: <tr><td></td>...</tr>. From the perspective of Dreamweaver MX, it's no more difficult to write repeating tables than it is to write a repeating line of text. From our perspective, however, it's pretty darn slick.

> **Tip**
>
> After all that work, I'm going to let you in on a little secret. You can *very* quickly create a simple table based on a query in your site by clicking the Dynamic Table object under Application. This tool works exactly like inserting a standard HTML table, but it will also ask you to choose one of the defined recordsets. It will then automatically add all of the necessary code to generate a table with appropriate headings and dynamic contents.

Still, is this table what you really want displayed to people who visit your page? It isn't incredibly attractive and doesn't present the information in a way that is natural for Web site layout. So, how can this table be "spiced" up?

An obvious way to do this would be to add some graphics to the mix and break up the monotony of the table. Dreamweaver MX, however, doesn't currently support the use of graphics embedded within a database—and shows no sign of doing so anytime soon. If you plan carefully, however, this isn't going to be much of a drawback.

Adding Graphics to the Recordset

It would be nice to show a picture of each doggy in the tblSimpleDoglist table. Without explicit Dreamweaver MX support, however, how can you use graphics within the database? The answer is simple; just store a URL to the location of the images within a directory on the server. Rather than storing the image itself, you store a reference to the image. This means you're going to need a slight variation of the table you're currently using, but nothing too serious.

> **Caution**
>
> If Dreamweaver MX ultimately adds embedded image support in the future, I would still think twice before using it. By employing the *blob* data type (Binary Large Object), it is possible to store images, files, and other binary data directly in a database table.

Keeping images in a database is at times useful and can speed up image retrieval from within a large library. Unfortunately, it also removes access to the files from the people who need it—namely, the designers. Depending on the system, the only person who might have access to the files is the database programmer. Because Dreamweaver MX tries to create a distributed editing environment, this works against one of the basic philosophies of the software.

I've personally worked on systems that stored all the graphics within a database. Each time a button, logo, or other element needed updated, the designers would call on me to retrieve the image. I would send it to them and then reimport the updated graphic. Not much fun, if you ask me.

For example, all we need to do to start storing images in our database is to add a new `imageurl` field to the existing `tblSimpleDoglist` structure. Within that field, you can store data such as `images/dog1.jpg`, and so on.

Table Definitions

Let's go ahead and define a new table for the `day10` database called `tblSimpleDogImagelist`. Again, this should already be defined in your system, but if you need to create it by hand, it's identical to the `tblSimpleDoglist` table you've been using up to this point, but with the addition of an `imageurl` field. Table 10.3 shows the new structure.

TABLE 10.3 The Definition of the `tblSimpleDogImagelist` Table

Fieldname	Description	SQL Data Type
AKCname	The registered AKC name of the dog.	varchar(250)
shortname	A short "family" name that the dog is typically called.	varchar(250)
breed	The dog's breed.	varchar(250)
birthday	The dog's birthday.	date
owner	The name of the owner.	varchar(250)
imageurl	A path to an image of the dog.	varchar(250)

Next, we need some slightly modified data for the new table. The sample information shown in Table 10.4 should be entered into the new `tblSimpleDogImagelist` table, if it isn't there already.

TABLE 10.4 Sample Data for the `tblSimpleDogImagelist` Table

AKCname	Shortname	Breed	Birthday	Owner	Imageurl
Maddy The Great	Maddy	Pomeranian	12/23/98	John Ray	images/maddy.jpg
Coco The Barking Queen	Coco	American Eskimo	11/12/00	Robyn Ness	images/coco.jpg
Abull King of the Danes	Abull	Great Dane	5/5/95	Kama Dobbs	images/abull.jpg
Shamrock of Wilmar	Sham	Irish Setter	2/13/97	Jack Derifaj	images/sham.jpg
Mojo bearded charcoal	Mojo	Scottish Terrier	7/4/98	Anne Groves	images/mojo.jpg

Each of the records now has the `imageurl` field that includes a directory and a filename that has a picture of the dog in the database. So, how do you get this on the Web? It's really very simple—use the `imageurl` field to construct the URL for an `<img>` tag.

Implementation

Create a new page called `simpleimages.asp`. We'll lay out the page exactly the same as the last table-based page, but with an extra cell (six columns) for the pictures.

You should be getting pretty good at this, but here are the steps you need to take to create this "picture-ready" version of the table:

1. Create `simpleimages.asp` and save it to your site folder.

2. Add a recordset `rsSimpleDogImagelist` to that document, including all the fields in the database.

3. Insert a two row, six column table. Enter the field names as the headings in the first row.

4. Fill in the first five table cells the same way as before. Drag the fields from the recordset into the document. The sixth cell will require some additional work. Do *not* add the Repeat Region yet.

Now that you've got a basic table constructed, how about adding those pictures? It's almost as simple as adding in a static image.

Adding a Dynamic Image to the Design

Go ahead and put the insert point in the last cell of the table to insert an image place-holder in that space. Configure the placeholder as seen in Figure 10.12—using the name myDogImage.

FIGURE 10.12

Add a placeholder for the dynamic image.

At this point, your document should look almost exactly like that of Figure 10.13. You may notice a slight difference in the look of the placeholder icons. I've already bound data to them, which is what you're about to do.

10

FIGURE 10.13

You should now have a basic six-column table with dynamic fields and an image placeholder.

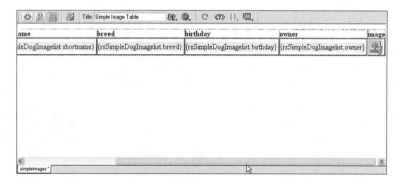

The next step is "binding" the placeholder image to the imageurl field in the database. Select the placeholder in the document design window, and then follow these steps:

1. Open the Data Bindings panel.

2. Expand rsSimpleDogImagelist so that you can see the imageurl field.

3. Highlight the imageurl field in the Data Bindings panel.

4. Use the Bind To pop-up menu at the bottom of the Data Binding panel to choose img.src. This means that the binding being created will connect the src attribute of the <img> tag in the document design window to the highlighted database field.

5. Click the Bind button in the Data Bindings panel to finalize the operation. Figure 10.14 shows the finished binding.

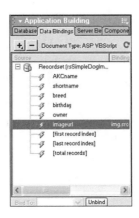

FIGURE 10.14

Bind the imageurl *field to the image placeholder.*

Now, to finish the document, select the entire second row in the table and add the Repeat Region server behavior as you did earlier. Finally, switch to the Live Data mode of viewing, if you haven't already. The finished simpleimages.asp document is shown in Figure 10.15.

FIGURE 10.15

The images are displayed along with the rest of the data.

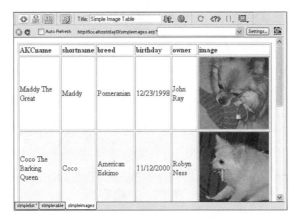

There's nothing to it. There's still a bit to be said for a more attractive layout, but you're the designer!

Note

In this example, you bound the image src to a dynamic field. You don't have to stop there. You could also store image widths and heights in the database and bind them to the width and height attributes.

Note

> Another way to bind database information to HTML element attributes is by using the Tag Inspector panel. Using this panel, you can find the tag whose elements you want to bind to the database, highlight it, and then choose among the different attributes you can bind. We'll look at this method of binding in a few seconds. You might find that it gives you access to a larger number of attributes than the Bindings panel.

The key to creating an attractive, but informative, page is to stop thinking that you're dealing with dynamic data. If this means that you need to lay out a page with static data first, so be it.

Take advantage of using different styles of fonts and table background colors. The end result is a something that looks slightly less computer generated and a little more appealing to the eye.

Try dropping the convention of using a repeating row in a table. You can repeat any elements you want—including entire tables—not just rows. There's no real rule to how you should set up your documents; just try designing them as you would any other HTML document.

Dynamic Attributes

You've already seen the effects of using a dynamic HTML attribute to place an image on a page. The image src attribute changed for each row in the database. But how far can you take this? You might be surprised to know that any attribute for an object can be set dynamically. This lets you create a document that is almost entirely laid out according to entries in a database.

Before moving on, let's take a look at one more method of laying out a page, this time using repeating layers. Suppose that you want to lay out a page in a manner that is completely nonlinear. In fact, we have five pictures, so how about laying out those pictures in a pentagon shape?

You can easily do this in static HTML using layers, but suppose that the supporting information for the pictures changes on a daily basis, and you want to provide a database backend to the Web site. One approach to this, which we'll take here, is to set up a repeating recordset that uses field data for the positioning and a few other attributes of the layers. To add a new layer to the page, you just add a record to the database. There's no need to bother with ever opening the HTML.

Note

> This exercise might not be incredibly practical for most Web sites, but it's fun and interesting nonetheless. The ability to bind to any tag attribute you want is what makes Dreamweaver MX an infinitely flexible application.

Table Layout

In order to dynamically create the layout of the layers, you need yet another field added to the `tblSimpleDogImagelist` table. This field, which we'll call `layerstyle`, will be bound to the style attribute of the layer. That means that it can hold anything used to stylize a layer—color, position, and so on. For our purposes, we'll just be using the positioning style information. Table 10.5 shows the new table, which we'll call `tblComplexDogImagelayout`. (I promise that on future projects, I'll cut down on the lengths of those names.)

If you didn't have this information automatically added to MySQL or aren't using the included Access database, you should create this new table in your `day10` database.

TABLE 10.5   The Definition of the `tblComplexDogImagelayout` Table

Fieldname	Description	SQL Data Type
AKCname	The registered AKC name of the dog.	varchar(250)
shortname	A short "family" name that the dog is typically called.	varchar(250)
breed	The dog's breed.	varchar(250)
birthday	The dog's birthday.	date
owner	The name of the owner.	varchar(250)
imageurl	A path to an image of the dog.	varchar(250)
layerstyle	Defines a style (in our case, a position) for the layer containing the image.	varchar(250)

We also need the `layerstyle` data for the new table. You can use the data provided in Table 10.6 (which, as always, should be in MySQL or the Access database downloadable from `http://downloads.cutelittledogs.com/`) or develop your own. This sample data should generate a pentagon shaped display. If you're wondering how I generated it, it was nothing more than positioning a few layers around the screen by hand, and then checking out the resulting HTML that was generated.

TABLE 10.6   Sample Data for the `tblComplexDogImagelayout` Table

AKCname	Shortname	Breed	Birthday	Owner	Imageurl	Layerstyle
Maddy The Great	Maddy	Pomeranian	12/23/98	John Ray	images/ maddy.jpg	position: absolute; left:220px; top:10px; width:150px; height:150px; z-index:1
Coco The Barking Queen	Coco	American Eskimo	11/12/00	Robyn Ness	images/ coco.jpg	position: absolute; left:0px; top:180px; width:150px; height:150px; z-index:1
Abull King of the Danes	Abull	Great Dane	5/5/95	Kama Dobbs	images/ abull.jpg	position: absolute; left:450px; top:180px; width:150px; height:150px; z-index:1
Shamrock of Wilmar	Sham	Irish Setter	2/13/97	Jack Derifaj	images/ sham.jpg	position: absolute; left:70px; top:350px; width:150px; height:150px; z-index:1
Mojo bearded charcoal	Mojo	Scottish Terrier	7/4/98	Anne Groves	images/ mojo.jpg	position: absolute; left:380px; top:350px; width:150px; height:150px; z-index:1

Besides just binding a style element to each layer, you should also bind a unique name. Luckily, the AKCname field will do just fine. After you've got your database tables ready, let's go ahead and start binding.

Implementation

Implementing this page is no more complicated than binding the image source attribute in the last exercise. Start by creating a new document, named `compleximages.asp`, and saving it to your site directory. Next, add a new recordset named `rsComplexDogImagelayout` that selects all of the records from the new table.

Now you need to add the two elements to the document that will be used to create the layout. First, a layer. The layer can be in any location and be any size—after all, you're going to set its final size/location dynamically with the `layerstyle` field values in the database.

Inside the layer, add a single image placeholder named `MyDogImage`, just as before. Your document should now similar to Figure 10.16 (but with a slightly different image place-holder icon).

FIGURE 10.16

Add a single layer with an image placeholder inside of it.

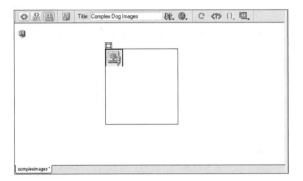

Now it's time to do the fun stuff—create your dynamic bindings. The first binding should be from the `img.src` attribute of the placeholder to the `imageurl` field in the Data Bindings panel. You've done this before, so we won't cover that here.

You should now be ready to bind dynamic information to the layer. Let's start with its name, which is the `layer id` attribute. Select the layer in the document design window, and then choose Tag Inspector from the Window menu. The Tag Inspector should appear, displaying all the attributes for the layer (an HTML `<div>` tag), as seen in Figure 10.17.

Find the `id` attribute in the list and click to highlight it. By default, it will have the value `Layer1`—you want to change this to be something dynamic. To bind data to an attribute, click the lighting bolt at the end of attribute line. Do this for the `id` attribute now. The dialog box shown in Figure 10.18 will let you configure the binding.

FIGURE 10.17

The Tag inspector allows you to bind any attribute to dynamic information.

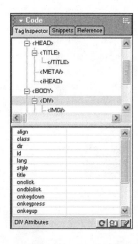

FIGURE 10.18

Choose the recordset and field to bind to.

Make sure the `rsComplexDogImagelayout` recordset is expanded, and then highlight the `AKCname` field and click OK. You've just created a new dynamic binding for the layer!

Repeat this same process for the `style` attribute of the layer. Choose the style attribute from the Tag Inspector panel, click the lightning bolt icon, and then bind it to the `layer-style` field in the recordset.

Not so difficult is it?

In fact, the Tag Inspector gives you more flexibility over what you can bind to than the Data Bindings panel does. It's perfectly reasonable to use this method for all future bindings if you want—it's entirely up to you.

Unfortunately, however, you aren't quite done with the document. There's still the matter of repeating the layer for all the images in the database. You can probably guess what you need—a repeating region.

10

To finish the page, simply highlight the layer in the document design window, and then add a Repeat Region server behavior. You're done! You should now be able to view the page in Live Data mode or in a Web browser and seen something similar to Figure 10.19.

FIGURE 10.19

The final output. Kind of cool for a page that really only has a single layer and image place-holder in it.

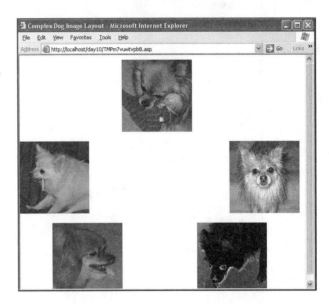

Additional Functionality on Dynamic Screens

You're probably thinking "This is nice, but I really want to do more…" Never fear, there's much more that you can do, but not all in one day. Using what you've learned so far today, you can actually create a system that lets you sort or filter the records in a recordset based on the information in one of the columns. The method for doing this that you're about to learn is not the most efficient way, but it is straightforward and should give you something to work with until the advanced techniques are discussed later in the week.

Sorting

Sorting records is simple. When you are defining a recordset, take notice of the Sort parameter at the bottom of the recordset definition window. Figure 10.20 shows the rsSimpleDoglist recordset definition you used earlier in the simpletable.asp file. This version of the recordset, however, allows you to sort on the AKCname field. The pop-up menu to the right of the sorting field allows you to choose whether the sorted records will be listed in ascending (A-Z) or descending (Z-A) order. If you change simplelist.asp or simpletable.asp to sort based on AKCname, you'll see the records appear in a different order.

FIGURE 10.20

*Sorting alters the way
records are returned in
a result set.*

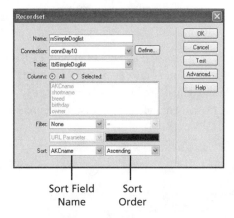

Sort Field   Sort
   Name   Order

10

Given the information you currently have, you can create a Web site that offers sorting of the database results based on a click of the heading in the table cells.

For example, if you have four columns in the database that you want to sort by, here's a quick-and-dirty way to establish a sorting system for the HTML:

1. Create four copies of the main HTML file that contains your dynamically generated page.

2. Modify the recordset in each of the documents so that it sorts based on a different field name.

3. Save each of the files based on the sorting parameter that the recordset is configured with.

4. Use a standard HTML link to connect the files so that the data can be displayed sorted in any format by moving between the documents.

The drawback to this approach is that you end up with a different file for each of the fields that you want to sort by.

Each of these files would need to be updated separately from one another—not very desirable if you have 50 files or so. There are better (programmatic) ways of sorting documents that you'll learn about later in the book. If you want to practice, however, this is a good way to start.

Filters

Similar to the sorting parameters, there is also a filter setting in the recordset definition. This allows you filter the information being returned from the database based on input from a server variable, cookie, session variable, and so on. Many of these won't be of much use to you unless you start programming directly, because Dreamweaver MX doesn't have any way to work with most of these values.

You can, however, set up a simple search using a filter and a URL parameter. On Day 6 you learned that Web applications pass information around on the URL by adding things like ?name=maddy to the Web address. You can use the filter function to quickly set up a search of a database using this technique. Take a look at Figure 10.21.

FIGURE **10.21**

Filters allow for simple searches to be configured.

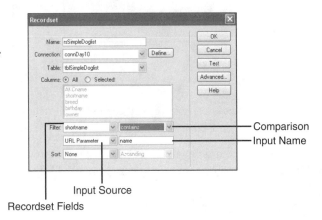

Here, the recordset used in `simpletable.asp` is modified with a filter. I've chosen to set up a filter that will only return records where the table field `shortname` must contain the text found in the URL parameter `name`. For example, if I call up the Web page with ?name=coco added to it, only the record for the dog with the short name Coco will be displayed. If I wanted to be a bit less specific, I could add ?name=a to the URL, and only dogs whose short names contained the letter "a" would be displayed. Using the first two filter pop-up menus, you control the field used for a match in the recordset and what type of match you want to make (are the values equal, greater than, less than, contained in one another, and so on). The third pop-up menu chooses where the filter information will come from (in this case, a URL parameter), whereas the field beside it is used to specify the name of the input source. For this example, I used a URL parameter named `name` to get the filter information into the program.

 Tip

You can test the filter URL parameter using a Web browser, or by using the URL field at the top of the Live Data view.

As you look at more complicated projects, you learn how sorting and searching can add a great deal of functionality to a Web site.

Summary

Developing database-driven pages in Dreamweaver MX is as simple as setting up a database connection, developing a recordset, and dragging and dropping the fields you need onto a page.

Dreamweaver MX also makes previewing your final page extremely easy—the Live Data view is a feature offered in few other Internet application design packages. By actually deploying a designed page on a remote server and running it, Dreamweaver MX can create an environment that, even when using dynamic data, truly is "what you see is what you get."

The challenge in setting up dynamic pages is in creating something visually appealing while still being functional. When designing dynamic pages in Dreamweaver MX, you can use the entire Dreamweaver MX tool palette to lay out the screens.

10

The Dreamweaver MX data bindings can be applied to any object's attributes, allowing a database to determine any setting for any object that you can add to an HTML page. This makes it possible to create a completely dynamic page in which the database can determine the visual appearance of the site.

Workshop

The Workshop area is meant to reinforce your reading with a series of questions and exercises.

Q&A

Q Do I have to use Live Data previews in order to design a site?

A Absolutely not. The Live Data preview works best on low latency networks and fast systems. If you are stuck using a dial-in line and don't have a local Web server that contains a copy of the content, the Live Data preview will really slow down your development. You can design without live data, but you'll need to get used to the abstract *recordset.fieldname* representation of the live data.

Q What attributes can be bound to dynamic data?

A Any attribute of an HTML object can be bound to dynamic data. Even if the attribute cannot be bound using the Bindings panel, the Tag Inspector still makes it possible.

Q What sorts of data can be stored in a database?

A Dreamweaver MX can only handle data stored as text. There are currently no provisions for handling binary data such as images. That doesn't mean, however, that you can't use the database to provide references to the objects.

Q **What do I do if the Dreamweaver MX-generated code becomes "confused"?**

A The easiest way to solve this problem is to avoid it completely. Dreamweaver MX will try to warn you if it thinks you're about to do something that will corrupt the automatically maintained source code. As a general rule of thumb, *always* use the Server Behaviors panel to handle removing database-driven code from your Web page.

Quiz

1. What two components must be in place before a dynamic Web page can be created?

2. How does Dreamweaver MX generate its Live Data view?

3. How do you create a repeating region?

4. Which attributes can be bound to dynamic data?

5. How can images be used inside of a database?

6. What happens when a recordset is sorted?

Quiz Answers

1. A connection to the application server and a database connection.

2. By sending the page to the application server, executing it, and then displaying the results locally.

3. Using the Repeat Region server behavior.

4. Anything! Sometimes you'll need to use the Tag Inspector, but you truly can make any part of an HTML object dynamic.

5. Images can be used by providing references to the image files and using those references as a dynamic data source for image tags.

6. The contents are returned in the order of the sort parameters.

Exercises

1. Create your own back-end database and develop a front end to it. Experiment with adding images to the database and referencing them on your dynamically generated pages. Try to lay out the page using something other than a simple table. Remember to take advantage of all the Dreamweaver MX development tools.

2. Expand your dynamically generated page to include database-bound attributes. Try setting table cell sizes, colors, and so on, based on attributes stored in your database.

DAY 11

Storing, Editing, and Updating Data

Yesterday you learned how to create pages that are driven by a database, all from within the Dreamweaver MX point-and-click interface. Now, instead of creating static HTML, you can build Web sites that pull data from your live corporate (or not-so-corporate) databases. Think of the amount of time you'll save rekeying information. Unfortunately, the only *input* interface that you have to this data is the database itself. In today's lesson, you'll learn how to build additional Web pages in Dreamweaver MX that will allow you to insert, update, and delete records in your online application—from anywhere on the Internet. In this chapter, you will learn how to:

- Create forms. So far you haven't had much use for the form tools of Dreamweaver MX because you haven't had a reason to use them. Today, you will.

- Connect a form to a database to save user-created data.

- Delete data from a database. Unless you're a perfect typist and your data never needs to be replaced, you'll also want to know how to remove information from databases.

- Modify database entries. Although the process of deleting and inserting can be used as a crude form of modifying data, wouldn't it be nice to be able to change the existing values and resave them? Of course it would!

The Dreamweaver MX Application Framework

In order to plan your Web applications, you should understand the way that Dreamweaver MX auto-generates code. Dreamweaver MX builds online applications based on a predetermined flow; the control of the application flows from one program to another, rather than building all the functionality into a single embedded file. For example, Dreamweaver MX's strength lies in its ability to create systems based on this flow:

1. Display a list of elements in a database.
2. Provide a link from each element to an update/detail page.
3. When visiting a detail page, provide options for updating or deleting the record.
4. After an update/delete action is performed, move to a new URL to confirm the results or get ready for the next action. Often this URL will be the URL where the user started in step 1.

Don't worry too much if this doesn't sound as if it offers much flexibility for your Web site's design. You'll find that most sites actually do operate using this same pattern, but have hidden it rather well. The key is taking these rather dull steps and using them in an interesting way; next week's chapters are devoted to building real-world systems using Dreamweaver MX.

 Note

> If you've never worked with embedded programming languages before, you might wonder why the previously outlined sequence of events is unusual. The reason is that embedded programming languages offer a great range of flexibility. An entire Web application can easily be built in to a single file. When building applications by hand, I typically build the listing, updating, and deleting functionality in to the same file. Without modifying the Dreamweaver MX code by hand, you won't be able to do this very easily.

The first thing you'll need to do before inserting data into a database is create a form that corresponds to the fields in the database.

Creating an Input/Output System

In Day 10, "Creating Database-Driven Web Pages," we created the dog database view that lists the dogs' names in the database along with their pictures. Table 11.1 shows the `tblSimpleDogllist` as we originally designed it.

TABLE 11.1 The Definition of the `tblSimpleDoglist` Table

Fieldname	Description	SQL Data Type
AKCname	The registered AKC name of the dog.	varchar(250)
shortname	A short family name that the dog is typically called.	varchar(250)
breed	The dog's breed.	varchar(250)
birthday	The dog's birth date.	date
owner	The name of the owner.	varchar(250)

The first step is to design an input screen that will collect information for each of these fields, and then store the data back into the database. To get ready, download the Day 11 materials from `http://downloads.cutelittledogs.com`, unarchive it, and copy the contents to a new folder on your computer. Create a Day 11 site definition using this folder as your site root.

Today's database, named day11, contains the `tblSimpleDoglist` that we'll work to put online. If you followed the instructions in Day 7 "Preparing a Server for Dreamweaver MX," this data should already be accessible in either a MySQL or Access data source on your test server. If not, create your own day11 database. As always, it is important that we work with the same data. I've taken the liberty of adding the data from Table 10.2 to the new `tblSimpleDoglist` table.

Start by creating another `simpledoglist.asp` page (just like yesterday) that displays all the information available in the `tblSimpleDoglist` table. Unlike yesterday, let's take full advantage of the automated Dynamic Table object to quickly create the document. Define a new connection to the day11 database:

1. Open the Databases panel.
2. Click the "+" button and choose Data Source Name (DSN).
3. Create a new `connDay11` connection to the day11 data source.

Now add a simple recordset (`rsSimpleDogList`) to the page that selects all of the records in the `tblSimpleDoglist` database table, as shown in Figure 11.1. This is identical to what you did yesterday.

11

FIGURE 11.1

Add the
`rsSimpleDogList`
recordset.

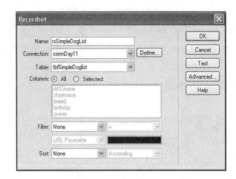

Insert the Dynamic Table object into the page. You can find this element under the Insert panel's Application category, or the Insert menu's Application Object selection. Figure 11.2 shows the Dynamic Table dialog box.

FIGURE 11.2

Add a dynamic table to display the new data.

Choose the `rsSimpleDogList` recordset and to show all records. Click OK and the `simpledoglist.asp` page is finished. Its sole purpose is to display information we've added to the database, so you can put it away for now. It's time to create the input form.

We'll need to create a form that has all five fields in it. When users submit the form, their dog's information will be added to the site.

HTML forms are one of my least favorite things to lay out. This might be part of the reason that this will be your first *serious* use of forms in the book. The rendering of forms makes them one of the least cross-browser/cross-platform elements in the HTML language. On Windows systems, for example, `<font>` tags alter the size of `<input>` fields and other form elements in both Internet Explorer and Netscape. The Macintosh, however, displays form elements at one consistent size in Netscape. Some browsers use special "skins" to generate the look and feel of the buttons; others use the operating system defaults.

Be sure that you know what your forms look like on different systems before declaring them done.

> **Note**
>
> Some of you will identify this as a bit of a rant, but I feel that it's important to bring up at this point anyway. One of the key features of a good user interface is consistency. User input elements should be of a consistent size and shape. When HTML alters the basic user interface, there's a problem. HTML was designed to provide a platform-independent layout of information on any screen. Changing elements of the operating system's user interface removes some of this independence.
>
> A good example of this is the implementation of buttons in OmniWeb (http://www.omnigroup.com) for Mac OS X versus Internet Explorer. Mac OS X users recognize their buttons by the translucent aqua appearance. In OmniWeb, all form submit buttons take on this appearance and even pulse if they are the default button. In Internet Explorer, however, the buttons look like Mac OS 8 or 9 "grayscale" blocks. For the users of OmniWeb, online forms are simply an extension of the Mac user interface. Internet Explorer users, however, must recognize a different interface and work within it.

Start a new ASP document within your site named `addtodoglist.asp`. Next, switch to the Form category of the Insert panel, and click the Form button. (The panels are documented in Chapter 1, "Getting Started," for your reference.) Make sure the Properties panel is open; name the form `frmInsertDoglist`, as seen in Figure 11.3. There is no need to set the form's action. Dreamweaver MX will do it for you.

11

FIGURE 11.3

Name the form `frmInsertDoglist`!

Now, making sure your cursor is inside the form within the design window, insert a 6-row×2-column table. Tables are often used to lay out user input screens. Lining up form elements is extremely difficult without the use of tables because of the varying sizes of the elements. I typically start all my user input screens with a two-column form that has the same number of rows as it has fields.

After you've added your table, go ahead and add all the field identifiers to the left column of the table—AKCname, shortname, breed, birthday, and owner. I've capitalized these labels in my table, simply for appearance sake. The last row in the table is for the submit button, which we'll add in a moment.

Now, here's the fun part—adding in the fields. Position your cursor in the top cell of the right table column—this will be the AKCname field. Add a text field by clicking the Text

Field icon in the Insert panel or by choosing Text Field from the Form Object submenu under Insert. Once the field is added, select it in the design view, and then use the Properties panel to set its name to match the corresponding tblSimpleDoglist table. Figure 11.4 shows the AKCname field properly configured in the panel.

FIGURE 11.4

Set the field names to match their database counterparts.

Position your cursor in the next empty cell and repeat this step until the entire form is filled in. When you're done, your page should resemble Figure 11.5.

FIGURE 11.5

Create a basic table with text input fields for each of the database fields.

Adding the Insert Behavior

An insert server behavior creates a new record in a database using information that was submitted from a Web browser—most likely from a form. Because we've designed a form to add records to the tblSimpleDoglist table in the day11 database, let's go ahead and add the necessary behaviors to connect the two.

Define an Insert Record behavior by following these steps:

1. Open the Server Behaviors panel.
2. Click the "+" button.
3. Choose Insert Record from the available server behaviors.

The Insert Record dialog box will be shown, as in Figure 11.6. This lets you tell Dreamweaver MX where data should be stored and how to store it.

FIGURE 11.6

The Insert Record behavior must be configured so that the form data matches the fields in the receiving table.

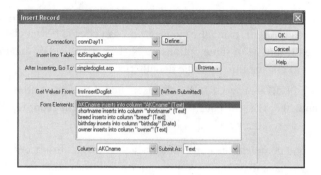

You'll need to fill out all the sections of this screen in order for your Insert Record behavior to work appropriately. Dreamweaver MX does a good job of guessing how a form should be matched up with a database table based on the names of the fields in both objects, so only a small amount of work will actually have to be done by hand. Make sure that each of the behavior attributes are set up appropriately for your application:

- **Connection**—The database connection that you want to use to store the data—in this case, connDay11. If you haven't defined a connection to the database yet, you can click the Define button to set up a connection now.

- **Table to Update**—Choose the table in the database that will hold the information you are submitting from the form (tblSimpleDoglist). This table should have a matching field for every field that is being submitted from the HTML form.

- **Form**—The HTML form that is providing the user input to be stored. If you named your form appropriately (frmInsertDoglist), you should have no problem making the right selection here.

- **Form Elements/Column**—The Form Elements configuration is the most important part of configuring the behavior. This is where one matches the form field name (listed on the right) with the database field name (on the left). To start, all the form fields are shown on the right. Dreamweaver MX makes default matches by comparing the names of the form fields to those in the database and pairs those that are the same. When a match cannot be made, the tag <ignore> appears in the right column. To attach a form field to a column, make sure that the field name is selected in the Form Elements list, and then choose the table field to attach it to from the Column pop-up menu. For this example, you should match AKCname in the form with AKCname in the database, shortname with shortname, and so on.

- **Column/Type**—Next to the Column pop-up is a second pop-up menu that lets you choose the type of data that is being saved. If you are saving a date, for example, choose Date from the pop-up menu. Because check boxes are commonly used for Boolean (on/off, true/false) values, you can choose how a check box on/off state is saved from one of three options (Y/N, 1/0, or –1/0). For this example, you won't need to change this from the default text value.

- **Go To URL**—The URL that the user should be sent to after the insert action is completed. For this page, just send the user to simpledoglist.asp, which is, (obviously), the simple dog listing.

Go ahead and complete the configuration screen for the Insert behavior. You should now have a single page that enables you to enter new information into the tblSimpleDoglist table, and then transports you to the simpledoglist.asp page to verify that the data was indeed added.

Give your new application a test run. First, open the newly designed addtodoglist.asp page in a Web browser and try typing in some information. Click the Submit button and the screen will refresh with the new data shown in the dynamic table. If, for some reason, this doesn't work, make sure that you've done the following:

1. Synchronized the remote server and the local server.
2. Filled in *at least* the field designated as the primary key. In the tblSimpleDoglist definition that you're using, the AKCname field is the primary key.
3. Specified a *unique* value for the primary key.

These are really just common sense rules, but they're also easy to overlook. If an error occurs during the process of inserting a record, the embedded language processor will display an error. For example, trying to insert multiple records with the same AKCname generated this error in my ASP application:

```
Microsoft OLE DB Provider for ODBC Drivers error '80004005'
[TCX][MyODBC]Duplicate entry '' for key 1
/Test1/TMP8kprugf0ye.asp, line 49
```

That's about all you need for inserting records. As always, take advantage of the Dreamweaver MX design tools. Don't assume that you're stuck with plain tables.

Note

As you will learn later, many times the primary key is generated automatically behind the scenes by the database server. This keeps the responsibility of "uniqueness" on the server and not on the user—making it very unlikely that you'll ever see an error message such as the one just shown.

Generating Detail Pages and Deleting Records

Now that you can add information to your database, how about deleting it? With the ability to add and delete, you gain complete control of your information from within a Web interface. In many applications, before deleting data, the details of a record are shown, and the user is given the option of deleting it. In this part of the lesson, you'll learn how to create a detail screen and delete information—a "twofer."

Detail Pages

Let's start with a detail page. Right now, we only know how to display a list of records in the database. How can we single out a specific record for display? The answer is a *detail* screen. This is slightly different from the behaviors we've seen thus far and will require a few additions to your current knowledge of what Dreamweaver MX has to offer—most notably, how do we tell Dreamweaver MX what record we want displayed on the detail screen?

First things first: Design a basic detail screen. Think of how you'd create a single screen that did nothing more than display the AKCname, shortname, breed, birthday, and owner fields for a single record. Don't worry too much about the design now—you know the layout tools, and you can certainly alter the screen after you have it up and running. Create a new file called dogdetail.asp that displays each of the five field labels with space to display their values. I prefer to do this with a two-column, five-row table. Figure 11.7 shows a vertical "single record" detail screen.

FIGURE 11.7

Create a screen that will do nothing more than display a single record from the tblSimpleDoglist *table.*

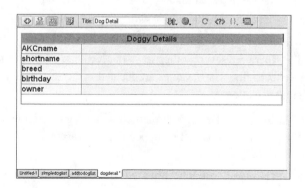

Now you need to design a recordset that properly describes the data you want to retrieve and display. Previously, our recordsets selected *all* the information in the database. This time you have a very specific set of information you need to retrieve—a single record.

11

The easiest way to retrieve a single record is to apply a filter to the search. Create a new recordset by opening the Server Behaviors panel, clicking "+" and adding a Recordset (query) behavior. Name the new recordset rsDetail using the connDay11 connection. Set the table to tblSimpleDoglist. Finally set the filter to AKCname = URL Parameter AKCname.

Figure 11.8 shows a filter that is configured for the AKCname field and the URL parameter AKCname.

FIGURE 11.8

The filter can be used to select information based on a URL parameter.

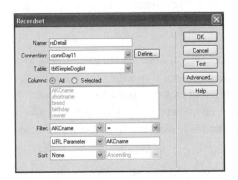

So, what exactly does this mean? It means that, in order for a record to be part of the rsDetail recordset, the AKCname database field must equal a parameter named AKCname specified in the URL. As you recall, the variable-passing methods discussed on Day 6, "Introduction to Dynamic Web Applications and Database Design" and in Day 10, you can pass variables by appending their value to the URL. In order to pass the value SuperDoggy in the AKCname parameter, the URL might resemble http://www.someurl.com/dogdetail.asp?AKCname=SuperDoggy.

This is the easiest and most common way to pass a value to the page that displays the record details. There are several other ways that you can pass information to a recordset or other server behavior. These values are located under the variable-passing pop-up menu in the filter section:

- **URL Parameter**—The default method of getting a variable to the server behavior. A URL parameter is passed by appending the variable name and its value to the URL.
- **Form Variable**—A variable submitted from a form. If you are using the POST method in a form, you'll need to use this setting to access its value.
- **Cookie**—If a cookie is set and returned to the server application, it is accessible through this variable passing type.

- **Session Variable**—Like a cookie, a session variable, if set, is available throughout the Web application. We'll use session variables to create login systems in Day 12, "Writing Advanced Database Queries."

- **Application Variable**—An application variable is accessible throughout the entire Web application. This type of variable isn't accessible in all server models.

- **Entered Value**—A value that is defined prior to the program running.

Not all these variable-passing types are accessible in all the server models. The most useful of these are the URL parameters and session variables that we'll be using extensively in the rest of the book. Unfortunately, Dreamweaver MX doesn't offer server behaviors to *set* many of these types of variables, so they're of little use to nonprogrammers.

Back to the matter at hand: selecting a specific record from `tblSimpleDoglist` to display in the detail screen. In the simple recordset dialog box, I've set a filter to select records based on a dog's `AKCname`.

We're about done, and are almost ready to test the detail screen. You've configured a recordset, but you haven't used any of the data from it yet. Open the Data Bindings panel and, one-by-one, drag the fields from the data bindings into the document design window to match the corresponding field labels. The final detail view that I've defined is shown in Figure 11.9.

FIGURE 11.9

The detail screen is finished!

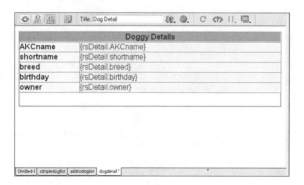

After setting up the detail page, you can test it using one of the cooler features of the Dreamweaver MX interface—the Live Data view, but with dynamic variable values supplied through the URL parameters:

1. Switch to the Live Data mode under the View menu.

2. Immediately, click "Stop."

3. In the empty URL field at the top of the document design view, add the URL parameter: `AKCname=Maddy%20The%20Great`. (Of course this is assuming you're using

the sample data and have a dog named Maddy The Great in the database; if not use a different name.) The result is shown in Figure 11.10.

4. The data for that record is now displayed in the detail screen.

5. Try this for the other records in your database.

FIGURE 11.10

*Use the Live Data view
to test the detail page.*

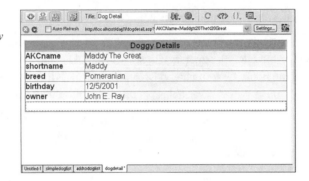

The Live Data view also allows you to add default values that will be passed to the pages as they are executed on the application server. Clicking the Settings button in the Live Data view toolbar or choosing Live Data Settings from the View menu will open a window where you can define the URL parameters you are passing (such as AKCname) and the values they take on (such as Maddy The Great).

 Do not expect robust error handling. Dreamweaver MX writes the code to do the job, but don't expect magic. If you request a record that doesn't exist, you'll get an error from the application server. This isn't really a fault in Dreamweaver MX because it is impossible for the software to know exactly what is going to happen or what kind of errors it can expect to occur in the database. In order for robust error handling to be implemented, you'll need to edit the code by hand. Luckily, this won't often be necessary because the links to the detail page will eventually be generated automatically.

What's with the %20 in the URL Parameter?

The name Maddy The Great includes spaces that must be *URL encoded* before being passed to the Web application. A hex-encoded space is simply %20.

Deleting Records

The detail screen is now complete, and you can focus on providing a means of deleting the record that is being displayed. This is actually a very simple process that will only take a few minutes to set up and test.

The record deletion server behavior requires that a form be submitted—this process is what triggers the execution of the DELETE command on the database server. Now, add a new form to the dogdetail.asp screen. Be sure to get in the habit of naming the form something appropriate—in this case, frmDelete. All you need to add to the form is a single submit button named Delete, and you're ready to go. Figure 11.11 shows the modified detail page.

Add a form with a Delete button to the page. This will trigger a delete action for the record displayed on the detail page.

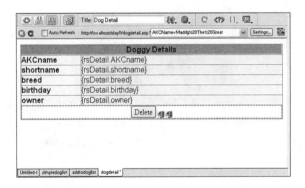

Now add the Delete Record server behavior. Click the "+" button in the Server Behaviors panel and choose Delete Record.

Configure the dialog box, shown in Figure 11.12, according to the following standards:

- **Connection**—The connection to the database server to use. Use the same connection you used for the detail screen: connDay11.

- **Delete from Table**—Once again, use the same table used to build the detail screen: tblSimpleDoglist. This is the table that the record will be deleted from.

- **Select Record From**—This is where things get interesting. This is the recordset that contains the record you want to delete. In the case of the detail screen, the *only* record in the recordset is the record you want to delete. Select the rsDetail recordset used in the detail screen.

- **Unique Key Column**—The unique column is set as the primary key in the database. Set this to the primary key column AKCname. Click the Numeric box if the column holds numeric values, which, in this case, it doesn't.

- **Delete By Submitting**—Choose the form that will delete the record after it is submitted. This should be the frmDelete form with the Delete submit button on it. It's the only form on the page, so the default value is probably a safe choice.
- **When Done Deleting/Go To URL**—Choose the URL to go to after the record has been deleted. I want to send the user back to the simpledoglist.asp file. You can do the same, or point to a new page with a "Your Record Has Been Deleted" message.

FIGURE 11.12

Configure the form that, when submitted, will delete the record.

Once configured, click OK and open one of the records in the database using the same technique shown earlier (specifying parameters in the URL), but within a Web browser. You can now click the Delete button on the page, and the record will be deleted. There's nothing to it.

Caution

> When testing behaviors that involve submitting a form, be sure to use your Web browser rather than the Live Data view; otherwise, the behavior might appear to be broken.

Linking to a Detail Page

Dreamweaver MX automates the process of linking to a detail screen with the Go To Detail Page behavior. This enables you to add a link from the main simpledoglist.asp page directly to the detail page, where the record can be deleted—no more typing URL parameters by hand!

Open the simpledoglist.asp document and highlight the dynamic text in the AKCname column (that is, the text labeled {rsDetail.AKCname}). The dog's name will be used as the link text to connect to the detail page.

Add the details link to your document by following these steps:

1. Open the Server Behaviors panel.
2. Click the "+" button and choose Go To Detail Page.

3. Set up the details link configuration dialog box, seen in Figure 11.13. (We'll discuss the fine points next.)

FIGURE 11.13

Dreamweaver MX automates the process of linking to the detail page.

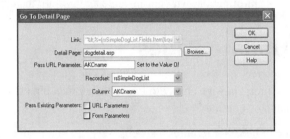

Configure the Go To Detail Page dialog box with these parameters:

- **Link**—The link to use to the detail page. If you selected the dynamic AKCname text before adding the server behavior, this should already be set.
- **Detail Page**—The detail page you created, dogdetail.asp.
- **Pass URL Parameter**—The URL parameter name to be transferred to the detail page, AKCname.
- **Recordset/Column**—The recordset that contains the data to pass to the detail page (rsDetail), and the database field that will be passed in the URL parameter. Because the detail page filter is based on the AKCname field, that's the column to choose.
- **Pass Existing Parameters**—Lets you pass all the currently set URL parameters and any form-submitted parameters to the detail page. There's no reason to use that functionality here.

Click OK when you've finished adding the Detail Page server behavior.

Note

You might notice that Dreamweaver MX doesn't allow you to go to a detail page by passing multiple URL parameters. If you're dealing with multiple keys in database tables, this is a serious limitation that can only be overcome by manually editing the embedded code.

Your record display and deletion system is done. You should now have a screen created that allows you to insert new records (addtodoglist.asp), one that displays all your records (simpledoglist.asp), and one that shows record details and offers the option to delete that record (dogdetail.asp).

Although this certainly does give you control over your data, it is still missing something—the ability to update data that is already in your database. Rather than having to delete and re-enter information, why not just update it within the database?

Creating Update Pages

Creating update screens is a combination of the techniques you've already learned, coupled with a new function—the ability to load existing data directly into a form, allowing it to be edited and resubmitted.

The Update server behavior requires a specific record to be loaded, edited, and saved back to the database. Like the detail screen that you created earlier, the update screen must select a particular record using a filtered recordset. It must also include a form, much like the `addtodoglist.asp` document we created earlier. In fact, the easiest way to build an update screen is to start with an insert screen and make some modifications.

Open the `addtodoglist.asp` screen and save a copy as `updatedoglist.asp`. Switch to the Server Behavior panel and select the Insert Record behavior that was added for the `frmInsertDoglist` form. Click the "-" button to remove the behavior. We're going to replace the Insert behavior with the Update behavior.

In the Server Behavior panel, click the "+" button and add the Recordset (query) behavior to your document. Like the detail screen, this behavior must select a specific record in a table. Name the new recordset `rsUpdate` using the `connDay11` connection. Set the table to `tblSimpleDoglist`. Finally set the filter to AKCname = URL Parameter AKCname. Again, this should be identical to the recordset defined for `dogdetail.asp` and is shown in Figure 11.8.

Now, let's add the Update Record server behavior. Again in the Server Behavior panel, click the "+" button and choose Update Record from the pop-up menu.

The Update Record dialog box, displayed in Figure 11.14, is a hybrid of the Detail and Insert dialog boxes.

Add the appropriate values to the Update configuration, much as you did with the past two server behaviors we've covered:

- **Connection**—The database connection containing the recordset you're updating: `connDay11`.
- **Table to Update**—Well…, the table to update: `tblSimpleDoglist`.
- **Select Record From**—Choose the recordset that defines the record being updated. As in the detail screen, this recordset only contains a single record. In this case, the recordset is `rsUpdate`.

FIGURE **11.14**

FIGURE 11.14

The Update Record dialog box is a combination of the Detail and Insert dialog boxes.

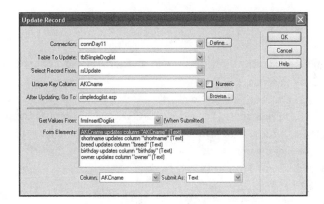

- **Unique Key Column**—The column in the database that is used as the primary key: AKCname.

- **Get Values From Form**—The form that, when submitted, will contain the updated values to be stored in the database: frmInsertDoglist.

- **Form Elements/Column**—Match the form text fields (listed on the right) with the database field names (on the left). To start, all the form fields are shown on the right. To attach a form field to a column, make sure that the form field name is selected in the Form Elements list, and then choose the database field to attach it to from the Column pop-up menu.

- **Go To URL**—The page to transfer the user to after a record has been updated. As with the other pages (insert and detail/delete) returning to simpledoglist.asp is a good idea.

Click OK when you've finished with the configuration, but don't sit back just yet. The server action you've just created does nothing but update a record based on the information you provide in a form. It does not, sadly, fill in the form with the record data that you're updating. In order to do that, you need to bind the form fields to data in the recordset.

Creating Dynamic Forms

To update a record, it is useful to have the original data filled in to the form we're using to make the update. To do this, we can bind the value attribute of the input fields to the fields in the tblSimpleDoglist.

Binding a form element to a database record is simple. Using the Bindings panel, we can select an object in the design screen, pick the database field that will supply data to the element, and then click the Bind button. Alternatively, using the Tag Inspector panel, you can bind an HTML tag or any of its attributes to dynamic data. You learned both of these

11

techniques in yesterday's lesson when you bound data to the `<img>` tag's `src` attribute and the `<div>` (layer) `style` attribute.

Let's bind the database to the form input fields using the same method we explored yesterday. Click the first field (`AKCname`) in the `updatedoglist.asp` design view. Next, open the Bindings panel and click the `AKCname` field in the `rsUpdate` recordset. The Bind To value should automatically be set to `input.value`—if not, use the pop-up menu to choose `input.value`. This will ensure that the default value of the `AKCname` input field is set to the `AKCname` value in the recordset. Figure 11.15 shows the properly bound `AKCname` field.

FIGURE 11.15

Bind each text field's value attribute to the corresponding record-set field.

Repeat these steps for the first *four* fields in `tblSimpleDoglist`. Why not all five fields? Because we're going to address the last field, `owner`, in a slightly different manner.

By now you should be getting used to the idea that there are 1, 2, 3, or maybe 50 ways to do something in Dreamweaver MX. In addition to the two binding methods you've used, there are special server behaviors created for the sole purpose of creating form elements that are bound to database information.

Dynamic Forms through Server Behaviors

The server behavior method of creating a dynamic form element is quite straightforward. After creating the form and the fields you want to fill in (which we've done), follow these steps:

1. Click the "+" button in the Server Behaviors panel.
2. Choose Dynamic Form Elements then Dynamic Text Field.
3. In the dialog box shown in Figure 11.16, set the text field to the form field that you want to be filled. In this example, choose the form item `owner` in form `frmInsertDoglist`.

FIGURE 11.16

A built-in server behavior exists for creating dynamic form elements.

4. Click the lightning icon in the Set Value To field to open up a view of your defined recordsets.

5. Choose the rsUpdate recordset and owner database field to be bound to the text field's value.

6. Click OK to close the recordset window.

7. Click OK to finish defining the dynamic field value.

8. Repeat these steps for all the form elements in the update document.

After this final dynamic field is added, your form is complete, and should look something similar to mine, shown in Figure 11.17.

FIGURE 11.17

The completed update form is shown here.

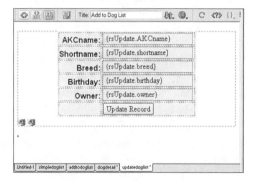

11

> **Note**
>
> When you added the dynamic text field to the document, you probably noticed that Dreamweaver MX can also create database-driven check boxes, menus, and other form elements. These are set up in a very similar manner to the text field that we just used. We'll use these additional behaviors on future projects in the book.

Linking to the Update Page

You created an update page, but it isn't connected to anything! Like the Detail page, you must pass a URL value to updatedoglist.asp. Like dogdetail.asp, you must use a Go To Detail Page server behavior to link to the update page. As we're nearing the end of the chapter and this is absolutely identical to the `dogdetail.asp` link you created earlier, it is left as an exercise to try on your own.

I recommend editing the `simpledoglist.asp` page and adding, perhaps, an Edit link directly following the `AKCname`, or create an extra column in the table to hold an edit link. Using the Go To Detail Page server behavior, create a link to the `updatedoglist.asp` page. Refer to the earlier section "Linking to a Detail Page" for step-by-step instructions.

Auto-Generating Forms and Pages

For the past two days, you've created database listings, and detail, insert, and update pages by hand. You've probably also noticed that there is a great deal of repetition when writing the HTML. You might remember yesterday that, after making you do a significant amount of work (aka "learning"), I introduced you to a dynamic table object that quickly inserts a dynamic table into a Web page. Guess what I'm about to do?

To give you a head start, Macromedia has included several entities in the Insert panel's Application category that let you generate generic versions of today's forms very, very quickly.

Although these features are time savers, you might find that you prefer creating your own screens by hand. I don't like trying to adapt existing designs into what I'm visualizing in my head. However, if you just need to get a simple database access site online quickly, these objects can give you everything you need in seconds.

Caution

It is very important that you understand the server behaviors we've discussed today if you plan on expanding the automatically generated documents that these objects create. After they are added to a site, you must work directly with their underlying server behaviors to edit their functionality. Only the creation phase is automated—editing is up to you.

Switch to the Application category within the Objects panel. We'll be looking at the Master Detail Page Set, Record Insert Form, Record Update Form objects. Because we've created quite a few pages already today, this section will serve as a basic guide to these features. There's no need to re-create what we've worked to accomplish today.

Note

As with just about everything in Dreamweaver MX, these objects are accessible from the menu system as well as the Insert panel's Application category. You can use Application Objects under the Insert menu to access these

> prebuilt forms if you don't want to clutter your screen space with the
> Insert panel.

Master-Detail Pages

To create the record listing and detail pages that we've already seen using these template objects, you must first create a new document that contains nothing but the recordset that you want to attach to. To try this, create and save a new document named `automaster.asp`. Add a new recordset—the `rsSimpleDoglist` recordset we've been using for the past two days.

Next, click the Master Detail Page Set icon in the Application table of the Insert panel, or use the Application Objects submenu of the Insert menu to add the Master Detail object to the current page. You'll be prompted to enter some information about the records you want to display, as seen in Figure 11.18. Configure these areas as follows:

FIGURE 11.18

Configure the Master Detail object with the connection, form, and fields you need.

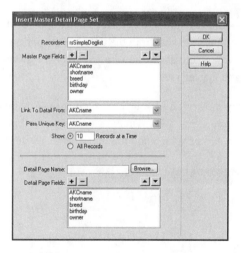

11

Recordset—The recordset defined for the document.

Master Page Fields—Using the "+" and "–" buttons, you can add and delete columns from the display that will be generated for the main record listing. You can also use the up and down arrows to change the ordering of the column display.

Link to Detail From—Choose from the pop-up menu which column should provide the link to the detail page. Remember how we used the AKCname to link to the detail page? This is the same thing.

Pass Unique Key—Select the column that uniquely identifies each record. This will be passed in the URL when the user clicks the field chosen in Link to Detail From. `tblSimpleDoglist` used `AKCname`.

Show—Choose to show only a few records or all the records at a time. If you choose to limit the number of records displayed, a navigation bar will be added automatically to allow the user to move to additional records. You'll learn more about navigation bars and how they work in Day 14, "Advanced Components: Catalogs, Searches."

Detail Page Name—Enter a name to use for the auto-generated detail page or click Browse to choose an existing file. For this test, simply use `autodetail.asp`.

| Caution | Be sure to include the appropriate file extension (`.ASP`, `.JSP`, and so on) when choosing the detail page name. If you don't, Dreamweaver MX will create the file without an extension and then proceed to open it in Code view because it cannot identify it. |

Detail Page Fields—Like the previous Master Page Fields configuration, here you can choose which columns are shown in the detail page, and in what order they are shown. Presumably you would show the same number (or more) of fields in the detailed view as in the master view.

When you've configured the screen to your liking, click the OK button and sit back. After a few moments of chugging away, Dreamweaver MX will present you with your two new documents: the master screen and the detail page, as shown in Figure 11.19.

FIGURE 11.19

Master and detail screens will be generated after a few moments.

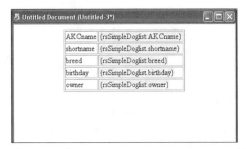

| Note | As mentioned earlier, any changes you want to make in these documents will have to be made by hand. After the initial pages are generated, you must work directly within the Server Behaviors and Bindings panels. |

As you can see, this simple-to-use object lays out the master record listing and detail screens extremely quickly. Using the other two objects, you can create the Insert and Update pages just as quickly.

Record Insert Forms

To create a new insert form that will add information to a database table, create a new empty document, autoinsert, and choose the Record Insert Form entity from the Insert panel or the Insert menu. The configuration screen shown in Figure 11.20 will be displayed.

FIGURE 11.20

Choose the fields and captions you want displayed on the insert form.

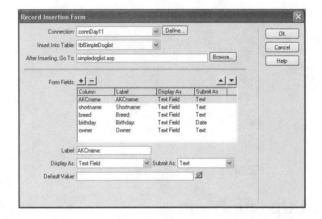

Choose the settings you need to connect to the database:

Connection—Choose the database connection to use.

Insert Into Table—Select the table that should receive the incoming data.

After Insert, Go To—Enter the name of the page to go to after inserting data, or click the Browse button and choose the file. Chances are, you'll want to return to the master record listing page.

Form Fields—The Form Fields area lists all the text fields that will be included in the HTML form, the labels that will be placed in front of them, the type of field used to collect the data, and the format that should be used when the data is submitted to the server. Use the "+" and "–" buttons to remove or add fields to the form and the up/down arrows to rearrange the positioning of the elements in the form. Dreamweaver MX will automatically fill in these values for you, but you can change them at any time. To change a value, highlight it, and then modify the Label, Display As, and Submit As fields.

Label—The label that should be included in the form for the highlighted field. Click an item in the Form Field's list, and then change its label in this field.

Display As—The type of form element that should be used to represent the selected field.

Submit As—The format of the data that is being submitted.

Click OK when you've finished configuring the Insert form. After a few moments, your newly generated form will appear, much like Figure 11.21, which was configured to insert into tblSimpleDoglist.

FIGURE 11.21

The resulting form isn't necessarily pretty...but it's functional!

Record Update Forms

The Record Update form is very similar in operation and configuration to the Insert form, but like the Master Detail object, requires a recordset to be defined before it can be added.

Assuming that you're continuing to work with the same site, start a new document, autoupdate.asp, and then add the exact same recordset (rsSimpleDoglist) to the document that you did for the updatedoglist.asp page created earlier.

With the recordset defined, add the Record Update Form object to your document from the Insert menu or the Insert panel. Shown in Figure 11.22, the configuration is almost identical to the Record Insert Form object.

A few minor differences exist in the configuration, which are documented here:

Table to Update—Choose the database table that will be receiving the updated information.

Select Record From—Select the filtered recordset that you've created to "seed" the form.

Unique Key Column—Pick the database column that uniquely identifies the record. This should be the same column you are using to filter the recordset. Click the Numeric box if this is a numeric column.

FIGURE 11.22

The Update and Insert forms share a similar setup.

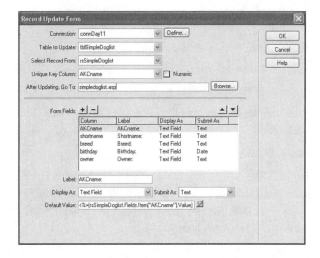

Click OK to save the configuration and auto-generate the server behaviors that you need. The result is a generic update form, demonstrated in Figure 11.23.

FIGURE 11.23

Your update form is automatically added to the document.

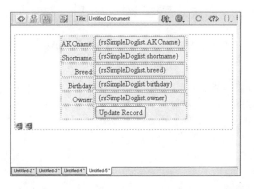

11

In a matter of five minutes or less, you can create the same screens you built over the course of this chapter.

Making the Final Connection

All that remains is to add a link from the auto-generated master listing page to the update page, and you've got yourself a complete working online database system. To do this, you'll need to modify the master listing slightly and add one more server behavior.

First, open the master listing page, `automaster.asp`, click inside the right column of the table (any cell), and then use the Modify, Table, and Insert Column to add a new column to your master listing table. Next, add a label to the new cell that will be used to link to the update page, such as `Click Here to Edit`, and select that label in the design window.

Finally, use the Go To Detail Page server behavior to link to the update page:

1. Click "+" in the Server Behaviors panel.
2. Choose Go To Detail Page.
3. Enter the name of the update page to transfer to.
4. Pass the unique identifier as the URL parameter. This is the same URL parameter you defined as the filter for update form's recordset, such as `AKCname`.
5. Click OK to add the behavior to your document.

You should now have a fully functional system that allows you to list records, view details, update individual records, and insert new records—all without touching the HTML design tools. You can use these prebuilt template objects at any time or build the forms yourself—it's entirely up to you!

Summary

Following up on yesterday's lesson of displaying data, today you learned how to insert data into a form, pass variables between pages in order to display details, and update existing records. Dreamweaver MX provides built-in server behaviors for all these different actions and makes it very simple to create sites that work based on a basic screen-by-screen flow.

Although today's page designs are purely functional, you must keep in mind that all the HTML design tools function perfectly when creating dynamic data. Experiment with the screens you've already created to adjust them to your particular look and feel.

Workshop

The Workshop area is meant to reinforce your reading with a series of questions and exercises.

Q&A

Q Can I use a text link rather than a button to submit a form?

A Yes. You can use a link to `"javscript:document.forms[<yourformindex>].submit()"` to get around having to use the Form button.

Q I inserted the form elements onto the page, but when I look at it in my browser, I see nothing. It looks fine in Dreamweaver MX's design view. What's going on?

A You've left out the <form> tag. If the <form> tag is missing, some browsers don't bother to render the fields on the page. Dreamweaver MX will warn you if you attempt to insert form elements without a <form> tag, but it won't prevent you from doing so. Additionally, the <form> tags that Dreamweaver adds for you might not automatically encompass all the fields on your page, so be careful!

Q Why doesn't Dreamweaver MX handle multiple field primary keys?

A Dreamweaver MX relies on a very specific set of conditions being true in order to generate code in a point-and-click manner. If these conditions aren't met, the code will need to be customized, or a workaround will be needed. As you might have noticed, the server behaviors are set up to work with single field primary keys. Go over this limit, and you'll need to edit the generated code by hand.

Q When will I get to attach the other form elements to a database?

A Soon. Many of the projects in the last week will push Dreamweaver MX to its limits. If you're anxious to get started, go ahead and practice with the other elements now. The interface is very similar to what you've already worked with, and you should have no problem connecting other elements to your document recordsets.

Quiz

1. How can you set the size of a form field for design purposes?
2. How can you test dynamic pages, such as detail screens, from within the design view?
3. How many primary key fields can Dreamweaver MX work with in the server behaviors?
4. Besides using server behaviors, what's another way to bind form elements to a database?
5. How can you quickly create master detail page sets and supporting insert/update pages?

Quiz Answers

1. You can set the size of a form field using the Properties panel.
2. The Live Data view with URL parameters can simulate a basic Web browser. This, however, does not work will with pages expecting the results of a form submission.
3. One. If you need more, you'll need to edit the code manually.
4. The Data Bindings panel and Tag Inspector can both bind HTML objects to dynamic data.

5. The Application category of the Insert panel and the Server Objects selection under the Insert menu can both be used to create these special objects.

Exercises

1. Create an entire linked database system using your own HTML design. The design, thus far, has been driven by functionality. It's wise to keep in practice with the Dreamweaver MX HTML tools and learn to integrate them into the creation of dynamic sites.

2. Modify the existing Update screen so that it also offers the option to delete the existing record. Be careful, just adding a server behavior to the existing update screen might cause disastrous results. Hint: you'll need to create *two* forms on a single page to do this properly.

DAY 12

Writing Advanced Database Queries

So far, you've seen what Dreamweaver MX can do if you stick to the simple queries. You can retrieve information from the database and display it. Many times, you'll find that the simple query mode is all you need to make your site. For advanced applications, however, you'll want to tap the power of SQL to handle some of your program logic. This chapter provides a short SQL tutorial so that you can harness the power of your MySQL database server. In many ways, this is a continuation of the lesson on Day 6, "Introduction to Dynamic Web Applications and Database Design." Today, you will learn:

- How to set up database tables using SQL
- Different techniques for writing SQL queries that perform functions beyond what is possible in Dreamweaver MX
- How to point and click your way to an advanced query within Dreamweaver MX

Why We Need SQL

For the past few days, you've been using Dreamweaver MX's simple queries and server behaviors to write Web pages that have dynamic functionality. Unfortunately, there is a limit to the amount of flexibility you can achieve with the built-in behaviors. For example, if you allow users to input a first and last name on a form, and then want to search the database for those names, you won't be able to do it with a simple Dreamweaver MX query.

Simple recordsets, such as the one shown in Figure 12.1, only allow you to select data based on a single parameter passed to the behavior. If you want to use multiple pieces of information in a simple query, you're out of luck.

FIGURE 12.1

A simple query is limited to data selection based on a single input parameter.

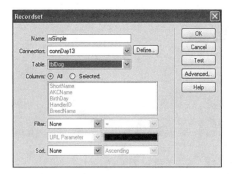

That's just the tip of the iceberg. Using the SQL directly, you can select database records based on multiple attributes, sort by multiple attributes, perform mathematical and logical functions on field values, randomize information, and a whole lot more.

Today's lesson will give you a working knowledge of SQL, which will allow you to create truly advanced applications, all without leaving the comfort of the Dreamweaver MX environment. Although Dreamweaver MX does provide a means of clicking to create a few limited advanced queries, you'll probably find it easier to type the queries directly into the application. This also gives you access to database functions beyond what is built into Dreamweaver MX.

Note

In case the term SQL is new to you, it stands for *Structured Query Language*. SQL is a language that was developed for querying relational database systems. It has become a widely accepted standard and is used in almost all commercial database systems, as well as several Open Source applications, such as MySQL, which is what we're using in this book.

I'm Not Sold...Why Do I Need to Learn this Stuff?

If you don't learn SQL, you'll need to learn one of the application server languages (VBScript, PHP, and so on) to create advanced functionality. If you want to be able to write applications for a number of server platforms, you'll need to learn a number of different languages.

If you learn SQL, on the other hand, you'll find that you can put a great deal of your application logic in your database, which makes it transportable to *any* server language. For example, if you are building an online shopping cart that needs to calculate tax, shipping, and total cost, you could either build the math into the application (which you would have to do outside of the Dreamweaver server behaviors), or use SQL functions in your database server to perform the calculations and return the results—which would be made available as a recordset in Dreamweaver MX—regardless of whether you're deploying on PHP, ASP, JSP, and so on.

Let's start by looking at the SQL needed to create a database. You've already seen the SQL statements used to do this, but do you know how to write your own? After mastering the basic tools for creating databases, tables, and other structures, we'll move on to queries. Make sure that you have a database server installed before continuing—you'll need to be able to type commands into your server console in order to follow along.

 Note

If you're using Access, you can still use SQL to create a query. Create a new query and then choose SQL from the View menu. You can type SQL directly into the resulting dialog box. Microsoft Access, however, isn't a full-featured SQL system, so some queries might fail.

12

The Database Objects

Four primary objects need to be defined before you can start creating SQL. This might seem a bit trivial if you're used to working with databases, but if this is all new to you, it might help clarify things a little bit. Within Dreamweaver MX, you have access to four database structures:

Databases—These are the container elements, which are defined when creating a connection. A database itself doesn't contain data—it does, however, contain other elements that actually hold the information.

Tables—They hold the actual data in the database. The type of information held in a database table is defined when the table is created. Multiple tables can exist within a single database and can be related to one another to form a normalized structure.

Views—Think of a view as a virtual table. If you perform a single complex query repeatedly, it might be easier to define it as a view. A view is nothing more than a query that, for all intents and purposes, appears to the outside world as a table. Each time this table is accessed, the SQL query used to create it is executed and the data returned, as if it were a *real* table.

Stored Procedures—These are program subroutines that are stored on the remote database server. Like a view, a stored procedure isn't a storage place for actual data, but a virtual construct. Stored procedures can be used to process data and return the result directly into Dreamweaver MX as if the data were a standard recordset. Unfortunately, different database servers support different programming languages for writing stored procedures. If you want to remain truly portable, keep as much of the code as possible written in SQL.

The dynamic applications in this book will work mainly with tables. Views and stored procedures are dependent on the database server you've chosen. Because *every* SQL database supports tables, you shouldn't have any problem applying this to any Dreamweaver MX compatible database system.

Creating Databases and Tables

The first step in working with a database system is creating the database container itself. This will hold all the tables, views, and so on for an entire collection of data. Remember, when you say the word *database*, you're referring to a collection of data, not the individual pieces of data themselves. What you might not have realized is that you actually created a number of databases and tables when you set up MySQL in Day 6. This was all performed "behind the scenes" by having MySQL run a simple import script. In this section you'll learn exactly what happened, and how you can do it by hand, if need be.

Assuming you installed MySQL on your system in Day 6, you're ready to go—you will need to use the MySQL command-line tool `mysql`, activated by typing `C:\mysql\bin\mysql` on your Windows machine, or just `mysql` on Mac OS X. Otherwise you should find out how to access the SQL console for your database server before continuing. Your server documentation should provide the information to get to this point. If you're using a more visually oriented tool, you'll need to find the equivalent functions to these commands.

First, create a database:

```
CREATE DATABASE <database name>
```

> **Note**
>
> Because SQL statements often grow quite large, most systems allow them to stretch across several lines and require a terminator character to tell them to execute the statement. In the case of MySQL and Access, which are used in this book, the semicolon is the terminating character.

The creation command will create a completely empty database. After a database has been created, depending on your system, you might need to explicitly tell your database server that you want to *use* the database, like this:

```
USE <database name>
```

For example, let's start simple by actually creating the database we're working with today, day12. If you're using MySQL, you'll need to use the username dreamweaver and the password 21days to invoke the mysql command-line client, because these were set up in Day 6 (mysql -udreamweaver -p21days):

```
[carrot3:~] jray% mysql -udreamweaver -p21days
Welcome to the MySQL monitor.  Commands end with ; or \g.
Your MySQL connection id is 927 to server version: 3.23.42

Type 'help;' or '\h' for help. Type '\c' to clear the buffer.

mysql>
```

The command-line client is now ready and waiting for input. Type **create database day12;** to create the database, followed by **use day12;** to switch to the new database.

```
CREATE database day12;
Query OK, 1 row affected (0.07 sec)

USE day12;
Database changed
mysql>
```

12

If you want to delete the database that you've defined, you can use the DROP command, just like CREATE:

```
DROP DATABASE <database name>
```

> **Tip**
>
> If you're using the MySQL data that was seeded into the system in Day 6, all the "work" of this chapter has already been done for you! Part of the purpose of today is to get you used to working with SQL and understanding the syntax. Because of this, you might want to DROP DATABASE day12, and then CREATE DATABASE day12 to get a fresh start and complete the different exercises along with the text. If you want to rebuild the complete database structure, repeat the seeding process that you followed in Day 6.

After a database has been created, you need to set up the internal tables that will actually hold the data that you want to store.

When making a table, you'll use another CREATE command to tell the system what type of data you want to store—if any.

```
CREATE TABLE <tablename> (<columns…>,<columns…>)
```

For example, let's go ahead and create the tables for keeping track of a dog show, just like those defined in Day 6. See Listing 12.1.

LISTING 12.1   Create the Database Structure Used Throughout Day 12

```
1 create table tblBreed {
2       BreedName varchar(250) not null,
3       BreedStandards text,
4       primary key (BreedName)
5 }
6
7 create table tblResult {
8       AKCName varchar(250) not null,
9       WinDate date not null,
10       primary key (BreedName,WinDate)
11 }
12
13 create table tblDog {
14       ShortName varchar(100),
15       AKCName varchar(250) not null,
16       Birthday date,
17       HandlerID int,
18       BreedName varchar(250),
19       primary key (AKCName)
20 }
21
22 create table tblHandler (
23       HandlerID int not null,
24       FirstName varchar(150),
25       LastName varchar(100),
26       primary key (HandlerID)
27 )
```

Tip

In many ways, today's lesson really is a continuation of Day 6. Refer back to that lesson if you need to get an idea of what we're doing.

This lesson is the closest you'll get to a programming language in the text, so don't be too frightened.

This simple multi-table database is designed to keep track of dog breeds and results from dog shows that you've visited, including the types of dogs and their handlers.

Data Types

When tables are defined, each field must have a name and a *data type*. The data type determines what kind of information that database will hold. Let's take a look at some common data types that you'll see in Dreamweaver MX projects:

`int`—Integers (1,2,3,–1,–2,–100, and so on)

`char(#)`—Holds a specified number of characters. This particular data type will always use the same amount of space, no matter how many characters are actually stored.

`varchar(#)`—Holds a variable number of characters up to a specified limit. Unlike the char data type, `varchar` only stores as much data as needed.

`float`—Floating point numbers (or numbers with decimal places). Typically used for representing money or the results of floating-point-based calculations.

`date`—Quite simply, stores the date.

`text`—Holds a large amount of text information (gigabytes)—more than `varchar` or `char`. Useful for storing comments or large amounts of information from forms.

> **Tip**
>
> Many more data types are available within different database systems. For example, you might have access to small integers under the type name `tinyint`, or fields that store the date and time `datetime`. Check your database documentation to find out what types are available to you.

12

> **Caution**
>
> If you've worked with databases before, you might want to use binary fields to embed binary information, such as photographs, into a database. Unfortunately, this is not currently possible in Dreamweaver MX. There are, however, workarounds, which we'll discuss over the next few days.

Along with the field definitions are two other pieces of information, the first is the modifier attribute NOT NULL. Adding NOT NULL to the end of a field name tells the database system that the field *must* not have a null value in it—that is, it *must* contain some sort of information. This is not the same as an empty string (`""`), which *is* information. A NULL value is considered to be a complete lack of data.

The second piece of non-field declaration information is the *primary key*. As you learned on Day 6, a primary key is used to uniquely identify a piece of information in a table. Obviously, this particular field (or fields) must contain information and therefore is typically declared NOT NULL in the corresponding table definition.

Tip

> Many database systems will assume that any fields used in the primary key are implicitly defined as NOT NULL. MySQL does not take this approach and forces you to add NOT NULL to the primary key fields.
>
> To maintain compatibility between different database systems, you should include NOT NULL in your table definitions.

Similar to the database DROP command, you use

```
DROP TABLE <table name>
```

to completely remove a table from the database. This removes the table and all the information it might contain from the database. We haven't actually entered any data into the tables yet, so now is the time to test a DROP command or two, if you so desire.

Adding/Changing Data

Entering data into a database is quite simple—you use the INSERT command. You'll use two forms for inserting data—one for inserting a partial record, another for inserting a complete record into a table:

```
INSERT INTO <table name> [(<field1,field2,...>)] VALUES
(<'value1','value2',...>)
```

Using the first variation of the command (that is, including the field name list), you can provide a comma-separated listing of field names and the corresponding data that they should receive. For example:

```
insert into tblDog (ShortName,AKCName,Birthday,HandlerID,BreedName) values
➥('Maddy','Maddy The Great','2000-12-05','1','Pomeranian');
```

The second variation assumes you will insert all the fields at once and accepts the values in the order of the fields as defined when creating the tables.

```
insert into tblDog values ('Maddy','Maddy The Great','2000-12-
05','1','Pomeranian');
```

Caution

The first form of the INSERT command is often confusing because it gives the implication that you can store any data you want, whenever you want. In reality, you must obey the same NOT NULL rules that you set when creating the table.

Furthermore, you cannot re-run the INSERT command with additional field names to add information that was missing the first time around. You must either delete the partial record or use the UPDATE command to change the field values.

Try inserting some records into the tables that we've created. See Listing 12.2.

LISTING 12.2   Insert the Sample Data into the Database

```
1 INSERT INTO tblBreed VALUES ('Pomeranian',
2  'Small fuzzy dog, no teeth, walks with a limp');
3 INSERT INTO tblBreed VALUES ('American Eskimo',
4  'Small fuzzy dog, white, known for it's ferocious bark and poisonous teeth');
5 INSERT INTO tblBreed VALUES ('Great Dane',
6  'Large muscular dog, easily operates heavy machinery');
7 INSERT INTO tblBreed VALUES ('13 inch Beagle',
8  'Only two inches tall, the 13 inch beagle has an enormous 23inch tail');
9
10 INSERT INTO tblDog VALUES ('Maddy','Maddy The Great Hair Clump',
11  '1999-12-05','1','Pomeranian');
12 INSERT INTO tblDog VALUES ('Norman','Psycho Norman',
13  '2001-11-15','2','Pomeranian');
14 INSERT INTO tblDog VALUES ('Abull','Abull eats children',
15  '1995-01-01','1','Great Dane');
16 INSERT INTO tblDog VALUES ('Coco','Coco is not spelled with an a',
17  '2001-01-23','3','American Eskimo');
18 INSERT INTO tblDog VALUES ('Sham','Long ears elite',
19  '1999-12-05','3','American Eskimo');
20 INSERT INTO tblDog VALUES ('Ginger','An inch too short',
21  '1997-06-23','4','13 inch Beagle');
22
23 INSERT INTO tblResult VALUES ('Maddy The Great Hair Clump','2002-05-15');
24 INSERT INTO tblResult VALUES ('Abull eats children','2002-05-15');
25 INSERT INTO tblResult VALUES ('Coco is not spelled with an a','2002-06-21');
26 INSERT INTO tblResult VALUES ('Maddy The Great Hair Clump','2002-06-21');
27
28 INSERT INTO tblHandler VALUES ('1','John','Ray');
29 INSERT INTO tblHandler VALUES ('2','Russ','Schelby');
30 INSERT INTO tblHandler VALUES ('3','Robyn','Ness');
31 INSERT INTO tblHandler VALUES ('4','Diane','Babulak');
```

12

This data adds several dog breeds, dogs, dog handlers, and the results of dog shows to the system. Although it might seem like a discontinuous mess right now, in a few minutes we'll look at queries that pull it all together.

Note

> No, those aren't real dog breed descriptions. Most breed standards are long and boring. I decided that your typing fingers are more important.

Tip

> An advanced feature of the INSERT command is the use of a SELECT statement (a query) to replace the VALUES (<value1...>) portion of the INSERT command. This enables you to insert data that can be retrieved from other tables (in the form of a query) directly into a given table. Read ahead for information about the SELECT syntax.

After you have data in your system, you can use two commands to modify it: UPDATE and DELETE.

Update

UPDATE does exactly what its name implies—it updates existing records in the SQL database. The format of an UPDATE is simple, but also very powerful:

UPDATE <table name> SET <field name 1>=<expression 1>,<field name 2>=<expression 2>,<field name n>=<expression n> [WHERE <search expression>]To use UPDATE, you must supply a table name, as well as the names of the fields that need to be updated, and the new values that they should take on. For example, this is a *partial* UPDATE statement, which will update the last name of all the dog handlers in the tblHandler table. **Do not execute this command!**

```
UPDATE tblHandler SET LastName='Smith';
```

This is a valid UPDATE command but what is missing? Hopefully, it should be obvious that this is lacking any way to identify the records that it is updating. In fact, if you were to run this command on the database, and then display the results, you might be a bit surprised. *Each* of the handler's last names will have been changed to Smith. Without being able to differentiate between any of the records, it simply updates all of them!

INPUT
```
UPDATE tblHandler SET LastName='Smith';

SELECT * FROM tblHandler;
```

OUTPUT

```
+———————+———————+———————+
| HandlerID | FirstName | LastName |
+———————+———————+———————+
|         1 | John      | Smith    |
|         2 | Russ      | Smith    |
|         3 | Robyn     | Smith    |
|         4 | Diane     | Smith    |
+———————+———————+———————+
4 rows in set (0.57 sec)
```

Thank goodness you didn't use the command! You didn't did you? If you did, don't worry, you can just use UPDATE correctly to fix the records.

The lesson to be learned from this is that without the WHERE clause, SQL will assume that you mean to operate on *all* the records. The same holds true for the DELETE and SELECT statements, which you'll learn about in a few minutes.

So, the next question is, how do you fill in the search expression for the WHERE clause? The search expression must evaluate to a true or false condition, which will indicate whether or not a record can be selected. You can use typical Boolean algebra to create the search expression:

<fieldname> = <value>—Selects records based on a direct comparison to a value.

<fieldname> > <value>—Selects records where the value of a field is greater than a given value.

<fieldname> < <value>—Selects records where the value of a field is less than a given value.

<fieldname> >= <value>—Selects records where the value of a field is greater than or equal to a given value.

<fieldname> <= <value>—Selects records where the value of a field is less than or equal to a given value.

<fieldname> LIKE <value>—Selects records based on a simple SQL pattern-matching scheme. The character % matches any number or characters, whereas _ matches a single character. Check your database documentation for additional information on its pattern matching capabilities.

These basic expressions can be combined to form more complex searches:

NOT <expression>—Evaluates to true when the expression evaluates to false.

<expression> OR <expression>—Evaluates to true if either of the expressions is true.

<expression> AND <expression>—Evaluates to true if both of the expressions are true.

12

(**<expression>**)—Uses parentheses to combine expressions to force an order of evaluation.

To make things even more complicated (or "feature-ific," if you prefer), you can use a variety of SQL mathematical and string operations to manipulate field values within expressions, all on-the-fly. For example, if you have fields named a and b, you can create an expression to determine if the combined total of the fields is greater than 10, by using "a+b > 10" as the search expression.

Each database system offers different levels of functionality, so, again, be sure to check your database documentation for its exact specifications. We're going to use a few of the more common functions today, but it's likely that you might have access to many more.

Now, back to the matter of updating the `tblHandler` table. Suppose you want to change the last name of the dog handler whose `HandlerID` is 4 because she recently got married and her name is now Burkholder. Using the `WHERE` clause, you could just write

```
UPDATE tblHandler SET LastName='Burkholder' WHERE HandlerID='4'
```

Caution

> With the data that we have in the `tblHandler` table, you could just have easily written the search expression to check for a `LastName` field equal to `'Babulak'`. Unfortunately, there is a chance (however small) that you'll find another 'Babulak' in the table and accidentally change that name too. In a database of a few hundred thousand people, you're likely to have a few that match.
>
> In a production system, if you're trying to update a single record (rather than a group of records), you should base your search expression on the primary key for the table.

After updating the record, it should be visible in the `tblemployee` table:

INPUT
```
UPDATE tblHandler SET LastName='Burkholder' WHERE HandlerID='4';
Query OK, 1 row affected (1.20 sec)
```

OUTPUT
```
SELECT * FROM tblHandler;
+----------+-----------+------------+
| HandlerID | FirstName | LastName   |
+----------+-----------+------------+
|        1 | John      | Ray        |
|        2 | Russ      | Schelby    |
|        3 | Robyn     | Ness       |
|        4 | Diane     | Burkholder |
+----------+-----------+------------+
4 rows in set (0.10 sec)
```

Sure enough, Diane's last name is now "Burkholder."

Deleting Data

Because you've already learned about creating search expressions with WHERE, understanding how the DELETE command works should be no problem. In fact, you'll be happy to know that many of the available SQL commands use the same search expression to select records from database tables.

When using DELETE, you are deleting an entire record, not just fields from a record. All you need to supply is the name of a field and a search expression to select the records.

```
DELETE from <table name> [WHERE <search expression>]
```

Similar to UPDATE, the DELETE command *can* be used without the WHERE and search expression. As you saw before, this will result in all the records being selected. If all the records are selected in a DELETE command, they'll all be deleted! Be careful to define your delete search expression, otherwise you might find that you're deleting records you hadn't intended to touch.

You might find that testing the search expression with a SELECT statement is a good way to find out what you're about to delete before you delete it.

You now have enough background to create and work with database structures and information. The real power of SQL hasn't been tapped, but that's what we're going to do now.

12

Querying Database Tables

After you have information in your database tables, the true power of SQL can finally become apparent by learning how to query that data.

SQL databases were designed to be relational. This means that you can take multiple tables and relate information from one table to another. In the example tables, we can relate dogs to breeds, handlers to dogs, and dogs to winners.

By combining information from multiple locations, you can build truly powerful queries that aren't possible in single table flat-file database systems.

All queries are performed using the SELECT command to select records from a table, or multiple tables, based on a search expression. A simplified model of the SELECT syntax looks similar to this:

```
SELECT <field name1>,<field name2>,...FROM <table name 1>,<table name 2>,...
[WHERE <search expression>] [ORDER BY <expression> ASC|DESC]
```

If you want to select all the fields in a table or tables, you don't have to list each field name—instead, you can just use the * character as shorthand for all fields.

The simplest query (which you've already seen) selects all the records from a single table:

```
SELECT * FROM <table name>
```

For example:

INPUT

```
SELECT * FROM tblHandler;
```

OUTPUT

```
+--------+-----------+------------+
| HandlerID | FirstName | LastName  |
+--------+-----------+------------+
|      1 | John      | Ray        |
|      2 | Russ      | Schelby    |
|      3 | Robyn     | Ness       |
|      4 | Diane     | Burkholder |
+--------+-----------+------------+
4 rows in set (0.10 sec)
```

> **Note**
>
> Try selecting all records from more than one table (SELECT * FROM tblBreed,tblDog,tblHandler); you might be interested in the results. Rather than one table followed by another, you will get a combination of the three tables (called a *Cartesian join* or *product*)—each record in each table is matched with each record in every other table.

Sorting Information

To sort the information based on one of the fields, use ORDER BY with an expression (often one or more comma separated field names) and ASC for ascending order or DESC for descending order. For example, ordering the tblDog table by the Birthday field in descending order will give you a list of the dogs, from youngest to oldest:

INPUT

```
SELECT * FROM tblDog ORDER BY Birthday DESC;
```

OUTPUT

```
+ — — — — —+— — — — — — — — — +— — — — — — +— — — — —+— — — — — — — —·+
| ShortName | AKCName          | BirthDay   | HandlerID | BreedName       |
+ — — — — —+— — — — — — — — — +— — — — — — +— — — — —+— — — — — — — —·+
| Norman    | Psycho Norman    | 2001-11-15 |         2 | Pomeranian      |
| Coco      | Coco is not spelled| 2001-01-23 |        3 | American Eskimo |
| Maddy     | Maddy The Great Hai| 1999-12-05 |        1 | Pomeranian      |
| Sham      | Long ears elite  | 1999-12-05 |         3 | American Eskimo |
| Ginger    | An inch too short| 1997-06-23 |         4 | 13 inch Beagle  |
| Abull     | Abull eats children| 1995-01-01 |        1 | Great Dane      |
+ — — — — —+— — — — — — — — — +— — — — — — +— — — — —+— — — — — — — —·+
```
6 rows in set (0.03 sec)

This is great for retrieving all the information in a particular table, but it doesn't really do *that* much. In order to put SQL to work for you, you need to write queries that combine and use the data in multiple different tables and produce results that can't be duplicated in a simple query.

Joining Tables

To really start to see how an advanced query can work, you need to *join* the information in multiple different tables. This means that you create a relationship between the different available tables and combine the information in an intelligent manner.

For example, suppose that we wanted to display a list of each dog's short name and his or her handler's name. Because these fields are stored in many different tables, "joining" them is the only way to do this. By using the HandlerID field common to both the tblDog and tblHandler tables, you can create an advanced query that returns exactly what you want:

INPUT

```
SELECT FirstName,LastName,Shortname FROM tblHandler,tblDog WHERE
tblHandler.HandlerID=tblDog.HandlerID;
```

OUTPUT

```
+ — — — — —·+— — — — — —+— — — — —·+
| FirstName | LastName  | Shortname |
+ — — — — —·+— — — — — —+— — — — —·+
| John      | Ray       | Maddy     |
| Russ      | Schelby   | Norman    |
| John      | Ray       | Abull     |
| Robyn     | Ness      | Coco      |
| Robyn     | Ness      | Sham      |
| Diane     | Burkholder | Ginger   |
+ — — — — —·+— — — — — —+— — — — —·+
```
6 rows in set (0.25 sec)

12

In this query, the relationship between the tables is defined by

```
WHERE tblHandler.HandlerID=tblDog.HandlerID
```

The search expression, however, doesn't have to stop at a single relationship—it can include any of the other expressions that we've mentioned today. For example, how about a query that selects all the dogs who have handlers with the last name Ray?

Try this:

INPUT
```
select Shortname from tblHandler,tblDog
WHERE tblHandler.HandlerID=tblDog.HandlerID AND
tblHandler.LastName='Ray';
```

OUTPUT
```
+———————+
| Shortname |
+———————+
| Maddy     |
| Abull     |
+———————+
2 rows in set (0.50 sec)
```

It works, but notice that the dog handler names aren't displayed? This is by design, and is intended to demonstrate that although only a few fields might be returned from a query, the search expression itself has access to all the field information.

Now we're starting to get somewhere—but we're really only scratching the surface. How about a query that gives us the dogs' short names and ages in years?

INPUT
```
SELECT shortname,YEAR(NOW())-YEAR(Birthday) FROM tblDog;
```

OUTPUT
```
+———————+———————————————+
| shortname | YEAR(NOW())-YEAR(Birthday) |
+———————+———————————————+
| Maddy     |                          3 |
| Norman    |                          1 |
```

```
| Abull     |                         7 |
| Coco      |                         1 |
| Sham      |                         3 |
| Ginger    |                         5 |
+ — — — — —.+ — — — — — — — — — — — —+
```

6 rows in set (0.65 sec)

This query uses two new functions to perform some simple math: NOW(), which returns the current date and time, and YEAR() which returns the year, given a date. To calculate a numeric age, we just take the current year and subtract the birthday year. Suddenly, with a little bit of math, we have access to information that was never really stored in the database—and if *we* have access to it by writing a query, Dreamweaver MX has access to it by creating an advanced recordset.

Calculations in a Query

When including calculations in a query, it is often easier to give them a real field name rather than just taking a name based on the function. For example, rather than show the function ' YEAR(NOW())-YEAR(Birthday)' in the results, wouldn't it be nice to just see 'Age'? This makes Dreamweaver happier and will make you a little saner if you're working with documents that have dozens of recordsets and hundreds of fields.

By changing the query slightly to include a SQL variable, you can have the calculation value returned as if it were any other field in the database. The format for this virtual field is

```
<expression> AS '<variable name>'
```

Let's say that we now want to show the dog's age in dog years. The calculation is simply ((YEAR(NOW())-YEAR(Birthday))*6). To display this in a table with the dog's short name, you can write this query:

INPUT
```
SELECT shortname,((YEAR(NOW())-YEAR(Birthday))*6) AS 'DogAge' FROM
tblDog;
```

OUTPUT
```
+ — — — — —.+ — — —+
| shortname | DogAge |
+ — — — — —.+ — — —+
| Maddy     |     18 |
| Norman    |      6 |
| Abull     |     42 |
| Coco      |      6 |
| Sham      |     18 |
| Ginger    |     30 |
+ — — — — —.+ — — —+
```
6 rows in set (0.01 sec)

12

By working with the functions in your SQL database server, you can use your existing data to create new information based on the relationships between the tables. Careful database planning makes this possible. Your alternative is to learn how to perform these actions in the programming language used on the server—yuck.

Summarization Tools

Summarizing data is another very useful part of any query. Using the summarization functions, you can easily find totals for numeric columns, or count the number of records of a particular type. Let's take a look at a few of these functions now:

MAX()—The maximum of a given field. Used to match the highest value. For example, if you use MAX() on the Birthday field of the tblDog table, it should return the highest (most recent) birthday in the list, which is the youngest dog in the group.

INPUT

```
SELECT MAX(Birthday) FROM tblDog;
```

OUTPUT

```
+ — — — — — — —.+
| MAX(Birthday) |
+ — — — — — — —.+
| 2001-11-15    |
+ — — — — — — —.+
1 row in set (0.01 sec)
```

> **Note**   Depending on your mathematical calculation, you might want to use the round function to strip off trailing decimal places and create "prettier" output. On the other hand, Dreamweaver MX can do this for you by setting format values when binding with dynamic data.

MIN()—The minimum of a given field. It is the exact opposite of the MAX() function. Used on the dog's Birthday field, it should give you the birthday of the *oldest* dog.

INPUT

```
SELECT MIN(Birthday) FROM tblDog;
```

OUTPUT

```
+ — — — — — — —.+
| MIN(Birthday) |
+ — — — — — — —.+
| 1995-01-01    |
+ — — — — — — —.+
1 row in set (0.54 sec)
```

SUM()—Sums the values of a given (or calculated) field. For example, to find the sum of all the dog's ages in doggy years:

INPUT

```
SELECT SUM((YEAR(NOW())-YEAR(Birthday))*7) AS 'TotalDogAge' FROM tblDog;
```

OUTPUT

```
+ — — — — — — ·+
| TotalDogAge |
+ — — — — — — ·+
|         140 |
+ — — — — — — ·+
1 row in set (0.04 sec)
```

COUNT()—Provides a count of the number of occurrences of a given field. Suppose for example, we want to count the number of dogs each dog handler is taking care of. We might type something like this:

INPUT

```
SELECT COUNT(HandlerID) FROM tblDog;
```

OUTPUT

```
+ — — — — — — — —+
| COUNT(HandlerID) |
+ — — — — — — — —+
|               6 |
+ — — — — — — — —+
1 row in set (0.56 sec)
```

At first glance, the output might not seem at all useful. After all, this is simply a count of the number of records returned by a search, and Dreamweaver MX actually makes that number available to you without having to resort to a separate query. You're quite right; it *isn't* useful at all!

What you can do to make all these summarization tools more useful is to combine them with the GROUP BY function to organize data into groups for summarization. For example, to actually generate a list of handlers and the number of dogs they work with, first try generating just a list of dogs and their handlers. This is pretty easy; just relate the tblHandler and tblDog tables together based on the HandlerID field in each:

INPUT

```
SELECT tblHandler.HandlerID,FirstName,LastName,shortname
FROM tblDog,tblHandler WHERE tblDog.HandlerID=tblHandler.HandlerID;
```

OUTPUT

```
+ — — — — ·+ — — — — ·+ — — — — — + — — — — — ·+
| HandlerID | FirstName | LastName  | shortname |
+ — — — — ·+ — — — — ·+ — — — — — + — — — — — ·+
|         1 | John      | Ray       | Maddy     |
|         1 | John      | Ray       | Abull     |
|         2 | Russ      | Schelby   | Norman    |
```

12

```
|     3 | Robyn   | Ness       | Coco   |
|     3 | Robyn   | Ness       | Sham   |
|     4 | Diane   | Burkholder | Ginger |
+———.+———.+———-+————-+
```
6 rows in set (0.65 sec)

This relates the two tables as we would hope, and it shows that John Ray and Robyn Ness both have two dogs that they handle. We can, however, only see this *visually*. Dreamweaver MX wouldn't be able to look at the results and see, "Oh, two people manage two dogs." To make the information into something that Dreamweaver can handle, *now* we use the COUNT and GROUP BY features. The COUNT function's role should be obvious; we want to count the number of occurrences of a specific field, so let's count the number of times HandlerID appears. To do this, you also need to add a GROUP BY clause so that the SQL server knows that it should be grouping equal HandlerIDs together and then COUNTing them:

```
SELECT COUNT(tblHandler.HandlerID),FirstName,LastName,shortname
FROM tblDog,tblHandler WHERE tblDog.HandlerID=tblHandler.HandlerID
GROUP BY tblHandler.HandlerID;
```

OUTPUT

```
+———————————+————+————+—————+
| COUNT(tblHandler.HandlerID) | FirstName | LastName   | shortname |
+———————————+————+————+—————+
|                           2 | John      | Ray        | Maddy     |
|                           1 | Russ      | Schelby    | Norman    |
|                           2 | Robyn     | Ness       | Coco      |
|                           1 | Diane     | Burkholder | Ginger    |
+———————————+————+————+—————+
```
4 rows in set (0.35 sec)

From that, almost magically, we get a table of each of the dog handlers followed by the number of dogs that they handle. Doing this programmatically in Dreamweaver MX would require that you retrieve the tblHandler table and store each handler in memory (in a variable or an array), and then you would have to retrieve the tblDog table and cycle through it, incrementing the handler variables each time you saw that they were working with a dog in the table. Using database relationships and functions can save you time and effort, and result in code that is easily portable to other systems. Sounds like a good thing, huh?

Other Advanced Techniques

Entire volumes have been written that present SQL and the commands that you can use with it. Obviously, we can't do that here. Today's goal is to provide you with enough background in query writing to add advanced functionality to your applications without having to resort to manually editing your embedded code.

Before seeing how all this integrates into the Dreamweaver MX environment, let's take a look at what else awaits within the wondrous world of SQL. These are a few of the functions that you might be interested in checking out on your database server. The 3.x series of MySQL releases do not support these features, but if you'd like to try the MySQL 4.x betas (`http://www.mysql.com`), you'll find that many of these advanced functions are available.

Views

As I mentioned earlier, a view is essentially a virtual table that is based on a query. After a view is created, you can access it exactly as you would any other table. The syntax for creating a view is simple, but requires that you already understand how to create complex queries:

```
CREATE VIEW <view name> [<field name1>,<field name2>,…] AS <select statement>
```

The field names can be added to provide new names for existing fields, or, if left out, the view will take on the names of the fields in existing tables. As you'll see later in the book, Dreamweaver MX has some problems referring to identically named fields, so you might want to keep views in mind if your database system supports them.

As with databases and tables, you get rid of a view by dropping it:

```
DROP VIEW <view name>
```

12

Stored Procedures

Stored procedures let you write application logic directly within your database server and have it executed as a query. There are both advantages and disadvantages to using stored procedures, and surprisingly, they're interchangeable.

Most database servers let you write stored procedures using SQL or another language. SQL does not lend itself to programming and can only be used to perform functions that could normally be performed in a query. Therefore, the true power comes from writing the procedures in the language native to the database server. Unfortunately, because this is generally specific to the server, it is not portable to other systems. Your code becomes locked to the SQL server platform that it was written on.

The advantage of stored procedures is that they eliminate much of the need to provide custom embedded code in your Web pages to handle application logic. This means that if you write your Web application using stored procedures, you can redeploy on any server platform (ASP, JSP, and so on) using the same programming techniques as long as you're using the same SQL server platform.

As you can see, stored procedures both increase and decrease platform dependence in different ways. Which dependencies are more important to you is entirely your choice. In this book, I've chosen to modify the embedded server code where necessary—otherwise this would have to become a book on database languages as well as the Dreamweaver MX environment.

> **Tip**
>
> A good use of stored procedures is when you are processing secure information. Keeping the application logic as far away from the Web browser is the best strategy when implementing routines that require secure access. For example, rather than embedding credit card processing information into an Active-X control on your Web page, it makes a *lot* more sense to have it handled by a stored procedure in a database.

Sub-queries

An interesting feature of SQL is the capability to embed SELECT statements within other statements.

For example, earlier you saw how to select the minimum birthday (and thus the oldest dog) from the tblDog table:

INPUT
```
SELECT MIN(Birthday) FROM tblDog;
```

OUTPUT
```
+-----------+
| MIN(Birthday) |
+-----------+
| 1995-01-01    |
+-----------+
1 row in set (0.54 sec)
```

Unfortunately, after you've found out the oldest dog's birthday, you're still a query away from finding out *who* the poor aging doggy is:

```
SELECT * FROM tblDog WHERE Birthday='1995-01-01';
```

Using a subselect, you can rewrite the both queries into a single line, like this:

```
SELECT * FROM tblDog WHERE Birthday=(SELECT MIN(Birthday) FROM tblDog);
```

The inner-most query is executed first and used in the upper query. You can embed multiple levels of queries—each one returns its results to the one before.

The level of complexity of the query is entirely in your hands. Sub-queries are very similar to joins, but offer the ability to accomplish in one step what can sometimes take several.

Advanced Queries and Dreamweaver MX

So, exactly what counts as an advanced query, and how can you use Dreamweaver MX to perform it? The answer to the first question is simple—anything that involves more than a single table is considered an advanced query within Dreamweaver MX. The simple query dialog allows you to display information from the fields of only one table.

The interface for specifying an advanced query is a bit convoluted, probably to the point where you'll find it easier to enter the SQL by hand than to point and click to enter it.

As a final exercise, let's enter one of the queries developed today into Dreamweaver MX.

Open Dreamweaver MX and create a new project for the day (Day 12) with a new document named advanced.asp. You're just going to be using this to test some queries, so the details of this page aren't particularly important.

Next, use the Database panel to add a connection named connDay12 to the day12 database that you've been working with directly today.

Now you're ready to play. Open the Data Binding panel, and click the + button to add a new recordset to the page. Your screen should look similar to Figure 12.1. The first thing you should do is click the Advanced button to switch to the advanced recordset (query) mode. The dialog box should update itself, as demonstrated by Figure 12.2.

The SQL query field accepts a plain text SQL query which you can simply type in. If you're interested in saving yourself some typing, you can add objects to the database query by using the Database Items area of the advanced query configuration.

There are three items to work with:

- Tables
- Views
- Stored procedures

12

FIGURE 12.2

Advanced mode is where we want to be.

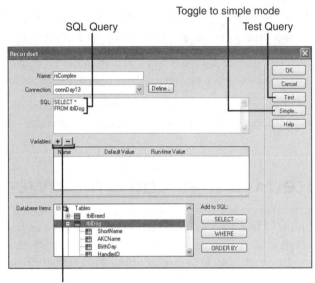

Each of these can be expanded by clicking the disclosure arrow to the left to show the items underneath them. For example, the tables and views categories contain all the tables and views from the current connection. Stored procedures contain the available stored procedures.

Each of these categories can be opened further to reveal additional database information, such as individual fields.

To incorporate these elements into a query, there are three buttons to the right of the database items area. By clicking one of these buttons when the appropriate element is selected in the database, Dreamweaver MX will insert the corresponding SQL into the query window.

Each of the buttons can be used with a particular type of database item:

SELECT—Inserts a Table, View, Column (field name), or Procedure into the SELECT `<field name>` or FROM `<table/view/procedure name>` portion of the code.

WHERE—Inserts a field name into the WHERE clause of the SQL.

ORDER BY—Inserts a field name into the ORDER BY clause of the query. Rather than typing SELECT * from tblDog, for example, you could open the Tables category, highlight the tblDog table, and then click the Select button. You can be the judge as to whether that is easier or just plain silly.

The Variables section of the advanced query dialog box is used to control variables that are passed into a query. If, for example, you wanted to use the input of a form in an advanced query, this is where you could do it. We'll be looking at this feature tomorrow, so you'll be learning a lot more about it shortly.

Possibly the most useful feature of the advanced recordset screen is the Test button. Clicking Test will display the results of whatever query you've currently entered into the system. For example, type the reasonably advanced query into the SQL field:

```
SELECT COUNT(tblHandler.HandlerID),FirstName,LastName,shortname
FROM tblDog,tblHandler
WHERE tblDog.HandlerID=tblHandler.HandlerID
GROUP BY tblHandler.HandlerID;
```

Now, click Test. You should see results much like Figure 12.3.

FIGURE 12.3

Use the Test button to test your advanced queries.

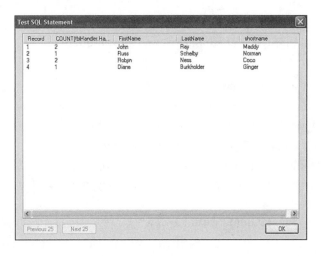

You should now have a tool for testing queries without resorting to the command line. I recommend that you play around with the day12 database and the advanced recordset window so that you can get a feel for how queries are constructed and what information they will produce. You'll need advanced queries from here on out, so take the time to understand SQL and appreciate its capabilities.

Summary

In today's lesson, you learned how to create SQL databases, tables, and queries, and how to enter them directly into Dreamweaver MX to create a far more powerful system than what is allowed with the simple queries.

12

SQL is a very flexible relational database query language that makes it possible to work with data in ways that would be impossible with other systems. The basic syntax is extremely easy to grasp, but allows even the most experienced programmer the ability to develop complex relational systems.

All the projects in this book are implemented using MySQL. If you want to learn more about the specific functions available in MySQL, you might want to skip to Appendix B, "MySQL Quick Function Reference," before continuing on to tomorrow's lesson.

Workshop

The Workshop area is meant to reinforce your reading with a series of questions and exercises.

Q&A

Q Will MySQL ever support views and sub-queries?

A Yes, both of these features are available in MySQL 4.x.

Q How can I compare dates within SQL?

A Use the same comparison operators that you use with other data types (=, <, >, and so on). The SQL Server will handle doing the hard work for you.

Q Is it possible to join more than two tables?

A Absolutely. The reason the examples consist of a single table is to limit the amount of space they take up. You can just as easily join three, four, or more tables within SQL.

Q Can I update data within a view?

A It depends on the features of your database server. Many servers offer the feature of allowing you to update view data just like any other table and even *reject* updates if the updated data would no longer be included within the view.

Quiz

1. How do you create a database within SQL?

2. Why is the phrase "insert data into the database" syntactically wrong?

3. What does * do in a SELECT statement?

4. How can you refer to a specific field name within a specific table?

5. What happens if you do not supply a WHERE clause when selecting records?

Quiz Answers

1. Use the database CREATE command.

2. Although I probably use the same phrase in several places of the book, it isn't entirely correct. A database is the wrapper for one or more tables, views, and so on. These internal structures hold the actual records and are the object of the INSERT command.

3. Selects all the fields, rather than a named subset.

4. Use the format <table name>.<field name>. Although it is possible to use just the field name in many cases, this leads to ambiguities when dealing with multiple tables with identical names.

5. If a query, delete, and so on receive an empty search expression, they will select all the records in the database. This can be a bit distressing for a first-time SQL author who guesses (incorrectly) that an empty search expression would match zero records.

Exercise

Because today's text is mostly about becoming accustomed to the flexibility and power of SQL, all that you need to do is practice using some of the techniques that you learned today. Try building your multi-table database and develop advanced queries for it.

If you're not up to the challenge, use the existing day12 database to practice creating and testing queries in Dreamweaver MX. It's possible to relate *all* the tables in the day12 database to create a list of winning dogs including information about their breeds and handlers. Try writing and testing a query to do this.

12

DAY 13

Restricting User Access

Something has been missing from everything that we've looked at up until this point. You've learned how to create interactive sites and various other database-driven screens, but there's one area that hasn't even been touched—user logins. How many times have you been to a Web site and been asked to create a user profile or been required to log in before you can use any of the features? The ability to know who the users are when they are interacting with a Web site is paramount in providing true personalized interactive services.

Dreamweaver MX offers its own authentication system, but in order to better understand how and why it works, today's lesson will focus on building a similar system by hand. Today you'll learn:

- What login systems are good for, and why you need them.
- How to set up basic login functionality based on an existing user database.
- Security concerns that you should worry about on production Web sites.

Login Systems

There are several ways that you can handle login systems for a Web site, depending on the purpose of your site. If you want a secure site that keeps track of users, you'll need some form of session tracking. Otherwise, you might be able to get away with one of the less secure methods.

HTTP Authentication

Using the basic authorization functions offered by the HTTP protocol, you can pop up a basic username and password window and retrieve the information for your Web site. This procedure, however, uses the standard browser-defined authentication dialog box and doesn't offer the flexibility of designing the interface yourself.

Typically, you can set this up on your Web server using its basic configuration tools without any interaction in Dreamweaver MX. I rarely see this used as the primary form of authentication on a Web site. Instead, it is commonly used to provide limited access to portions of your Web site, such as administrative tools. Because the functionality of the authentication can be handled at the server level, there is no need to make any changes to your existing code in order for it to work. You simply tell the server which directory to protect and which username/password combinations are allowed to access that directory.

Web-Based Login

A Web-based login gives you the greatest control over the way that users interact with your site. Using an HTML-based login page, the system can identify a *good* user versus a *bad* user and give users the option to continue into the system based on their status.

Suppose, for example, you want to create a site from which several users can access a particular section, but the system doesn't need to differentiate *who* the users are—all it needs to do is verify that a user has logged in to the system. In this particular instance, all that you need is a screen that blocks invalid logins and allows valid users to continue.

In addition, each subsequent page that is a privileged page must also include code to verify that a user has logged in correctly. Otherwise invalid users would be able to guess a URL behind the protection screen and have access to it—regardless of the existence of a login screen.

The second way to handle HTML-based logins is to verify the user information in the same manner as the first method. Then instead of just passing a "Yes, this person is allowed to be here" value to the other Web pages, the server sends an identifier that uniquely identifies the person who moves through the Web page. This lets you develop a Web site that is built around the users, and adapts to the users, rather than requiring the users to reconfigure the Web site each time they access it.

Take the example of a store where you can purchase items from an online catalog with your credit card. For me, this store is generally dvdexpress.com—an e-commerce site that stocks just about every DVD on the planet. When I make my biweekly visit to the site, I don't want to have to fill in all of my shipping or billing information again. Instead, I want the system to remember who I am, so I can shop without having to worry about spending 10–15 minutes searching for my credit card and filling in forms.

The system used by dvdexpress.com and other sites allows me to give a username and a password that will retrieve my account information at any point in time. This is far more convenient than having to type it repeatedly.

Unfortunately, although this method of handling logins offers that greatest power, it also offers the greatest challenge—keeping track of user information while the user is logged in. If you're offering a simple "remember me" service such as dvdexpress.com, you don't have to worry about keeping track of what the user is doing from page to page. You simply ask for the username and password, and then retrieve the information from the database, displaying it on the next screen. The trouble is that many times you'll want users to be able to log in as soon as they reach the site. This enables you to access information about them (and, if you desire, to *store* information about them) as they work their way through your Web site.

So, the obvious question is where do we begin? The answer—with the easiest part. The first variation of a login system will be extremely simple. From there, we'll build on that system until we have something that will work almost anywhere!

Because there are two types of login-based systems (secure and not-so-secure), we'll do our best to be as secure as possible on the Web sites. For example, on sites that could pull information out of a database, the sensitive information will only be used when necessary. On pages that do not require high-level security, the login techniques will be more relaxed. Additionally, we'll use a little "home-brewed" authentication, as well as the Dreamweaver MX user authentication behaviors. Don't worry—this will all make sense when you start using it. Let's start by seeing how to build an authentication system by hand.

13

Login SQL and Passwords

The SQL that you need for a user authentication system is trivial. You can keep your basic user information in one table and store additional information in a separate table, relating the two based on a common user ID. If you follow this structure, you only have to build the user authentication once, and you can use it anywhere you'd like without changes.

What information will you need in your user authentication table? Just a few pieces of information:

- User identifier
- Username
- Password

The user identifier is needed to provide a simple single key for determining whether a record is unique. You could, of course, use the username or username *and* password as primary key, but a significant drawback to this approach is that users then cannot change their passwords; the primary key can never change. In addition, Dreamweaver MX doesn't support multiple primary keys directly in its server behaviors. Table 13.1 shows a common database table for user authentication. Throughout the exercises in the book, we'll commonly refer to this table (and minor variations to it) as tblUserInfo.

TABLE 13.1   The tblUserInfo Table Stores Account Information

Fieldname	Description	SQL Data Type
userID*	An auto-incrementing number that identifies a specific user.	int auto_increment
username	The login username.	varchar(250)
password	The login password.	varchar(250)

In any login system, you must pay close attention to the Web site's security requirements.

If the user's password is kept in plain text in the database, and the database is compromised, the information tied to that record could be exposed. If you've ever called a company to ask for your password, and they've been able to look it up, this should have set off a warning alarm in your head! The most information that anyone should ever store about your unencrypted password is a phrase to remind you of what your password is. Encrypted passwords should be stored with a one-way encryption that cannot be decrypted with a single master password. This level of encryption prohibits even the server operators from retrieving a password—they can reset it, but not recover the original information. One-way encryption means that even if a password database is "stolen," the passwords themselves are likely to remain secure.

Passwords should also never be stored in a plain text format if the Web application must be secure. Although one user's account could be compromised if his password is guessed, *all* of the passwords won't be visible if the database table is (somehow) dumped to the Web.

So, how is the password field protected? There are two ways: either through a built-in function in the database system or by writing a stored procedure on the database server itself.

MySQL offers a special function that handles encoding passwords and other sensitive information. Called `password`, this function encrypts the information that is passed to it into something that isn't easily decrypted by a user. For a production Web site, it's probably good to use a commercial grade encryption on the password. For practice, however, the `password` function should be more than sufficient.

Note

A question that might be fluttering around in your head right now is "How in the world do you check to see whether the password that the user enters is correct if the field you need to compare it to is encrypted?" The answer is simple. Before comparing the password field to the value that the user entered, you must encrypt the entered value. If the values are equal, the password is correct.

Inserting records into MySQL using the `password` function requires only a slight variation on the standard method of inserting data. For example, to insert a record for myself into the `tblUserInfo` table, I'd use a command like this:

```
INSERT INTO tblUserInfo VALUES ('','jray',password('mypass'));
```

The `password` function takes as its argument the string that you want to encrypt (in this example it's the password `'mypass'`).

To query the database to determine whether a given username/password combination exists (for example, Whether a valid login is occurring), one would simply use the `password` function to encrypt the plaintext password being compared against the database.

```
SELECT * FROM tblUserInfo WHERE username='jray'
    AND password=password('mypass');
```

13

Note

For the sake of maintaining the highest degree of compatibility between database servers, the examples in this book will *not* include the MySQL `password` function to encrypt data. You are welcome to include them on your own using the instructions given here.

Sample Data

To demonstrate a working login system, obviously we'll need some sample data stored in the system. Table 13.2 shows a few records stored in the `tblUserInfo` table that we can use to verify that the system is working. This information is stored in the day13 database that should have been loaded onto your system in Day 7.

TABLE 13.2 The tblUserInfo Database Table Needs a Few Sample Entries So We Can Test the System

UserID	Username	Password
1	test	test
2	hairy	dog
3	agroves	badmovie
4	robyn	nester

A Simple Login

To create a simple login system, we'll need to set up a new ASP site in Dreamweaver MX (Day 13—Logins), and then create a few pages that query the tblUserInfo table.

Define the Day 13 site, and then open and save a new ASP document named login.asp. This page will have no dynamic behaviors—its purpose is to collect a username and password, and then submit the information to another page for processing.

A Login Screen (login.asp)

Build your page by creating a form named frmLogin that contains two fields with the names username and password, and a submit button. The form's action should be set to verify.asp. The verify.asp page will process the login information, determine whether it is correct, and then react appropriately.

When setting up the form, it's probably easiest to place it inside a three-row, two-column table. The first row should contain a username label and the username HTML field; the second row's cells should be the label password and HTML field password. Finally, the third row's cells can be merged and the submit button inserted. A sample login page is shown in Figure 13.1. There's nothing much to the basic login screen.

 Note

If you want, you can use the password field type for the Password field. Although this doesn't offer any real server security, it does have two purposes. First, it protects a user's password from being seen as it is typed. Second, it offers peace of mind to users. Using the password style for a field shows the users that you (the Web site) recognize that data is sensitive.

FIGURE 13.1

FIGURE 13.1

The login screen is simple.

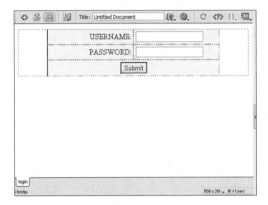

So, how do you actually log in to something? It's all fine and well to have a login form, but it needs to do something!

The form that you've created needs to submit its data to a page for processing. For a change, there's actually no server behavior on this page—its purpose is to supply data to the *next* page in the login system—verify.asp.

Processing the Login Information

Create the next page, verify.asp, now. Remember yesterday how you learned to use the advanced query features of Dreamweaver MX? This is precisely what is going to be used today to handle the login.

Start by adding a connection to your site, named connDay13. This process is probably starting to get familiar:

1. Open the Databases panel in the Application panel group.
2. Click the "+" button and choose Data Source Name (DSN).
3. Create a new connDay13 connection to the day13 data source.

Now, prepare the advanced query that will select all of the records that match both the username and password entered on the login.asp page. This query will also make use of *Dreamweaver variables,* named values that are bound to URL parameters, form values, and so on, which can be used in advanced queries.

To prepare a recordset for the page, follow these steps:

1. Open the Server Behaviors panel.
2. Click the "+" button and choose the Recordset (query) option.
3. Switch to the Advanced mode by clicking the Advanced button.

13

4. Name the recordset `rsLogin` and choose the `connDay13` connection.

5. Add a `varUsername` variable, using a default value of `none`, and the runtime value of `Request("username")`.

6. Add a `varPassword` variable, using a default value of `none`, and the runtime value of `Request("password")`.

7. Finally, add the following SQL statement to the document:

```
SELECT *
FROM tblUserInfo
WHERE username='varUsername' AND password='varPassword'
```

The final recordset configuration should look very similar to Figure 13.2.

FIGURE 13.2

Define the advanced `rsLogin` *query so that it looks like this.*

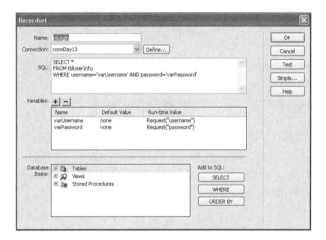

What Do the "Default Values" of the Dreamweaver Variables Do?

The default values are used in the query if values aren't otherwise defined. In the `rsLogin` query, for example, we're expecting two form variables to be passed into the page—username and password. If, for some reason, the `verify.asp` page is called without having these values passed to it, the query will still be performed, but using the values none and none. To be completely safe, we should technically add a user named none with a password set to something *other* than none to the `tblUserInfo` database. This will make certain that the default query *never* returns a valid login. I recommend *always* verifying default values for your queries. If you don't you're likely to find that at one time or another you've left a backdoor open in one of your queries.

If you set default values that match values in the database for the purpose of testing, be sure you remove them before deploying! In the case of the login system, using a valid default username and password as default variable values creates a situation in which *no* username or password needs to be given to gain access to the protected pages.

Now, the fun part—checking to see whether the login information was valid. You can probably guess how we're going to do this. The recordset rsLogin was defined so that it would find a record that matches a username and a password. If the login is incorrect, rsLogin will be empty. To verify this, you can use the Test button inside the query definition to show that the rsLogin query is empty when using the default (and obviously invalid) username and password values of none and none.

To set up your verify.asp document so that it can tell whether a login is valid, you need to define the content for your valid and invalid logins. Create these two areas of content directly within the verify.asp document.

For one region, add the text:

You've logged in successfully!

For the next, use:

Your login information is invalid.

A simple way to do this is to set up both content areas within two different tables. For example, Figure 13.3 shows both a successful message and an unsuccessful login message.

FIGURE 13.3

Set up both the successful and unsuccessful messages from within the single view.

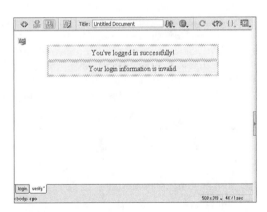

Now that there are two content regions on your screen, you need to set the page so that only the appropriate region is displayed when the user attempts to log in to the page. You can easily do this by setting up the Show Region server behavior based on the status of the recordset.

For the successful login message:

1. Select the successful message. If you inserted this into a table, select the entire table.

2. Open the Server Behaviors panel.

3. Click the "+" button and, from the Show Region submenu, choose Show Region If Recordset Is Not Empty.

4. Choose the rsLogin recordset.

5. Click OK when finished.

The Show Region behavior is shown in Figure 13.4.

FIGURE 13.4

Show the successful login message only if the recordset is not empty.

Likewise, you need to configure the unsuccessful login message so that it is shown when rsLogin *is* empty. Do this now. Because the rsLogin recordset cannot be empty and not empty simultaneously, only the appropriate message is displayed at the appropriate time.

> In case you're concerned that just "hiding" the successful login page content might not be a good way to protect the page, don't worry. The Show Region behavior does not pose a security risk in that it *doesn't* actually hide/show a region on a page by making it visible or invisible. Instead of conditionally showing data, a better way to think of it is as a *delete* region behavior that *doesn't* delete a specific region if the appropriate condition is met. The server dynamically writes the Web page before it is sent to the user's browser.

Testing

Go ahead and try the login system. Transfer both the login and the verification screens to your application server and test them. As part of the testing process, you need to test all the options that are available on the form:

- Invalid username and password
- Invalid username and valid password
- Valid username and invalid password
- Invalid username and empty password
- Valid username and empty password

- Valid username and password
- Empty username and password

As you develop more and more applications, you should run through testing procedures similar to this in order to make sure that your application works as expected under all circumstances.

Maintaining a Session

With the user properly logged in to the system, the problem becomes one of maintaining the user information as users pass from page to page on the site. There are two ways to maintain the identity of users as they make their way through the Web site.

First, the user identifier can be passed from page to page as a portion of the URL, or embedded in a form. This method of session management is useful in that it does not rely on cookies to keep track of users. You'll find that if you implement a site using cookies to handle session management, eventually someone will complain.

The drawback to this approach is that the client is constantly reminding the remote computer who it is. Without custom programming, the user will be able to bookmark a page after logging in to the system and immediately return to the logged-in state. (Although you might see this as a benefit.) Because the user identifier that is being passed between pages never changes, there's no way to tell whether the user has freshly logged in to the system, or is returning from a previous visit.

A popular way to get around this problem is to use *session variables*. Session variables work by using a cookie to store a randomly generated session ID and then use that session ID to store any additional information about the user on the application server itself. After a certain length of inactivity, the server can remove this session ID. When that takes place, the cookie will be worthless, regardless of whether it has expired. Session variables (and the associated cookies they set) are entirely managed by the application server.

Alternatively, you, as the programmer, could simply use cookies to store all of the information you need to track. Typically, you just need to track the userID or another unique identifier, so this is a perfectly viable solution as well.

Unfortunately, Dreamweaver MX provides no support for setting either cookies *or* session variables.

13

Note There is really very little difference (programmatically) between using cookies and passing information from URL to URL. Cookies are more transparent from the user's point of view, but, by requiring that the users have cookie support, are less compatible with customized browser configurations.

So, which technique will we be using here? Let's try both.

Variable Passing

Let's go ahead and implement session management through URL parameter passing. We're going to pass the userID of the logged in user so that we can identify who is using the site. There's very little you'll need to do to achieve this. You will, however, need to learn a new server behavior so that you can implement this feature site-wide.

Create a placeholder page for the rest of the site, called online.asp. Add a "Welcome to our Web site" message to the page; this is just an example of a page that would exist behind the login system.

Open the Dreamweaver MX verify.asp document that includes both the valid and invalid regions. The region that you need to work with is the valid area. In order to let the rest of the site know who we are, we must provide a link from this region to the online.asp document.

Follow the steps to link to the online.asp document while passing the userID identifier:

1. Add a line of text, such as continue, to the portion of the page that contains the valid login region. This will be the linked object.

2. Select the link text and choose Make Link from the Modify menu.

3. Highlight the online.asp file that you've created and saved.

4. Click the Parameters button. You need to add a dynamic parameter to the link that passes the userID information.

5. Add a new parameter that will be used to pass the user ID. As shown in Figure 13.5, this parameter should be named userID.

FIGURE 13.5

Add a new parameter that will pass the user ID.

6. To set the value for the parameter, click inside the `value` field, and then click the lightning bolt icon that appears.

7. Expand the `rsLogin` recordset, choose the `userID` field, and then click OK.

8. Your dynamic URL parameter should now be added to the link configuration dialog box, as shown in Figure 13.6. Click Choose to exit all of the dialog boxes.

FIGURE 13.6

The dynamic parameter will be added to the end of your link.

That should do it. Now, when the user clicks the link to connect to the rest of the site, his or her user ID will be passed through the link to the next page. This parameter can then be used on the subsequent page to look up or store account information, and so on.

There's actually a server behavior specifically for creating links to other pages while passing all existing URL and form parameters. For this very first link, however, we must manually define the parameter passing because the value doesn't yet exist as a URL parameter or form element!

Go ahead and test the page. Notice that when you connect with a valid username and password, the link to the new site page will contain the URL parameter that you want to pass.

Unfortunately, although the page might seem to be complete, there's actually a bit of work that still needs to be done. Easy work, but work nonetheless.

There's a serious problem with the system we've designed. Try playing around with your pages and see what happens. If you follow the logic flow through your site, you'll find that everything is working perfectly. However, this depends entirely on the *assumed* site logic. Put yourself in the shoes of a hacker, however—does a hacker *need* to follow the flow of logic that you've defined for yourself? Of course not! To verify that a problem exists, bypass the login screen and load the `online.asp` page directly in your browser.

Do you realize what the problem is now?

13

You've accessed the "secure" Web page with absolutely no login information. This isn't exactly what you intended, is it?

Luckily, you already know what you need to do in order to fix this problem—use the Show Region server behavior. By defining a simple recordset, `rsVerify`, that selects the `tblUserInfo` user information based on the passed `userID` parameter, you can then use it with a Show Region behavior. If the `userID` doesn't pull up a valid user account, the region should be hidden. Try doing this on the simple `online.asp` page you created. An example of the `rsVerify` recordset is shown in Figure 13.7.

FIGURE 13.7

The `rsVerify` *record-set can be used to with a Show Region behavior to check usernames and passwords on internal Web pages.*

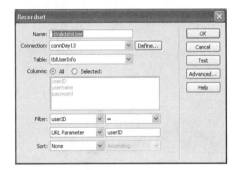

<table>
<tr><td colspan="2">**Caution**</td></tr>
</table>

> These examples should be used as a proof of concept, not something to use on a high-security production system. The trouble with what we're doing here is that the `userID` is an auto-incrementing number that is very easy to guess. On a production server, you'd want to use your database server to create a more difficult to decrypt value that uniquely identifies the user. For example, on MySQL, one could use the function `password(userID+user-name+password)` within the `SELECT` statement to generate a pseudo unique (and difficult to guess) user identifier from the fields in the `tblUserInfo` table. This function could then be used in place of the current `userID` comparisons shown throughout the chapter.
>
> Because this requires working directly with the database server or programming language, it is not covered here.

Tip

> Besides just hiding the content of the page so that it isn't visible when the user isn't logged in, you might want to provide a warning message. You can add an Invalid Access region to the page that is shown when the recordset *is* empty. This provides the page content to people who have logged in correctly and a warning message to people who have tried to bypass the security system.

You'll need to use the Show Region behavior on all pages that are protected from the general public. It might be tempting to not protect pages that only execute queries based on input from pages that *are* protected. This, however, is bad practice because it may reveal enough about your code for a potential intruder to cause damage. The less information a potential hacker has to work with, however, the better.

Moving to a Related Page

If you're using URL parameters to pass a user identifier from the login system into the site itself, you'll be glad to know that there is another easier way to move data from page to page.

An alternative way to transfer URL parameters between pages is to use a server behavior. This isn't really any faster than choosing a dynamic parameter for a link if you're transferring a single parameter (as you did from `verify.asp` to `online.asp`). It does come in handy, however, if you have an entire sequence of parameters that needs to be transferred. You've submitted a form to a page, and then want to transfer all the variables to another page. You could do this by setting a few dozen dynamic URL parameters to transfer.

To use the Go To Related Page behavior, select the text or HTML object that you want to use as the link, and then choose Go To Related Page from the Server Behaviors panel. Fill in, or choose the related page that you're linking to, and choose the parameters that you want to pass.

You can choose to pass URL parameters and form parameters to the related page. The URL parameters are the options that you've been passing back and forth on the URL line—such as the `userID` that you passed to `online.asp`.

The second type of parameter that you can pass is the *form* parameter. These are the variables generated when a form is submitted. If the page you're on is the result of a form submission, you can pass the submitted information to another page by clicking this option.

To test this server behavior, create a new page called `online2.asp`. We'll link from the `online.asp` page to the new page to verify that the `userID` url parameter is passed.

After creating the `online2.asp` document, open the `online.asp` page. Add a text string that you can use as a link to take the user to the new `online2.asp` page. Now, select that text string, open the Server Behaviors panel, click "+", and choose the Go To Related Page. For the related page, enter `online2.asp` and choose to pass URL parameters. Because we aren't using any forms, there's no point in transferring form parameters.

Figure 13.8 shows the Go To Related Page server behavior definition.

13

FIGURE **13.8**

Choose the page you
want to pass existing
parameters to.

> A common stumbling point for first-time users is that the Go To Related
> Page behavior can't be used until URL or Form parameters exist. It's impor-
> tant to note that the contents of a recordset *are not* part of the URL or form
> parameters. Although they are available to be worked with on a page (just
> like form or URL parameters) they are different beasts altogether.
>
> Only *after* you've passed the userID manually to subsequent pages (as you
> did from verify.asp to online.asp) can you use the Go To Related Page
> behavior to pass the value to additional pages. For the test pages we've cre-
> ated, you could use the Go To Related Page behavior to link to all the rest
> of the site pages (if there were more!) from online.asp.

Using Cookies

Rounding out today's work will be a look at the use of cookies to maintain user information. This is not exactly the best-integrated feature of Dreamweaver MX, so we'll do
what we can do within Dreamweaver MX and step outside when we need to.

So far, we've seen a fairly simple way to maintain information about who is logged in,
but it involves passing a lot of data across the URL. Using cookies to do the same thing
is even easier, and you can define a cookie for an entire project—not just a single page.

We're going to look at a bit more advanced use of cookies—namely session variables. As
mentioned earlier, a session variable stores a particular piece of information based on the
session ID stored in a cookie. What makes this incredibly useful is that the cookie set on
the client computer stores only a randomly generated session ID—this is the *only* information stored on the client. The session ID is used to identify other session values that
are stored on the server. This means that there are no security problems created by passing data back and forth between the client and the server.

Unfortunately, as we've already mentioned, the use of cookies (and thus session variables) is not trivial in Dreamweaver MX. It requires editing code by hand. In addition,
your Web site customers must have cookie support turned on in their browsers.

If you're planning on running a cookie-based site, you should probably supply a dis-
claimer somewhere on the site so that users understand how and why they are being

used. A common misconception of many people is that cookies are inherently evil and will be used to store their credit card numbers, their children's social security numbers, and detailed plans for a burglary of their homes. In reality, cookies, properly used, are a fantastic, and mostly benign tool for building secure and powerful Web sites.

In this exercise, we'll adapt the login pages we've already made to use cookies. We'll use the existing login.asp page, and add a cookie (by way of session variable) to the verify.asp document.

Note

> Here's a nice, typical cookie disclaimer that you can use:
>
> This site uses cookies only to maintain your information as you move throughout this site. A *cookie* is a small piece of information usually used to identify an individual when that person is accessing a site. At no time is any personal information stored in a cookie, nor is any tracking information made available to other sites for any reason.
>
> To configure your browser for cookies, follow these instructions.
>
> Internet Explorer:
>
> In IE 4.0, choose Edit from your pull-down menu and select Preferences. If you're using IE 6.0 or greater, use the Tools menu to access Internet Options. Under Receiving Files, select Cookies. Next to When Receiving Cookies, you can select either Never Ask, Ask for each site, or Ask for each cookie. This controls whether your browser prompts you for incoming cookies, or accepts them.
>
> Netscape Navigator:
>
> Choose Edit from your pull-down menu and select Preferences. Select Advanced and click on the appropriate cookie option.

Setting a Session Variable

If you've decided to set a session variable in your application, you'll need to choose the appropriate place to do it. Luckily, you've already learned how to do this. In the verify.asp page, by using the Show Region behavior, you've defined exactly where the session variable should be defined. If the user had a valid login, you can then set a session variable so that it contains the userID. This variable, in turn, will then be accessible from any Web page in the site—without the site needing to pass any of the information between pages *and* without needing to encrypt or generate complicated "unguessable" user IDs.

For example, to set a session variable with the userID after a user has successfully logged in, open the verify.asp page that you created with the valid login and invalid login regions.

13

Look for the section that defines the valid-login region:

```
1  <% If Not rsLogin.EOF Or Not rsLogin.BOF Then %>
2  <table width="100%" border="0" cellspacing="0" cellpadding="0">
3    <tr align="center" bgcolor="#00FF00">
4      <td>
5        <p><font face="Arial, Helvetica, sans-serif" size="+2">
6        You've Logged in Successfully!</font></p>
7        <p><font face="Arial, Helvetica, sans-serif" size="+2">
8        <a href="online.asp?userID=<%=(rsLogin.Fields.Item("userID").Value)%>">
9        CONTINUE</a>
10       </font></p>
11     </td>
12   </tr>
13 </table>
14 <% End If ' end Not rsLogin.EOF Or NOT rsLogin.BOF %><br>
```

In defining the show region in line 1, Dreamweaver MX has set up the conditions under which the session variable should be set. If you set the session variable in this area, only valid users will have a session ID generated.

So, how exactly do you do this? Simple—by inserting this piece of code into the appropriate area:

```
<% Session("userID")=<your user ID query> %>
```

You'll need to replace the *<your user ID query>* with the actual query that returns the userID field from your database. For our document, with a recordset named rsLogin that returns the userID field, use this command:

```
<% Session("userID")=rsLogin.Fields.Item("userID").Value %>
```

The final block of HTML (and embedded language) code should look like this:

```
1  <% If Not rsLogin.EOF Or Not rsLogin.BOF Then %>
2  <% Session("userID")=rsLogin.Fields.Item("userID").Value %>
3  <table width="100%" border="0" cellspacing="0" cellpadding="0">
4    <tr align="center" bgcolor="#00FF00">
5      <td>
6        <p><font face="Arial, Helvetica, sans-serif" size="+2">
7          You've Logged in Successfully!</font></p>
8        <p><font face="Arial, Helvetica, sans-serif" size="+2">
9        <a href="online.asp?userID=<%=(rsLogin.Fields.Item("userID").Value)%>">
10         CONTINUE</a></font></p>
11     </td>
12   </tr>
13 </table>
14 <% End If ' end Not rsLogin.EOF Or NOT rsLogin.BOF %><br>
```

Note

The code samples shown here are for the ASP server platform. You'll want to look to Appendix A for more information on how to set session variables in ColdFusion and Java server pages.

If you choose not to use session variables, you maintain greater compatibility with browsers that have disabled cookies but will have a harder task of programming your sites.

Using Session Variables

After a session variable has been defined, you can use it anywhere in Dreamweaver MX—just like a piece of data in a recordset. To do this, you'll need the Bindings panel and these simple instructions:

1. Open the Bindings panel.

2. Click the "+" button and choose Session Variable.

3. Supply the name of the variable (such as userID) that you used in the session variable assignment on your Web page and click OK, as seen in Figure 13.9.

FIGURE 13.9

Enter the name of the session variable that you've defined in the code.

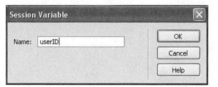

The session variable that you defined is now accessible from any page in the site. You can use the session variable exactly as you would any other piece of bound data. The session variables and the recordset values are listed under separate sources. Figure 13.10 displays the Bindings panel with the userID session variable added.

FIGURE 13.10

Session variables have their own place under the Bindings panel.

13

Session Variables in Queries

Session variables can be used in queries, much like the normal request variables (URL or Form). However, instead of using runtime value of `Request("<variablename>")` to assign the session variable to an Dreamweaver MX variable, you'll need to use runtime values of `Session("<variablename>")`. For simple queries, it's just a matter of choosing Session Variable from a pop-up menu.

For example, open the `online.asp` document that represents the "inside" of the Web site. Currently this page is configured with the query (`rsVerify`) that compares the `userID` that is passed as a URL parameter to one that is stored in the database. To convert this page to use the session variable we've set in `verify.asp`, simply edit the recordset `rsLogin` query by double-clicking its name in the Server Behaviors panel. Switch to simple mode, if necessary. Finally, use the filter settings to create a filter of `userID = Session Variable userID`, as shown in Figure 13.11.

FIGURE 13.11

Adjust the existing `rsVerify` *query to compare against the session variable* `userID`.

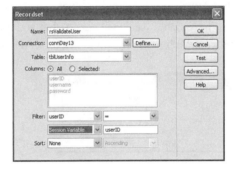

Using this technique, you can do exactly what you normally do with URL parameters, except, instead of having to pass things to every single page where they might be needed, the values are accessible everywhere.

Once again, passing information through session variables is actually safer than using URL parameters. Instead of having data being sent back and forth, it is stored on the server, and the client application is only used to store a session ID that identifies the values on the server.

We're going to use session variables for several of the Week 3 projects. Using them is both cleaner and more efficient than URL parameter passing. If you'd rather keep things compatible with all browsers, you'll need to use URL parameters as the session-management system on your sites.

The Dreamweaver MX Authentication System

The purpose of this chapter is to introduce you to the process of user authentication and maintaining a user's state across different Web pages. Dreamweaver MX's built-in user authentication behaviors help automate this process, but it is important that you understand how the underlying process works so that you are aware of the shortcomings and benefits. You'll use the techniques discussed here, and the Dreamweaver MX authentication system in depth.

Dreamweaver MX will perform the same actions you've learned here, including setting a session variable—all without editing the code once. One of the problems with the behavior, though, is that it forces you to use the username as the primary key for the user table. Although this is fine for most cases, it eliminates the possibility of allowing the users (or an administrator) to modify their usernames.

There are four server behaviors that comprise the Dreamweaver MX system:

Log In User—Inserted onto a page with a username and password field, this behavior compares the form values to those stored in a database and redirects the user's browser to either a "successful" or "invalid" login page.

Restrict Access to Page—"Locks" a page unless a user has successfully been processed by the Log In User behavior.

Log Out User—Ends the user's login session.

Check New Username—If you're offering the ability for users to register themselves with your site, this behavior provides a convenient means of verifying that they've picked a new username.

As we work through the examples in the final week, such as Days 17, "Advanced Techniques: Tracking and Using User Data," 18, "Online Testing and Surveys," and 19, "Advanced Techniques: Complex Query Systems," we'll take a look at several user information tables—from those that match the User ID system we've worked with today, to a hybrid User ID/username system, and a pure username-based system. You'll get the full treatment in user authentication!

It is very important to note, however, that the parameter-passing method of maintaining user state is the *only* way to create a site that's accessible by *all* users. This form of session management is *not* supported by the Dreamweaver MX authentication system in any form, but you've seen how to do it by hand earlier in this chapter. Additionally, some

13

server deployment platforms, such as PHP and ASP.NET, do not support *any* of the built-in behaviors. For these users, you'll need to use a system very much like what we worked with today in order to successfully control access to the pages.

Real Web Site Security

If you're using a Web-based login to any site, you're inevitably transmitting a username and password across the Internet using plain text. This is not a good thing if you're trying to run a secure operation.

In order to fix this problem, you should look into running a secure, *SSL (Secure Sockets Layer)* based Web server. If you use a secure Web server to handle your login information, all transactions between the client and the server are encrypted before they take place. This means that a site that uses simple login schemes can become significantly more secure without any additional programming.

Unfortunately, there is no perfect solution for Web security. A combination of good Web site authorship and intelligent server operation makes for the best defense against hackers.

Summary

Today's lesson covered one of the most important functions that exist on Web sites—login pages. By combining the use of hidden regions (Show Region behaviors that *aren't* being shown) and standard queries, you can develop a login engine for your Web sites. The Show Region behavior can be used to hide information as well as to show information based on the results of a recordset query.

After the user has successfully logged in, how does the system maintain the user's information? It's not as easy as it might seem! In order for the system to remember who has logged in, it needs to pass information from page to page and look up the needed user information from the database as it goes. The Related Page server behavior can be used to transfer existing parameters from page to page.

Another way of keeping session information after a successful login is to use session variables. Session variables are maintained on the server and are not transferred back and forth during each request like URL parameters. Session variables rely on a session ID cookie that is set on a client's machine. The drawback to this approach is that the client computer *must* have cookies enabled in order for the program to work.

On the up side, the built-in Dreamweaver MX authentication behaviors automate many of the techniques in this chapter—*if* you're using a supported server platform and *if* you're willing to accept Macromedia's user database definition. This process will be covered in several projects next week. Understanding the underlying techniques, however, is very important in developing secure sites that perform as expected.

Workshop

The Workshop area is meant to reinforce your reading with a series of questions and exercises.

Q&A

Q   What sorts of Web sites should logins be used for?

A   Logins can be used in many different Web sites, regardless of whether they contain sensitive information. For example, you can provide customizable Web content (news, surveys, and so on) based on who the user is at your site. Although the information might not need to be secure, providing a way for the site to customize itself based around a user is a value-added feature than you can easily employ with a login screen.

Q   How can I tell whether I should use a URL parameter-passing method or session variables?

A   First, you need to identify the users of your site. If you have control over your clientele, you can use session variables without fear. Unfortunately, if you *must* cater to as wide of an audience as possible, you should use URL parameter passing. Be aware, however, that if the data based on the URL is sensitive, the parameters themselves must encrypted.

Q   How do session variables work if the information isn't stored in a cookie?

A   Session variables are actually kept on the server. They are referenced based on a session ID that *is* stored in a cookie on the client machine. If the client does not accept cookies, you'll be unable to set session variables.

Q   Why do you have to use session variables or URL parameter passing?

A   The Web is a stateless environment. Each request to a Web site is separate and unique. If the Web server does not receive some sort of information from the client computer, it cannot identify who the client is. Cookies and parameter passing are the two methods by which you can maintain information about a user accessing your site.

13

Quiz

1. How can you use a Show Region behavior to hide information?

2. What are login systems used to secure?

3. How can you protect pages from being viewed without a valid username or password?

4. What does the Go To Related Page behavior do?

5. Are recordset values passed by the Go To Related Page behavior?

6. If a user cannot navigate through a session variable-based site, what is the likely cause?

Quiz Answers

1. You can "hide" information with the Show Region behavior by "showing" the region if the opposite of a given condition is true. For example, to hide a region if a recordset is empty, you would choose to show the region if the recordset is not empty.

2. Login systems can secure intranets and private pages, or simply provide a way for a public system to recognize a given user.

3. Use the Show Region server behavior to hide page content that the user should not have access to.

4. Transfer URL or Form parameters to subsequent Web pages.

5. No. The only values that are transferred are those that were passed to the page with URL or Form parameters.

6. The user likely has cookies disabled in his or her browser.

Exercises

1. Create your own login system based on the one seen today. You can modify the user database as you see necessary. For an added challenge, add a user profile to the system so that users can change their passwords if they want. This is common on many login-based systems.

2. Experiment with the use of the Show Region behavior to show and hide Web page content based on login information. You'll quickly realize that this behavior, although very simple to use, can be far more flexible that one might initially believe. It could be used, for example, be used to create a page that displays specialized content (sports, weather, news, and the like) depending on a user's preferences.

3. Rewrite the login system you wrote in exercise 1 so that it uses a session variable to maintain user state. Session variables will greatly speed up your application development time and will reduce the chances of error caused by not passing state information in URL parameters.

Advanced Components: Catalogs, Searches

Today's advanced topic involves creating a *catalog* system. A catalog can be any listing of items that is displayed on the computer—usually featuring item details and other information. The contents of the catalog are completely up to you. In this example, however, the catalog will be very much like a product catalog, containing product descriptions and other information.

You have already looked at a basic catalog system that listed various types of dogs. This system, however, will include advanced features beyond those in the earlier system. Today, you'll learn how to:

- Create and test a catalog database system.
- Create an advanced interface that explores new server behaviors.
- Set up search functionality for a database.
- Find items based on keywords in their descriptions.
- Navigate between detail screens without returning to a search window.

A Product Catalog

Before starting programming today's lesson, you'll need to set up a working catalog database. This isn't necessarily as easy as it seems. What functionality do you want to include in your catalog? What tables are necessary, and how do you implement them? These are the sorts of questions that are going to be asked (and hopefully answered) at the start of every day for the rest of the book. For the past few days you've been building small components using the different available server behaviors. Today you'll build a rather large project using several different behaviors and multiple database tables. This will give you a feel for how Dreamweaver MX can be used to create real-world systems and prepare you for the full projects you'll be building over the next few days. To keep things tied into the general theme used throughout the book, this will be a catalog of pet toys, just in case `www.cutelittledogs.com` wants to become the next big online pet store.

 Note

> Although this day shares some common ground with previous days, don't skip this or future lessons without looking through them first. There are plenty of new concepts introduced to keep you occupied.

Site Map

The features that you'll be adding to today's doggy product catalog are common in online information directories:

- **Catalog searches**—Search for a keyword in the catalog, and retrieve only the applicable records.
- **Related items**—Find items that are tagged as *related* to a given item.
- **Thumbnail/expanded images**—Thumbnail and expanded images for each product.
- **Limited Search results**—Limit the number of results that are returned and enable the users to browse the catalog.

The catalog will consist of three different screens: a search screen (`search.asp`), a results screen (`results.asp`), and a detail screen (`detail.asp`). Unlike the previous examples, you'll integrate all of these features so that the users are presented with a seamless experience. MySQL supports everything you need to follow this chapter completely. A site map for the system is shown in Figure 14.1.

Figure 14.1

The site map for the catalog system is very simple.

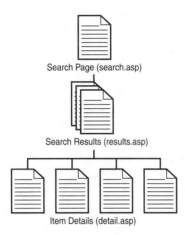

The database model that I have developed for this basic catalog system follows.

Table Definitions

Catalogs store lists of information about products. The products in this particular catalog are going to be dog-related toys and accessories. To hold all of this information we'll use a product table, tblProduct. Specifically, the product table will contain product descriptions, prices, and links to small and large product images. Table 14.1 shows the layout for tblProduct.

Table 14.1   The tblProduct Table Stores Product Information

Fieldname	Description	SQL Data Type
prodID*	A unique product identifier.	varchar(250)
prodName	The name of the product (such as Little orange dog ball).	varchar(250)
prodDesc	An extended product description.	text
prodPrice	The product's price.	real
prodThumbPic	A URL to a product thumbnail.	varchar(250)
prodPic	A URL to a detailed product picture.	varchar(250)

Related Items

A nice feature of online catalog systems is the capability to relate one product to another. This can create a *related-item* feature that displays other items users might be interested in. For noncommercial applications, such as a dog breed database, it could offer the

14

capability to show records with characteristics similar to the one specifically selected. Because we're money hungry, we'll build this as if it were becoming an e-commerce application. To add a related item feature to the this system, we'll need another table, tblRelated, which will simply create a relation between two product IDs, as seen in Table 14.2.

TABLE 14.2 The tblRelated Table Relates Two Product IDs

Fieldname	Description	SQL Data Type
prodID1*	A unique product identifier.	varchar(250)
prodID2*	The product ID that is similar.	varchar(250)

There's actually another way to set up this same functionality that I like slightly better. Unfortunately, it technically breaks the normalization rules, but, at the same time, is more efficient because less information needs to be stored in the database. In the alternative implementation of the Related Items functionality, the entire tblRelated table could be dropped, and the product table would be implemented with a simple prodRelated text field that would contain a comma-separated list of related product IDs. SQL can easily be written to parse this field and find the matching catalog entries.

Normalization aside, sometimes it's best to use common sense when designing your tables. There's no shame in breaking some of the rules of normalization if you end up with a product that is easier to use. Beginners, however, should stick to the normalization rules until they are comfortable with database design and realize the long-term consequences of the design decisions.

Sample Data

As you already know, Day 7, "Preparing a Server for Dreamweaver MX" discussed how to set up MySQL or MS Access data sources for all of the exercises in the book. As with the other days, the sample data for this chapter (day14) should already be loaded on your system and ready to use. Table 14.3 shows the sample tblProduct product information.

TABLE 14.3 Sample Products in the `tblProduct` Database

ProdID	ProdName	ProdDesc	ProdPrice	ProdThumbPic	ProdPic
T001	Fuzzy Giraffe	This brightly colored stuffed chew toy will delight any dog. Squeaker included.	$8.95	`images/T001s.jpg`	`images/T001.jpg`
T002	Fuzzy Bone	A simple bone-shaped chew toy.	$4.95	`images/T002s.jpg`	`images/T002.jpg`
T003	Mini Orange Tennis Ball	A pint-sized orange tennis ball, just the right size for little dogs.	$2.00	`images/T003s.jpg`	`images/T003.jpg`
T004	Mini Purple Tennis Ball	A pint-sized purple tennis ball, just the right size for little dogs.	$2.00	`images/T004s.jpg`	`images/T004.jpg`
T005	Rope Bone Toy	Stringy and meaty. What makes a better bone than string?	$6.50	`images/T005s.jpg`	`images/T005.jpg`
T006	Holiday Dog Suit	The perfect cape for Thanksgiving or Christmas dog dressing.	$14.95	`images/T006s.jpg`	`images/T006.jpg`
T007	Lion Dog Pillow	Where else would a dog like to sleep but on a lion? This fluffy dog pillow makes a perfect bed.	$25.95	`images/T007s.jpg`	`images/T007.jpg`

14

TABLE 14.3   continued

ProdID	ProdName	ProdDesc	ProdPrice	ProdThumbPic	ProdPic
T008	Plaid Dog Bed	The complete sleeping solution for elegant little dogs. Stitched in bright red plaid, this bed is the ultimate in comfort.	$35.95	images/T008s.jpg	images/T008.jpg
T009	Rawhide Chew	Release the animal instincts in your dog; feed him a rawhide. This chew toy will last through at least a week of constant chewing.	$4.00	images/T009s.jpg	images/T009.jpg
T010	Regular Tennis Ball	Play tennis; play with your dog. Do everything at once with this regulation tennis ball.	$0.50	images/T010s.jpg	images/T010.jpg

Finally, to indicate a few related products, the tblRelated table contains the sample data shown in Table 14.4.

TABLE 14.4   The tblRelated Table Contains Some Sample Relations

ProdID1	ProdID2
T003	T004
T003	T010
T007	T008

The first two lines of sample data relate the orange tennis ball (Product ID T003) to the purple tennis ball (T004) and the regular tennis ball (T010). The last line relates the Lion Dog Pillow (T007) to the Plaid Dog Bed (T008).

In addition, it creates a relationship from the dog pillow (T007) to the dog bed (T008) .

The SQL Queries

With some sample data, you're ready to construct the queries that will make your database function. Why aren't we doing this in the design phase? Simple—wouldn't you rather design your site than worry about the logic? Get the nasty stuff out of the way first, and then the actual Dreamweaver MX work becomes a much more enjoyable activity.

Most of the queries in this database system are simple—just a SELECT statement from one of the tables. For example, to display the product table, use the query SELECT * FROM tblProduct.

Searching the Product Database

The first trouble comes in when we search the description field for a keyword. In some circumstances, a simple search—which compares a field in the database to a value—will work. A simple search won't, however, look in the field for the value ANYWHERE, which is what you need. Depending on your SQL implementation, you might have to do this a bit differently. The easiest way to perform the query with MySQL is to use a pattern-matching function to see whether one string is contained within another—namely, if the search string is contained in the description field.

For example, a search on chew toy would work like this:

```
SELECT * FROM tblProduct WHERE prodDesc LIKE "% chew toy%"
```

In plain English, the SELECT statement is looking for anything "like" the words "chew toy" with anything on the right or left of it. The results would look like this:

INPUT

```
mysql> SELECT * FROM tblProduct WHERE prodDesc LIKE '%chew toy%' \G
```

OUTPUT

```
*************************** 1. row ***************************
     prodID: T001
   prodName: Fuzzy Giraffe
   prodDesc: This brightly colored stuffed chew toy will
             delight any dog. Squeaker included.
  prodPrice: 8.95
prodThumbPic: images/T001s.jpg
    prodPic: images/T001.jpg
*************************** 2. row ***************************
     prodID: T002
```

14

```
        prodName: Fuzzy Bone
        prodDesc: A simple bone-shaped chew toy.
       prodPrice: 4.95
    prodThumbPic: images/T002s.jpg
         prodPic: images/T002.jpg
*************************** 3. row ***************************
          prodID: T009
        prodName: Rawhide Chew
        prodDesc: Release the animal instincts in your dog,
                  feed him a rawhide. This chew toy will last through
                  at least a week of constant chewing.
       prodPrice: 4
    prodThumbPic: images/T009s.jpg
         prodPic: images/T009.jpg
3 rows in set (0.00 sec)
```

Precisely as intended, only the records containing chew toy were returned!

Showing Related Products

The biggest problem with the product catalog is defining the query that shows the related
products. The related products table is a start, but it doesn't contain the information you
want. For example, to show the items related to product ID T003, you might try a query
like SELECT * FROM tblRelated WHERE prodID1='T003'.

INPUT

```
mysql> SELECT * FROM tblRelated WHERE prodID1='T003';
```

OUTPUT

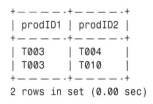

```
+--------+--------+
| prodID1 | prodID2 |
+--------+--------+
| T003    | T004    |
| T003    | T010    |
+--------+--------+
2 rows in set (0.00 sec)
```

These are the correct product numbers, but they aren't the information you need to build
a dynamic page. For each of the prodID2 fields returned, you need to retrieve the given
record.

**Why Are the Query Results Laid Out Differently in the Output of the Last Two
Examples?**

Because tblProduct is a rather large table with a great deal of information, I used the \G
option at the end of the SQL so that the results would be output in a long format. This
format is more appropriate for this book. This is an option available to those of you
using MySQL to test your queries.

At first, this might seem like a two-step process—retrieve related product IDs, and then look up the full record corresponding to the product ID. You could certainly program this feature using that logic, but it would be a lot of work, and it wouldn't be supported in Dreamweaver MX's recordset model. Unless the information can be returned in a single query, Dreamweaver MX cannot work with it.

As chance would have it, this query is possible by using this syntax SELECT tblProduct.* FROM tblProduct,tblRelated WHERE tblProduct.prodID=tblRelated.prodID2 AND tblRelated.prodID1='T003';.

Before trying this, let's break apart the query to see the logic:

SELECT tblProduct.*—Select all fields from the tblProduct database. Because this is a multiple table query (a JOIN), you need to be specific about what information you want to see.

FROM tblProduct,tblRelated—These are the tables that the data is pulled from. Both the Product and Related tables are needed for the query.

tblProduct.prodID=tblRelated.prodID2—Return records where the product ID of the Product table is equal to the prodID2 field of the Related table.

tblRelated.prodID1='T003'—Finally, limit the records to those where the main product field (ProdID1) of the Related table is equal to what we're looking for.

Seemingly magic, this query performs exactly as we had hoped and returns all items related to the given prodID (T003 in this example) .

INPUT

```
mysql> SELECT tblProduct.* FROM tblProduct,tblRelated
       WHERE tblProduct.prodID=tblRelated.prodID2
       AND tblRelated.prodID1='T003' \G
```

OUTPUT

```
*************************** 1. row ***************************
      prodID: T004
    prodName: Mini Purple Tennis Ball
    prodDesc: A pint sized purple tennis ball,
              just the right size for little dogs.
   prodPrice: 2
prodThumbPic: images/T004s.jpg
     prodPic: images/T004.jpg
*************************** 2. row ***************************
      prodID: T010
    prodName: Regular Tennis Ball
    prodDesc: Play Tennis, Play with your dog. Do everything
              at once with this regulation tennis ball.
   prodPrice: 0.5
prodThumbPic: images/T010s.jpg
     prodPic: images/T010.jpg
2 rows in set (0.00 sec)
```

14

Tip

Always try to make your database server do your work for you. Although it might seem that a query is impossible without additional programming, SQL is a very powerful language and can be adapted to handle just about anything you throw at it. Additionally, the speed at which the SQL server can handle the data processing is likely to be significantly faster than the embedded language you're using.

That completes the SQL that you'll need for today's project. As you can see, getting the queries out of the way can make the rest of the development go far faster and gives you the knowledge that what you're going to build is actually going to work.

 Note

Earlier in the day, I mentioned that I would consider implementing the related items differently. As an unofficial exercise, try writing the query to do this. You can get a good idea of what you need to do by looking at the section on the keyword search in "Searching the Product Database." The related items could be implemented using the SQL comparison LIKE in a very similar manner.

Implementing the Application

This site is actually going to be a bit different from the previous dynamic applications. The design will draw together the different elements (search, results, and so on) into a look and feel that is similar across all the functions.

 Note

Before you can start designing the pages, define new site (Day 14—Catalog) and a new database connection called connDay14 to the data source, day14. Make sure that you have Dreamweaver MX talking to your Web server and database server before continuing.

There are many ways that you can lay out the screen, but I've chosen to use a simple table design, as seen in Figure 14.2. This is the basis for all the pages that will be designed today. The top of the page is reserved for title information, whereas the right side provides navigation throughout the site. Design the initial table layout shown in Figure 14.2 as a template file named catalog.dwt.

FIGURE 14.2

*A simple layout will
work perfectly for the
application.*

If you don't remember the steps for creating a template, refer back to Day 5, "Creating Reusable Components."

Because all of the pages will share a common look and feel, the template will contain the navigation. These are going to be very special links, because they'll trigger events on other pages. You've already learned about URL passing to transfer data from page to page. The links will pass simple search terms to the results page, giving the user some "quick clicks" to certain types of products. Add these links to the navigation portion of your template:

Search catalog—search.asp

Browse catalog—results.asp

Balls—results.asp?prodDesc=ball

Chew toy—results.asp?prodDesc=chew%20toy

Bedding—results.asp?prodDesc=bed

The first link provides a jump to the search page. The other four links, however, are special in that they call the results.asp, which is a dynamic page that uses the prodDesc URL parameter to pass a search term to the dynamic behaviors on the results.asp page.

After creating the initial template, start a new page with the template that you've created. This will be the search.asp page.

Search Form (search.asp)

We've already discussed the use of LIKE and % to perform a basic search on the text of a field, but we can take this a few steps further when we design the form. Any of the fields in the database are fair game for a search, but there are only a few that would be useful to the users, such as:

14

Product name—prodName

Product description—prodDesc

Price limit—prodPrice

The search form will submit its values to the results.asp page which, in turn, will display all the matching items. Create your search form (frmSearch) with the action results.asp and two text fields, prodName and prodDesc. These are named to correspond with the database field names in tblProduct. Add a submit button named Search to the form so that the users can send the values to the results.asp page.

A basic search screen is shown in Figure 14.3. Leave some room for a Price Limit label and a corresponding pop-up menu.

FIGURE 14.3

Lay out a simple search screen.

Add a Price Limit label to the form and a corresponding selection menu (prodPrice) by clicking the List/Menu item in the Insert panel's Form category.

Define a few price limits for the Price Limit pop-up menu. To do this, highlight the prodPrice menu and open the Properties panel. Click the List Values button to open the list item definition screen, shown in Figure 14.4. You can add items to the list by clicking the "+" button and setting values for each field.

FIGURE 14.4

Add price limits for a simple price search function.

Add the items 1.00, 5.00, 15.00, 25.00, and 999999 to the list. To make the list more visually appealing, format numbers using dollar signs in the labels, but not in the values. For the value 999999, use the label All.

Search Results (results.asp)

Building the search results page, results.asp, will follow very much in line with the record listing pages that you've built in the past, but with a twist. Because there are potentially hundreds of items in this catalog, it would be nice to be able to step through them without having to worry about overwhelming your browser with 10,000 records on a single page. This is a very typical process for online databases and is, without a doubt, a necessity on a site that has any reasonable volume of data to manage.

To set up the search results, go ahead and create a new page named results.asp that will contain a basic layout for the data. Be sure that you base this page on the catalog.dwt template.

To aid in the design, you'll probably want to access the data in the database so you can see how it fits. This means it's time to write the master search query!

There are three conditions to the search—the keyword, category, and price. Each of these attributes must be used in the WHERE clause of the SQL in order to correctly retrieve *only* the records that match the search from the database. The following query will do the job nicely:

```
SELECT * FROM tblProduct WHERE prodName LIKE 'varProdName' AND prodDesc
➥LIKE '%varProdDesc%' AND prodPrice<'varProdPrice'
```

This query is simple but powerful. It is powered by three conditions that are driven from the defined form:

1. **prodName LIKE '%varProdName%'**—Matches the tblProduct field prodName against a Dreamweaver MX variable containing the product name, as submitted from the search.asp form. Matches all occurrences of the name.

2. **prodPrice<'varProdPrice'**—Quite simply, the product price (prodPrice) must be less than the price listed on the form (varProdPrice). In order to give the users the ability to match any of the prices, we added the All selection with a very large value. If you know of a pet supply that costs $999,999, please let me know!

3. **prodDesc LIKE '%varProdDesc%'**—Finally, the product description database field (prodDesc) needs to contain the varProdDesc value, submitted from the search form.

14

Switch to the Server Behaviors panel, click the "+" button, and then add a new Recordset (query) server behavior to the `results.asp` document. Make sure you click the Advanced button to enter the advanced query mode.

Name the new recordset `rsResult` and select the `connDay14` connection.

Now, type the SQL query directly into the advanced recordset definition. You'll also need to set up some Dreamweaver MX variables that capture the data being submitted by the search form on `search.asp`.

Click the "+" button within the query definition window and add each Dreamweaver MX variable—`varProdName`, `varProdPrice`, and `varProdDesc`—to the corresponding runtime values of `Request(prodName)`, `Request(prodPrice)`, and `Request(prodDesc)` respectively. Add the default values of `%`, `99999`, and `%` (respectively) to each of the Dreamweaver MX variables. Figure 14.5 shows the advanced query setup with the properly defined variables.

FIGURE 14.5

The search query uses three form values submitted from the search.asp *page.*

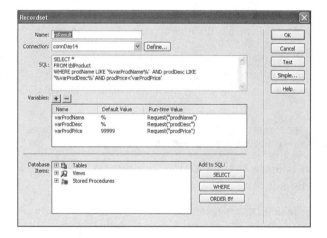

After the `rsResult` query is set up on your page, add the `prodName`, `prodPrice`, `prodDesc`, and `prodThumbPic` fields to a result table within your document design window. The text fields should be old hat—simply drag them from the Data Bindings panel to the design window. In the case of the price (`prodPrice`), after dragging it to the design, use the Format menu in the Data Bindings panel to format the price to Currency with two decimal places.

The thumbnail image should be added to the design by first inserting an image placeholder named `prodThumbnail`, and then using the Data Bindings panel to bind the placeholder's image source to the `prodThumbPic` field in the `rsResult` recordset. To do this, make sure that the placeholder is selected in the design window, and then switch to the Bindings panel. Expand the rsResult recordset so that you can see the prodThumbPic and select it. Finally, make certain that the Bind To pop-up menu is set to img.src, and then click the Bind button. The data binding can be seen in Figure 14.6.

FIGURE 14.6

Bind the prodThumbPic *placeholder to the* rsResult prodThumbPic *field.*

Now add a Repeating Region server behavior so that more than one record is displayed at a time. However, unlike previous instances of the application, change the repeating region so that it repeats only three times, as seen in Figure 14.7.

FIGURE 14.7

Repeat only three records at a time.

Not showing everything at once keeps the display clean and doesn't overwhelm the users.

Check to make sure that your page is working by uploading the pages to your server, accessing the search.asp page, and performing a search on all the items in the database. You should see a display similar to that of Figure 14.8.

Unfortunately, the display, although clean, isn't complete. The users are left without the ability to view the rest of the records in the database.

Recordset Paging

The server behaviors that you've used up to this point rely on a specific set of data being present, either a complete record or a set of records. They haven't offered the capability to move throughout the records. There are, however, a set of server behaviors that *do* let you move between individual records and groups of records in the database.

14

FIGURE 14.8

With only three records available per screen, we'll need to add a means of navigating the database.

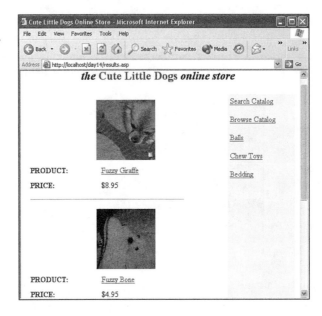

These behaviors are located under the Recordset Paging heading of the Server Behavior panel:

- **Move to First Record**—Moves within the given recordset to the first record in the set.

- **Move to Previous Record**—Moves to the previous record in the recordset. If the recordset is within a group of records, this behavior moves to the previous group.

- **Move to Next Record**—Moves to the next record or group of records for a recordset.

- **Move to Last Record**—Moves to the last record in a recordset.

- **Move to Specific Record**—Moves to a specific record in the set.

> **Note**
>
> There is some confusion about the difference between moving to a detail record and a specific record. Moving to a detail record sets up the passing of values to a *detail* page, which typically has a new recordset that selects a single record based on the passed value. The Move to Specific Record server behavior can be used to jump to a single record in the middle of a recordset on any page. The recordset does not have to be set up to select a single record—limiting the results is all handled internally. If this doesn't make sense, don't worry. You'll see it in action shortly.

Add recordset paging to the `results.asp` document by creating two links near the bottom of the content region—Previous and Next.

To create the Next behavior, select the Next label and then add the Move To Next Record server behavior. The configuration for this behavior is seen in Figure 14.9.

Set the behavior's recordset to `rsResult` so that it knows which set of records it is moving through. Because we only have a single recordset, this shouldn't be a mystery. It's actually *amazingly* simple.

After you set up the behavior for the Next button, do the same for the Previous button. The setup is exactly the same, but it uses a slightly different server behavior—the Move To Previous Record behavior. Test the behaviors by pulling up your Web page in a browser. You should be able to click through the different pages and browse the entire contents of the catalog!

Figure 14.10 shows the catalog in action on my computer.

FIGURE 14.10

The Next and Previous buttons should now page through the search results.

14

Tip

There's an alternative to the Previous server behavior that might be better suited for your application. Although the server behavior appears to be almost instantaneous when moving back through records, it really must perform a query on the database each time it is used. On large datasets, this can take time. An alternative method is to use the browser's history to move back to the previous screen. Using the link `javascript:history.back();`, you can move backward through records that you've already visited.

Finally, you must provide a link from each of the search results to the `detail.asp` page, which will show a full product description.

1. Select the `prodName` dynamic text to use as a link to the detail page.

2. Open the Server Behaviors panel.

3. Click "+" and select Go To Detail Page from the pop-up menu.

4. Configure the link so that the product ID (`prodID`) is transferred to the `detail.asp` page using the URL parameter `prodID`.

5. Be sure to check both of the Pass Existing Parameters options. This ensures that the search is carried through to the detail page. The final configuration is shown in Figure 14.11.

6. Click OK to save the behavior.

Caution

If you *don't* transfer the existing parameters to your detail page, you might end up pulling your hair out later. The Next and Previous links on the detail page will move through the entire recordset rather than just the results from the search. Additionally, any links to other pages will lose the results of the search—this is important if you plan on expanding the functionality of the catalog.

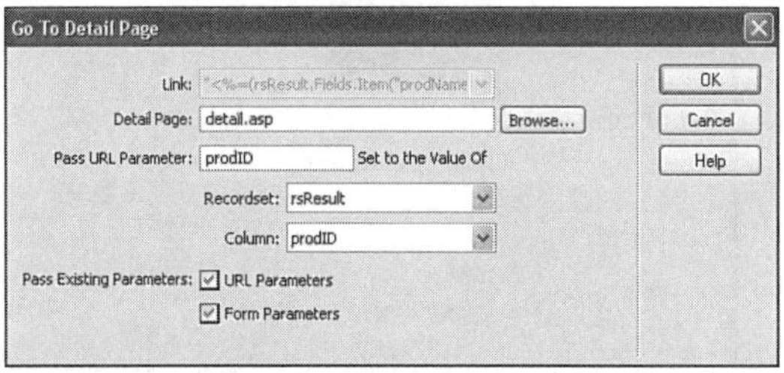

FIGURE 14.11

Use the Go To Detail Page behavior to transfer to the product detail.asp *page.*

You now have a working search system.

There are two areas, however, that still need to be addressed. The first of these, of course, is the detail screen.

Detail Screen (`detail.asp`)

The catalog detail screen (`detail.asp`) is actually the easiest portion of the site to build because, in essence, you've already built it! The search results page is 99% of what you need for a new detail page. To prepare it for use as a detail page, follow these instructions:

1. Open the search results page, and use File, Save As to copy it to a new file named `detail.asp`. Open the new `detail.asp` page.

2. Delete the Repeating Region behavior. This behavior was only necessary when more than one record is going to be shown on the page.

3. Add the Move To Specific Record behavior to the new `detail.asp` document. Figure 14.12 displays this new behavior configuration.

Setting the Move To Specific Record configuration is simply a matter of choosing a recordset, the column that uniquely identifies a record, and a URL parameter that is used to pass a value for that column.

FIGURE 14.12

Tell Dreamweaver MX which column in the database should be matched with which URL parameter.

For example, in this catalog system, we're using the `rsResult` recordset with the primary key of `prodID`. The URL parameter must be set to the same identifier that is used in the search results page (`results.asp`) for the Go To Detail Record behavior—`prodID` again.

Finally, lay out the detail screen so that it displays the large image of the product (`prodPic`) as well as its full description (`prodDesc`). My final layout is shown in Figure 14.13. Of course, you can alter the page as you see fit.

Note

Notice that I've left the Next and Previous links in the body of the page. This provides a way for the users to casually browse the catalog from the detail view—without any additional server behaviors!

14

FIGURE 14.13

Lay out the detail screen with the larger version of the catalog picture and the full description of the catalog item.

Related Items

Remember how we originally set up a complex query so that related items could be shown for an item? It's time to add this query to the detail.asp page. Open the Server Behaviors panel, click "+" to add a new Recordset (query), and then switch to the Advanced mode.

Configure the query as recordset rsRelated using the connection connDay14. For the SQL query, type:

```
SELECT tblProduct.* FROM tblProduct,tblRelated
WHERE tblProduct.prodID=tblRelated.prodID2
AND tblRelated.prodID1='varProdID'
```

A Dreamweaver MX variable needs to be added to pick up the URL parameter prodID and feed it to the recordset definition. Click the "+" button within the query definition to add a new Dreamweaver variable named varProdID, and then set its runtime value to Request(prodID). The finished query is shown in Figure 14.14.

Next, you need to modify your detail screen so that the records from the rsRelated recordset are shown on the screen. Make some space at the bottom of the content area, and then drag the prodName field from the new recordset over to the design view. Insert a <br> after the newly created dynamic text.

Finally, select the dynamic Product Name field that you've added to the design ({rsRelated.prodName}) and add a repeating region server behavior. Set the behavior to repeat for all the records in the rsRelated recordset. This will produce a list of related product names on the screen. The final page design should look like Figure 14.15.

FIGURE **14.14**

Because the SQL was designed earlier, showing related records is easy.

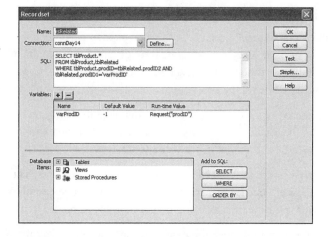

FIGURE **14.15**

The related items should be added as a repeating region to the bottom of the content area in the design view.

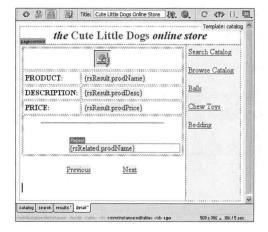

Caution

Be sure to choose the right recordset when defining the related items repeating region. This is the first time there have been multiple recordsets in a single document, so you can no longer just let Dreamweaver pick the appropriate recordset for you.

When you load the page in your browser, it will show a list of related items at the bottom of the screen—based on the `tblRelated` database table.

14

Showing/Hiding Page Elements

After the users perform a search on the `search.asp` page, they are taken to the `results.asp` page. They can navigate through the search results by clicking the Next and Previous buttons at the bottom of the screen. What happens, however, if they click the Previous link while on the first page of results, or the Next link on the last page?

Clicking these links will take the users to the page that they are already on, but, at the same time, they'll also requery the database. This adds an extra load on the server system and creates a false link that is presented to the users.

Yesterday you were introduced to the Show Region behaviors. These enable you to highlight a region of your HTML code and show it only when certain conditions are met during a database query, such as being on the first or last record in a recordset.

To apply this behavior, open the `results.asp` page and select the Next link (be sure to select the *entire* text of the link). Then open the Server Behaviors panel and choose Show Region If Not Last Record from the list of available options under the Show Region submenu. There isn't much additional configuration, just choose the repeating `rsResult` recordset and click OK, as shown in Figure 14.16.

FIGURE 14.16

The Show Region behavior can show regions only if the recordset meets certain conditions.

Repeat this same procedure for the Previous button, except use the Show Region If Not First Record option.

Automating the Navigation Bar

Today you experimented with recordset navigation for the first time. As you've discovered in the past, Dreamweaver MX provides some quick-and-dirty tools to build common collections of server behaviors.

Two tools you might want to use in future projects that can help streamline the process of recordset paging are the Recordset Navigation Bar and Recordset Navigation Status. These are located under the Application category in the Dreamweaver MX Insert panel.

Navigation Status

Navigation status is nothing more than a string of text showing which record is being viewed out of the total number of records in a recordset. This allows the users to gauge how far into the database they are. To insert this information into your document, simply click the numbers icon in the Application category of the Insert panel. Alternatively, you could insert the object directly from the Application Objects submenu of the main Insert menu.

Configuration is easy, as shown in Figure 14.17. Choose the recordset that you'd like to show the status of, click OK, and the appropriate information is inserted directly into your document design view.

FIGURE 14.17

Choose the recordset that you want to provide status information for.

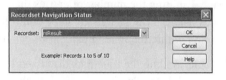

You can accomplish the same thing by hand by dragging the [first record index],[last record index], and [total records] fields out of the Data Bindings panel for a given recordset. These three items show the first record in the recordset, the last record, and the total number of records, respectively.

Navigation Bars

Earlier today you inserted Next and Previous buttons to provide navigation through the recordset. You also added Show Region behaviors to these links in order to show them only when it was appropriate. You can automate this entire process by clicking the Recordset Navigation Bar object in the Server Objects category of the Insert panel.

As with the navigation status, you will be prompted for the recordset that you want to provide navigation for, as well as whether you want to use graphic or text links. The setup screen can be seen in Figure 14.18. Click OK when you are finished.

FIGURE 14.18

Choose your recordset, and whether you want HTML or graphic links.

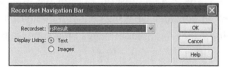

14

The recordset navigation that is inserted into your document will contain the Next and Previous behaviors you added by hand, as well as First and Last buttons to jump to the first and last record in a recordset. In addition, the Show Region behaviors are also added to the document so that the navigation is only displayed when appropriate.

Although you can still use the individual server behaviors to build these features, the prebuilt application objects make providing basic record status and paging as easy as a single click.

Summary

In today's lesson, you created a unified layout for a catalog system and developed an easy-to-navigate result page. Limiting the number of entries that can be shown at a time makes it easier to build sites where the appearance can be controlled. The Move To server behaviors enable navigation within the limited amount of data that is being shown.

If you are having any difficulty finding the functions discussed in the text, I urge you to look over the past week's material. Moving into the final week of projects requires that you understand the Dreamweaver MX layout and the available server behaviors. We'll still cover tools on a case-by-case basis, but by now you should be getting pretty comfortable with the Server Behaviors and Server Bindings panels.

Each of the remaining days will follow the general flow of this day—including the back-end database development and then the design of the site itself. Remember, although this is a *21 Day* text, there is no time limit for actually reading it.

Workshop

The Workshop area is meant to reinforce your reading with a series of questions and exercises.

Q&A

Q Why shouldn't I show all the returned records in a recordset?

A Returning *all* the records in a recordset is fine for the limited applications that we've built so far, but consider what happens if a database contains a few thousand records? Displaying 2,000 thumbnail images on a single page is likely to slow a user's browser to a crawl.

Q How can I use the Next and Previous buttons to browse the entire database table rather than just a subset?

A The only reason that Next and Previous are constrained to a few records is because the recordset is defined by the search parameters. Using Next and Previous actions without any search parameters will cause the entire database table to become browseable.

Q Why didn't we use the Move To Specific Record option previously?

A The Move To Specific Record option is only needed if there are multiple records in the recordset. When we created the last detail record page, only a single record existed in the recordset—eliminating the need to go to a specific record.

Q What good are the Show Region behaviors except for navigation?

A You'll actually be surprised by how useful these regions can be, especially if you use them to create code that you later modify. For example, you can set up code that performs certain actions other than show regions. Create the basic framework using the server behavior to show/hide a generic region on the document, and then insert custom code into the document.

Quiz

1. How do you match *any* substring in SQL?
2. What is an alternative method for handling the related items' functionality?
3. How do you add Next and Previous functionality to a recordset?
4. What happens if you forget to name a file with the appropriate .asp extension?
5. What is the fastest way to create a navigation bar?

Quiz Answers

1. Using the LIKE keyword and wildcard characters.
2. Using a single text field containing comma-separated values.
3. Using the Recordset Paging server behaviors.
4. A misnamed file will not be properly executed by the application server.
5. Using the Recordset Navigation Status object found in the Application category of the Insert panel.

Exercises

1. Add recordset status to the previously static search.asp page. This will let your visitors know how many products are in your tblProduct table.

14

2. Create a hidden region on the `results.asp` page that appears when *no* search results are returned. This region can provide an explanation to the user, and a link back to the `search.asp` page.

3. As a final exercise, change the related items that are listed in the catalog so that they are clickable and will take the users to the detail page for each of the entries.

   Hint: This involves adding one more server behavior to the `detail.asp` page—it *is* a behavior you've used before!

WEEK 2

In Review

Completing the second week of *Sams Teach Yourself Dreamweaver MX Application Development in 21 Days* means that you should have a good understanding of the dynamic tools that Dreamweaver MX offers. The final week will use server behaviors extensively, so you should spend as much time practicing with these behaviors as possible:

Recordsets—The recordset is the most common server behavior that you'll use. Recordsets put you in touch with the data in your database. A working knowledge of SQL is necessary in order to create advanced recordsets that do more than just select information from a database and display it.

Repeating Regions—Similar to `Do While` loops in traditional programming languages, repeating regions let you loop over the contents of a recordset, displaying each record as you go. You must understand the use of these regions in order to display more than a single record at a time.

Update/Insert/Delete—Showing the contents of a database isn't extremely useful without the ability to work with the data. The Insert, Update, and Delete server behaviors enable Web pages to modify the database in real-time.

Show Regions—Any element on a Web page can be shown or hidden based on the state of a recordset. You can use the Show Region behavior to deliver status messages to the user, or hide information that isn't applicable. Remember, hiding a region is the same as showing a region based on the *opposite* condition being true.

User Authentication—Checking a username and a password is a very common activity on a Web site. With the Dreamweaver MX authentication tools, you can add this functionality to your site in minutes. If you want greater control over the process, you can build your own authentication routines using recordsets and hidden regions.

As practice for the upcoming week, try building the following application from scratch—a movie tracking system:

1. Design a multi-table database that includes a main movie information table and an actor/actress table.

2. Use the recordset, dynamic element, and repeating region behaviors to display all the available movies in the database.

3. When viewing a movie, also show the actors and actresses in the movie.

4. Include administrative pages where you can add to the movie information, add actors and actresses, and attach actors and actresses to a movie. (Hint: You'll need a third table to relate a movie to its stars.)

You should be able to build this system with your current knowledge. In the final week you'll see more of the server behaviors in action, so if you can't complete this exercise now, try again in a week.

Week 3

At a Glance

You've reached the final week of the text and should now be a Dreamweaver MX expert in terms of understanding the server behaviors, connections, data bindings, and other dynamic elements. This final week is dedicated to building a series of sites that draw together the different techniques you've learned into functional sites. Within the next seven days, you'll create:

Randomized Banner Ads—As you've certainly seen before, banner ads are very popular. You can easily add similar randomly chosen images to your system using Dreamweaver MX and a simple database structure.

Seasonal Theme Images—Similar to the banner ads, you can even swap out images on your site based on a day or date. Instead of having a site that remains the same all year long, you can create one that includes images that change site-wide with the seasons.

Guestbooks—Let your users add a name and a comment to a Web page. A simple Dreamweaver MX application will give you online guestbooks in minutes.

Bulletin Boards—Expanding the guestbook concept, you can create a fully functioning bulletin board system where the users can post/read messages, reply, and delete any message that they've submitted.

Dynamic, User Specified Content Pages—Many Web sites include "my Web page" functionality, letting the users choose what content should be on a page and how it should be shown. Dreamweaver MX can even author applications like this.

15

16

17

18

19

20

21

Online Testing Applications—With more and more schools and organizations turning to the Web for quizzing, it is important to be able to quickly produce online tests and quizzes. Using Dreamweaver MX, you'll quickly create a system that dynamically generates tests and even scores them online.

Complex Query Systems—Trying to create systems that allow searching available data in a way that isn't exact is a bit of a problem within Dreamweaver MX. Using the power of your database server and advanced queries, you can easily add "fuzzy matching" to your sites.

Each of these projects can be combined with other projects, or expanded upon as you see fit. Every aspect of the application's creation will be covered, from start to finish.

Wrapping up the week will be information about what can and will go wrong when creating Web sites within the Dreamweaver MX environment and a look at some advanced tools you can work with in the future. Although Dreamweaver MX is an excellent environment, things can and do go wrong. Learning what to expect can keep you from quietly (or not so quietly) going nuts.

DAY **15**

Advanced Techniques: Static to Dynamic

If you've been involved with creating Web sites before you picked up this book, you've already experienced some situations where you could have used dynamic tools to improve the functionality or add to the appeal or commercial viability of your site. Today we will look at several short Dreamweaver MX applications that you can use to supplement or replace existing portions of your "now stale" sites. I've tried to choose some applications that might not be immediately obvious as being database driven, but certainly can be. Today, you will learn how to:

- Use and follow the final week's projects in the most efficient manner.
- Add randomly chosen banner ads to your site.
- Automatically adjust your site's images depending on the season or time of day.
- Replace e-mail feedback with a filtered online guestbook.

Making the Static to Dynamic Transition

The hardest part of getting started with dynamic Web page programming is getting used to breaking the rules that you've come to know and despise. Rather than having static links on your pages, or static objects, suddenly you have the ability to change all the pages in your site each time a user visits them.

The most complex online applications are covered in detail later this week, but you'll find that many of the most compelling Web sites use very simple dynamic functionality to make them interesting. For example, how many times have you visited the Dilbert Web site? (If the answer is none, I can only wonder what you're doing with a computer book.) Many people visit the site daily. The same goes for sites such as CNN, or computer sites such as versiontracker.com. I'm guessing that you visit at least one Web site on a daily basis. So, the question is, "why do you visit these sites so frequently?"

Think about that for a little bit. The answer is that you keep going back to the site because the content changes. Each day there is a new Dilbert comic posted on the Dilbert Web site. Every time you go to CNN, updated news stories are posted (sometimes those that you'd rather not see!). Providing new and fresh content is an excellent way to keep visitors interested in your site.

So, what if you don't want to have to update your site everyday? You can still provide dynamic information and visuals to your readers. Many sites pre-seed content into their databases that is triggered at a specific time or date. Although this wouldn't work well for a news site, it *does* work well for other types of content that can be generated before they are needed, such as images, weekly recipes, or monthly newsletters.

Introduction to the Exercises

Today you'll complete some little projects that you can use on your Web site to replace traditional static elements. These are common modules of Web sites and can be used to supplement sites that you already have in place. Here's a brief overview of what you'll be doing:

- Random banners/images—Common on many sites, banners offer a way to advertise other sites. Each time the user visits a Web page, the image on the page changes. You can use this for banners or any image that you put on a page.

- Seasonal/time-based images—Do you like updating your Web site for different seasons of the year? Do you like changing your graphics to reflect the color of the leaves on the trees? Changing your site graphics adds variation and interest and requires no interaction on your part, beyond the initial graphic setup and creating an image-rotation schedule.

- Guestbook—A popular Web site feature is a feedback forum. You can add this to your site very easily. You can also add a "neat" feature to the guestbook that filters out messages that are rude or include language that you feel is inappropriate.

Setting up these mini projects will get you into the swing of things, and you'll be ready for the big projects that we're going to be building the rest of the week. You might want to go through your existing sites to see if they lend themselves to incorporating these features.

Before we get started, let me spend a few moments describing what you're going to see while reading these last few chapters in the book. My philosophy is simple—learn by doing. Dreamweaver MX itself is simple. You've already seen all the common server functions and how to access them through the Bindings and Server Behaviors panels. In fact, the HTML layout capabilities of Dreamweaver MX are in many ways more complicated than the dynamic database connection tools. Because of this, the final week in this book is dedicated to providing real-world examples that demonstrate the flexibility and many possibilities of Dreamweaver MX coupled with a SQL server. Even though these examples are only "certified" on the MySQL/Access databases and ASP combination we set up in Day 7, "Preparing a Server for Dreamweaver MX," they should work with very few modifications on the other database/application server platforms. These chapters are presented in three parts:

- **Database Design**—The most important part of any project is designing the back-end. Certain limitations of the Dreamweaver MX behaviors can be overcome by writing queries in the right way. Even if you're experienced with databases, you might find yourself running into walls unless you pay close attention here. If you've worked through Day 7, this data is already stored in MySQL or Access databases. If you're using another database system, check out Appendix D for the SQL statements required to create and populate the sample databases, or look in the Day 7 file archive, available on `http://downloads.cutelittledogs.com/`.

- **Site Design**—Before the HTML and programming, there is a matter of deciding how the site is going to be laid out. You learned this in Day 2, and you'll put it to use this week. This usually doesn't take long, but it must be taken seriously. Don't start coding pages before thinking the project through. Lack of structure is another sure-fire way to end up at a dead end.

- **Implementation**—Each lesson wraps up with the actual implementation of the project—the HTML design, the addition of the server behaviors, and so on. Sometimes this will require editing the source code manually. After the implementation is finished, you will have a fully functional Web application capable of being deployed on a production server. You'll need to generate your own content, but the framework will be ready to go.

You're more than welcome to skip around, but I recommend reading each chapter and not jumping between sections until you understand the material fully. At times, we're going to be "tricking" Dreamweaver MX into doing things that it wasn't designed to do. Learning a few tips and tricks is essential for getting what's in your head into

As you work through each project today, be aware of the following conventions and assumptions:

- For each project (even the "mini" projects), you should define a new site. I, personally, have based my site names on the day and project name.

- After a short introduction, I will name the files that you should copy from `http://downloads.cutelittledogs.com` into your project folder.

- I will also give you the name of the database that was created for the project. You'll still get to learn the how/why of defining the database; but everything will be in place if you want to skim ahead; the text will also prompt you when to make the connection to the database.

- If you are creating the database by hand, use the record information contained in Appendix D or the SQL import file covered in Day 7. You should have a functioning database *before* creating the first Web page of the site.

- If you want to test the queries along with the text, you can use the command-line `mysql` client utility found at `C:\mysql\bin\mysql` on Windows or accessible directly from the Terminal application in Mac OS X. If you're using MS Access, create a new query, and then choose SQL View from the View menu and enter the query into the window.

This information will be set off in a sidebar, so it will (with luck) grab your attention.

Let's start!

Randomizing Banner Ads

Okay, they're annoying, but they're popular. Banner ads can be sold for an amazing amount of money if your site is well-traveled. You've seen how to dynamically show a series of images, but you haven't created a *single* image that is dynamic. Using a dynamic table with a collection of images gets you halfway there, but we want a single image that changes randomly instead.

Note

Yes, for you ASP programmers out there, ASP already has functions for banner ads. These aren't, however, available through Dreamweaver MX's interface. Obviously you can open the Dreamweaver files and edit the code however you like. The goal for this week, however, is to stretch the application authoring limits of Dreamweaver MX. Learning how to program is a process you'll need to undertake on your own!

Table Definitions

The key to setting up the changing image is writing a recordset that returns a different record each time. This is easier than you might think, but before you can define this magical query, you need to create a basic database to drive it.

In order to randomize the selection of an image, you need multiple images to choose from, so obviously the database should store image filenames. Additionally, most banners link to other sites, so you need to provide a means by which the application can set a link for the image that it is displaying.

The table definition (tblBanner) only needs to take two fields into account (filename and url). Because we're assuming that you'd have different image names for each of the banners, we'll use the filename as the primary key. Table 15.1 shows the layout for the tblBanner database table.

TABLE 15.1   The Definition of the tblBanner Table

Fieldname	Description	SQL Data Type
filename*	String containing the name of the file.	varchar(250)
url	URL that the image should link to.	varchar(250)

As you've already learned, you can't actually work with images stored directly in a database, but you can store the filenames in the table and then insert that filename into an `<img>` tag. Place that image in the middle of a dynamically generated link and you're done!

Sample Data

For sample data, let's try a few banners for www.cutelittledogs.com and some of the outstanding daily sites that we've built throughout the book. Obviously you'll want to place these on your own Web pages. Figure 15.1 shows the images that we'll use to test the system.

FIGURE 15.1

Advertise
www.cutelittledogs.c
om*! (No, you'd don't
really have to.)*

Table 15.2 contains the sample data for the `tblBanner` table. Each of the images is located in the `images` folder of your project. Like the filename, the URL is arbitrary and could point anywhere as long as it is a valid location.

TABLE 15.2 Sample Data for the `tblBanner` Table

Filename	URL
images/cutelittledogs.gif	http://www.cutelittledogs.com/
images/day2cutelittledogs.gif	http://day2.cutelittledogs.com/
images/day3cutelittledogs.gif	http://day3.cutelittledogs.com/

Again, this information should already be stored in the database on your system. If it isn't you should catch up using Table 15.2 or the data in Appendix D.

The SQL Queries

So, how can you get a single random image to appear? Obviously, you can select all the data with a simple select query, such as `SELECT * FROM tblBanner`:

INPUT

```
mysql> SELECT * FROM tblBanner;
```

OUTPUT

```
+----------------------------+------------------------------+
| filename                   | url                          |
+----------------------------+------------------------------+
| images/cutelittledogs.gif  | http://www.cutelittledogs.com |
| images/day2cutelittledogs.gif | http://day2.cutelittledogs.com |
| images/day3cutelittledogs.gif | http://day3.cutelittledogs.com |
+----------------------------+------------------------------+
3 rows in set (0.00 sec)
```

Unfortunately, the information always comes back in the same order each time the query is performed. What would be ideal is changing the order of the records being returned. By adding an ORDER BY clause to do the search, coupled with MySQL's RAND() function, you can randomize the return order of these records:

INPUT

```
mysql> SELECT * FROM tblBanner ORDER BY RAND();
```

OUTPUT

```
+----------------------------+------------------------------+
| filename                   | url                          |
+----------------------------+------------------------------+
| images/day2cutelittledogs.gif | http://day2.cutelittledogs.com |
| images/cutelittledogs.gif  | http://www.cutelittledogs.com |
| images/day3cutelittledogs.gif | http://day3.cutelittledogs.com |
+----------------------------+------------------------------+
3 rows in set (0.02 sec)
```

This is much better. However, the problem with this query is that all the records are returned, not just one. Because we're only interested in displaying a single image, the rest of the records being returned are not important. The clean way to limit the number of results returned is to add a LIMIT to the end of the query. Using LIMIT 1 will limit the number of returned records to one. The final query becomes SELECT * FROM tblBanner ORDER BY RAND() LIMIT 1.

INPUT

```
mysql> SELECT * FROM tblBanner ORDER BY RAND() LIMIT 1;
```

OUTPUT

```
+----------------------------+------------------------------+
| filename                   | url                          |
+----------------------------+------------------------------+
| images/day3cutelittledogs.gif | http://day3.cutelittledogs.com |
+----------------------------+------------------------------+
1 row in set (0.00 sec)
```

Note

You don't need to include the LIMIT 1 clause unless you want super-neat code. With the way the Dreamweaver MX recordset works, the only record that you immediately have access to is the first record returned in the recordset unless you explicitly tell the program to loop through all the records in the database. I've left the LIMIT 1 clause out of the examples in this chapter.

Caution

If you're using the MS Access database, the RAND function is slightly different. Replace RAND() with RND(LEN([filename])). See http://support.microsoft.com/default.aspx?scid=kb;en-us;Q208855 for a full explanation as to why this is necessary.

That's it for the SQL. Now we'd typically move on to the generation of a site map. However, this project is a bit different from others in that it adds functionality to images that can be placed on any page in any site. For that reason, we're going to skip the site map because it really could resemble anything.

Implementation

To implement the randomized banners, open a new ASP document in Dreamweaver MX. Using the database panel, click the "+" button and create a connection to the day15banner database; name it connBanner. Save your empty and "connected" document with the name banner.asp. You'll need three Dreamweaver MX-authored elements in the page to make the system come to life:

- A recordset containing the image being displayed—This recordset will provide us with the image that we need to show. Because the SQL has already been developed, it should be no problem defining the query within Dreamweaver MX.
- An image with its source bound to the image field of the recordset.
- A link surrounding the image that is set to the URL field.

Start by adding the recordset to the page. Because all the other elements are driven from the recordset, it makes little sense to start elsewhere.

Configure the advanced query as shown in Figure 15.2:

1. Set a recordset query named rsBanner.
2. Choose the current connection that you've created for the Banner project (connBanner).
3. Enter the following as your query: SELECT * FROM tblBanner ORDER BY RAND().

15

Click the test button to try the query out a few times—you shouldn't see any discernible pattern in the records that are being returned. If you are not using MySQL or Access, check your database server's manual for an equivalent randomization function.

FIGURE 15.2

You need to manually define the query in advanced mode. The use of the RAND function is prohibited in the simple query configuration screen.

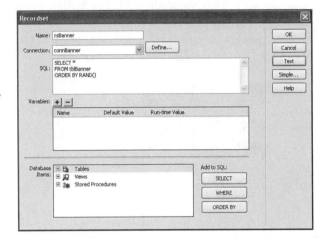

Random Events

If you happen to see a record coming up more than once in a row, it doesn't necessarily mean that anything is wrong. Although it is unlikely that a long string of repetitions will be generated, each individual event is equally likely to occur. This means that if you have three images, each time you choose one, you have a one in three chance of choosing the same one.

Now you'll need to add the banner image to the document. Move to the Insert panel and click the image placeholder icon, or choose Insert Image Placeholder from the Insert menu. Because we don't actually have a single image file, the placeholder will represent all the possible banner images that we could display. Provide a reasonable name for the image, such as MyBanner, as seen in Figure 15.3.

FIGURE 15.3

Add an image placeholder to your page.

The next step is "binding" the image name in the database to the image that is displayed onscreen. Make sure that the placeholder is selected in the document design window, and then open the Bindings panel. Expand the rsBanner recordset so that you can see the filename and url fields. Next, highlight the filename field and use the Bind To pop-up menu to choose the img.src element (the source for the image). Finally, click the Bind button. The image placeholder should now be bound to the filename field in the database. Figure 15.4 shows the correctly configured binding.

FIGURE 15.4

Bind the filename to the image placeholder.

Because Dreamweaver MX doesn't have an actual image to work with in the code, you'll only see an icon to represent the image. You can, however, activate the Live Data option under the View menu to poll the database and display one of the randomly selected images. Click the refresh button at the top of the window a few times—each time you click, a new image will be selected. Remember, the selection is random, so you might see the same image reappearing a few times.

Now you need to add the link from the banner to an external URL. Select the entire banner image (you can do this while in Live Data mode, if you want), and then choose Make Link from the Modify menu. This time you'll be prompted for the file that you should link to. Because we don't actually have a file to link to, click the Select File Name From Data Sources button in the dialog box. You should now see a window similar to that in Figure 15.5. Here you will bind the URL of the link to the url field in the database.

Be sure that the recordset is expanded by clicking the disclosure arrow in front of it, and then highlight the url field in the list. Finally, click OK to make the connection, and then click Choose to dismiss the file selection dialog box.

Tip

On my computer, Dreamweaver MX will often refuse to let me dismiss the dialog box until I choose a file in the file selection list. Unfortunately, when you're working with dynamic data, choosing a file will override the data

15

bindings you make! To get around this "quirk", choose a file (*any* file) from the file list before clicking the Select File from Data Source button. Doing so will make everything work as you'd expect.

FIGURE 15.5

This data binding will connect the link's URL to the url *database field.*

Note

As soon as you highlight the field in the recordset, you'll see the code that will be added in place of the URL appear in the lower half of the window. Additionally, you can use the Parameters button to add additional parameters to the `<a href>` tag that is being created behind the scene. For example, you might want to use a `target` attribute and value to cause a click on the banner image to open a new browser window.

With that step, you've completed the basic banner program. Try loading the page in your browser and see what happens. You now have a completely randomized image on your document. It isn't an obvious use of Dreamweaver MX, but it's certainly a valid application!

Note

The recordset order is randomized each time the database is queried. This doesn't mean, however, that you can copy and paste your dynamic image to different places within a single page and have the multiple occurrences each be randomized. In order to do this, you'll need to define multiple recordsets based on the same query. Each of these recordsets, in turn, can drive a single randomized image.

Tip

> The project is lacking a feature—the ability to remember which image a user last saw and *not* load that image the next time the user visits the page. You could implement this feature by setting a cookie equal to the filename that is chosen, and then filtering the recordset where the image filename is not equal to the cookie value. This is an advanced function that involves manually editing the ASP code—you'll learn how to do this later in the week.

Rotating Seasonal/Time-Based Images

Another popular type of dynamic image that you can add to your Web site is an image that changes with time. This is popular when you want to predefine content and have it automatically updated when a certain date passes. For example, having your Web graphics change with the seasons or even on a monthly basis provides the illusion that the site is under continual development, even though you don't need to pay any attention to the pages at all. It's a great way to make your boss think that you're always working to keep the site fresh and up-to-date (of course, you're already doing that, right?).

This project is very similar to the random banner ads, but requires a slightly modified query and database table definition.

What Do I Need to Get Started?

Before reading any further into today's lesson, you'll need to prepare your computer by downloading support files from the `http://downloads.cutelittledogs.com/` Web site and use them to create a new site on your hard drive.

- You should define a new site named after the project (such as Day 15—Time Images)
- You should copy the files from inside the `timeimages` folder of Day 15 archive on `http://downloads.cutelittledogs.com` into the project directory.
- The database used for the time-based image system should be set up as a data source named `day15timeimages`.

Table Definition

As in the previous project, the table definition for these dynamic images is simple. You'll want to store the image filename along with a date or time. The implementation that we'll be looking at here is based on a certain image being triggered after a given date. After reading this section, you might want to rework the database tables and base the image change on time of day, week, month, or several other options. Table 15.3 shows

15

the time-based table layout (tblTimeimage) used in day15timeimages. The important piece of information stored here is the golivedate field, which will be used to "trigger" an image.

TABLE 15.3 The Definition of the tblTimeimage Table

Fieldname	Description	SQL Data Type
filename*	String containing the name of the file.	varchar(250)
golivedate	The day that an image should "go live."	date

Sample Data

The images for this project are stored (as usual) in the images directory as part of the Day 15 archive on http://downloads.cutelittledogs.com/ in your project folder. These correspond to the sample data shown in Table 15.4. If you are creating the database by hand, make sure this information is in it before continuing.

TABLE 15.4 Sample Data for the tblTimeimage Table

Filename	Golivedate
images/spring.gif	2003-03-21
images/summer.gif	2002-06-21
images/fall.gif	2002-09-21
images/winter.gif	2002-12-21

If the dates in this example have expired, you can modify the MS Access files or MySQL databases to increase the dates until they're relevant.

The SQL Queries

MySQL provides a series of functions that lets you quickly manipulate data based on dates. You can combine these functions to easily create time- and date-based queries in any system that you develop:

DAYOFWEEK(<date>)—Returns a numeric value to represent the day of the week. 1=Sunday, 2=Monday, and so on.

DAYOFYEAR(<date>)—Returns the day of the year. For example, January 1st is day 1 of the year, whereas December 31st is the 365th day.

DAYNAME(<date>)—The name of the day of the week, rather than a numeric value.

MONTHNAME(<date>)—The name of the month in the given date.

WEEK(date)—A numeric result is returned containing the week (1–52) of the year that the given date occurs within.

CURDATE()—The current date.

CURTIME()—The current time.

NOW()—The current date and time.

> **Tip**
>
> For a more complete list of the functions that MySQL supports, be sure to check out Appendix B, "MySQL Quick Function Reference," for a quick MySQL function reference.

The trick is getting the query to work. Obviously you need to know the current date—as returned by CURDATE() or NOW()—but you can't just compare for equality between the stored date and the results of the NOW() function. This would result in the record being returned only when it is a certain date. What we're trying to accomplish is building a system that selects an image after the target date has passed. To do this, select records in the database that are greater than the current date using the query SELECT * FROM tblTimeimage WHERE golivedate > now() ORDER BY golivedate provides a series.

INPUT

```
mysql> SELECT * FROM tblTimeimage WHERE golivedate > now() ORDER BY
golivedate;
```

OUTPUT

```
+———————————+———————+
| filename          | golivedate |
+———————————+———————+
| images/summer.gif | 2002-06-21 |
| images/fall.gif   | 2002-09-21 |
| images/winter.gif | 2002-12-21 |
| images/spring.gif | 2003-03-21 |
+———————————+———————+
4 rows in set (0.00 sec)
```

The ORDER BY clause ensures that the closest date is at the top of the table. If you leave this value out, you'll get the results that match in whatever order they were added to the table.

Similar to random banner images, you're only interested in the first result of the query. Either ignore this technicality and use only the first record in the recordset, or limit the query using the LIMIT clause: SELECT * FROM tblTimeimage WHERE golivedate > now() ORDER BY golivedate LIMIT 1.

15

```
mysql> SELECT * FROM tblTimeimage WHERE golivedate > now() ORDER BY
golivedate LIMIT 1;
```

```
+ — — — — — — — — —.+ — — — — — —+
| filename          | golivedate |
+ — — — — — — — — —.+ — — — — — —+
| images/summer.gif | 2002-06-21 |
+ — — — — — — — — —.+ — — — — — —+
1 row in set (0.00 sec)
```

This gives you a specific image that becomes active at a certain date provides a series.

Implementation

You can now follow the same steps as with the randomized banner image to add it to your page:

1. Create a new document for your project named timeimage.asp.

2. Use the database panel to add a connection (connTimeimage) to the day15timeimages database.

3. Add a rsTimeimage recordset to your document that contains the query you've just defined—remember, you can leave out the LIMIT 1 clause. Figure 15.6 shows a properly defined recordset.

4. Insert an image placeholder (MyTimeimage) onto the page.

5. Use the Data Bindings panel to bind the img.src attribute of the image to the filename field in the rsTimeimage recordset.

6. Save the timeimage.asp file.

FIGURE 15.6

Define an advanced query to select images based on dates.

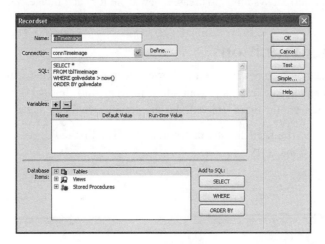

After saving the document, try loading the page or switching to live data view. The image you see should be the one that falls *after* the closest date in the database. If you have direct access to the server, try changing the system's date and see what happens.

 Note

> In case you're wondering, the images document the growth of a puppy over the course of a year. The puppy was born in the winter.

As you can see, this is actually a little bit easier than the randomized banner image we created earlier today. Unfortunately, this is a simple implementation that suffers from a *large* drawback—the inability to handle multiple different images per page.

Managing Multiple Seasonal/Time-Based Images

What makes time-based images so useful is that you don't have to pay attention to them in order for the changes to take place. You can set up the potential site images and a schedule for their implementation, then forget about it. Your server will take care of altering the look of your site for you.

The problem with the seasonal image, as we've defined it so far, is that it works for a single image. All images in the tblTimeimage table are considered different variations of the same graphic. What would be ideal is a theme-based system in which different images could be stored in a table and related to a group of dates. The only way to do this with the current system is to create a new table for each image. We definitely need a new technique.

Table Definitions

For example, you could have a Halloween theme that, coupled with the right queries, would replace the images in your site with scary stuff. Instead of a single image being replaced from the main table, all the site graphics could be managed within the table.

To do this, you need slightly different tables. The first table, tblMultiTimeimage, is shown in Table 15.5.

TABLE 15.5 The Definition of the `tblMultiTimeimage` Table

Fieldname	Description	SQL Data Type
filename	A string containing the name of the file.	varchar(250)
name*	An abstract name to describe the "type" of image.	varchar(250)
themeID*	A unique theme "name" that a given image belongs to.	varchar(250)

The table `tblMultiTimeimage` includes a `themeID`, which will be defined in the second table (discussed shortly), and a `name`. The `name` field is used to identify an image by an abstract name rather than a filename. This will let you call up an image called `MainGraphic` (or some such thing) for any theme, even though the actual filename might vary between the different themes.

The `tblTheme` table relates a `ThemeID` to an activation date. For example, you might want to add in a Christmas theme that is keyed to the date 12/25/20XX. The database structure for this `tblTheme` is shown in Table 15.6.

TABLE 15.6 The Definition of the `tblTheme` Table

Fieldname	Description	SQL Data Type
themeID*	A unique theme "name" for defining collections of images.	varchar(250)
golivedate	The date that a theme should "go live."	date

The two elements work together by relating the `themeID` between the two tables. This is everything you need for your "advanced" multi-image time-based system!

Sample Data

In order to understand how the time and "theme" based image system works, you'll need to make sure there is some sample data in the database. We'll work with a very simple version of the system that defines a single image name (a "header" graphic), which exists in four themes: spring, summer, fall, and winter. The system could be expanded beyond the single header image by adding more graphics with other name designations.

Table 15.7 defines the sample data for `tblTheme`, whereas Table 15.8 shows the information that should be stored in `tblMultiTimeimage`. If you aren't using the pre-seeded MySQL or MS Access data source, enter this information into your own database system now.

TABLE 15.7 Sample Data for the tblTheme Table

ThemeID	Golivedate
spring	2003-03-21
summer	2002-06-21
fall	2002-09-21
winter	2002-12-21

TABLE 15.8 Sample Data for the tblMultiTimeimage Table

Filename	Name	ThemeID
images/headspring.gif	header	spring
images/headsummer.gif	header	summer
images/headfall.gif	header	fall
images/headwinter.gif	header	winter

The SQL Queries

The sample data sets up four themes (spring, summer, fall, and winter) and four header graphics to go with them. What makes this system better than the previous table structure is that it allows you to store different images in the same table.

To use this new layout, you just need to modify the previous SQL to relate the two tables together and select an image based on its abstract name. For this particular example, there is only one "named" image to worry about—header. The SQL becomes:

```
SELECT * FROM tblMultiTimeimage,tblTheme
    WHERE tblMultiTimeimage.themeID=tblTheme.themeID
    AND tblTheme.golivedate > NOW()
    AND tblMultiTimeimage.name='header'
    ORDER BY tblTheme.golivedate
    LIMIT 1
```

Ack! Looks a bit scary, doesn't it? Because you haven't had much experience with complex queries yet, let's break this down and clarify what's going on:

- tblMultiTimeimage.themeID=tblTheme.themeID—Relates the two tables (the image table and the theme table) together based on the themeID.

- tblTheme.golivedate > NOW() —Compares the current date to the activation date in the tblTheme table.

15

- `tblMultiTimeimage.name='header'`—Selects the image based, not only on the `golivedate`, but also on the abstract name (`header`) that you defined for your set of images.

Implementation

To use this revised system, create a new `multitimeimage.asp` document, and then follow the same process you used with the single time-based image created earlier:

1. If you didn't work through the earlier example, use the Database panel to add a connection (`connTimeimage`) to the `day15timeimages` database. If you *did* try the earlier version of the time-based image system, this connection should already exist.

2. Add a `rsMultiTimeimage` recordset to your document that contains the query you've just defined—leave out the `LIMIT 1` clause if you want. This is an advanced query, so make sure you click the Advanced button.

3. Insert an image placeholder (`MyMultiTimeimage`) onto the page.

4. Use the Data Bindings panel to bind the `img.src` attribute of the image to the `filename` field in the `rsMultiTimeimage` recordset.

5. Save the `multitimeimage.asp` file.

The advanced time-based image system should now be working! You can easily add other images to the four themes—navigation, footers, photos, and so on—as long as they share a common `name` for each grouping and have a corresponding image file for each of the themes. For each image that you add to a page, you simply add another query (recordset) to the page and bind the `filename` field to the image's source.

Getting Your User's Feedback

The final mini-project for the day is a guestbook. The benefits of providing a guestbook for your users is so they don't feel that their feedback is "going nowhere." How many times have you visited a Web site and clicked a link to leave feedback, only to find that it opens your e-mail program so you can send a message to a nameless/faceless person who will never reply. A guestbook lets the users leave their mark on a Web site—something that can't easily be ignored.

I'm sure that you have some concerns about the messages a user can leave in a guestbook, and you should. It's not uncommon for an unfriendly person to take advantage of a public forum to display his or her immaturity. Inappropriate language, embedding images, and inappropriate HTML tags in plain text, and so on—there are plenty of potential problems. We'll see if this guestbook can't overcome some of downfalls.

> **What Do I Need to Get Started?**
>
> Before reading any further into today's lesson, you'll need to prepare your computer by downloading support files from the `http://downloads.cutelittledogs.com/` Web site and use them to create a new site on your hard drive.
>
> - You should define a new site named after the project (such as Day 15—Feedback)
> - You should copy the files from inside the `feedback` folder of Day 15 archive from `http://downloads.cutelittledogs.com/` into the project directory.
> - The database used for the feedback system should be set up as a data source named `day15feedback`.

Table Definitions

The contents of the guestbook table are really up to you. How much information do you want to store? The sample guestbook in this chapter is going to store a user's name, e-mail address, and comment.

A database table to hold this is defined in Table 15.9.

TABLE 15.9   The Definition of the `tblFeedback` Table

Fieldname	Description	SQL Data Type
messageID*	An auto-incrementing number that identifies a message.	int auto_increment
name	User's name or "handle."	varchar(250)
email	User's e-mail address.	varchar(250)
message	The contents of the message.	text

If this is the first time you've seen the `auto_increment` field type, don't worry; it isn't difficult to understand. This feature will automatically increment the field's value each time a record is added. You don't need to worry about manually generating this number. Unfortunately, this varies from database to database and might not be denoted in the same manner with your system.

Sample Data

The feedback system that we're going to create is unique in that it will allow you, the administrator, to filter inappropriate content from being displayed. To get an idea of how this is going to work, you need some sample data. The data that is seeded in your `tblFeedback` sample table is shown in Table 15.10.

TABLE 15.10   Sample Data for the `tblFeedback` Table

MessageID	Name	E-mail	Message
1	John Ray	jray@cutelittledogs.com	This is the greatest dog Web site ever! I have very low standards!
2	Robyn Ness	robyn@cutelittledogs.com	Not true. This isn't a very good Web site at all! The dogs are UGLY!
3	Bad Dude	badguy@someplacethatisevil.com	Forget this place! go <a href="http://mydogsarebetter.com"> here </a>guestbook

The SQL Queries

The SQL needed to select and display all the available comments in the guestbook should be immediately apparent: `SELECT * FROM tblFeedback`.

A recordset could be defined that contains all messages, and then a repeating region applied to the fields to create a list of all the messages. This doesn't address a big problem—namely, the fact that a given message might include content that you'd rather not show.

For the sake of being polite, the sample data that we're using here is just going to be filtered based on rather tame rules, which we'll establish shortly. Obviously, you'll want to adjust the filter to include actual naughty language if you deploy the system on your server. For the sample data, only the first message is considered "clean."

The second message, although not too bad in its current form, contains the inappropriate word "ugly." Similarly, the third message has a link to any outside site—and we don't want to display any messages in which the users have embedded their own HTML.

To filter the messages, you can use a partial match in the query to block out root words that you don't want to appear.

For example, the query `SELECT * FROM tblFeedback WHERE message NOT LIKE '%UGL%'` will choose any message that doesn't contain the letters `UGL`:

INPUT
```
mysql> SELECT * FROM tblFeedback WHERE message NOT LIKE '%UGL%' \G
```

OUTPUT
```
*************************** 1. row ***************************
messageID: 1
      name: John Ray
     email: jray@poisontooth.com
   message: This is the greatest dog website ever!  I have very low
standards!
*************************** 2. row ***************************
messageID: 3
      name: Bad Dude
     email: badguy@someplacethatisevil.com
   message: Forget this place! go <a href="http://mydogsarebetter.com">
here </a>
2 rows in set (0.00 sec)
```

The key part of the query is the to select pattern consisting of the letters UGL surrounded by "anything"—as represented by the % symbol. You can combine as many of these conditions together as you want.

For example, to filter based on the letters ugl, lamp, and kitten, you could use

```
SELECT * FROM tblFeedback WHERE message
     NOT LIKE '%UGL%'
     AND message NOT LIKE '%LAMP%'
     AND message NOT LIKE '%KITTEN%'
```

As you can see, the query just needs to be expanded with the new conditions to check. Because we wanted to filter out any message that had an HTML tag in it, the original query should be rewritten as SELECT * FROM tblFeedback WHERE message NOT LIKE '%UGL%' AND message NOT LIKE '%<%>%'.

INPUT
```
mysql> SELECT * FROM tblFeedback WHERE message NOT LIKE '%UGL%' AND
message NOT LIKE '%<%>%' \G
```

OUTPUT
```
*************************** 1. row ***************************
messageID: 1
      name: John Ray
     email: jray@poisontooth.com
   message: This is the greatest dog website ever!  I have very low
standards!
1 row in set (0.00 sec)
```

That's it, that's what we're looking for. The message containing the HTML is blocked based on a pattern that matches <> with anything in the middle and anything on either side. A final step you might want to take is to add ORDER BY messageID DESC to the end of the query so that the newest messages will appear first.

Note   The query defined here will match anything that resembles an HTML tag. In fact, it will match anything that has a < followed by > in it. You can't possibly define every HTML tag as a pattern, but you could, if you want, define some of the ones you want to filter out, such as `<a href>` or `<img>`.

It's time to create the HTML to get the guestbook online.

Implementation

Like the other two projects in this chapter, we're going to skip the creation of a site map because the guestbook is going to take up a single page. This page will have a short form for submitting comments, and, directly beneath it, the comments themselves.

Start by creating a new file called `feedback.asp` and setting up the form for inputting new comments. Open the Insert panel and switch to the form elements. As with any page that contains a form, you first need to insert the form object itself—without the `<form>` tag, the elements themselves won't appear. The document will look fine in the design view, but it won't show up in your Web browser. Insert a new form into your document, and name it `frmFeedback`—you'll be saving the contents of this form in the guestbook database. If you don't remember how to name a form, follow these instructions:

1. Click the form tag in the status bar of the document design window or Dreamweaver MX workspace to select the form.
2. Change the Form Name to `frmFeedback` in the Properties panel.

While you're at it be sure to set the form's action to the value `feedback.asp`. This may seem strange, but the form will submit information to itself for processing.

Next, insert the elements of the form that you need. You might want to add a table to help structure the layout of the form. You will need three fields with these names:

- `name`
- `email`
- `message`

Add these to the document by using the text field object in the form tab of the Insert panel. The `name` and `email` fields are normal text fields (the default field type that Dreamweaver MX inserts), whereas you need to adjust the `message` field so that it is a multiline field. Select the message field in the document design view, and then, within the Properties panel, click the multiline radio button to change the field type.

Finally, add a submit button to the form. Clicking this button will save the new comment to the database. A final version of the form is shown in Figure 15.7.

FIGURE **15.7**

This is a sample comment form; yours doesn't have to resemble it, but you're more than welcome to copy its stunning design.

The last step in making the form functional is adding the Insert Record server behavior. There are two parts to this task, adding a connection to the day15feedback database and then defining the server behavior that will store information in it. Because you should be getting used to defining the database connections, go ahead and create one called connFeedback now. I'll assume you're familiar with the process by now.

Once the connection is in place, you're ready to add the Insert server behavior, which will add the new comments to the database:

1. Open the Server Behaviors panel.

2. Click "+" and choose Insert Record.

3. Set the connection to the connFeedback connection defined for this project.

4. Choose the tblFeedback table to insert into.

5. In the Get Values From: pop-up, choose the frmFeedback form (it should be selected by default).

6. Each of the form elements should match up with the columns in the database. If they aren't matched, select one of the columns, and then use the Value pop-up menu to set the form value it corresponds to. The messageID column doesn't need to match with a form element since it will automatically be assigned a number.

7. Finally, fill in feedback.asp into the After Insert, Go To field at the bottom of the dialog box. This will send the browser to feedback.asp after the insert occurs. Click OK to save the behavior.

The appropriately defined behavior is shown in Figure 15.8.

FIGURE 15.8

Match the form elements with the database columns so that new messages can be inserted.

Now, the only thing that remains is adding a recordset to retrieve the available comments, and then display them. Because we've already defined the SQL, all that remains to be done is entering it into the system:

1. Open the Bindings panel.

2. Click "+" and choose Recordset (query).

3. Click the Advanced button to go into advanced mode. If you see a button labeled "Simple", you're already there.

4. Name the new recordset `rsFeedback`.

5. Select the `connFeedback` database connection.

6. Add the following SQL into the query window: `SELECT * FROM tblFeedback WHERE message NOT LIKE '%UGL%' AND message NOT LIKE '%\<%\>%' ORDER BY messageID DESC.`

7. Click OK.

Why Are There \ (Slashes) in the Query?

The slashes are necessary to "escape" the greater-than and less-than symbols. Because <% and %> are the start and end tags for ASP code, you must escape them with the slash character so as not to confuse Dreamweaver MX.

Once the recordset is defined, the very last step is to add a layout for the feedback listing. Below the form that you created, add a two-by-two table. The first row of the table will be the headings Author and Message. The second row will be turned into a repeating region and hold the individual messages. The e-mail address is stored for the administrator's benefit and is not visible in the guestbook. An example of this layout can be seen in Figure 15.9.

FIGURE **15.9**

Create the layout in which the messages will be displayed.

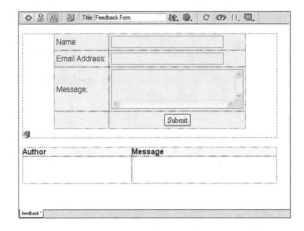

Now, open the Bindings panel and expand the `rsFeedback` recordset. The Bindings panel will resemble Figure 15.10.

FIGURE **15.10**

Your Data Bindings panel should resemble this.

Drag the `name` field from the Bindings panel into the table cell directly below the `Author` heading. Repeat the process for the `message` field. This will display the first record in the defined recordset, but what about the others?

To show multiple records, you need to add a Repeat Region server behavior:

1. Select the area you want to repeat (the name and message row in the table). Highlight both cells or click in front of the first cell to choose the entire row.

2. Open the Server Behaviors panel.

3. Click "+" and choose Repeat Region.

4. In the Repeat Region configuration dialog box, shown in Figure 15.11, choose the `rsFeedback` recordset.

5. Set the maximum number of messages (repetitions) you want displayed, or choose All to display all the available messages.

6. Click OK.

7. Save the finished `feedback.asp` document.

FIGURE 15.11

Choose the number of records to display.

The final document design is shown in Figure 15.12. Test the system—try adding a few comments to the database. Be sure to experiment with the filtering options as well. In fact, now would be a good time to go back and add real words that you want filtered from the system.

FIGURE 15.12

A final design of the comment board.

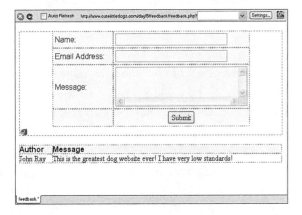

You've now successfully completed the first project day! Hopefully you've learned something that can be applied to your own sites.

Summary

Today's projects are meant to be quick and easy pieces of code that you can add to existing static Web sites to increase their appeal and functionality. Although not necessarily something you haven't seen before, the chapter provides information on how to do some things that might not be considered obvious for the beginner.

The use of SQL functions greatly increases the amount of flexibility you have within Dreamweaver MX. As it exists now, Dreamweaver MX is a tool that lets you display information in a database and insert it. Nothing more, nothing less. It's up to you to combine the strengths of the Dreamweaver MX environment with the strengths of your database server.

Today's lessons were clean and didn't require touching the HTML or ASP by hand. The rest of this week will consist of defining and implementing full Web applications. Sometimes you'll have to get your hands a bit dirty, but I'll do my best to keep it to a minimum!

Remember, as with each day's creations, these sample projects can be seen at http://day15.cutelittledogs.com/.

Workshop

The Workshop area is meant to reinforce your reading with a series of questions and exercises.

Q&A

Q Can banner images be set to not show the same one twice in a row?

A Through the use of cookies, you can have a browser remember (and tell the server) which image it saw last. You'll learn more about this later in the week.

Q How can time-based images be applied to more than a single year?

A In the example that we've provided, the themes expire after a certain date and cannot be reused. However, as discussed in the chapter, MySQL provides functions for comparing dates based on the month or day of the year. Either of these functions could work for multiple years.

Q Now can I expand the comment board into a full messaging system?

A Just wait until tomorrow because that's exactly what you're going to be doing.

Quiz

1. What does % do in an SQL LIKE query?
2. Why do randomized images come up repeatedly?
3. What image element should you bind the dynamic data to in order to change the displayed graphic?
4. Why isn't it important that multiple images are returned in the randomized banner and time-based image applications?
5. What does the RAND() function do in MySQL or RND() in MS Access?

15

Quiz Answers

1. When used in a `LIKE` clause, the `%` character matches any string of characters.

2. Random numbers occur randomly; the system has no idea which images it chose previously.

3. Use the `img.src` element to bind dynamic data to an image's source.

4. Dreamweaver MX, by default, uses the first element of a recordset unless a repeat region is applied.

5. `RAND()` and `RND()` generate random numbers; see Appendix B for more SQL functions.

Exercises

1. Alter the seasonal theme queries so that the image selection is based on the day of the year. This will let you pick specific dates (New Year's Day, and so on) as well as general times of the year (spring, summer, fall).

2. Using the knowledge you have from Day 14, "Advanced Components: Catalogs, Searches," add the ability to navigate through multiple screens of user comments.

DAY **16**

Applied Techniques: Data Collection and Reporting

Thus far, you've learned how to input data and display queries from a database—but there has been very little integration of these two processes. When a Web site is displaying dynamic data, there is often a back end to that Web site that is used to update the stored data.

Today's lesson will focus on creating a message board system that uses both data collection and reporting techniques. This will draw together almost all of Dreamweaver MX's capabilities into a single application. You'll find out how to:

- Design a Web message board system from the ground up—including the support databases
- Implement a user-based message system without the need for a separate user database
- Create a system that can easily be expanded and reused

Input and Output, a Messaging System Overview

Assuming the site www.cutelittledogs.com becomes wildly popular, it might be nice to add the capability for readers to communicate with one another, trade stories about their pets, and the like. One of the most common Web applications that exists is the *messaging board*, a forum for users to exchange messages. A few years ago, as a student, I sold a message board program (written in C) for more than $1,000. Fortunately for anyone needing such a system now, it can be built in Dreamweaver MX in an hour or two.

Today's lesson will pull together many of the standard Dreamweaver MX behaviors that we've seen throughout the book. The result will be a messaging application that offers many of the features of commercial packages, but you'll be able to build it yourself. Most notably, you'll offer users and administrators the capability to:

- Post messages without a signup procedure
- Post the popular message icons with each message
- Delete messages on the server
- Search and sort messages

After the past few days' activities, you should now be familiar with the concepts of *recordsets, server behaviors, site definitions,* and, of course, the design tools. Today's lesson picks up the pace and skips many of the fine points of laying out the pages. Don't worry, you'll still be given instructions on what to do and when, but how the pages look will largely be up to you.

What Do I Need to Get Started?

1. You should define a new site named after the project (such as Day 16—Message Board)

2. You should copy the Day 16 materials from http://downloads.cutelittledogs.com, unarchive them, and copy them to your site folder.

3. The database used for the message system should be set up with a data source named day16 as defined in Day 7, "Preparing a Server for Dreamweaver MX."

Defining the Site Map

Because this is a reasonably complex multi-page application, the first place to start is a site map. The site map defines all the screens that we will need to build, and lays out the basic interaction between them. In the case of the message board project, there are really very few pages needed. Although there is a great deal of functionality in the final product, only a handful of Web pages are needed to do the trick because the content changes. Here's what we're looking at:

Message listing (`listing.asp`)—A list of all the messages that are available in the bulletin board. This page can include an integrated search feature as well as column headings that can be clicked for sorting. Instead of separate pages for each of these features (sorting/searching), we'll just use a single display and several server behaviors.

Message viewing (`view.asp`)—When a user finds a message she wants to view, she can open it in a viewing window. One of the unique features of this bulletin board system is that it will also show the responses to a message that is being viewed. If the user posted a message, she'll be able to delete it after viewing.

Message composition (`compose.asp`)—The final portion of the site is for message composition. There are two ways to reach the message composition screen—either through the message viewing page, for replies, or from the main message listing.

We'll develop these pages one by one so that each component can be tested before moving on. The more you work with Dreamweaver MX, the more you'll realize that *a lot* can be done in very few files. Figure 16.1 shows the site map for the messaging board.

FIGURE 16.1

The site map for the messaging system is remarkably simple.

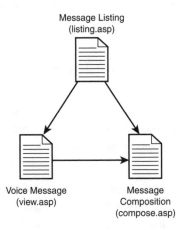

Message Listing
(listing.asp)

Voice Message
(view.asp)

Message
Composition
(compose.asp)

After the site map is developed, you'll need to create the back end for the system. Keep track of the features you want to add because they'll be very important in determining the structure of the database itself.

16

Table Definitions

The database for the message system is really very simple, but requires some important decisions to be made in the design process.

First off, let's make note of the information that we know for certain needs to be stored:

- Message subject
- Message image icon
- Message author
- Message body

Unfortunately, none of these fields makes an appropriate primary key because none can be considered a "unique" identifier. We can fix the problem by adding a unique "auto-incrementing" message ID field (the same as yesterday's "feedback" mini-project). Another problem is that the message board should be able to display a list of all the responses to a given message. To do this, there needs to be a second message ID stored in the database as well.

What? Two message IDs? Why in the world is that necessary?

The first ID will be the unique identifier for the message, and the second ID will be equal to the value of a parent message. For example, if you're replying to a message with the ID 325, the new message would have the parentID of 325. When the parent message is displayed, any messages that have the parentID equal to that message's ID will be displayed as a list of responses.

Another feature of this system is the ability of the users to delete a message that they have posted.

Because I'm writing this book, I get to do things my way—that's the truly fun part about writing. I do not enjoy going to a Web site and trying to participate in a discussion only to find that I have to go through a long registration process in order to post a single message.

What's the point? There's absolutely no reason to force someone to register in order to participate in a discussion! It doesn't *force* the users to enter in accurate information—it just slows them down. I'd rather just post my thoughts and be on my way. Because of this, we're going to do this message board my way—no long registration processes in order to post! (You're welcome to change it to suit your own opinions though.)

My preferred technique for giving the users the ability to delete messages is to store a simple password with each message. When the message is being viewed, a small password field and delete button form will be shown at the bottom of the window. Just enter the message's password and click a Delete button. Poof, it's gone!

So, that final piece of information brings the database table definition, tblMessage, to its final form, shown in Table 16.1.

TABLE 16.1 The Definition of the tblMessage Table

Fieldname	Description	SQL Data Type
messageID*	An auto-incrementing number that identifies a message.	int auto_increment
parentID	The messageID of the message that this message is a reply to.	int
subject	The subject for the message posting.	varchar(250)
iconURL	The URL for an icon that is included with the message. It's used to "personalize" the posting.	varchar(250)
author	Author's name or "handle."	varchar(250)
body	The contents of the message.	text
password	A password that can be used to delete the message.	varchar(250)

Note

Later you might realize that this table structure isn't entirely normalized. We'll be using the same icons over and over for each record, so, technically, the iconURL field should be in its own table.

That said, this structure opens up the possibility of users being able to post their own icons/images to accompany a message, whereas a second table would not.

Sample Data

The messages shown in Table 16.2 should already be included in the MySQL or Access database included with your system. If not, be sure to add them to your database before continuing.

TABLE 16.2 Sample Message Board Data for the `tblMessage` Table

messageID	parentID	Subject	iconURL	Author	Body	Password
1	0	First Post	images/icon1.jpg	John Ray	I had the first post of the message system! Cute Little Dogs are cool!	ihartdogs
2	0	Lame	images/icon2.jpg	Admin	People who make first posts with no real content really get on my nerves.	madadmin
3	0	Cool	images/icon1.jpg	Pom Gal	This new message system is wonderful. I plan to use it every day.	loveit
4	2	Re: Lame	images/icon3.jpg	Rude Dude	I think that first posts are great; stop being mean!	nodelete
5	2	Re: Lame	images/icon3.jpg	Nice Guy	I agree entirely. Listen to the admin and post real content please.	cutedogcool
6	2	Grumble	images/icon2.jpg	Anonymous	Let's drop this discussion and talk about something important!	frustrated

Note To give the message board some "bulk", the sample data shown here has been added several times over to the database files available for download.

Building the Main List View (`listing.asp`)

Each portion of this site can be built up from simple components—it's just a matter of putting the building blocks in the right place and keeping your fingers crossed.

Now, it's time to get started. The page that you'll be designing now, `listing.asp`, is the main message listing. This is the home page for the site and will be the primary browsing page for users of the Web application. Create this page now. As with all sites, try to keep it simple. If you're going to be browsing a thousand messages or so, you'll want to keep the load time as fast as possible. Also, take into account the features that this page will need to have:

Sorting—Provides column headings (`messageID`, `author`, `subject`, and so on) to click for sorting.

Message composition—A simple link to `compose.asp` for creating new messages.

Message listing navigation—Links for jumping among pages of the message listing—we'll do this all at once, so just leave some room on the page for the navigation.

Searching—Creates a single-field search form named `frmSearch`. It should be added with a single text field name `searchterm`, an action of `listing.asp`, and a submit button.

A message list—The formatted message list itself!

Because I promised you these features at the beginning of the chapter, I'd better deliver. Figure 16.2 shows a simple layout for the message listing page. We're just setting up the *look* of the page right now, not any dynamic behavior, so design away.

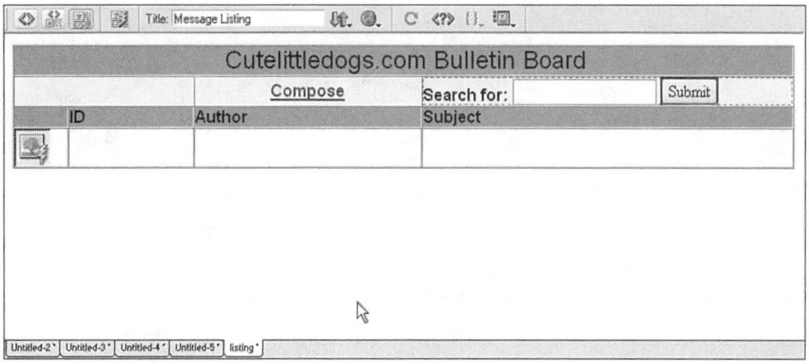

FIGURE 16.2

Design your message listing page so that all the elements you'll need for the site are included.

Once the page is set up, start adding dynamic functionality by adding the connection connDay16 to the day16 datasource. Because the connection is shared between all of the documents in the site, you'll only need to do this once, even though the site consists of multiple pages.

Now, let's create a recordset that will list all the messages. Because we need to plan ahead and build in the ability to sort the messages in the list, this isn't as straightforward as using SELECT * FROM tblMessage.

Creating the Message Listing

What makes the recordset we're creating unique is its ability to sort the message list by clicking on the column headings and search by submitting a simple form. Although the search is easy to implement, the sorting is a bit more involved. What we're going to need to do is link each of the column headings to the page itself, passing a parameter that will signal the recordset and let it know what to sort by. (If that didn't make any sense, don't worry, it will.) For example, there are three headings that we want to sort by:

- MessageID
- Author
- Subject

These headings correspond to three fields in the database. By some stroke of coincidence, these fields are also named identically to the headings. Select each of the column headings on your message listing page and set their respective links to:

- listing.asp?sortby=messageID
- listing.asp?sortby=author
- listing.asp?sortby=subject

Figure 16.3 shows the Properties panel when the messageID column heading is selected in the document design window.

FIGURE 16.3

Set the links for each of the column headings so that they pass their name to listing.asp.

This, amazingly, completes the *most* of the work we'll need to do on the page to enable sorting. Of course, we don't have a recordset yet, but now that we know that we're going to be passing a URL parameter called sortby that contains the name of the database column to sort by, we can create the recordset.

Using the Data Bindings panel, create a new recordset (query) called rsMessages, and then switch to advanced mode and follow these steps:

1. Enter the SQL SELECT * FROM tblMessage WHERE subject LIKE '%varSearchterm%' OR author LIKE '%varSearchterm%' OR body LIKE '%varSearchterm%' ORDER BY 'varSortby'.

2. Click the "+" button to add a new variable to the query named varSortby. Its initial value should be messageID and the runtime value should be Request("sortby"). Setting the default value to messageID will ensure that the listing is sorted intelligently, regardless of whether a heading has been clicked on.

3. Add another variable, varSearchterm, with the initial value % and a runtime value of Request("searchterm"). The % initial value ensures that if no search text is entered, all of the results will be returned.

4. When finished, your recordset definition should look like the one in Figure 16.4.

FIGURE 16.4

Create the message listing recordset with sorting capabilities.

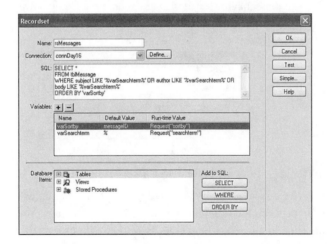

Now, add the dynamic data to the message listing by following these steps:

1. Open the Bindings panel.

2. Expand the rsMessages recordset so you can see the available fields.

3. Drag the messageID, author, and subject fields into the appropriate location on the design view.

4. For the iconURL field, insert a new image placeholder where you'd like the icon to appear on your screen, and then select the placeholder and bind the image.src attribute to the iconURL column, as seen in Figure 16.5.

FIGURE 16.5

Add a binding from the image placeholder to the iconURL field in the tblMessage table.

One final server behavior must be added before the message listing is functional—a repeating region that will display all of the records in the database. Select the table row in the listing.asp page that contains the message information (messageID, author, subject, and the image placeholder), open the Server Behaviors panel and add the Repeating Region behavior for the rsMessages recordset. Configure the behavior to operate over 10 records, as shown in Figure 16.6.

FIGURE 16.6

Add a repeat region so that all the message headings are shown.

Setting Up Message List Navigation

Because we're displaying only 10 messages at a time, there must be a way for the users to navigate between the different screens of message listings. You've already learned about the Hide/Show server behaviors as well as recordset navigation links, so, rather than bother with all of the Go To behaviors and Hide/Show region behaviors, we can accomplish the same thing by inserting the recordset navigation object from the Application category of the Insert panel. Find an appropriate location for the navigation object, and click the Recordset Navigation Bar in the Insert panel. Configure the bar to use the rsMessages recordset, and text or images. Your choice, as demonstrated by Figure 16.7.

FIGURE 16.7

Add a recordset navigation bar to the page.

> **Tip**
>
> While we're on the topic of hiding and showing regions, you might want to consider adding two conditional regions to your document design.
>
> The first region to hide is the message listing itself! If there are no messages available, why show the message headings at all? Apply this Show Region behavior if the `rsMessages` recordset is not empty. This will keep all the column headings from being shown unless there's an actual message being listed.
>
> The second region is a bit less obvious because you haven't created it yet. If there aren't any messages, why not tell the users so they aren't staring at the screen confused? Add a new `There are no messages available` message to the content portion of the screen—but outside of the repeating region (hidden regions cannot overlap repeating regions). Apply the Show Region behavior to this message text with the condition that it will be shown if you select the option If Recordset is Empty.

Unfortunately, there is a teensy weensy problem induced by adding this feature to our page. The sorting feature will "break" the recordset navigation because when we click on a link, it won't pass all of the information needed to keep track of which messages are being viewed. As a result, if you're on the second set of messages and you change the sorting, the message list will jump back to the first page.

To get around this, we can employ the Go To Related Page server behavior in a way that wasn't quite intended. This behavior adds a very nice variable, `MM_keepBoth`, that contains all the form and URL parameters that were passed to the page.

Add some text to the page that you can use as a link. It doesn't matter what it is; you'll be erasing it in a few moments. Select this text, and then using the Server Behaviors panel, add the Go To Related Page behavior to the document, as shown in Figure 16.8. As soon as it is added to the page, select the link in the design view and erase it. Do *not* delete the server behavior; just erase the link it created. The point of adding the behavior is to get some supporting code added to the document so we can use the `MM_keepBoth` variable.

FIGURE 16.8

Add the Go To Related Page behavior for a "fake" link.

Now, select each of the headings in the listing.asp document to modify the URL's slightly in the Properties panel. Add the following text after each URL: &<%= MM_keepBoth %>.

Be sure you put the & between the sortby=subject and the <%= MM_keepBoth %> code. If you're missing this symbol, the results will be very unpredictable.

This is all that's needed to get the links working correctly. Of course, this is less than perfect because it isn't completely automated within the Dreamweaver MX environment. It does illustrate the fact that you can frequently get around Dreamweaver MX's limitations by building the code as much as possible from within the interface, and then "fixing up" the rest.

If you've followed my basic design, your screen will look like Figure 16.9.

FIGURE 16.9

The final message listing is displayed.

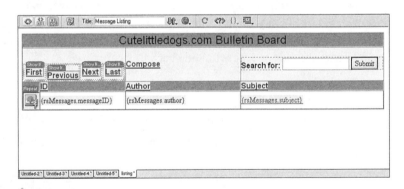

After you've designed your listing, switch into the live data viewing mode to see the message listing in action. You should also test the screen inside a browser so that you can verify that the message sorting and searching work.

Linking to the Message

Before putting away listing.asp, let's add one more server behavior that will link from the subject line of each message to the view.asp screen to read that message.

Select the dynamic text that the users should click on in order to see the full message—{rsMessages.subject}. Add a Go To Detail Page server behavior to create the link, as follows:

1. Open the Server Behaviors panel and click the "+" button.

2. Add the Go To Detail Page server behavior.

3. Configure the behavior, as seen in Figure 16.10, so that it passes an URL parameter `messageID` set to the `messageID` column in the recordset `rsMessages` to the page `view.asp`.

4. Pass along existing URL and form parameters for good measure.

5. Click OK when you're done.

FIGURE 16.10

Pass the message ID to the new message page.

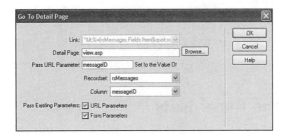

Congratulations! You just survived the toughest part of today's lesson. The `listing.asp` page is complete. Next, we'll move on to reading messages, and then, finally, to message composition. These last two segments are significantly easier to complete than the message listing!

Reading Messages (`view.asp`)

Although it actually is possible to implement the capability to read messages within the same document as the message listing, it'll be easier to implement this in a new document. To keep things easy to remember, create and save a new document named `view.asp`.

As with the message listing, there'll be no hand holding during the design of message viewing page. This is a reasonably basic "detail" page, which you've seen before. You need to take into account these three features of the message view:

- A list of replies to the message being viewed. This list will be a simplified message listing—no need for sorting, and so on—just a basic list of `messageID`, `subject`, and `author`.

- The view of the message itself.

- A small password/delete form named `frmDelete` that contains a single text field named `password` and a submit button with the label `Delete`. Entering a message's password and clicking delete will (eventually) remove the message from the system.

Figure 16.11 shows a basic layout for a message display screen. Yours, of course, can be as ornate or as simple as you'd like.

FIGURE 16.11

The message view screen needs to include the three functional elements we've defined for the site.

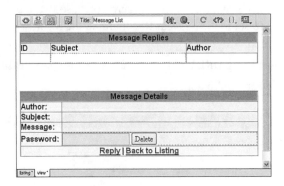

Creating the Recordsets

There are two recordsets that need to be defined for view.asp: a recordset that contains the message itself and one that contains a list of all the available replies to that message.

These are really extremely simple to define, so you can be up and running in a matter of minutes. First, define the recordset that contains the message being displayed:

1. Add a recordset (query) behavior to the document named rsMessageDetail.
2. If you aren't in Simple mode, switch to it now by clicking the Simple button in the recordset definition window.
3. Set your connection to connDay16 and table to tblMessage.
4. Leave all fields selected.
5. Set a filter for the query. The messageID should equal the URL parameter messageID, as passed in the Go To Detail Page behavior defined in listing.asp.

The completed recordset for the message being displayed is shown in Figure 16.12.

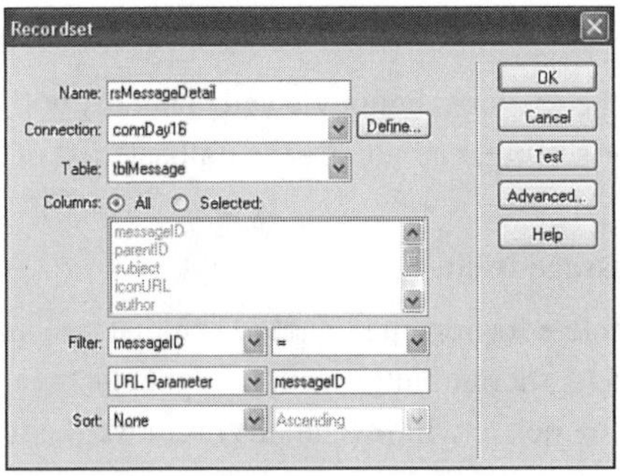

FIGURE 16.12

Make sure you filter based on the message ID.

The second recordset you should create, rsReplies (containing all the replies to the message being shown), is almost identical to rsMessageDetail. Add this new recordset to your document. However, this time, the filter needs to change slightly. Because we want to select all the messages where parentID is equal to the messageID (passed as a URL parameter), the filter should reflect this. Figure 16.13 shows the rsReplies recordset.

FIGURE 16.13

Only the filter needs to change for the second query.

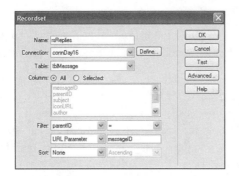

Adding the Dynamic Data

Creating this page is cut and dried—by now you're used to dragging elements from the recordsets that you've defined and into the document design view. Go ahead and drag the author, subject, and body portions of the rsMessageDetail recordset into their appropriate positions in the design view. Remember, you're dragging from the rsMessageDetail recordset, not rsReplies.

Handling the view of replies is a little more complicated, but nothing that you haven't seen before. For my version of the page, I'm just going to add a simple repeating region at the top of the page that has the messageID, subject, and author for each of the replies:

1. First, drag each of these fields from the rsReplies recordset into the design window.
2. Select the fields in the design view.
3. Open the Server Behaviors panel.
4. Click "+" and add a repeating region to the document. Have the region repeat all the available records in the rsReplies recordset.

Caution

Be absolutely certain that you select the appropriate recordset when defining your repeating region. If you choose the recordset that contains the message being displayed, the program will fail to run correctly and might be difficult to debug.

If all has gone according to plan, you should be almost done with the viewing screen. Switch to the live data mode and supply messageID=2 on the URL line to see whether both the message view and the reply list is visible.

Let's go ahead and finish the reply listing. Because the replies are listed, you should be able to click them and move to a page that contains that message, much as you can with the master message listing.

1. Select the dynamic text from the list of replies that you want the users to click in order to view the reply—such as {rsReplies.subject} or {rsReplies.author}, or both.

2. Add the Go To Detail Page server behavior.

3. Configure the behavior, as seen in Figure 16.14, so that it passes a URL parameter messageID that is set to the messageID column in the rsReplies recordset. It should be passed back to the message detail page view.asp for display. Don't pass URL or form parameters.

4. Click OK when completed.

FIGURE **16.14**

Pass the messageID *of the replies back to the message page.*

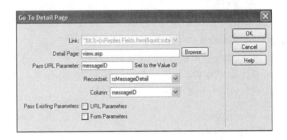

When viewing replies, you should not pass the existing URL or form parameters. If you do, you'll end up with multiple messageID= parameters on a single URL. This can confuse the server and cause unexpected results.

You should now be able to click the link of one of the replies to view it.

Handling Message Deletion

The final step needed to complete the functionality of this page is to implement message deletion. Hopefully, you designed the screen with this function in mind by adding the form discussed at the start of this section.

The desired behavior of this feature is that, if a users want to delete a message that they own, they can type in the message's password, click the Delete button, and the message will be instantly removed from the database. You might remember that there is a server behavior that can automate most of this process for us!

Open the Server Behaviors panel and add the Delete Record behavior to the document. Configure the behavior as follows:

- **Connection**—The Message board database connection, `connDay16`.
- **Delete From Table**—The message will be deleted from the message table, `tblMessage`.
- **Select Record From**—Choose the main recordset for the page, `rsMessageDetail`.
- **Unique Key Column**—The key for the message field—this should be set to `messageID` and the Numeric check box should be selected.
- **After Deleting, Go To**—Take the users back to the main message listing, `listing.asp`.
- **Delete By Submitting**—The form `frmDelete` that you've created.

After you've completed the Delete behavior, shown in Figure 16.15, click OK.

FIGURE 16.15

Add the delete behavior so that messages can be removed from the system.

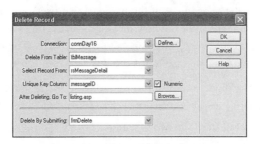

Unfortunately, there's no way that we can tell Dreamweaver MX that the password in the `frmDelete` form must match the password in the database in order for the delete to take place. This means that *anyone* can delete *anything* just by clicking the Delete button. To fix the problem, we need to directly edit the ASP code a teensy bit. Switch to the code view and look for the following line:

```
MM_editQuery = "delete from " & MM_editTable & " where "
               & MM_editColumn & " = " & MM_recordId
```

This builds the delete SQL query. In order to make it work, we must add the additional clause `AND password='<the password field>'`. To do this, add the following to the end of the existing line:

```
& " and password='" & Request("password") & "'"
```

The delete command will now operate only if the password is filled in correctly.

In addition to this small fix, the delete command will attempt to pass all of the existing URL parameters back to the main page after it executes. Unfortunately, that will cause errors during execute. Again, switch to the code view and look for this line:

```
Response.Redirect(MM_editRedirectUrl)
```

Replace it with:

```
Response.Redirect("listing.asp")
```

That's it. You can switch back to the design view.

Adding the Reply and Return Links

Functionally, the message viewing screen is done—but there are two loose ends that should be taken care of before we design the composition window. First, there needs to be a way to reply to a message, and, second, there should be a link back to the main message listing.

Of these two links, only one is out of the ordinary—the link to the reply screen. In this link, we need to pass the `messageID` of the message that users are currently reading. This will be stored as the `parentID` of the new message—indicating that it is a reply. Add a Reply link to your message view, and then follow these steps. The message composition page will be called `compose.asp`, so that's the link URL we'll use.

1. Select the text or object you want to link to the reply feature. I'm just adding a label named `Reply` to my screen.
2. Choose Make Link from the Modify menu.
3. Enter `compose.asp` manually in the URL field.
4. Click the Parameters button to show the recordsets and their fields.
5. Add a new parameter named `messageID` to the parameter list.
6. Click the lightning bolt in the value field to set a dynamic value for the `messageID` parameter.
7. Choose the `messageID` column from the `rsMessageDetail` recordset.
8. Click OK to exit from each of the dialog boxes.

With that link out of the way, just add a normal link (no dynamic parameters) back to the main message listing, `listing.asp`. Providing a user the ability to go back is always very important when the branch of the site you're working on is a dead end. The final version of the message view screen is shown in Figure 16.16.

FIGURE 16.16

All the necessary features have been added to the viewing screen.

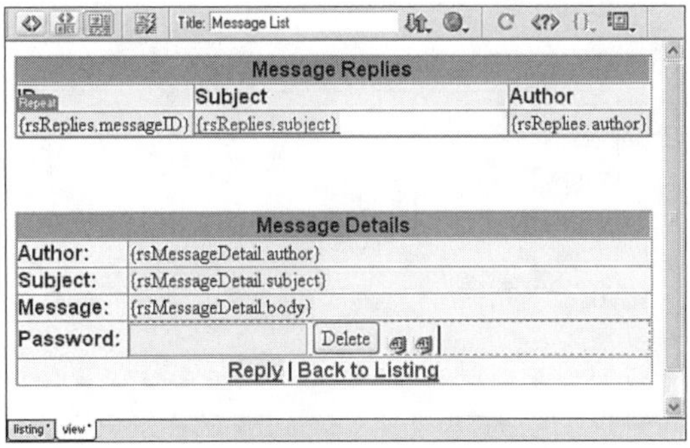

16

Creating the Composition Screen (`compose.asp`)

The message composition screen is the last piece of the puzzle—and the easiest. This is simply a form where users can enter their messages to submit back to the server. Keep track of the fields that we need to store:

parentID—This value is being passed in as the URL parameter ID. We'll need to create a *hidden* field that is set to this value.

subject—The subject of the message.

iconURL—The filename/URL of the icon to display with the message. For the composition screen, we're simply going to create a series of radio buttons to choose the value for the iconURL.

author—The name of the message's author.

body—Message content.

password—A password that can be used to delete the message.

Create the form now, and try to keep things simple by naming your HTML fields the same as the database fields. Also, be sure to name the form itself—frmCompose. When you get to the radio buttons for the iconURL field, simply insert an image, followed by a radio button for each of the images icon1.jpg, icon2.jpg, and icon3.jpg, all found within the images folder of your current site definition. The radio buttons should all share the name iconURL with the values images/icon1.jpg, images/icon2.jpg, and images/icon3.jpg. These corresponding to the image URLs of the images that they will sit beside.

Figure 16.17 shows the layout I've created for my compose.asp page.

FIGURE **16.17**

Create the message composition form.

Adding a Hidden Field

There is a single hidden field that you need on the form—parentID. In order to add this field to the document, you need to add a new data binding for a request variable. We've mostly dealt with bindings to recordsets—this will be a binding to the request variable messageID. To add this to your system, open the Bindings panel and follow these steps:

1. Click "+" in the Bindings panel.

2. Choose Request Variable.

3. Enter messageID into the request variable binding configuration screen. This is the URL parameter we need to access. See Figure 16.18.

4. Click OK to save the binding.

FIGURE **16.18**

Add a binding to a request variable.

Now you have direct access to the ID parameter that is being passed to the page. You can use this to define the value of the hidden form field:

1. Use the Insert menu's Form Objects submenu or Insert panel's Forms category to add a hidden field to the document design.

2. Select the hidden field's tag, and then open the Properties panel.

3. Click the lightning bolt icon at the end of the value field.

4. In the Bindings panel, expand the Request object.

5. Select the request value `messageID` (see Figure 16.19).

6. Click OK

FIGURE 16.19

Bind the hidden field to the request value `messageID`.

16

The form is now ready to be used for the Insert Record behavior. We're only a few minutes from being done for the day!

Saving the Message

To save the message, you need to insert the message as a record into the database. Everything has already been configured for the form, but one last server behavior needs to be added.

Open the Server Behaviors panel and add the Insert Record behavior to the document. Choose the `connDay16` connection and the `tblMessage` table to update. In the Get Values From portion of the configuration, choose the `frmCompose` form being submitted with the new message data, and then match the form elements with the column name and data type. As a final step, set the Go To URL to the main message listing—`listing.asp`. Figure 16.20 shows the complete configuration for the Insert behavior.

FIGURE 16.20

All that remains is to add the capability to insert records into the database.

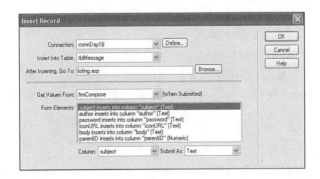

You should now have a fully functional message board!

Summary

We covered a lot of ground today, and built a reasonably complicated application. Many of the available server behaviors came into play on the message listing and viewing screens. Hopefully you have a better idea of how server behaviors work together and how they can be combined to perform complex feats of Web programming!

As you saw today, sometimes you can take advantage of Dreamweaver behaviors in ways that were never intended by Macromedia. Often this is required to get around limitations in the software itself.

If you run into a wall with Dreamweaver MX, determine whether combinations of other server behaviors can get you out of trouble. If not, you'll need to edit the source code directly.

Workshop

The Workshop area is meant to reinforce your reading with a series of questions and exercises.

Q&A

Q Why is the searching so slow?

A If you're searching across multiple fields in multiple different records, the search can take a while. You can always add a pop-up menu to choose the field that is being searched.

Q What's the best way to handle the problem with link values not being passed unless a Dreamweaver function is used?

A If you're creating links by hand, you'll need to use the techniques demonstrated today or you'll lose URL and form data as you move from page to page. If you *always* use the Go To Related Page or Go To Detail Page server behaviors, you can pass the information with you.

Q How can I expand my site?

A There's actually quite a bit of room for improvement—message dates, message editing—these are all features you can add with your existing knowledge.

Quiz

1. What is the `parentID` field for?
2. Why shouldn't you pass all parameters in the Go To Detail Page behavior when they are applied to the list of replies?

3. On multiple recordset pages, what do you need to watch out for?

4. What is an effective shortcut for defining Go To Record behaviors and Show/Hide regions to navigate a recordset?

Quiz Answers

1. The `parentID` field contains the `messageID` number of a message that is the parent of another message. If, for example, a message has a `parentID` of 15, it was created as a reply to the `messageID` 15.

2. If you pass the ID parameter on a page that's already passed the ID parameter, you'll end up with two copies of the ID being passed through the URL. This will cause headaches for the server.

3. Make sure you've chosen the right recordset when adding server behaviors to the pages. If your code doesn't act the way you think it should, you might be working within the wrong recordset.

4. The Recordset Navigation Bar can be used to quickly insert a "prepackaged" setup of all these behaviors.

Exercises

1. Modify the system so that it includes more information for the messages—such as the date and a topic. This could then be used to make a multiple board message system based on the topic.

2. Add editing capabilities to the system. This would be a fourth page with a form added to the existing site map. Use the password field to determine whether the user should be allowed to edit messages. Chapter 11's record updating tutorial should provide a good reference for getting started.

16

DAY 17

Advanced Techniques: Tracking and Using User Data

When users enter data into a form on a Web site, it isn't always just for an online survey, or to complete an order form—it could, in fact, be information that the users want to store for themselves. For example, it is possible to create a Web site that allows users to set up custom home pages for themselves by filling in a few forms. Too often the assumption is made that if a Web site is collecting data, its only purpose is marketing.

Today's lesson will show you how to create Web sites that collect information from users, and then use that information to customize the users' browsing experiences. In a way, you give users the ability to author their own customized version of the Web site. Today, you will learn how to:

- Let users log in to the system and create a new account with their preferences.
- Set a cookie so that the users are remembered each time they visit the site.
- Alter the appearance of a Web site so that it is customized for the user browsing it.

Customized Web Sites

Have you ever been to a Web site and seen the option of customizing the site based on your own personal preferences? This is an extremely popular technique that, when used correctly, gives the users an incredible amount of control over a site's environment. If you have a Web site that offers more than one service (various types of news, shopping, and so on), you can win repeat visitors by showing them only what they want to see on a page.

For example, I visit a popular Internet DVD site at least two or three times a week. In the beginning, I was forced to view their weekly specials before reaching the New Releases section to find what I was looking for. I thought if I could browse to their home page and see the content I want, when I want, I'd be much happier. Luckily, they've implemented this feature in a revision of their site. Now, instead of clicking through pages I'm not interested in, the "good stuff" appears as soon as I load the first page.

In today's lesson, you'll learn how to create the same behavior on your Web site. You can later apply this to any site you create in order to give it value above and beyond a traditional site.

The first question that you need to ask yourself is, "What portions of the site should I make customizable?" There are several levels of service that you can give to the viewer, depending on the nature of your site. For example, as you've already learned, any tag attribute on a page is easily made into a dynamic element simply by selecting the object in the design window and binding it to a database field in the Tag Inspector or Bindings panel.

Anything that you can set manually in a tag can be set dynamically from the database:

Color

Images

Text

Fonts

You can quite literally set up a site that pulls its entire look and feel from a remote database—without hard-coding anything at all.

Note

> You must take into consideration one slight drawback when designing a dynamic site—if you are adding a dynamic component to the site, it cannot contain any dynamic elements itself. For example, if you're storing the HTML to generate an entire table in a database table record, you can't turn around and add dynamic tags to that record—the tags will not be interpreted recursively.

The extreme case of a customizable Web site is one that allows the content of the site, not just tag attributes, to be changed. This is common on *portal* sites that offer customized news based on what the users have chosen. Today's lesson will attempt to follow this model and provide a completely customizable portal site where the users can control the information that is being displayed.

17

What Do I Need to Get Started?

1. You should define a new site named after the project (such as Day 17—Custom Portal).

2. You should copy the Day 17 materials from http://downloads.cutelittledogs.com, unarchive them, and copy them to your site folder.

3. The database used for the portal system should be set up with a data source named day17 as defined in Day 7, "Preparing a Server for Dreamweaver MX."

Defining the Site Map

Surprisingly, the majority of the work in this site will be handled by the database server and a few simple queries. Providing the interface through which the users can customize their software will actually take longer than designing the portal page itself. In order to use the site, users must take their browsers through a series of registration steps where they will set their preferences for the Web site. At the end of the registration, a cookie will be saved on their computers to allow the users to return to the site and have it appear exactly the way they want—at any time. A basic site map for the registration system and portal is shown in Figure 17.1.

Note

> Some of you might want to build Web sites that offer these services without the trouble of having to deal with a login system. Although this is certainly possible by more or less leaving out the registration system (only a cookie would be used to identify the user), it doesn't give the users the ability to go back to the site and change their settings. If the users move to another computer, they won't be able to recover the previous settings.

Figure 17.1

*The major portion of
the site is the registra-
tion section.*

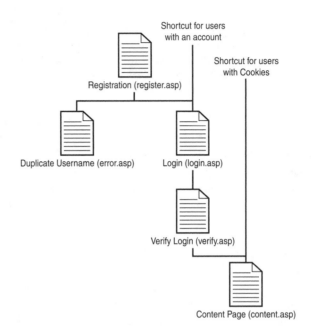

A question that you should be asking yourself is "Why can't we just store all this stuff in cookies rather than bothering with a database?" In order to fully answer the question, you must consider the number of elements that you want to make dynamic on your site. Is it one? Two? Ten? Five hundred? At what point do you stop allowing the users to customize their environments?

By resorting to cookies for the means of storing the configuration data, you place a limit on the amount of data that you can manipulate dynamically. Cookies are best suited for storing small amounts of information, such as user IDs. Additionally, each time you add a new element, you'll need to modify the code that supports that element, or write a somewhat sophisticated, generic cookie configuration utility before you start. Don't get me wrong—if you want to store a value or two, cookies are great—but enough values to configure an entire Web site? That might be a bit excessive.

A cookie-only approach also forces the users to re-register their preferences if they change browsers or computer systems—not a very user-friendly way to handle things. Using a database tied to a single user ID *within* a cookie creates a much more flexible and extensible system. Only a single value is stored on the client's machine—that value, however, is tied to as many database entries as you need to create your perfect site.

Caution Using cookies to store a user ID is a great way to handle something such as Web site preferences, but it shouldn't be used for secure-access sites. One of the fun things about today's lesson is that the resulting site doesn't need to be *totally* secure. No private information is being stored, or anything that a user would truly want to mess with. If there were, we could use a more random method of coming up with a user ID than just letting the database auto-sequence record numbers for us. Typically, secure cookies contain encrypted information that is valid only for a very short period of time.

Table Definitions

The table definitions for the site are going to be interesting, to say the least. Let's start with the simple stuff first—the user information table.

User Authentication and Preferences

Users need the ability to log in to the system and register their preferences. This is accomplished by a simple user table that will auto-generate user IDs and store them with usernames and passwords, as shown in Table 17.1.

TABLE 17.1   The `tblUserInfo` Table Stores Account Information

Fieldname	Description	SQL Data Type
userID*	An auto-incrementing number that identifies a specific user.	int auto_increment
username	The login username.	varchar(250)
password	The login password.	varchar(250)

The second table to build is also related to the users, but will store all the preferences that the users set when interacting with the site. One's first thought in making a table to store user preferences might be to create a table with a field for each feature that you want to be able to store a dynamic value for. This certainly would work, but it doesn't allow for the sort of flexibility that we're looking for. Instead, we need an approach that allows the number of options in the system to grow without the need to constantly add fields to the system.

Preferences

So, what values make up a dynamic option? Let's try to enumerate the things we'll need to track in the preferences table:

1. The feature that we're storing a preference for (page color, image location, whatever), which we'll call the featureID.

2. The userID of the person storing the feature.

3. The option that is chosen for that feature, which we'll call, surprise, optionID.

If this sounds confusing, don't worry, it really isn't that bad. Imagine that you want to make the background of the Web site a configurable user preference. This feature could be assigned a featureID of, say 1. For that given featureID (1), suppose there were three options that the background color could take on: red, green, or blue. Each of these color options is also assigned a unique number, such as 1, 2, and 3, respectively—this is their optionID.

So, when the user sets a preference, what gets stored in the preference table is the ID that identifies them (userID), the feature they're modifying (featureID), and the option it is set to (optionID). If that still doesn't make sense, keep following along. As the pages are built, the process should become clear. Table 17.2 shows the tblPreference table definition.

TABLE 17.2   The tblPreference Table Matches FeatureIDs and OptionIDs

Fieldname	Description	SQL Data Type
userID*	An integer that identifies a specific user.	int auto_increment
featureID	An integer that denotes a configurable feature.	int
optionID	The stored option associated with a given feature.	int

Note

Although the approach I'm taking for the system offers the highest degree of flexibility, it is also the most taxing on the server. Instead of a single query being able to return multiple preferences, each preference must be returned by a separate query.

If your server and site can handle the increased database traffic, use this method. If not, you should probably switch to an entirely flat table structure for storing the field values.

Features and Options

There are still two other tables that will need to be a part of the database, and a third that's *optional*. Let's start with the optional table—it is simply a lookup table that keeps track of each of the feature IDs and what the feature is. You'll only need this to keep things straight in *your* mind; this table isn't used by the application itself.

For this site, what are the features that we want to offer to the users?

- Alter the background color of the site
- Set the background color of each content area
- Choose the content areas of the sites
- Choose the font style of the content areas

The first two items are self-explanatory—you'll just be dynamically altering some of color tags in the document. The others are not (seemingly) so simple.

Multiple content areas exist that users can choose to display on their pages when they visit the site. These content areas are divided into individual table cells that contain the variable information.

The critical decision becomes one of choosing how to implement the multiple cells that must be present in order to offer the users the choice of picking any content at any time. You can approach the problem in one of the following two ways:

- Add several static tables to the site and implement the users' preferences to change their location and visibility. Each page contains all the information that could possibly be displayed, and this is modified by the dynamic settings made by the users.
- Use table content that is also pulled from a database, just like any other attribute.

Obviously the preferred technique is to have everything in the database. This provides a completely centralized point for updating the page's content. Using the first approach, the page would constantly need to be edited in order to provide new content. I find it highly unlikely that news sources such as CNN have an HTML editor open and waiting for a story to break.

Our page design is going to consist of two columns (created with a two-column table) of varying color, content, and style. Using a preferences page, the users will be able to set each of the values in Table 17.3. This is our feature "lookup" table, which can be stored in the database if you'd like, but isn't necessary.

TABLE 17.3 What the Features Actually Mean

FeatureID	Function
1	The background color of the main Web page.
2	The color of the content regions.
3	Content of the first region.

TABLE 17.3   continued

FeatureID	Function
4	Content of the second region.
5	Font style of the first region.
6	Font style of the second region.

Next, we'll need a table of options that can exist for each of the two regions. Because it's possible that a generic option such as a color could be applied to several different feature IDs, the option table—`tblOption`—will simply describe each possible option, and we'll use a final table to relate options to features. Table 17.4 shows the `tblOption` table.

TABLE 17.4   The `tblOption` Table Stores Each Possible Option and Its Value

Fieldname	Description	SQL Data Type
optionID*	An integer that identifies a specific option.	int auto_increment
optionName	The name of an option, like "The Color Red," and so on.	varchar(250)
optionValue	The content/html/tags associated with the given option.	text

Finally, we need to create one last table—`tblFeatureOption`. This table will contain records that match a given `featureID` to an `optionID`. This is how we "let the system know" which options are available to which features. The table definition is shown in Table 17.5.

TABLE 17.5   The `tblFeatureOption` Table Stores a List Relating Features to Their Possible Options

Fieldname	Description	SQL Data Type
featureID*	An integer that identifies a specific feature.	int
optionID*	An integer that identifies a specific option for a feature.	int

Sample Data

To prepare the site, our databases need to be seeded with users, passwords, and some appropriate options and the features that they "belong" to. As always, this data should already be in the database files that you set up in Day 7. Table 17.6 shows the default entries in the `tblUserinfo` table.

TABLE 17.6 Sample `tblUserinfo` Data

UserID	Username	Password
0	default	notgonnaguessme
1	test	test

The first user (`userID 0`) will be used to store the "default" look and feel of the site. The second `userID` will be for testing purposes.

Next, let's move to options and features. Table 17.7 contains the sample data for the `tblOption` database table.

 Note

Table 17.7 includes an extra field "description" that's included solely for the purpose of describing what is stored and why. It is not included in the actual database file and is provided here for your reading benefit.

TABLE 17.7 Sample `tblOption` Data

OptionID	OptionName	OptionValue	Description
1	Blue	#0000FF	The color blue.
2	Yellow	#FFFF00	The color yellow.
3	White	#FFFFFF	The "color" white.
4	Black	#000000	The "color" black.
5	Arial	Arial	The font Arial.
6	Helvetica	Helvetica	The font Helvetica.
7	Times	Times	The font Times.
8	Dog Training Tip	Tip: To get your dog to lay down and stay lying down, wait until late at night, quietly issue the command "down", then watch. You'll be amazed by the results.	A possible content piece.

17

TABLE 17.7 continued

OptionID	OptionName	OptionValue	Description
9	Breed News	A new breed of dog was discovered today in Estonia. The small, brown creature is primarily a tree-dweller and has developed a primitive language based on pop music from the eighties.	A possible content piece.
10	Famous Dog Quotes	Yesterday I was a dog. Today I'm a dog. Tomorrow I'll probably still be a dog. Sigh! There's so little hope for advancement.	A possible content piece.
		Charles M. Schulz, (Snoopy)	
		Outside of a dog, a book is man's best friend. Inside of a dog it's too dark to read.	
		Groucho Marx (1890–1977)	
11	Upcoming Dog Shows	2003/01/03—Winter Carnival dog show, Fargo, ND.	A possible content piece.
		2003/03/25—Blue Island Celebrity Dogs, Blue Island, IL.	
		2003/05/12—Summer Dog Sizzler, Wakeman, OH.	
		2003/06/17—Gator Dog Dinners, Melbourne, FL.	

Tip

Although not shown here, the records in the database include HTML for the line breaks, and the like. Although this might seem strange at first, there is nothing wrong with storing HTML in your database. It is rendered the same as static HTML pages after it is retrieved from the database and inserted into your document.

Now the `optionID`s must be tied to the `featureID`. The data in the `tblFeatureOption` takes care of this. Table 17.8 shows the relationship between our `optionID` and `featureID` values.

TABLE 17.8   The `tblFeatureOption` Table Relates `OptionID` to `FeatureID`

FeatureID	OptionID
1	1
1	2
1	3
1	4
2	1
2	2
2	3
2	4
3	8
3	9
3	10
3	11
4	8
4	9
4	10
4	11
7	5
7	6
7	7
8	5
8	6
8	7

Tip

Before you start scratching your head and asking, "What in the world just happened?", just think about matching the feature numbers to the options and what each number stands for.

Feature 1, for example, is the background of the Web page, and can be set to any of the colors we defined in the `tblOption` table. There are four

> possible colors with the optionIDs of 1, 2, 3, and 4. So, stored in the
> tblFeatureOption table are records that related featureID 1 to optionID 1,
> featureID 2 to optionID 2, featureID 3 to optionID 3, and so on.

Default Preferences

The final step in the preparation of the database is setting up a generic userID that will
be used as the default userID for all the available preference queries. Doing this will
allow users to browse the site using a default set of preferences before they set any of
their own. The tblUserinfo table already has the user created, userID 0, so all that
remains is adding in default values that will determine the look and feel for registered
visitors to your site. Table 17.9 shows the default values set in the sample database.

TABLE 17.9   Default Preferences for the Default User

UserID	FeatureID	OptionID
0	1	1
0	2	3
0	3	9
0	4	10
0	5	5
0	6	5

Note

As an exercise, you might want to match the features with the options to
see exactly what the default pages will look like. For those without the
patience, the answer is a blue page with white content regions, one set to
Breed News and the other showing "Famous Dog Quotes." The Arial font is
used throughout.

With the setup out of the way, we're finally ready to start building the actual site. Three
components to the finished site need to be built—the login system, preferences, and content page. You might be surprised to learn that the login pages are actually the key to the
site and will take the longest to create. The second most difficult portion is setting the
preferences. Although not exactly simple, this is still just a matter of a few applied server
behaviors.

Developing the Registration and Login System

The login system for this site will require four pages—two for the login process, and two for the user's registration. At the end of the registration process, the users will be allowed to view the site with a default set of preferences, or they can begin to set their own. The functions of the four pages that we need in order to set up and log into the user account are as follows:

register.asp—Asks the users to enter a username and password for their accounts. Each account will be forced to have a unique username, so we'll want to check it before saving the user's account information. If the check *fails*, the error.asp file will be displayed; otherwise, the username and password will be stored, and the users will be sent to the login.asp page.

error.asp—This is a static page that displays an error message if the users enter a username that already exists.

login.asp—Collects the username and password for a valid user account.

verify.asp—Verifies the username and password. If the username and password are valid, a cookie is set on the user's computer, and the user is provided with a link to the content page.

There is a teensy bit of customization that will need to take place on a few of these pages, but, for the most part, the design and implementation are very straightforward.

Creating the Registration Pages

The first page to complete is the register.asp page. This collects a potential username and a password that will be used to query the tblUserinfo database table.

Create the register.asp page now; it should consist of a form, frmRegister, and fields named username and password, as well as a submit button to submit the data for processing. Your form should be no more complicated than the one shown in Figure 17.2.

1. Open the Server Behaviors panel.
2. Click "+" and choose the Insert Record behavior.
3. Choose the connDay17 connection and tblUserInfo table to receive updates.
4. Make sure that all the frmRegister fields from the form match up with the columns in the database.
5. Configure the behavior so that it goes to the login.asp page after inserting the record.

FIGURE **17.2**

*The first form will only
collect a username and
password for testing.*

Your behavior should end up looking very similar to the configuration page shown in
Figure 17.3.

FIGURE **17.3**

*Insert the username
and password into the*
tblUserInfo *table.*

Now it's time to deal with the possibility that a duplicate username has been entered.
This is performed via a server behavior, and is keyed to the Insert behavior you just cre-
ated. Add the Check New Username server behavior from the User Authentication group.
The setup dialog box is displayed in Figure 17.4.

FIGURE **17.4**

Choose the username
*field; if it already
exists go to* error.asp.

Choose the username field, as it needs to be checked against the database to make sure it
is unique. If the username *does* exist, send the browser to the error.asp.

> **How Does the Server Behavior Know What to Compare Username To?**
>
> The Check New Username behavior matches the chosen form field name with the database column that it was matched with when creating the Insert Record behavior. It is simply using the information from the previously defined behavior. You cannot have a Check New Username behavior without a corresponding Insert Record behavior.

To finish the registration process, we have to deal with the possibility that a user has entered a username on the `register.asp` page that already exists in the user database. If this happens, the user is redirected to the static `error.asp` page.

 Note

> If the error page contains no server behaviors, why name it `error.asp` and make it an Active Server Pages behavior?
>
> The answer is, no reason at all; just a personal preference for naming all application pages with the same scheme. If you want to make a simple `.html` page, feel free.

17

Create the `error.asp` page however you see fit. Include a message to the user explaining what was done wrong (such as `"You've entered a duplicate username, please try again."`) along with a link back to the `register.asp` page to try again. Figure 17.5 shows a basic version of the page.

FIGURE 17.5

Create an error page to tell your users what has gone wrong.

The registration system is finished.

Writing the Login Pages

The first login page (login.asp) is nothing but a form with a username and password field that submits data to the verify.asp page, which in turn handles the majority of the processing. Create this page now; name the form frmLogin and include the username and password fields. Be sure to use the Properties panel to set the form's action to verify.asp.

Figure 17.6 shows an example of how the completed login page should look.

FIGURE 17.6

The first login page contains the username and password fields.

The second login page (verify.asp) uses the Show Region server behaviors and a recordset to show different messages for valid and invalid login attempts.

Create verify.asp. Add two regions (tables, layers, lines, whatever you'd like) to the document that contain these two different messages:

```
Thank you for logging into the system. Click here to continue.
Your username or password is incorrect. Click here to retry.
```

The first message should link to the content.asp screen that we'll be creating in the next section of this chapter, whereas the second notification links back to the login.asp screen.

In order to hide and show these documents, we'll need to define a recordset to select the user information that has been registered by filtering based on the input of the username and password on the login form. If the recordset turns up empty, the username or password is incorrectly defined. Add this recordset now:

1. Open the Server Behaviors panel.

2. Click the "+" button and choose Recordset (query).

3. Switch to the Advanced view, and name the recordset rsLogin.

4. Choose the connDay17 connection for this project.

5. Add the SQL: SELECT * FROM tblUserInfo WHERE username='varUsername' AND password='varPassword'.

6. Click "+" and add a new Dreamweaver MX variable named varUsername to the query.

7. Set the default value of the variable to a nonexistent username and the runtime value to Request("username").

8. Repeat steps 6 and 7 for the varPassword variable—make sure that you use varPassword in place of varUsername.

9. Click OK. The final recordset definition is shown in Figure 17.7.

FIGURE 17.7

Define an advanced query to select records based on the supplied username and password.

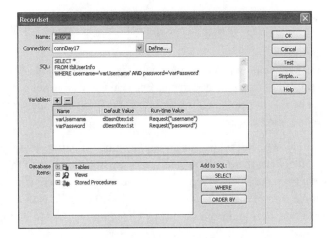

To finish the page, select the valid login region on the verify.asp page, and then add a new Show Region If Recordset Is Not Empty server behavior to the document. Choose the rsLogin recordset, as seen in Figure 17.8.

FIGURE 17.8

Choose the rsLogin recordset.

The invalid login region is set up in a similar way. Select this information and apply the Show Region If Recordset Is Empty behavior so that the area is displayed when the recordset *is* empty. The final design view of the verify.asp screen is shown in Figure 17.9.

FIGURE 17.9

The final design for the verify.asp *screen should incorporate valid and invalid login messages.*

With these behaviors in place, the document is as good as done. We still need, however, to add a tiny addition to the document. Because we need to set a cookie, it makes sense to add the cookie information directly into the document in the same place where the Valid Login region is shown.

Unfortunately, we can't do that. A cookie must be set before anything else is sent to the browser; otherwise, there will be an error. A possible solution to this would be to pass the userID from the selected record in the recordset to the content page—setting the cookie at the start of the content page itself. This, however, isn't a good idea—it allows one user to take over another's ID just by changing the userID on the URL line (session hijacking).

Even though this is a low security site, we really want to avoid session hijacking if possible. Let's take a different approach—set a sessionID on this page, and then set the cookie to equal the sessionID when the user goes to the content page. This is an easy fix to our problem.

Search your verify.asp code for the valid region—it should look similar to the following:

```
1 <% If Not rsLogin.EOF Or Not rsLogin.BOF Then %>
2     <table width="100%" border="0" cellspacing="0" cellpadding="2">
3         <tr>
4             <td><font face="Arial, Helvetica, sans-serif">Congratulations,
```

```
5              you've successfully logged in! <br>
6              Please enter the system by clicking <a href="content.asp">here.
7              </a></font></td>
8          </tr>
9      </table>
10 <% End If ' end Not rsLogin.EOF Or NOT rsLogin.BOF %><br>
```

Add into this area (between lines 1 and 2) a session variable named `tempUserID` set to the `userID` field in the `rsLogin` recordset with a piece of code such as this:

```
<% Session("tempUserID")=(rsLogin.Fields.Item("userID").Value) %>
```

The final piece of code representing a valid login will resemble this:

```
1 <% If Not rsLogin.EOF Or Not rsLogin.BOF Then %>
2      <% Session("tempUserID")=(rsLogin.Fields.Item("userID").Value) %>
3      <table width="100%" border="0" cellspacing="0" cellpadding="2">
4          <tr>
5            <td><font face="Arial, Helvetica, sans-serif">Congratulations,
6              you've successfully logged in! <br>
7              Please enter the system by clicking <a href="content.asp">here.
8              </a></font></td>
9          </tr>
10     </table>
11 <% End If ' end Not rsLogin.EOF Or NOT rsLogin.BOF %><br>
```

The session variable `tempUserID` is set in line 2 of the code sample.

The login pages are now officially done. We're ready to build the content page itself. Because we've already set up a temporary user with preferences, we can design this page based on those temporary preferences—then finish up the project with the preferences settings.

Note

> You might have noticed that we did not use the Log In User server behavior. For our purposes, we don't really want to lock users out of pages (which is the purpose of the Log In behavior), rather remember who they are.
>
> The login system we've created here, however, is actually easier to set up than the built-in behavior.

Generating the Content Screen (`content.asp`)

It's time to set up the content screen—this is what the users see after they log in to the system, or if they have a cookie set on their machines. It is nothing but a series of queries that are embedded into the HTML code. The majority of this screen is simple to build but will require some custom code before we can start writing queries. Create a new ASP document, content.asp, now.

In the previous section, we let the user log in and create a new account, and then set a session variable (tempUserID) based on his or her userID in the tblUserInfo database table. Before we can do anything else on this page, we need to set a cookie named userID that will store the tempUserID value for future visits. We also need to redirect the users to login.asp if they don't have a cookie currently set.

To break this down into pseudo-code, what we're trying to accomplish is this:

```
if (session("tempUserID") exists) then
    set cookie("UserID")=session("tempUserID")
    set strUserID=session("tempUserID")
end if
if (cookie("UserID") doesn't exist) then
    redirect to the login.asp page
else
    set strUserID=Cookie("UserID")
end if
```

Let's go ahead and translate it into ASP code that you should add to the top of the content.asp page, beneath the ASP language declarations:

```
1 <% If (not (Session("tempUserID")="")) Then
2     Response.Cookies("UserID")=Session("tempUserID")
3     Response.Cookies("UserID").Expires=#12/31/2030#
4     strUserID=Session("tempUserID")
5 End If
6 If (Request.Cookies("UserID")="") Then
7     Response.Redirect("login.asp")
8 Else
9     strUserID=Request.Cookies("UserID")
10 End If
11 %>
```

 Note

Sadly, Dreamweaver MX makes no provisions for setting cookies within the development environment. You'll need to enter this code by hand each time you have to set a cookie or a session variable. Remember that the Snippets library was created to hold pieces of code like this!

This code actually handles the bulk of the work on this site. It essentially guarantees us that the variable strUserID is set by the time we reach the Web page (line 2), or the user is redirected to the login screen (lines 6–7). The cookie's expiration date is set to 12/31/2030 (line 3)—which should be sufficiently far in the future for most applications.

With this code entered into top of the `content.asp` page, create a two-column table that will hold the page content. After creating the table, place your cursor in one of the cells, choose a default font from Properties panel, and then press the spacebar. This will insert a `<font>` tag into cell, which we'll need later. Repeat this for the second cell as well.

Don't spend too much time on the design of the document because it will eventually end up being driven by the database anyway. All you really need is something similar to Figure 17.10.

FIGURE 17.10

Set up a simple two-column page similar to this.

17

Now comes the fun part—setting the queries for all the preferences that the users can set. This isn't tough, but it is slightly tedious. To make matters simpler, let's enumerate the recordsets that need to be created as they correspond to a `featureID`:

- `rsPageColor`
- `rsContentColor`
- `rsRegion1Content`
- `rsRegion2Content`
- `rsRegion1Font`
- `rsRegion2Font`

We'll set up the `rsPageColor` recordset now, and then you can follow the same pattern for the others. This is an advanced query that uses the `strUserID` variable we created directly in the code. The only portion of the recordset that varies from feature to feature is the `featureID` and the recordset name.

Open up the Server Behaviors panel and add a new recordset to the document. Immediately switch to the advanced mode by clicking the Advanced button. Be sure to name the recordset based on the feature that it will be supporting; for this example, use `rsPageColor`. Enter this SQL into the recordset:

```
SELECT tblOption.optionValue FROM tblPreference,tblOption
WHERE tblPreference.featureID='1'
AND  tblPreference.optionID=tblOption.optionID
AND (tblPreference.userID='varUserID'
OR tblPreference.userID=0)
ORDER BY tblPreference.userID DESCNext, define the varUserID variable.
```

Click the "+" button inside the advanced query view to add a new Dreamweaver MX variable. Set the name of the variable to varUserID, the default value to 0, and the runtime value to strUserID. The strUserID value, to refresh your memory, was set at the start of the content.asp page when we checked for and set the userID cookie.

The final recordset definition is shown in Figure 17.11.

FIGURE 17.11

Define the
rsPageColor *recordset*
like this.

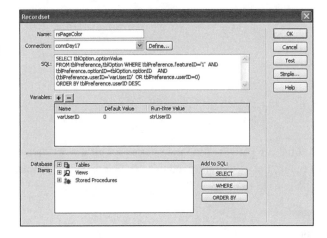

Test the query. After verifying that it works, click OK to save the recordset.

Our new rsPageColor recordset selects the current userID's preferences as well as the preferences for the userID 0 (which we already entered into the Preference table). Because we don't know whether the user will actually have any preferences set, we'll need *something* to use in order to display the page. By selecting from both of these records, we're guaranteed to always have a value. Although multiple values might be returned, we won't be using a repeating region, so only the first record in the set is displayed. But how do we know which record comes first? This ORDER BY code handles that little problem:

```
ORDER BY tblPreference.userID DESC
```

This will order the records in descending order by userID. Because any user will certainly have a userID greater than the default 0 user, the user's preference record, if it exists, will be the first in the recordset.

The rest of the query is pretty straightforward. The `featureID` is selected:

```
featureID='1'
```

The `userID` is compared to `varUserID` to select the option corresponding to the preferences stored for the user viewing the site:

```
tblPreference.userID='varUserID'
```

Now that you've completed the first recordset, you need to do the same thing with the other five recordsets (listed earlier in the chapter). When you're done, your Bindings panel should look similar to mine—shown in Figure 17.12.

Tip

Recordsets can be copied using Copy from the Edit menu. This can greatly speed up the process of making multiple similar recordsets. If you do copy one recordset repeatedly, make sure that you change the recordset name and featureID appropriately.

17

FIGURE 17.12

Your finished document will have a total of six recordsets.

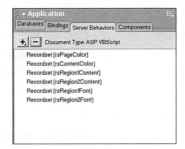

With all six recordsets in place, you can start attaching attributes to objects. The first attribute is the background color of the Web page itself.

Open the Tag Inspector panel (found in the Code panel group), and highlight the `<BODY>` element. Find the `bgcolor` attribute in the lower portion of the panel, as seen in Figure 17.13.

FIGURE 17.13

Use the Tag Inspector to set the body's `bgcolor` *attribute.*

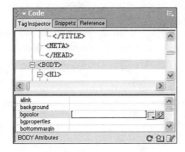

Highlight the value field to the left of the `bgcolor` attribute, and then click the lightning bolt icon to bind to a dynamic attribute. Dreamweaver MX will prompt you for the recordset—choose `rsPageColor`, and then `OptionValue` as seen in Figure 17.14.

FIGURE 17.14

Choose optionValue *from the* rsPageColor *recordset.*

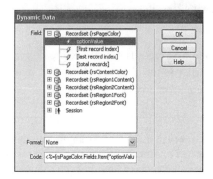

That's one out of the way. Now the other attributes need to be done. You can set these up in exactly the same way, just make sure that you use all the possible `featureID` values, as defined in Table 17.3. Using the Tag Inspector, you can set dynamic attributes for the `<td>` tag's `bgcolor` attribute, and the `<font>` tag's `face` attribute. When you get to the step of defining the recordsets for the region 1 and region 2 content, simply drag the `OptionValue` fields from the Bindings panel into the first and second `<td>` cells, respectively.

Guess what? You've just finished the content page. You still need one more thing though—a link to the configuration page. Near the bottom of the page, add a link called Preferences that goes to the page `preferences.asp`.

You should now be able to go through the registration process and view the content page (with the default `userID 0` settings). All that remains is the ability to set preferences. The final view resembles Figure 17.15. Obviously you could do a little bit to make it prettier, but it works, doesn't it?

 Caution

Before continuing, open the source code of the document and make sure that the custom programming to set the cookie is still at the top of your document. If it isn't, cut and paste it so that it falls above any of the other Dreamweaver MX-generated code. You may also want to comment the cookie code so you can easily find it within the document.

Now on to the final part of the site—the preferences.

FIGURE 17.15

The content page should now be functional, although not terribly attractive.

Finishing the Preferences (`preferences.asp` and `storepref.asp`)

The first preferences page (`preferences.asp`) doesn't actually set the attributes, but it does provide the links to the page that does set the preferences (`storepref.asp`). These links need to pass an identifier to a second page, which identifies what the user wants to set. For example, a link called "Page Background Color" would link to:

```
storepref.asp?featureID=1
```

This passes a URL parameter `featureID` set to 1 to the `storepref.asp` page. Set up your list of links for all six `featureID`s now. A sample page that lists all the available preferences is shown in Figure 17.16.

FIGURE 17.16

The features are listed, along with a link to the `storepref.asp` page.

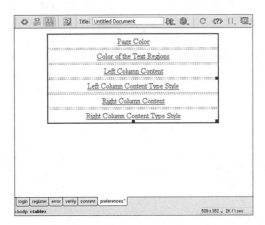

Make sure that all your links are correctly set before continuing. The storepref.asp page is the final page that we need to design in this document, and it would be a good idea if everything was working before we design it.

Note

> In this application, we must manually pass featureID to the second preferences page. If there were a table in the database that listed feature name and ID, we could dynamically generate the table of links. You might want to think about adding that later.
>
> Additionally, the method we are using to set links is fast, but if you'd rather stay in the Dreamweaver MX interface, you can use Make Link under the Modify menu and then click the Parameters button to set the featureID parameter.

Let's go on to the final page, storepref.asp. Create this new document now. This page should be built to contain a very simple form (frmPreferences) containing a database-driven pop-up menu, two hidden fields with the userID and featureID, and a submit button. Create the form now, inserting the userID and featureID hidden fields and a submit button.

To generate the pop-up menu, we need to write a query to select all the available options for the featureID that were passed to the page:

1. Open the Server Behaviors panel.
2. Click "+" and add a new recordset (query) behavior.
3. Switch to the Advanced Query mode.
4. Name the recordset rsFeatureOptions and set the project connection to connDay17.
5. Set the SQL to: SELECT tblOption.optionID,tblOption.optionName FROM tblFeatureOption,tblOption WHERE tblFeatureOption.optionID=tblOption.optionID AND tblFeatureOption.featureID='varFeatureID'.
6. Add a new Dreamweaver MX variable varFeatureID variable that is set to the run-time value "Request("featureID")" and uses a default value of 1.
7. Click OK.

Now, add a new List/Menu from the Form category of the Insert panel—this will be the dynamically generated pop-up list of available options. Set the name of this pop-up menu to optionID.

To bind the pop-up menu to the rsFeatureOptions recordset, select the pop-up menu, and then open the Properties panel and click the button labeled Dynamic. The setup dialog box shown in Figure 17.17 will appear.

FIGURE 17.17

Pop-up menus can be bound to recordset columns.

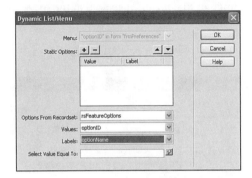

Leave the menu and static options settings alone; they are used to choose between multiple pop-up menus and add static pop-up options, neither of which we need to do. Set the Options From Recordset value to the rsFeatureOptions query. Values and Labels should both be set to OptionID. Click OK to continue.

Next, we need to set the values of the two hidden fields.

First add the userID cookie and featureID request variable as Data Bindings.

1. Open the Bindings panel.
2. Click "+" and choose Request Variable.
3. Enter userID and click OK.

Repeat this for the featureID request variable. Both variables should now be shown in the Bindings panel.

Bind the value of the userID and featureID form fields to the bound featureID and userID data. Select the tag for the appropriate hidden field in the document design view, and then click the corresponding item in the Bindings panel. Choose input.value as the binding, and then click Bind.

The last thing you need to do is actually save the data to the preferences database. Add the Insert Record behavior now:

1. Open the Server Behaviors panel.
2. Click "+" and choose the Insert Record behavior.
3. Set the connection to your project's data source, connDay17.

4. Choose `tblPreference` to update.

5. Select the form you defined on the page, and then match the elements in the form to the columns in the database.

6. When done inserting, go to `content.asp` so that the users can immediately see their changes.

Figure 17.18 shows the completed Insert Record action.

FIGURE 17.18

Insert the preference into the user preference database.

Wait! What if the user has already chosen a preference for the page? The system will generate an error if the user already has saved a preference for one of features and then tries to save over that preference. If you prefer, you could choose to work an Update Record option into the system. A simpler approach is to delete an existing preference before adding a new one.

Look for the insert code in your document:

```
' execute the insert
  Set MM_editCmd = Server.CreateObject("ADODB.Command")
  MM_editCmd.ActiveConnection = MM_editConnection
  MM_editCmd.CommandText = MM_editQuery
  MM_editCmd.Execute
```

Directly *before* this code, add the following:

```
  ' finish the sql and execute it
  Set deleteRec = Server.CreateObject("ADODB.Command")
  deleteRec.ActiveConnection = MM_editConnection

  deleteRec.CommandText = "delete from tblPreference where userID='" &
      Request("userID") & "' AND featureID='" & Request("featureID") & "'"
  deleteRec.Execute
```

This block of ASP will connect to the database and delete an existing parameter record if one exists.

As a final step, add a `Click Here to Set Your Preferences` link from somewhere on the `content.asp` page to the `preferences.asp` page. Figure 17.19 shows the `storepref.asp` page in action.

FIGURE 17.19

The `storepref.asp` page presents and saves feature options.

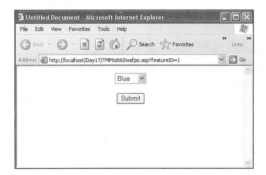

17

Now the system should be fully functional. Try going through and setting a few options: Quit out of your browser, restart it, and load the content page. All your preferences are retrieved with no interaction.

The technique I used for deleting a record before attempting to add a new one is only employed because of the trivial nature of the data being stored. If this were a system in which the information were extremely important, you would use the Update Record behavior or manually add the new preference into a temporary record and then move it to the correct spot after it has been saved properly. As it stands now, if the program were to crash in between the DELETE and INSERT commands, the users would lose their previous setting. It's very unlikely, but possible.

Summary

Today's lesson was more about a concept than providing a fully working news portal. Using cookies to customize a user's Web browsing experience provides an environment where users can feel at home and get the information and features they need. At the same time, you can use the collected preferences to better gauge what users like on your site and how they like it presented.

Obvious areas are open to improvement, but the overall concept is what's important. You could easily expand this idea into more interesting layouts. Additionally, you should now consider how you can make other projects remember and react to individual users on-the-fly using similar techniques.

Workshop

The Workshop area is meant to reinforce your reading with a series of questions and exercises.

Q&A

Q Why can't all the preferences be set at once?

A This is the biggest problem, in my mind, with the site. Because of the extensibility of the system, the table structure does not lend itself to showing all the attributes on a single page. If we had built a system that used a single table entry to store all the user's preferences, you could build a page that sets all attributes at once.

Q What happens if a user tries to access the site from a computer other than the one with a cookie?

A The site will force the user to log in again. This will set a new cookie with the userID on the client's browser.

Q What happens if the user has cookies turned off?

A If the user does not have cookies turned on, the site is inaccessible. The cookie is checked when the content page is shown. If it doesn't exist, the browser is redirected to the login page.

Quiz

1. What is the session variable used for in this project?
2. How do you add a cookie data binding?
3. How long will the server remember a user's preferences?
4. Why aren't the user's preferences all stored in a single long record?

Quiz Answers

1. The tempUserID session variable is set to the userID.
2. The cookie is bound using a Request Variable binding, the same as a form variable.
3. Until 12/31/2030, which hopefully is far enough in the future that you won't have to worry about the example itself expiring.
4. This would work just fine, but the system wouldn't be nearly as extensible. In order to add new preferences, you would have to modify the database structure itself.

Exercises

1. Update the preferences selection screen so that the currently selected feature option is visible when the user is presented with the pop-up option menu.

2. Add an additional feature table that matches feature IDs to a description of that feature. This will let you add a dynamically generated preference screen rather than the static table version currently used.

3. Modify one of your existing sites to use the features we've discussed today. For example, you could modify the message board so that it remembers what messages are yours, or what your name and e-mail address are.

17

DAY 18

Advanced Techniques: Online Testing and Surveys

One of the hottest topics in schools around the country is *distance education*—creating courses where children and adults alike can learn without needing to be in a classroom. The World Wide Web is an excellent medium to make distance education accessible to a very large number of users.

This chapter discusses the creation of an online testing forum that could easily be adapted to many academic and non-academic uses. Today you will learn:

- How to create an extensive survey/testing system.
- How to control the interaction of Dreamweaver MX with several database tables.
- How to use SQL to handle the scoring of tests in real-time—as the answers are submitted.

Survey and Testing Systems

I've spent hours setting up online testing courses for university faculty and government employees. Entire businesses are founded on providing distance education and certification. If you work to build internal (intranet) sites, eventually you too will find yourself in the position of creating some sort of online test, survey, or other training materials.

In some cases this is just a matter of creating a few HTML forms that e-mail the student's answers to the professor or save the results for the professor to grade later. Generating these HTML forms repeatedly gets to be a bit tedious, and can quickly become a hassle to modify and maintain. A better way to handle the task is to set up an extensible system where the HTML is separate from the questions being asked.

The system that you'll be developing today can do just that—record a series of questions and their answers, and then "play back" the questions to students. In order to access the site, the students will log in to the system and complete the questions. When finished, the administrator will be able to view the statistics for each of the students.

What Do I Need to Get Started?

1. You should define a new site named after the project (such as Day 18—Online Tests).

2. You should copy the Day 18 materials from http://downloads.cutelittledogs.com, unarchive them, and copy them to your site folder.

3. You should set up the database used for the testing system with a data source named day18, as defined in Day 7, "Preparing a Server for Dreamweaver MX."

Site Map

The development of this system takes a bit of forethought. Unlike some of the other applications we've developed, some interaction here might not be obvious at first glance. Surprisingly, however, the site map will be *very* small. As we've done before, let's list the features that must be in place in this system:

- Multiple arbitrary questions
- Multiple arbitrary answers
- A login page to authenticate users
- Immediate scoring of correct answers
- An administrative backend to view students scores

So, let's think about the site map. Obviously, there must be a login page (login.asp) and a question page (question.asp), as well as administrative pages (admin.asp and admin-results.asp) to search for a user and display the result data. In addition, we'll need a login page (login.asp) and an error page if the login fails (error.asp). You'll need to create a total of five pages, but the majority of the program's functionality will be contained within question.asp.

The finished site will support multiple questions and multiple answers. This means that there can be an arbitrary number of questions, and each question can have any number of answers. A single screen will handle displaying this information. Many people I've known who have set up online testing have developed individual pages for each of the questions—don't worry, we're not going to have to do that with *our* system!

The site map for the testing system being developed today is shown in Figure 18.1.

FIGURE 18.1

There are five pages in the testing site map.

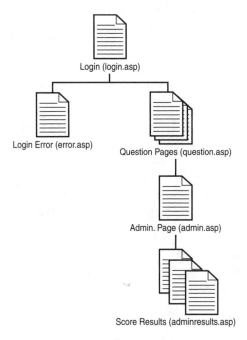

Login (login.asp)

Login Error (error.asp)

Question Pages (question.asp)

Admin. Page (admin.asp)

Score Results (adminresults.asp)

18

Table Definitions

When developing the database that we need for this section, we need to make sure that the tables are created in a way that doesn't limit the extensibility of the system.

User Authentication

The first table that we need is the username and password table—this will handle logins to the system. We won't bother creating a registration screen because we assume here that the administrator will be directly entering the users who should have access to the system. In today's exercise, we're going to rely fully upon the Dreamweaver MX authentication system; this will look a little different from previous user tables because we will also provide access levels for basic users and administrative control. Table 18.1 shows the authentication tblUserInfo table.

TABLE 18.1 The tblUserInfo Table Stores Testing Account Information

Fieldname	Description	SQL Data Type
username*	The login username.	varchar(250)
password	The login password.	varchar(250)
userlevel	An access level to identify users (student) and administrators (teacher).	varchar(250)

Tip

> The Dreamweaver MX authentication system does not make provisions for the use of an arbitrary field (such as userID) to identify a user. Unlike other days, today we'll stick with a tblUserInfo table that is based on a primary key of the username. I prefer to use a UserID, but for this exercise, we'll let Macromedia win out.

In Day 17, "Advanced Techniques: Tracking and Using User Data," you created a preference system that used two tables to define a preference type and to define different values that the preference can have.

Today's lesson will be much the same—instead of using a single table for the question *and* answers, two tables are needed. One table will hold the question itself, and another table will hold the answers to the question.

Quiz Questions

In order to relate the two tables, the answer table will hold a questionID for each of the answers. Because we need to implement online scoring, the system also needs to know when an answer is correct. To implement this feature, add the ID of the correct answer to the question table. The question table, tblQuestion, is shown in Table 18.2.

TABLE 18.2 The `tblQuestion` Table Stores Questions and an ID of the Correct Answer

Fieldname	Description	SQL Data Type
questionID*	The login username.	int
questionTitle	A title to identify the question (such as "The worlds smallest dog breed.").	varchar(250)
questionText	The text for the question that is being asked.	text
answerID	The ID of the correct answer.	int

Quiz Answers

The `tblAnswer` table, defined in Table 18.3, simply stores an answer ID number, the `questionID` it corresponds to, and the text that should be displayed for the answer.

TABLE 18.3 The `tblAnswer` Table Stores Possible Answers for Each Question

Fieldname	Description	SQL Data Type
answerID*	The ID that identifies each answer.	int auto_increment
questionID	The ID of the question that the answer corresponds to.	int
answerText	The text of the answer.	varchar(250)

User Responses

Finally, we need some place for user data to be stored. The `tblResponse` table, shown in Table 18.4, stores an `answerID` for each `username` and `questionID`.

TABLE 18.4 The `tblResponse` Table Stores User Responses to the Questions

Fieldname	Description	SQL Data Type
username*	The unique username.	varchar(250)
questionID*	The question identifier.	int
answerID	The answer that the user has chosen for the particular question.	int

Sample Data

For there to be an online test, we obviously need users, questions, and answers. This information is already entered into the day18 database, which should have been set up in Day 7's lesson.

Table 18.5 shows the same `tblUserInfo` data.

TABLE 18.5 Sample `tblUserInfo` Data

Username	Password	Userlevel
teststudent	studentpass	student
testteach	teachpass	teacher

Of course, the test needs questions. Of course, these questions must be related to cute little dogs. Table 18.6 shows the `tblQuestion` sample data. Note that the `answerID` column is already populated. The answers are defined in Table 18.7.

TABLE 18.6 Table `tblQuestion` Defines the Sample Test Questions

QuestionID	QuestionTitle	QuestionText	AnswerID
1	Animal Type	What type of animal is a dog?	2
2	Hazardous Food	You should never feed a dog one of these types of food. It could make the dog very ill, or even worse.	7
3	Animal Doctor	What type of doctor should you take your dog to?	10

TABLE 18.7 The Answers Are Stored in `tblAnswer`

AnswerID	QuestionID	AnswerText
1	1	Reptile
2	1	Mammal
3	1	Plant
4	1	Mineral
5	2	Potato
6	2	Meat
7	2	Chocolate
8	2	Cat food
9	3	Dentist
10	3	Veterinarian
11	3	Podiatrist
12	3	Optometrist

> **Note**
>
> In the sample data, there are only three questions and four answers per question. The system is created to handle any number of questions or answers. In fact, each of the questions can have an arbitrary number of answers. You can easily move from multiple-choice questions, for example, to true and false.

The SQL Queries

One of the hardest parts of this lesson is calculating the number of correct responses the user has made. Before we start building the pages themselves, let's determine exactly how this process is going to take place. As I've said all along, before you start building the site, you should have a good grasp on how it's actually going to work. Our sample database has a few responses already added for a username `example`, shown in Table 18.8.

TABLE 18.8 A Few Sample Responses, Just for Testing

Username	QuestionID	AnswerID
example	1	2
example	2	7
example	3	9

This sample data assumes that `example` has answered all three questions—two of them correctly and one of them incorrectly.

How can we determine the number of correct user responses?

We can use a bit of clever SQL, that's all:

```
SELECT * FROM tblResponse,tblQuestion
WHERE tblResponse.username='example'
AND tblResponse.answerID=tblQuestion.answerID
AND tblResponse.questionID=tblQuestion.questionID;
```

This statement, when executed, returns a set of records that contain all the responses the user entered that *are* correct.

INPUT

```
mysql> SELECT * FROM tblResponse,tblQuestion
       WHERE tblResponse.username='example'
       AND tblResponse.answerID=tblQuestion.answerID
       AND tblResponse.questionID=tblQuestion.questionID \G
```

18

```
************************ 1. row **************************
     username: example
   questionID: 1
     answerID: 2
   questionID: 1
questionTitle: Animal Type
 questionText: What type of animal is a dog?
     answerID: 2
************************ 2. row **************************
     username: example
   questionID: 2
     answerID: 7
   questionID: 2
questionTitle: Hazardous Food
 questionText: You should never feed a dog one of these types of food.
               It could make the dog very ill, or even worse...
     answerID: 7
2 rows in set (0.14 sec)
```

To look up the incorrect responses in the database, you can just invert the test condition `tblResponse.answerID=tblQuestion.answerID`. The new "incorrect response" query becomes:

```
SELECT * FROM tblResponse,tblQuestion
WHERE tblResponse.username='example'
AND tblResponse.answerID!=tblQuestion.answerID
AND tblResponse.questionID=tblQuestion.questionID;
```

These two pieces of SQL, coupled with the [total records] Dreamweaver MX recordset parameter, will give you the capability to display the total number of responses that were correct and what they were. It can also do the same thing for the responses that are *not* correct.

This should be everything that we need to get started. The rest of the process will be handled in the Dreamweaver MX application itself.

Let's start building! Be sure to set up your database and server connection.

Building the Login Pages (login.asp and error.asp)

As mentioned earlier, the testing screen is the primary screen for handling the interactions with the users. It is not, however, the first screen that we need to build. In order to store the information that a user enters on the Web site, the system must first know *who* the user is. This needs to be a somewhat secure system, so we'll build this login system using Macromedia's authentication routines and the MM_username session variable that you've seen in previous chapters.

There's nothing special about this login page. All we really need is a form (frmLogin) with the username and password fields and a submit button to test them. Create a new file within your site named login.asp, and then design a basic login form. A sample login screen is shown in Figure 18.2.

Next, add a database connection named connDay18 to the site. The connection should be to the day18 data source, which was set up in Day 7.

The real work of authentication comes into play when you add the Log In User server behavior to verify a user account. This will check to make sure that a username and password combination is valid and redirect the browser based on the outcome:

1. Open the Server Behaviors panel.
2. Click the "+" button and choose Log In User from the User Authentication submenu.
3. Choose the frmLogin form you created as well as the username and password fields.
4. Select the connDay18 database connection and the table (tblUserInfo) and fields within it that will be matched to the fields in your form.
5. If the login succeeds, send the users to question.asp. Otherwise, they should go to an error screen named error.asp.
6. Choose to restrict access based on the Username, Password, and Access Level option.
7. Select the userlevel field as the database field to retrieve the user's access level from. The final configuration should look very much like Figure 18.3.

With the server behavior defined, we can go ahead and create the error.asp page to provide error messages if the username or password is incorrect.

The error.asp page doesn't need to be anything fancy—just an error message with a link back to the login screen so that the users can try again. Depending on your application of the system, you might want to provide a warning message for unauthorized users. A sample error.asp is seen in Figure 18.4.

18

FIGURE 18.3

Match the username and password fields from your login form with the database fields to create a working authentication system.

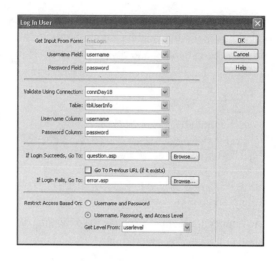

FIGURE 18.4

Provide an error message for the user, as well as a link back to the login screen.

That's all we need for the login pages. Before moving on, however, let's go ahead and add in the session variable into the data bindings so that we can access the current username from anywhere in the site:

1. Open the Bindings panel.

2. Click "+" and choose Session Variable.

3. Type in the name of the Macromedia authentication session variable MM_username, as shown in Figure 18.5.

4. Click OK.

FIGURE 18.5

Enter the name of the session variable to track.

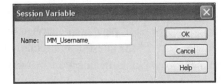

Remember, you can define a session variable anywhere in your site and access it from anywhere else. The session variable is active until the users start a new browser session (quit and restart the browser).

Of course the users must have cookies enabled for this site to work—if they don't, the site will be unable to determine who has logged in.

Creating the Question Form (`question.asp`)

The quiz form is the most difficult of the program to implement, and is obviously the most important. Before getting started, let's take a few minutes to determine exactly what we need to do and how we're going to do it. This page is actually very similar to some of the pages you've created before. So, what exactly does the `question.asp` portion of the site need to do? It must perform the following:

- **Maintain the user login information**—We've tested to see if the users should be able to access a Web site, but we need to do this throughout the entire site. This will be the last feature we add to the pages—but one of the most important. If the users can access the page without a login and password, they can preview the questions and cheat.

- **Ask questions**—Obviously. The purpose of the site is to create an online quiz, but there are a few things that make this slightly confusing. For example, there are an arbitrary number of answers for an arbitrary number of questions. The responses need to be stored for *everything*.

- **End the quiz**—Because we aren't just browsing back and forth between records, what happens when the users reach the last question? The system must be able to tell when the quiz is done and react appropriately.

So, how are we going to handle these requirements? Let's determine how the quiz page is going to work before we start building it. The most important part of the quiz is asking the questions—so how do we accomplish this? We create a basic catalog system that contains questions instead of products. Imagine the product catalog that we've already developed (Day 14), but with a forced browsing sequence rather than a full catalog system.

18

The question system is actually a crippled form of the catalog system—no searching, no browsing, and so on. The responses for each page are generated based on the questionID that is being shown. Each of the questions is actually a dynamic form. The form consists of the pop-up menu containing the question answers and a submit button. When a form is submitted, the system must store the answer in a database for future use by the administrator.

Finally, we'll use hidden regions (basically a Show Region behavior, written by hand) to implement a few features of the quiz screen. For example, when the quiz ends, the users will be notified by a hidden region (it remains hidden until the users reach the last record). At the same time, the entire page needs to be hidden if the users haven't correctly logged into the system. Let's go ahead and start creating the quiz screen.

We won't be adding all the functionality at once, so just get a basic screen design in place for now. Add a form frmAnswer to the page, and then create a table-based quiz screen inside of it. My display consists of a two-column by four-row table. The top two columns are merged and contain the text Quiz Question Topic:. We'll dynamically generate the text that follows it. Down the left column of the table are the labels: The Question, Your Answer, and Submit Answer. The only form elements inserted into the page so far are the submit button and the <form> tag itself.

Figure 18.6 shows the basic question.asp screen.

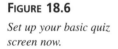

FIGURE 18.6

Set up your basic quiz screen now.

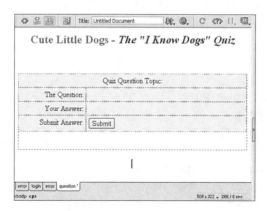

The first step in hooking up the quiz screen is connecting to the database. We need to develop a recordset for the page. This requires a bit of explanation. The difficulty with the quiz is that we need the questions and the answers to stay in sync. This means that we need to select a question in the same way we choose the set of answers to display.

Luckily, we can take advantage of one very important fact—tblAnswer and tblQuestion share a common index. When we're viewing tblQuestion where tblQuestion.QuestionID=1, we also want to be viewing tblAnswer where tblAnswer. QuestionID=1. To keep track of both, what we're going to do is pass a parameter index between each page, incrementing it each time. The only "unusual" part about this is that the first time the user pulls up the question.asp page, the index value will equal 0; therefore, this value will always trail the QuestionID by 1.

We're actually in a good spot here—this isn't nearly as difficult as it sounds. The record-set for the questions is an advanced query that uses connDay18 and selects all of the fields from the tblQuestion database table.

Set up a new recordset in the document named rsQuestion as an advanced query. Choose the connDay18 connection, and then type in the following SQL:

```
SELECT * FROM tblQuestion WHERE questionID='varQuestionID'
```

Now, add a Dreamweaver MX variable to the query by clicking the "+" button. Set the Dreamweaver MX variable's name to varQuestionID and the runtime value set to Request("index")+1; the default value should be set to 1, identical to the definition shown in Figure 18.7.

FIGURE 18.7

The question recordset selects based on an index parameter that we will create shortly.

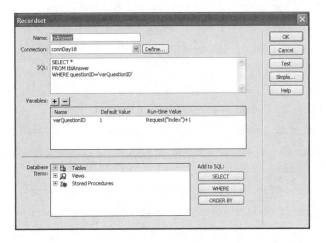

Next, open the Bindings panel and expand the rsQuestion recordset. Drag the questionTitle into the heading area (Quiz Question Topic:) of the question.asp table. Insert the question text into the document as well by dragging questionText into the appropriate table cell.

This is one of the few instances in which we don't need to use a repeating region to view all the questions in the database. When the recordset is defined and the record fields are inserted into the document, they refer to the current record in the database. Because only one question can be onscreen at a time, this is all that we need.

Dynamic Answers

The next step in setting up the quiz screen is creating the answer pop-up menu. In order to do this, you'll need to create an advanced query based on the answer table of the database. Like the tblQuestion query, this SQL selects the answer we need based on the common index shared between the recordsets.

```
SELECT * FROM tblAnswer WHERE questionID=<whatever question we're currently viewing>
```

Create a new recordset in the document named rsAnswer. This will be set up as an advanced query, so switch to the advanced mode if you aren't already in it. Choose the connDay18 connection, and then type in the following SQL:

```
SELECT * FROM tblAnswer WHERE questionID='varQuestionID'
```

Next, add a Dreamweaver MX variable to the query by clicking the "+" button. The variable's name should be set to varQuestionID and the runtime value set to Request ("index")+1; the default value should be set to 1.

After you've added the recordset, create a pop-up menu that is driven from this recordset:

1. Insert a list/menu form element named answerID into the question.asp document where you want the question's answers to appear. The list/menu elements are found under the Form category of the Insert panel.
2. Select the pop-up menu, and then open the Server Behaviors panel.
3. Click the "+" button and choose Dynamic List/Menu from the Dynamic Form Elements menu.
4. Set the Menu field to the answerID pop-up menu that you added to the system.
5. Set the Options From Recordset value to the rsAnswer recordset.
6. Set the values for the elements in the pop-up field to the answerID field.
7. Retrieve the Labels from the answerText field. (Static Options are left empty.)
8. Click OK after configuring the behavior completely, as seen in Figure 18.8.

At this point, the page should be ready for a casual inspection of functionality.

FIGURE 18.8

Configure the pop-up menu so that it is generated dynamically from the answer recordset.

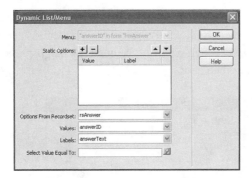

You should be able to do two things with the current pages:

- Browse the available questions.
- View the appropriate answers for each of the questions.

Be sure to test both of these functions before continuing. If anything is not working, go back through the steps that we've completed so far and make sure that you've followed the steps completely. If you add additional functionality before correcting any errors, it's only going to lead to confusion later when you try to debug the system.

Saving the Response

The most important part of the quiz system is saving the user's response back into the database. This is what we will deal with next. With this part of the system out of the way, all we'll need to do is work on the administrative screens, which is a bit more fun because they aren't "mission critical" to the application. So, how are we going to save the response? The form is already set up, but all the data isn't accessible.

To refresh your memory, the structure of the `tblResponse` table is shown in Table 18.9.

TABLE 18.9 The Table `tblResponse` Stores User Responses

Fieldname	Description	SQL Data Type
username*	The unique username.	varchar(250)
questionID*	The question identifier.	int
answerID	The answer that the user has chosen for the particular question.	int

18

Before values can be inserted into this table, it needs to be defined as a recordset. Set up a simple `rsResponse` recordset (query) that selects all the fields in the response table, as shown in Figure 18.9. Although we won't be querying this recordset, it is necessary for the Insert Record server behavior.

FIGURE 18.9

The response recordset must be defined in order to use the Insert action.

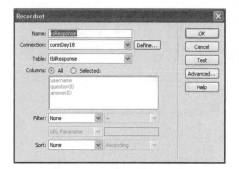

The form that we've created has the `answerID` in it, but what about the `username` and the `questionID`? You can most easily add these values by using hidden fields in the existing form `frmAnswer`.

Add two hidden fields to the `frmAnswer` form in `question.asp`—`questionID` and `username`. Next, you'll need to provide the values for these fields to take on.

Select the `username hidden` field in the document, and switch to the Bindings panel. Expand the Session object to show the `MM_username` variable. Bind `MM_username` to the `input.value` attribute of the `username` hidden form field. The completed binding is shown in Figure 18.10.

FIGURE 18.10

Bind `MM_username` *to the hidden field's value attribute.*

For the `questionID` form field, we need to do exactly the same thing. Highlight the hidden `questionID` form field, and then expand the `rsQuestion` recordset in the Bindings panel and bind the `questionID` database column to the form field's `input.value` attribute. Figure 18.11 displays the completed binding for the `questionID`.

FIGURE 18.11

Bind the database column questionID *to the corresponding hidden field's value attribute.*

We're ready to add the Insert Record server behavior:

1. Open the Server Behaviors panel.
2. Click "+" and choose Insert Record.
3. Choose the connDay18 connection and rsResponse recordset. Match up each of the frmAnswer form fields with the database table fields, as demonstrated in Figure 18.12. Don't worry about the Go to URL field—leave it blank.
4. Click OK to save the behavior.

FIGURE 18.12

Create the behavior that adds the response to the database.

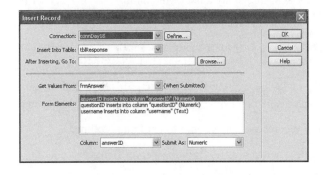

18

The Insert Record behavior has a feature that we *don't* want to inherit in our code. By leaving the Go To URL field blank when inserting a record, we tell Dreamweaver MX to send the user back to the quiz page. But won't this just result in the same question being asked over and over?

Remember, each time the form is submitted, we want to send the current index value plus 1. As you've learned, in ASP, the value of a passwd parameter is Request(<*parameter name*>). Therefore, on each subsequent page, we want index to equal Request ("index")+1. Specifically, the frmAnswer action must be set to question.asp?index= <% =Request("index")+1 %>, like this:

```
<form name="frmAnswer" method="post" action="question.asp?index=
    <% =Request("index")+1 %>">
  <table width="100%" border="0" cellspacing="0" cellpadding="2">
    <tr align="center" bgcolor="#CCCCFF">
      <td> </td>
```

Tip

> If you don't want to manually edit the HTML, you can just select the form, open the Properties panel, and change the `frmAnswer` form's action to be `question.asp?index=<% =Request("index")+1 %>`.

Try the page now; the program should work exactly as we want. Note: you'll need to clear answers from the database between "tests." For MySQL, this is as simple as using the command `DELETE from tblResponse`; MS Access users can use the Access interface to remove stored responses.

Measuring Correct Responses

While the users are taking the test, they are building up a table of information containing all the responses. These answers could be used at any time to determine the number of correct responses the users have given. Providing this information to the users might be a good thing, depending on how you view online testing. Remember that earlier we came up with this SQL to display a list of the number of correct user responses:

```
SELECT * FROM tblResponse,tblQuestion
WHERE tblResponse.username='<username>'
AND tblResponse.answerID=tblQuestion.answerID
AND tblResponse.questionID=tblQuestion.questionID
```

This is the code that we'll need now. Using this SQL and the `MM_username` session variable, we can display real-time scoring within the `question.asp` page.

Add a new recordset to the system to get things rolling:

1. Create a new recordset from the Server Behaviors panel.
2. Switch to the advanced query mode.
3. Define a new `rsCorrect` recordset using the `connDay18` connection. It will contain all the valid user responses.
4. Enter `SELECT * FROM tblResponse,tblQuestion WHERE tblResponse.user-name='varUsername' AND tblResponse.answerID=tblQuestion.answerID AND tblResponse.questionID=tblQuestion.questionID` into the SQL field.
5. Add a new Dreamweaver MX variable named `"varUsername"` with a runtime value of `Session("MM_username")` and a default value of `none`.
6. Click OK.

Figure 18.13 shows the completed recordset.

FIGURE 18.13

Define this advanced query in order to calculate the current user's number of correct responses.

Add the [Total Records] dynamic text to your design window by switching to the Bindings panel and dragging [Total Records] from the rsCorrect recordset. This will be the count of correct responses that the user has entered. Such a small page—so many server behaviors! Add an explanatory message by the [Total Records] that tells the user that the indicated number is how many questions they've answered correctly.

> **Note** You may want to also add an indicator of the total number of questions in the system and the question currently being asked. These correspond to the values [Total Records] and QuestionID values in the rsQuestion recordset.

18

Ending the Quiz

We're to the point in the system where the users can work their way through the quiz material until the last question. Unfortunately, after they answer the last question, there's nothing left for them to do but keep answering it (which is impossible because they would already have a response for that question).

In order to end the quiz, we need to use a Show Region behavior that will hide the Quiz form when we run out of questions. To do this, add a message to your bottom of your document that says "Congratulations, you've finished the test."

Next, select the question/answer form (frmAnswer), switch to the Server Behaviors panel, and add the Show If Recordset is Not Empty server behavior. Configure the behavior to use the rsQuestion recordset.

Repeat this process, using the "Congratulations" message area, and the Show If Recordset is Empty server behavior.

Obviously, you can put anything you want inside these regions. Finish up the HTML code for this area of the quiz, and you're done! This is certainly a complicated page, but you've made it through.

Protecting the Quiz

Although the question.asp page is finished from a functionality standpoint, we still need to keep prying eyes away. To protect the page, you must apply the Restrict Access To Page server behavior. Follow these steps to limit access to your page:

1. Click "+" in the server behaviors panel, and choose Restrict Access To Page from the User Authentication menu.

2. Choose to restrict access based on the Username, Password, and Access Level.

3. Define two access levels, student and teacher, by clicking the Define button and using the "+" button to add the new levels.

4. Restrict access to both the student and teacher levels by making sure both are selected in the Select Levels list—this means that anyone can take the quiz—even someone with teacher-level access.

5. If access is denied, send the user back to the login page. In this case, login.asp.

6. When you're finished, the behavior should be configured like Figure 18.14. Click OK to finish the definition.

FIGURE 18.14

Restrict access to the page based on user-name, password, and access level.

To provide easy access to the administration section, create an Admin link from within the question.asp document that links to the administrative section you're about to create (admin.asp)—otherwise administrators will have to enter the URL by hand. Make sure this link falls outside the "Show Region" server behavior on the question.asp page.

On a production site, the link to the admin page should either be hidden by checking to see if the logged in user (Session("MM_username")) is a student, or left off the page entirely. This is left as an exercise for the reader.

Administrative Access

We're finally ready to wrap up the day by creating the administrative interface to enable the test administrator to easily view the score of anyone who took the test.

The first administrative page, `admin.asp`, contains a single form where you can enter a user's name to look up information. Create the `admin.asp` page now. Add a form, `frmAdmin`, a single field `username` and a submit button, that's all. The form's action should be set to `adminresults.asp`. This page will not have any server behaviors. A sample `admin.asp` page is shown in Figure 18.15.

FIGURE 18.15

The first screen of the administrative backend is extremely simple.

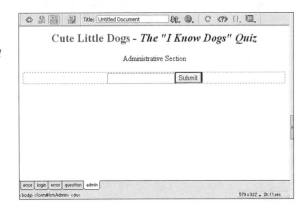

Creating the Results Screen

After you've finished the first admin page, create the second document, `adminresults.asp`. This page will receive the form value `username` from the `admin.asp` page and will perform a few lookups to show how the users answered the different questions.

Before you can design this screen, you need to create two recordsets. These queries will generate lists of the correct user responses and the invalid user responses. We already have a query that does this:

```
SELECT * FROM tblResponse,tblQuestion
WHERE tblResponse.username='<username>'
AND tblResponse.answerID=tblQuestion.answerID
AND tblResponse.questionID=tblQuestion.questionID
```

For incorrect responses, the SQL is very similar; only the comparison between `response` `answerID` and `question` `answerID` must change:

```
SELECT * FROM tblResponse,tblQuestion
WHERE tblResponse.username='<username>'
AND tblResponse.answerID!=tblQuestion.answerID
AND tblResponse.questionID=tblQuestion.questionID
```

Go ahead and design a `rsCorrect` and `rsIncorrect` recordset now:

18

1. Open the Server Behaviors panel.

2. Click "+" and choose the Recordset behavior.

3. Switch to the Advanced query mode if you aren't currently there.

4. Name the recordset `rsCorrect` and use the `connDay18` connection.

5. Enter the SQL: `SELECT * FROM tblResponse,tblQuestion WHERE tblResponse.username='varUsername' AND tblResponse.answerID=tblQuestion.answerID AND tblResponse.questionID=tblQuestion.questionID`.

6. Define an Dreamweaver MX variable `varUsername` with the runtime value of `Request("username")`.

7. Click OK.

8. Repeat this process for the `rsIncorrect` recordset. Be sure to use the `!=` comparison for `tblResponse.answerID!=tblQuestion.answerID`.

Figure 18.16 shows the query definition for the recordset containing correct responses.

FIGURE 18.16

Define both of your recordsets for this page based on this model.

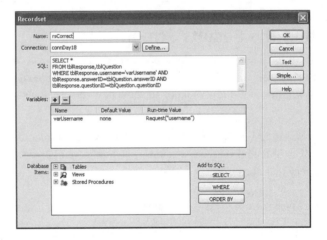

Now you can design your `adminresults.asp` page using the two recordsets you've defined. The `[Total Records]` field can be used to show the total number of responses that are correct, or the total number that are wrong (depending on if you insert them from the `rsCorrect` or `rsIncorrect` recordset, obviously).

It would be helpful to show the actual question titles that the users got right or wrong. You can add this feature to your page by dragging the `questionTitle` database fields from the `rsCorrect` recordset in the Bindings panel to your document design view, and then applying a Repeat Region server behavior to the fields using the `rsCorrect` recordset. As a final nicety, add a link to the page that sends the users back to `admin.asp` so that they can look up another user.

My final administrative results (`adminresults.asp`) page is shown in Figure 18.17.

FIGURE 18.17

Add the features and information you want to the administrative summary page.

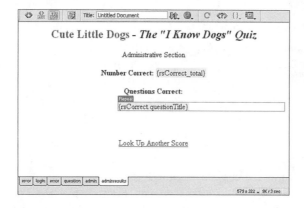

Protecting the Pages

As a last step, follow the same sequence you used to protect the `question.asp` file to restrict access to the administrative screens—`admin.asp` and `adminresults.asp`. Because the `admin.asp` page does nothing but submit a form to `adminresults.asp`, protecting it is optional. There is little concern of it being exploited.

1. Open the Server Behaviors panel.
2. Click "+" and choose Restrict Access To Page from the User Authentication submenu.
3. Configure the restriction to base access on Username, Password, and Access level.
4. Restrict the access level to `teacher` only. This will prevent students from looking up scores and answers.
5. If the login is incorrect, send the users back to the login page (`login.asp` in this case). The completed behavior can be seen in Figure 18.18.
6. Click OK when finished.

FIGURE 18.18

Restrict access to the teacher-*level users.*

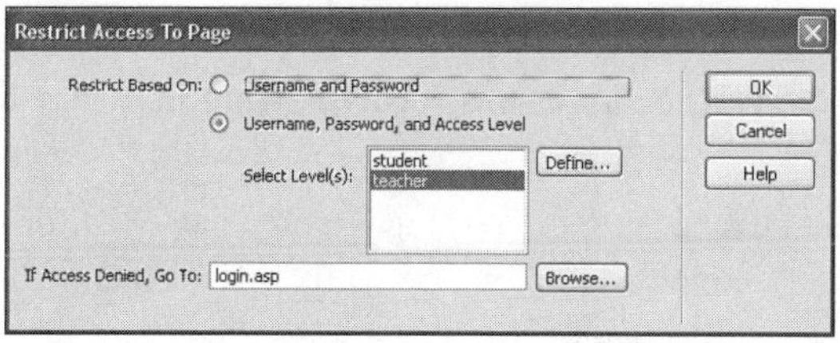

That's it. You have more than enough experience to extend this example to a full-blown testing system, or use it as is.

Summary

Today's exercise created an application with some unique features that we haven't seen before in an Dreamweaver MX application. For example, bypassing the Go To URL behavior after a data insert is performed. The more you work with Dreamweaver MX, the more you'll find that in order to make it do what you want, you need to break the rules a bit. Dreamweaver MX, of course, can't read our minds, so it does the best it can. Tomorrow's lesson will show you how to push the limits of the Dreamweaver MX environment by using simple logic on your SQL server.

On a final thought, I want to point out that today's project, although a working system, is definitely open for expansion. A full testing site could include actual education material that is presented before the tests, and so on. Feel free to expand on what we've created today to fit your own educational or recreational applications.

Workshop

The Workshop area is meant to reinforce your reading with a series of questions and exercises.

Q&A

Q **The quiz's security…how secure is it?**

A It's secure to the point of handling the questions correctly, but it has the problem of allowing users to potentially fake their identity by changing the username within the form. If you're security minded, you should replace the hidden field submitted with this value so that it is handled entirely by the MM_username session variable.

Q **Why didn't we use a Go To Next Record server behavior to page through the quiz questions?**

A It's possible to munge the Go To Next Record server behavior to move through the question set. Unfortunately, it requires extensive "tweaks" to the code. It is much easier to maintain our own index value and pass it from page to page.

Q **What happens if the users answer a question that they have already answered?**

A The system fails because only a single record can exist for a user. Take a look at the exercise section for a tip on how to fix this problem.

Quiz

1. Why did we have to bypass the Go To URL behavior that is inherent to the Insert Record behavior?

2. How is security of the administration section handled?

3. How did we increment the common index between `rsQuestion` and `rsAnswer`?

Quiz Answers

1. This was necessary to force the quiz to jump to the next question rather than redisplaying the current question.

2. The Dreamweaver MX authentication behavior protects this page from anyone who does not have teacher-level access.

3. Using the parameter index plus 1 (`Request("index")+1`).

Exercises

1. The program, in its current state, will fail if the user tries to answer a question more than once. The optimal way to handle this is to only display questions that do not have a corresponding user response. Go ahead and modify the SQL so that it works in this manner. You'll need to see if a `QuestionID` has been stored in `tblResponse`.

2. Add an administrative frontend for creating question and answer sets. This should be a matter of creating a few simple insert pages and tying them together, but it will create a friendlier system for the people running the tests.

3. Fix the security problem with the username being accessible on the quiz form. You can do this by using `Session("MM_username")` directly when the data is being stored for a particular question.

18

Day 19

Advanced Techniques: Complex Query Systems

Many of the most difficult tasks that your Web sites will perform can be made easier by using the features of your SQL server to do the work for you. The capabilities of your database server can greatly increase the complexity of the applications that you build. Today's lesson will discuss one such case in which the query makes a seemingly impossible task quite easy. Today, you will learn:

- Alternative ways to think about problems. Approaching from the side is often better than approaching head-on.
- A technique for implementing a "fuzzy" search that lets you write a "non-exact" query for users who aren't quite sure what they are looking for.
- How to develop matching Web sites that lets users specify criteria to use in finding an "imperfect" (or perfect) match.
- Get hands-on experience using the Dreamweaver MX authentication system and the `MM_username` session variable.

Complex Searches

Spaced reasonably evenly apart throughout this book have been lessons that build on your SQL skills and reinforce the idea that Dreamweaver MX's abilities can be greatly enhanced by your SQL server. Because this is the last project in the book, it's only appropriate that we leave you with something interesting to think about. Today explores Dreamweaver MX, SQL, and how their happy marriage can create complex site searches beyond simply matching some text.

As you build Web sites that collect user information, you'll discover that providing searching features for the databases is a necessity. SQL, by its very nature, provides an excellent system for querying tables of information. Unfortunately, what if the user wants to search the system based on parameters outside a direct SQL query? Even worse, what if the search needs to match some items but not all of them?

For example, consider a search on a database of dogs. The user is searching for a dog that is under 10 pounds with a tan coat, but he wouldn't mind black—if there aren't any black 10 pound dogs, he'll settle for a 20 pound gray dog. This is an example of logic that's very difficult to represent in a search that isn't directly written for the user making the query.

So, how can a system be created that allows "shades" of an answer to be matched?

Let's build this up by looking at a few cases—each one increasing in complexity. By starting slow and getting complicated, hopefully you'll see what I'm getting at. You can follow along with MySQL if you want.

First, let's create the situation in which you are trying to match a number in a table that is close to a number you've chosen. Table 19.1 shows a list of numbers in a table `tblNumber` that is stored in your `day19` database (installed on Day 7, "Preparing a Server for Dreamweaver MX"). The `tblNumber` database table stores a single number for each record in the field a. Because it's so absurdly simple, we won't define the table here.

TABLE 19.1 Contents of the day19 Database

a (An Integer)
5
6
1
15
9
8

TABLE **19.1** continued

a (An Integer)
21
500
10
50

Now, let's pick a number that we want to search for. Try just picking a number in the range of 1–500 off the top of your head…oh, say, 6.

So, we want to match records that are *like* the number six. The first query to try is a direct selection:

INPUT

```
select * from tblNumber where a=6;
```

OUTPUT

```
+ — — —+
| a    |
+ — — —
|    6 |
+ — — —+
1 row in set (0.05 sec)
```

This query found 6, but it isn't very effective in finding numbers that are *similar* to 6. So, how can we manage this feat of magic? We could *modify* the selection with an or condition to find numbers that are around 6:

INPUT

```
select * from tblNumber where a=6 or a=5 or a=7;
```

OUTPUT

```
+ — — —+
| a    |
+ — — —+
|    5 |
|    6 |
+ — — —+
2 rows in set (0.02 sec)
```

This is a better approach, but it isn't perfect. The search is still limited to what can be specified directly in the query. We could do a bit better by adjusting the selection to a range of numbers around 6, but it still doesn't solve the overall problem.

It's time to shift your way of thinking. The WHERE clause of the query sets a condition that limits the search based on the parameters set, but how can we be certain how limited

19

the users wants to make their search? Do they want to find a number within the range of 6 +/– 5, or 6 +/– 500? By focusing on how we select the data, we're actually overlooking a somewhat simple solution.

The correct approach is to analyze the relationship between six and all the other numbers in the table. Take, for example, the number 7. How closely related to 6 is it? It is within one position of the number 6 (7–6 = 1). Likewise, how close to 6 is the number 10? It is 4 away from 10 (10–6 = 4). The answer to all our problems is subtraction. By subtracting the values in the table from the chosen value, we've established a relationship between a given number and the other entries in a table.

That's nice, but how exactly do we work this knowledge into a query? It's not as difficult as you might think. The most important thing to realize is that *all* numbers are related to the chosen number—it's just a matter of how closely they're related. Are you catching on yet? The trick isn't limiting how you choose records, it's limiting how the chosen records are displayed. The working portion of the query is handled by a custom ORDER BY clause added to the query.

Let's draft a first attempt for the new query:

INPUT

```
SELECT *,(6-a) as 'difference' FROM tblNumber ORDER BY difference;
```

OUTPUT

```
+ — — +— — — — — +
| a   | difference |
+ — — +— — — — — +
|  500 |      -494 |
|   50 |       -44 |
|   21 |       -15 |
|   15 |        -9 |
|   10 |        -4 |
|    9 |        -3 |
|    8 |        -2 |
|    6 |         0 |
|    5 |         1 |
|    1 |         5 |
+ — — +— — — — — +
10 rows in set (0.04 sec)
```

This query defines a variable `difference` that contains the expression (6-a), which is evaluated for each of the records in the database—the results are then ordered by this parameter. The problem is that numbers under the chosen number result in a positive response, whereas the larger values are negative. This won't do. According to this result, the numbers 1 and 9 are equally similar to the number 6. In reality, 9 (9–6 = 3) is closer than one (6–1 = 5). The negative and positive distances must be treated equally. One function in particular lends itself to being used in the query: ABS, or absolute value. The absolute value of a negative number is its positive counterpart. Adding this function to the query, we get something similar to this:

INPUT

```
SELECT *,ABS(6-a) as 'difference' FROM tblNumber ORDER BY difference;
```

OUTPUT

```
+———+—————+
| a   | difference |
+———+—————+
|   6 |          0 |
|   5 |          1 |
|   8 |          2 |
|   9 |          3 |
|  10 |          4 |
|   1 |          5 |
|  15 |          9 |
|  21 |         15 |
|  50 |         44 |
| 500 |        494 |
+———+—————+
10 rows in set (0.05 sec)
```

That's *exactly* what we want! The listing of results shows how closely related all the numbers in the table are to the number 6. The further down the table you go, the more distant the number is from the chosen value.

So, how is this related to the real world, where you aren't usually asking a user to pick a number? That's easy to explain—although the user might be picking a non-numeric response from a pop-up menu or something, that response can probably be represented by a number.

For example, choose your preferred dog behavior:

1. Passive

2. Passive, playful

3. Playful, guard dog

4. Guard dog

Here, the possible selections are ranked numerically in relation to one another. Querying a database to find potential matches for your desired dog behavior can use these values and the technique that we've developed for ranking similar responses to find dogs that "kinda" match your preferences but don't necessarily have a 100% match. The world isn't black and white—your queries shouldn't be either.

In the real world, however, multiple questions need to be answered—that's our ultimate goal.

19

The system needs to be expanded so that you can take a group of responses and determine how close they are to other responses. To model this case, let's use a slightly expanded table that can hold two values to represent the two responses we want to match. For this example, let's use the table tblTwoNumber with two integer fields, a and b. Sample data is shown in Table 19.2.

TABLE 19.2   The tblTwoNumber Table Contains Two Numbers

a (An Integer)	b (An Integer)
2	5
10	5
9	1
15	50
1	2
20	5
2	5
11	2
3	7
6	6

Pick two numbers to use as the values that you're trying to find a close match for. I'll pick 8 and 12 as values for a and b, respectively.

Using the same procedure used with a single answer, we come up with two lists of results that show the ranking of the other records in relation to the numbers we've chosen:

INPUT

```
mysql> SELECT *,ABS(8-a) as 'difference' FROM tblTwoNumber ORDER BY
difference;
```

OUTPUT

```
+———+———+————————+
| a    | b    | difference |
+———+———+————————+
|    9 |    1 |          1 |
|   10 |    5 |          2 |
|    6 |    6 |          2 |
|   11 |    2 |          3 |
|    3 |    7 |          5 |
|    2 |    5 |          6 |
|    2 |    5 |          6 |
|   15 |   50 |          7 |
|    1 |    2 |          7 |
|   20 |    5 |         12 |
+———+———+————————+
10 rows in set (0.02 sec)
```

and

INPUT

```
SELECT *,ABS(12-b) as 'difference' FROM tblTwoNumber ORDER BY
difference;
```

OUTPUT

```
+———+———+——————+
| a   | b   | difference |
+———+———+——————+
|   3 |   7 |          5 |
|   6 |   6 |          6 |
|   2 |   5 |          7 |
|  10 |   5 |          7 |
|  20 |   5 |          7 |
|   2 |   5 |          7 |
|   1 |   2 |         10 |
|  11 |   2 |         10 |
|   9 |   1 |         11 |
|  15 |  50 |         38 |
+———+———+——————+
10 rows in set (0.01 sec)
```

Notice that the listing of selected matches when looking at the a field is very different from looking at b. This highlights the problem we need to overcome. How do you take into account both of the variables when performing the query? No problem—all you need to do is modify the query so that it sorts by the combined error (or distance from the original number) in the two queries.

INPUT

```
SELECT *,(ABS(8-a)+ABS(12-b)) as 'difference'
FROM tblTwoNumber ORDER BY difference;
```

OUTPUT

```
+———+———+——————+
| a   | b   | difference |
+———+———+——————+
|   6 |   6 |          8 |
|  10 |   5 |          9 |
|   3 |   7 |         10 |
|   9 |   1 |         12 |
|   2 |   5 |         13 |
|   2 |   5 |         13 |
|  11 |   2 |         13 |
|   1 |   2 |         17 |
|  20 |   5 |         19 |
|  15 |  50 |         45 |
+———+———+——————+
10 rows in set (0.00 sec)
```

19

By adding the two absolute values, you get a measurement of how far off each of the records is from the two chosen numbers.

This model can be expanded to handle checking as many values as you need simply by following the same pattern and using the combined differences between the desired and actual values.

Thresholds

Wait…you don't really want to have to deal with showing everything that even *remotely* comes close to the desired values. These queries are different from the other queries you've used for searching because they match *all* the records in the table being searched. Because of this, you will generally want to impose some sort of cut-off on the number of records displayed. The records near the end of the list are likely to be of little importance to the users.

There are two ways you can limit what the users see when they perform the query— either by imposing a limit on the returned records, or by imposing an upper threshold for the results.

Limiting the results to a certain number of records is usually fine, but it doesn't give the users much control over what they see. Suppose you decide that you're going to generate a top 10 list for the users, which shows them the top ten matches. Unfortunately, that doesn't really do much good if the first 50 records are perfect matches. They will miss 40 other results that might satisfy the query just as well as the first 10. Still, limiting the results to a range of values is often more than sufficient for the task and is easily accomplished directly through the Dreamweaver MX Repeating Region behavior.

A more advanced way to limit the results shown is to impose a threshold on the search, such as an upper limit on the amount of error that can exist in order for a record to be returned. Suppose that we want to check for a combined error of less than 20; we can modify the last query to include a WHERE clause, similar to this:

INPUT
```
mysql> SELECT *,(ABS(8-a)+ABS(12-b)) as 'difference'
       FROM tblTwoNumber WHERE (ABS(8-a)+ABS(12-b))<20 ORDER BY difference;
```

OUTPUT
```
+———+———+—————————+
| a    | b    | difference |
+———+———+—————————+
|    6 |    6 |          8 |
|   10 |    5 |          9 |
|    3 |    7 |         10 |
|    9 |    1 |         12 |
|    2 |    5 |         13 |
|    2 |    5 |         13 |
|   11 |    2 |         13 |
|    1 |    2 |         17 |
|   20 |    5 |         19 |
+———+———+—————————+
9 rows in set (0.00 sec)
```

> **Note**
>
> The redundancy of the calculation of difference for both the ORDER BY and WHERE clauses is a limitation of MySQL. Your database server might provide a more efficient means of performing the query so that the error value isn't calculated twice.

Setting a threshold doesn't force the number of results users can see—instead, it forces a certain *quality* of response to be shown to the users.

When allowing the users to set a threshold, you probably want to present the value selection in a user-friendly manner. Asking the user to "type in a threshold level" isn't very nice. A real-world solution would be to provide a percentage of allowable errors that users could set. The question then becomes, how do you relate the amount of error to a percentage?

For each of the questions you use to define your query, add the maximum amount of error between the first and last response. For example, if I have these two questions:

What is your favorite dog color?

1. Black
2. Black and brown
3. Brown
4. White

and

How large of a dog would you like?

1. 10 pounds
2. 50 pounds
3. 100 pounds

There are two questions; the first one has four possible responses, whereas the second has three.

> **Note**
>
> This entire query system is based on providing answers that vary from one end of the spectrum to another. This lets us evaluate how far off from a desired response we are. It also imposes a strict ordering on the response lists. Each possible option must be assigned a value that is only slightly changed from its closest variant. For example, in the dog color list, we

> cannot number White as 2. If we did, this would be implying that White fur is closely related to Black fur. If you have a white dog, you'll know that this isn't the case.

The worst-case scenario for the first question is that the user wants a match for the first Black response, and it is compared to the White response. The distance between these two options is three—so that is the maximum amount of error possible in the first question.

In the second problem, the maximum amount of error is, once again, the difference between the first and last responses—or two.

Combining these, we see that the total amount of error possible is 5—so 100% error is equal to 5, 50% error is 2.5, 0% is 0, and so on. After calculating these values, you can provide a pop-up menu for the user that correlates percentage error to a threshold value, thus limiting the number of values returned.

 Tip

> If you're wondering whether you can provide a *percentage match* instead of percentage error, of course you can! Inverting the values will give you what you're looking for. For example, using the same scenario we just set up—if you wanted to match with 100% confidence, you want a threshold of 0. Likewise, if you wanted 0% confidence, you'd use a threshold of the maximum amount of possible error—or, in this case, 5.

Weighing Responses

Another useful tool for the query system we've been working our way through is a way to weight responses if they are of higher importance than others. This places more importance on the question's response than other questions, or other options within a response. For example, if you have a question that tries to match the role a dog will take in your life, such as:

What role would you like your new dog to play?

1. Family pet
2. Hunting dog
3. Attack dog

These values are *not* closely related, but they're the only options we have. Rather than numbering them sequentially, we can impose a penalty for choosing anything other than the one that would result in a direct match, but simply renumber the options.

What role would you like your new dog to play?

1. Family pet
20. Hunting dog
100. Attack dog

This numbering expresses the relationship between these canine occupations. A family pet and a hunting dog are somewhat related, whereas an attack dog is *very* different. Using weighted responses coupled with thresholds, we can provide more accurate results to the users.

Note

The querying system we've developed over the past few pages should not, by any stretch of the imagination, be considered the pinnacle of searching technology. This is merely a starting place for developing your own complex query systems.

You can add additional conditions and other features to the SQL in order to fit it to your needs. Remember—make your database server do the work for you. Any custom programming you can avoid, the better.

Complex Queries: Finding Your Perfect Match

19

So, how are we going to use all this in a site? By developing a "dog match" site to help users find potential play-pals for their furry friends. Let's go ahead and start developing the site map and strategy now. The layout will be very simple—a login and registration system, and a query/results screen.

What Do I Need to Get Started?

1. You should define a new site named after the project (such as Day 19—Query System).
2. You should copy the Day 19 materials from http://downloads.cutelittledogs.com, unarchive them, and copy them to your site folder.
3. The database used for the query system should be set up with a data source named day19, as defined in Day 7.

Defining the Site Map

The login and registration screens are very much the same as what you created in yesterday's project. In addition, we need pages for the search, search results, and a place where users can create a "default search" profile for logging into the site.

>   `register.asp`—Asks the user to enter a username and password for the account. Each account will be forced to have a unique username, so we'll want to check it before saving the user account information. If the check *fails*, the `error.asp` file will be displayed; otherwise, the username and password will be stored, and the user will be sent to the `login.asp` page.

>   `error.asp`—This is a static page that displays an error message if the user enters a username that already exists.

>   `login.asp`—Collects the username and password for a valid user account. If the login fails, the user is sent to an error page called `error2.asp`.

>   `error2.asp`—A static page that displays an error if the login information is incorrect.

>   `search.asp`—The complex query screen that's used to set the parameters of the search.

>   `results.asp`—Results of the complex search.

>   `profile.asp`—A page where the users can update their own personal preferences for future searches.

When all is said and done, the site map should resemble Figure 19.1.

The Table Definitions

The tables that we need to complete the site are *really*, simple. Most of the information we need is stored in a single table. A second table relates the answers of the questions to the values that will be used to calculate the error between different profiles.

We've spent more time discussing the theory behind this project than the others, so we're going to take less time to build it.

First, let's address the authentication and "preference" table, `tblUserInfo`. This database table stores the username and password as well as a profile of the search that a user wants to perform. This feature would be very helpful if, for example, the Web site was updated constantly. If you're building the next `Monster.com`, you don't want to force the users to redefine their perfect job each time they log in. In addition, each user's preferences create a new profile in the database that others can search against. Think of this as a dating service for dogs.

FIGURE 19.1

Today's lesson will demonstrate the principles of our fuzzy search engine.

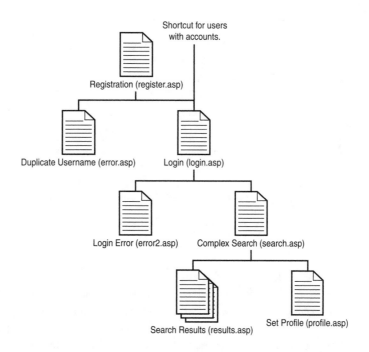

So, in order to set up the preferences, we first need to decide how many questions there are. The user table will include a field for each question—this field will contain a `responseID` that is matched to a given answer.

For the example system, four questions will be used in the queries, so four responses (`q1Response`, `q2Response`, and so on) must be stored for the users. We'll also collect the user's e-mail address so that other users can contact potential matches. The `tblUserInfo` definition is shown in Table 19.3.

TABLE 19.3 The `tblUserInfo` Table Stores Account Information

Fieldname	Description	SQL Data Type
userID*	An auto-incrementing number that identifies a specific user.	int auto_increment
username	The login username.	varchar(250)
password	The login password.	varchar(250)
email	An e-mail address for the user.	varchar(250)
fullname	The full name of the user.	varchar(250)
q1Response	The response to question 1.	int
q2Response	The response to question 2.	int

19

TABLE 19.3 continued

Fieldname	Description	SQL Data Type
q3Response	The response to question 3.	int
q4Response	The response to question 4.	int

Note

In other chapters we've kept the user's preferences in a separate table so that the preferences could easily be expanded in the future. Because this system is constantly collecting information, adding additional preferences would pose a problem because the existing profiles would suddenly be incomplete. In addition, because only a single record can be inserted at a time in Dreamweaver MX, the only way to display/set all the preferences simultaneously on a single screen is to include them in a single record.

In order to allow the user's preferences to fill the search form with default values, we need to store more than just the value of the response. Because of this requirement, a second table must be used to store all the information about all the possible responses (its label, value, and ID). Unfortunately, things will get very complicated very quickly if we try to do this all in one table. Our queries will need to create multiple relationships to a single table. This can be done in MySQL with table aliases, but it's best just to avoid it for fear of creating a page-long query string.

To get around the problem, we'll use a different option table for each of the questions—then each question can be related to a separate table, eliminating the problem. There are four tables—tblOption1, tblOption2, tblOption3, and tblOption4—that follow the pattern shown in Table 19.4.

TABLE 19.4 Each tblOption Database Table Stores These Values

Fieldname	Description	SQL Data Type
optionName1*	The name of a given response to a question.	varchar(250)
optionValue1	The value of a given response.	int

Note

Each of the fields in the four option tables is named uniquely (optionName1, and so on) so it can be differentiated between the other option table fields. Near the end of the project, you will be querying all five tables simultaneously and will need to have access to all five optionName values. You could use the same field names, but you'd have to specify the name of the table that holds each one. We're just trying to avoid a gargantuan query.

Sample Data

The final piece we need before getting started is the sample data—a few entries in the tblUserInfo database table along with the different possible tblOption values. This site is going to be a dog play-pal match site, so I've attempted to come up with some questions and options that are somewhat reasonable. Obviously a production site would have a larger list of questions and options, but this will suffice:

1. What breed is your dog?

    1. Jack Russell Terrier

    2. Pomeranian

    3. American Eskimo

    8. Irish Setter

    9. Golden Retriever

    10. Great Dane

Note

> Notice that several numbers are skipped in the middle. This will help weigh the query so that the type (and thus, the size) of the dog is very important.

2. How active is your dog?

    1. Lazy as can be

    2. Moves occasionally

    3. Plays frequently

    4. Never stops running

3. What is your dog's temperament?

    1. Shy

    2. Easily befriended

    3. Loves everyone

4. How old is your pet?

    1. Puppy

    2. Adolescent

    3. Full grown

Each question and answer group translates directly into one of the tblOption database tables. Tables 19.5, 19.6, 19.7, and 19.8 show the sample data as stored in the day19 database.

19

TABLE 19.5 The Possible Answers and Values for "What Breed Is Your Dog?" (tblOption1)

OptionName1	OptionValue1
Jack Russell Terrier	1
Pomeranian	2
American Eskimo	3
Irish Setter	8
Golden Retriever	9
Great Dane	10

TABLE 19.6 The Possible Answers and Values for "How Active Is Your Dog?" (tblOption2)

OptionName2	OptionValue2
Lazy as can be	1
Moves occasionally	2
Plays frequently	3
Never stops running	4

TABLE 19.7 The Possible Answers and Values for "What Is Your Dog's Temperament?" (tblOption3)

OptionName3	OptionValue3
Shy	1
Easily befriended	2
Loves everyone	3

TABLE 19.8 The Possible Answers and Values for "How Old Is Your Pet?" (tblOption4)

OptionName4	OptionValue4
Puppy	1
Adolescent	2
Full grown	3

Finally, we need some records for the tblUserInfo table. Without these, there will be no way to test the system! Table 19.9 contains a few sample records. You've heard this a dozen times so far, but, once again, all of this information should already be in your database—loaded during the Day 7 lesson.

TABLE 19.9 The `tblUserInfo` Database Table Needs a Few Sample Entries For Testing

UserID	Username	Password	E-mail	Fullname	q1Response	q2Responseq	3Response	q4Response
1	test	test	test@testing.com	Test User	1	3	2	3
2	hairy	dog	hairy@poisontooth.com	Bob Dawg	10	4	3	3
3	agroves	badmovie	agroves@poisontooth.com	Anne Groves	3	2	1	3
4	robyn	nester	robster@poisontooth.com	Robyn Ness	2	4	2	3
5	julie	vujgirl	julie@poisontooth.com	Julie Vuje	2	3	1	2
6	jackd	nrri	jackd@poisontooth.com	Jack Derifaj	9	4	2	1
7	maddy	marty	maddy@poisontooth.com	Maddy Darg	10	4	3	3
8	Cindy	sandy	cindy@poisontooth.com	Cynthia Sands	3	3	3	3
9	Carl	fuzzy	carl@poisontooth.com	Carl Winds	8	1	1	1
10	Martha	homemade	martha@poisontooth.com	Martha Clipper	1	1	2	2

19

This is a good start, and should give you everything you need to build and test the system.

Creating the Login System

The login system is virtually *identical* to the system that we built in Day 17. Four pages will collect the system data, store it, and then allow the users to log in by setting a session variable (MM_username). An additional screen, update, will let the users update their profiles.

Handling Registration and Initial Profile (`register.asp` and `error.asp`)

A user visiting the site for the first time will want to be able to register with the system and set up his or her profile—so let's get the registration working first.

The registration screen works in much the same way as earlier projects—it consists of a small form that prompts the user for a new username, password, and some other basic information,   and then submits it for processing. If the username is *not* unique, the user must be asked to pick a new username.

Create a new page named register.asp, and then create a registration form named frmRegister that includes the username, password, fullname, and email text fields—all the basic information you want to collect. Also add a submit button that will be used to process the registration.

Next, because the user's profile should contain some data before he or she is allowed to search, add five hidden fields to hold the default profile. These fields should be named q1Response, q2Response, q3Response, and q4Response and contain a default value of 1 (or whatever option value you want to be the default). These are not dynamic fields in any way; they're just five hidden fields hardcoded with a single value.

Figure 19.2 shows a completed register.asp document.

Finally, you need to add two server behaviors to the registration page in order to make sure that the username is unique and then insert the registration information into the tblUserInfo table. Remember, Dreamweaver MX requires that you add the Insert Record behavior before adding the behavior to check the username.

Add the insert behavior now:

1. Open the Server Behaviors panel.
2. Click "+" to add a new Insert Record behavior.

FIGURE 19.2

The first registration page will check the username for uniqueness and save the registration information if it is correct.

3. Choose the `connDay19` connection and match the form elements to the fields in `tblUserInfo`, as seen in Figure 19.3.

4. After inserting values, configure the behavior to direct the users to the login (`login.asp`) page.

FIGURE 19.3

Make sure that the fields from the registration page are matched to the `tblUserInfo` fields.

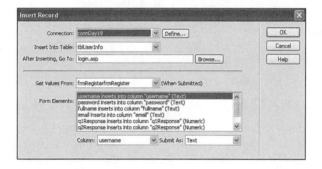

Now insert the Check New Username behavior to verify that the username is new to the database:

1. Open the Server Behaviors panel if it isn't already.

2. Click "+" and choose Check New Username from the User Authentication submenu.

3. When prompted, configure the behavior so that it checks the `username` field for uniqueness.

4. If the `username` already exists, have the behavior go to `error.asp`, as seen in Figure 19.4.

5. Click OK when finished.

19

FIGURE 19.4

The username *field will be checked for uniqueness. If it* isn't *unique, the users should be redirected to* error.asp.

Finally, as in day 17's example, we need to provide a "that username is taken" message that appears when the visitor has chosen a name identical to one already in the system. Because the Dreamweaver MX behaviors will automatically redirect the user to a new page if a duplicate exists, all you need to do is provide an informative message on your error.asp page and a link back to the registration screen so that the user can try again. Figure 19.5 gives an example of what your error page might look like. To save time, feel free to use the error.asp page included with the Day 19 example files.

FIGURE 19.5

Warn the users when they have chosen a duplicate username.

Designing Login Pages (`login.asp` and `error2.asp`)

Similar to the registration process, logging in to the system also takes two pages—one to collect and check the user information (login.asp), and another to display a message if an error occurs (error2.asp). We'll be using a session variable to track the users after they've logged in. The Dreamweaver MX authentication system uses the internal MM_username session variable, saving us the time of setting it up it by hand.

Design the login.asp page. The sole requirement is that it contains a form (frmLogin) with a username field, password field, and a submit button. An example of this screen is shown in Figure 19.6.

FIGURE 19.6

The login screen should contain the username and password fields for processing by the user authentication behavior.

With the form completed, open the Server Behaviors panel and add the Log In User behavior to handle verifying the username and password that has been provided.

1. Within the Server Behaviors panel, click "+".

2. Choose Log In User from the User Authentication submenu.

3. Choose the frmLogin form that is submitting the login information, as well as the username and password fields from the form.

4. Set the connDay19 connection. Pick the tblUserInfo table and username/password columns from tblUserInfo.

5. On a successful login, the users should be sent to the search.asp page so that they can start searching the system.

6. If a login fails, send the user to error2.asp.

7. When completed, the Log In User form should look very similar to Figure 19.7. Click OK when you are satisfied with your work.

19

FIGURE 19.7

Choose the username/password fields from both the login form and the tblUserInfo database table.

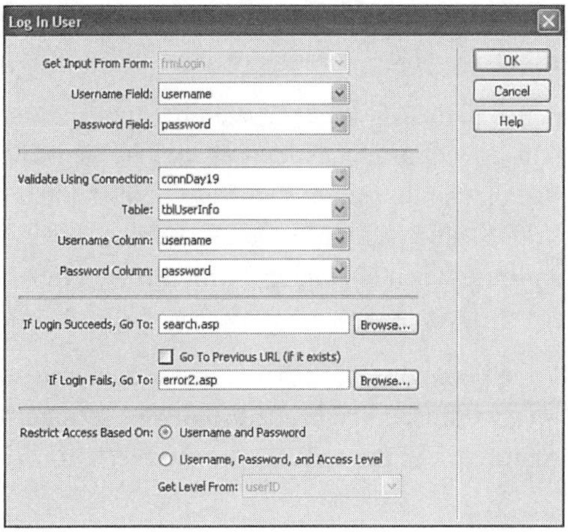

You now need to create your error2.asp page that the users will be redirected to if their information is incorrect. Be sure to provide links back to the login and registration pages from this screen.

An example error2.asp page is shown in Figure 19.8.

FIGURE 19.8

The error2.asp *page should contain an error message for an invalid username/-password.*

That's it; the login and registration systems are finished. Time to get started on the fun stuff—writing the profile management and search engine pages.

Creating the Update Profile Page (profile.asp)

The Update Profile page, profile.asp, is the most difficult page you will create today—not because it is hard to write or uses any complex behaviors, but because the coding is monotonous. This page allows the users to update any information in their profiles—password, e-mail address, and the default responses to the four questions. Create and save profile.asp within your Day 19 site now.

Start by setting up a form named frmUpdate with the four questions defined earlier and four corresponding pop-up menus (List/Menu objects in the Insert panel's form category) named q1Response through q4Response —include fields named email and password for updating the e-mail address and password. Finally add a submit button that will save the user's changes to his profile when he's happy with the selections. The page layout can be seen in Figure 19.9.

All these fields need to be bound to data that is in the database—that's where the work comes in. A total of *five* recordsets are needed to drive the page. The first recordset selects the user information from the tblUserInfo table. This is used to fill the e-mail address and password form fields. Define this query, named `rsUserInfo`, now. You can define this as a simple query that selects all the fields in `tblUserInfo` based on a filter where the session variable `MM_username` must equal the `username` field within the database. Figure 19.10 shows the `rsUserInfo` recordset.

FIGURE 19.9

The `profile.asp` *page should include four questions, four menus, and fields for updating the e-mail and password.*

FIGURE 19.10

Select the `tblUserInfo` *record that matches the* `MM_username` *field.*

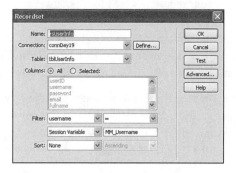

19

> **Note**
>
> The `MM_username` session variable is set automatically when the user successfully completes the Log In server behavior. You can use it as you would use a session variable that you set yourself.

Next, bind the e-mail address to the e-mail address form field. Select the e-mail address text field in the document design, and then choose the `email` field within Bindings. Set the binding type at the bottom of the panel to `input.value`, and then click the Bind button. Repeat this procedure for the password field. You've been doing this everyday for the last week, so if you're having trouble, you might be skipping too far ahead!

Now you need to create four additional recordsets that contain the options for each of the four questions. Define these recordsets, rsOption1 through rsOption4, as simple queries that select everything in the corresponding tblOption tables (tblOption1 through tblOption4). This should take a few minutes to set up; the configuration for the rsOption1 recordset is displayed in Figure 19.11.

FIGURE 19.11

Define four rsOption
*recordsets similar to
this one.*

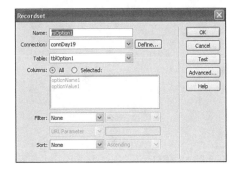

After you've created these four recordsets, add four popup (List/Menu) menus (Option1, Option2, Option3, and Option4) to the document. These will serve as the "answers" to the four questions and do not need to contain any static content. Use the Server Behavior panel to add four Dynamic List/Menu (from the Dynamic Form Elements submenu) to bind the Option1-4 menus to each of the four rsOption recordsets.

For the first menu, choose Option1 as the Menu setting in the server behavior. Ignoring the Static Options, set rsOption1 for the Options From Recordset value. Finally, set the Values field to OptionValue and the Labels field to OptionName. Click OK to save the dynamic behavior. Figure 19.12 shows the properly configured behavior.

Repeat this for all four pop-up menus. The result will be four dynamic menus that are bound to the corresponding option tables in the database.

FIGURE 19.12

Your rsOption *record-
sets will drive the four
pop-up menus.*

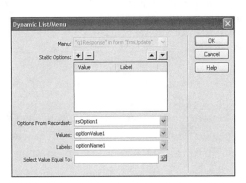

When you've had a chance to catch your breath after creating the bindings for the pop-up menus, prepare yourself to do it all over again. To show the items that the user has selected, you must bind the `item.selected` attribute of each of the option menus to the corresponding response field in the `rsUserInfo` recordset. For example, the `item.selected` attribute of form's `q1Response` pop-up menu should be bound to the `q1Response` database field in `rsUserInfo`, and so on. This ensures that the items stored in the user's profile are shown as the default selection in the database.

The last step in setting up the page is adding the server behavior to update the user's profile after he clicks submit. Add this behavior to the `profile.asp` page now:

1. Open the Server Behaviors panel.
2. Click "+" to add an Update Record behavior.
3. Select your connDay19 connection.
4. Set `tblUserInfo` as the table to update.
5. Choose `username` as the unique key column. Although our standard database tables use the `UserID` as the unique column, the user authentication system we're using assumes unique usernames.
6. Make sure that all form fields and database columns match up in the Get Values From section.
7. Finally, set the Go To URL value to `search.asp`.
8. Click OK.

Good job! You've finished the hardest page in today's lesson. A final design for the profile page is shown in Figure 19.13.

19

FIGURE 19.13

A simple page, but a ton of supporting recordsets.

The final portion of the site that you'll be creating is the search page and results form. The `search.asp` page will be set up the same as the `profile.asp` page, but without the additional `email`, `password`, and `userID` form fields.

Writing the Search and Results Pages (`search.asp` and `results.asp`)

The search and result pages are simple to build—mainly because you already did the *real* work on the `profile.asp` page. Make a copy of the `profile.asp` page named `search.asp`. Open this new page in the document design window. Because `search.asp` requires most of the behaviors that were already implemented in the profile page, all we really need to do is trim the page a bit.

First, clean out the form so that it only includes the four questions and their response pop-up menus. Delete the hidden `userID`, `email`, and `password` form fields. Next, open the Server Behaviors panel, select the *existing* Update Record behavior from the list, and then click the "-" button to remove it from the project. No hidden fields should be left in the form—so if you happen to see any, it's because Dreamweaver MX missed something —remove them manually.

 Tip

> The best way to keep Dreamweaver MX from "getting confused" when removing server behaviors is to remove everything you can from the Bindings panel or Server Behaviors panel before manually editing the document. Even so, you might still find yourself in a situation where a few straggler fields need your attention.

Finally, select the form in the document (`frmUpdate`) and set its action to `results.asp`. Also add an Update Your Profile link to the page that links the users to `profile.asp` for easy access to their profile information. Because the `MM_username` session variable identifies the person browsing the site, there is no need to pass any additional values to the page. A final view of the search page is displayed in Figure 19.14.

Create the project's final page `results.asp`. This page will show the contents of a recordset; nothing more than what you learned back in Day 10, "Creating Database-Driven Web Pages." Lay out a basic screen design for your results by adding a six-column, two-row table that contains the following headings in the first row:

- Name
- E-mail

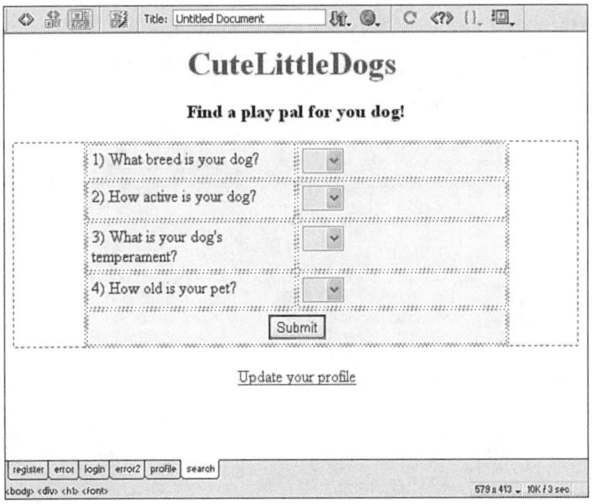

FIGURE 19.14

The search screen is nothing but a stripped down version of the user profile management page.

- Breed
- Activity
- Temperament
- Age

Only a single query in this document is needed to handle the search, but it's a *real* beauty. Remember the basic search pattern that we set up early in the day? We want to combine the absolute values of the differences between the desired response and the actual response. The full SQL of the query for the search is

```
SELECT *,abs('varQ1'-tblOption1.OptionValue1)
+abs('varQ2'-tblOption2.OptionValue2)+abs('varQ3'-tblOption3.OptionValue3)
+abs('varQ4'-tblOption4.OptionValue4) as 'difference' FROM
tblUserInfo,tblOption1,tblOption2,tblOption3,tblOption4 WHERE
tblUserInfo.q1Response=tblOption1.OptionValue1
AND tblUserInfo.q2Response=tblOption2.OptionValue2
AND tblUserInfo.q3Response=tblOption3.OptionValue3
AND tblUserInfo.q4Response=tblOption4.OptionValue4 ORDER BY difference
```

Note that a WHERE clause is set up to match the responses for each of the tblUserInfo records to the corresponding record in each of the tblOption tables. This is required so that we can use the OptionName fields to show the responses that the users gave to the survey.

Create an rsResults advanced query that includes this SQL. You will also need to define Dreamweaver MX variables varQ1 through varQ4 and set them to the runtime values Request("q1Response") through Request("q4Response") with default values of 1. Be

19

absolutely certain that the query is defined correctly before clicking OK. Click the Test button to verify that the query works. Figure 19.15 shows the properly defined query.

FIGURE 19.15

Be very careful when entering the query; it's a handful.

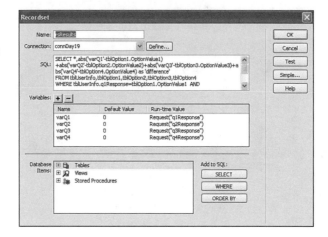

Open the Bindings panel and drag the fields you want into the appropriate columns of your document design's HTML table.

The last step in creating the page is to select the row of dynamic data that you've inserted into the document and add a Repeat Region server behavior so that multiple matches are shown. If you want, you can display either all the records, or a specific number. Limiting the responses to a certain threshold of error is left as an exercise to the reader, but it was covered earlier and shouldn't be too difficult.

Go through your Web site and test the functionality. If everything is working correctly, you should get a result listing that is similar to that of Figure 19.16. You've finished your site.

Note

A quick test to show that everything is working is to verify that the profile you've logged in with shows up at the top of the search results, because obviously your dog matches itself perfectly!

FIGURE 19.16

Your dynamic search result should look a bit similar to this.

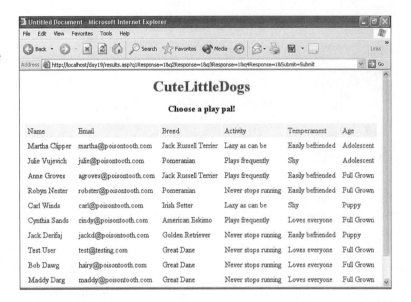

Protecting Your Pages

A final step that you can take for your site is to protect the search.asp, results.asp, and profile.asp pages. After all, these pages shouldn't even be accessible by someone who hasn't registered with the system. Because this isn't exactly a high-security Web site, you might not find this necessary. If you choose to protect them, however, it's a very simple process to complete.

1. Open a page you want to protect, such as profile.asp.

2. Open the Server Behaviors panel.

3. Click "+" and Choose Restrict Access To Page from the User Authentication submenu.

4. Configure the behavior, as seen in Figure 19.17, to restrict access based on user-name and password.

5. If access is denied, send the user to the login.asp page.

6. Click OK when finished.

7. Repeat this process for the other pages (search.asp and results.asp) you want to protect.

If users try to access any protected page before logging in, they will immediately be sent to the login.asp page. Simple, but effective.

19

Figure 19.17

Restrict access to the pages that unauthorized users shouldn't see!

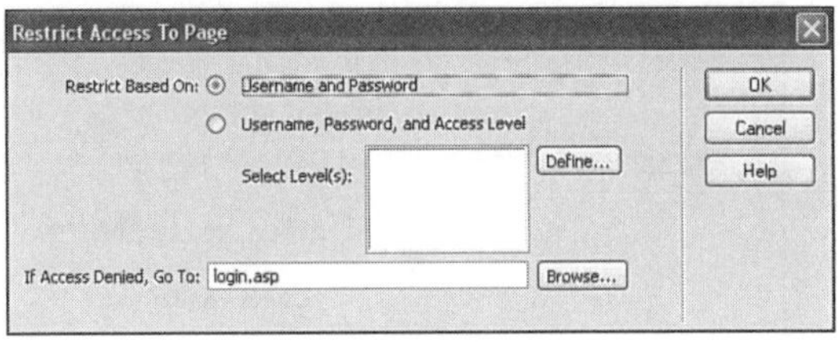

Summary

Today's lesson covers one of the most powerful tools that you have at your disposal—Dreamweaver MX's authentication system and your database server! The Dreamweaver MX authentication behaviors greatly speed up the process of developing protected sites, whereas the database makes it possible to perform minor miracles by creating advanced SQL queries.

The query system that you've just developed is useful, but it is also limited because it places equal emphasis on all the queries. You can refine the process that we've created today by adding weights to the various elements of the query. Additionally, traditional search elements can be used to limit the recordset to values that are exact matches. For example, rather than matching all the records, you could modify the query in the WHERE clause. If people wanted exact matches based on breed, this comparison would be moved out of the absolute value calculation into the WHERE portion of the SQL.

My hope is that after reading this chapter, you have some new ideas on how to create your own searches. It's too easy to think that all the queries have to match records by filtering based on the attributes used with WHERE. Breaking out of the traditional query mold opens up the manipulation of your Web site data to a whole new world of complex queries.

Workshop

The Workshop area is meant to reinforce your reading with a series of questions and exercises.

Q&A

Q How many questions can this query handle?

A You can add as many questions to this recordset as your SQL server can handle in a single query. Unfortunately, Dreamweaver MX seems to have some problems with extremely lengthy queries.

Q What sorts of applications can this be used with?

A Anything. Although today's lesson used the search technique to match dogs, you can use it anywhere. For example, you could provide attribute rankings for products in a shopping catalog that could be queried. Essentially, anywhere you have a search, you could consider using this technique.

Q Do I have to set up the separate option tables all the time?

A These tables are only needed because we wanted to display the names of the options that the users selected. If that information wasn't important, we could make do with just the `tblUserInfo` table.

Quiz

1. What is the absolute value?
2. Why do we add the absolute values together?
3. How can query items be weighted?
4. What is a threshold?

Quiz Answers

1. The absolute value function returns the positive distance between a given value and zero. This can be used to determine how far off two values are from each other.

2. The combined absolute values are representative of the total amount of error in the query. The less total error, the better the match overall.

3. You can weight certain elements of a query by changing the distance between the option values.

4. The threshold for a search is the maximum allowable amount of errors that a result item can have to be included in the search results. You can relate a threshold value to a percentage by calculating the total distance between all the responses and relating that number to 100% error.

Exercises

1. Add a threshold value to the search. You will need to calculate the total amount of error possible in the query.

2. Fix the search so that the results do not include your own record. You'll have to add a condition to the WHERE clause of your search query to accomplish this.

3. If you're feeling truly adventurous, you can provide even more advanced search capabilities by combining multiple SELECT statements using unions. This will allow you to group the error into categories, and then join the results of these queries. It might be more appropriate than combining all the error together in a single query.

19

DAY **20**

Testing and Deploying Dynamic Applications

As we approach the end of this three week guide to Dreamweaver MX, we'll take a look at one of the most overlooked but important aspects of setting up any Web site—the process of testing and debugging. Even on static Web sites, there are times when something that you *think* should be happening isn't. The key to keeping your sanity and not cursing your Web server is to understand what can go wrong and why. Today, you will learn how to:

- Diagnose common HTML-based problems
- Test dynamic applications thoroughly
- Use Dreamweaver MX tools for debugging Web pages
- Find additional resources for your problems

Coding Problems

Part of creating a Web site is an understanding that it is extremely unlikely that a page or program is going to work correctly the first time you view it. Many times, this will be nothing more than a table cell width being off, and the change will take a few seconds to detect and correct. Unfortunately, there are also cases in which you can stare at your HTML page for hours and never determine what is going wrong.

When you take the already finicky HTML and toss in an embedded programming language, the result can be even more painful. What happens when you dynamically add HTML to the screen, but there is an error in the HTML code? Instead of having to debug in one place, suddenly you need to make the determination of whether the HTML code or the embedded language is causing the problem. Sometimes, it might even be both!

By using Dreamweaver MX's automatic code generation, you're pretty much guaranteed that the underlying code will be correct. But even with a hands-off code approach, you can still get errors on your site. The only way to get rid of these problems is to understand where they come from, and that is the point of what you're going to learn today. The following three areas in particular need attention:

- **HTML design errors**—Problems that occur directly within the HTML, whether dynamically generated or not.
- **Server behavior problems**—Errors that might occur with some Dreamweaver MX added server behaviors.
- **Testing regimens**—How to test your site to ensure that it works every time for everyone.

Browser Issues

Whether generated by a program or generated by hand, HTML cross-browser compatibility is a common problem, even on commercial Web sites. In some cases, the browser guesses what you intended to do and often renders the page correctly even though the HTML is wrong. This is nice if you happen to be using a browser that has correctly fixed the problem, but if you're not, the results can be very difficult to debug.

Table Rendering

Let's start with the most common design problem that you'll run into—especially if you end up tweaking your HTML by hand. Rather than give away what the problem is, try entering the HTML found in Listing 20.1 into a text file, and then view it using a Netscape 4.x browser.

LISTING 20.1 See What Kind Of Tables You Get With This in Netscape 4.x

```
1 <table border=1 bgcolor="#FF0000">
2   <tr>
3   <td>Hello World</td>
4   <td><table border=1 bgcolor="#FFFF00">
5       <tr><td>Hello World</td></tr>
6       </table>
7   </td>
8   </tr>
9   <tr>
10   <td><table border=1 bgcolor="#FF00FF">
11       <tr><td>Hello World</td></tr>
12       </table>
13   </td>
14   </tr>
```

As you can see in Figure 20.1, although three tables are defined that contain Hello World, there is absolutely *no* content appearing in the Netscape window.

FIGURE 20.1

The code contains three tables, but where are they?

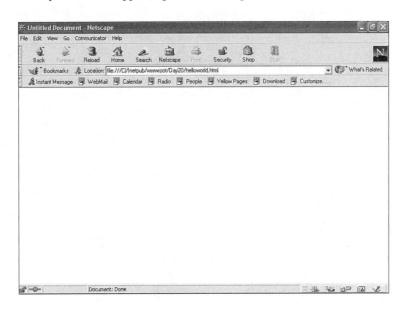

Now, if you happen to have a copy handy (that is, you're using any computer that shipped in the past four years), open Internet Explorer and take a look at the same HTML document. Suddenly, the tables are there. A view of the same document from within Internet Explorer is shown in Figure 20.2. What in the world is going on?

20

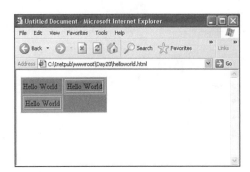

FIGURE 20.2

Three tables, and they're all here.

If you haven't caught on already, the trouble with the code is that there is a missing `</table>` tag in the document. There are three start tags, but each does not have a corresponding end tag.

When Netscape encounters a table like this, it doesn't render it. There isn't enough data, in its opinion, to lay out the table without knowing where it ends. Internet Explorer, on the other hand, automatically assumes that there is a missing end tag and renders the table anyway.

So, Which Browser Is Misbehaving?

Although it might seem that Internet Explorer is behaving better, I would strongly disagree. By compensating for a human error, Internet Explorer is allowing bad HTML to go unnoticed. Netscape 4.x, although not making it immediately obvious what the problem is, does demonstrate that there is definitely a problem with the page.

So, the question is, where does it stop? How sloppy can the coders get without having to be accountable for their own HTML? How many users will be unable to view the Web site because of it?

Luckily for everyone, Dreamweaver MX does notice the missing end tag and can highlight erroneous HTML that it finds in the code view, as shown in Figure 20.3. To activate this feature, use Highlight Invalid HTML from the Code View Options selection of the View menu. Alternatively, you can access the View Options pop-up menu shortcut at the right side of the design window toolbar.

Besides just showing that there is a problem with a tag, Dreamweaver MX can also give you information so that you can fix the issue. Click the highlighted tag in the code view and the Properties panel, shown in Figure 20.4, will describe exactly what the problem is.

FIGURE 20.3

Dreamweaver MX will highlight problem tags directly within the design view.

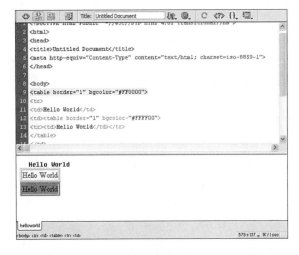

FIGURE 20.4

Clicking a highlighted tag will show exactly what is wrong with it.

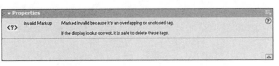

Tip

One of the most common explanations for empty pages that appear as though they should have content is an incomplete table. This can commonly happen when using a Repeat Region server behavior if the area being repeated is a table row. If something goes wrong during the loop, the application server might die before it has a chance to spit out the rest of the page, including the end table tag. As a result, you're left wondering exactly what happened because nothing is appearing onscreen.

The simple solution to the invisible content problem is to always use your browser's View Source feature to look directly at the HTML if you feel something is missing. You're likely to see the start of a table, followed by an error message from your server describing what went wrong.

20

Forms Inconsistencies

A similar, but more bizarre, problem is that of the vanishing form. Again, demonstration through example is the best way to explain exactly what I'm talking about. Try entering the HTML fragment given in Listing 20.2 into a new page.

LISTING 20.2 This Markup Will Produce Very Different Results in Netscape and Internet Explorer

```
 1 <table border="1">
 2 <tr>
 3      <td>Enter your name:</td>
 4      <td><input type="text" name="name"></td>
 5 </tr>
 6 <tr>
 7      <td>Choose your favorite color:</td>
 8      <td><select name="color">
 9          <option>Red</option>
10          <option>Blue</option>
11          <option>Yellow</option>
12          <option>Black</option>
13          <option>Green</option>
14          </select>
15      </td>
16 </tr>
17 <tr>
18      <td colspan="2"><input type="submit" name="submit"></td>
19 </tr>
20 </table>
```

As you can tell, I've been very careful with the formatting and all the tags and end tags are definitely in place. Everything looks fine, right?

Now, try Internet Explorer. Again, as you can see in Figure 20.5, everything looks completely fine. It isn't exactly the most wonderful form in the world, but it looks functional. Because we're on a roll, go ahead and open the document in Netscape 4.x.

FIGURE 20.5

Again, all is well in Internet Explorer.

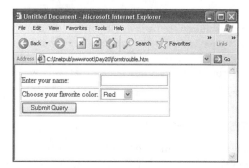

Whoa! What in the world is that? Seen in Figure 20.6, Netscape renders the form in an entirely unpredictable manner. The input field is missing, the submit button is missing, but the selection list is just a big bunch of jumbled words that come from the option tags.

FIGURE 20.6

Netscape makes a bit of a mess of the form.

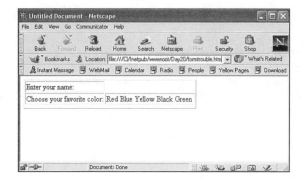

So, if Dreamweaver MX doesn't detect anything wrong and it looks fine in Internet Explorer, what's up with Netscape? Again, Netscape 4.x is the "outcast." The explanation for this rather peculiar activity is that the document is missing the <form> tags. It isn't necessarily the wrong behavior, but it does seem to be inconsistent when compared to other browsers (Internet Explorer, Opera, iCab, and so on). Inserting the appropriate <form> tags will immediately solve the problem.

Tip

It's actually easier to find yourself in this position than you might think. Dreamweaver MX will warn you (until you tell it not to) that you need to insert a <form> tag upon adding a form element—it will even do it for you. The funny thing is, subsequent fields might not insert within the same form.

The easiest way to make sure that all your <form> tags end up in the correct place is to insert a <form> tag before adding form elements. Then, check the HTML after the form is created and make sure that all the fields are within the <form> and </form> tags by moving the form elements manually.

Trouble with Layers

Layers are fun. They enable the HTML designer to place objects with pixel-point precision and can be combined with JavaScript to create dynamic Web pages that run entirely within the client browser. Best of all, layers work with almost all current browsers. If your users have a 4.0 or greater browser version, they can view your layered site, right? Not necessarily.

Create a simple layered page within Dreamweaver MX, or enter the HTML from Listing 20.3 into a text editor.

20

LISTING 20.3 Use This Markup to Test Layer Behavior in Different Browsers

```
1 <body bgcolor="#FFFFFF">
2 <div id="Test" style="position:absolute; width:225px;
3     height:261px; z-index:1; left: 45px; top: 43px;
4     background-color: #CCCCFF; layer-background-color: #CCCCFF;
5     border: 1px none #000000">
6   <div align="center">
7     <br>
8     <br>
9     <br>
10    <br>
11    <br>
12    <p>I'm a test too!</p>
13   </div>
14 </div>
15
16 <div id="Layer1" style="position:absolute; width:247px;
17    height:242px; z-index:2; left: 170px; top: 183px;
18    background-color: #CCFFCC; layer-background-color: #CCFFCC;
19    border: 1px none #000000">
20   <div align="center">
21    <br>
22    <br>
23    <br>
24    <br>
25    <br>
26    <p>This is a test!</p>
27   </div>
28 </div>
29 </body>
```

This code defines two overlapping layers, one green, one blue, and both with a test message as their content. Within the Dreamweaver MX design view, these layers should look similar to Figure 20.7.

After the past two examples, you've probably figured out that what is going to go wrong will only go wrong in Netscape. So, if you're waiting for the Internet Explorer figure, don't bother. It looks exactly as you would expect.

So, go ahead and load the page in Netscape. What do you see? There is an extremely good chance that it looks absolutely perfect in your document. This doesn't mean that all is well because a very simple change in your Netscape 4.x preferences can completely ruin the layout of the layers. What makes this even more interesting is that the change *isn't* related to layers at all.

Figure 20.7

Two overlapping layers should work fine in a 4.0 version browser, right?

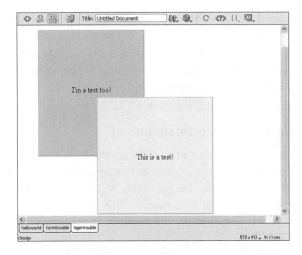

Turn off Netscape's capability to run JavaScript:

1. From within Netscape 4.x, choose Preferences from the Edit menu.
2. Choose the Advanced category from the left scrolling list.
3. Uncheck Enable JavaScript.
4. Exit the Preferences window.

Now, ask yourself, what JavaScript did I insert into the Web page? Take a look at the source code—you'll find that absolutely no JavaScripting is present. So, with no JavaScript in the code, it shouldn't make any difference that it is turned off. Go ahead and load the layered page now. As you can see in Figure 20.8, it isn't at all like what we laid out. The layers are gone, and only the text within them remains.

Figure 20.8

Where did the layers go?

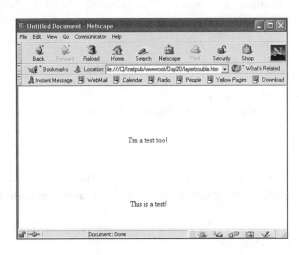

20

If you're like me, you occasionally get tired of having JavaScript windows pop up all over the place. Imagine my surprise when, in one of these instances, I visited a site that was originally laid out in layers. Instead of a Web site, I was greeted with a blank page. Checking the source code showed that the HTML was present, but it wasn't being displayed. This can be especially unnerving if you've never run into the problem before. Your page is fine, but doesn't show up in a Web browser. Isn't that lovely?

Netscape and Relative Positioning

You haven't seen the last problem that comes from using layers in Netscape 4.x browsers. Another problem is as bizarre as it is annoying. This is the use of relative positioning in an HTML document. Dreamweaver MX doesn't support the use of relative positioning directly within the Dreamweaver MX interface. It does the best it can to represent the layer, but it isn't perfect.

If you haven't used relative positioning, don't worry too much about this. If, however, you're a big fan of layers, it's only a matter of time before you need relative positioning. Instead of *absolute* positioning, which places the layer at an exact pixel coordinate, *relative* positioning places the layer an exact distance relative to another object. If you want to create a group of layers that center on the page, this is the only way to accomplish it. Unfortunately, Netscape has a problem with this. To see what happens, add the code from Listing 20.4 to another new page.

LISTING 20.4   Use This Markup to Test How Relative Positioning Works in Netscape

```
1 <body bgcolor="#FFFFFF">
2
3 <div id="Layer1" style="position:relative; left:240px; top:100px;
4      width:200px; height:170px; z-index:1; background-color: #FFFFCC;
5      layer-background-color: #FFFFCC; border: 1px none #000000">
6   <div align="center"><br>
7     <br>
8     <br>
9     <br>
10     <br>
11     <br>
12     <a href="http://www.poisontooth.com/">
13         Click Here to Jump to Poisontooth</a></div>
14 </div>
15 </body>
```

This is nothing more than a layer that is moved in from the edge of the page. Inside the layer is a single link. Open the page in Netscape. Your screen should look similar to Figure 20.9.

Figure 20.9

The screen looks fine...but is it?

> **Note**
>
> In this example, the use of relative positioning yields the same visual results as absolute positioning. This is because the layer is positioned relative to its parent object—the page itself.

Everything looks fine, but all is not well. Take your cursor and position it over the link. Give it a click or two. Notice that nothing happens. In fact, the link does not behave like a link at all. The destination URL does not show in the status bar of the browser as it normally would. So, what is going on? Netscape does not render links within relative positioned layers correctly.

Picture the layer as if it were positioned in the upper-left corner of the Web browser. Now, move your cursor over the area where the link would be if the layer were in that position. Surprise! The link is indeed there—invisible, but there.

The layer attributes are actually part of a larger problem with Netscape's cascading style sheet implementation. Positioning attributes are inconsistently handled, and often lead to problems.

20

> **Note**
>
> Don't get me wrong, I like Netscape. In fact, Netscape 6.0 is set as the primary browser on all the computers I use. Unfortunately, a large percentage of my page viewers are still using the Netscape 4-series browsers, which contain a number of issues, just like the ones you've seen today.

Validating Code

One of the easiest ways to make sure that your pages are going to work is to use the Dreamweaver MX code validation tools to check them. Dreamweaver can validate against a number of code standards, reporting each error it finds along the way. In fact, tests are included for testing against different browser models as well as coding standards.

Checking the Target Browser

One of the most frequent tests you might want to perform is a browser check, which will help identify HTML issues that occur on different versions of browsers, including Explorer, Netscape, and Opera. To activate the check, select File, Check Page, and then Check Target Browsers. Dreamweaver MX will open a list of possible browser models to validate against, as seen in Figure 20.10.

FIGURE 20.10

Check your document against your target audience before even deploying.

Click the Check button to start the check.

After a few moments the results of the test will be shown in the Target Browser panel (located in the Results panel group, or under the Results selection in the Window menu). An example is shown in Figure 20.11.

FIGURE 20.11

The test results display details of every problem found.

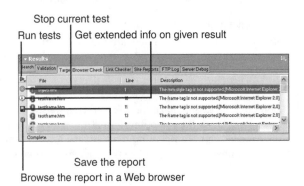

Stop current test

Run tests   Get extended info on given result

Save the report

Browse the report in a Web browser

Each line in the result panel shows the line number and error. Double-clicking an error will take you to the correct line in the code view. The icons to the right of the window can be used to run additional tests on the entire site or on selected files, stop the current test, display extended error information, or save and view the report externally.

Unfortunately, although this is extremely helpful, it's still up to you to actually *fix* the problems that are found.

Checking Markup

Dreamweaver's error-checking toolkit has a few more tricks beyond a target browser validation. Another valuable feature is the ability to check your code against the recognized Web standards such as HTML 4.0, XHTML 1.0 Transitional, and so on.

To run a markup validation, first configure the Dreamweaver MX Validator preferences so that the standards you want to use are selected. Figure 20.12 shows the Validator preferences.

FIGURE 20.12

Choose the standards to use as a basis of the validation.

Click the Options button to set additional parameters for the validation, such as the level of error messages being displayed. Many pages will display warning messages that you'd rather not see. They can be disabled in the Options dialog box.

To run the actual test, save your settings and then select File, Check Page, and then Validate Code. Within a few moments, a window identical to the Target Browser check will list all of the validation errors. All of the Dreamweaver MX validation tools use the same interface, so learn one, and you'll know how to use them all.

20

Checking Links

Another page and site check that you'll want to use frequently is the Link Checker. This tool will verify that the links in your site are still working and that you haven't accidentally *orphaned* any files.

What Is an Orphaned File?

An orphaned file has no links connecting it to the rest of the site. It is reachable only by directly referencing it through a URL.

To run a link check, select File, Check Page, and then Check Links. Unlike the other code-checking tools, the Link Check results panel contains a Show pop-up menu that can be used to select one of three types of links: broken links to files on your computer, external links, and orphaned files.

Sadly, external links are *not* verified by Dreamweaver. The are simply displayed so that you can check them on your own.

Verifying Accessibility

A final check that you can run on your pages is the accessibility test. These checks are used to verify whether your pages meet the section 508 accessibility standards, as required for federal organizations. Very few commercial Web sites meet these accessibility requirements, so don't feel too bad if yours doesn't either. Tomorrow's lesson (Day 21), "Advanced Dreamweaver MX Features" shows how the accessibility tools are used.

To run an accessibility test on your existing page, choose File, Check Page, and then Check Accessibility. If you've never seen an accessibility check before, don't be surprised to see entries such as "Avoid Causing the Screen to Flicker" if you are using layers and JavaScript. You're *not* going to be able to create a 508-compliant Web site using DHTML—it simply isn't going to happen.

Finding Server Behavior Problems

As you've read through the book, you've probably noticed that there are some cases in which you need to "finesse" the Dreamweaver MX output a little bit. The problems are generally not with the code itself, but with some very special cases that you must learn to avoid. By following some general guidelines, you can usually keep yourself out of trouble.

Removing Leftovers

The first problem is easy to avoid, but difficult to remember to do. Dreamweaver MX has a bit of a problem cleaning up after itself, especially if you have manually inserted HTML or embedded programs above and beyond what is already in the document.

You often might add server behaviors to your page, only to decide that they need to be removed. Removing portions of the code from the HTML results in an unstable document that might not be able to function properly upon adding new behaviors. Dreamweaver MX does what it can to force you to remove behaviors in the correct order, but sometimes it just doesn't work out the way you would hope.

I *highly* recommend that you either become comfortable with manually removing embedded code from within the HTML view, or start fresh each time you need to revise your server behavior. Users of ASP and JSP should have no problem locating the embedded tags in the HTML—although CFML tends to blend a bit more. Dreamweaver MX, however, should highlight the code for you, making it easy to find and remove.

Problems with Advanced Queries

One of the most common places for something to go wrong is the specification of an advanced query. A number of troublesome events can take place, and little can be done to stop them. These problems will usually force you to manually edit the embedded SQL in order to fix them.

Identical Field Names

When developing one of the chapters in the book, I laid out a series of tables that I wanted to link. Each of the tables carried common field names—optionText and optionID.

The SQL for joining them was simple:

```
SELECT tblOption1.optionText,tblOption2.optionText,tblOption3.optionText FROM
tblAnswer,tblOption1,tblOption2,tblOption3 WHERE
tblAnswer.question1=tblOption1.optionID AND
tblAnswer.question2=tblOption2.optionID AND
tblAnswer.question3=tblOption3.optionID
```

From this, you should have access to the fields tblOption1.optionText, tblOption2.optionText, and so on—but, within the Data Bindings window, all these fields become nothing more than three copies of optionText. Choosing any one of these optionText fields from the bindings gives the same value.

It isn't uncommon to run into tables that have multiple fields that are named similarly. If you're working with legacy data, the problem is compounded by the inability to alter the database design. If you do have control over your data, the easiest solution is to make sure that all your fields have unique names—at least in the tables that you plan to relate.

20

If you have no option other than working with the existing data, you could use MySQL's as alias feature to alter the field names on-the-fly. As you might recall from Day 19, "Advanced Techniques: Complex Query Systems," you can use as with a query to store an expression in a variable and make it available as a field within a query.

Query Length and Complexity

Another stumbling block in the creation of the advanced queries is the awkward behavior that Dreamweaver MX displays when working with extended queries and queries that use advanced SQL techniques. It's annoying to spend 15 minutes designing a query within the advanced query builder and save, only to come back a few minutes later find that it has been butchered beyond recognition. Unfortunately, this happens all too often within Dreamweaver MX.

The first problem appears to be related to the length of the query. At times, I've been happily entering SQL into the advanced query field, only to find that I can no longer scroll to the end of the query or correctly position my cursor. Although I have no doubt that this is a bug in the current version of Dreamweaver MX, it becomes extremely difficult to take the advanced query builder seriously.

I highly recommend that any queries that you build be created in a text editor outside the Dreamweaver MX environment, and then be pasted back into the query window when you want to use them. The benefits of this approach are two-fold. First, you have a copy of the query saved in case anything goes wrong. Second, pasting lengthy queries into Dreamweaver MX seems to circumnavigate the troubles with long queries. In all honesty, the advanced query builder really only saves a few keystrokes here and there, and, from my perspective, has never really been that much of a time saver after you become familiar with SQL.

Caution

If you do save your queries in an external editor, try to make it a text-only editor. If you use a traditional word processor, such as MS Word or WordPerfect, you're likely to inadvertently paste smart quotes back into the query window. These are very hard to detect in the mono font used in the query builder and will cause you nothing but headaches as you wonder why your perfect query is failing repeatedly.

Rather than maintaining metadata in a separate file and correlating that information to the page, Dreamweaver MX only uses the page to keep track of server behaviors and data bindings.

What this means to you, the developer, is that it is very simple to transfer files from one system to another. In fact, you can even add simple embedded code to the document and have it show up in the Bindings panel. In order to provide this functionality, Dreamweaver MX must parse the page and determine which code is a server behavior, which is a query, and so on. As you can imagine, this involves some pretty heavy-duty pattern matching. When you manually alter the code so that it no longer fits Dreamweaver MX's view of what a behavior should look like, it can no longer track or work with it. Sometimes, just entering complex query elements can cause this to happen.

The best way to handle the problem of lengthy and complex queries is to use an SQL view to simplify things. If you don't remember, a view is best defined as a virtual table. It is the product of a standard SQL query, but it is accessible as if it were its own entity. You can learn more about views in Day 12, "Writing Advanced Database Queries."

Note

Views, unfortunately, are not a supported feature in the current version of MySQL. They're on the "coming attractions" list, but haven't quite appeared yet. Most commercial databases support views, and some noncommercial products, such as PostgreSQL, also have this feature. Check your database documentation to see if they are supported.

Issues with Multiple Primary Keys

Dreamweaver MX does not support the use of multiple primary keys in many of its server behaviors. This is usually just a matter of semantics. You can force Dreamweaver MX to insert and delete records from a subset of a table by defining a query that selects records based on the appropriate keys. Unfortunately, it is not currently possible to tell the software about multiple primary keys. Again, this is an instance in which a view can be extremely useful. Using a view, you can limit the amount of data that Dreamweaver MX has access to, and only update the data that is contained in the view.

20

Note

Unfortunately, using views in this manner presents a problem in some database systems. First, your database system must support views, and second, it must support inserting data into a view. Again, your database documentation is going to be the best place to find this information.

Keep It Simple

If you're a programmer, you'll recognize some of the functions that Dreamweaver MX offers and you might try to use one or two of them in a traditional programming construct. For example, consider repeating regions. If you have programming experience, you'll recognize these as a limited sort of loop.

A common trick used in programming is embedded loops. For example, you can easily manually program two embedded loops that lay out a series of photos, and so on in a table format. One loop would handle laying out the columns of cells, whereas another would loop through all the rows. Using Dreamweaver MX, you *can* embed two loops, but let's look at exactly how those two loops work:

```
<%
Dim Repeat1__numRows
Repeat1__numRows = 3
Dim Repeat1__index
Repeat1__index = 0
rsTest_numRows = rsTest_numRows + Repeat1__numRows
%><%
Dim Repeat2__numRows
Repeat2__numRows = 10
Dim Repeat2__index
Repeat2__index = 0
rsTest_numRows = rsTest_numRows + Repeat2__numRows
%>
```

The first part of the program sets up the loop limits. The first loop should run for 3 iterations, whereas the second should run for 10.

```
<%
While ((Repeat2__numRows <> 0) AND (NOT rsTest.EOF))
%><%
While ((Repeat1__numRows <> 0) AND (NOT rsTest.EOF))
%><%=(rsTest.Fields.Item("featureID").Value)%>
<%=(rsTest.Fields.Item("optionID").Value)%>
<%
Repeat1__index=Repeat1__index+1
Repeat1__numRows=Repeat1__numRows-1
rsTest.MoveNext()
Wend
%><%
Repeat2__index=Repeat2__index+1
Repeat2__numRows=Repeat2__numRows-1
rsTest.MoveNext()
Wend
%>
```

Here, the two loops are nested. Unfortunately, there is one slight problem. For both of the loops, the counter (numRows) is initialized in the same place. After the first loop has finished running, it cannot run again because the looping variable has already reached its limit. Because of the way that Dreamweaver MX handles these behaviors, you cannot simply apply programming knowledge to the Dreamweaver MX way of doing things. You must do what you can inside of Dreamweaver MX, and handle the rest manually.

Testing

The most important part of any application is testing. Because all the Dreamweaver MX code is dynamically generated, you have little to fear with something going wrong programmatically. If you decide to add your own code to the system, it's up to you to debug it.

What can go wrong, however, are the queries that you've defined for the system. If you go with the assumption that everything in Dreamweaver MX is correct, the problems can be limited to what you, as the developer, are providing the program to work with; namely, the SQL and the database definitions. Let's look at a couple of situations where the results you get aren't what you expect, and what steps you should take to test your system before deploying it.

Tip

Use the Live Data View whenever possible. If an error occurs while in Live Data View, Dreamweaver MX will show an error window with a More Info button. Clicking this button will take you to Macromedia's debugging Web site for fixing common problems.

Check for NULL Values

As you designed each of the databases throughout the book, you've noticed that certain fields are denoted as not null—this *always* applies to the primary keys. The MySQL database forces you to include the not null attribute for the primary key, but some systems might not. It's important to keep in mind that even if your primary keys are not defined as being not null, it *is* implied.

So, what does this mean to you? Any field that is defined as not null must have a value. If you've never built database-driven systems before, this can be slightly confusing. For example, consider a table that includes a username and password field with a very strict limit of 10 characters for each, and the additional requirement that the fields *must* contain data.

If you create a form that submits data to this table, you must make sure that all of the prerequisite requirements are met. You cannot expect Dreamweaver MX to come back

20

with a message explaining that the form needs to be filled in. Instead, the user would get an error message from the server describing (in programming terms) the problem. You need to intercept this problem before it happens.

The easiest way to do it is to use the Validate Form behavior, shown in Figure 20.13 (not *server* behavior):

1. Create a form that submits data to the database.
2. Determine which fields must have values and make a note of them.
3. Open the Behaviors panel.
4. Click "+" and choose Validate Form.
5. Select a field from the list that you want to force a value for.
6. Choose whether the field is required, or if it should accept a particular type of data (number, e-mail address, or number range).
7. Click OK.

FIGURE 20.13

Choose the fields that you want to force a value into.

Using a form validation behavior forces certain form elements to have values before they are submitted to the Insert or Update server behavior. This eliminates the potential problem of having users submit a form with fields that are empty, but are required to have a value in the database.

Always check your forms to see what happens when a form that collects user input is submitted blank. This is the most extreme case of testing not null values, and should demonstrate any problems if they exist.

Validate Using Duplicate Data

The second type of problem that you might encounter with the server behaviors is the matter of duplicate data within forms. You cannot use an Insert behavior to replace existing data in the database. Although this is probably obvious, it does present a potential problem when a system bases records and queries off user input. Throughout this final week of projects, there have been a few records that give the users the ability to create their own account on the system.

In creating these systems, you had the user input the data that could not be duplicated (such as the username) one step at a time. By doing the registration process in steps, you can check for duplicate data before it becomes a problem. If you try to input all the data at once and it is in conflict with existing data, the database server will generate an error and cause the Web application to crash.

Even if you don't think this problem affects you, you should always test your application (if it accepts user input) by entering multiple identical records and verifying that no server errors are generated.

Test Maximum Lengths

How does your database server handle values that exceed the maximum length? Does it cut them off? Does it generate an error? What happens? There's no way to tell without testing. MySQL, for example, will truncate the data if it is longer than the allowed field. This is yet another one of the extreme cases that needs to be tested.

Tip

Remember, you can limit the amount of data that an input field can accept by adjusting the max chars attribute in the Property Inspector. Unfortunately, this only works for basic single-line input fields. Multi-line input fields (text areas) cannot be limited.

If you follow a basic testing regimen using these three conditions, you're very likely to find everything that can and will go wrong with your Web application. To summarize, each application could go through several stress tests:

- **Empty (null) values**—What happens when an application that accepts data receives empty values? Can it handle them? You might find that forcing field input using a JavaScript behavior is an excellent way to eliminate this potential hang-up.

- **Duplicate values**—Likewise, what will your program do if you submit the same data twice? You must make sure that your database structure can handle multiple identical field values (an auto incrementing field could be useful here), or that you test values as they are submitted to eliminate any chance for conflict.

- **Size limits**—Make sure that your database is large enough to handle the amount of data that it is getting. Force input field limits where you can.

Even if you think you know how your application will react to these conditions, test them anyway. It's easy to make a mistake, and you might end up paying for it later.

20

> **Tip**
>
> Some of the restrictions that you might be forced to place on a form might not be obvious to the users. Be sure to include instructions in the form that document the required fields, size limits, and so on.

Additional Troubleshooting Resources

A wealth of information is available on the Internet that can make solving problems much easier. As much as I would have liked, this book simply cannot be made large enough to cover ASP, JSP, CFML, and SQL programming in an in-depth manner. Although I've done what I can to provide an informative overview of these topics, sometimes you'll need more information:

- `http://www.blooberry.com/`—BlooBerry is, in my mind, the definitive site for information on HTML and cascading style sheets. Beyond just defining what the tags and attributes are, BlooBerry shows examples of the tags, as well as provides information about the browsers that support them, and what potential problems you might encounter.

- `http://www.mysql.com/`—To effectively use Dreamweaver MX as a development tool, you must know your database server because it will be providing a great deal of the application logic. If you decide to use MySQL, be sure to check out the home page, which has extensive documentation on how to run the server and use SQL.

- `http://jsptags.com/`—The everything reference to JSP, including links to the official Sun documentation and reader forums to ask questions. JSPtags is an excellent site for anyone who uses JSP, whether amateur or professional.

- `http://www.macromedia.com/support/coldfusion/md]`There's no better reference for the ColdFusion Markup Language than Macromedia's own Web site. Providing detailed information on all the available tags and functions, you'll want to bookmark this site if you're a CF developer.

- `http://aspfree.com/`—This site has examples, online tutorials, and free Active Server Pages help. If you've never programmed ASP before, the complexity can be a bit overwhelming—this site will make everything clear.

Summary

As you set out to create your own applications and projects, keep in mind that Dreamweaver MX is only a tool, and it does have limitations. The best way to use the software to its fullest is to know your database server and the Dreamweaver MX environment. Together, these are the two components that make everything possible.

Everything is not always going to go smoothly, but I hope that the special cases you've seen throughout this text will prepare you for the potential problems that can come from server behavior problems or the need to expand the code beyond the built-in functions that Dreamweaver MX currently offers.

Workshop

The Workshop area is meant to reinforce your reading with a series of questions and exercises.

Q&A

Q What is the best approach to development, considering all the problems with Netscape 4.x?

A Develop for the problem child (which currently is Netscape), and deploy everywhere. If you develop for the browser with the most problems, you won't have to go back and adjust your code later.

Q Is there any definitive way to identify a query that is going to confuse Dreamweaver MX?

A Beware of queries that use the tag identifiers for the embedded language you're using. For example, using <%> to match HTML tags in a SQL query is dangerous.

Q If I test the document the way you described, is it going to be perfect?

A Maybe, maybe not! That depends on how you defined your database, the server behaviors you used, and what you intended the final product to be. I can only give you hints to point you in the right direction. It's up to you to do the rest. There is no way to perfectly predict the actions of users—they're likely to follow link paths, resize windows, and change preferences in ways you never thought of.

Quiz

1. What happens when you try to display a table with no end tag in Netscape 4.x?
2. Which feature of cascading style sheets should be avoided at all costs?
3. How can you prevent a `not null` error on an input form?
4. How can you limit the amount of input so that it doesn't exceed the limits of the database?

20

Quiz Answers

1. The contents of the table are not displayed on the screen. This is different from Internet Explorer, which assumes that you wanted to end the table and adds the end tag for you.

2. Relatively positioned objects that have links in them. Netscape 4.x renders the links in relatively positioned objects as if they were located in the upper-right corner of the document. The layout looks right, but is nonfunctional.

3. Validate the form using the Validate Form JavaScript behavior. This will guarantee that the form is filled in before the data is sent to the server.

4. Using simple input fields, you can do this with the max chars attribute of the field. Unfortunately, this is not available for multi-line fields, which is where it actually counts.

Exercise

1. Work through the Dreamweaver projects you've already designed and test for potential problems with link paths, input field lengths, and the like. Breaking the code before it goes online will help you save face if something goes wrong later.

DAY 21

Advanced Dreamweaver MX Features

Every large product that serves many purposes will have features that don't
necessarily fit into the flow of a tutorial text. Dreamweaver MX is hardly an
exception. This book is written for those who want to become accustomed to its
features without having to learn how to program—yet there are advanced features for programmers and Web developers working on advanced projects. This
chapter is the "catch all" for these features, and provides a reference for those
of you who might be interested in taking Dreamweaver MX to the next step.
Today's lesson will round out the three weeks with Macromedia Dreamweaver
MX by:

- Examining unique and specialized HTML tools.
- Exploring the creation of server behaviors
- Discussing how the Dreamweaver MX environment can be modified, cus-
  tomized, and changed down to the very files that make up the interface.

Advanced HTML Tools

Days 2, "Creating Your First Web Site," and 3, "Advanced HTML and Site Tools," taught you most everything you need to know to create and HTML pages and sites within the Dreamweaver MX environment. There are a few additional tools that can be used when creating your pages.

Tag Editor

When an object or a tag is highlighted in the document design, the Properties panel can be used to set the attributes for the object. Alternatively, you can use the Tag Inspector panel. True to form, Macromedia gives you yet another option for defining tag attributes—the Tag Editor.

The Tag Editor is most easily invoked by highlighting an HTML tag within the code window, and then choosing Edit Tag from the Modify menu, or by invoking a contextual menu on the selected HTML. The Tag Editor for the <body> tag is shown in Figure 21.1.

FIGURE 21.1

The Tag Editor can be used to set tag attributes.

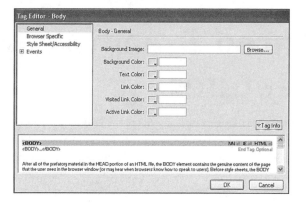

Along the right side of the window are the different attribute categories that can be "explored"—such as general attributes, browser specific, accessibility, and the Events (JavaScript Events) that are accepted by the particular object. You can click the Tag Info toggle in the lower-right corner of the window to view extended information on the tag and its use—the same as you can find in the Reference panel.

Use the attribute settings in the Tag Editor just as you would within the Properties panel. The corresponding HTML code will be automatically inserted into your document.

You might be wondering why the Tag Editor is necessary. The Tag Editor provides the friendly interface of the Properties panel with the attribute-editing capabilities of the Tag

Inspector and the code reference of the Reference panel. Could Macromedia have come up with a more consistent implementation? Is the redundancy needed? Be your own judge.

Accessibility Issues

There is an ever-increasing trend to make Web sites accessible to everyone. The government's Section 508 guidelines (`http://www.section508.gov/`) place accessibility requirements on federal institutions such that their pages *must* be accessible to the handicapped. If you are in the position in which you must create pages matching these guidelines, Dreamweaver MX can help automate the process.

When you learned the HTML tools, such as the `table` tool, in Chapters 2 and 3, you saw the standard form of the tools. Dreamweaver MX also provides "accessible" versions of forms, frames, media, images, and table objects. You can activate these alternative forms of the tools by opening the Dreamweaver Preferences, switching to the Accessibility category, and choosing the objects to activate, as seen in Figure 21.2.

FIGURE 21.2

Activate the Dreamweaver MX accessibility preferences.

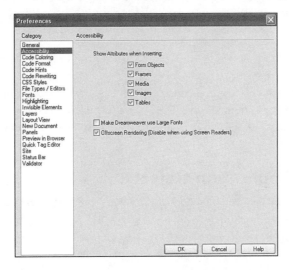

For example, if you've activated the accessibility attributes for tables, you'll see the two setup dialog boxes when inserting a table. The first configuration dialog box contains the basic table settings you know and love. The second, however, contains the accessibility options shown in Figure 21.3.

As you can see, there are additional attributes, such as `caption`, that help page-reading devices identify and parse table information. For more information on the section 508 guidelines, be sure to check out `http://www.section508.gov`.

21

FIGURE 21.3

FIGURE 21.3

Accessibility attributes change the setup dialog boxes for several basic HTML objects.

> ### Should My Page Be Accessible?
>
> Although I believe that pages should be made available to as large an audience as possible, this is not standard practice for the Web in general. The Dreamweaver MX environment does little more than provide basic support for a few accessibility features—but at the same time provides extensive tools so that you can instantly insert Flash, DHTML animations, and table/layer-driven pages—each of which could be considered the *antithesis* of accessibility.
>
> To be honest, if you're using Dreamweaver MX to its full capacity, you're probably not creating pages that follow accessibility guidelines. On the other hand, neither are any major computer Web sites, network news sites, or online superstores.

Server Code

If you want to modify the embedded code in Dreamweaver MX, or learn how to program, those things are up to you. There are a few additional programming tools that you might want to explore if you decide to take the next step and become a full-fledged Web developer.

Server Application Objects

As you've learned over the past 14 days, server behaviors insert complete pieces of code into your pages—no editing required on your part. In Appendix A, "Inside the Supported Languages," you will learn some of the basics of the common supported Dreamweaver MX languages. To get a quick start on inserting code, you can use the different application objects found on the Insert menu. For each of the supported languages, there are one or more application object menus that insert code fragments directly into the page's code.

For example, choosing If from the ASP Application Objects submenu will insert `<% If Then %>` into your document code. By itself, this is of little use—it requires you to fill in the details correctly for the appropriate programming language. Keep in mind that there are *five* implementation languages available. Providing a reference that applies to all five is unfeasible. I recommend that you purchase a book on the language you intend to use for the majority of your projects.

> **Note**
>
> Some of the application server platforms support *components* (encapsulated "chunks" of program logic). These application objects can be inserted and modified using the Component panel, accessed from the Window menu. As with the other application server objects, you must create or find pre-written components—Dreamweaver MX will not write them for you.
>
> JSP developers can use the Components panel to add and view JavaBeans, and then browse and view their Properties and Methods and add them to the document.
>
> ASP/VBScript does not support components, so it was not used in the writing of this book. You should check the documentation of your application server programming language to learn how it interacts with component technologies.

Editing/Creating Server Behaviors

Dreamweaver MX includes a built-in server behavior editor that allows you to very quickly create new server behaviors and alter existing behaviors to suit your needs. I highly discourage *everyone* from modifying existing behaviors on the system. It is much safer to copy existing behaviors and change them.

Let's work through a quick example so that you get an idea of how the system works. To access the Server Behavior editor, click the "+" button and choose Edit Server Behavior to change an existing behavior (not recommended), or New Server Behavior to add a new behavior or copy and edit an existing behavior.

Assume that you want to add a server behavior to the ASP behaviors that sets a session variable based on a request variable. Syntactically, it would look like this:

```
<% Session("MySessionVariable")=Request("MyRequestVariable") %>
```

First, choose New Server Behavior from the pop-up menu in the Server Behavior panel. You'll be greeted by the initial naming screen, shown in Figure 21.4.

FIGURE 21.4

Choose the server model and name for your new behavior.

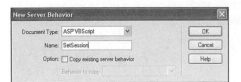

Select the appropriate server model (ASP, in this case), and a name for your new behavior, such as Set Session. If you check the Copy Existing Server Behavior option, you can also choose from the many existing behaviors to modify, rather than starting from scratch.

21

Click OK when you've chosen your name and scripting model.

The second step in defining your behavior is adding the code to the system in the Server Behavior Builder dialog box, shown in Figure 21.5.

FIGURE 21.5

The Server Behavior Builder is where you define all your ASP/JSP/CFML code.

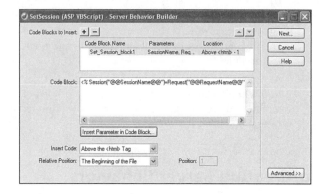

Each behavior can have multiple blocks of code, and each block of code can fall in a somewhat arbitrary location in the document. Because this is a relatively simple server behavior (it only has a single block of code), it should be easy to define:

1. Click the "+" button to add a new code block. Name it Set_Session_block1 (the default name).

2. Make sure that the Insert Code and Relative Position pop-up menus are set to "Above the <html> Tag" and "The Beginning of the File," respectively. These two configuration options control where the code will be inserted into the document, and where, relative to that location, it will be written.

3. Change the Code Block to resemble <% Session("")=Request("") %>.

4. Position your cursor inside the quotes of the Session("") portion of the code, and click the Insert Parameter In Code Block button. You will be prompted for a new parameter. Name it SessionName.

5. Position your cursor inside the quotes of the Request("") portion of the code, and click the Insert Parameter In Code Block button again. You will be prompted for a new parameter. Name it RequestName.

6. You've just defined the basis for the server behavior. Click the Next button to continue.

The final step of defining the server behavior is creating the dialog box that will be shown to configure it. Not surprisingly, this step, like most everything in Dreamweaver MX, is automated. As shown in Figure 21.6, you can change the ordering of the fields that will be created in the behavior configuration form, and, by clicking in the Display As field, you can provide a link to the recordset menu, allowing dynamic data to be used to fill one or more of the parameters.

FIGURE 21.6

Choose the order of the Server Behavior configuration fields and decide how they should be displayed.

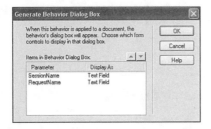

When you're satisfied with the display, click OK to continue.

After a few seconds, your server behavior will be generated and added to the menu within in the Server Behaviors panel. The screen for the behavior you just created is shown in Figure 21.7.

FIGURE 21.7

The new server behavior is ready to use.

As you work your way through the book, you'll notice that there are several instances in which the code needs to be customized in order to work correctly. These are *not* good places to use customized server behaviors. Although it would work, it would take longer to alter an existing behavior to include the new functionality than to just edit the code. The best candidates for new behaviors are actions that you find yourself repeating again and again—not the occasional oddball case. That said, the server behavior authoring tool is a fantastic addition to the Dreamweaver MX product. It is extremely valuable to the hardcore programming crowd.

Dreamweaver MX Extensions

If you cannot find something that you want within the Dreamweaver MX environment, it might not be possible. More likely, however, the solution is just an extension away. Dreamweaver MX supports a variety of add-ons from simple HTML objects like pull-down menus to dynamic tools such as shopping carts. To jump directly to the add-on download site, choose Get More Commands from the Commands menu. As you can see in Figure 21.8, there is no doubt you'll find something that interests you.

21

Figure 21.8

*Macromedia's site has
a wealth of packages
for the Dreamweaver
MX environment.*

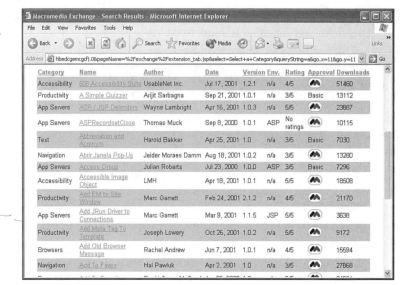

After using the Web site to locate a package that you want, be sure to verify that it works
on the platform of your choice (Macintosh or Windows) and is compatible with
Dreamweaver MX. This information should be readily available on the product detail
pages.

Follow these simple steps to install a package:

1. Find the package you want to download.

2. Click the download link for the appropriate platform (Macintosh or Windows).

3. Unarchive and uncompress the file if necessary. Dreamweaver extensions are distributed with the extension `.mxi`.

4. Open the Macromedia Extension Manager.

5. Choose Install Extension from the File menu.

6. Select the `.mxi` file and click Choose.

7. Read any license agreements and instructions thoroughly. Some extensions are *not*
   free products and have licensing and deployment costs associated with them.

After a short pause while the extension is installed, the Extension Manager will display
the new module seen in Figure 21.9.

If you want to remove an installed package, use Remove Extension from the File menu.
To disable a package temporarily, use the check box in front of the package to turn it on
or off.

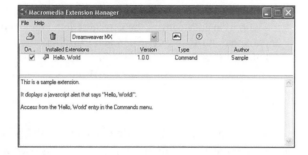

FIGURE 21.9

Macromedia Extension Manager handles all the installed packages.

There are literally hundreds of new features that you can add to Dreamweaver MX just by browsing Macromedia's Web site and downloading the appropriate package files. Before you decide that Dreamweaver MX *can't* do something you need, check out the rest of the freely available tools.

Note

Macromedia's Extension Manager is shared by different Macromedia products, including Dreamweaver MX and Flash MX. If you use other Macromedia software, don't be surprised if you start the Extension Manager and see packages not associated with Dreamweaver.

Besides just extending Dreamweaver MX, you can also modify the environment to match your tastes. If you aren't turned off by the thought of editing JavaScript, you can create a truly custom environment.

Customizing the Dreamweaver MX Environment

What makes Dreamweaver MX truly unique among modern complex applications is that almost *all* the files that Dreamweaver MX uses to configure its interface and behaviors are text-based. This means that with a bit of tinkering, you can change almost anything you want.

The best place to get started with modifying the Dreamweaver MX system is by reading the "Extending Dreamweaver" portion of the online help system. This will give you a good idea of what you can and cannot do. If you're impatient and just want to tinker, open the configuration directory within your main Dreamweaver MX program directory and take a look around.

21

> **Tip**
>
> It is wise to make a copy of the Configuration directory before you make any changes. If Dreamweaver MX fails to work properly, just replace the modified files with a copy of the original.

Menus

An interesting place to start fiddling is the Menus subdirectory. Within this directory is a `menus.xml` file that contains the definitions for all the menus used in the system. Near the bottom of the file, for example, you can find the XML definition of the Window menu—it should look something similar to this:

```
<menu name="_Window" id="DWMenu_Window">
    <menuitem name="_Insert" key="Cmd+F2"
        enabled="dw.getFocus() != 'browser'"
        command="dw.toggleFloater('objects')"
        checked="dw.getFloaterVisibility('objects')"
        domRequired="false" id="DWMenu_Window_Insert" />

        <menuitem name="_Properties" key="Cmd+F3"
         enabled="dw.getFocus() != 'browser'"
         command="dw.toggleFloater('properties')"
         checked="dw.getFloaterVisibility('properties')"
         domRequired="false" id="DWMenu_Window_Properties" />
...
</menu>
```

This is a much-abbreviated copy of the complete file, but you get the overall picture.

Each line is made up of a `<menuitem>` that has a name and a keyboard shortcut equivalent. You can actually go into these values and modify them to whatever you prefer. The only danger is in changing the command that executes a Dreamweaver JavaScript function and makes a window appear or disappear.

> **Tip**
>
> Although this is indeed a good way to edit keyboard shortcuts, an even easier way is to choose Keyboard Shortcuts from the Edit menu within Dreamweaver MX.

If you feel so inclined, you can copy menu items from one menu to another, or rearrange the menu system entirely. All you have to do is make sure that your tags are intact and valid.

Dialog Boxes and Windows

Open the Behaviors folder in the Dreamweaver MX Configuration folder. Here you'll find the majority of the window and command definitions for Dreamweaver MX's many windows and dialog boxes. For example, open the Popup Message.js file within the Behaviors/Actions directory. An annotated copy of the functions in the file is included here.

Set up the behavior function that will be included in the HTML. Here, the function is just a rehash of the already existing alert function:

```
//****************** BEHAVIOR FUNCTION ********************

//Passed a expression string, pops it up in an alert.

function MM_popupMsg(msg) { //v1.0
  alert(msg);
}
```

It defines the events that can be used with the function. The onClick event is set to be the default.

```
//****************** API ********************


//Can be used with any tag and any event

function canAcceptBehavior(){
  var retVal = "onClick,onMouseUp,onMouseDown,(onClick)";
  return retVal;
}
```

The previous code defines the function from the behavior document (this document) that will be included in the HTML. In this case, it's the MM_popupMsg function.

```
//Returns a JavaScript function to be inserted in HTML head with script tags.

function behaviorFunction(){
  return "MM_popupMsg";
}
```

The previous code creates the function call string, including the message to display as taken from the user interface form.

```
//Returns fn call to insert in HTML tag <TAG... onEvent='thisFn(arg)'>

function applyBehavior() {
  var index,frameObj,presBg,msgStr="",retVal;
  with (document.theForm) {
    msgStr = escExprStr(message.value,false);
  }
```

21

```
  if (msgStr == null) retVal = MSG_BadBraces;
  else if (msgStr) retVal = "MM_popupMsg('"+msgStr+"')";
  else retVal = MSG_NoMsg;
  return retVal
}
```

The previous code sets the value of the message field in the user interface form in case the behavior is edited.

```
function inspectBehavior(fnStr){
  var argArray, msgStr;

  argArray = extractExprStr(fnStr);
  if (argArray.length == 1) { //expect 1 arg
    document.theForm.message.value = unescExprStr(argArray[0],false);
  }
}
```

Finally, the `initializeUI` function sets any initial conditions in the user interface that must be addressed.

```
//***************** LOCAL FUNCTIONS  ******************


//Load up the frames, set the insertion point

function initializeUI(){
  document.theForm.message.focus(); //set focus on textbox
  document.theForm.message.select(); //set insertion point into textbox
}
```

As you can see, using JavaScript as the behavior/command programming language, Macromedia has opened the extension of Dreamweaver MX to anyone who has a text editor and the patience to script.

Supporting the behavior code is the user interface. Open the user interface file that corresponds to the JavaScript behavior file—Popup Message.htm. Amazingly, the interface itself is also defined in a text format that you might be familiar with—HTML. You can actually edit the interface of Dreamweaver MX within Dreamweaver MX itself.

The source code for this simple UI is shown here:

```
1 <HTML>
2 <HEAD>
3 <SCRIPT LANGUAGE="JavaScript"
4       SRC="Popup Message.js"></SCRIPT>
5 <SCRIPT LANGUAGE="JavaScript"
6       SRC="../../Shared/MM/Scripts/setText.js"></SCRIPT>
7 <SCRIPT LANGUAGE="JavaScript"
8       SRC="../../Shared/MM/Scripts/CMN/string.js"></SCRIPT>
9 <!— Remove the following SCRIPT tag
```

```
10      if you are modifying this file for your own use. —>
11 <SCRIPT SRC="../../Shared/MM/Scripts/CMN/displayHelp.js"></SCRIPT>
12 <!— End removal area. —>
13 <SCRIPT LANGUAGE="javascript">
14 // Copyright 1999 Macromedia, Inc. All rights reserved.
15
16 //———————· LOCALIZEABLE GLOBALS ———————·
17
18 var MSG_NoMsg = "Please enter a message or click Cancel.";
19 var MSG_BadBraces = "Curly braces are reserved for
20     embedding variables and must be matched correctly.\n
21     Please fix the braces or click Cancel.";
22 //———————·    END LOCALIZEABLE    ———————·
23 //———————·    END JAVASCRIPT      ———————·
24 </SCRIPT>
25 <TITLE>Popup Message</TITLE>
26 <META HTTP-EQUIV="Content-Type" CONTENT="text/html">
27 </HEAD>
28 <BODY onLoad="initializeUI()">
29   <FORM NAME="theForm">
30     <DIV ALIGN="center">
31       <TABLE BORDER=0>
32         <TR>
33           <TD HEIGHT=8></TD>
34           <TD ALIGN="left" VALIGN="top" NOWRAP ROWSPAN="2">
35             <TEXTAREA NAME="message" ROWS="5" COLS="50" WRAP="VIRTUAL">
36             </TEXTAREA><BR>
37         </TR>
38         <TR>
39           <TD ALIGN="right" VALIGN="TOP" NOWRAP>Message:</TD>
40         </TR>
41       </TABLE>
42     </DIV>
43   </FORM>
44 </BODY>
45 </HTML>
```

The key to understanding the connection between this document and the JavaScript is the message field. Named message in the HTML (line 35), this field is accessed directly within the JavaScript behavior definition.

Dreamweaver MX inserts a series of default buttons into the right side of the configuration window that are not shown in the dialog box's HTML. These buttons (typically OK and Cancel) signal the behavior to insert the JavaScript code into the document or forgo making any changes.

The best way to create your own behaviors (as a beginner) is to duplicate and edit existing behaviors. You can truly customize Dreamweaver MX into an application that bears no resemblance to its original self.

21

As your aspirations grow, you can check out the extending Dreamweaver MX help information, which describes the process of authoring your own additions. The Macromedia Web site also includes a wealth of information for developers.

Summary

Throughout the course of this book, we've done our best to avoid becoming programmers. The point of Dreamweaver MX is to provide a common interface for building applications, regardless of the languages you choose to use.

Today's lesson gave you a glimpse of some of the tools you might want to use if you decide to work directly with the code and take the next step in Web development. I highly recommend following the reading of this book with an application server specific text. Although you *can* develop complete applications in Dreamweaver MX, you're eventually going to need to get your hands dirty with the code in order to make things work exactly the way you want.

Well folks, that's it. You've made it through the full text of *Sams Teach Yourself Macromedia Dreamweaver MX in 21 Days.* Today's lesson wrapped up the final week with a look at a few of the tools that you might encounter as you become more experienced with developing Web applications.

If you have any questions about the projects in the book, I'd be more than happy to answer them. Feel free to e-mail me at jray@poisontooth.com.

Good luck, have fun, and play nice.

Workshop

The Workshop area is meant to reinforce your reading with a series of questions and exercises.

Q&A

Q Why are these tools mentioned at the end?

A It was a difficult choice to decide what to place in the book and when. Dreamweaver MX is a very large program with an outrageously large number of options. My goal was to provide the information in order of logical progression. Hopefully the vast majority of the audience of this book found the appropriate information in the appropriate places.

Q What limits does the Server Behavior Creation utility have?

A You can build reasonably complex behaviors with the built-in tools, but not nearly as extensive as what can be developed by reading Macromedia's documentation on extending Dreamweaver.

Q Which Macromedia extensions are available in Dreamweaver MX?

A You can find shopping carts, additional application server implementations, and many other tools. The only drawback to using these is that there is limited, if any, support. Although some extensions have a very loyal following and excellent support, with others you'll be on your own and responsible for maintaining the source code as needed.

Quiz

1. What are section 508 guidelines?

2. What are the application server object menus?

3. What Web language was used to develop a large portion of the Dreamweaver MX interface?

4. How are the Dreamweaver extensions installed?

Quiz Answers

1. The government's section 508 guidelines are designed to make Web site elements accessible to the handicapped. Because the Web was originally designed to provide content rather than animation and other extraneous fluff, you might want to consider accessibility requirements for your own sites.

2. These menus provide an easy way to insert basic programming building blocks into the HTML.

3. JavaScript and HTML are used to define many of the interface actions.

4. The Macromedia Extension Manager is used to install, remove, and temporarily disable extensions.

Exercises

1. Go outside and enjoy the sunlight or play in the snow, depending on when you read this :)

21

WEEK 3

In Review

This week's lessons introduced you to new and different ways of using and combining the Dreamweaver MX behaviors. There are still many areas where the projects can be improved, however. Try revisiting the past week's projects and adding the following features:

Day 16—Alter the message board system so that it allows the users to set a default password to use on all their messages. Store this value in a cookie by manually editing the code. You should be able to enhance the functionality even further using this cookie by allowing users to have one-click deleting of e-mail messages that they've posted.

Day 17—Add an administrative interface to the system so that the site content can be controlled from a centralized location. You might also want to add additional information that the users can customize. With the database structure developed in this chapter, the sky is the limit.

Day 18—Add an interface for the instructor to add questions to the database system. To make things more interesting, you can also add a point value system to the database so that questions can have different weights.

Day 19—The complex query system presents a good start on a fully functional matching system. In order to turn this into a more commercially viable system, you can add the capability for users to store messages directly in the private mailbox for other users. This is commonly used on systems that pair people together in order to protect their privacy and not distribute e-mail addresses publicly.

20

Obviously, you could expand many other portions of the projects. These are just a few additions that I think would be worthwhile and beneficial to the operation of the system.

I certainly hope that this book has been beneficial to you in using the Dreamweaver MX environment effectively. I've enjoyed developing project lessons that I feel are both useful and interesting. I hope you find them to be helpful in your Web programming endeavors. Remember to check out the `http://www.cutelittledogs.com` site for updates and corrections.

Good luck!

John Ray

APPENDIX **A**

Introduction to the Dreamweaver MX Languages

In the main text of this book, we looked at how to use the Dreamweaver MX tools without needing a degree in Computer Science. Unfortunately, there are occasions when you'll need to understand the code that has been added to a page. In this appendix, we'll take a look at the actual structure of the most popular Dreamweaver MX languages and how they operate. This is not meant to be a complete programming reference by any stretch of the imagination. Instead, it will hopefully give you enough information so that you can find your way around the auto-generated server behaviors and modify them to do your bidding.

You can consider this appendix a basic reference to some of the code you'll see generated by Dreamweaver MX. If you're a non-programmer, you might want to look into a full programming manual, many of which are listed at the end of this guide. Most readers with a general understanding of programming languages will be able to use the following information to help them better understand the structure of the Dreamweaver MX languages.

Programming Concepts

Several concepts apply to all programming languages at a base level. Although each of the supported programming languages is different, they all have certain fundamental elements in common. The best way to understand a language you've never used before is to understand these fundamental building blocks and how they appear within the language you are using. This appendix covers a few of the basics of the following application server languages:

- ASP VBScript
- ColdFusion Markup Language (CFML)
- PHP
- JSP

 Note

> Although JavaScript is one of the supported programming languages, it will not be discussed here. The structure of JavaScript at the level we're discussing is similar to Java and therefore would be redundant.

Basics

Before looking at the actual languages, here are some basics to keep in mind as you look at the code:

Tags—ASP and JSP tags are denoted by <% *tagname* %>. ColdFusion tags are embedded directly within HTML and look identical to existing HTML tags. PHP tags fall within <? *tagname* ?> brackets.

Comments—Comments can be added to ASP code by starting the line with an ' character. Likewise, Java and CFScript lines can be commented with //. PHP comments are typically set off with the # mark. Because all the languages are embedded directly into HTML, you can always use the standard <! — — > HTML comment tags to denote a comment.

End of Line—VBScript lines end with a carriage return. ColdFusion Script, Java, and PHP terminate a command line with a semicolon.

Variables

Variables store information during the execution of an application. They can be used to store text, numbers, and other more abstract concepts such as time. Each programming

A

language deals with variables in a different way and offers different capabilities for working with the variables that you define.

ASP—VBScript

VBScript, or Visual Basic Script, is a very simple language that mirrors Microsoft's popular Visual Basic development environment. Variables are defined when they are used within a VBScript program. Additionally, you can store text or numeric data in a variable without needing to differentiate between the data types.

For example,

```
myVar=3
```

and

```
myVar="Four"
```

are both valid variable assignments. Occasionally, you'll see VBScript that includes the Dim (Dimension) command:

```
Dim myVar
```

This simply declares that the variable myVar exists but doesn't assign a value to it. Because variables are automatically declared when they are first used, this keyword is rarely employed.

Java

Java is a tighter language than VBScript. You cannot add variables wherever you want them in the code. Instead, you must tell the system the name and type of variable you're using before it appears in the source code.

For example,

```
int myInt;
float myFloat;
String myString="This is a string value";
myInt=3;
myFloat=4.5;
```

As seen with myString, you can set the value of a variable when it is first declared. Also notice that each line ends in a ; character. Within Java and JavaScript, these characters are used to denote the end of a command. You can break code across several lines as long as a ; falls at the end of the code segment.

Arrays in Java work similarly to those in VBScript. The difference is that you must declare the array (int myInts[50];) before using it.

CFML/CFScript

ColdFusion suffers from a bit of an identity crisis when it comes to nailing down the programming language. CFML allows you to do most of your programming very quickly, but is often a stumbling point for those who want to write code in a traditional style. Because of this, ColdFusion provides a second language called CFScript, which can be embedded in a page. Dreamweaver MX uses both types of programming when writing its server behaviors.

Within CFML, declaring a variable is performed like this:

```
<CFSET myVar="Test Value">
```

Within CFScript, however, the variables are declared and used in a fashion that is identical to VBScript:

```
myVar="Test"
myInt[50]=75
```

Within CFML, you can access CFScript variables using "#variablename#". It's a bit confusing, but it works.

PHP

If you've used Perl, you'll recognize the variable conventions of PHP. Variables are not "typed," which means that any variable can contain anything and PHP will automatically attempt to convert between types. Variables are prefaced by the $ character:

```
$myVar="Test";
$myInt=75;
```

Arrays can be indexed based on numbers, letters, or any combination:

```
$myArray[1]="Hello";
$mySecondArray["one"]="Howdy";
```

PHP does not require that you initialize variables before you use them. This makes it extremely flexible and also a bit dangerous. In large applications, it's very easy to lose track of what variables you've used.

Conditionals and Looping Constructs

In order to do work, applications need to make decisions and adjust their activities to the data that they are processing. For example, if you have an unknown amount of records in your database table and you want to display them all, you will need to loop through the records until you find the end. Additionally, if you don't have any records to display, you might want to add a message to the screen that will warn the users that no information is available.

Both of these activities require the program to adjust its logic flow depending on a several different things. Let's take a look at these programming constructs and how to recognize them in the available languages.

VBScript

There two types of loops you're likely to see in Dreamweaver MX server behaviors—for...next loops and while loops. The for...next loop counts over a range of values until an upper or lower value is reached. The while loop, however, continues to execute code repeatedly while a condition remains true.

For example,

```
For x=1 To 5
    ' Do Something five times
Next
```

and

```
Do While (x<5)
    ' Continue as long as variable x is less than 5.
Loop
```

In addition to looping, applications also need to make decisions about where to go when certain conditions are met. This is typically handled by an If...Then...Else construct that checks a condition before executing a piece of code:

```
If x=5 Then
    ' Do something useful!
Else
    ' Do something else!
End If
```

Using this conditional statement, you can alter the logic flow of the program so that it performs new actions based on the conditions you specify.

Java

Looping within Java is done according to the C style syntax. Unlike the verbose VBScript code, Java keeps the loops to a minimum:

```
for (x=0;x<5;x=x+1) {
    // Do something 5 times
}
```

The initial line of the for loop does three things; it initializes the variable x to zero, it sets the condition under which the loop will continue to run (x<5), and finally it tells the program what to do each time the loop executes (increase $x by one).

Code segments within Java are always contained within curly brackets {} rather than several different constructs as in VBScript.

For example, the `while` loop varies from the `for` loop only in the initial line:

```
while (x<5) {
    // Do Something!
}
```

This same structure also carries over to the `if` statement:

```
if (x==5) {
    // Do something useful!
} else {
    // Do something else!
}
```

As you can see, this is a more consistent programming style, but can be difficult to debug if you have several nested conditionals.

CFML/CFScript

As luck would have it, CFScript follows the same syntax as Java, so you don't need to look at it here. What you do need to check, however, are the CFML tags that handle looping and conditionals.

The `<CFLOOP></CFLOOP>` tags handle both a counting style `for...next` loop and the conditional `while` loop:

```
<CFLOOP INDEX="x"
 FROM="1"
 TO="5"
 STEP="1">
    <!- Do Something Here! ->
</CFLOOP>
```

This example would loop from 1 to 5, just as the previous ASP and JSP code fragments do.

 Note   The `CFLOOP` tag is spread across multiple lines here to show its components. It could just as easily be on a single line.

To perform a conditional loop, you just modify the tags slightly:

```
<CFLOOP CONDITION="x LESS THAN 5">
    <!-Do Something Here Too! ->
</CFLOOP>
```

As you can see, ColdFusion aims to make creating dynamic pages as simple as coding HTML.

Creating an IF statement is just as simple—another set of tags <CFIF><CFELSE></CFIF> control the login flow. For example,

```
<CFIF x EQ 5>
<!— Do something useful —>
<CFELSE>
<!— Do something else useful —>
</CFIF>
```

CFML isn't difficult to work with, but it does take some getting used to!

PHP

Like Java, PHP loops are based on the C syntax. In fact, they're almost identical to Java, aside from the changes in the variable notation:

```
for ($x=0;$x<5;$x=$x+1) {
    // Do something 5 times
}
```

As with Java, the initial line of the for loop does three things; it initializes $x to zero, it sets the run condition ($x<5), and finally it tells the program what to do each time the loop executes (increase $x by one).

Likewise, the while loop also has the same structure:

```
while ($x<5) {
    // Do Something!
}
```

...and the if statements:

```
if ($x==5) {
    // Do something useful!
} else {
    // Do something else!
}
```

Most people with experience in Java, C, or Perl will pick up PHP almost immediately.

Dynamic Elements

Dynamic elements, for the sake of discussion here, are elements that receive their contents from the client browser. This includes things such as sessions, cookies, and form fields.

Each of the programming languages covered here offers a different way to access these elements because they are *not* a common feature of traditional languages and were implemented as an addition to the core syntax.

ASP—VBScript

Accessing dynamic client-specific values, such as sessions, cookies, or form results is very simple within Active Server Pages. In fact, if you've ever used Perl or another traditional language to develop server-based CGIs from scratch, you'll be astounded by the ease of ASP.

Setting a session variable is as easy as assigning any other variable value:

```
Session("myVar")="My Value"
```

Likewise, setting a cookie is equally simple:

```
Response.Cookies("myVar")="My Other Value"
```

You can even modify the expiration date of the cookie by adding another line:

```
Response.Cookies("myVar").Expires=#12/31/2030#
```

 Caution | Although setting a cookie is indeed very easy, you must set the cookie before any other information is sent to the client computer. Failing to do this will result in an error.

Within Dreamweaver MX, you can easily read the contents of any of these elements by adding a data binding, as you'll learn in Day 9, "Introducing the Dreamweaver MX Server Behaviors." Unfortunately, if you want to *set* a value, you'll need to do it manually.

Java

Setting session variables in Java is similar to ASP, but with a slightly different syntax:

```
session.putValue("myVar", "My Value!")
```

To set a cookie within JSP, you must add the cookie to the Response header that is sent to the client computer. This is identical (conceptually) to the ASP example—and it explains why the ASP command contains the word Response.

```
myCookie = new Cookie("myVar", "My value!"));
myCookie.setMaxAge(50000);
response.addCookie(myCookie);
```

What is a bit different here is that there is an extra step to the creation of the cookie.

First, you must create the Cookie object (myCookie in the example). Next, if you want, you can set a maximum age that the cookie can reach in seconds. Finally, the correctly configured cookie object is added to the response header.

CFML

Before you can use session variables within ColdFusion, you must use the `<CFAPPLICATION>` tag to activate session management. This tag is held in the primary `application.cfm` file for your project and should be used only in the `<CFAPPLICATION>` tag in any of the pages.

```
<CFAPPLICATION NAME="My Application" SESSIONMANAGEMENT="Yes">
```

After session management is enabled for the project, you can set session variables using `<CFSET>` much the same way you set any other variable:

```
<CFSET session.myVar="My Value!">
```

Cookies, however, get their own special tag `<CFCOOKIE>` that can be used to store a browser-based value:

```
<CFCOOKIE NAME="myCookie" VALUE="My Value!" EXPIRES="12/30/2010">
```

PHP

PHP Session variables and cookies are remarkably easy to use because they appear in the application as normal variables. To use sessions, you should start the PHP script with `session_start()`, although PHP will do this for you if it's configured properly. You can then "store" a session variable using its name and the `session_register()` function. For example:

```
session_start();
$myVar="My Value!";
session_register(myVar);
```

Here, `$myVar` is registered as a session variable. On subsequent pages, it can be accessed just like any other variable. Note that the `session_register` function uses only the base name of the variable, not including the $.

Cookies are equally simple to work with—just use `setcookie()`:

```
setcookie("MyCookie","My Value!", time()+3600);
```

Here, the cookie is set with an expiration of 3600 seconds (1 hour) in the future. Unlike the other languages, PHP requires a time setting in seconds. You use the `time()` function to generate the current time, and then add the desired interval (yes, even if it's *huge*) to it.

That's it! These are the basic constructs that Dreamweaver will use when building your pages. If you can understand this information, you can probably also understand how to dissect the server behaviors and modify them to do your bidding.

Note

If you'd like to learn more (a lot more!) about the languages Dreamweaver MX can use, check out the following titles:

Sams Teach Yourself Visual Basic .NET Web Programming in 21 Days by Peter Aitken and Phil Syme.

Sams Teach Yourself Macromedia ColdFusion in 21 Days by Charles Mohnike.

Sams Teach Yourself Java 2 in 21 Days by Laura Lemay and Rogers Cadenhead.

PHP Developer's Handbook by Luke Welling and Laura Thomson.

APPENDIX B

MySQL Quick Function Reference

This appendix contains a summary of the data types that are currently supported within MySQL as well as many functions you can use within your queries to further advance the capabilities of your application.

The descriptions given are a simplified and abbreviated version of those on the MySQL Web site (`http://www.mysql.com/`). Please refer to the official documentation for more detailed information.

Common Data Types

The following data types can be used when defining tables within MySQL.

TINYINT [UNSIGNED]—A very small integer. The signed range is –128 to 127. The unsigned range is 0 to 255.

SMALLINT [UNSIGNED]—A small integer. The signed range is –32,768 to 32,767. The unsigned range is 0 to 65,535.

MEDIUMINT [UNSIGNED]—A medium-size integer. The signed range is –8,388,608 to 8,388,607. The unsigned range is 0 to 16,777,215.

INT [UNSIGNED]—A normal-size integer. The signed range is –2,147,483,648 to 2,147,483,647. The unsigned range is 0 to 4,294,967,295.

INTEGER [UNSIGNED]—This is a synonym for INT.

BIGINT [UNSIGNED]—A large integer. The signed range is –9,223,372,036,854,775,808 to 9,223,372,036,854,775,807. The unsigned range is 0 to 18,446,744,073,709,551,615.

FLOAT—A small (single-precision) floating-point number. Cannot be unsigned. Allowable values are –3.402823466E+38 to –1.175494351E-38, 0 and 1.175494351E-38 to 3.402823466E+38

DOUBLE—A normal-size (double-precision) floating-point number. Cannot be unsigned. Allowable values are –1.7976931348623157E+308 to –2.2250738585072014E-308, 0 and 2.2250738585072014E-308 to 1.7976931348623157E+308.

DECIMAL—An unpacked floating-point number. Cannot be unsigned. Behaves like a CHAR column: "unpacked" means that the number is stored as a string, using one character for each digit of the value.

DATETIME—A date and time combination. The supported range is '1000-01-01 00:00:00' to '9999-12-31 23:59:59'. MySQL displays DATETIME values in 'YYYY-MM-DD HH:MM:SS' format, but allows you to assign values to DATETIME columns using either strings or numbers.

TIMESTAMP—A timestamp. The range is '1970-01-01 00:00:00' to sometime in the year 2037.

YEAR—A year in 2- or 4-digit formats (default is 4-digit). The allowable values are 1901 to 2155, and 0000 in the 4-year format and 1970-2069 if you use the 2-digit format (70-69).

CHAR(M) [BINARY]—A fixed-length string that is always right-padded with spaces to the specified length when stored. M can range from 1 to 255 characters. Trailing spaces are removed when the value is retrieved. CHAR values are sorted and compared in case-insensitive fashion according to the default character set unless the BINARY keyword is included.

VARCHAR(M) [BINARY]—A variable-length string. Note: Trailing spaces are removed when the value is stored. M can range from 1 to 255 characters. VARCHAR values are sorted and compared in case-insensitive fashion unless the BINARY keyword is included.

TINYBLOB/TINYTEXT—A BLOB or TEXT column with a maximum length of 255 (2^8-1) characters.

BLOB/TEXT—A column with a maximum length of 65,535 ($2^{16}-1$) characters.

MEDIUMBLOB/MEDIUMTEXT—A BLOB or TEXT column with a maximum length of 16,777,215 ($2^{24}-1$) characters.

LONGBLOB / LONGTEXT—A BLOB or TEXT column with a maximum length of 4,294,967,295 ($2^{32}-1$) characters.

Arithmetic Operations

Rather than hard coding mathematical operations into your Web pages, use the SQL database's arithmetic functions to do the dirty work.

+—Addition

-—Subtraction

*—Multiplication

/—Division

Logical Operations

Logical operations are used to tie multiple conditions together in complex queries.

! or **NOT**—Logical NOT

OR or ||—Logical OR

AND or &&—Logical AND. Returns 0 if either argument is 0 or NULL; otherwise returns 1.

Basic Comparisons

When writing query conditions, basic value comparisons often come into play. Use these operators to develop your queries.

=—Equal

<> or !=—Not equal

<=—Less than or equal

<—Less than

B

>=—Greater than or equal

>—Greater than

IS NULL/IS NOT NULL—Tests whether a value is NULL.

<expr> BETWEEN <min> AND <max>—Tests an expression to determine whether it is between two values.

<expr> IN (<value 1>,<...>)—Compares an expression to a list. Returns true if the expression matches any of the values in the list.

<expr> NOT IN (<value 1>,<...>)—Performs the inverse of the previous function.

ISNULL(<expr>)—Returns true if the expression is a NULL value.

String Comparison Functions

When comparing strings, there are several additional functions that provide advanced pattern matching features:

<expr> LIKE <pat>—Pattern matching using SQL simple regular expression comparison.

<expr> NOT LIKE <pat>—The opposite of the previous comparison.

<expr> REGEXP <pat> / <expr> RLIKE <pat>—Performs a pattern match of a string expression expr against a pattern pat.

<expr> NOT REGEXP <pat> / <expr> NOT RLIKE <pat>—The opposite of the previous comparison.

STRCMP(<expr1>,<expr2>)—Returns 0 if the strings are the same, -1 if the first argument is smaller than the second according to the current sort order, and 1 otherwise.

MATCH (<field name1>,<field name2>,<...>) AGAINST <expr>—MATCH ... AGAINST() is used for full-text search and returns *relevance*—a similarity measure between the text in the fields and the expression.

Mathematical Functions

As always, use your SQL server to its fullest potential. If you can force it to perform your calculations, you'll end up with much more portable code.

ABS(X)—Returns the absolute value of X.

SIGN(X)—Returns the sign of the argument as -1, 0, or 1, depending on whether X is negative, zero, or positive.

MOD(N,M)—% Modulo (like the % operator in C). Returns the remainder of N divided by M.

FLOOR(X)—Returns the largest integer value not greater than X.

CEILING(X)—Returns the smallest integer value not less than X.

ROUND(X)—Returns the argument X, rounded to the nearest integer.

ROUND(X,D)—Returns the argument X, rounded to a number with D decimals. If D is 0, the result will have no decimal point or fractional part.

EXP(X)—Returns the value of e (the base of natural logarithms) raised to the power of X.

LOG(X)—Returns the natural logarithm of X.

LOG10(X)—Returns the base-10 logarithm of X.

POW(X,Y) or **POWER(X,Y)**—Returns the value of X raised to the power of Y.

SQRT(X)—Returns the non-negative square root of X.

PI()—Returns the value of PI.

COS(X)—Returns the cosine of X, where X is given in radians.

SIN(X)—Returns the sine of X, where X is given in radians.

TAN(X)—Returns the tangent of X, where X is given in radians.

ACOS(X)—Returns the arc cosine of X, that is, the value whose cosine is X. Returns NULL if X is not in the range −1 to 1.

ASIN(X)—Returns the arc sine of X, that is, the value whose sine is X. Returns NULL if X is not in the range −1 to 1.

ATAN(X)—Returns the arc tangent of X, that is, the value whose tangent is X.

ATAN2(X,Y)—Returns the arc tangent of the two variables X and Y. It is similar to calculating the arc tangent of Y / X, except that the signs of both arguments are used to determine the quadrant of the result.

COT(X)—Returns the cotangent of X.

RAND() or **RAND(N)**—Returns a random floating-point value in the range 0 to 1.0. If an integer argument N is specified, it is used as the seed value.

LEAST(X,Y,...)—With two or more arguments, returns the smallest (minimum-valued) argument.

GREATEST(X,Y,...)—Returns the largest (maximum-valued) argument.

RADIANS(X)—Returns the argument X, converted from degrees to radians.

TRUNCATE(X,D)—Returns the number X, truncated to D decimals. If D is 0, the result will have no decimal point or fractional part.

String Functions

Much as mathematical functions operate on numbers, string functions can be used to combine, add to, or subtract from text strings.

ASCII(str)—Returns the ASCII code value of the leftmost character of the string str. Returns 0 if str is the empty string. Returns NULL if str is NULL.

CONV(N,from_base,to_base)—Converts numbers between different number bases. Returns a string representation of the number N, converted from the base called from_base to the base called to_base.

BIN(N)—Returns a string representation of the binary value of N.

OCT(N)—Returns a string representation of the octal value of N.

HEX(N)—Returns a string representation of the hexadecimal value of N.

CHAR(N,...)—Interprets the arguments as integers and returns a string consisting of the characters given by the ASCII code values of those integers.

CONCAT(str1,str2,...)—Returns the string that results from concatenating the arguments.

CONCAT_WS(separator, str1, str2,...)—CONCAT_WS() stands for *CONCAT with separator* and is a special form of CONCAT(). The first argument is the separator for the rest of the arguments.

LENGTH(str)—Returns the length of the string str.

LOCATE(substr,str) or **POSITION(substr IN str)**—Returns the position of the first occurrence of substring substr in string str. Returns 0 if substr is not in str.

LOCATE(substr,str,pos)—Returns the position of the first occurrence of substring substr in string str, starting at position pos. Returns 0 if substr is not in str.

INSTR(str,substr)—Returns the position of the first occurrence of substring substr in string str. This is the same as the two-argument form of LOCATE(), except that the arguments are swapped.

LPAD(str,len,padstr)—Returns the string str, left-padded with the string padstr until str is len characters long.

RPAD(str,len,padstr)—Returns the string str, right-padded with the string padstr until str is len characters long.

LEFT(str,len)—Returns the leftmost len characters from the string str.

RIGHT(str,len)—Returns the rightmost len characters from the string str.

SUBSTRING(str,pos,len) or **MID(str,pos,len)**—Returns a substring len characters long from string str, starting at position pos.

SUBSTRING(str,pos)—Returns a substring from string str starting at position pos.

LTRIM(str)—Returns the string str with leading space characters removed.

RTRIM(str)—Returns the string str with trailing space characters removed.

SOUNDEX(str)—Returns a soundex string from str. Two strings that sound about the same should have identical soundex strings.

SPACE(N)—Returns a string consisting of N space characters.

REPLACE(str,from_str,to_str)—Returns the string str with all occurrences of the string from_str replaced by the string to_str.

REPEAT(str,count)—Returns a string consisting of the string str repeated count times. If count <= 0, returns an empty string. Returns NULL if str or count are NULL.

REVERSE(str)—Returns the string str with the order of the characters reversed.

INSERT(str,pos,len,newstr)—Returns the string str, with the substring beginning at position pos and len characters long replaced by the string newstr.

LCASE(str) or **LOWER(str)**—Returns the string str with all characters changed to lowercase.

UCASE(str) or **UPPER(str)**—Returns the string str with all characters changed to uppercase.

Date and Time Functions

Many applications sort or store information based on a day or time. These MySQL functions provide an easy means of working with dates without having to learn calendar mathematics.

DAYOFWEEK(date)—Returns the weekday index for date (1 = Sunday, 2 = Monday, ... 7 = Saturday).

WEEKDAY(date)—Returns the weekday index for date (0 = Monday, 1 = Tuesday, ... 6 = Sunday).

DAYOFMONTH(date)—Returns the day of the month for date, in the range 1 to 31.

DAYOFYEAR(date)—Returns the day of the year for date, in the range 1 to 366.

MONTH(date)—Returns the month for date, in the range 1 to 12.

DAYNAME(date)—Returns the name of the weekday for date.

MONTHNAME(date)—Returns the name of the month for date.

QUARTER(date)—Returns the quarter of the year for date, in the range 1 to 4.

WEEK(date) / WEEK(date,first)—With a single argument, returns the week for date, in the range 0 to 53.

YEAR(date)—Returns the year for date, in the range 1000 to 9999.

YEARWEEK(date) or YEARWEEK(date,first)—Returns year and week for date.

HOUR(time)—Returns the hour for time, in the range 0 to 23.

MINUTE(time)—Returns the minute for time, in the range 0 to 59.

SECOND(time)—Returns the second for time, in the range 0 to 59.

TO_DAYS(date)—Given a date, returns a daynumber (the number of days since year 0).

FROM_DAYS(N)—Given a daynumber N, returns a DATE value

CURDATE() or CURRENT_DATE—Returns today's date.

CURTIME() or CURRENT_TIME—Returns the current time.

NOW()—Returns the current date and time.

SEC_TO_TIME(seconds)—Returns the seconds argument, converted to hours, minutes, and seconds.

TIME_TO_SEC(time)—Returns the time argument, converted to seconds.

Summarization Functions for Use with GROUP BY Clauses

When using a GROUP BY clause, these functions can be employed to summarize information about the query.

COUNT(<expr>)—Returns a count of the number of non-NULL values in the rows retrieved by a SELECT statement.

COUNT(DISTINCT <expr>,[<expr...>])—Returns a count of the number of different non-NULL values.

AVG(<expr>)—Returns the average value of expr.

MIN(<expr>)—Returns the minimum value of expr.

MAX(<expr>)—Returns the maximum value of expr.

SUM(<expr>)—Returns the sum of expr. Note that if the return set has no rows, it returns NULL.

STD(<expr>) or STDDEV(<expr>)—Returns the standard deviation of expr.

B

APPENDIX C

Dreamweaver MX CSS Style Reference

Dreamweaver MX provides extensive cascading style sheets (CSS)—editing capabilities—beyond what reasonably fits into a chapter. This appendix takes a close look at the different CSS categories available.

Tip

> Remember that Dreamweaver MX offers an extensive help section for HTML as well as cascading style sheets. Any time you need more detailed information, just turn to the Help menu.

Table C.1 examines the Type attributes.

TABLE C.1 Type Attributes

Attribute	Description
Font	The font faces to be applied to the object.
Size	Font size can be specified in pixels for cross-platform consistency.

TABLE C.1　continued

Attribute	Description
Weight	The level of the bold applied to the font.
Style	Standard font styles.
Variant	Allows small caps to be used for lowercase.
Line Height	The line spacing for the text object. Determines the amount of space between lines.
Case	Converts the case in the text object to all uppercase, lowercase, or capitalizes the first letter of each word.
Decoration	Additional styles beyond the standard HTML Styles such as strikethrough. The None setting is commonly used to remove underlines from hyperlinks.
Color	Color.

The Background category sets background colors, graphics, and their attributes for objects such as tables and layers. Table C.2 looks at the available Background attributes.

TABLE C.2　Background Attributes

Attribute	Description
Background Color	The background color of an object.
Background Image	The background image of an object.
Repeat	Controls how a background image repeats (horizontally, vertically, both, or none).
Attachment	Determines whether a background image is attached to the page or doesn't scroll with the page.
Horizontal Position	The horizontal offset of the background image.
Vertical Position	The vertical offset of the background image.

Block attributes control text alignment and spacing attributes for text block objects such as paragraphs. Table C.3 looks at the Block attributes.

TABLE C.3　Block Attributes

Attribute	Description
Word Spacing	The amount of space between words. Negative space collapses the space.
Letter Spacing	Spacing between letters. Again, use negative numbers to tighten spacing.
Vertical Alignment	How an object is arranged in relation to its peers.

TABLE C.3 continued

Attribute	Description
Text Align	Controls text justification within an object.
Text Indent	The amount of indent for the first line of a text area, such as a paragraph.
Whitespace	Controls how whitespace is handled. Unlike standard HTML rendering, which condenses strings of spaces into a single space, pre shows all spaces, whereas nowrap prevents all wrapping.
Display	Sets how an element is displayed. Using None will not display the element.

Margin and padding information can be set by altering bounding box attributes for objects. Table C.4 looks at these attributes in detail.

TABLE C.4 Box Attributes

Attribute	Description
Width	The width of an object.
Height	The height of an object.
Float	Sets the object position to the right or left and lets other objects float around it.
Clear	Sets a side of the object that does not allow floating. This side remains clear.
Padding	The amount of padding between the boundary of an object and its content.
Margin	The space held between an object and other objects.

The Border attributes control border sizes and colors for tables. Table C.5 examines the available Border attributes.

TABLE C.5 Border Attributes

Attribute	Description
Style	How the border is drawn (solid or dashed lines).
Width	Thickness of object borders—for objects such as layers and tables.
Color	The color of the border being drawn.

List attributes for ordered and unordered lists include bullet and number styles. Table C.6 looks at the List attributes in more detail.

TABLE C.6   List Attributes

Attribute	Description
Type	The shape/appearance of bulleted items in lists.
Bullet Image	An image to be used in the place of the character-based bullet point.
Position	Sets the manner in which list item wrapping occurs.

The `Positioning` attributes control positioning and determining clipped regions of layers. Table C.7 looks at the `Positioning` attributes.

TABLE C.7   Positioning Attributes

Attribute	Description
Type	The manner in which a layer is positioned. Relative position places the layer relative to its parent object. `Absolute` defines the layer's position in reference to the top of the page, whereas `Static` places the layer in relation to the document flow.
Width	The width of the element.
Height	The height of the element.
Visibility	Whether a layer is hidden or visible in its initial state.
Z-Index	The front-to-back ordering of the layer in reference to other layers in the document.
Overflow	How content that doesn't fit in the element should be handled. Layers can be configured to allow all content to be visible, hidden, or scrollable (if the browser allows).
Placement	Location and size settings for a layer.
Clip	Sets a clipping region for a layer.

`Extensions` include attributes that are not consistent across browsers such as visual Photoshop-like filters and cursor shapes. Table C.8 looks at the `Extensions` attributes in more detail.

TABLE C.8   Extensions Attributes

Attribute	Description
Before	Sets the space at the top of a page (for printing).
After	Sets the space after a page (for printing).
Cursor	Sets the cursor when it is positioned over an object. This is supported only in Internet Explorer.
Filter	Another Internet Explorer specific option. Filters apply Photoshop-like filters to portions of a Web page. It's unlikely that these are going to become a standard anytime soon.

APPENDIX D

Support Database Definitions

This appendix contains the SQL database definitions used for each of the projects in the book. Because Dreamweaver MX is "database agnostic," it will work with hundreds of data sources. If the MySQL or MS Access data files (available on `http://downloads.cutelittledogs.com`) don't fit your needs, you can re-create the examples on other SQL servers using these statements to create the tables and store the default data sets.

Day 8

Listing D.1 shows the table structure for `tblConnTest`.

LISTING D.1 Table Structure for `tblConnTest`

```
1 CREATE TABLE tblConnTest (
2   looks int(11) default NULL,
3   good int(11) default NULL,
4   to2 int(11) default NULL,
5   me int(11) default NULL
6 );
```

Day 10

Listing D.2 shows the table structure for `tblComplexDogImagelayout`.

LISTING D.2 Table Structure for `tblComplexDogImagelayout`

```
1 CREATE TABLE tblComplexDogImagelayout (
2   AKCname varchar(250) NOT NULL default '',
3   shortname varchar(250) default NULL,
4   breed varchar(250) default NULL,
5   birthday date default NULL,
6   owner varchar(250) default NULL,
7   imageurl varchar(250) default NULL,
8   layerstyle varchar(250) default NULL,
9   PRIMARY KEY  (AKCname)
10 );
```

Listing D.3 contains the data for the table `tblComplexDogImagelayout`.

LISTING D.3 Sample Data for `tblComplexDogImagelayout`

```
1 INSERT INTO tblComplexDogImagelayout VALUES
2 ('Maddy The Great','Maddy','Pomeranian','1998-12-23','John Ray',
3  'images/maddy.jpg','position:absolute; left:220px; top:10px; width:150px;
4  height:150px; z-index:1');
5 INSERT INTO tblComplexDogImagelayout VALUES
6 ('Coco The Barking Queen','Coco','American Eskimo','2000-11-12',
7  'Robyn Ness','images/coco.jpg','position:absolute; left:0px;
8  top:180px; width:150px; height:150px; z-index:1');
9 INSERT INTO tblComplexDogImagelayout VALUES
10 ('Abull King of the Danes','Abull','Great Dane','1995-05-05',
11  'Kama Dobbs','images/abull.jpg','position:absolute; left:450px; top:180px;
12  width:150px; height:150px; z-index:1');
13 INSERT INTO tblComplexDogImagelayout VALUES
14 ('Shamrock of Wilmar','Sham','Irish Setter','1997-02-13',
15  'Jack Derifaj','images/sham.jpg','position:absolute; left:70px; top:350px;
16  width:150px; height:150px; z-index:1');
17 INSERT INTO tblComplexDogImagelayout VALUES
18 ('Mojo bearded charcoal','Mojo',
19  'Scottish Terrier','1998-07-04','Anne Groves','images/mojo.jpg',
20  'position:absolute; left:380px; top:350px; width:150px;
21  height:150px; z-index:1');
```

Listing D.4 contains the structure for `tblSimpleDogImagelist`.

LISTING D.4   Table Structure for `tblSimpleDogImagelist`

```
1 CREATE TABLE tblSimpleDogImagelist (
2   AKCname varchar(250) NOT NULL default '',
3   shortname varchar(250) default NULL,
4   breed varchar(250) default NULL,
5   birthday date default NULL,
6   owner varchar(250) default NULL,
7   imageurl varchar(250) default NULL,
8   PRIMARY KEY  (AKCname)
9 );
```

Listing D.5 shows the sample data for the table `tblSimpleDogImagelist`.

LISTING D.5   Sample Data for `tblSimpleDogImagelist`

```
1 INSERT INTO tblSimpleDogImagelist VALUES
2 ('Maddy The Great','Maddy','Pomeranian','1998-12-23',
3  'John Ray','images/maddy.jpg');
4 INSERT INTO tblSimpleDogImagelist VALUES
5 ('Coco The Barking Queen','Coco','American Eskimo','2000-11-12',
6  'Robyn Ness','images/coco.jpg');
7 INSERT INTO tblSimpleDogImagelist VALUES
8 ('Abull King of the Danes','Abull','Great Dane','1995-05-05',
9  'Kama Dobbs','images/abull.jpg');
10 INSERT INTO tblSimpleDogImagelist VALUES
11 ('Shamrock of Wilmar','Sham','Irish Setter','1997-02-13',
12  'Jack Derifaj','images/sham.jpg');
13 INSERT INTO tblSimpleDogImagelist VALUES
14 ('Mojo bearded charcoal','Mojo','Scottish Terrier','1998-07-04',
15  'Anne Groves','images/mojo.jpg');
```

Listing D.6 shows the table structure for `tblSimpleDoglist`.

LISTING D.6   Table Structure for `tblSimpleDoglist`

```
1 CREATE TABLE tblSimpleDoglist (
2   AKCname varchar(250) NOT NULL default '',
3   shortname varchar(250) default NULL,
4   breed varchar(250) default NULL,
5   birthday date default NULL,
6   owner varchar(250) default NULL,
7   PRIMARY KEY  (AKCname)
8 );
```

D

Listing D.7 contains sample data for the table tblSimpleDoglist.

LISTING D.7   Sample Data for tblSimpleDoglist

```
1 INSERT INTO tblSimpleDoglist VALUES
2 ('Maddy The Great','Maddy','Pomeranian','1998-12-23',
3  'John Ray');
4 INSERT INTO tblSimpleDoglist VALUES
5 ('Coco The Barking Queen','Coco','American Eskimo',
6  '2000-11-12','Robyn Ness');
7 INSERT INTO tblSimpleDoglist VALUES
8 ('Abull King of the Danes','Abull','Great Dane','1995-05-05',
9  'Kama Dobbs');
10 INSERT INTO tblSimpleDoglist VALUES
11 ('Shamrock of Wilmar','Sham','Irish Setter','1997-02-13',
12  'Jack Derifaj');
13 INSERT INTO tblSimpleDoglist VALUES
14 ('Mojo bearded charcoal','Mojo','Scottish Terrier',
15  '1998-07-04','Anne Groves');
```

Day 11

Listing D.8 shows the table structure for tblSimpleDoglist.

LISTING D.8   Table Definition for tblSimpleDoglist

```
1 CREATE TABLE tblSimpleDoglist (
2  AKCname varchar(250) NOT NULL default '',
3  shortname varchar(250) default NULL,
4  breed varchar(250) default NULL,
5  birthday date default NULL,
6  owner varchar(250) default NULL,
7  PRIMARY KEY  (AKCname)
8 );
```

Listing D.9 contains the sample data for the table tblSimpleDoglist.

LISTING D.9   Sample Data for tblSimpleDoglist

```
1 INSERT INTO tblSimpleDoglist VALUES
2 ('Maddy The Great','Maddy','Pomeranian','1998-12-23',
3  'John Ray');
4 INSERT INTO tblSimpleDoglist VALUES
5 ('Coco The Barking Queen','Coco','American Eskimo',
6  '2000-11-12','Robyn Ness');
```

LISTING D.9 continued

```
7  INSERT INTO tblSimpleDoglist VALUES
8  ('Abull King of the Danes','Abull','Great Dane','1995-05-05',
9   'Kama Dobbs');
10 INSERT INTO tblSimpleDoglist VALUES
11 ('Shamrock of Wilmar','Sham','Irish Setter','1997-02-13',
12  'Jack Derifaj');
13 INSERT INTO tblSimpleDoglist VALUES
14 ('Mojo bearded charcoal','Mojo','Scottish Terrier',
15  '1998-07-04','Anne Groves');
```

Day 12

Listing D.10 shows the table structure for tblBreed.

LISTING D.10 Table Structure for tblBreed

```
1 CREATE TABLE tblBreed (
2   BreedName varchar(250) NOT NULL default '',
3   BreedStandards text,
4   PRIMARY KEY  (BreedName)
5 );
```

Listing D.11 contains the sample data for the table tblBreed.

LISTING D.11 Sample Data for tblBreed

```
1 INSERT INTO tblBreed VALUES
2 ('Pomeranian','Small fuzzy dog, no teeth, walks with a limp');
```

Listing D.12 shows the table structure for tblDog.

LISTING D.12 Table Structure for tblDog

```
1 CREATE TABLE tblDog (
2   ShortName varchar(100) default NULL,
3   AKCName varchar(250) NOT NULL default '',
4   BirthDay date default NULL,
5   HandlerID int(11) default NULL,
6   BreedName varchar(250) default NULL,
7   PRIMARY KEY  (AKCName)
8 );
```

D

Listing D.13 shows sample data for the table tblDog.

LISTING D.13   Sample Data for tblDog

```
 1 INSERT INTO tblDog VALUES
 2  ('Maddy','Maddy The Great Hair Clump','1999-12-05',1,'Pomeranian');
 3 INSERT INTO tblDog VALUES
 4  ('Norman','Psycho Norman','2001-11-15',2,'Pomeranian');
 5 INSERT INTO tblDog VALUES
 6  ('Abull','Abull eats children','1995-01-01',1,'Great Dane');
 7 INSERT INTO tblDog VALUES
 8  ('Coco','Coco is not spelled with an a','2001-01-23',3,'American Eskimo');
 9 INSERT INTO tblDog VALUES
10  ('Sham','Long ears elite','1999-12-05',3,'American Eskimo');
11 INSERT INTO tblDog VALUES
12  ('Ginger','An inch too short','1997-06-23',4,'13 inch Beagle');
```

Listing D.14 contains the table structure for tblHandler.

LISTING D.14   Table Definition of tblHandler

```
1 CREATE TABLE tblHandler (
2   HandlerID int(11) NOT NULL default '0',
3   FirstName varchar(150) default NULL,
4   LastName varchar(100) default NULL,
5   PRIMARY KEY  (HandlerID)
6 );
```

Listing D.15 shows sample data for the table tblHandler.

LISTING D.15   Sample Data for tblHandler

```
1 INSERT INTO tblHandler VALUES (1,'John','Ray');
2 INSERT INTO tblHandler VALUES (2,'Russ','Schelby');
3 INSERT INTO tblHandler VALUES (3,'Robyn','Ness');
4 INSERT INTO tblHandler VALUES (4,'Diane','Burkholder');
```

Listing D.16 shows the table structure for tblResult.

LISTING D.16   Table Definition of tblResult

```
1 CREATE TABLE tblResult (
2   AKCName varchar(250) NOT NULL default '',
3   WinDate date NOT NULL default '0000-00-00',
```

LISTING D.16 continued

```
4   PRIMARY KEY  (AKCName,WinDate)
5 );
```

Listing D.17 shows sample data for the table `tblResult`.

LISTING D.17 Sample Data for `tblResult`

```
1 INSERT INTO tblResult VALUES ('Abull eats children','2002-05-15');
2 INSERT INTO tblResult VALUES ('Coco is not spelled with an a','2002-06-21');
3 INSERT INTO tblResult VALUES ('Maddy The Great Hair Clump','2002-05-15');
4 INSERT INTO tblResult VALUES ('Maddy The Great Hair Clump','2002-06-21');
```

Day 13

Listing D.18 shows the table structure for `tblUserInfo`.

LISTING D.18 Table Definition of `tblUserInfo`

```
1 CREATE TABLE tblUserInfo (
2   userID int(11) NOT NULL auto_increment,
3   username varchar(250) default NULL,
4   password varchar(250) default NULL,
5   PRIMARY KEY  (userID)
6 );Listing D.19 shows sample data for the table tblUserInfo.
```

LISTING D.19 Sample Data for `tblUserInfo`

```
1 INSERT INTO tblUserInfo VALUES (1,'test','test');
2 INSERT INTO tblUserInfo VALUES (2,'hairy','dog');
3 INSERT INTO tblUserInfo VALUES (3,'agroves','badmovie');
4 INSERT INTO tblUserInfo VALUES (4,'robyn','necster');
```

Day 14

Listing D.20 shows the table structure for `tblProduct`.

LISTING D.20   Table Definition of `tblProduct`

```
1 CREATE TABLE tblProduct (
2   prodID varchar(250) NOT NULL default '',
3   prodName varchar(250) default NULL,
4   prodDesc text,
5   prodPrice double default NULL,
6   prodThumbPic varchar(250) default NULL,
7   prodPic varchar(250) default NULL,
8   PRIMARY KEY  (prodID)
9 );
```

Listing D.21 displays the sample data for the table `tblProduct`.

LISTING D.21   Sample Data for `tblProduct`

```
1 INSERT INTO tblProduct VALUES
2  ('T001','Fuzzy Giraffe','This brightly colored stuffed chew toy will delight any
3   dog. Squeaker included.',8.95,'images/T001s.jpg','images/T001.jpg');
4 INSERT INTO tblProduct VALUES
5  ('T002','Fuzzy Bone','A simple bone-shaped chew toy.',4.95,
6   'images/T002s.jpg','images/T002.jpg');
7 INSERT INTO tblProduct VALUES
8  ('T003','Mini Orange Tennis Ball','A pint sized orange tennis ball, just the
9   right size for little dogs.',2,'images/T003s.jpg','images/T003.jpg');
10 INSERT INTO tblProduct VALUES
11  ('T004','Mini Purple Tennis Ball','A pint sized purple tennis ball, just the
12   right size for little dogs.',2,'images/T004s.jpg','images/T004.jpg');
13 INSERT INTO tblProduct VALUES
14  ('T005','Rope Bone Toy','Stringy and meaty. What makes a better bone than
15   string?',6.5,'images/T005s.jpg','images/T005.jpg');
16 INSERT INTO tblProduct VALUES
17  ('T006','Holiday Dog Suit','The perfect cape for Thanksgiving or Christmas
18   dog dressing.',14.95,'images/T006s.jpg','images/T006.jpg');
19 INSERT INTO tblProduct VALUES
20  ('T007','Lion Dog Pillow','Where else would a dog like to sleep but on a
21   lion? This fluffy dog pillow makes a perfect bed.',25.95,'images/T007s.jpg',
22   'images/T007.jpg');
23 INSERT INTO tblProduct VALUES
24  ('T008','Plaid Dog Bed','The complete sleeping solution for elegant little
25   dogs. Stitched in bright red plaid, this bed is the ultimate in
26   comfort.',35.95,'images/T008s.jpg','images/T008.jpg');
27 INSERT INTO tblProduct VALUES
28  ('T009','Rawhide Chew','Release the animal instincts in your dog, feed him
29   a rawhide. This chew toy will last through at least a week of constant
30   chewing.',4,'images/T009s.jpg','images/T009.jpg');
```

LISTING D.21   continued

```
31 INSERT INTO tblProduct VALUES
32 ('T010','Regular Tennis Ball','Play Tennis, Play with your dog. Do
33   everything at once with this regulation tennis ball.',0.5,
34   'images/T010s.jpg','images/T010.jpg');
```

Listing D.22 shows the table structure for tblRelated.

LISTING D.22   Table Definition of tblRelated

```
1 CREATE TABLE tblRelated (
2   prodID1 varchar(250) NOT NULL default '',
3   prodID2 varchar(250) NOT NULL default '',
4   PRIMARY KEY  (prodID1,prodID2)
5 );
```

Listing D.23 shows sample data for the table tblRelated.

LISTING D.23   Sample Data for tblRelated

```
1 INSERT INTO tblRelated VALUES ('T003','T004');
2 INSERT INTO tblRelated VALUES ('T003','T010');
3 INSERT INTO tblRelated VALUES ('T007','T008');
```

Day 15: Banner

Listing D.24 shows the table structure for tblBanner.

LISTING D.24   Table Definition of tblBanner

```
1 CREATE TABLE tblBanner (
2   filename varchar(250) NOT NULL default '',
3   url varchar(250) default NULL,
4   PRIMARY KEY  (filename)
5 );
```

Listing D.25 shows sample data for the table tblBanner.

D

LISTING D.25   Sample Data for `tblBanner`

```
1 INSERT INTO tblBanner VALUES
2 ('images/cutelittledogs.gif','http://www.cutelittledogs.com');
3 INSERT INTO tblBanner VALUES
4 ('images/day2cutelittledogs.gif','http://day2.cutelittledogs.com');
5 INSERT INTO tblBanner VALUES
6 ('images/day3cutelittledogs.gif','http://day3.cutelittledogs.com');
```

Day 15: Feedback

Listing D.26 shows the table structure for `tblFeedback`.

LISTING D.26   Table Definition of `tblFeedback`

```
1 CREATE TABLE tblFeedback (
2   messageID int(11) NOT NULL auto_increment,
3   name varchar(50) default NULL,
4   email varchar(80) default NULL,
5   message varchar(250) default NULL,
6   PRIMARY KEY  (messageID)
7 );
```

Listing D.27 shows sample data for the table `tblFeedback`.

LISTING D.27   Sample Data for `tblFeedback`

```
1 INSERT INTO tblFeedback VALUES
2 (1,'John Ray','jray@poisontooth.com','This is the greatest dog website ever!
3   I have very low standards!');
4 INSERT INTO tblFeedback VALUES
5 (2,'Robyn Ness','robyn@cutelittledogs.com','Not true. This isn\'t a
6   very good website at all! The dogs are UGLY!');
7 INSERT INTO tblFeedback VALUES
8 (3,'Bad Dude','badguy@someplacethatisevil.com',
9   'Forget this place! go <a href=\"http://mydogsarebetter.com\"> here </a>');
```

Day 15: Time Images

Listing D.28 contains the table structure for `tblMultiTimeimage`.

LISTING D.28   Table Definition of tblMultiTimeimage

```
1 CREATE TABLE tblMultiTimeimage (
2   filename varchar(250) default NULL,
3   name varchar(250) NOT NULL default '',
4   themeID varchar(80) NOT NULL default '',
5   PRIMARY KEY  (name,themeID)
6 );
```

Listing D.29 lists the sample data for the table tblMultiTimeimage.

LISTING D.29   Sample Data for tblMultiTimeimage

```
1 INSERT INTO tblMultiTimeimage VALUES
2 ('images/headspring.gif','header','spring');
3 INSERT INTO tblMultiTimeimage VALUES
4 ('images/headsummer.gif','header','summer');
5 INSERT INTO tblMultiTimeimage VALUES
6 ('images/headfall.gif','header','fall');
7 INSERT INTO tblMultiTimeimage VALUES
8 ('images/headwinter.gif','header','winter');
```

Listing D.30 shows the table structure for tblTheme.

LISTING D.30   Table Definition of tblTheme

```
1 CREATE TABLE tblTheme (
2   themeID varchar(80) NOT NULL default '',
3   golivedate date default NULL,
4   PRIMARY KEY  (themeID)
5 );
```

Listing D.31 shows sample data for the table tblTheme.

LISTING D.31   Sample Data for tblTheme

```
1 INSERT INTO tblTheme VALUES ('spring','2003-03-21');
2 INSERT INTO tblTheme VALUES ('summer','2002-06-21');
3 INSERT INTO tblTheme VALUES ('fall','2002-09-21');
4 INSERT INTO tblTheme VALUES ('winter','2002-12-21');
```

Listing D.32 shows the table structure for tblTimeimage.

LISTING D.32　Table Definition of `tblTimeimage`

```
1 CREATE TABLE tblTimeimage (
2   filename varchar(250) NOT NULL default '',
3   golivedate date default NULL,
4   PRIMARY KEY  (filename)
5 );
```

Listing D.33 shows the table structure for `tblTimeimage`.

LISTING D.33　Table Definition of `tblTimeimage`

```
1 INSERT INTO tblTimeimage VALUES ('images/spring.gif','2003-03-21');
2 INSERT INTO tblTimeimage VALUES ('images/summer.gif','2002-06-21');
3 INSERT INTO tblTimeimage VALUES ('images/fall.gif','2002-09-21');
4 INSERT INTO tblTimeimage VALUES ('images/winter.gif','2002-12-21');
```

Day 16

Listing D.34 shows the table structure for `tblMessage`.

LISTING D.34　Table Definition of `tblMessage`

```
1 CREATE TABLE tblMessage (
2   messageID int(11) NOT NULL auto_increment,
3   parentID int(11) default NULL,
4   subject varchar(250) default NULL,
5   iconURL varchar(250) default NULL,
6   author varchar(250) default NULL,
7   body text,
8   password varchar(250) default NULL,
9   PRIMARY KEY  (messageID)
10 );
```

Listing D.35 shows sample data for the table `tblMessage`.

LISTING D.35　Sample Data for `tblMessage`

```
1 INSERT INTO tblMessage VALUES
2 (1,0,'First Post','images/icon1.jpg','John Ray','I had the first post
3  of the message system! Cute Little Dogs are cool!','ihartdogs');
4 INSERT INTO tblMessage VALUES
5 (2,0,'Lame','images/icon2.jpg','Admin','People who make first posts
```

LISTING D.35   continued

```
 6   with no real content really get on my nerves.','madadmin');
 7 INSERT INTO tblMessage VALUES
 8  (3,0,'Cool','images/icon1.jpg','Pom Gal','This new message system is
 9   wonderful. I plan to use it every day.','loveit');
10 INSERT INTO tblMessage VALUES
11  (4,2,'Re: Lame','images/icon3.jpg','Rude Dude','I think that first
12   posts are great, stop being mean!','nodelete');
13 INSERT INTO tblMessage VALUES
14  (5,2,'Re: Lame','images/icon3.jpg','Nice Guy','I agree entirely.
15   Listen to the admin and post real content please.','cutedogcool');
16 INSERT INTO tblMessage VALUES
17  (6,2,'Grumble','images/icon2.jpg','Anonymous','Lets drop this discussion
18   and talk about something important!','frustrated');
19 INSERT INTO tblMessage VALUES
20  (7,0,'First Post','images/icon1.jpg','John Ray','I had the first post
21   of the message system! Cute Little Dogs are cool!','ihartdogs');
22 INSERT INTO tblMessage VALUES
23  (8,0,'Lame','images/icon2.jpg','Admin','People who make first posts
24   with no real content really get on my nerves.','madadmin');
25 INSERT INTO tblMessage VALUES
26  (9,0,'Cool','images/icon1.jpg','Pom Gal','This new message system
27   is wonderful. I plan to use it every day.','loveit');
28 INSERT INTO tblMessage VALUES
29  (10,0,'First Post','images/icon1.jpg','John Ray','I had the first post
30   of the message system! Cute Little Dogs are cool!','ihartdogs');
31 INSERT INTO tblMessage VALUES
32  (11,0,'Lame','images/icon2.jpg','Admin','People who make first posts
33   with no real content really get on my nerves.','madadmin');
34 INSERT INTO tblMessage VALUES
35  (12,0,'Cool','images/icon1.jpg','Pom Gal','This new message system is
36   wonderful. I plan to use it every day.','loveit');
37 INSERT INTO tblMessage VALUES
38  (13,0,'First Post','images/icon1.jpg','John Ray','I had the first
39   post of the message system! Cute Little Dogs are cool!','ihartdogs');
40 INSERT INTO tblMessage VALUES
41  (15,4,'Howdy Dooty','images/icon1.jpg','Test Person','There
42   aren\'t enough smiley faces!','testing');
```

Day 17

Listing D.36 contains the table structure for tblFeatureOption.

LISTING D.36 Table Definition of tblFeatureOption

```
1 CREATE TABLE tblFeatureOption (
2   featureID int(11) NOT NULL default '0',
3   optionID int(11) NOT NULL default '0',
4   PRIMARY KEY  (featureID,optionID)
5 );
```

Listing D.37 shows the sample data for the table tblFeatureOption.

LISTING D.37 Sample Data for tblFeatureOption

```
 1 INSERT INTO tblFeatureOption VALUES (1,1);
 2 INSERT INTO tblFeatureOption VALUES (1,2);
 3 INSERT INTO tblFeatureOption VALUES (1,3);
 4 INSERT INTO tblFeatureOption VALUES (1,4);
 5 INSERT INTO tblFeatureOption VALUES (2,1);
 6 INSERT INTO tblFeatureOption VALUES (2,2);
 7 INSERT INTO tblFeatureOption VALUES (2,3);
 8 INSERT INTO tblFeatureOption VALUES (2,4);
 9 INSERT INTO tblFeatureOption VALUES (3,8);
10 INSERT INTO tblFeatureOption VALUES (3,9);
11 INSERT INTO tblFeatureOption VALUES (3,10);
12 INSERT INTO tblFeatureOption VALUES (3,11);
13 INSERT INTO tblFeatureOption VALUES (4,8);
14 INSERT INTO tblFeatureOption VALUES (4,9);
15 INSERT INTO tblFeatureOption VALUES (4,10);
16 INSERT INTO tblFeatureOption VALUES (4,11);
17 INSERT INTO tblFeatureOption VALUES (7,5);
18 INSERT INTO tblFeatureOption VALUES (7,6);
19 INSERT INTO tblFeatureOption VALUES (7,7);
20 INSERT INTO tblFeatureOption VALUES (8,5);
21 INSERT INTO tblFeatureOption VALUES (8,6);
22 INSERT INTO tblFeatureOption VALUES (8,7);
```

Listing D.38 lists the table structure for tblOption.

LISTING D.38 Table Definition of tblOption

```
1 CREATE TABLE tblOption (
2   optionID int(11) NOT NULL default '0',
3   optionName varchar(250) default NULL,
4   optionValue text,
5   PRIMARY KEY  (optionID)
6 );
```

Listing D.39 shows the sample data for the table tblOption.

LISTING D.39   Sample Data for tblOption

```
1 INSERT INTO tblOption VALUES (1,'Blue','#0000FF');
2 INSERT INTO tblOption VALUES (2,'Yellow','#FFFF00');
3 INSERT INTO tblOption VALUES (3,'White','#FFFFFF');
4 INSERT INTO tblOption VALUES (4,'Black','#000000');
5 INSERT INTO tblOption VALUES (5,'Arial','Arial');
6 INSERT INTO tblOption VALUES (6,'Helvetica','Helvetica');
7 INSERT INTO tblOption VALUES (7,'Times','Times');
8 INSERT INTO tblOption VALUES
9  (8,'Dog Training Tip','Tip: To get your down to lay down
10   and stay lying down, wait until late at night, quietly issue
11   the command \"down\", then watch.  You\'ll be amazed by the
12   results. ');
13 INSERT INTO tblOption VALUES
14  (9,'Breed News','A new breed of dog was discovered today in Estonia.
15   The small, brown creature is primarily a tree-dweller and has
16   developed a primitive language based on pop music from the
17   eighties.');
18 INSERT INTO tblOption VALUES
19  (10,'Famouse Dog Quotes','Yesterday I was a dog. Today I\'m a
20   dog. Tomorrow I\'ll probably still be a dog. Sigh! There\'s so little
21   hope for advancement.<br><b>Charles M. Schulz, (Snoopy)</b><br><br>
22   Outside of a dog, a book is man\'s best friend. Inside of a dog it\'s
23   too dark to read.<br><b>Groucho Marx (1890 - 1977)</b>');
24 INSERT INTO tblOption VALUES
25  (11,'Upcoming Dog Shows','<b>2003/01/03</b> - Winter Carnival
26   dog show, Fargo, ND.<br><br><b>2003/03/25</b> - Blue Island Celebrity
27   Dogs, Blue Island, IL.<br><br><b>2003/05/12</b> - Summer Dog Sizzler,
28   Wakeman, OH.<br><br><b>2003/06/17</b> - Gator Dog Dinners,
29   Melbourne, FL.');
```

Listing D.40 shows the table structure for tblPreference.

LISTING D.40   Table Definition of tblPreference

```
1 CREATE TABLE tblPreference (
2   userID int(11) NOT NULL default '0',
3   featureID int(11) NOT NULL default '0',
4   optionID int(11) default NULL,
5   PRIMARY KEY  (userID,featureID)
6 );
```

Listing D.41 shows the sample data for the table tblPreference.

D

LISTING D.41 Sample Data for `tblPreference`

```
1 INSERT INTO tblPreference VALUES (0,1,1);
2 INSERT INTO tblPreference VALUES (0,2,3);
3 INSERT INTO tblPreference VALUES (0,3,9);
4 INSERT INTO tblPreference VALUES (0,4,10);
5 INSERT INTO tblPreference VALUES (0,5,5);
6 INSERT INTO tblPreference VALUES (0,6,5);
```

Listing D.42 displays the table structure for `tblUserInfo`.

LISTING D.42 Table Definition of `tblUserInfo`

```
1 CREATE TABLE tblUserInfo (
2   userID int(11) NOT NULL auto_increment,
3   username varchar(250) default NULL,
4   password varchar(250) default NULL,
5   PRIMARY KEY  (userID)
6 );
```

Listing D.43 contains the sample data for the table `tblUserInfo`.

LISTING D.43 Sample Data for `tblUserInfo`

```
1 INSERT INTO tblUserInfo VALUES (1,'default','notgonnaguessme');
2 INSERT INTO tblUserInfo VALUES (2,'test','test');
```

Day 18

Listing D.44 displays the table structure for `tblAnswer`.

LISTING D.44 Table Definition of `tblAnswer`

```
1 CREATE TABLE tblAnswer (
2   answerID int(11) NOT NULL default '0',
3   questionID int(11) default NULL,
4   answerText varchar(250) default NULL,
5   PRIMARY KEY  (answerID)
6 );
```

Listing D.45 contains the sample data for the table `tblAnswer`.

LISTING D.45 Sample Data for tblAnswer

```
1 INSERT INTO tblAnswer VALUES (1,1,'Reptile');
2 INSERT INTO tblAnswer VALUES (2,1,'Mammal');
3 INSERT INTO tblAnswer VALUES (3,1,'Plant');
4 INSERT INTO tblAnswer VALUES (4,1,'Mineral');
5 INSERT INTO tblAnswer VALUES (5,2,'Potato');
6 INSERT INTO tblAnswer VALUES (6,2,'Meat');
7 INSERT INTO tblAnswer VALUES (7,2,'Chocolate');
8 INSERT INTO tblAnswer VALUES (8,2,'Cat Food');
9 INSERT INTO tblAnswer VALUES (9,3,'Dentist');
10 INSERT INTO tblAnswer VALUES (10,3,'Veterinarian');
11 INSERT INTO tblAnswer VALUES (11,3,'Podiatrist');
12 INSERT INTO tblAnswer VALUES (12,3,'Optometrist');
```

Listing D.46 displays the table structure for tblQuestion.

LISTING D.46 Table Definition of tblQuestion

```
1 CREATE TABLE tblQuestion (
2   questionID int(11) NOT NULL default '0',
3   questionTitle varchar(250) default NULL,
4   questionText text,
5   answerID int(11) default NULL,
6   PRIMARY KEY (questionID)
7 );
```

Listing D.47 contains the sample data for the table tblQuestion.

LISTING D.47 Sample Data for tblquestion

```
1 INSERT INTO tblQuestion VALUES
2  (1,'Animal Type','What type of animal is a dog ?',2);
3 INSERT INTO tblQuestion VALUES
4  (2,'Hazardous Food','You should never feed a dog one of these
5   types of food. It could make the dog very ill, or even worse...',7);
6 INSERT INTO tblQuestion VALUES
7  (3,'Animal Doctor','What type of doctor should you take your dog to?',10);
```

Listing D.48 displays the table structure for tblResponse.

LISTING D.48 Table Definition of tblResponse

```
1 CREATE TABLE tblResponse (
2   username varchar(250) NOT NULL default '',
```

D

LISTING D.48 continued

```
3   questionID int(11) NOT NULL default '0',
4   answerID int(11) default NULL,
5   PRIMARY KEY  (username,questionID)
6 );
```

Listing D.49 contains the sample data for the table tblResponse.

LISTING D.49 Sample Data for tblResponse

```
1 INSERT INTO tblResponse VALUES ('example',1,2);
2 INSERT INTO tblResponse VALUES ('example',2,7);
3 INSERT INTO tblResponse VALUES ('example',3,9);
```

Listing D.50 displays the table structure for tblUserInfo.

LISTING D.50 Table Definition of tblUserInfo

```
1 CREATE TABLE tblUserInfo (
2   username varchar(250) NOT NULL default '',
3   password varchar(250) default NULL,
4   userlevel varchar(250) default NULL,
5   PRIMARY KEY  (username)
6 );
```

Listing D.51 displays the table structure for tblUserInfo.

LISTING D.51 Table Definition of tblUserInfo

```
1 INSERT INTO tblUserInfo VALUES ('teststudent','studentpass','student');
2 INSERT INTO tblUserInfo VALUES ('testteach','teachpass','teacher');
```

Day 19

Listing D.52 displays the table structure for tblNumber.

LISTING D.52 Table Definition of tblNumber

```
1 CREATE TABLE tblNumber (
2   a int(11) default NULL
3 );
```

Listing D.53 contains the sample data for the table tblNumber.

LISTING D.53   Sample Data for tblNumber

```
1 INSERT INTO tblNumber VALUES (5);
2 INSERT INTO tblNumber VALUES (6);
3 INSERT INTO tblNumber VALUES (1);
4 INSERT INTO tblNumber VALUES (15);
5 INSERT INTO tblNumber VALUES (9);
6 INSERT INTO tblNumber VALUES (8);
7 INSERT INTO tblNumber VALUES (21);
8 INSERT INTO tblNumber VALUES (500);
9 INSERT INTO tblNumber VALUES (10);
10 INSERT INTO tblNumber VALUES (50);
```

Listing D.54 displays the table structure for tblOption1.

LISTING D.54   Table Definition of tblOption1

```
1 CREATE TABLE tblOption1 (
2   optionName1 varchar(250) NOT NULL default '',
3   optionValue1 int(11) default NULL,
4   PRIMARY KEY  (optionName1)
5 );
```

D

Listing D.55 contains the sample data for the table tblOption1.

LISTING D.55   Sample Data for tblOption1

```
1 INSERT INTO tblOption1 VALUES ('Jack Russell Terrier',1);
2 INSERT INTO tblOption1 VALUES ('Pomeranian',2);
3 INSERT INTO tblOption1 VALUES ('American Eskimo',3);
4 INSERT INTO tblOption1 VALUES ('Irish Setter',8);
5 INSERT INTO tblOption1 VALUES ('Golden Retriever',9);
6 INSERT INTO tblOption1 VALUES ('Great Dane',10);
```

Listing D.56 displays the table structure for tblOption2.

LISTING D.56   Table Definition of tblOption2

```
1 CREATE TABLE tblOption2 (
2   optionName2 varchar(250) NOT NULL default '',
3   optionValue2 int(11) default NULL,
4   PRIMARY KEY  (optionName2)
5 );
```

Listing D.57 contains the sample data for the table tblOption2.

LISTING D.57 Sample Data for tblOption2

```
1 INSERT INTO tblOption2 VALUES ('Lazy as can be',1);
2 INSERT INTO tblOption2 VALUES ('He moves occasionally',2);
3 INSERT INTO tblOption2 VALUES ('Plays frequently',3);
4 INSERT INTO tblOption2 VALUES ('Never stops running',4);
```

Listing D.58 displays the table structure for tblOption3.

LISTING D.58 Table Definition of tblOption3

```
1 CREATE TABLE tblOption3 (
2   optionName3 varchar(250) NOT NULL default '',
3   optionValue3 int(11) default NULL,
4   PRIMARY KEY  (optionName3)
5 );
```

Listing D.59 contains the sample data for the table tblOption3.

LISTING D.59 Sample Data for tblOption3

```
1 INSERT INTO tblOption3 VALUES ('Shy',1);
2 INSERT INTO tblOption3 VALUES ('Easily befriended',2);
3 INSERT INTO tblOption3 VALUES ('Loves everyone',3);
```

Listing D.60 displays the table structure for tblOption4.

LISTING D.60 Table Definition of tblOption4

```
1 CREATE TABLE tblOption4 (
2   optionName4 varchar(250) NOT NULL default '',
3   optionValue4 int(11) default NULL,
4   PRIMARY KEY  (optionName4)
5 );
```

Listing D.61 contains the sample data for the table tblOption4.

LISTING D.61   Sample Data for tbl0ption4

```
1 INSERT INTO tbl0ption4 VALUES ('Puppy',1);
2 INSERT INTO tbl0ption4 VALUES ('Adolescent',2);
3 INSERT INTO tbl0ption4 VALUES ('Full Grown',3);
```

Listing D.62 displays the table structure for tblTwoNumber.

LISTING D.62   Table Definition of tblTwoNumber

```
1 CREATE TABLE tblTwoNumber (
2  a int(11) default NULL,
3  b int(11) default NULL
4 );
```

Listing D.63 contains the sample data for the table tblTwoNumber.

LISTING D.63   Sample Data for tblTwoNumber

```
1 INSERT INTO tblTwoNumber VALUES (2,5);
2 INSERT INTO tblTwoNumber VALUES (10,5);
3 INSERT INTO tblTwoNumber VALUES (9,1);
4 INSERT INTO tblTwoNumber VALUES (15,50);
5 INSERT INTO tblTwoNumber VALUES (1,2);
6 INSERT INTO tblTwoNumber VALUES (20,5);
7 INSERT INTO tblTwoNumber VALUES (2,5);
8 INSERT INTO tblTwoNumber VALUES (11,2);
9 INSERT INTO tblTwoNumber VALUES (3,7);
10 INSERT INTO tblTwoNumber VALUES (6,6);
```

D

Listing D.64 displays the table structure for tblUserInfo.

LISTING D.64   Table Definition of tblUserInfo

```
1 CREATE TABLE tblUserInfo (
2   userID int(11) NOT NULL auto_increment,
3   username varchar(250) default NULL,
4   password varchar(250) default NULL,
5   email varchar(250) default NULL,
6   fullname varchar(250) default NULL,
7   q1Response int(11) default NULL,
8   q2Response int(11) default NULL,
9   q3Response int(11) default NULL,
10  q4Response int(11) default NULL,
11  PRIMARY KEY  (userID)
12 );
```

Listing D.65 contains the sample data for the table `tblUserInfo`.

LISTING D.65   Sample Data for `tblUserInfo`

```
1  INSERT INTO tblUserInfo VALUES
2  (1,'test','test','test@testing.com','Test User',10,4,3,3);
3  INSERT INTO tblUserInfo VALUES
4  (2,'hairy','dog','hairy@poisontooth.com','Bob Dawg',10,4,3,3);
5  INSERT INTO tblUserInfo VALUES
6  (3,'agroves','badmovie','agroves@poisontooth.com','Anne Groves',1,3,2,3);
7  INSERT INTO tblUserInfo VALUES
8  (4,'robyn','nester','robster@poisontooth.com','Robyn Nester',2,4,2,3);
9  INSERT INTO tblUserInfo VALUES
10 (5,'julie','vujgirl','julie@poisontooth.com','Julie Vujevich',2,3,1,2);
11 INSERT INTO tblUserInfo VALUES
12 (6,'jackd','nrri','jackd@poisontooth.com','Jack Derifaj',9,4,2,1);
13 INSERT INTO tblUserInfo VALUES
14 (7,'maddy','marty','maddy@poisontooth.com','Maddy Darg',10,4,3,3);
15 INSERT INTO tblUserInfo VALUES
16 (8,'cindy','sandy','cindy@poisontooth.com','Cynthia Sands',3,3,3,3);
17 INSERT INTO tblUserInfo VALUES
18 (9,'carl','fuzzy','carl@poisontooth.com','Carl Winds',8,1,1,1);
19 INSERT INTO tblUserInfo VALUES
20 (10,'martha','homemade','martha@poisontooth.com','Martha Clipper',1,1,2,2);
```

INDEX

Symbols

+ (addition operation), 643
+ button, 385
/ (division operation), 643
\<form\> tag, 22, 103
* (multiplication operation), 643
\<param\> tag, Dreamweaver MX interface, 26
– (subtraction operation), 643

A

ABS(X), mathematical function, 644
absolute positioning, 598
access
  databases access (HTML embedded languages), 198
  restricted to Web pages, 586

Access
  installing, 238
  ODBC data sources, 242-244
  queries, creating (SQL), 365
accessibility
  HTML design errors, 602
  HTML tools, 615-616
Accessibility preferences, 37
ACOS(X), mathematical function, 645
actions
  Behaviors Panel, 136-138
  Drag Layer action, 148-150
    advanced properties, 150-152
  HTML editor search features, 112
  Open Browser Window action, 145-147
Active Server Pages (ASP), 223-224, 259
  application servers on Windows XP, 232

ActiveState, Perl add-on, 197
ActiveX, Dreamweaver MX interface, 26
adding
  keyframes to timelines, 155-156
  server behavior to Update Profile page, 581
addition operation (+), 643
administrative interface (online testing systems), 550-552
  administrative pages, 550
  security, 553
  results screen, 552-553
ADO ODBC, database connections, 270-271
Advanced button, 385
advanced queries, 385-386
  configuring, 452
  errors, 603-605

TRUNCATE(X,D), mathematical function, 646
Type attributes (styles), 651-652
Type definition screen, 96
types, assets, 173
    Favorite Assets, 174-175
    Site Assets, 174

U

UltraDev
    DSN, connections, 271
    extending, 187-188
        recording commands, 188-189
UltraDev 4-Style connections, 274-275
unique identifiers, 207
    attributes, entities (second normal form normalization), 212
    entities (first normal form normalization), 210
unique incrementing numbers, 211
UNIX, comparing to Windows NT, 229-232
    performance/cost ratio, 230
    reliability, 230
    services, 229-230
    support, 231-232
    user friendliness, 229
update command, 372-375
update page
    linking, 353
    linking to master listing page, 359-360

Update Profile page
    creating, 578-581
    recordsets, 581
    server behavior, adding, 581
Update Record behavior, 350-351
Update Record server behavior, 288
update screens, 350-352
    dynamic form elements, 351-352
        creating with server behaviors, 352-353
    Update Record behavior, 350-351
updating
    data in databases, 372-375
    library items, 177
    templates, 185
    Web pages, 177
URL parameter passing (session management), 402-405, 413
URLs, identifying, 276
user authentication, data passing, 202
User Authentication server behaviors, 295
    Check New Username behavior, 296-297
    Log In User behavior, 294-295
    Log Out User behavior, 296
    Restrict Access To Page behavior, 295-296
user identifiers, session management (login systems), 401-403

user logins, 392-399, 405
    HTTP authentication, 392
    login checking query, 397-399
    login screen, 396-397
    passwords, 395
    security, 412
    session management, 401-405
        cookies, 406-410
        Go To Related Page server behavior, 405
        user identifiers, 401-403
        variable passing, 402-405, 413
    Show Region behavior, 399-400
    SQL, 393-395
        creating, 396
        sample data, 395
    testing, 400-401
    verification screen, 397-400
    Web-based logins, 392-393
user names, MySQL connections, 277
user preferences, tables, 570
user preferences (customized Web sites), 503-504
user response table (online testing systems), 537-538
username and password table (online testing systems), 534-537
username fields, 577
    checking, 575
username variables (customized Web sites), detecting, 513